Charles Campbell Prinsep

Record of services of the Honourable East India Company's civil

servants

In the Madras presidency, from 1741 to 1858 - from records in the possession of

the Secretary of state for India

Charles Campbell Prinsep

Record of services of the Honourable East India Company's civil servants
In the Madras presidency, from 1741 to 1858 - from records in the possession of the Secretary of state for India

ISBN/EAN: 9783337191535

Printed in Europe, USA, Canada, Australia, Japan

Cover: Foto ©Andreas Hilbeck / pixelio.de

More available books at **www.hansebooks.com**

RECORD OF SERVICES

OF THE

HONOURABLE EAST INDIA COMPANY'S
CIVIL SERVANTS

IN THE

MADRAS PRESIDENCY.

FROM 1741 TO 1858.

Including Chronological Lists of

*GOVERNORS, COMMANDERS-IN-CHIEF, CHIEF JUSTICES AND JUDGES,
OF THE MADRAS PRESIDENCY, BETWEEN 1652 AND 1858.*

AS WELL AS

*LISTS OF THE DIRECTORS OF THE EAST INDIA COMPANY;
CHAIRMEN AND DEPUTY CHAIRMEN OF THE DIRECTION;
AND PRESIDENTS OF THE BOARD OF CONTROL.*

Compiled and Edited, from Records in the Possession
of the Secretary of State for India,

BY

CHARLES C. PRINSEP,

STATISTICAL REPORTER, AND LATE SUPERINTENDENT OF RECORDS, INDIA OFFICE.

LONDON:

TRÜBNER & CO., LUDGATE HILL.

1885.

[*All rights reserved.*]

CONTENTS.

*

PREFACE.

—♦—

THE past History of the Old East India Company's service is too well known to require any description in this place; suffice it to remark, that it has produced a class of public servants not to be equalled by any other nation. No reader of Indian History can pronounce this eulogy as undeserved, for whether in peace or in war, rebellion or famine, its truth has been amply demonstrated.

The Indian Civil Service may be said to have commenced from the time when the Right Hon. Warren Hastings, who had previously served on the Council of the Government of Madras, was appointed Governor of Bengal in 1772, and subsequently became the first Governor-General under an Act passed (13 Geo. III., cap. 63) in 1773, when the East India Company first determined to take the country's revenues into their own hands. It was also resolved that the Presidencies of Madras and Bombay should be subject to the Governor-General in political matters. At this date the stupendous fabric of the Indian Civil Service fairly began, although from that time to the present day each Presidency has had its distinctive functions.

The first English Company for the purpose of trading with India was incorporated by Queen Elizabeth on 31st December

1599 under the title of " *The Governor and Company of Mer-chants of London trading to the East Indies.*" Courten's Association, *the Assada Merchants*, established in 1635, united with the *London Company* in 1650. The " *Merchant Adven-turers*," chartered in 1654–55, united with the *London Com-pany* in 1656–57. The " *English Company* " (or " *the General Society*") trading to the East Indies was incorporated in 1698. The aforesaid Company of Merchants of London, and the English Company, were finally incorporated under the title of " *The United Company of Merchants of England trading to the East Indies*" in 1708, and thus was founded the East India Company, which title it maintained until 1858 (an unbroken period of one hundred and fifty years), when the transfer of Indian affairs to the Crown was effected.

Fort St. George, Madras, was erected in the year 1640, and in 1653 the possessions of the East India Company along the Coromandel Coast, comprising the settlements (as they were then termed) of Fort St. George, Fort St. David, Viza-gapatam, and Mechlipatam (Masulipatam), were raised to the rank of a Presidency.

In offering to the public a record of the services of the Madras Covenanted Civilians the compiler has no desire to credit himself with being the first to have initiated such a work, for Messrs. Dodwell and Miles prepared a similar register (now out of print and unobtainable), commencing with civilians who were in the service in 1780 and ending with the year 1839, the date of publication; but notwith-standing its excellence, there is a want of completeness as a work of reference at the present time to the general reader, thus rendering further work necessary, which it has been the object of the compiler herein to achieve.

The present register will be found to contain the names and services of all Civil servants who were on the Madras establishment of the East India Company in 1766 (which is the earliest date of the Indian Registers), and of all those who subsequently entered the service up to, and were in the service in, 1858, when the change of Government took place. In the case of those officers who continued in the service after that date, the appointments held by them up to retirement or death have also been included. It is to be regretted that the present work is still not so complete as it might have been made, for since going to press manuscript lists of services of civilians from 1700 have been discovered to exist, too late however for insertion in the present volume; but it may be hoped that these new sources of information will be placed before the public at some future time.

In all cases the dates of death have been given where the information has been accessible.

The services of civilians not recorded in this work will be found in a "History of Services of all Gazetted Officers in the Civil Department," covenanted, uncovenanted, and military officers in civil employ, annually published by each administration or province in India.

Further information of a varied character, extracted from the Old Court Books of the East India Company, public consultations of the respective Governments in India, and other valuable records in the India Office, has been appended, so as to render the work a more useful one for general reference, and to increase the interest of officers still living, as well as of relatives of deceased persons, in those who have played their parts so prominently, and

*

added lustre to a record of services performed by civil servants, in India.

In conclusion, the compiler desires to express his sense of the valuable and willing assistance rendered by Colonel Laurie, of the Royal (late Madras) Artillery, in the laborious searches that had to be made in following up each individual name through nearly 200 volumes of registers and other books of reference, and without whose practical experience of India, and of Madras in particular, the publication of this record of services would have been much retarded.

India Office, 19th February 1885.

ALPHABETICAL LIST

OF

DIRECTORS OF THE UNITED COMPANY OF MERCHANTS OF ENGLAND TRADING TO THE EAST INDIES

(*Incorporated under Act, Queen Anne, in 1708*),

OTHERWISE ENTITLED THE EAST INDIA COMPANY,

FROM 1708 TO 1858.

NOTE.—Previous to the year 1773, the twenty-four Directors were elected every year, and the day of election was in the month of April. In 1773 (Act 13 Geo. III. cap. 63) the system of election was changed. It was then provided that six Directors should be chosen for 4 years, six for 3 years, six for 2 years, and six for 1 year, and at every Annual Election six new Directors were to be chosen for the term of 4 years, and no longer. Subsequently, Act 17 Geo. III. cap. 8, of 1777, fixed the second Wednesday in April as the date of the Annual Election. The qualification of a Director was £2000 East India stock. In the event of a vacancy by death or otherwise, another Director had to be chosen within 40 days of the declaration of such vacancy, the new Director succeeding to the unexpired portion of his predecessor's term of office. The salaries of Directors were regulated by the Bye-laws. In earlier years each Director received £150 per annum, in 1794 the amount was increased to £300, and in 1854 to £500, a year.

Names.	Period of Service as Director.
ADAMS, ROBERT . . .	1736 ; 1737.
Addams, Abraham . . .	1721 to 1739.
Agnew, Patrick Vans (C.B.) .	1833 ; 1835 to 1842 (Lt.-Col. in 1840). Died in June 1842.
Aislabie, William . .	1719 to 1726.
Alexander, Josias du Pré .	(M.P., Old Sarum) ; 1820 to 1839. Died in Sept. 1839.
Alexander, Henry . .	(M.P., Barnstaple) 1826 to 1853. Died in Jan. 1861.
Allan, Alexander .	(M.P., Berwick) ; 1814 to 1819 (Bart. in 1819). Died in Oct. 1820.
Allen, Edward . . .	(Director of English Company) 1709.
Amyard, George . . .	1760 ; 1763.
Andrews, Sir Jonathan (Knt.) .	(Director of English Company) 1709 ; 1711 ; and 1712 to 1716.

Names.	Period of Service as Director.
Astell, William . . .	(1807 to 1845 (M.P., Bridgewater, 1809). Died March 1847.
Astell, John Harvey . .	1851 to 1858.
BAKER, WILLIAM . .	(Alderman) 1741 to 1752.
Baillie, Colonel John .	(M.P., Hedon) 1823 to 1833. Died in May 1833.
Bance, John	1722 to 1730.
Bannerman, John Alexander .	1807 to 1816. Disqualified in 1817.
Baring, Francis . .	1779 to 1810 (Bart. in 1799). Died in Oct. 1810.
Barne, Miles . . .	1733; and 1736 to 1739.
Baron, Christopher . .	1759; and 1761 to 1767.
Barrington, Fitzwilliam .	1759 to 1767.
Barwell, William . .	1753 to 1766.
Bateman, Sir James (Knt.) .	(Director of English Company) 1709; 1710, Alderman.
Bayley, William Butterworth .	1834 to 1858. Died in May 1860.
Baylis, Sir Robert (Knt.) .	(Alderman) 1731; 1732.
Beake, Abraham . .	(Director of London Company) 1709.
Bebb, John . . .	1805 to 1829. Disqualified in 1830.
Becher, Richard . .	1775 to 1783.
Beck, Justus . . .	1714.
Bensley, William . .	1786 to 1810 (Bart. in 1801). Died in Jan. 1810.
Benyon, Richard . .	1745 to 1748.
Betts, William . .	1709 to 1711.
Billers, William . .	(Alderman) 1724 to 1742 (Knight in 1727) (Lord Mayor in 1734).
Bisse, Stephen . .	1732; 1735 to 1741.
Blount, Richard . .	1730 to 1743.
Blunt, John . . .	1709.
Boddam, Charles . .	1769; 1772 to 1782.
Boehm, Edmund . .	1784 to 1787.
Boone, Charles . .	1729 to 1735.
Booth, Benjamin . .	1767 to 1783.
Bootle, Capt. Robert .	1741 to 1749; 1752; 1753; 1755.
Bosanquet, Jacob (1) .	1759.
Bosanquet, Jacob (2) .	1790 to 1827. Disqualified in 1827.
Bosanquet, Richard .	1768 to 1772.
Bosanquet, Joseph . .	1785 to 1788.
Boulton, Capt. Richard .	1718 to 1736.
Boulton, Henry Crabb .	1753 to 1773. Died in Sept. 1773.
Boyd, John . . .	1753 to 1764.
Braddyll, Dodding .	1728 to 1748.
Baund, William . .	1745 to 1753.
Brisco, Robert . .	1712 to 1720.
Bristow, Robert . .	1716; 1717.
Browne, Capt. John .	1714 to 1720.
Browne, John . . .	1757 to 1763.

Names.	Period of Service as Director.
Bryant, Maj.-Gen. Sir Jeremiah (C.B.)	1841 to 1845. Died in June 1845.
Burgess, John Smith	1791 to 1802 (Bart. in 1801). Died in 1803.
Burrow, Christopher	1735 to 1761.
Burrow, Robert	1762 to 1764.
Burton, Richard	1741 to 1746.
CAMPBELL, ROBERT	1817 to 1852 (Bart. in 1832). Died in 1858.
Carnac, James Rivett	1827 to 1839 (Bart. in 1836). Appointed Governor of Bombay in 1839.
Caulfield, Maj.-Gen. James, C.B.	1848 to 1851. Died in Nov. 1852.
Chambers, Charles (senr.)	1755 to 1757; 1763 to 1768.
Chambers, Charles (junr.)	1770; 1773.
Chauncey, Richard	1737 to 1754.
Cheap, Thomas	1780 to 1793.
Child, Robert	1709 to 1720 (Alderman in 1714) (Knight in 1715).
Child, Francis	1718; 1722 (Alderman); 1732 (Lord Mayor); 1733 (Knight).
Clarke, William Stanley	1815 to 1843. Died in Jan. 1844.
Clerk, Robert	1812 to 1815. Died in Aug. 1815.
Cock, Peter	1725 to 1730.
Cockburn, Sir James (Bart.)	1767 to 1772.
Cooke, Richard	(Director of London Company) 1709 to 1711.
Colborne, Charles	1734 to 1737.
Colebrooke, Sir George (Bart.)	1767 to 1772.
Cooke, John	(Director of London Company) 1709 to 1734.
Cornelison, William Henry	1713 to 1715.
Cotesworth, William	Director of English Company) 1710 to 1713.
Cotesworth, Dr. Caleb	1721 to 1734.
Cotton, Joseph	1795 to 1823. Disqualified in 1823.
Cotton, John	1833 to 1853. Died in July 1860.
Coupland, John	1713.
Coulson, Thomas	(Director of English Company) 1709 to 1712.
Creed, Sir James (Bart.)	1749; 1755 to 1758; 1761.
Creswicke, Joseph	1765 to 1768.
Cruttenden, Edward Holden	1765 to 1771.
Cuming, George	1764 to 1782, and 1785 to 1788.
Currie, Sir Frederick (Bart.)	1854 to 1858. Died in Sept. 1875.
Cust, Peregrine	1767 to 1769.
Cutts, Charles	1749 to 1754; 1758 to 1766.
DANIEL, JAMES	1810 to 1824.

Names.	Period of Service as Director.
Darell, Lionel	1780 to 1803 (Bart. in 1800). Died in 1803.
Davis, Samuel . .	1810 to 1819. Died in July 1819.
Dawsonne, William .	(Director of English Company) 1710 to 1722.
Decker, Matthew . .	1714 to 1732 (Bart. in 1717).
Dempster, George . .	1769 ; 1772.
Dent, William . .	1851 to 1853. Died in Dec. 1877.
Dethick, Thomas . .	1772.
Devaynes, William . .	1770 to 1805 (1802, M.P., Barnstaple).
Dorrien, John . . .	1755 to 1763.
Drake, Roger . . .	1738 to 1758.
Drummond, John . .	1722 to 1733.
Ducane, Peter (senr.) .	1750 to 1753.
Ducane, Peter (junr.) .	1764 to 1773.
Dudley, George . .	1757 to 1767 ; 1770 and 1771.
Du Pré, Josias . .	1765 ; 1766.
Dutry, Sir Dennis (Bart.) .	1724 to 1727.
EASTWICK, CAPTAIN WILLIAM JOSEPH . . .	1849 to 1858.
Ecclestone, John . .	1721 to 1735.
Edmonstone, Neil Benjamin .	1820 to 1840.
Ellice, Russell . .	1832 to 1858.
Elphinstone, Hon. William Fullarton . . .	1791 to 1824.
Elwick, John . . .	1713 to 1720.
Emmerson, John . .	1735 to 1745.
Ewer, Walter . . .	1792 to 1795.
Eyles, Francis . . .	(Director of English Company) 1709.
Eyles, John . . .	1710 to 1713 ; and 1717 to 1720 (Bart. in 1717).
Eyles, Joseph . . .	1714 to 1716 ; and 1721.
FARQUHAR, SIR ROBERT TOWNSEND (Bart.) . . .	M.P., Hythe, 1826 to 1828.
Feake, Samuel . .	1733 to 1751.
Fergusson, Robert Cutlar .	1830 to 1834 (1832, M.P., Kirkcudbright).
Fitzhugh, Thomas . .	1787 to 1800. Died in 1800.
Fleet, Sir John (Knt.) .	(Director of London Company and Alderman) 1709 and 1711. Died in July 1712.
Fletcher, Henry . .	1769 to 1774 ; and 1777 to 1785 (Bart. in 1783.
Forbes, John . . .	(M.P., Malmesbury) 1831 to 1839.
Fonnereau, Abel . .	1749 to 1752.
Fonnereau, Zachary Philip .	1753 and 1754.
Fraser, Simon . . .	1793 to 1807.
Freeman, William George .	1769 ; and 1774 to 1781.
Fryer, Sir John, Bart. .	1719 (Alderman).

Names.	Period of Service as Director.
GALLOWAY, Maj.-Genl. ARCHIBALD, C.B.	1842 to 1849 (K.C.B. in 1849). Died in April 1850.
Gibbon, Edward . . .	(Director of London Company) 1709 to 1711.
Gildart, Richard . .	1759.
Gill, Leonard . . .	1724 to 1732.
Godfrey, Peter . . .	1710 to 1717 and 1734 to 1760.
Gosselin, William . .	1714 to 1743.
Gough, Richard . . .	(Director of English Company) 1713 to 1720 (Knight in 1715).
Gough, Capt. Harry (senr.) .	1730 to 1733 and 1736 to 1751.
Gough, Harry (junr.) . .	1735 to 1751.
Gough, Charles . . .	1749 to 1762.
Gould, John (senr.). . .	1710 to 1712 and 1715 to 1735.
Gould, Nathaniel . . .	(Director of English Company) 1714.
Gould, John (junr.). . .	1724 to 1735.
Grant, Charles . . .	1797 to 1823 (M.P., Inverness-shire in 1802). Died in November 1823.
Gregory, Robert . .	1769 to 1772 and 1775 to 1783.
HADLEY, HENRY . . .	1757 to 1765.
Hall, Richard . . .	1773 to 1789.
Hall, Urban	(Director of London Company) 1709.
Harrison, Sir Edmond (Knt.) .	(Director of English Company) 1710, 1711.
Harrison, Edward . . .	1718 to 1731.
Harrison, John . . .	1758 to 1771 and 1774 to 1782.
Harrison, Samuel . .	1759; 1761; and 1762.
Hawkesworth, John . .	1773.
Heath, Thomas . . .	1713 to 1715 and 1719 to 1721.
Heathcote, John . . .	1716 to 1724 and 1728 to 1731.
Heathcote, Henry . .	1725 to 1727.
Herne, Joseph . . .	1719 to 1722.
Herne, Frederick . . .	1709 to 1713.
Herne, Nathaniel . . .	(Director of London Company) 1710 to 1718.
Hewer, William . . .	(Director of London Company) 1709 to 1712.
Hodges, Joseph . . .	1714 to 1716 (Baronet in 1715).
Hodges, Sir William (Bart.) .	1712.
Hogg, James Weir . . .	(M.P., Beverley) 1839 to 1858 (1846, Baronet), (1850, M.P., Honiton). Died in May 1876.
Hope, John . . .	1738 to 1741 and 1744 to 1752.
Huddlestone, John . . .	1803 to 1826 (1805, M.P., Bridgewater). Disqualified in 1826.
Hudson, Capt. Robert . .	1721 to 1729; 1732 to 1734; and 1745 to 1748.
Hume, Alexander . . .	1737 to 1748.
Humphreys, Sir William (Knt.)	(Alderman) 1711 to 1714.
Hunter, John	1781 to 1802.

Names.	Period of Service as Director.
Hurlock, Joseph . . .	1768 ; and 1770 to 1773.
Hyde, Samuel	1734 to 1747.
IMPLY, MICHAEL . . .	1736 to 1757.
Inglis, Hugh	1784 to 1812 (Baronet in 1801) (M.P., Ashburton in 1802).
Inglis, John . . .	1803 to 1821.
Irwin, James . . .	1797 to 1800.
JACKSON, WILLIAM ADAIR .	1803 ; and 1804.
Jackson, John	1807 to 1820 (1808, M.P., Dover) (Baronet in 1815). Died in June 1820.
James, William . . .	1768 to 1786 (1779, Baronet).
Janssen, Abraham . .	1725 to 1728.
Jenkins, Richard . .	1833 to 1853 (M.P., Shrewsbury in 1837) (G.C.B. in 1839). Died 30th Dec. 1853.
KELSEY, HENRY . . .	1709 to 1712 ; and 1715 to 1727.
LASCELLES, HENRY .	1737 to 1745.
Lascelles, Peter . .	1770 to 1775.
Law, Stephen . . .	1746 to 1756.
Lethieullier, Benjamin .	1730 to 1733.
Lemesurier, Paul . .	(Alderman) 1784 to 1802 ; and 1805 (Lord Mayor in 1794). Died in 1806.
Lindsay, Honble. Hugh .	1814 to 1844 (1826, M.P., Forfar). Died in May 1844.
Linwood, Nicholas . .	1749 to 1754.
Loch, John . . .	1821 to 1853.
Lock, Sir John (Knt.) .	1733.
Loribond, Edward . .	1736 ; and 1737.
Lumsden, John . .	1817 ; and 1818. Died in Dec. 1818.
Lushington, Stephen .	1782 to 1802. (Bart. in 1792) ; (M.P. for Penrhyn in 1802). Died in 1807.
Lushington, James Law .	(M.P., Carlisle), 1827 to 1853; (C.B. in 1830) ; (1837, Major-Gen. and K.C.B.); (1847, G.C.B.) Died in 1859.
Lyall, George . . .	1830 to 1850; (1842, M.P., London). Disqualified in 1851.
Lyell, Henry . .	(Director of English Company), 1710 to 1730.
Lyell, Baltzar . .	1723 to 1740.
MABBOTT, CAPTAIN WILLIAM .	1741 to 1756.
Macnaghten, Elliot . .	1842 to 1858.
Mangles, Ross Donnelly .	(M.P., Guildford), 1847 to 1858. Died in Aug. 1877.

Names.	Period of Service as Director.
Manship, John . . .	1755 to 1758; 1762 to 1809. Disqualified in 1809.
Marjoribanks, Campbell . .	1807 to 1840. Died in Sept. 1840.
Marjoribanks, Dudley Coutts .	1853.
Martin, Matthew . .	1722 to 1729; and 1732 to 1740.
Masterman, John . . .	1824 to 1853; (1842, M.P., London).
Mathew, Sir George (Knt.) .	1710 to 1713.
Mead, Richard . . .	1709; and 1712.
Melville, Hon. William Henry Leslie	1845 to 1855.
Metcalfe, Thomas Theophilus .	1789 to 1812; (1802, M.P., Abingdon); (1803, Bart.) Died in 1813.
Michell, Robert . . .	1712 to 1718.
Michie, John	1770 to 1780; and 1783 to 1791.
Millett, George . . .	1806 to 1812.
Mills, William . . .	1778 to 1785. Disqualified in 1785.
Mills, Charles (senr.) . .	1778 to 1781; 1793 to 1815 (1802, M.P., Warwick). Disqualified in 1815.
Mills, Charles (junr.) . .	1823 to 1858 (Bart. in 1868). Died in 1872.
Moffat, James . . .	1774 to 1782; and 1787 to 1790.
Money, William . . .	1789 to 1797.
Money, William Taylor . .	(M.P., Wotton Basset), 1818 to 1825. Disqualified in 1826.
Moore, Arthur . . .	(Director of London Company) 1709.
Moore, Major James Arthur .	1850 to 1853. Died in July 1860.
Morris, John	1814 to 1837. Disqualified in 1838.
Motteux, John . . .	1769; and 1784 to 1787.
Muspratt, John Petty . .	1824 to 1853. Died in Aug. 1855.
NEWNHAM, NATHANIEL . .	1738 to 1758.
Nightingale, Robert .	1712 to 1722 (Bart. in 1715).
OLIPHANT, MAJOR JAMES .	1844 to 1856 (Lieut.-Col. in 1856). Died in June 1881.
Owen, Edward . . .	1722 to 1729.
PAGE, AMBROSE . . .	1714.
Page, Gregory (senr.) . .	(Director of London Company), 1709 to 1722; (Knt. in 1715).
Page, Gregory, junr. . .	1719 to 1722.
Page, John . . .	1730 to 1732.
Paggen, Captain Peter .	1709.
Pardoe, John	1765 to 1768.
Parry, Thomas . . .	1783 to 1806.
Parry, Edward . . .	1800 to 1826. Died in July 1827.
Parry, Richard . . .	1815 to 1816. Died in July 1817.
Pattison, James . . .	1806 to 1829. Disqualified in 1830.
Pattle, Thomas . . .	1787 to 1795.
Payne, John . . .	1741 to 1757.

Names.	Period of Service as Director.
Peach, Samuel . . .	1773 to 1784.
Peers, Sir Charles (Knt.) .	(Director of English Company and Alderman) 1712 to 1714.
Phipps, Thomas . .	1742 to 1758.
Pigou, Frederick . .	1758 to 1776.
Plaut, Henry . . .	1745 to 1758.
Plowden, Richard Chicheley .	1803 to 1829. Died in Feb. 1830.
Plowden, Wm. Henry Chicheley	1841 to 1853. Died in March 1880.
Pollock, Lieut.-Gen. Sir George, G.C.B. .	1854 to 1858. Died in Oct. 1872.
Pomeroy, William . .	1736 to 1744.
Prescott, Charles Elton .	1820 to 1832. Died in June 1832.
Prinsep, Henry Thoby .	1850 to 1858. Died in Feb. 1878.
Purling, John . . .	1763 to 1771 ; and 1777 to 1780.
RAIKES, GEORGE . .	1817 to 1836. Disqualified in 1836.
Ravenshaw, John Goldsborough	1819 to 1839. Died in June 1840.
Rawlinson, Lieut.-Col. Sir Henry Creswicke, K.C.B. .	1856 to 1858.
Raymond, Jones . .	1734 to 1757.
Raymond, John . .	1757 to 1760.
Reid, Thomas . . .	1805 to 1824. (Baronet in 1824.) Died in March 1824.
Rider, William . .	1738 to 1754.
Robarts, Abraham . .	1788 to 1814 (1802, M.P., Worcester.) Disqualified in 1815.
Roberts, John . . .	1764 to 1772 ; 1775 to 1778 ; 1784 to 1787 ; and 1790 to 1808.
Robertson, Major-Gen. Archibald	1841 and 1844 to 1847. Died in June 1847.
Robinson, George Abercrombie	1808 to 1829 (M.P., Honiton in 1813) (Baronet in 1825). Disqualified in 1829.
Rokeby, Benjamin . .	1720.
Rooke, Giles . . .	1758 to 1764.
Rous, William . .	1733 to 1741 (Knight and Alderman in 1738).
Rous, Thomas . . .	1745 to 1771.
Rous, Thomas Bates .	1773 to 1779.
Rumbold, Thomas . .	1772 to 1778.
SATTER, JOHN .	Alderman 1734 to 1744 ; (Knight in 1736) ; (Lord Mayor in 1740).
Saunders, Thomas . .	1757 ; and 1765 to 1767.
Savage, Charles . .	1725 to 1728 ; and 1731 (Disqualified for transferring part of his stock).
Savage, John . . .	1733.
Savage, Henry . .	1755 to 1762 ; 1765 to 1767 ; and 1770 to 1782.
Seawen, Sir William (Knt.) .	(Director of English Company) 1710 to 1711.

Names.	Period of Service as Director.
Scott, David	1793 to 1801; 1814 to 1819 (Baronet in 1819). Disqualified in 1820.
Scrafton, Luke	1765 to 1768.
Seward, Richard	1759 to 1763.
Shank, Henry	1831 to 1853.
Shepheard, Samuel (1)	(Director of English Company) 1709 to 1710.
Shepheard, Francis	1712 to 1714.
Shepheard, Samuel (2)	1717 to 1719.
Shepherd, John	1836 to 1858. Died in January 1859.
Smith, Richard	1759 to 1764.
Smith, Joshua	1771; 1772.
Smith, John	1773 to 1789.
Smith, Nathaniel	1774 to 1795.
Smith, Samuel	1783 to 1786.
Smith, George	1797 to 1832 (M.P., Midhurst in 1802). Disqualified in 1833.
Smith, Martin Tucker	1840 to 1858 (M.P., Wycombe in 1848). Died in October 1880.
Snell, William	1742 to 1764; 1767 to 1769.
Sparkes, Joseph	1773 to 1789.
Stables, John	1774 to 1781.
Steele, William	1742 to 1748.
Steevens, George	1757 to 1763.
Stephenson, John	1765 to 1768.
Stewart, Sir William (Knt.)	(Alderman) 1716 to 1719.
Stuart, James	(M.P., Huntingdon) 1826 to 1833. Died in April 1833.
Styleman, John	1716 to 1718.
Sulivan, Laurence	1755 to 1758; 1760 to 1764; 1769 to 1772; 1778 to 1781; 1783.
Sykes, Lieut.-Col. William Henry	1840 to 1858 (Colonel in 1857). Died in June 1872.
Tatem, George	1772 to 1784; 1788 to 1801.
Taylor, John Bladen	1810 to 1819.
Thellusson, George Woodford	1799 to 1807.
Theunemans, Simon	1720 to 1732.
Thompson, St. Quentin	1732 to 1736.
Thornhill, John	1816 to 1840. Died in February 1841.
Thornton, John	1749; 1750.
Thornton, William (1)	1759 to 1764.
Thornton, Robert	1790 to 1813 (1802, M.P., Colchester)
Thornton, William (2)	1800 to 1805.
Toone, Sweny	1800 to 1830. Disqualified in 1831.
Tourton, Nicholas	(Director of London Company) 1710 to 1712.
Townson, John	1785 to 1798.
Travers, John	1786 to 1809. Died in October 1809.
Trenchfield, Elihu	1723.
Tucker, Henry St. George	1826 to 1851. Died in June 1851.

Names.	Period of Service as Director.
Tullie, Timothy . . .	1750 to 1763.
Turner, Edward . . .	1717 ; 1718 ; and 1721 to 1723.
Turner, Whichcott . . .	1742 to 1755.
Twining, Richard . .	1810 to 1816. Disqualified in 1817.
VAN NECK, GERRARD . .	1729 to 1731.
Vansittart, Henry . . .	1769.
Verelst, Harry . . .	1771.
Vivian, Maj.-Gen. Sir John Hussey (K.C.B.) . .	1856 to 1858.
WALKER, JOHN . . .	1732.
Wallis, James . . .	1714 to 1716.
Walpole, Thomas . . .	1753 ; and 1754.
Walton, Bourchier . .	1759 to 1762.
Ward, John (Senr.). . .	(Alderman, and Director of English Company) 1709 to 1711 ; and 1718.
Ward, John (Junr.). . .	1712 to 1715 ; and 1718 to 1726.
Ward, Edward . . .	1762.
Warden, Francis . . .	1838 to 1851. Disqualified in 1851.
Warner, Richard . . .	1760 to 1763.
Waters, Thomas . . .	1759 to 1762.
Webber, William . . .	1762 to 1765.
Webster, Sir Thomas (Bart.) .	1715 ; 1716.
Webster, Sir Godfrey (Knt.) .	1717 to 1719.
Western, Maximilian .	1755 to 1757.
Wheler, Edward . .	1765 to 1777.
Whiteman, John Clarmont .	1844 to 1852. Died in Aug. 1866.
Wier, Daniel . . .	1768 to 1776.
Wigram, William . .	1809 to 1812 (1810, M.P., New Ross) ; 1815 to 1853 (M.P., Wexford, in 1825).
Wilberforce, William . .	1753 ; and 1754.
Wilkinson, Jacob . .	1782 to 1785.
Williams, Stephen . .	1791 to 1804. Died in 1805.
Williams, Robert . .	1809 to 1812. Died in July 1812.
Willock, Sir Henry (K.L.S.) .	1838 to 1858.
Willoughby, John Pollard .	1854 to 1858 (1857, M.P., Leominster). Died Sept. 1866.
Willy, William . . .	1746 to 1754.
Winter, Capt. James . .	1737 to 1754.
Withers, Sir William . .	1709.
Wombwell, George . .	1766 to 1768 ; and 1775 to 1783 (Bart. in 1780).
Woodhouse, John . .	1768 to 1781 ; and 1788 to 1791.
Wordsworth, Josias (Senr.) .	1712 to 1739.
Wordsworth, Josias (Junr.) .	1721 to 1736.
YOUNG, Sir WILLIAM (Bart.) .	1829 to 1846.

LIST OF

CHAIRMEN AND DEPUTY CHAIRMEN

OF THE

UNITED COMPANY OF MERCHANTS OF ENGLAND TRADING TO THE EAST INDIES.

1714 TO 1858.

[NOTE.—The Chairman and Deputy Chairman were first elected by the Directors permanently for a whole year in 1714. Previous to this date a Chairman was appointed on each occasion of a meeting of the Court. The salaries of the Chairman and Deputy Chairman in earlier years were under the Bye-laws £200 a year each. In 1794 they were increased to £500, and in 1854 to £1000 a year each.]

Years Elected.	Chairman.	Deputy Chairman.
1714	Sir Charles Peers (Knt.).	Robert Child (Alderman).
1715	Sir Robert Child (Knt.)	Josias Wordsworth.
1716	Sir Gregory Page (Bart.)	Henry Lyell.
1717	Josias Wordsworth.	Henry Lyell.
1718	Henry Lyell.	Sir Robert Nightingale (Bart.)
1719	Sir Robert Nightingale (Bart.)	William Dawsonne.
1720	William Dawsonne.	Sir Mathew Decker (Bart.)
1721	Henry Lyell.	Thomas Heath.
1722	Josias Wordsworth.	Joseph Herne.
1723	Josias Wordsworth.	Edward Harrison.
1724	Edward Harrison.	Abraham Addams.
1725	Sir Mathew Decker (Bart.)	Henry Lyell.
1726	Henry Lyell.	John Gould.
1727	John Gould.	Josias Wordsworth.
1728	Josias Wordsworth.	Edward Harrison.
1729	Edward Harrison.	Sir Mathew Decker (Bart.)
1730	Sir Mathew Decker (Bart.)	Josias Wordsworth.
1731	Sir Mathew Decker (Bart.)	Edward Harrison.
1732	Sir Mathew Decker (Bart.)	Josias Wordsworth.
1733	Josias Wordsworth.	John Gould.
1734	Josias Wordsworth.	Abraham Addams.
1735	Josias Wordsworth.	Sir William Billers (Knt. and Alderman).]

Years Elected.	Chairman.	Deputy Chairman.
1736	Sir William Billers (Knt.)	Harry Gough.
1737	Harry Gough.	Josias Wordsworth.
1738	Josias Wordsworth.	Sir William Rous (Knt. and Alderman).
1739	Sir William Rous (Knt.)	Samuel Feake.
1740	Samuel Feake.	Harry Gough.
1741	Harry Gough.	Sir John Salter (Knt. and Alderman).
1742	Sir John Salter (Knt.)	Harry Gough.
1743	Harry Gough.	Samuel Feake.
1744	Samuel Feake.	Dodding Braddyll.
1745	Dodding Braddyll.	Harry Gough.
1746	Harry Gough.	Samuel Feake.
1747	Harry Gough.	Richard Chauncey.
1748	Richard Chauncey.	Dodding Braddyll. (Died in Jan. 1748–9.)
1749	William Baker.	Richard Chauncey.
1750	Richard Chauncey.	Harry Gough.
1751	Roger Drake.	William Baker.
1752	William Baker.	Richard Chauncey.
1753	Richard Chauncey.	Roger Drake.
1754	Roger Drake.	Richard Chauncey.
1755	Roger Drake.	Peter Godfrey.
1756	Peter Godfrey.	John Payne.
1757	John Payne.	Laurence Sulivan.
1758	Laurence Sulivan.	Roger Drake.
1759	Peter Godfrey.	John Boyd.
1760	Laurence Sulivan.	Thomas Rous.
1761	Laurence Sulivan.	Thomas Rous.
1762	Thomas Rous.	John Dorrien.
1763	John Dorrien.	Laurence Sulivan.
1764	Thomas Rous.	Henry Crabb Boulton.
1765	Henry Crabb Boulton.	George Dudley.
1766	George Dudley.	Thomas Rous.
1767	Thomas Rous.	Thomas Saunders.
1768	Henry Crabb Boulton.	Sir George Colebrooke (Bart.)
1769	Sir George Colebrooke (Bart.)	Peregrine Cust.
1770	Sir George Colebrooke (Bart.)	John Purling.
1771	John Purling.	George Dudley.
1772	Sir George Colebrooke (Bart.)	Laurence Sulivan.
1773	Henry Crabb Boulton. (Died in October 1773.) Edward Wheler.	Edward Wheler. John Harrison.
1774	Edward Wheler.	John Harrison.
1775	John Harrison.	John Roberts.
1776	John Roberts.	William James.
1777	George Wombwell.	William Devaynes.
1778	George Wombwell.	William James.
1779	Sir William James (Bart.)	William Devaynes.
1780	William Devaynes.	Laurence Sulivan.

Years Elected.	Chairman.	Deputy Chairman.
1781	Laurence Sulivan.	Sir William James (Bart.)
1782	Robert Gregory.	Henry Fletcher.
1783	Sir Henry Fletcher (Bart.)	Nathaniel Smith.
1784	Nathaniel Smith.	William Devaynes.
1785	William Devaynes.	Nathaniel Smith.
1786	John Michie.	John Motteux.
1787	John Motteux.	Nathaniel Smith.
1788	Nathaniel Smith.	John Michie.
1789	William Devaynes.	Stephen Lushington.
1790	Stephen Lushington.	William Devaynes.
1791	John Smith Burges.	Francis Baring.
1792	Francis Baring.	John Smith Burges.
1793	William Devaynes.	Thomas Cheap.
1794	William Devaynes.	John Hunter.
1795	Sir Stephen Lushington (Bart).	David Scott.
1796	David Scott.	Hugh Inglis.
1797	Hugh Inglis.	Jacob Bosanquet.
1798	Jacob Bosanquet.	Sir Stephen Lushington (Bart.)
1799	Sir Stephen Lushington (Bart.)	Hugh Inglis.
1800	Hugh Inglis.	David Scott.
1801	David Scott.	Charles Mills.
1802	John Roberts.	Jacob Bosanquet.
1803	Jacob Bosanquet.	John Roberts.
1804	Hon. Wm. Fullarton Elphin-stone.	Charles Grant.
1805	Charles Grant.	George Smith.
1806	Hon. Wm. Fullarton Elphin-stone.	Edward Parry.
1807	Edward Parry.	Charles Grant.
1808	Edward Parry.	Charles Grant.
1809	Charles Grant, M.P.	William Astell, M.P.
1810	William Astell, M.P.	Jacob Bosanquet.
1811	Jacob Bosanquet.	Sir Hugh Inglis (Bart.)
1812	Jacob Bosanquet.	Sir Hugh Inglis (Bart.)
1813	Robert Thornton.	Hon. Wm. Fullarton Elphin-stone.
1814	Hon. Wm. Fullarton Elphin-stone.	John Inglis.
1815	Charles Grant, M.P.	Thomas Reid.
1816	Thomas Reid.	John Bebb.
1817	John Bebb.	James Pattison.
1818	James Pattison.	Campbell Marjoribanks.
1819	Campbell Marjoribanks.	George Abercrombie Robinson.
1820	George Abercrombie Robinson.	Thomas Reid.
1821	Thomas Reid.	James Pattison.
1822	James Pattison.	William Wigram.
1823	William Wigram, M.P.	William Astell, M.P.
1824	William Astell, M.P.	Campbell Marjoribanks.
1825	Campbell Marjoribanks.	Sir George Abercrombie Robinson (Bart.)

Years Elected.	Chairman.	Deputy Chairman.
1826	Sir George Abercrombie Robinson, (Bart.)	Hon. Hugh Lindsay, M.P.
1827	Hon. Hugh Lindsay, M.P. (Bart.)	James Pattison.
1828	William Astell, M.P.	John Loch.
1829	John Loch.	William Astell, M.P.
1830	William Astell, M.P.	Robert Campbell.
1831	Robert Campbell.	John Goldsborough Ravenshaw.
1832	John Goldsborough Ravenshaw.	Campbell Marjoribanks.
1833	Campbell Marjoribanks.	William Wigram.
1834	Henry St. George Tucker.	William Stanley Clarke.
1835	William Stanley Clarke.	James Rivett Carnac.
1836	Sir James Rivett Carnac, (Bart.)	John Loch.
1837	Sir James Rivett Carnac, (Bart.)	Major-Gen. Sir James Law Lushington, K.C.B.
1838	Major-Gen. Sir James Law Lushington, K.C.B.	Richard Jenkins, M.P.
1839	Sir Richard Jenkins, G.C.B., M.P.	William Butterworth Bayley.
1840	William Butterworth Bayley.	George Lyall.
1841	George Lyall.	Major-Gen. Sir James Law Lushington, G.C.B.
1842	Major-Gen. Sir James Law Lushington, G.C.B.	John Cotton.
1843	John Cotton.	John Shepherd.
1844	John Shepherd.	Sir Henry Willock, K.L.S.
1845	Sir Henry Willock, K.L.S.	James Weir Hogg, M.P.
1846	Sir James Weir Hogg, Bart., M.P.	Henry St. George Tucker.
1847	Henry St. George Tucker.	Lieut.-Gen. Sir James Law Lushington, G.C.B.
1848	Lieut.-Gen. Sir James Law Lushington, G.C.B.	Major-Gen. Archibald Galloway, C.B.
1849	Major-Gen. Sir Archibald Galloway, K.C.B.	John Shepherd.
1850	John Shepherd.	Sir James Weir Hogg, (Bart.), M.P.
1851	John Shepherd.	Sir James Weir Hogg, (Bart.), M.P.
1852	Sir James Weir Hogg, (Bart.), M.P.	Russell Ellice.
1853	Russell Elice.	Major James Oliphant.
1854	Major James Oliphant.	Elliot Macnaghten.
1855	Elliot Macnaghten.	Lieut.-Col. Wm. Henry Sykes.
1856	Colonel Wm. Henry Sykes.	Ross Donnelly Mangles, M.P.
1857	Ross Donnelly Mangles, M.P.	Sir Frederick Currie, (Bart.)
1858	Sir Frederick Currie, (Bart.)	Capt. Wm. Joseph Eastwick.

LIST

OF

PRESIDENTS OF THE BOARD OF CONTROL.

[The Board of Control was established by Law on the 13th August 1784, and abolished with the East India Company in 1858.]

Date of assuming charge of Office.	Names of Presidents of the Board of Control.
September 5, 1784 .	Right Hon. Henry Dundas (afterwards Viscount Melville).
April 25, 1801 .	Viscount Lewisham (afterwards Earl Dartmouth).
July 12, 1802 .	Viscount Castlereagh.
February 11, 1806 .	The Earl of Minto.
July 15, 1806 .	Right Hon. Thomas Grenville.
September 30, 1806 .	Right Hon. George Tierney.
April 4, 1807 .	Right Hon. Robert Dundas.
July 11, 1809 .	Earl of Harrowby.
November 7, 1809 .	Right Hon. Robert Dundas (afterwards Viscount Melville).
April 4, 1812 .	The Earl of Buckinghamshire.
June 4, 1816 .	Right Hon. George Canning.
January 12, 1821 .	Right Hon. Charles Bathurst.
February 5, 1822 .	Right Hon. Charles Watkins Williams Wynn.
February 4, 1828 .	Viscount Melville.
September 17, 1828 .	The Earl of Ellenborough.
November 22, 1830 .	Right Hon. Charles Grant (afterwards Lord Glenelg).
December 15, 1834 .	The Earl of Ellenborough.
April 23, 1835 .	Right Hon. Sir John Cam Hobhouse, Bart. (afterwards Lord Broughton).
September 4, 1841 .	The Earl of Ellenborough (became Governor-General of India).
October 23, 1841 .	Lord Fitzgerald and Vesey (died 11th May 1843).
May 17, 1843 .	The Earl of Ripon.
July 6, 1846 .	Lord Broughton.
February 5, 1852 .	Right Hon. Fox Maule.
February 27, 1852 .	Right Hon. John Charles Herries.
December 28, 1852 .	Right Hon. Sir Charles Wood, Bart. (afterwards Viscount Halifax).
February 28, 1855 .	Right Hon. Robert Vernon Smith.
February 26, 1858 .	The Earl of Ellenborough.
May 31, 1858 .	Lord Stanley (became First Secretary of State for India).

CHRONOLOGICAL LIST

OF

GOVERNORS OF THE MADRAS PRESIDENCY

FROM 1652 TO 1858,

When the Affairs of the East India Company were transferred to the Imperial Government.

Date of Arrival at Madras.	Date of Assuming Charge of Office.	Names.
...	1652	AARON BAKER. At first Agent for the settlement of Madras, which was under the jurisdiction of the Presidency of Bantam in Java, from its foundation in 1639 till it was created a Presidency in 1653.
...	1659	Sir THOMAS CHAMBERS.
...	1661	Sir EDWARD WINTER. Made over charge 22d Aug. 1668, and embarked for England 19th Jan. 1672.
June — 1665	Aug. 22, 1668	GEORGE FOXCRAFT. Three months after his arrival with a commission to supersede Sir E. Winter, Mr. Foxcraft was, on a charge of disloyalty, placed in confinement by Sir E. Winter, who resumed the Governorship and retained it until Mr. Foxcraft was released and reinstated by commissioners from England. Mr. Foxcraft made over charge in 1670, and embarked for England the same year.
———— 1668	1670	Sir WILLIAM LANGHORN, Bart. Made over charge 27th Jan. 1678, and embarked for England.
July 7, 1676	Jan. 27, 1678	STREYNSHAM MASTER. Made over charge 3d July 1681.
July 3, 1681	July 3, 1681	WILLIAM GYFFORD. By the East India Company's commission dated 14th Nov. 1681, received 17th July 1682. The Bengal Agency, hitherto attached to Madras, became a separate Government.

Date of Arrival at Madras.	Date of Assuming Charge of Office.	Names.
June 23, 1672	July 25, 1687	ELIHU YALE. Also Acting Governor in Mr. Gyfford's absence in Bengal, 8th Aug. 1684 to 26th Jan. 1685.
Mar. 19, 1684	Oct. 3, 1692	NATHANIEL HIGGINSON. Made over charge 7th July 1698, and embarked for England 25th Feb. 1700.
July 7, 1698	July 7, 1698	THOMAS PITT. Made over charge 18th Sept. 1709, and embarked for England 26th Oct. 1709.
Feb. 3, 1693	Sept. 18, 1709	GULSTON ADDISON. Died at Madras 17th Oct. 1709.
—	1684	Oct. 17, 1709 EDMUND MONTAGUE. Acting Governor; made over charge 3d Nov. 1709.
May 31, 1685	Nov. 3, 1709	WILLIAM FRASER. Acting Governor; made over charge and embarked for England 11th July 1711.
July 11, 1711	July 11, 1711	EDWARD HARRISON. Made over charge on 8th Jan. 1717, and embarked for England.
Aug. 28, 1716	Jan. 8, 1717	JOSEPH COLLET. Made over charge on 18th Jan. 1720, and embarked for England.
July 16, 1701	Jan. 18, 1720	FRANCIS HASTINGS. Acting Governor; made over charge and embarked for England 15th Oct. 1721.
Feb. 25, 1719	Oct. 15, 1721	NATHANIEL ELWICK. Made over charge 15th Jan. 1725, and embarked for England 17th Jan. 1725.
Aug. 30, 1724	Jan. 15, 1725	JAMES MACRAE. Made over charge 14th May 1730; embarked for England 21st Jan. 1731.
Dec. 26, 1724	May 14, 1730	GEORGE MORTON PITT. Made over charge 23d Jan. 1735, and embarked for England.
June 28, 1733	Jan. 23, 1735	RICHARD BENYON. Made over charge 17th Jan. 1744, and embarked for England.
June 25, 1718	Jan. 17, 1744	NICHOLAS MORSE. Taken prisoner on the capture of Fort St. George by the French in 1746. The Government devolved on Mr. Hinde, Deputy Governor of Fort St. David.
Aug. 22, 1713	Sept. 10, 1746	JOHN HINDE. Deputy Governor at Fort St. David, where he died on 14th April 1747, previous to receipt of Court's despatch, dated 24th Jan. 1747, creating Fort St. David the head settlement, and appointing him Governor and President.

Date of Arrival at Madras.	Date of Assuming Charge of Office.	Names.
May 23, 1730	April 16, 1747	CHARLES FLOYER. Dismissed from service under Court's despatch received 6th July 1750.
July 14, 1732.	Sept. 19, 1750	THOMAS SAUNDERS. Made over charge and embarked for England 14th Jan. 1755. (The seat of government was re-established at Fort St. George on 5th April 1752, four years after its restoration under the Treaty of Aix la Chapelle.)
July 26, 1737	Jan. 14, 1755	GEORGE PIGOTT. Made over charge and embarked for England 14th Nov. 1763. Became Lord Pigot (see below).
Oct. 2, 1761	Nov. 14, 1763	ROBERT PALK. Made over charge and embarked for England 25th Jan. 1767.
Dec. 30, 1741	Jan. 25, 1767	CHARLES BOURCHIER. Made over charge 31st Jan. 1770, and embarked for England 8th Feb. 1770.
June 10, 1752	Jan. 31, 1770	JOSIAS DU PRÉ. Made over charge and embarked for England 2d Feb. 1773.
July 12, 1768	Feb. 2, 1773	ALEXANDER WYNCH. Made over charge 11th Dec. 1775, and embarked for England 15th Feb. 1776.
Dec. 9, 1775	Dec. 11, 1775	Right Hon. Lord PIGOT. Governor for second time. Placed under arrest by order of Mr. Geo. Stratton and the majority of the Council, and detained at St. Thomas' Mount on 24th Aug. 1776; allowed to return to Garden House for change of air on 24th April 1777, and there died on 20th May 1777.
June 17, 1751	Aug. 23, 1776	GEORGE STRATTON. Suspended from service 31st Aug. 1777.
Aug. 3, 1752	Aug. 31, 1777	JOHN WHITEHILL. Acting Governor. Made over charge 8th Feb. 1778.
Feb. 8, 1778	Feb. 8, 1778	Sir THOMAS RUMBOLD, Bart. Was second in Council under Mr. Warren Hastings in Bengal. Made over charge, and embarked for England 6th April 1780.
(See above)	April 6, 1780	JOHN WHITEHILL. Acting Governor for second time, but suspended by order of the Governor-General of Bengal and his Council under sec. ix of the Regulations. Made over charge 8th Nov. 1780.

Date of Arrival at Madras.	Date of Assuming Charge of Office.	Names.
July 10, 1753	Nov. 8, 1780	CHARLES SMITH. Acting Governor. Made over charge 22d June 1781, and embarked for England.
June 22, 1781	June 22, 1781	Lord MACARTNEY, K.B. Embarked for the Northern Ports and Bengal 4th June 1785, and resigned 8th June by letter from Vizagapatam.
Sept. 8, 1760.	June 18, 1785	ALEXANDER DAVIDSON. Acting Governor. Made over charge 6th April 1786. Died in Madras 1791.
...	April 6, 1786	Major-Gen. Sir ARCHIBALD CAMPBELL, K.B. Made over charge, and embarked for England 7th Feb. 1789.
July 26, 1760	Feb. 7, 1789	JOHN HOLLAND. Acting Governor. Made over charge and embarked for England 13th Feb. 1790.
June 5, 1769	Feb. 13, 1790	EDWARD HOLLAND. Acting Governor. Made over charge 20th Feb. 1790.
Feb. 20, 1790	Feb. 20, 1790	Major-General WILLIAM MEDOWS. Made over charge and embarked for England 1st Aug. 1792.
Oct. 15, 1790	Aug. 1, 1792	Sir CHARLES OAKELEY, Bart. Date of arrival as writer in Madras 6th June 1767. Resigned Governorship 7th Sept. 1794, and embarked for England 29th Sept. 1794.
Sept. 7, 1794	Sept. 7, 1794	Lord HOBART. Made over charge and embarked for England 20th Feb. 1798.
Mar. — 1797	Feb. 21, 1798	Lieutenant-General GEORGE HARRIS. Commander-in-chief and Acting Governor. Made over charge 21st Aug. 1798.
Aug. 21, 1798	Aug. 21, 1798	Lord CLIVE (The Second). Made over charge 30th Aug. 1803, and embarked for England 12th Sept. 1803.
Aug. 30, 1803	Aug. 30, 1803	Lord WILLIAM CAVENDISH BENTINCK. Made over charge 11th Sept. 1807, and embarked for England 27th Sept. 1807. Died 17th June 1839.
Jan. 23, 1765	Sept. 11, 1807	WILLIAM PETRIE. Acting Governor. Made over charge 24th Dec. 1807. Died 27th Oct. 1816 at Prince of Wales Island.
Dec. 24, 1807	Dec. 24, 1807	Sir GEORGE HILARO BARLOW, Bart., K.C.B. Made over charge 21st May 1813, and embarked for England 26th Aug. 1813.

Date of Arrival at Madras.	Date of Assuming Charge of Office.	Names.
March 6, 1813	May 21, 1813	Lieutenant-General the Hon. JOHN ABERCROMBY. Commander-in-chief and Acting Governor. Made over charge 16th Sept. 1814, and embarked for England 20th Oct. 1814.
Sept. 16, 1814	Sept. 16, 1814	Right Hon. HUGH ELLIOT. Made over charge 10th June, and embarked for England 16th June 1820.
June 10, 1820	June 10, 1820	Major-General Sir THOMAS MUNRO, Bart., K.C.B. Died at Pattikonda, in the Kurnul district, 6th July 1827.
Feb. 3, 1798	July 10, 1827	HENRY SULLIVAN GRÆME. Acting Governor. Made over charge 18th Oct. 1827. Died 14th July 1850.
Oct. 18, 1827	Oct. 18, 1827	STEPHEN RUMBOLD LUSHINGTON. Made over charge and embarked for England 25th Oct. 1832.
Oct. 25, 1832	Oct. 25, 1832	Lieutenant-General Sir FREDERICK ADAM, K.C.B. Made over charge and embarked for England 4th March 1837.
Aug. 29, 1803	March 4, 1837	GEORGE EDWARD RUSSELL. Acting Governor. Made over charge 6th March 1837. Died 20th Oct. 1863.
March 6, 1837	March 6, 1837	Lord ELPHINSTONE, G.C.H. Made over charge 24th Sept. 1842, and left the Presidency on the 29th Sept. for Bangalore and Nilgiri Hills en route to Europe. Died 19th July 1860.
Sept. 24, 1842	Sept. 24, 1842	Lieutenant-General the Most Honourable the Marquis of TWEEDDALE, K.T. and C.B. Also Commander-in-chief. Made over charge and embarked for England 23d Feb. 1848. Died 10th Oct. 1876.
July 5, 1809	Feb. 23, 1848	Major-General HENRY DICKINSON. Acting Governor. Made over charge 7th April 1848.
April 7, 1848	April 7, 1848	Right Hon. Sir HENRY POTTINGER, Bart., G.C.B. Made over charge and embarked for England 24th April 1854. Died 18th March 1856.
Aug. 3, 1817	April 24, 1854	DANIELL ELIOTT. Acting Governor. Made over charge 28th April 1854. Died 30th Oct. 1872.
April 28, 1854	April 28, 1854	Lord HARRIS. Made over charge 28th March and embarked for England 31st March 1859. Died 23d November 1872.

CHRONOLOGICAL LIST

OF

COMMANDERS-IN-CHIEF IN THE MADRAS PRESIDENCY

FROM 1697 TO 1858,

When the Affairs of the East India Company were transferred to the Imperial Government.

[In the earlier years the Commissions of Governors also bore the title of Commanders-in-Chief.]

Date of Commission.	Date of Assuming Command.	Names.
Jan. 5, 1697	July 7, 1698	THOMAS PITT. Also Governor. Embarked for England 20th Oct. 1709.
Jan. 20, 1708	Sept. 18, 1709	GULSTON ADDISON. Also Governor. Died at Madras 17th Oct. 1709.
Dec. 22, 1710	July 11, 1711	EDWARD HARRISON. Also Governor. Embarked for England 8th Jan. 1717.
Dec. 19, 1719	Jan. 18, 1720	FRANCIS HASTINGS. Also Governor. Embarked for England 15th Oct. 1721.
April 14, 1721	Oct. 15, 1721	NATHANIEL ELWICK. Also Governor. Embarked for England 17th Jan. 1725.
Jan. 27, 1724	Jan. 15, 1725	JAMES MACRAE. Also Governor. Embarked for England 21st Jan. 1731.
Dec. 5, 1729	May 14, 1730	GEORGE MORTON PITT. Also Governor. Embarked for England 23d Jan. 1735.
Jan. 29, 1735	Jan. 23, 1735	RICHARD BENYON. Also Governor. Embarked for England 17th Jan. 1744.
July 24, 1747	Sept. 10, 1746	JOHN HINDE. Also Governor at Fort St. David, where he died 14th April 1747, previous to receipt of commission and the orders creating Fort St. David the head settlement, in consequence of the capture of Fort St. George by the French.

Date of Commission.	Date of Assuming Command.	Names.
Dec. 24, 1747	April 16, 1747	CHARLES FLOYER. Also Governor. Dismissed the service 6th July 1750.
Aug. 21, 1751	Sept. 19, 1750	THOMAS SAUNDERS. Also Governor. Embarked for England 14th Jan. 1755.
Feb. 15, 1754	Jan. 14, 1755	GEORGE PIGOT. Also Governor. Embarked for England 14th Nov. 1763. (See below.)
Nov. 14, 1764	...	Brigadier - General JOHN CAILLAND. Commander of the Forces on the Coromandel Coast.
Jan. 4, 1765	Nov. 14, 1763	ROBERT PALK. Also Governor. Embarked for England 25th Jan. 1767.
Jan. 12, 1768	Jan. 25, 1767	CHARLES BOURCHIER. Also Governor. Embarked for England 8th Feb. 1770.
Mar. 17, 1769	Jan. 31, 1770	JOSIAS DU PRÉ. Also Governor. Embarked for England 2d Feb. 1773.
April 12, 1774	Feb. 2, 1773	ALEXANDER WYNCH. Also Governor. Embarked for England 15th Feb. 1776.
April 12, 1774	...	Brigadier - General JOSEPH SMITH. Commander of the Forces on the Coromandel Coast.
April 4, 1775	Dec. 11, 1775	Right Hon. Lord PIGOT. Also Governor. Placed under arrest by the majority of his Council. Died 20th May 1777. (See under Governors.)
June 25, 1777	...	Major-General HECTOR MUNRO. Commander of the Forces on the Coromandel Coast.
Jan. 5, 1781	June 22, 1781	Lord MACARTNEY, K.B. Also Governor. Resigned 8th June 1785.
Nov. 24, 1784	June — 1785	Lieutenant-General Sir ROBERT SLOPER, K.B. Died 13th August 1802 at West Green, Hants.
Sept. 21, 1784	July 21, 1785	Lieutenant-General Sir JOHN DALLING, Bart., K.B. Commander of the Forces at Madras. Commission revoked 21st April 1786.
Sept. 7, 1785	April 6, 1786	Lieutenant-General Sir ARCHIBALD CAMPBELL, K.B. Also Governor. Embarked for England 7th Feb. 1789. Died March 1791 in London.
Nov. 25, 1789.	Feb. 20, 1790	Major-Gen. Sir WILLIAM MEDOWS, K.B. Also Governor. Was Commander-in-Chief in Bombay. Quitted command and embarked for England 1st Aug. 1792. Died 14th Nov. 1813 in England.

Date of Commission.	Date of Assuming Command.	Names.
June 3, 1790	Aug. 1, 1792	Sir CHARLES OAKELEY, Bart. Also Governor. Embarked for England 29th Sept. 1794.
Feb. 12, 1794	Sept. 7, 1794	Right Hon. Lord HOBART. Also Governor. Embarked for England 20th Feb. 1798.
May 1, 1795	Jan. 15, 1796	Major-Gen. Sir ALURED CLARKE, K.B. Commander of the Forces Madras. Governor of Bengal 6th Aug. 1796. Governor-General of Bengal and Commander-in-Chief of India 17th May 1798. Died Sept. 1832 in England.
Oct. 11, 1797	Mar. 27, 1797	Major-Gen. GEORGE (afterwards Lord) HARRIS, G.C.B. Commander of the Forces; also Governor 21st Feb. 1798. Quitted command 21st Aug. 1798. Died 31st May 1829 at Belmont, Kent.
Dec. 10, 1800	Aug. 1, 1801	Lieut.-Gen. JOHN STUART. Quitted command 17th Oct. 1804.
Mar. 16, 1803	Aug. 30, 1803	Lord WILLIAM CAVENDISH BENTINCK. Also Governor. Embarked for England 29th Sept. 1807. Died 17th June 1839.
May 7, 1804	Oct. 17, 1804	Major-Gen. Sir JOHN FRANCIS CRADOCK, G.C.B., K.H. (afterwards Lord HOWDEN). Commander of the Forces. Quitted command 17th Sept. 1807. Died July 1839 in England.
June 3, 1807	Sept. 17, 1807	Lieut.-Gen. Sir HAY M'DOWALL. Commander of the Forces. Quitted command 10th April 1810.
Jan. 6, 1807	April 10, 1810	Lieut.-Gen. Sir GEORGE HEWITT, G.C.B. Quitted command 27th Sept. 1810.
Mar. 23, 1810	Sept. 27, 1810	Major-Gen. Sir SAMUEL AUCHMUTY, G.C.B. Commander of the Forces. Governor and Commander-in-Chief 15th Oct. 1811. Quitted command 21st May 1813. Died 31st Aug. 1822 while in command at Dublin.
May 3, 1809	May 21, 1813	Lieut.-Gen. the Hon. JOHN ABERCROMBY, G.C.B. Also Governor. Was Commander-in-Chief at Bombay. Quitted command 25th May, and embarked 20th Oct. 1814. Died Feb. 1819 in England.
Dec. 21, 1813	May 25, 1814	Lieut.-Gen. Sir THOMAS HISLOP, G.C.B. Was Commander-in-Chief at Bombay. Captured on his voyage to

Date of Commission.	Date of Assuming Command.	Names.
		Madras. Governor and Commander-in-Chief, Fort St. George, 2d July 1817. Quitted command 15th June 1821. Died 3d May 1843 at Charlton, Kent.
Dec. 6, 1819	June 10. 1820	Major-Gen. Sir THOMAS MUNRO, Bart., K.C.B. Also Governor. Died at Pattikonda in Kurnul district 6th July 1827.
Feb. 12, 1821	June 15, 1821	Lieut.-Gen. Sir ALEXANDER CAMPBELL, Bart., K.C.B. Commander of the Forces. Died 11th December 1824.
Dec. 11, 1824	Dec. 11, 1824	General BOWSER. Assumed command as senior officer.
May 25, 1825	Mar. 3. 1826	Lieut.-Gen. Sir GEORGE TOWNSEND WALKER, Bart., G.C.B. Quitted command 11th May 1831. Died Governor of Chelsea Hospital 15th Nov. 1842.
Oct. 17, 1830	May 11, 1831	Lieut.-Gen. Sir ROBERT WILLIAM O'CALLAGHAN, G.C.B., K.C.H. Quitted command 11th Oct. 1836. Died 9th June 1840 in London.
April 17, 1836	Oct. 11, 1836	Lieut.-Gen. Sir PEREGRINE MAITLAND, K.C.B. Quitted command 21st Sept. 1838. Governor at the Cape of Good Hope 19th Dec. 1843. Died 30th May 1854 in London.
July 4, 1838	Dec. 21, 1838	Lieut.-Gen. Sir JASPER NICOLLS, K.C.B. Quitted command 7th Dec. 1839, and became Commander-in-Chief of India. Died 4th May 1849 at Goodrist, Reading.
Sept. 18, 1839	Aug. 1, 1840	Lieutenant-General Sir SAMUEL FORD WHITTINGHAM, K.C.B., K.C.H. Died 19th Jan. 1841 at Madras.
July 3, 1841	Jan. — 1841	Major-General Sir HUGH GOUGH (afterwards Lord GOUGH), G.C.B. Appointed temporarily, but did not assume command. Became Commander-in-chief of India 11th Aug. 1843. Died 2d March 1869 at Dublin.
Jan. 20, 1841	Jan. 20, 1841	Major-General Sir JAMES ALLEN, K.C.B. Temporary command. Died 17th Feb. 1853 at Cheltenham.
Feb. 11, 1841	Feb. 11, 1841	Major-General Sir ROBERT HENRY DICK, K.C.B., K.C.H. Temporary command. Killed at Sobraon 10th Feb. 1846.

Date of Commission.	Date of Assuming Command.	Names.
April 20, 1842	Sept. 20, 1842	Lieutenant-General the Marquis of TWEEDDALE, K.T., G.C.B., G.C.H. Also Governor. Embarked for England 23d Feb. 1848. Died 10th Oct. 1876.
Sept. 29, 1847	Mar. 13, 1848	Lieutenant-General Sir GEORGE HENRY FREDERICK BERKELEY, K.C.B. Quitted command 29th Sept. 1851. Died 12th Feb. 1863.
May 20, 1851	Sept. 29, 1851	Lieutenant-General Sir RICHARD ARMSTRONG, K.C.B., K.T., and S. Quitted command 27th Oct. 1853. Died 3d March 1854 on his voyage home on board the "Barham."
Sept. 7, 1853	Oct. 27, 1853	Lieutenant - General Sir WILLIAM STAVELEY, K.C.B. Died at Ootacamund 4th April 1854.
Sept. 23, 1854	Sept. 23, 1854	Lieutenant-General the Hon. GEORGE ANSON. Removed to Bengal. Commander-in-chief of India 23d Jan. 1856. Died of cholera 27th May 1857.
Jan. 23, 1856	Jan. 23, 1856	Major-General MARCUS BERESFORD. Temporary command. Died 16th March 1876 at Leamington.
April 24, 1856	June 10, 1856	Lieutenant - General Sir PATRICK GRANT, K.C.B.

LIST

CHIEF JUSTICES AND PUISNE JUDGES OF THE MADRAS PRESIDENCY.

FROM 1800 TO 1858.

[The Mayor's Court, which existed at Madras for many years, was abolished in 1797, and in its place was established a Recorder's Court, under Act 37 of George III., cap. 142. In 1800 a Supreme Court of Judicature was established, under 39 and 40 of George III., cap. 79, to consist of a Chief Justice and two Puisne Judges. Letters Patent granting a Charter of Justice were issued on the 26th December 1801.]

Date of Appointment.	Names.
	CHIEF JUSTICES.
Dec. 26, 1800	Sir THOMAS A. STRANGE, Knt. Resigned 4th June 1817.
Sept. 6, 1815	Sir JOHN H. NEWBOLT, Knt. Resigned 31st Aug. 1820. Died March 1823.
May 17, 1820	Sir EDMUND STANLEY, Knt. Resigned 28th Jan. 1825.
Jan. 28, 1825	Sir RALPH PALMER, Knt. Resigned 25th Oct. 1835 Died 25th Jan. 1838.
Dec. 31, 1831	Sir ROBERT BUCKLEY COMYN, Knt. Resigned 17th Jan. 1842. Died 23d May 1853.
May 22, 1842	Sir EDWARD J. GAMBIER, Knt. Resigned — June 1848. Died 31st May 1879.
April 15, 1850	Sir CHRISTOPHER RAWLINSON, Knt. Resigned 14th Feb. 1859.
Mar. 11, 1859	Sir HENRY DAVIDSON. Died at Ootacamund, 4th Nov. 1860.
	PUISNE JUDGES.
Dec. 26, 1800	Sir HENRY GWILLIM, Knt. Resigned 28th Oct. 1808. Died 12th Sept. 1837.
Dec. 26, 1800	Sir BENJAMIN SULLIVAN, Knt. Resigned 7th May 1809. Died — Nov. 1810.

Date of Appointment.	Names.
May 7, 1809	Sir FRANCIS M'NAUGHTEN, Knt. (Baronet in 1836). Removed to Bengal 3d July 1815. Resigned 2d March 1825. Died in 1876.
May 30, 1810	Sir JOHN H. NEWBOLT, Knt. Chief Justice 6th Sept. 1815.
July 3, 1815	Sir EDMUND STANLEY, Knt. Chief Justice 17th May 1820.
Sept. 6, 1815	Sir ANTHONY BULLER, Knight. Removed to Bengal 10th April 1816. Resigned 1st Jan. 1827. Died in June 1866.
April 15, 1817	Sir ANDREW GEORGE COOPER, Knt. Died 30th Aug. 1821.
May 17, 1820	Sir CHARLES E. GREY, Knt. Removed to Bengal 18th Aug. 1824. Chief Justice 29th June 1825. Resigned 2d July 1832. Died June 1865.
April 12, 1822	Sir WILLINGHAM FRANKLIN, Knt. Died May 1824.
Aug. 18, 1824	Sir RALPH PALMER, Knt. Chief Justice 28th Jan. 1825. Resigned 25th Oct. 1835.
Jan. 28, 1825	Sir ROBERT BUCKLEY COMYN, Knt. Chief Justice 31st Dec. 1831. Resigned 17th Jan. 1842.
Mar. 7, 1825	Sir GEORGE W. RICKETTS, Knt. Died at Sea 14th July 1832.
Nov. 28, 1836.	Sir EDWARD J. GAMBIER, Knt. Chief Justice 22d May 1842. Resigned June 1848. Died 31st May 1879.
April 5, 1842	Sir JOHN DAVID NORTON, Knt. Died at sea 24th Sept. 1843.
Aug. 29, 1844	Sir WILLIAM WESTBROOKE BURTON, Knt. Resigned 15th March 1857.
Mar. 16, 1857	Sir HENRY DAVIDSON, Knt. Chief Justice 11th March, 1859.
July 26, 1858	Sir ADAM BITTLESTON, Knt. Pensioned 3d April 1870.

RECORD OF SERVICES

OF

CIVIL SERVANTS IN THE MADRAS PRESIDENCY.

FROM THE YEAR 1740 TO THE YEAR 1858.

N.B.—See also Supplementary List, page 161, and Addendum, page 209.

ABERCROMBY, ROBERT.—1802: Writer; Acting Assistant to Secretary to the Special Commission. 1803: Assistant to the Collector of the Northern Division of Canara. 1805: Register of Canara. 1806: Register of the Zillah of the Southern Division of Canara. 1808: *At home.* 1809: *Resigned, 8th November, in England.* (*Annuitant,* 1836.) *Died, 6th July* 1855.

ADAMSON, WILLIAM DAVID.—1813: Writer. 1816: Second Assistant to Collector and Magistrate of Nellore. 1817: Register of the Zillah of Guntoor. 1819: Head Assistant to Collector and Magistrate of Guntoor. *Died, 5th June,* 1820, *at Guntoor.*

AGNEW, JOHN VANS.—1801: Writer. 1802: Assistant to Chief Secretary in Secret, Political, and Foreign Departments. 1803: Secretary and Accountant to the Commissioners of the Sinking Fund. 1804: *At home.* 1808: *Out of the service.*

ALCOCK, DAVID.—1766: Writer. 1771: Factor and Assistant at Masulipatam. 1774: Junior Merchant. *No trace after this date.*

ALEXANDER, ROBERT.—1790: Writer; Assistant to the Secretary to the Board of Revenue. 1791: Assistant at Vizagapatam. 1794: Assistant and Accountant under Mr. Chamier in the Vizianagram Zemindary. 1796: Assistant to the Collector in the Northern Division of Vizianagram. 1797: Assistant to the Resident at Ceylon. 1798: Assistant to the Collector in the Second Division of Vizagapatam District. 1800: Sub-Secretary to the_

*

Public Commercial and Revenue Departments; Collector in the First Division of the Vizagapatam Districts. 1803: Judge of the Zillah of Vizagapatam. 1806: Collector in the Zillah of Ganjam. 1808: Second Member of the Board of Revenue. 1812: Senior Member of the Board of Revenue. 1814: Member of Council and President of the Board of Revenue. 1818: *At home.* 1821: *Resigned, 21st December, in England.* (*Annuitant,* 1819.) *Died, 15th July* 1861.

ALEXANDER, JOSIAS DU PRE.—1796: Writer. 1798: Assistant under the Secretary to the Board of Trade. 1799: Deputy Commercial Resident at Colombo. 1801: Assistant to the Collector of Government Customs. 1803: *Leave to Bengal.* 1818: *At home. Out of the service in* 1820, *and elected a Director of the East India Company,* 16th *August* 1820. (*Annuitant,* 1822.) *Died,* 20th *August* 1839.

ALEXANDER, HENRY STEWART.—1854: Writer. 1856: Assistant to Collector and Magistrate, Coimbatore. 1857: Third Assistant to Accountant-General. 1858: *Proceeded on furlough ; died,* 6th *April, in England.*

ANDERSON, ROBERT.—1807: Writer. 1810: Assistant to Secretary in the Revenue and Judicial Department. 1811: Fixed Examiner in the Office of Register of the Sudder and Foujdarry Adawlut. 1813: Persian Translator to the Carnatic Commissioners. 1816: Assistant Register to the Sudder and Foujdarry Adawlut, and Deputy Persian Translator to Government. 1818: *At home.* 1821: *Resigned,* 28th *December, in England.* (*Annuitant,* 1843.) *Died,* 22d *March* 1843.

ANDERSON, WILLIAM BENSLEY. — 1815: Writer. 1818: Assistant to the Accountant-General. 1821: Register of the Provincial Court, Western Division. 1826: *At home on absentee allowance.* 1828: *Returned to India per "Lyndoch."* 1829: Sheriff of Madras, &c., and Acting Senior Deputy Register of the Sudder Court. 1830: Judge and Criminal Judge of Canara. 1832: Acting Judge of the Provincial Court, Western Division; Third Judge of the Provincial Court, Western Division. 1838: Second Judge of the Provincial Court, Western Division. 1842: *Resigned the service. Died,* 16th *July* 1863.

ANDERSON, FINDLAY.—1825: Writer. 1827: Assistant to the Principal Collector of Malabar. 1829: Head Assistant to the Principal Collector of Malabar. 1832: Additional Sub-Collector and Joint Magistrate of Canara. 1834: Sub-Collector and Joint

Magistrate of Canara. 1835: Acting Sub-Collector of Canara. 1836: Sub-Collector and Joint Magistrate of Canara. 1837: *At home on absentee allowance.* 1841: *Returned to India.* 1842: Judge and Criminal Judge, Canara. 1844: Civil and Sessions Judge, Mangalore. 1856: Civil and Sessions Judge, Calicut. 1857: *Resigned the service, 28th April. (Annuitant on Company's Fund.)*

ANDERSON, STUART MURRAY.—1851: Writer. 1853: *Proceeded on furlough ; Died, 9th December in England.*

ANDREWS, JOHN.—1768: Member of the Council of the Governor. 1774: *Out of the service.*

ANDREWS, ROBERT.—1778: Writer. 1790: Senior Merchant. 1791: Second in Council at Cuddalore. 1792: Collector in the Trichinopoly District. 1804: *At home.* 1808: *Returned to India.* 1810: Acting Judge of the Provincial Court of Appeal and Circuit for the Southern Division. 1813: Postmaster-General. 1815: First Judge of the Provincial Court of Appeal, Southern Division. *Died, 13th November 1821, at Trichinopoly.*

ANGELO, ANTHONY EDWARD.—1815: Writer. 1819: Assistant to the Collector of Madras. 1822: Assistant to the Collector of Sea Customs at Madras. 1825: *At home.* 1829: *Returned to India.* 1832: Assistant Judge and Joint Criminal Judge of Guntoor. 1834: Judge and Criminal Judge of Chicacole. 1836: Judge and Criminal Judge of Bellary ; Acting Judge and Criminal Judge of Cuddapah. 1837: Judge and Criminal Judge of Cuddapah ; Judge and Criminal Judge, Bellary. 1840: Judge and Criminal Judge, Chittoor. 1843: *Resigned the service, 1st January. Died, 28th July* 1855.

ANSTEY, THOMAS.—1789: Writer. 1790: Assistant under the Military Secretary. 1791: Assistant under the Secretary to the Board of Assumed Revenue. 1793: Assistant Commercial Resident at Ganjam. 1794: Assistant Export Warehouse-keeper. 1796: Deputy Commercial Resident at the Presidency. 1800: Head Assistant to the Collector of Salem. 1801: Malabar Translator to Government. 1802: Third Judge of Court of Circuit and Appeal, Southern Division. 1806: Commercial Resident at Tinnevelly. 1811: Commercial Resident at Ingeram. 1813: *At home.* 1815: *Resigned, 1st December, in England.*

ANSTEY, JOHN THOMAS.—1812: Writer. 1816: Assistant to the Magistrate of Guntoor. 1817: Head Assistant to the Collector of Guntoor. 1819: Head Assistant to the Collector and Magistrate of Bellary. 1821: *At home.* 1824: *Returned to India ;* Sub-

Collector and Assistant Magistrate of Ganjam. 1827: Collector and Magistrate of Rajahmundry. 1830: *At home. (Retired on the Annuity Fund in* 1839.)

ANSTRUTHER, Thomas Andrew.—1828: Writer. 1831: Second Assistant to Principal Collector and Magistrate of Southern Division of Arcot. 1832: Head Assistant to Principal Collector and Magistrate of Northern Division of Arcot; Acting Head Assistant to the Principal Collector and Magistrate of Madura. 1835: Acting Sub-Collector of Coimbatore. 1837: Sub-Collector and Joint Magistrate of the Southern Division of Arcot; Sub-Collector and Joint Magistrate of Coimbatore; Acting Assistant Judge and Joint Criminal Judge of Salem. 1838: Acting Judge and Criminal Judge of Madura. 1839: *At home on absentee allowance.* 1841: *Returned to India.* 1842: Judge and Criminal Judge, Rajahmundry. 1844: Civil and Sessions Judge, Honore. 1845: Civil and Sessions Judge, Rajahmundry. 1855: *On furlough.* 1856: *Resigned the service, 2d April in England. Died,* 14th April 1876.

ANTROBUS, Thomas.—1781: Writer. 1783: Assistant to the Secretary to the Select Committee; *Leave to China for health. Not traced after* 1784.

ARBUTHNOT, William Urquhart.—1825: Writer; Temporary Sub-Collector of Vizagapatam. 1827: Assistant to the Principal Collector of South Arcot. 1828: Head Assistant to the Principal Collector of South Arcot. 1833: Temporary Sub-Collector of Vizagapatam. 1836: Acting Judge and Criminal Judge of Chicacole. 1837: Acting Collector and Magistrate of Vizagapatam. 1838: Collector and Magistrate of Vizagapatam. 1840: Collector and Magistrate, Vizagapatam, and Agent to Governor. 1846: *Resigned the service,* 16th April. 1858: Member of Council of the Secretary of State for India. *Died,* 11th December 1874, *in England.*

ARBUTHNOT, Coutts Trotter.—1837: Writer. 1840: Assistant to Collector and Magistrate, Coimbatore. 1843: Head Assistant to Collector and Magistrate, Arcot. 1847: *On furlough.* 1850: *Returned to India.* 1852: Head Assistant to Collector and Magistrate, Nellore. 1853: *On furlough.* 1855: *Resigned the service,* 19th December.

ARDLEY, Samuel.—1749: Writer. 1768: Member of the Council of the Governor. 1774: *Out of the service.*

ASHTON, William.—1816: Writer. 1818: *At Home.* 1822: *Returned to India.* 1823: Assistant to the Collector and Magistrate of Masulipatam. 1824: *At home.* 1827: *Returned to India;* Subordinate Collector and Joint Magistrate of Tanjore. 1828: Deputy Collector of Sea Customs at Madras, and Acting Superintendent of Civil Pensions. 1830: Joint Magistrate on the Beach. 1832: Collector of Sea Customs at Madras; Member of the Marine Board. 1836: Acting Principal Collector and Magistrate of the Southern Division of Arcot. 1838: Collector and Magistrate, afterwards Principal Collector and Magistrate of the Southern Division of Arcot. 1842: Principal Collector and Magistrate, Cuddapah. 1845: *On furlough; resigned the service, 5th December.*

ATKINSON, EDWARD.—1783: Writer. 1785: Assistant to the Secretary of the Select Committee. 1786: Assistant to the Secretary in the Military Department. 1787: Clerk to the Court of Requests, and under the Secretary in the Secret Department. 1788: Secretary to the Hospital Board. 1789: Muster-Master of the Troops on the Guntoor Sircar. 1790: Muster-Master of the Troops with the Centre Army. 1791: Assistant to the Collector of Trichinopoly. 1793: *Out of employ.* 1794: Assistant under Mr. Gregory in the Vizianagram Zemindary. 1796: Commissary of Provisions, with Expedition under General Stewart. 1798: Commissary of Provisions at Colombo. 1800: *At home. Not traced after* 1808.

AUFRERE, THOMAS NORRIS.—1792: Writer. 1793: Assistant under the Accountant-General. 1794: Assistant under the Secretary to the Board of Revenue. 1796: Assistant under the Collector in the 4th Division of Masulipatam. 1799: *At home for health.* 1800: *Returned to India;* Assistant under the Collector of Ganjam. 1803: Judge of the Zillah of Salem. 1810: *At home.* 1814: *Out of the service.*

AYLMER, HENRY.—1773: Writer. 1780: Promoted to Factor. *Not traceable after this date.*

BABINGTON, JOHN.—1804: Writer. 1805: Assistant under the Secretary in the Revenue and Judicial Departments. 1807: Malabar Translator to Government; Assistant to the General Agent for the Salt Monopoly. 1810: Cashier to the Government Bank. 1815: Deputy Collector, afterwards Collector of Sea Customs at Malabar and Canara. 1823: Collector and Magistrate of Chingleput. 1824: Principal Collector and Magistrate of Canara. 1829: *At home on absentee allowance. (Retired on the Annuity Fund from 1st May 1833.)*

BABINGTON, BENJAMIN G.—1812: Writer. 1814: Assistant to the Secretary to the Board of Revenue. 1815: *At home.* 1817: *Returned to India;* Assistant to the Secretary to the Board of Revenue. 1819: *At home.* 1822: *Out of the service.*

BABINGTON, WILLIAM HENRY.—1821: Writer. 1824: Assistant to the Principal Collector and Magistrate of Canara. 1827: *At home on absentee allowance.* 1831: *Returned to India;* Sub-Collector and Joint Magistrate of the Northern Division of Arcot. 1834: Member of the Committee to Report upon the Export, Import, and Transit Duties of the three Presidencies. 1836: Sub-Collector and Joint Magistrate of Cuddapah. 1838: Placed temporarily under the Board of Revenue; Acting Principal Collector and Magistrate of Coimbatore. 1839: Sub-Collector and Joint Magistrate of Cuddapah; Sub-Collector and Joint Magistrate of Malabar. 1841: Judge and Criminal Judge, Madura. 1842: Third Judge of the Provincial Court of Appeal and Circuits, Centre Division. 1844: Civil and Session Judge, Cuddalore. 1849: *Resigned the service, 30th June, in India.* (*Annuitant on the Fund,* 1849.) *Died,* 17th September 1867.

BAINE, DUNCAN ANDREW.—1771: Writer. 1776: Factor. 1780: Junior Merchant. 1782: Senior Merchant. *No trace after this date.*

BAKER, CHARLES.—1783: Writer; Assistant in the Civil Department. 1785: One of the Company's Solicitors. 1791: Assistant to the Senior Member of the Board of Revenue in the Management of the Beetle Farm. 1792: Manager of the Company's Exclusive Privilege for Supplying Beetle Tobacco and Ganja. 1801: Collector of Revenue on the Sale of Arrack, Toddy, and other Spirituous Liquors. 1803: *At home.* 1807: *Out of the service.*

BAKER, JOSEPH.—1771: Writer. 1776: Factor and Assistant at Masulipatam. 1780: Junior Merchant; *In England; No trace after this date.*

BALFOUR, JAMES.—1793: Writer. 1796: Assistant under the Secretary in the Public Commercial and Revenue Department. 1797: Assistant under the Collector of Polygar Peishcush. 1799: *Out of employ.* 1800: Deputy Commercial Resident at the Presidency; *Suspended the service; Ordered to proceed home.* 1802: *Returned to India.* 1812: *At home.* 1815: *Out of the service.*

BALFOUR, JOHN.—1772: Writer. 1778: Factor. 1780:

Junior Merchant. 1790: Senior Merchant; *At home.* 1795: *Out of the service.*

BALFOUR, WALTER.—1777: Writer. 1782: Factor. 1790: Senior Merchant and Paymaster at Chingleput and Permacoil. 1792: Collector in the Southern Division of the Jaghir. 1800: Civil Paymaster-General. 1801: Collector of Government Customs. 1809: *At home.* 1811: *Out of the service.*

BALFOUR, WILLIAM.—1778: Writer. 1790: Senior Merchant. 1791: Secretary to Board of Revenue, and Agent for Clothing Troops. 1792: Member of the Board of Revenue. 1795: *Out of the service.*

BALMAIN, GEORGE.—1789: Writer. 1790: Assistant under the Secretary in the Military, Political, and Secret Departments. 1793: Assistant under the Collector of the Peishcush in the Southern Polygars. 1796: Collector in the Mannargoody Districts of the Tanjore Country. 1799: Collector at Peddapore, in the 1st Division of Masulipatam. 1803: *At home.* 1805: *Returned to India. Died, 16th January 1807, at Fort St. George.*

BANNERMAN, DAVID.—1815: Writer. 1818: Assistant to the Secretary to Government. 1819: Register of the Zillah of Masulipatam. 1821: *Leave to the Cape of Good Hope.* 1822: Register to the Zillah of Madura. 1824: Sub-Collector and Assistant Magistrate of Madura. 1826: *At home on absentee allowance.* 1829: *Returned to India, per "Brunswick."* 1830: Judge and Criminal Judge of Chicacole. *Died, 1st September 1832, at Guntoor.*

BANNERMAN, EDWARD.—1816: Writer. 1819: Second Assistant afterwards Head Assistant to Collector and Magistrate of Masulipatam. 1821: Head Assistant to Collector and Magistrate of Tinnevelly. 1825: Acting Deputy Persian Translator to Government. 1826: Assistant to the Chief Secretary to Government. 1828: Senior Deputy Register of the Sudder Court. 1830: Judge and Criminal Judge of Madura. 1833: Judge and Criminal Judge of Salem. 1835: *Out of employ.* 1836: Acting Judge and Criminal Judge of Cuddapah; Acting Judge and Criminal Judge of Salem. 1837: Judge and Criminal Judge of Salem. 1840: *Out of employ.* (*Retired on the Annuity Fund,* 1843.) 1844: *Died on his passage to England.*

BANNERMAN, ROBERT ALEXANDER.—1821: Writer. 1824: Assistant to the Principal Collector of Tanjore. 1826: Head Assistant to the Collector and Magistrate of Tinnevelly. 1828:

Junior Deputy Secretary to the Board of Revenue. 1830: Senior Deputy Secretary to the Board of Revenue. 1832: Secretary to the Commissioners for the Government of Mysore; Acting Secretary to the Board of Revenue; Joint Magistrate and Deputy Collector of Salem. 1834: *At home on absentee allowance.* 1837: *Returned to India, via Egypt.* 1838: Collector and Magistrate of Ganjam and Commissioner of Goomsoor. 1840: Agent to Governor, and Collector and Magistrate of Ganjam, and Commissioner of Goomsoor. 1849: *Resigned the service, 6th June.* (*Annuitant on the Fund,* 1849.) *Died, 29th June* 1851.

BARCLAY, ANDREW.—1796: Writer. 1799: Assistant in the Military Secret and Political Departments. 1800: Assistant to the Import Warehouse-Keeper; Head Assistant under the Collector of Dindigul. *Died, 29th March* 1801, *at Dindigul.*

BARCLAY, ROBERT.—1763: Writer. 1776: Senior Merchant and Paymaster at Chicacole. *No trace after this date.*

BARKER, WILLIAM.—1755: Writer. 1768: Senior Merchant and third in Council at Vizagapatam. 1771: *Out of the service.*

BARLOW, NATHANIEL.—1763: Writer. 1776: Senior Merchant. 1790: *Out of the service.*

BARNARD, THOMAS.—1765: Writer. 1776: Senior Merchant. 1790: *Out of the service.*

BARNETT, CHARLES JAMES.—1817: Writer. *Appointed but never joined the service; Resigned in England, 7th January* 1820.

BARRINGTON, FITZWILLIAM.—1771: Writer. 1776: Factor, and Assistant at Ganjam. 1780: Junior Merchant. 1782: *Out of the service.*

BASKERVILLE, HARRY.—*See* VIVEASH, HARRY.

BAYARD, ROBERT.—1807: Writer. 1808: Deputy Commercial Resident at Maddepollam; Assistant to the Register of the Zillah of Ganjam. 1811: Register of the Zillah of Ganjam. 1819: Sub-Collector in charge of the Hill Zemindaries in Ganjam. 1824: Collector and Magistrate of Vizagapatam. 1827: Collector and Magistrate of Ganjam. 1830: *At home on absentee allowance.* (*Annuitant on the Fund,* 1*st May* 1833.)

BAYLEY, EDWARD THOMAS.—1775: Writer. 1780: Factor. 1790: Senior Merchant and Assistant at Tanjore. *Died in* 1790.

BAYLEY, WILLIAM HENRY.—1831: Writer. 1834: Assistant to the Principal Collector and Magistrate of South Arcot. 1837: Acting Head Assistant to the Principal Collector and Magistrate of

South Arcot. 1838: Acting Head Assistant to the Principal Collector and Magistrate of Salem. 1839: Deputy Secretary to Government under the Chief Secretary's Department; Commissioner for Drawing Government Lotteries. 1843: Commissioner in Kurnool. 1844: *Proceeded on furlough.* 1848: *Returned to India.* 1849: Sub-Collector and Joint Magistrate of the North Division of Arcot. 1850: Secretary to the Board of Revenue; Tamil Translator to Government; Member of the College Board. 1851: Secretary to the Board of Revenue; Tamil Translator to Government; Member of the Mint Committee. 1855: Secretary to the Board of Revenue; Tamil Translator to Government; Member of the College Board; Third Member of the Board of Revenue. 1856: Third Member of the Board of Revenue; Member of Mint Committee; *Proceeded on furlough.* 1857: *Returned to India;* Third Member of the Board of Revenue; Member of Mint Committee. 1860: *Proceeded on furlough.* 1861: *Resigned the service,* 10th *June.* (*Annuitant on the Fund,* 1861.)

BAYNES, CHARLES ROBERT.—1828: Writer. 1831: Assistant to the Collector of Rajahmundry. 1832: Assistant in the Accountant-General's Office; Commissioner for Drawing Government Lotteries; Second Assistant in the Accountant-General's Office; Acting Head Assistant to the Accountant-General. 1834: Head Assistant in the Accountant-General's Office. 1835: Acting Sub-Collector of Nellore. 1836: Acting Sub-Collector and Joint Magistrate of Cuddapah. 1837: Acting Assistant Judge and Joint Criminal Judge of Chingleput. 1838: Assistant Judge and Joint Criminal Judge of Chingleput. 1842: *Proceeded on furlough.* 1844: *Returned to India.* 1845: Subordinate Judge, Calicut. 1846: Assistant Judge, Calicut. 1847: Civil and Session Judge, Madura. 1856: *Proceeded on furlough.* 1857: *Returned to India;* Civil and Session Judge, Madura. 1858: Puisne Judge of the Sudder Dewannee and Sudder Foujdarry Adawlut. 1859: *Resigned the service in January.* (*Annuitant on the Fund,* 1859.)

BEAUCHAMP, GEORGE THOMAS.—1830: Writer. 1833: Assistant under Principal Collector, Nellore; Assistant to Principal Collector, North Arcot. 1834: Second Assistant to the Accountant-General, and Commissioner for Government Lotteries. 1836: Register of the Provincial Court, Northern Division. 1838: Acting Assistant Judge and Joint Criminal Judge, Rajahmundry; Acting Head Assistant to the Accountant General; and Commissioner for Government Lotteries. 1840: Acting Assistant Judge and Joint Criminal Judge, Guntoor. 1843 : Acting Assistant Judge and Joint Criminal Judge, Trichinopoly ; Extra Assistant to Collector, and Magistrate at Trichinopoly ; Acting Sub-Judge, and afterwards Civil and Sessions Judge, Combaconum. 1844 : Sub-Judge at Combaconum. 1845 : Acting Civil and Sessions Judge at Combaconum. 1849 : Register to the Court of Sudder and Foujdaree Adawlut. 1851 : Member of the College Board. 1852 : Acting, afterwards Civil and Sessions Judge, Tinnevelly. 1855 : Civil and Sessions Judge, Combaconum. 1859 : Officiating Assistant Judge of the Sudder and Foujdaree Adawlut. 1861 : Officiating Puisne Judge of same Court. 1862 : *Resigned the service, 1st May.* (*Annuitant on the Fund*, 1862.)

BELL, WILLIAM.—1807 : Writer. 1808 : Assistant to the Chief Secretary in the Secret, Political, and Foreign Departments. 1810 : Assistant to the Collector of Salem ; Assistant to the Collector of Coimbatore. 1811 : Persian Translator to the Carnatic Commissioners. 1812 : *At home.* 1814 : *Returned to India ;* Head Assistant to the Collector of Trichinopoly. 1816 : Head Assistant to the Collector of Chingleput ; Assistant to the Magistrate of Chingleput. *Died 30th July* 1817, *at St. Thomas's Mount.*

BELL, JAMES HAMILTON.—1829 : Writer. 1832 : *At home on absentee allowance.* 1834 : *Returned to India, per "Duke of Buccleuch."* 1835 : Assistant to the Collector and Magistrate of Rajahmundry. 1836 : Acting Head Assistant to the Collector and Magistrate of Guntoor ; Head Assistant to the Collector and Magistrate of Rajahmundry. 1837 : Charge of the Zillah of Rajahmundry. 1838 : Acting Deputy Collector of Sea Customs at Madras ; Commissioner for Drawing Government Lotteries. 1840 : Assistant Judge and Joint Criminal Judge, Malabar. 1842 : Assistant Judge and Joint Criminal Judge, Chingleput. 1844 : Subordinate Judge, Chittoor. 1850 : Civil and Sessions Judge, Guntoor. *Died at Guntoor, in India, 25th August* 1851.

BENFIELD, PAUL.—1765 : Writer. 1776 : Senior Merchant. *Recalled,* 1776. *Suspended,* 1790. 1792 : *Out of the service.*

BIGSBY, THOMAS.—1797 : Writer. 1798 : Assistant in the Military, Secret, and Political Departments. *Died at sea in* 1798.

BINNING, ROBERT BLAIR MONRO.—1833 : Writer. 1835 : Assistant to the Collector and Magistrate of Masulipatam. 1837 : Acting Head Assistant to the Collector and Magistrate of Rajahmundry. 1839 : *At home on absentee allowance.* 1842 : *Returned to India.* 1843 : Assistant, afterwards Head Assistant, to Collector and

Magistrate, Northern Division of Arcot. 1850 : Sub-Collector and Joint Magistrate, Northern Division of Arcot. 1856 : *Proceeded on furlough.* 1861 : *Resigned the service in England.* (*Annuitant on the Fund,* 1860.) *Died in England.*

BINNY, EDWARD DYER.—1852 : Writer. 1855 : Assistant to Collector and Magistrate, Canara. 1858 : Head Assistant to Collector and Magistrate, Canara. 1860 : *Proceeded on furlough; Died,* 13*th January, at Cheltenham.*

BIRCH, RICHARD.—1779 : Writer. 1782 : *Out of the service.*

BIRCH, SYLVESTER DOUGLAS.—1830 : Writer. 1833 : Doing duty under the Collector of Chingleput. 1834 : Assistant to Collector and Magistrate, Chingleput. 1835 : Assistant to Principal Collector and Magistrate, Tanjore. 1838 : Acting Cashier at Government Bank, and Assistant to Sub-Treasurer. 1839 : Cashier at Government Bank, and Assistant to Sub-Treasurer. 1841 : Commissioner for Government Lotteries, and Acting Sub-Treasurer and Superintendent and Treasurer of Government Bank. 1843 : Secretary and Treasurer of the Bank of Madras. 1845 : Acting Sub-Treasurer, Director of the Bank of Madras, and Acting Member and Secretary to the Mint Committee. 1847 : Head and Special Assistant to the Accountant-General. 1848 : Sub-Collector and Joint Magistrate, North Arcot. 1849 : Sub-Treasurer and Member of the Mint Committee ; and Director of the Incorporated Bank of Madras. 1859 : Accountant-General at Bombay ; President of the Mint Committee ; and Government Director of the Bank of Bombay. 1865 : *Resigned the service,* 28*th February.* (*Annuitant on the Fund,* 1865.) *Died* 4*th February* 1881, *in England.*

BIRD, JOHN.—1801 : Writer. 1805 : Assistant under the Principal Collector of Tanjore. 1806 : Assistant under the Principal Collector of the Ceded Districts ; Register of the Zillah of the Western Division of Ceded Districts. 1814 : Secretary to the Board of Trade and Reporter of External Commerce ; Assistant Judge of Zillah of Coimbatore. 1815 : Judge and Magistrate of the Zillah of Canara. 1816 : Judge and Criminal Judge of Zillah of Salem. 1824 : Third Judge of Provincial Court in the Southern Division. 1828 : Second Judge of Provincial Court in the Southern Division. 1830 : First Judge of Provincial Court in the Southern Division. 1831 : Acting Third Puisne Judge of the Sudder and Foujdarry Adawlut. 1832 : Second Puisne Judge of the Sudder and Foujdarry Adawlut. 1838 : First Puisne Judge of the Sudder and Foujdarry Adawlut, and Provincial Member of Council. 1842 :

Member of Council, and Chief Judge of the Sudder Dewannee and Sudder Foujdarry Adawlut. 1845: *Resigned the service, 30th June, in India.* (*Annuitant on the Fund*, 1845.) *Died, in* 1850, *at Cheltenham.*

BIRD, CHARLES.—1806: Writer. 1809: Register to the Zillah of Bareilly. 1812: Register to the Zillah of Cuddapah. 1815: Register to the Zillah of Vizagapatam. 1818: Head Assistant to the Collector, and Assistant Magistrate, of Ganjam. *Died,* 23*d August* 1819, *near Ganjam.*

BIRD, GEORGE.—1821: Writer. 1824: Employed at Dharwar under the Bombay Government. 1829: *At home on absentee allowance.* 1832: *Returned to India;* Sub-Collector and Joint Magistrate of Bellary. 1833: Acting Assistant Judge of Chingleput. 1834: Assistant Judge of Guntoor; Judge and Criminal Judge of Combaconum. 1835: Judge and Criminal Judge of Canara. 1838: Acting Judge of the Provincial Court, Western Division. 1839: Judge and Criminal Judge of Canara. 1842: Third Judge, afterwards Second Judge, of the Provincial Court of Appeal and Circuit, West Division. 1844: Civil and Session Judge, Coimbatore. 1847: *Proceeded on furlough.* 1849: *Returned to India.* 1850: Civil and Session Judge, Coimbatore; *Proceeded on furlough.* 1851: *Resigned the service, 25th February, in India. Died, 20th July* 1880, *in England.*

BIRD, CHARLES JAMES.—1830: Writer. 1832: Assistant to the Commissioners for the Government of Mysore. 1833: Assistant to Principal Collector of North Arcot. 1835: Head Assistant to the Collector and Magistrate of Tinnevelly. 1836: Acting Joint Criminal Judge at Madura. 1838: Sub-Collector and Joint Magistrate of Tinnevelly. 1839: Sub-Collector and Magistrate of Tinnevelly. 1842: *Proceeded on Furlough.* 1844: *Returned to India.* 1845': Sub-Collector and Magistrate of Coimbatore. 1850: Collector and Magistrate of Southern Division of Arcot. 1851: Collector and Magistrate of Tinnevelly. 1856: *Proceeded on Furlough.* 1859: *Resigned the service, 8th February.* (*Annuitant on the Fund,* 1860.) *Died, 21st April* 1879, *in England.*

BIRD, JOHN.—1830: Writer. 1832: Second Assistant to the Collector and Magistrate of Chingleput. 1835: Head Assistant to the Collector and Magistrate of Chingleput. 1838: Acting Sub-Collector and Joint Magistrate of Nellore; Acting Sub-Collector and Joint Magistrate of Coimbatore; Sub-Collector and Joint Magistrate of Coimbatore. 1839: Sub-Collector and Magistrate of

Coimbatore. 1845 : *Proceeded on furlough.* 1848 : *Returned to India ;* Sub-Collector and Joint Magistrate, Tanjore. 1851 : Collector and Magistrate, Trichinopoly. 1860 : *Resigned the service 30th April, in India. (Annuitant on the Fund,* 1860.) *Died, 16th April* 1877, *in England.*

BISHOP, JOHN FITZ-SIMMONS.—1827 : Writer. 1829 : Assistant to the Collector of Trichinopoly. 1830 : Head Assistant to the Collector of Trichinopoly. 1831 : Head Assistant to the Collector of Tinnevelly. 1832 : Acting Head Assistant to Principal Collector and Magistrate of Coimbatore. 1835 : Sub-Collector and Joint Magistrate of Tinnevelly. 1838 : *At home on absentee allowance.* 1841 : *Returned to India.* 1842 : *Out of employ.* 1843 : Sub-Collector and Joint Magistrate, Tanjore. 1845 : Collector and Magistrate, Nellore. 1847 : Collector and Magistrate, Tanjore. 1854: *Proceeded on furlough.* 1856 : *Resigned the service,* 13*th November, in England. (Annuitant on the Fund,* 1858.)

BLACKBURN, JOHN.—1815 : Writer. 1818 : Second Assistant to the Collector and Magistrate of Tanjore. 1823 : Assistant to the Principal Collector and Magistrate, and Head Assistant to Principal Collector, Tanjore. 1826 : *At home on absentee allowance.* 1830 : *Returned to India.* 1831 : Acting Resident at Tanjore. 1832 : Acting Collector and Magistrate, afterwards Collector and Magistrate of Tinnevelly ; Collector and Magistrate of Guntoor. 1834 : Principal Collector and Magistrate of Madura. 1847 : *Resigned the service. (Annuitant on the Fund,* 1847.) *Died,* 17*th June* 1850, *Sloane Street, Chelsea.*

BLACKETT, ROBERT STEWART.—1848 : Writer. 1852 : *Name removed in England.*

BLAIR, WILLIAM THOMAS.—1808 : Writer. 1811 : Assistant to the Accountant-General. 1814 : Deputy Accountant-General in the Military Department. 1817 : *At home.* 1818 : *Returned to India ;* Assistant to the Accountant-General. 1819 : Sheriff of Madras. 1822 : Deputy Accountant-General in the Military Department of Accounts. 1826 : *At home on absentee allowance. (Retired on the Civil Service Annuity Fund from* 1*st January* 1828.)

BLAIR, HENRY MARTIN.—1818 : Writer. 1823 : Assistant to the Collector and Magistrate of Chingleput. 1825 : Register of the Zillah of Canara. 1826: Head Assistant to the Principal Collector and Magistrate of Malabar. 1829: *At home on absentee allowance.* 1831 : *Returned to India, " La Belle Alliance."* 1832 : Acting Secretary to the College of Public Instruction ; Collector and Magistrate of

Trichinopoly.   1838: Acting Principal Collector and Magistrate of Canara.   1839: Principal Collector and Magistrate of Canara.   1846: *Proceeded on furlough.*   1847: *Resigned the service. (Annuitant on the Fund,* 1847.)   *Died,* 16*th October* 1880.

BLAKE, ARTHUR GARLAND.—1796: Writer.   1799: Assistant in the Public Department at Colombo.   1800: Assistant to the Collector at Guntoor; Assistant under the Collector at Chicacole.   1802: Register to the Judge of the Zillah of Guntoor.   1803: Register to the Judge of the Provincial Court, Northern Division.   1806: *At home.*   1808: *Returned to India.*   1809: Assistant Judge at Masulipatam.   1812: Collector of Rajahmundry.   *Died,* 30*th November* 1812, *at Rajahmundry.*

BLAKE, EDWARD PARKER.—1797: Writer.   1799: Assistant under the Commercial Resident at Cuddalore.   1800: Assistant under the Commercial Resident at Maddepollam.   1802: Deputy Commercial Resident in the Ceded District.   1804: *Out of employ.*   1805: Register of the Zillah of Guntoor.   1808: *Out of employ.*   1809: Assistant Judge at Combaconum.   1811: Collector of Sea Customs at Malabar and Canara.   1816: *At home.*   1821: *Out of the service.*

BLANE, THOMAS LAW.—1826: Writer.   1828: Assistant to the Collector of Chingleput.   1830: Acting Head Assistant to the Collector of Tanjore; Head Assistant to the Principal Collector of Tanjore.   1832: Additional Sub-Collector and Joint Magistrate of Tanjore.   1835: Sub-Collector and Joint Magistrate of Bellary.   1837: Charge of Office of Principal Collector and Magistrate of Cuddapah.   1838: Acting Collector and Magistrate of Masulipatam; Acting Collector and Magistrate, afterwards Collector and Magistrate of Cuddapah.   1842: Collector and Magistrate of Southern Division, Arcot.   1843: *Proceeded on furlough.*   1845: *Returned to India.*   1846: Principal Collector and Magistrate, Canara.   1851: Third Member of Board of Revenue.   1854: *Resigned the service,* 1*st May. (Annuitant on the Fund,* 1854.)

BLANSHARD, JOHN.—1830: Writer.   1833: Placed under the Principal Collector of North Arcot.   *Died,* 6*th September* 1833, *at Chittoor.*

BOILEAU, JOHN PETER.—1765: Writer.   1776: Senior Merchant and Paymaster at Ishapore.   1790: *Out of the service.*

BOILEAU, THOMAS EBENEZER JOHN.—1815: Writer.   1818: Assistant Register of Provincial Court, Southern Division, and Acting Register.   1819: Acting Register of the Zillah of Trichinopoly. 1820: Acting Register of the Zillah of Salem. 1821: Register of the Zillah of Chingleput. 1824: Acting Judge of Chingleput. 1827: Assistant Judge and Joint Criminal Judge of the Zillah of Canara. 1832: Judge and Criminal Judge of Bellary. 1833: Acting Third Judge of Centre Circuit Provincial Court. 1835: Acting Third Judge of Northern Circuit Provincial Court. 1836: Third Judge of Northern Circuit Provincial Court, and Acting Second Judge. 1838: Third Judge of Western Circuit Provincial Court. 1841: Second Judge of the Provincial Court of Appeal and Circuit, Northern Division. 1842: First Judge of the Provincial Court of Appeal and Circuit, Northern Division. 1844: Civil and Session Judge, Masulipatam. 1846: Third Judge of the Court of Sudder Dewannee and Sudder Foujdarry Adawlut. 1847: Civil and Session Judge, Chingleput. 1848: *Proceeded on furlough.* 1850: *Returned to India.* 1851: Civil and Sessions Judge, Guntoor; *Resigned the service, 15th April, in India.*

BOLDERO, CHARLES.—1777: Writer. 1782: Factor. 1790: *Out of the service.*

BOURCHIER, CHARLES.—1741: Writer. 1768: Became Governor of the Madras Presidency. *Out of the service prior to* 1771.

BOURCHIER, JAMES.—1751: Writer. 1768: Member of the Council of the Governor. 1771: *Out of the service.*

✶ **BOURDILLON**, JAMES DEWAR.—1829: Writer. 1831: Second Assistant to the Collector of Trichinopoly. 1833: Head Assistant to the Collector of Trichinopoly. 1835: Acting Assistant Judge of Salem. 1836: Head Assistant to the Collector and Magistrate of Trichinopoly. 1837: Acting Sub-Collector and Joint Magistrate of Nellore. 1838: Sub-Collector and Joint Magistrate of Northern Division of Arcot. 1843: Secretary to the Board of Revenue. 1845: *Proceeded on furlough.* 1848: *Returned to India;* Sub-Collector and Joint Magistrate, Nellore. 1849: Collector and Magistrate of the Northern Division of Arcot. 1855: Third Member of the Board of Revenue; Secretary to Government Revenue and Judicial Departments. 1857: *Proceeded on furlough.* 1859: *Returned to India;* Secretary to Government Revenue Department. 1860: Secretary to Government Revenue and Public Works Departments. 1861: *Resigned the service in England.* (*Annuitant on the Fund,* 1860.)

BOUTFLOWER, SAMUEL.—1796: Writer. 1798: Assistant under the Collector in the First Division of Vizagapatam District. 1802: *At home.* 1804: *Returned to India;* Register to the

Zillah Judge of Ganjam. 1806: Register to the Zillah Judge of Vizagapatam. 1810: Assistant Judge at Canara. 1812: *Out of employ.* 1823: *Out of the service.*

BRANFILL, Benjamin.—1781: Writer. 1783: Assistant to the Secretary to the Select Committee; Assistant to the Secretary to the Committee of Circuit. 1789: *Out of employ.* 1790: Sheriff; Land Customer Deputy Commissary-General and Register of the Choultry Court. 1791: Assistant to the Collector of Nellore. 1793: Second Member of the Committee of Investigation at Nuzeed. 1794: Superintendent of the Nuzeed Zemindary; Collector in the Third Division of Masulipatam District. 1802: *Out of employ.* 1804: *At home.* 1807: *Out of the service.*

BREEKS, Richard.—1848: Writer. *Died, at Trichinopoly, 19th February* 1852.

BRETT, Harry Augustus.—1831: Writer. 1832: Assistant in Chief Secretary's Office. 1833: Assistant to Principal Collector, Madura. 1834: Assistant to Principal Collector and Magistrate, North Arcot. 1836: Acting Register of the Zillah Court of Salem; and Acting Register of the Provincial Court, Centre Division. 1837: Register of the Provincial Court, Centre Division. 1839: Register of the Zillah Court of Bellary; Acting Head Assistant to the Collector and Magistrate, Chingleput, and to the Principal Collector and Magistrate, Salem. 1840: Assistant to the Principal Collector and Magistrate, Salem. 1842: Acting Sub-Collector and Joint Magistrate, Salem. 1843: Sub-Collector and Joint Magistrate, Salem. 1844: In charge of the Salem Sub-Court. 1846: *Proceeded on furlough.* 1849: Acting Sub-Collector and Joint Magistrate, Madura; Acting, afterwards Sub-Judge, Chittoor. 1852: Acting Collector and Magistrate, North Arcot. 1853: Acting Collector and Magistrate, and afterwards Collector and Magistrate, Salem. 1858: *On medical leave to Europe for* 21 *months.* 1860: Collector of Salem. 1862: Member of the Board of Revenue, and President of the Income Tax Commission. 1865: President of the Income Tax Commission. 1867: *Resigned the service, 27th May.* (*Annuitant on the Fund,* 1867.) *Died, 20th December* 1867.

BRICKENDEN, Richard.—1752: Writer. 1768: Senior Merchant. 1771: Member of the Council of the Governor. 1774: *Out of the service.*

BRODIE, James.—1789: Writer. 1790: Assistant under the Secretary in the Public and Revenue Departments. 1793: Acting

Secretary to the Military Board. 1796: Garrison Store-keeper and Import Warehouse-keeper. *No trace after* 1801.

BRODIE, ALEXANDER.—1773: Writer. 1780: Factor. 1782: Junior Merchant. 1790: *Out of the service.*

BROOKE, HENRY.—1751: Writer. 1768: Chief of Cuddalore. 1771: Member of the Council of the Governor. 1774: Chief of Masulipatam. 1776: *Recalled.* 1780: *Suspended.* 1782: *Out of the service.*

BROOKE, ARTHUR.—1793: Writer. 1796: Assistant under the Secretary in the Military, Political, and Secret Departments. 1797: Land Customer. 1799: Assistant to the Military Paymaster-General. 1800: Assistant to the Collector of Government Customs. 1802: Head Assistant to the Commercial Resident at Cuddalore. 1803: *At home.* 1808: *Returned to India;* Deputy Commercial Resident at Salem. 1811: Commercial Resident at Cuddalore. 1815: *Out of employ.* 1817: Commercial Resident at Nagore. 1826: *At home on absentee allowance.* 1829: *Returned to India.* 1830: Deputy Warehouse-keeper. 1832: Officiating Superintendent of Stationery. 1836: Superintendent of Government Lotteries; Acting Cashier to the Government Bank, and Assistant to the Sub-Treasurer. 1837: Superintendent of the Government Lotteries. 1845: *Out of employ. Died, 11th January* 1850, *in Madras.*

BROWN, WILLIAM.—1783: Writer; Assistant to the Secretary to the Select Committee. 1786: Assistant at Masulipatam. 1787: Under the Secretary in the Secret Department. 1790: Paymaster to the Detachment serving with the Nizam. 1793: *Out of employ.* 1794: Assistant in the Vizianagram Zemindary. 1796: Collector in the Southern Division of the Vizianagram Zemindary. 1797: Collector in the Cashimcottah Havelly, the resumed Pergunnahs of Vizianagram and Vizagapatam Farms. 1798: Collector in the First Division of the Vizagapatam District. 1800: Collector in the First Division of the Ganjam. 1802: Third Judge of the Court of Circuit and Appeal, Northern Division. 1806: Second Judge of the Court of Circuit and Appeal, Northern Division. 1810: *At home.* 1816: *Returned to India;* Sheriff of Madraspatam. 1817: Commissioner at Rajahmundry. 1819: Acting Third Judge of the Provincial Court, Northern Division. 1820: Commercial Resident and Collector of Sea Customs, Vizagapatam and Ganjam. 1821: *Out of employ.* 1822: Second Judge of the Provincial Court, Centre Division. 1824: Senior Judge of the

B

Provincial Court, Centre Division. 1828: Additional Government
Commissioner for Carnatic Claims. 1831: Telugoo Translator to
Government. 1832: *Out of employ.* 1835: Persian Translator
to Government. *Died, 27th June* 1837, *at St Thome.*

BROWN, HENRY.—1789: Writer. 1790: Assistant under the
Secretary in the Public and Revenue Departments. 1792: Acting
Deputy Export Warehouse-keeper. 1793: Deputy Warehouse-
keeper. 1794: Export Warehouse-keeper. 1796: Commercial
Resident at the Presidency. 1801: Commercial Resident at Ram-
nad. *Died, 29th December* 1808, *at Madura.*

BROWN, CHARLES PHILIP.—1816: Writer. 1820: Assistant
to the Collector and Magistrate of Cuddapah. 1822: Register of
the Zillah of Masulipatam. 1824: Head Assistant to the Collector
and Magistrate of Rajahmundry. 1826: Register of the Zillah of
Cuddapah. 1829: Register to the Provincial Court, Southern
Division. 1830: Assistant Judge and Joint-Criminal Judge of
Rajahmundry. 1835: *At home on absentee allowance.* 1837:
Returned to India, per "Mary Ann." 1838: Persian Translator
to Government; Acting Secretary to the College Board, and to
the Native Education Committee; and Member of the College
Board. 1839: Acting Register to the Sudder and Foujdarry
Adawlut; Persian Translator to Government; Member of the
College Board. 1847: Persian, Tamul, and Telugoo Translator
to Government; Postmaster-General. 1854: *Resigned the service,
1st May, in India. (Annuitant on the Fund,* 1854.)

BROWN, CHRISTIAN JAMES.—1824: Writer. 1825: Assistant
to the Principal Collector and Magistrate of Cuddapah. 1828:
Head Assistant to the Accountant-General. *Died,* 10*th April*
1831, *on his passage to England.*

BRUCE, PETER.—1796: Writer. 1799: Assistant to the
Accountant-General. 1801: Assistant under the Principal Col-
lector in the Ceded District. 1803: Subordinate Collector in the
Ceded Districts. 1806: Judge and Magistrate of Bellary. 1820:
Third Judge of the Provincial Court, Southern Division; Second
Judge of the Provincial Court, Centre Division. *Died, 2d Septem-
ber* 1821, *at Gooty.*

BRUCE, FREDERICK HERVEY.—1808: Writer; Assistant to
Secretary in Judicial and Revenue Department. 1809: Assistant
to the Collector of Vizagapatam. 1811: Assistant to the Register
of the Provincial Court, Northern Division. 1813: Deputy Commercial Resident at Maddepollam and Masulipatam. 1815:

Register of the Zillah of Cuddapah. *Died, 10th September* 1817, *at Cuddapah*.

BRUCE, ALEXANDER FAIRLIE.—1817 : Writer. 1820 : Assistant to the Collector and Magistrate of Tanjore. 1824 : Register of the Zillah of Salem. 1825 : Head Assistant to the Principal Collector of the Northern Division of Arcot; *At home*. 1829 : *Returned to India;* Acting Sub-Collector of Nellore. 1830 : Sub-Collector and Joint-Magistrate of Nellore. 1834 : Acting Secretary to the Board of Revenue. 1835 : Mint Master. 1836 : Acting Collector, afterwards Collector and Magistrate of Guntoor. 1837 : Acting Police Magistrate at the Presidency ; Acting Civil Auditor ; Acting Superintendent of Stamps ; Member of Mint Committee. 1838 : Collector and Magistrate of Guntoor (resumed); Acting Collector and Magistrate of Chingleput; Collector and Magistrate of Cuddapah; Postmaster-General. 1847 : Civil Auditor, and Superintendent of Stamps. 1852 : *Resigned the service, 1st July, in India.* (*Annuitant on the Fund,* 1852.) *Died,* 26*th June* 1875, *in England*.

BRUERE, JAMES GRAHAM SADLEIR.—1826 : Writer. 1828 : Register of the Zillah of Chittoor. 1832 : Acting Assistant Judge and Joint Criminal Judge at Salem ; Acting Deputy Collector of Madras. 1833 : Secretary to the Marine Board. 1834 : Assistant Judge and Joint Criminal Judge of Rajahmundry. 1836 : Assistant Judge and Joint Criminal Judge of Chingleput. 1837 : *At home*. 1840 : *Returned to India.* 1841 : *Out of employ.* 1842 : Deputy Collector of Sea Customs, Madras; Judge and Joint Criminal Judge of Salem. 1844 : Civil and Session Judge, Salem. 1852 : Civil and Session Judge, Cuddalore. 1854 : *Resigned the service, 1st May.* (*Annuitant on the Fund,* 1854.) *Died,* 27*th September* 1865, *in England*.

BUCHAN, GEORGE.—1792 : Writer. 1794 : Assistant under the Secretary in the Military, Political, and Secret Department, and French Translator. 1795 : Assistant Manager for Supplying Beetle Tobacco and Ganja. 1796 : Paymaster to the Expedition against Malacca. 1799 : Sub-Secretary in the Military, Political, and Secret Department. 1801 : Secretary in the Public and Commercial Department ; Secretary in the Military Department. 1803 : Chief Secretary to Government. 1809 : Private Secretary to the Governor. 1810 : *At home.* 1814 : *Out of the service.*

BURLTON, JOHN PHILIP.—1777 : Writer. 1780 : *At home.* 1790 : Senior Merchant and Muster-Master of the Calcroon. 1795 :

Resident at Negapatam. 1800: Paymaster at Kistnagherry. 1801:
Out of the service.

BURY, JOHN FULLER.—1834: Writer. 1836: Assistant to the
Principal Collector and Magistrate of Malabar; Assistant to the
Principal Collector and Magistrate of North Arcot. 1840: Assistant to Agent to Governor; Collector and Magistrate, Vizagapatam.
1845: *Proceeded on furlough.* 1848: *Returned to India. Died,
11th May* 1848, *in India (Waltair).*

BUSHBY, HENRY TURNER.— 1811: Writer. 1817: Assistant
to the Register of the Sudder and Foujdarry Adawlut. 1818:
Register of the Zillah of Chittoor. 1823: Register to the Provincial Court, Centre Division. 1827: Assistant Judge and Joint
Criminal Judge of Cuddapah. 1829: Judge and Criminal Judge
of Bellary. 1832: Third Judge of the Provincial Court, Northern
Division; Third Judge of the Provincial Court, Nellore. 1834:
Third Judge of the Provincial Court, Rajahmundry; *Out of employ.*
1836: Acting Judge and Criminal Judge of Bellary; Acting Judge
and Criminal Judge of Salem. 1837: Judge and Criminal Judge
of Bellary; Acting Judge of Provincial Court, Centre Division.
Died, 17th May 1838, *at Cuddapah.*

BUSHBY, CHARLES MAITLAND.—1817: Writer. 1820: Assistant to the Collector and Magistrate of Salem. 1823: Register
of the Zillah of Chittoor. 1827: Register to the Provincial
Court, Western Division. 1832: Assistant Judge and Joint
Criminal Judge of Canara. *Died,* 30th January 1835, *at Mangalore.*

BYNG, JOHN.—1796: Writer. 1797: Assistant under the
Secretary in the Public, Revenue, and Commercial Departments.
1798: Deputy Postmaster-General; Paymaster at Malacca. 1805:
Acting Register and Assistant Magistrate to Act in the Zillah of
Masulipatam. 1806: Judge and Magistrate of the Zillah of Guntoor. 1807: Judge and Magistrate of the Zillah of Ganjam.
1810: Judge and Magistrate of the Zillah of Trichinopoly. *Died,
23d November* 1811, *at Trichinopoly.*

BYRNE, PATRICK.—1789: Writer. 1790: Assistant under the
Military Secretary. 1791: *At home. No trace after* 1791.

CADOGAN, HON. GEORGE.—1771: Writer. 1776: Factor.
1780: Junior Merchant. *No trace after* 1780.

CALL, JOHN.—1751: Writer. 1768: Member of the Council
of the Governor. 1771: *Out of the service.*

CALL, JAMES.—1766: Writer. 1771: Factor. 1774: Junior

Merchant. 1778 : Senior Merchant, and Provisional Member of Board of Revenue. 1792 : Sea Customer. 1800 : *Out of the service.*

CALL, JEWEL.—1771 : Writer. 1776 : Factor. 1780 : Junior Merchant. 1782 : Senior Merchant. 1790 : *Out of the service.*

CALLAND, JOHN.—1751 : Writer. 1768 : Senior Merchant; *Suspended from service.*

CAMERON, N. S.—1813 : Writer. 1816 : Head Assistant to the Collector, afterwards Assistant Magistrate, Canara. 1823 : Sub-Collector and Assistant Magistrate of Canara. 1825: *At home.* 1828: *Returned to India ;* Collector and Magistrate of Trichinopoly. 1831 : Principal Collector and Magistrate of Canara. 1833 : Principal Collector and Magistrate of Madura. *Died, 12th December* 1833, *at the Cape of Good Hope.*

CAMPBELL, FREDERICK.—1781 : Writer. 1782 : Assistant to the Secretary in the Select Committee. 1783 : Assistant to the Secretary in the Civil Department. 1784 : Secretary to General Campbell. 1786 : Deputy Import Warehouse-keeper ; Assistant to the Committee of Circuit. 1789 : Muster-Master of the Centre Division. 1790 : *Out of employ. Died, 26th March* 1791, *at Chingleput.*

CAMPBELL, WILLIAM.—1806 : Writer. 1808 : Assistant in the Secret, Political, and Foreign Departments. 1809 : Assistant to the Collector of Canara. 1816 : *Suspended. Dismissed, 16th December* 1818, *in England.*

CAMPBELL, ALEXANDER DUNCAN.—1807 : Writer. 1809 : Assistant under the Collector of Bellary ; Fixed Assistant under the Secretary to the Board of Revenue, and Assistant to the Superintendent of Stamps. 1811 : Secretary to the Board of Superintendence for the College of Fort St. George. 1812 : Deputy Secretary to the Board of Revenue. 1817 : Secretary to the Board of Revenue. 1820 : Collector and Magistrate of Bellary. 1824 : Third Judge of the Provincial Court, Centre Division. 1826 : Third Member of the Board of Revenue. 1827 : Principal Collector and Magistrate of Tanjore. 1828 : *Out of employ ;* Register to the Sudder and Foujdarry Adawlut. 1830 : Telugoo Translator to Government. 1831 : *At home on absentee allowance.* 1833 : *Returned to India per " Alfred."* 1834 : Acting Judge of the Sudder and Foujdarry Adawlut. 1835 : Superintendent of Stamps and Civil Auditor ; Acting Judge of the Sudder Adawlut. 1837 : Member of the Mint Committee ; Persian Translator to Government ; Acting Third Judge of the Sudder Foujdarry Adawlut. 1838 : Third Puisne Judge of the Sudder Foujdarry Adawlut, and Member of the College Board. 1840 : Second Puisne Judge of the Court of Sudder Dewannee and Sudder Foujdarry Adawlut, and Member of the College Board. 1842 : First Puisne Judge of the Court of Sudder Dewannee and Sudder Foujdarry Adawlut, and Member of the College Board ; *Resigned the service, 6th May, in India.* (*Annuitant on the Fund,* 1842.) *Died, 23d April* 1857, *in England.*

CAMPBELL, E. C.—1856 : Writer. 1859 : *Proceeded on furlough.* 1861 : *Resigned the service, 24th July, in England.*

CAPPER, JAMES.—1770 : Writer. 1776 : Factor. *Died, 31st August* 1776, *at Calcutta.*

CARPENTER, CHARLES.—1789 : Writer ; Assistant under the Secretary in the Secret Department. 1790 : Assistant under the Secretary in the Military Department. 1791 : Assistant under the Collector of Coimbatore. 1792 : *Out of employ.* 1793 : Assistant under the Resident at Maddepollam. 1794 : Commercial Resident at Salem. *Died, 4th June* 1818, *at Salem.*

CASAMAJOR, JAMES HENRY.—1762 : Writer. 1776 : Senior Merchant ; Paymaster at Vellore. *No trace after* 1782. *Died, 23d January* 1815, *in England.*

CASAMAIJOR, JOHN.—1792 : Writer ; Assistant under the Secretary in the Political, Secret, and Military Departments. 1794 : Assistant under the Commercial Resident at Tinnevelly. 1796 : Deputy Commercial Resident at Ramnad and Tinnevelly. 1800 : Commercial Resident at Tinnevelly. 1806 : Third Judge of the Court of Circuit and Appeal, Southern Division. 1809 : Third Member of the Board of Trade. 1813 : Acting General Superintendent of Investments. 1816 : Senior Member of the Board of Trade. *Died, 1st February* 1821, *at Singapore.*

CASAMAIJOR, JAMES ARCHIBALD.—1802 : Writer. 1803 : Assistant to the Secretary to the Board of Trade. 1804 : Secretary and Accountant to the Sinking Fund. 1806 : Deputy Secretary to the Board of Revenue. 1809 : Register of Seringapatam ; Judge, Magistrate, and Collector of Seringapatam. 1811 : Military Paymaster at the Presidency and of Extraordinaries. 1813 :

Judge, Magistrate, and Collector of Seringapatam. 1818: Assistant to the Resident at Mysore. 1827: Resident at Mysore. 1832: Occasional Member of Council, and Officiating President of the Revenue and Marine Board. 1834: Resident at Travancore and Cochin. 1836: *At home on absentee allowance. (Annuitant on the Fund from 1st May 1837.)*

CASAMAIJOR, GEORGE JAMES.—1812: Writer. 1816: Assistant to the Secretary in the Military Department. 1819: *At home.* 1823: *Returned to India;* Assistant to the Chief Secretary to Government. 1826: Register to the Sudder and Foujdarry Adawlut. 1828: Judge and Criminal Judge of Nellore. 1832: Second Judge of the Provincial Court, Northern Division. 1834: Second Judge of the Provincial Court, Centre Division. 1836: Acting Principal Collector and Magistrate of Cuddapah. 1838: Acting First Judge of the Provincial Court, Centre Division. 1839: Second Judge of the Provincial Court of Appeal and Circuit, Centre Division. 1840: First Judge of the Provincial Court of Appeal and Circuit, Centre Division. 1842: Third Judge, afterwards Second Judge, of the Sudder Dewannee and Sudder Foujdarry Adawlut. 1844: *Resigned the service, 3d December, in India. (Annuitant on the Fund, 1845.) Died, 31st May 1849, at Ootacamund.*

CATOR, FREDERICK SAWBRIDGE WRIGHT.—1843: Writer. 1846: Assistant to Collector and Magistrate, Tinnevelly. 1847: Assistant to Collector and Magistrate, Madura. 1852: Head Assistant to Collector and Magistrate, Madura; Head Assistant to Collector and Magistrate, Guntoor. *Died, 11th February 1854, at Cape Town.*

CATHCART, ROBERT.—1826: Writer. 1827: Assistant to the Principal Collector of Tanjore. 1829: Employed under the Bombay Government. 1832: Acting Additional Sub-Collector and Joint Magistrate of Salem. 1833: Special Assistant to the Collector and Magistrate of Chingleput. 1834: Acting Sub-Collector of Ganjam. *Died, 26th May 1834, at Ganjam.*

CAZALET, PETER READE.—1796: Writer. 1798: Assistant under the Accountant-General. 1799: Assistant under the Collector of the Fourth Division of Masulipatam. 1802: Assistant under the Collector of the Third Division of Masulipatam. 1803; Collector of the Zillah of Masulipatam. 1806: Collector of the Zillah of Carangoody. 1809: Judge and Magistrate of the Zillah of Rajahmundry. 1813: *At home.* 1816: *Returned to India.*

1817 : Acting Collector and Magistrate of Ganjam. 1819 : Collector and Magistrate of Ganjam. (*Annuitant on the Fund in* 1827.) *Died,* 27*th January* 1839, *at Bath.*

CHAMBERS, WILLIAM.—1765 : Writer. 1776 : Senior Merchant. 1780 : *In Bengal.* 1790 : Interpreter to Supreme Court of Judicature in Bengal. *No trace after* 1792.

CHAMIER (DESCHAMPS), JOHN. — 1772 : Writer. 1778 : Factor. 1780 : Junior Merchant. 1782 : *At home.* 1790 : Senior Merchant ; Secretary to the Military, Political, and Secret Departments, and Judge-Advocate-General. 1792 : Collector at Muglatore. 1795 : Chief of Vizagapatam. 1801 : Chief Secretary to Government. 1802 : Chief Secretary to Government, and Provisional Member of Council. 1803 : Full Member of Council. 1804 : President of the Board of Trade. 1806 : *At home.* 1809 : *Out of the service.*

CHAMIER, HENRY.—1812 : Writer. 1816 : Persian Translator to the Carnatic Commissioners. 1817 : Second Deputy Secretary to the Board of Revenue. 1818 : Temporary Assistant to the Chief Secretary to Government. 1820 : Assistant to the Chief Secretary to Government. 1821 : Sub-Collector and Assistant Magistrate of Chittoor. 1825 : Sub-Collector and Assistant Magistrate of South Arcot. 1827 : Secretary in the Public Department. 1828 : Secretary in the Military Department. 1829 : Acting Secretary in the Revenue and Judicial Department; Acting Secretary in the Military Department. 1831 : Secretary in the Revenue and Judicial Department ; Chief Secretary to Government. 1832 : Acting Persian Translator to Government ; Occasional Member of Council under the Provisions of the Act, 33 George III., cap. 52 ; Trustee for St. George's Church. 1837 : Chief Secretary to Government. 1842 : Chief Secretary to Government, and Provisional Member of Council. 1843 : Member of Council, and President of the Revenue, Marine, and College Boards. 1848 : President of the Revenue, Marine, and College Boards ; *Resigned the service,* 14*th January. Died,* 4*th February* 1867, *in England.*

CHAPLIN, WILLIAM.—1799 : Writer. 1804 : Register in the Ceded Districts. 1806 : Subordinate Collector in the Ceded Districts. 1807 : Collector in the Zillah of Cuddapah. 1809 : Collector in the Zillah of Bellary. 1818 : Employed in the late Peishwah's Dominions. 1823 : Commissioner in the Deccan. 1827 : *Out of the service.*

CHAPMAN, ROBERT.—1791 : Writer ; Assistant under the

Secretary to the Board of Revenue. 1792 : Assistant under the Resident at Ingeram. *Died, 15th December 1792, at Ingeram.*

CHARLTON, JASPER.—1778 : Writer. 1790 : Senior Merchant. 1791 : *Absent. No trace after 1792.*

CHASE, THOMAS.—1781 : Writer. 1783 : Assistant to the Secretary to the Select Committee. 1784 : Clerk to the Justices, and French Translator. 1786 : Assistant to the Secretary in the Military Department, and Clerk to the Committee of Stores. 1788 : Examiner to the Mayor's Court. 1790 : Secretary to the Board of Trade. 1796 : *Out of employ.* 1799 : *At home.* 1801 : *Returned to India. Died, 5th February 1808, at Vizagapatam.*

CHASE, THOMAS CURTIS.—1808 : Writer. 1809 : Second Assistant to the Collector of Nellore. 1812 : Head Assistant to the Collector of Nellore. 1817 : *At home. Died, 19th May 1818, at Kensington.*

CHATFIELD, JAMES.—1806 : Writer ; Assistant under the Secretary to the Board of Revenue. 1808 : *At home.* 1813 : *Out of the service.*

CHATFIELD, ROWLEY WINSLEY.—1832 : Writer. 1834 : Doing Duty under the Principal Collector and Magistrate, Madura. 1835 : Second Assistant to Principal Collector and Magistrate, Madura. 1836 : Assistant to Principal Collector and Magistrate, Canara. 1837 : Acting Register of the Zillah Court of Canara ; Acting Head Assistant to Principal Collector and Magistrate, Canara ; afterwards Register of the Zillah Court of Malabar. 1839 : Acting Assistant Judge and Joint Criminal Judge of Cochin ; Resumed charge of the Office of Register of the Zillah Court of Cochin. 1842 : Acting Senior Deputy Register to the Court of Sudder and Foujdarry Adawlut. 1843 : Commissioner for Government Lotteries ; Extra Assistant to Collector and Magistrate, Malabar. 1844 : Acting Additional Sub-Collector and Joint Magistrate of Canara. 1845 : Acting Additional Sub-Collector and Joint Magistrate of Malabar ; Special Assistant to Collector and Magistrate, Tinnevelly. 1846 : Sub-Collector and Joint Magistrate, Malabar. 1850 : Acting Civil and Sessions Judge, Tellicherry. 1851 : Acting Civil and Sessions Judge, Calicut. 1852 : Acting Civil and Sessions Judge, Mangalore. 1853 : *Proceeded to England on furlough.* 1856 : Acting Civil and Sessions Judge, Guntoor. 1857 : Civil and Sessions Judge, Mangalore. 1863 : *Resigned the service, 1st May. (Annuitant.)*

CHEAPE, ANSTRUTHER.—1819 : Writer. 1824 : Assistant to

the Collector and Magistrate of Bellary; Register of the Zillah of Bellary. 1829: Register of the Zillah of Cuddapah; Assistant Judge of Cumbum. 1830: Assistant Judge and Joint Criminal Judge of Malabar. *Died, 16th June 1831, at Tellicherry.*

CHERRY, PETER.—1789: Writer. 1790: Assistant under the Secretary in the Public and Revenue Department. 1791: Assistant under the Collector of the Ganjam Havelly. 1796: Assistant under the Collector in the Northern Division of the Vizianagram Zemindary. 1798: Paymaster to Detachment under Lieutenant-Colonel Roberts. 1799: Paymaster to the Army. 1800: Collector of the Third Division of the Vizagapatam District. 1804: Judge of the Zillah of Ganjam. 1806: Judge of the Zillah of Combaconum. 1807: *At home.* 1811: *Returned to India.* 1813: Paymaster at the Presidency and of Extraordinaries. 1815: Third Judge, afterwards Second Judge of the Provincial Court, Northern Division. 1821: Senior Judge of the Provincial Court, Centre Division. *Died, 26th November 1823, at the Cape of Good Hope.*

CHERRY, GEORGE FREDERICK.—1804: Writer. 1807: Assistant under the Chief Secretary to Government in the Secret, Political, and Foreign Department; Assistant to the Register of the Zillah of Tinnevelly. 1809: Register of the Zillah of Madura. 1821: Judge and Criminal Judge of Masulipatam. 1824: Judge and Criminal Judge of Combaconum. *Died, 10th February 1827, at Combaconum.*

CHERRY, ALEXANDER INGLIS.—1824: Writer. 1825: Assistant to the Principal Collector and Magistrate of Tanjore. 1827: Head Assistant to the Secretary to the Board of Revenue. 1828: Deputy Tamil Translator to Government; Assistant to the Collector of Sea Customs at Madras. 1829: *At home.* 1834: *Returned to India;* Deputy Secretary in the Chief Secretary's Department. 1836: Acting Secretary to Government. 1837: Cashier to the Government Bank, and Assistant to the Sub-Treasurer; Commissioner for Drawing Government Lotteries. 1838: Acting Sub-Treasurer and Superintendent Treasurer of Government Bank. 1839: Sub-Treasurer and Superintendent Treasurer of Government Bank. 1840: Superintendent and Treasurer to the Government Bank, and Sub-Treasurer to Government. 1844: Sub-Treasurer to Government, and Member of the Mint Committee. *Died, 26th October 1850, at the Cape of Good Hope.*

CHERRY, JOHN WILLIAM.—1839: Writer. 1840: Assistant to Principal Collector and Magistrate, South Arcot. 1841: Assistant to Chief Secretary to Government. 1842: Acting Head Assistant to Collector and Magistrate, Chingleput, and Assistant to Accountant-General. 1843: Second Assistant to Accountant-General. 1844: Commissioner for Government Lotteries. 1847: Head Assistant to Accountant-General. 1849: *Proceeded to Europe on furlough.* 1853: Acting Sub-Collector and Joint Magistrate, Salem; Acting Deputy Collector of Sea Customs, Madras; Sub-Collector and Joint Magistrate, Salem. 1855: Acting Civil and Sessions Judge, Salem. 1856: Acting Collector and Magistrate, Tanjore. 1857: Acting Collector and Magistrate, Acting Civil and Sessions Judge, and Sub-Judge, Salem. 1858: Acting Collector and Magistrate, Coimbatore. 1859: At first Acting, afterwards Civil and Sessions Judge, Salem. 1859: *On medical certificate to Europe for 24 months.* 1861: Assumed Charge of the Office of Civil Court of Salem. 1864: *Six months special leave, extended to sick leave to Europe.* 1865: Civil and Sessions Judge, Ootacamund. *Died, 3d December 1866, in India.*

CHESTER, John E.—1848: Writer. 1850: Assistant to Collector and Magistrate, Malabar. *Died, 28th April 1850, at Calicut.*

CHINNERY, John.—1792: Writer; Assistant under the Secretary in the Secret, Political, and Military Department. 1793: Assistant under the Resident at Cuddalore. 1796: Deputy Commercial Resident at Cuddalore. 1799: *Out of employ.* 1812: Commercial Resident in the Northern Division of Arcot. 1813: *Out of employ. Died, 15th November 1817, at Madras.*

CHURCHILL, Charles Henry.—1789: Writer. 1790: Assistant under the Export Warehouse-keeper. 1791: Assistant under the Export Warehouse-keeper at Masulipatam. 1796: Assistant to the Commercial Resident at Ingeram. 1797: Assistant to the Collector at Guntoor. 1800: *Out of employ.* 1801: Assistant under the Collector of the Third Division of Masulipatam. 1802: Assistant under the Collector of the First Division of Masulipatam. 1803: Collector of the Zillah of Rajahmundry. 1805: Collector of the Zillah of Vizagapatam. *Died, 16th April 1811, at Vizagapatam.*

CLARKE, Richard.—1804: Writer. 1807: Assistant under the Collector of Customs at Madras. 1808: *Proceeded to England on private affairs.* 1813: *Returned to India;* Assistant to the Secretary to Government, and to Revenue and Judicial Department. 1814 : Secretary to the Police Committee ; Register of Chingleput. 1815 : Junior Deputy Register of the Sudder and Foujdarry Adawlut ; Tamil Translator to Government. 1817 : Acting Register of the Sudder and Foujdarry Adawlut. 1819 : Secretary to the Board for Revising the Regulations. 1820 : Secretary to the Board of Revenue. 1824 : Third Member of the Board of Revenue. 1826 : *At home on absentee allowance.* (*Annuitant on the Fund from 1st January* 1828.)

CLARKE, SYDENHAM CHARLES.—1818 : Writer. 1820 : Assistant to the Collector and Magistrate of Malabar. 1824 : *At home.* 1827 : *Returned to India ;* Register of the Zillah of Nellore. *Died, 26th August* 1828, *at Madras.*

CLARKE, THOMAS.—1833 : Writer. 1835 : Assistant to Collector and Magistrate, Trichinopoly. 1838 : Acting Head Assistant and afterwards Head Assistant to Register of the Sudder and Foujdarry Adawlut ; also Commissioner for Government Lotteries. 1839 : Acting Senior Deputy Register of the Sudder and Foujdarry Adawlut. 1840 : Acting Tamil Translator to Government, Commissioner for Lotteries, and Acting Deputy Register of the Sudder and Foujdarry Adawlut. 1842 : Senior Deputy Register of the Sudder and Foujdarry Adawlut. 1845 : Acting Tamil Translator to Government. 1847 : Acting Sub-Collector and Joint Magistrate, Madura. 1848 : Acting Sub-Collector and Joint Magistrate, Tanjore. 1849 : Sub-Collector and Joint Magistrate, Madura. 1851 : Acting Civil and Sessions Judge, Tinnevelly. 1853 : Acting Collector and Magistrate, Madura. 1855 : Acting Civil and Sessions Judge, Madura, and Collector and Magistrate, Malabar. 1856 : *On medical certificate to Europe for* 21 *months.* 1858 : Collector and Magistrate, Madura. 1860 : Member of the Board of Revenue. 1863 : Member of the Board of Examiners, and of the Central Committee for the Examination of Assistants. 1867 : Additional Member of the Council of Fort St. George for Making Laws and Regulations, and First Member of the Board of Revenue ; also President of the Committee for the Examination of Assistants. 1868 : On Special Duty in the Famine Districts. 1869 : *Resigned the service, 3d September.* (*Annuitant.*)

CLARKE, RICHARD GWATKIN.—1839 : Writer. 1840 : Acting Head Assistant to Register of the Court of Sudder and Foujdarry Adawlut. 1841 : Assistant to Collector and Magistrate, Chingleput, Acting Cashier to the Government Bank, and Assistant to Sub-Treasurer. 1842 : Head Assistant to Register of the Court of

Sudder and Foujdarry Adawlut, and Commissioner for Government Lotteries. 1845: Deputy Secretary to Government. 1848: Private Secretary to the Governor of the Presidency. 1851: Acting Deputy Collector of Sea Customs, Madras ; Acting Sub-Judge, and afterwards Sub-Judge, Bellary. 1857 : Acting Civil and Session Judge, Tinnevelly. 1858 : Subordinate Judge, Combaconum ; Acting Civil and Sessions Judge at Salem, and afterwards at Trichinopoly. 1860 : At first Acting Civil and Sessions Judge at Combaconum ; afterwards Civil and Sessions Judge, Negapatam. 1861 : *On medical certificate to Europe for 21 months.* 1863 : *Returned to India.* 1867 : Acting Civil and Sessions Judge, Ootacamund. 1871 : Civil and Sessions Judge, Tranquebar ; *On furlough ; Resigned the service, 17th May, in England.* (*Annuitant.*)

CLEMENTSON, Frederick Fenby.—1817 : Writer. 1820 : Assistant to the Principal Collector and Magistrate of Coimbatore. 1825 : Head Assistant to the Principal Collector and Magistrate of Coimbatore. 1827 : Sub-Collector and Joint Magistrate of Coimbatore. 1828 : Deputy Accountant - General, and Commercial Accountant and Auditor. 1831 : Acting Mint Master. 1832 : Principal Collector and Magistrate of Malabar. 1842 : *On furlough.* 1846 : *Resigned the service, 24th February.* (*Annuitant on the Fund, 1846.*) *Died, 9th March 1881, in England.*

CLERK, John.—1778 : Writer. 1790 : Senior Merchant, and one of the Collectors of the Jaghire Revenue. 1793 : *At home.* 1795 : *Out of the service.*

CLERK, Robert.—1780 : Writer. 1790 : Junior Merchant, Deputy Secretary to Public and Revenue Department, Sea Gate, and Register and Clerk of the Peace. 1793 : *At home.* 1800 : Senior Merchant, and Junior Member of the Board of Trade. 1801 : *At home.* 1806 : *Out of the service.*

CLERK, Robert (1st).—1781 : Writer. 1782 : Assistant to the Secretary in the Civil Department. 1783 : Under Searcher of the Sea Gate. 1786 : Deputy Sea Customer, and Deputy Secretary Commercial and Revenue Departments, Sea Gate Register, and Clerk of the Peace. 1793 : Secretary in the Public, Revenue, and Commercial Department, Clerk of Appeals, and Clerk to the Committee of Treasury. 1796 : *At home.* 1799 : *Returned to India ;* Junior Member to the Board of Trade. 1800 : Second Member to the Board of Trade ; *At home.* 1805 : *Out of the service.*

CLERK, ROBERT (2D).—1816: Writer. 1819: Assistant to the Sub-Treasurer. 1820: Assistant to the Principal Collector and Magistrate of Tanjore. 1822: *At home.* 1824: *Returned to India ;* Second Assistant to the Principal Collector and Magistrate of Tanjore. 1826: Assistant to the Secretary in the Military Department. 1829: Acting Secretary in the Military Department, and Secretary to the Civil Fund. 1831: Secretary to Government in the Military Department. 1832: Acting Chief Secretary to Government, and Acting Director of the Government Bank; Trustee for St. George's Church. 1835: Secretary to Government in the Civil Department. 1836: Secretary to Government in the Secret, Political, and Public Departments. 1837: Secretary to Government in the Civil Department. 1844: *Resigned the service, 22d February, in India.* (*Annuitant on the Fund,* 1843.) *Died, 3d April* 1873, *in England.*

CLIVE, RICHARD.—1808: Writer. 1814: Assistant to the Chief Secretary to Government. 1816: Secretary to the Mint Committee. 1820: Secretary in the Military Department. 1824: Paymaster of Carnatic Stipends. 1828: Chief Secretary to Government. 1829: Acting Secretary in the Revenue and Judicial Department. 1831: Chief Secretary to Government. *Died, 6th August* 1831, *at Coimbatore.*

CLIVE, ROBERT HERBERT.—1816: Writer. 1819: Assistant to the Secretary in the Military Department. 1820: Assistant to the Secretary in the Civil Department; Assistant to the Collector and Magistrate of Madura. 1822: Head Assistant to the Collector and Magistrate of Coimbatore. 1825: Sub-Collector and Assistant Magistrate of Coimbatore. 1827: *At home on absentee allowance.* 1829: *Returned to India per* "*David Scott ;*" Acting Secretary in the Public Department. 1831: Collector of Sea Customs at Madras. 1832: *At home.* 1838: *Out of the service.*

CLUBLEY, THOMAS.—1796: Writer. 1798: Assistant to the Secretary to the Board of Revenue. 1799: Assistant under the Collector of Vizianagram. 1802: Assistant to the Collector in the First Division of Vizagapatam. 1803: Register of the Zillah of Vizagapatam. *Died,* 17*th May* 1805, *at St Thomé.*

CLULOW, JOSEPH.—1816: Writer. 1818: Second Assistant to the Collector and Magistrate of Rajahmundry. 1821: Head Assistant to the Collector and Magistrate of Guntoor. 1826:

Head Assistant to the Collector and Magistrate of Bellary. 1828 : *At home on absentee allowance.* 1830 : *Returned to India per* "*Neptune.*" 1831 : Acting Superintendent of Police. 1832 : Acting Treasurer and Secretary to the Government Bank ; Acting Sub-Treasurer. 1834 : *At home.* 1840 : *Absent from India five years.*

COCHRANE, Hon. Basil.—1769 : Writer. 1776 : Factor. 1778 : Junior Merchant. 1780: Senior Merchant. 1792 : Agent for the Management and Distribution of Liquors for the Use of the Army. 1795 : Agent for the Management and Distribution of Liquors for the Use of the Army, and Civil Paymaster. 1808 : *At home.* 1810 : *Out of the service.*

COCHRANE, James.—1794 : Writer. 1796 : Assistant under the Secretary in the Public, Commercial, and Revenue Department. 1797 : Assistant under the Sea Customer. 1798 : Deputy Persian Translator. 1799 : Senior Assistant under the Resident at Mysore, and Postmaster. 1800 : Subordinate Collector in the Ceded Districts. 1803 : Collector of Ramnad and Tinnevelly. 1806 : Judge and Magistrate of the Northern Division of Canara. 1807 : *At home.* 1811 : *Returned to India ;* Sub-Treasurer. 1812 : Superintendent of Government Lotteries. 1814 : Second Member of the Board of Revenue. 1819 : Senior Member of the Board of Revenue. 1824 : Acting Member of Council and President of the Board of Revenue. 1825 : Second Puisne Judge of the Sudder and Foujdarry Adawlut. 1830 : *At home on absentee allowance. Died, 8th August* 1830, *at Cheltenham.*

COCHRANE, John Henry.—1829 : Writer. 1831 : Assistant to the Principal Collector of Tanjore. 1832: Acting Head Assistant, afterwards Head Assistant, to the Principal Collector and Magistrate of North Arcot. 1837 : Acting Sub-Collector and Joint Magistrate of Cuddapah. 1839 : Sub-Collector and Joint Magistrate of Cuddapah. 1841 : *Proceeded on furlough.* 1844 : *Returned to India.* 1845: Sub-Collector and Joint Magistrate of Bellary. 1848: Collector and Magistrate, Cuddapah. 1851 : Collector and Magistrate, Chingleput. *Died, 28th August* 1854, *in Europe (Homburg).*

COCHRANE, William Edward. — 1838 : Writer. 1842 : Assistant to Collector and Magistrate, Nellore. 1843 : Head Assistant to Collector and Magistrate, Nellore. 1847 : *Proceeded on furlough.* 1850 : *Returned to India ;* Head Assistant to Collector and Magistrate, Madura. 1852 : *Out of employ.* 1853 :

Sub-Collector and Joint Magistrate, Salem. 1854 : *Out of employ.*
1855 : Deputy Collector of Sea Customs, Madras. 1859 : *Proceeded on furlough.* 1860 : *Returned to India;* Deputy Collector of Sea Customs, Madras. 1861 : Collector of Sea Customs, Madras. *Died, 7th May* 1861, *at Madras.*

COCKBURN, THOMAS.—1779 : Writer. 1790 : Senior Merchant ; Commissary-General of Grain and Provisions ; Accountant to Board of Revenue ; Register and Transfer Accountant of Debts of the Nabob and Rajah of Tanjore ; Bullock Contractor. 1795 : Member of the Board of Revenue. 1800 : Second Member of the Board of Revenue. 1801 : Senior Member of the Board of Revenue. 1803 : *At home.* 1807 : *Out of the service.*

COCKBURN, DAVID.—1796 : Writer. 1798 : Assistant under the Accountant to the Board of Revenue. 1799 : Second Assistant under the Collector of Salem. 1801 : Collector of Baramahl with District of Salem Kishnagherry, and conquered Territory lately under Major Graham's charge. 1803 : Collector of the Western Polygar Piesheush and of Arcot, north of the River Patar. 1804 : Judge of the Zillah of the North Division of Arcot. 1805 : Judge of the Zillah of Dindigul. 1806 : Judge of the Zillah of the Southern Division of Arcot. 1814 : *At home.* 1817 : *Out of the service.*

COCKBURN, MONTAGUE DUNDAS.—1807 : Writer. 1808 : Assistant under the Judge of Verdochellam. 1809 : Head Assistant to the Collector of the Southern Division of Arcot. 1816 : Assistant Magistrate of the Southern Division of Arcot. 1820 : Collector and Magistrate of Salem. 1829 : *Out of employ.* 1836 : Judge and Criminal Judge of Malabar. 1842 : Judge and Criminal Judge of Madura. 1843 : *Out of employ.* 1850 : *Resigned the service, 16th February.* (*Annuitant on the Fund,* 1850.) *Died, 28th September* 1869, *at Kotagherry (Neilgherries).*

COLE, THE HON. ARTHUR HENRY.—1801 : Writer. 1806 : Secretary to the Resident at Mysore. 1809 : Acting Resident at Mysore. 1812 : Resident at Mysore. 1818 : Superintendent of the Government Lotteries. 1827 : *At home on absentee allowance.* (*Annuitant on the Fund from* 1st *May* 1829.)

COLE, ARTHUR.— 1831 : Writer. 1834 : Assistant to the Principal Collector and Magistrate of Madura. *Died,* 1st *April* 1835, *at Madura.*

COLEMAN, GEORGE.—1790 ; Writer. 1791 : Assistant under

the Accountant-General. 1792 : Assistant under the Accountant-General to the Board of Trade. 1794 : Deputy-Accountant to the Board of Trade. 1797 : Assistant in the Export Warehouse. 1798 : Deputy Accountant to the Board of Trade. 1800 : Deputy Commercial Resident at Masulipatam. 1805 : Commercial Resident at Masulipatam. 1806 : Judge of the Zillah of Chingleput. 1816 : *At home.* 1818 : *Out of the service.*

COLLINS, John.—1793 : Writer. 1796 : Assistant under the Commercial Resident at Salem. 1800 : Deputy Commercial Resident at Salem. 1808 : Commercial Resident at Maddepollam. 1809 : *Out of employ. Died, 8th February* 1811, *at St Thomé.*

COLT, Oliver.—1779 : Writer. 1790 : Senior Merchant and Postmaster-General. 1794 : *At home. No trace after* 1795.

COMBE, Harvey.—1804 : Writer. 1807 : Assistant to the Principal Collector of Coimbatore. 1809 : Head Assistant in the Secret and Political Department. 1810 : *At home.* 1814 : *Out of the service.*

CONOLLY, Henry Valentine.—1824 : Writer. 1826 : Assistant to the Principal Collector and Magistrate of Bellary. 1828 : Head Assistant to the Principal Collector of Tanjore ; Deputy Secretary in the Military Department. 1831 : Canarese Translator to Government. 1834 : Cashier to the Government Bank. 1835 : Assistant to the Sub-Treasurer. 1836 : Acting Additional Government Commissioner for Carnatic Claims. 1837 : Cashier to the Government Bank and Assistant to Sub-Treasurer, and Canarese Translator. 1838 : *Proceeded on furlough.* 1840 : *Returned to India.* 1841 : Collector and Magistrate, Malabar. *Assassinated, 11th September* 1855, *at Calicut.*

CONWAY, Thomas Barlow A.—1831 : Writer. 1834 : Assistant to the Principal Collector and Magistrate of Nellore. 1835 : Assistant to the Collector and Magistrate of Ganjam. 1837 : Head Assistant to the Collector and Magistrate of Ganjam. 1840 : Head Assistant to Agent, Collector, and Magistrate, Vizagapatam. 1841 : Head Assistant to Agent, Principal Collector, and Magistrate, Vizagapatam. 1845 : Private Secretary to Governor. 1847 : *Proceeded on furlough.* 1850 : *Returned to India.* 1851 : Sub-Collector and Joint Magistrate, Salem. 1852 : Agent to the Governor, Kurnool. 1856 : *Out of employ.* 1859 : *Resigned the service, 1st August, in India.* (*Annuitant on the Fund,* 1861.)

C

COOK, WILLIAM.—1797 : Writer. 1800 : Assistant under the Secretary in the Military, Secret, and Political Department. 1802 : Assistant under the Collector of Government Customs. 1803 : Assistant to the Reporter of External Commerce at Fort St. George. 1808 : Acting Collector and Reporter of External Commerce ; Collector of Sea Customs and Reporter of External Commerce and in Charge of Government Grain. 1815 : Collector of Chingleput. 1820 : Collector and Magistrate of Chittoor. 1821 : Principal Collector and Magistrate of Chittoor. 1826 : *At home.* 1829 : *Out of the service.*

COOK, HENRY DAVID.—1835 : Writer. 1836 : Assistant to Principal Collector and Magistrate, Malabar. 1839 : Acting Head Assistant to Principal Collector and Magistrate, Tanjore. 1840 : Head Assistant to Principal Collector and Magistrate, Tanjore. 1843 : Head Assistant to Principal Collector and Magistrate, Malabar. 1847 : Acting Sub-Judge, Mangalore. 1848 : *Proceeded to Europe on furlough.* 1851 : Acting Sub-Judge, Calicut; Head Assistant to Collector and Magistrate, Madura ; subsequently Sub-Judge, Calicut. 1855 : Acting Civil and Sessions Judge, Salem ; later, at Madura. 1856 ; Acting Civil and Sessions Judge, Calicut. 1857 ; Civil and Sessions Judge, Calicut. 1866 : Civil and Sessions Judge, Coimbatore. 1868 : *On furlough to Europe for two years.* 1870: *Resigned the service,* 18*th September.* (*Annuitant.*) *Died,* 16*th June* 1882, *in England.*

COOPER, THOMAS.—1767 : Writer. 1776 : Junior Merchant. 1778 : Senior Merchant. 1790 : *At home.* 1791 : *Returned to India.* 1795 : Paymaster at Ganjam and Aska. 1800 : *Out of the service.*

COPLESTON, FRANCIS.—1831 : Writer. 1833 : Assistant to Principal Collector, Nellore. 1834 : Assistant to Principal Collector and Magistrate, Nellore. 1835 : Acting Register of the Zillah of Cuddapah. 1836 : Acting Head Assistant to Principal Collector and Magistrate, Cuddapah. 1837 : Head Assistant to Principal Collector and Magistrate, Cuddapah. 1838 : Acting Head Assistant to Principal Collector and Magistrate, Guntoor. 1839 : Head Assistant to Principal Collector and Magistrate, Guntoor. 1840 : Acting Head Assistant to Principal Collector and Magistrate, Coimbatore : Acting Assistant Judge and Joint Criminal Judge, Salem. 1841 : Acting Register of the Zillah Court of Madura ; Acting Judge and Criminal Judge, Madura; Acting Assistant Judge and Joint Criminal Judge, Trichinopoly. 1843: Acting Assistant

Judge and Joint Criminal Judge, afterwards Sub-Judge, Rajahmundry. 1845 : *Proceeded to Europe on furlough.* 1847 : Sub-Judge, Mangalore. 1851: Acting Civil and Sessions Judge, Honore. 1852 : Acting Civil and Sessions Judge, Mangalore. 1854: Acting Civil and Sessions Judge, Honore, subsequently Civil and Sessions Judge, Rajahmundry. 1856 : *On medical leave to Europe for 20 months.* 1857 : *Returned to India.* 1858 : Resumed Charge of the Civil Court of Rajahmundry. 1862 : *On sick leave for 12 months, forfeiting appointment ; Resigned the service, 1st December. (Annuitant.) Died, 28th March 1869.*

CORBETT, THEODORE.—1769: Writer. 1776: Factor. 1778: Junior Merchant. 1780: Senior Merchant. 1790: *At home.* 1793 : *Returned to India.* 1795 : Civil Storekeeper and one of the Justices. *Died in 1795.*

CORBETT, VINCENTIO.—1771: Writer. 1776: Factor. 1782: Senior Merchant. 1791 : Mayor of Madraspatnam. 1792 : Collector at Coimbatore. 1795 : Resident at Masulipatam. 1806 : Commercial Resident at Vizagapatam. *Died, 17th December 1808, at Vizagapatam.*

COTSFORD, EDWARD.—1756 : Writer. 1776 : Member of Council of the Governor and Chief of Masulipatam. 1780: *Came home.* 1790: *Out of the service.*

COTTON, JOHN.—1801 : Writer. 1802: Head Assistant to the Collector of Tanjore. 1805: Sub-Collector of Tanjore. 1808: *Out of employ ;* Senior Assistant to the Collector of Tanjore. 1813 : Collector and Magistrate of Tinnevelly. 1820 : Collector and Magistrate of Tanjore. 1821 : Principal Magistrate of Tanjore. 1827 : *At home on absentee allowance. (Annuitant on the Fund, 1st May 1830.)* 1833 : *Elected a Director of the East India Company, 30th April.* 1842 : Deputy Chairman of the Court of Directors. 1843 : Chairman of the Court of Directors. 1845 : *Went out of the Direction by Rotation. Died, 16th July 1860, in England.*

COTTON, CHARLES ROBERT.—1815 : Writer. 1818 : Second Assistant to the Collector and Magistrate of Canara. 1823 : Head Assistant to the Principal Collector and Magistrate of Canara. 1825: Sub-Collector and Assistant Magistrate of Canara. 1826 : *At home on absentee allowance.* 1829 : *Returned to India per "David Scott."* 1830 : Collector and Magistrate of Chingleput. 1832 : Acting Collector of Madras ; Member of the Police Committee ; Third Judge of the Provincial Court, Southern Division.

1835 : Principal Collector and Magistrate of Canara. 1836: Temporary Member of the Board of Revenue ; Member of the Marine Board and Commercial Committee. 1838: Acting Second Member of the Board of Revenue. 1839: Second Member of the Board of Revenue. 1842 : *On furlough.* 1843 : *Resigned the service, 24th February. (Annuitant on the Fund, 1843.) Died, 19th May 1873, in England.*

COTTON, JOSEPH JOHN.—1831 : Writer. 1833: Assistant to the Principal Collector, Malabar. 1834 : Assistant to the Principal Collector and Magistrate, Tanjore. 1836 : Assistant to the Principal Collector and Magistrate, Bellary and Tanjore. 1837 : Register of the Zillah of Combaconum. 1839 : Acting Assistant Judge and Joint Criminal Judge, Trichinopoly. 1841 : Acting Judge and Criminal Judge, Combaconum ; Sub-Collector and Joint Magistrate, Cuddapah. 1843 : Acting Sub-Collector and Joint Magistrate, Tanjore. 1845 : Sub-Collector and Joint Magistrate, Tanjore. 1848 : *Proceeded to Europe on furlough.* 1851 : Acting Sub-Judge, Combaconum, afterwards Sub-Judge, Rajahmundry. 1853 : Acting Civil and Sessions Judge, Masulipatam. 1854 : Civil and Sessions Judge, Masulipatam. 1859 : *Six months' leave in India.* 1860: *On medical leave to Europe for* 21 *months.* 1862 : *Resigned the service,* 13*th April, in England. (Annuitant.)*

COTTON, ROBERT ROLLAND.—1836 : Writer. 1838 : Under the Principal Collector of Tanjore. 1839 : Doing Duty as Assistant to the Principal Collector at Tanjore and at Trichinopoly, and Assistant to the Principal Collector at Tinnevelly. 1840 : Register of the Zillah Court of Cuddapah. 1841 : Acting Head Assistant to Collector and Magistrate, Trichinopoly. 1843 : Assistant to Principal Collector and Magistrate, Cuddapah. 1844 : Extra Assistant to Collector and Magistrate, Chingleput. 1845 : Acting Head Assistant to Collector and Magistrate, Chingleput ; Acting Sub-Judge of the Zillah of Combaconum ; Acting Sub-Collector and Joint Magistrate, North Arcot. 1849 : Acting Sub-Judge, Salem. 1850 : Head Assistant to Collector and Magistrate, Chingleput. 1851 : Sub-Judge, afterwards Acting Civil and Sessions Judge, Salem. 1853 : *Proceeded to Europe on furlough.* 1856 : Acting Civil and Sessions Judge, Rajahmundry. 1857 : Acting Collector and Magistrate, Guntoor. 1858 : Sub-Judge, Bellary, and Acting Civil and Sessions Judge, Madura. 1859 : Civil and Sessions Judge, Madura. 1864 : *On medical leave to*

Europe for 19 *months.* 1867 : *Resigned the service, 27th May.* (*Annuitant.*)

COURT, MATHEW. — 1769 : Writer. 1776 : Factor. 1768 : Junior Merchant. 1780 : Senior Merchant. *No trace after* 1782.

COURT, DAVID.—1797 : Writer. 1799 : Assistant in the Office of the Secretary to the Board of Trade. 1800 : Assistant under the Collector in the Jaghire. 1802 : Register to the Judge of the Zillah of Chingleput. *Died, 12th July* 1804, *at the Mount.*

COXE, EDWARD.—1796 : Writer. 1798 : Assistant in the Military, Political, and Secret Departments ; Acting Dutch Translator ; Assistant under the Commercial Resident at the Presidency. 1800 : Deputy Commercial Resident at the Presidency. 1802 : Deputy to the Superintendent of the Quality of Investment. 1806 : Assistant to the Superintendent of the Salt Monopoly. 1810 : Commercial Resident at Masulipatam. 1813 : *Out of employ.* 1814 : Commercial Resident at Ramnad. *Died, 17th July* 1818, *at Fort St. George.*

CRAIG, HEW ALEXANDER.—1771 : Writer. 1776 : Factor. 1780 : Junior Merchant. 1782 : Senior Merchant. 1791 : Chief of Cuddalore. 1795 : *Out of the service.*

CRAIG, ALEXANDER COBHAM.—1794 : Writer. 1797 : Assistant under the Secretary in the Public, Revenue, and Commercial Departments. 1798 : Assistant under the Commercial Resident at Amboyna. 1799 : Deputy Commercial Resident at Banda. *No trace after* 1800.

CRAUFORD, QUINTIN.—1761 : Writer. 1776 : Senior Merchant. 1780 : Member of Council. 1782 : *At home.* 1790 : *Out of the service.*

CRAWFORD, HENRY. — 1763 : Writer. 1776 : Senior Merchant. 1791 : Senior Merchant and Manager of the Havallies under Vizagapatam. 1792 : Chief of Ganjam. 1795 : *At home.* 1800 : *Out of the service.*

CRAWFORD, DANIEL.— 1789 : Writer. 1790 : Assistant under the Accountant. 1791 : Assistant under the Collector of Ongole and Palnaud. 1792 : Assistant under the Accountant to the Board of Revenue. 1793 : Assistant to the Superintendent of the Noozeed Zemindary. 1794 : Assistant under the Military Paymaster-General. 1796 : *At home.* 1801 : *Returned to India ;* Agent for Public Property at Tranquebar. 1802 : Secretary to the Board of Trade. 1803 : Collector of the Zillah of Guntoor and of

Palnaud. 1805 : Acting Zillah Judge of Guntoor. 1806 : Judge of the Zillah of Rajahmundry. 1807 : Judge and Magistrate of the Zillah of Guntoor. 1808 : *At home. Lost in the ship " Lady Jane Dundas," 14th March* 1809.

CRAWFORD, STEWART.—1824 : Writer. 1826 : Assistant to the Principal Collector and Magistrate of the Southern Division of Arcot. 1827 : Register of the Zillah of Chingleput. 1828 : Assistant to the Accountant-General. 1830 : Head Assistant to the Accountant - General. 1832 : Acting Deputy Accountant-General, afterwards Deputy Accountant-General and Commercial Accountant and Auditor. 1835 : Superintendent of the Government Lotteries. 1837 : Deputy Accountant - General. 1840 : Accountant-General. 1843 : *Out of employ.* 1848 : Secretary to the College Board. 1852 : *Proceeded on furlough.* 1853 : *Resigned the service,* 13*th July, in India.* (*Annuitant on the Fund,* 1853.) *Died,* 5*th June* 1876, *in England.*

CRAWLEY, AMBROSE.—1812 : Writer. 1817 : Assistant to the Collector of Chingleput. 1820 : Head Assistant to the Collector and Magistrate of Chingleput. 1826 : Sub-Collector and Assistant Magistrate of Salem. 1830 : Collector and Magistrate of Rajahmundry. 1835 : Judge and Criminal Judge of Chicacole. 1837 : *At home on absentee allowance.* 1840 : *Resigned the service,* 1*st December.* (*Annuitant on the Fund,* 1841.) *Died, in* 1849, *at Chepstow.*

CROZIER, FRANCIS HENRY.—1831 : Writer. 1833 : Assistant to Collector, Vizagapatam. 1834 : Assistant to Collector and Magistrate, Vizagapatam. 1835 : Acting Head Assistant to Collector and Magistrate, Masulipatam. 1837 : Head Assistant to Collector and Magistrate, Ganjam. 1838 : Head Assistant to Register of the Sudder and Foujdarry Adawlut ; *Proceeded to Europe on furlough.* 1841 : Acting Sub-Collector and Magistrate, and Acting Register to Zillah Court of Malabar. 1842 : Sub-Collector and Joint Magistrate, Malabar. 1846 : *Proceeded to Europe.* 1848 : Acting Deputy Secretary to Government. 1849 : Special Agent for the Management of the Vizianagram Zemindary, and to exercise within the Zemindary the Powers of Assistant to the Agent of the Governor of Madras in the Departments of Criminal Justice and Police. 1853 : Sub-Collector and Joint Magistrate, Tanjore ; Civil and Sessions Judge, Nellore. 1859 : *On medical leave to England for* 33 *months.* 1861 : *Resigned the service,* 14*th November, in England.* (*Annuitant.*)

CRUTTENDEN, Edward Holden.—1806 : Writer ; Assistant to the Principal Collector of the Southern Division of Arcot. 1809 : Register of the Zillah of Trichinopoly. 1820 : Judge and Criminal Judge of the Zillah of Trichinopoly. *Died, 30th March 1822, at Neilgherry Hills.*

CUMING, William.—1760 : Writer. 1768 : Junior Merchant. 1771 : Senior Merchant. 1782 : *Out of the service.*

CUNINGHAME, Alexander.—1791 : Writer ; Assistant under the Secretary in the Public and Revenue Department. 1792 : Assistant to Resident at Maddepollam. 1796 : Commercial Resident at Maddepollam. 1797 : Commissary and Paymaster at Amboyna and Patna. *Died, 3d April 1797.*

CUNLIFFE, Ellis W.—1806 : Writer. 1808 : Assistant to the Register, afterwards Fixed Register in the Sudder and Foujdarry Adawlut. 1810 : First Assistant to the Register in the Sudder and Foujdarry Adawlut. 1811 : Deputy Register in the Sudder and Foujdarry Adawlut. 1813 : *At home.* 1817 : *Out of the service.*

CUNLIFFE, Brooke, Sen.—1808 : Writer. 1809 : Assistant to the Secretary in the Revenue and Judicial Department. 1810 : Fixed Examiner in the Revenue and Judicial Department. 1811 : Assistant to the Collector of Salem. 1812 : Head Assistant to the Collector of Salem. 1814 : Register of the Zillah of Verdachellum. 1821 : Sub-Collector and Assistant Magistrate of the Southern Division of Arcot. 1825 : Collector and Magistrate of Chingleput. 1826 : Principal Collector and Magistrate of the Southern Division of Arcot. 1832 : *At home on absentee allowance.* (*Retired on the Annuity Fund from 19th May* 1835.)

CUNLIFFE, Brooke, Jun.—1833 : Writer. 1835 : Assistant to Principal Collector and Magistrate, South Arcot. 1836 : Assistant to Collector and Magistrate, Guntoor ; Acting Assistant to the Principal Collector and Magistrate, South Arcot. 1839 : Acting Head Assistant to the Principal Collector and Magistrate at Salem, and afterwards in South Arcot. 1841 : Assistant, and subsequently Head Assistant to Principal Collector and Magistrate, South Arcot. 1842 : Deputy Secretary to Government. 1844 : Commissioner for Government Lotteries. 1845 : *Proceeded to Europe on furlough.* 1849 : Acting Sub-Collector and Joint Magistrate, Coimbatore. 1850 : At first Acting, then Sub-Secretary to the Board of Revenue. 1853 : Acting Secretary to the Board of Revenue. 1854 : Acting Secretary to the Board of Revenue ; Acting Tamil Translator to Government ; Member of the Board of Examiners. 1855 :

Secretary to the Revenue Board, and Acting Collector, Madras. 1856 : Collector, Madras ; Member of the Board of Examiners. 1860 : Collector of the United Districts of Madras and Chingleput, and Magistrate of Chingleput. 1863 : *Resigned the service, 14th May. (Annuitant.)*

CUNLIFFE, FOSTER.—1845 : Writer ; *Died, 17th November, at Secunderabad.*

DACRE, JOSEPH.—1802 : Writer. 1803 : Assistant to the Collector of Tanjore. 1804 : *Out of employ.* 1805 : Register under the Judge of the Zillah of Dindigul. 1806 : Register under the Judge of the Zillah of Madura. 1808 : Acting Register of the Southern Circuit Court ; Register of the Provincial Court,' Centre Division. 1816 : Assistant Judge at Chittoor. 1818 : Judge and Criminal Judge of Chittoor. 1826: Third Judge of the Provincial Court, Centre Division. *Died, 22d February 1828, at Chittoor.*

DALLAS, DAVID.—1819 : Writer. 1822 : *At home.* 1827 : *Out of the service.*

DALRYMPLE, ALEXANDER. — 1775 : Member of Council. 1777 : *At home. (Recalled by order of the General Court of Proprietors, 9th May.)* 1782 : *Out of the service.*

DALZELL, JOHN ALLEN.—1811 : Writer. 1815 : Register of the Zillah of Guntoor. 1816 : Register of the Zillah of Bellary. 1819 : *At home.* 1821 : *Returned to India ;* Assistant to the Secretary in the Civil Department, and to the Secretary in the Military Department. 1822 : Postmaster-General. 1824 : Secretary to the Native Pension Fund. 1828 : Principal Collector and Magistrate of Cuddapah. 1831 : *At home on absentee allowance. (Retired on the Annuity Fund in* 1839.)

DANCE, CHARLES WHITWORTH ALLEN.—1839 : Writer. *Died, 11th February* 1840, *at Cuddalore.*

DANIEL, JAMES. — 1761 : Writer. 1768 : Factor. 1771 : Junior Merchant and Paymaster of the Circars. 1774 : Senior Merchant. 1776 : Senior Merchant and Paymaster at Madura. 1782 : Member of Council. 1790 : *Out of the service.*

DANIEL, THOMAS.—1797 : Writer. 1798 : Assistant in the Public, Commercial, and Revenue Department. 1799 : Assistant under the Collector of Mannargoody. 1800 : Assistant in the Public and Commercial Department. 1801 : Deputy Secretary to the Board of Trade. 1803 : Commercial Agent at Ceylon. 1808 : *At home.* 1811 : *Returned to India ;* Commissioner at Tranquebar. 1815 : *Out of employ.* 1817 : Police Magistrate and Commissioner for Recovery of Small Debts. 1820 : Secretary to the Board of Trade. 1822 : Superintendent of Government Lotteries. 1824 : Secretary to the Marine Board, and Deputy Warehouse-keeper. 1826 : Third Commissioner for the Recovery of Small Debts, and Police Magistrate. 1827 : Joint Officiating Magistrate on the Beach. 1830 : Commercial Superintendent and Warehouse-keeper, &c. 1831 : *Out of employ.* 1832 : Acting Cashier to the Government Bank ; Acting Collector of Madras. 1833 : Additional Government Commissioner for Carnatic Claims. 1835 : *At home on absentee allowance. (Retired on the Annuity Fund from 1st May 1837.)*

DANIELL, MURRAY PATTISON.—1832 : Writer. 1833 : Assistant under the Principal Collector of South Arcot. 1834 : Assistant to the Principal Collector and Magistrate of Coimbatore. 1837 : Acting Register of the Zillah of Cuddapah ; Acting Head Assistant to the Collector and Magistrate of Masulipatam. 1838 : Acting Head Assistant to the Principal Collector and Magistrate of Coimbatore. 1840 : Head Assistant to Collector and Magistrate of Coimbatore. 1843 : Head Assistant to Collector and Magistrate of Chingleput. 1845 : *Proceeded on furlough.* 1848 : *Returned to India. Died, 24th February* 1849, *at Madras.*

DANIELL, LINDSAY.—1835 : Writer. 1838 : Assistant to the Principal Collector and Magistrate of Nellore. 1841 : Register of the Zillah Court, Nellore. 1844 : Extra Assistant to Collector and Magistrate, South Division of Arcot. 1845 : Head Extra Assistant to Collector and Magistrate, South Division of Masulipatam. 1847 : Head Assistant to Collector and Magistrate, South Division of Masulipatam. 1848 : Sub-Collector and Joint Magistrate, Bellary. 1855 : Agent to the Governor, Kurnool. *Died, 7th March* 1856, *at Kurnool.*

DARVALL, ROGER.—1772 : Writer. 1776 : Writer and Assistant at Masulipatam. 1778 : Factor. 1780 : Junior Merchant. 1790 : Senior Merchant and Paymaster of the Sibbendies at Masulipatam. 1795 : Collector of the Northern Division of the Jaghire. 1800 : *At home.* 1804 : *Returned to India.* 1806 : Second Member of the Board of Trade. 1808 : *At home.* 1810 : *Out of the service.*

DASHWOOD, ROBERT.—1781 : Writer. 1790 : Junior Merchant, and Third in Council at Cuddalore. 1792 : Assistant at Cuddalore. 1795 : Commercial Resident in the Salem Country. 1800 : *Out of the service.*

DAVIDSON, JOHN.—1753 : Writer. 1768 : Senior Merchant, and Second in Council at Vizagapatam. 1776 : *Out of the service.*

DAVIDSON, ALEXANDER. — 1760 : Writer. 1768 : Junior Merchant. 1771 : Senior Merchant, and Second in Council at Cuddalore. 1776 : Senior Merchant, and Second in Council at Masulipatam. 1782 : Member of Council of the Governor. 1791 : Chief of Vizagapatam. *Died in* 1791.

DAVIDSON, ROBERT.—1827 : Writer. 1831 : Second Assistant to the Principal Collector and Magistrate of Nellore. 1833 : Head Assistant to the Collector of Ganjam. 1834 : Head Assistant to the Collector and Magistrate of Masulipatam. 1836: Acting Sub-Collector and Joint Magistrate of Madura. 1837 : Acting Assistant Judge and Joint Criminal Judge of Rajahmundry. 1838 : Sub-Collector and Joint Magistrate of Madura. *Died, 20th October 1841, at Madura.*

DAVIDSON, THOMAS HARDWICK. — 1831 : Writer. 1833 : Acting Assistant, afterwards Head Assistant to the Register of the Sudder and Foujdarry Adawlut. 1836 : Commissioner for Drawing Lotteries. 1838 : Senior Deputy Register of the Sudder and Foujdarry Adawlut, and Commissioner for Drawing Government Lotteries. 1839 : Acting Register of the Sudder and Foujdarry Adawlut. 1840 : Senior Deputy Register of the Court of Sudder and Foujdarry Adawlut. 1842 : *Proceeded on furlough.* 1845 : *Returned to India.* 1846 : *Out of employ.* 1847 : Member of College Board, and Tamil Translator to Government. 1848 : Register of the Sudder Dewannee and Sudder Foujdarry Adawlut, Member of the College Board, and Tamil Translator to Government. 1850 : Subordinate Judge, Combaconum. *Died, 11th May 1852, at Salem.*

DAVIS, WILLIAM DONE.—1815 : Writer. 1818 : Second Assistant to the Collector and Magistrate of the Southern Division of Arcot. 1822 : Head Assistant to the Collector and Magistrate of Salem. 1826 : Sub-Collector and Assistant Magistrate of the Northern Division of Arcot. 1828 : Sub-Collector and Assistant Magistrate of the Southern Division of Arcot. 1832 : Acting Collector and Magistrate of Chingleput ; afterwards Collector and Magistrate of Chingleput. 1833 : Third Judge of the Provincial Court, Centre Division. 1837 : Third Judge of the Provincial Court of Appeal and Circuit for the Centre Division. 1842 : *Out of employ.* 1844 : Collector and Magistrate, Southern Division of Arcot. 1850 : *Proceeded on furlough.* 1853 : *Resigned the service,*

1st May, in India. (*Annuitant on the Fund,* 1853.) *Died,* 17th *November* 1865, *in England.*

DAVISON, WILLIAM.—1817 : Writer. 1828 : *Out of the service.*

DAWES, HENRY.—1779 : Writer. 1790 : Senior Merchant. *Died in* 1790.

DAWSON, GEORGE.—1751 : Writer. 1768 : Member of Council of the Governor. 1771 : Member of Council of the Governor and Chief of Cuddalore. 1776 : *At home.* 1778 : *Out of the service.*

DAY, CHARLES.—1807 : *Transferred from the Bencoolen Establishment.* 1811 : *At home.* 1816 : *Out of the service.*

DAYRELL, FRANCIS B. V.—1796 : Writer. 1798 : Assistant under the Secretary to the Board of Revenue. 1803 : Register to the Adawlut in the Zillah of Masulipatam. *Died,* 26th *August* 1805, *at Madras.*

DE MIERRE, FERDINAND.—1812 : Writer. 1817 : Second Assistant to the Collector and Magistrate of Bellary. 1818 : Head Assistant to the Collector and Assistant to the Magistrate of Cuddapah. 1819 : Employed in the late Peishwah's Dominions. *Died,* 21st *March* 1821.

DENT, COTTON BOWERBANK.—1763 : Writer. 1768 : Factor. 1771 : Junior Merchant. 1774 : Senior Merchant. 1791 : Senior Merchant and Civil Storekeeper. 1792 : Senior Merchant and Civil Storekeeper ; Member of the Board of Trade. 1795 : Senior Merchant and Civil Storekeeper ; Senior Member of the Board of Trade. 1804 : *At home.* 1806 : *In India.* 1808 : Paymaster and Garrison Storekeeper at Vellore. *Died,* 11th *August* 1817, *at Vellore.*

DENT, JOHN.—1812 : Writer. 1815 : Second Assistant to the Collector of Malabar. 1816 : Assistant to the Collector of Sea Customs. 1820 : Malayalum Translator to Government ; Secretary to the Mint Committee. 1821 : Deputy Collector of Government Sea Customs at Madras. 1824 : Secretary to the Board of Trade. 1827 : Collector and Magistrate of Masulipatam and in Charge of the Treasury there. 1831 : Principal Collector and Magistrate of the Southern Division of Arcot. 1838 : First Member of the Board of Revenue. 1842 : First Member of the Board of Revenue ; Commissioner in Southern Division of Arcot. 1843 : Member of the Board of Revenue, and appointed Provisional Member of Council. *Died,* 17th *January* 1845, *at Calcutta.*

DESCHAMPS, John.—*See* Chamier.

DESVŒUX, Charles.—1763: Writer. 1768: Factor. 1771: Junior Merchant. 1774: Senior Merchant. 1776: Senior Merchant, and Third in Council at Masulipatam. 1778: *At home.* 1790: *Out of the service.*

DICK, Mungo.—1771: Writer. 1776: Factor and Assistant at Maddepollam. 1780: Junior Merchant. 1782: Senior Merchant. 1791: Senior Merchant and Resident at Maddepollam. 1795: Commercial Resident at Vizagapatam. 1800: Member of the Board of Trade. 1801: Member of Council of the Governor. 1803: Superintendent of Investments, and to have a Seat at the Board of Trade. 1809: *At home.* 1813: *Out of the service.*

DICKENSON, Henry.—1806: Writer. 1810: Assistant to the Register of the Provincial Court, Centre Division; Assistant to the Register of the Provincial Court of Chittoor. 1813: Register of the Zillah of Verdachellum; Register of the Zillah of Chittoor. 1816: Register of the Provincial Court, Centre Division. 1819: *At home.* 1821: *Returned to India;* Secretary in the Public Department. 1823: Judge and Criminal Judge of the Zillah of Nellore. 1826: Collector and Magistrate of Trichinopoly. 1828: Principal Collector and Magistrate of Canara. 1831: Second Judge of the Provincial Court, Southern Division. 1836: Acting First Judge of the Provincial Court, Southern Division. 1838: First Judge of the Provincial Court, Southern Division. 1839: Acting Puisne Judge of the Sudder and Foujdarry Adawlut. 1840: First Judge of the Provincial Court of Appeal and Circuit for the Southern Division; Third Puisne Judge of the Court of Sudder Dewannee and Sudder Foujdarry Adawlut. 1842: Second Puisne Judge of the Court of Sudder Dewannee and Sudder Foujdarry Adawlut; afterwards First Puisne Judge of the Court of Sudder Dewannee and Sudder Foujdarry Adawlut. 1845: First Puisne Judge of the Court of Sudder Dewannee and Sudder Foujdarry Adawlut, and appointed Provisional Member of Council. 1846: Member of Council, and Chief Judge of the Sudder Dewannee and Sudder Foujdarry Adawlut. 1850: *Resigned the service, 16th February. (Annuitant on the Fund, 1850.) Died, 29th November 1859.*

DIGBY, Kenelm.—1772: Writer. 1778: Factor. 1780: Junior Merchant. *No trace after 1780.*

DIGHTON, Richard.—1771: Writer. 1776: Factor. 1780: Junior Merchant. 1782: Senior Merchant. 1791: Senior Merchant, and one of the Collectors of the Jaghire Revenue. 1792 : Collector in the Nellore District. 1795 : *At home.* 1799 : *Out of the service.*

DILLON, RICHARD.—1781 : Writer. 1783 : Assistant to the Secretary to the Select Committee. 1784 : Assistant to the Secretary at Vizagapatam. 1787 : Assistant to the Secretary at Ingeram. 1789 : Muster-Master of the Troops in the Itchapore and Chicacole Districts. 1794 : Assistant to the Commercial Resident at Vizagapatam. 1796 : Deputy Commercial Resident at Masulipatam, and in Charge of the Factory of Maddepollam. 1800 : Commercial Resident at Maddepollam. 1806 : *At home.* 1811 : *Out of the service.*

DOBBYN, WILLIAM AUGUSTUS.—1767 : Writer. 1774 : Factor and Assistant at Madura. 1776 : Junior Merchant and Assistant at Masulipatam. 1778 : Senior Merchant. 1791 : In Council at Masulipatam, and Salt Farmer there. *No trace after* 1791.

DODWELL, WILLIAM.—1797 : Writer. 1798 : Assistant in the Military, Political, and Secret Department. 1799 : Assistant under the Resident at Mysore. 1801 : Head Assistant under the Collector in the Jaghire. 1802 : Assistant to the Resident at Mysore. 1804 : Assistant to the Secretary to the Board of Trade and to the Superintendent of the Quality of Investments. 1806 : *At home.* 1808 : *Returned to India ;* Deputy Commercial Resident at Maddepollam. 1810 : Commercial Resident at Maddepollam. 1813 : Commercial Resident at Maddepollam and Masulipatam. 1818 : Commercial Resident at Vizagapatam. 1820 : *At home. (Annuitant on the Fund in* 1824.)

DOLBEN, GEORGE.—1752 : Writer. 1768 : Senior Merchant, and First in Council at Ingeram. 1771 : *Out of the service.*

DOUGLAS, ROBERT.—1800 : Writer. 1802 : Assistant to the Secretary in the Public and Commercial Department ; Deputy Commercial Resident at Tinnevelly. 1808 : Commercial Resident at Ingeram. 1811 : Commercial Resident at Tinnevelly. *Died, 17th September* 1814, *at Tuticorin.*

DOUGLAS, WILLIAM.—1824: Writer. 1827: *At home on absentee allowance.* 1828 : *Returned to India, per "Fairlie."* 1829 : Senior Assistant to the Register of the Sudder Court. 1830 : Senior Deputy Register to the Sudder and Foujdarry Adawlut. 1832 : *At home.* 1833 : *Returned to India ;* Acting Senior Deputy Register of the Sudder and Foujdarry Adawlut. 1834 : Additional Government Commissioner for Carnatic Claims. 1835 :

Register of the Sudder and Foujdarry Adawlut. 1843: Judge and Criminal Judge, Madura. 1844: Civil and Sessions Judge, Tinnevelly. 1853: Civil Auditor and Superintendent of Stamps; *Resigned the service, 1st July, in India.* (*Annuitant on the Fund,* 1853.)

DOWDESWELL, WILLIAM.—1826: Writer. 1829: *At home on absentee allowance.* 1831: *Returned to India, per "Minerva;"* Head Assistant to the Collector, Guntoor. 1832: Head Assistant to the Collector, Chingleput. 1833: Acting Register of the Zillah Court of Chingleput. 1834: Register of the Zillah Court of Chingleput; Acting Sub-Collector and Joint Magistrate, Nellore. 1835: Acting Assistant Judge and Joint Criminal Judge, Rajahmundry. 1836: Register of the Zillah Court of Madura; Acting Register of the Zillah Court of Nellore; Acting Assistant Judge and Joint Criminal Judge, Guntoor; Register to the Provincial Court for the Centre Division. 1837: Acting Assistant Judge and Joint Criminal Judge, afterwards Assistant Judge and Joint Criminal Judge, subsequently Acting Judge and Joint Criminal Judge, Rajahmundry; Acting Judge and Joint Criminal Judge, Chingleput. 1838: Assistant Judge and Joint Criminal Judge, Chicacole. 1839: Acting Judge and Joint Criminal Judge, Rajahmundry. 1840: Assistant Judge and Joint Criminal Judge, Madura. 1841: Acting Judge and Criminal Judge, Nellore. 1843: *Proceeded to Europe on furlough.* 1845: Acting Civil and Sessions Judge, Coimbatore; Acting Civil and Sessions Judge, Madura; Civil and Sessions Judge, Masulipatam. 1846: Commissioner for the Northern Division. 1854: Civil and Sessions Judge, Chingleput; *Absent on medical certificate.* 1860: Collector and Magistrate, Trichinopoly; *Absent on medical certificate for 21 months.* 1861: *Resigned the service, December, in England.* (*Annuitant.*) *Died, 12th December* 1870.

DOWSETT, ROBERT.—1754: Writer. 1768: Senior Merchant, and Second in Council at Cuddalore. 1776: *Out of the service.*

DRAKE, DAWSONNE.—1742: Writer. 1768: Member of the Council of the Governor. 1771: *Out of the service.*

DRAKE, FRANCIS HENRY.—1777: Writer. 1782: Factor. 1790: Senior Merchant; *At home.* 1795: *Out of the service.*

DROZ, BENJAMIN.—1813: Writer. 1817: Second Assistant to the Collector and Magistrate of the Northern Division of Arcot. 1818: Acting Register of the Zillah of Vizagapatam. 1820: *Out* *of employ ;* Head Assistant to the Collector and Magistrate of Guntoor. *Died, 7th May 1821, at Guntoor.*

DRUMMOND, ANDREW J.—1807 : Writer. 1808 : Assistant to the Chief Secretary in the Secret, Political, and Foreign Department ; Assistant under the Collector of Coimbatore. 1813 : *Out of employ.* 1814 : Head Assistant to the Collector of Tinnevelly. 1817 : Deputy Commercial Resident at Ramnad. 1819 : *Out of employ.* 1823 : Assistant to the Collector of Madras ; Deputy Collector of Madras, and Superintendent of the Custody and Issue of Stationery. 1828 : Judge and Criminal Judge of Bellary. 1829 : *Out of employ. Died, 1st May 1834, at Cuddalore.*

DRURY, GEORGE DOMINICO.—1812 : Writer. 1815 : Head Assistant to the Collector of Madura. 1816 : Assistant Magistrate of Madura. 1823 : Sub-Collector and Assistant Magistrate of Salem. 1826 : Sub-Collector and Assistant Magistrate, Southern Division of Arcot. 1828 : Collector and Magistrate of Tinnevelly. 1832 : Commissioner for the Government of Mysore ; Acting Member of the Board of Revenue ; Principal Collector and Magistrate of Coimbatore. 1842 : Second Member of the Board of Revenue. 1843: Chief Secretary to Government. 1845: Member of the Board of Revenue. 1847 : First Member of the Board of Revenue. 1850 : *Resigned the service, 1st July, in India.* *(Annuitant on the Fund, 1850.) Died, 5th August 1870.*

DUFF, WILLIAM.—1767: Writer. 1774: Factor and Assistant at Maddepollam. 1776 : Junior Merchant and Factor and Assistant at Maddepollam. 1778 : Senior Merchant. 1790 : *Out of the service.*

DUMERGUE, HENRY FRANCIS.—1824 : Writer. 1827 : *At home on absentee allowance.* 1828 : *Returned to India per " Wellington."* 1829 : Register of the Zillah of Madura ; Assistant to the Collector of Sea Customs at Madras. 1831 : Cashier to the Government Bank. 1835 : Assistant Judge of the Adawlut in the Zillah of Canara. 1837 : Acting Judge and Criminal Judge of Malabar and Canara. 1838 : Acting Judge and Criminal Judge of Canara. 1839 : Assistant Judge of the Zillah of Canara. *Died at sea, 8th April 1840, on board " Reliance."*

DUMERGUE, CHARLES.—1829 : Writer. 1832 : Second Assistant to the Collector of Chingleput ; Head Assistant to the Collector of Guntoor. 1833 : Head Assistant to the Collector and Magistrate of Rajahmundry. *Died at sea, 22d May 1837.*

DUMERGUE, GEORGE PENRICE.—1832: Writer. 1834: Assistant

to the Principal Collector and Magistrate of North Arcot. 1836: Acting Second Assistant to the Accountant-General; Assistant to the Principal Collector and Magistrate of Canara. 1837: Commissioner for Drawing Government Lotteries. 1838: Second Assistant to the Accountant-General. *Died, January* 1839, *at the Cape of Good Hope.*

DUNDAS, WILLIAM.—1778: Writer. 1782: *At home. No trace after* 1782.

DU PRÉ, JOSIAS.—1768: Appointed Member of the Council of the Governor. 1771: Became Governor of the Presidency. *Retired before* 1774.

DUTTON, JOHN.—1770: Writer. 1776: Factor. *Died, 8th November* 1776.

DYNELEY, THOMAS.—1763: Writer. 1768: Factor. 1771: Junior Merchant. 1774: Senior Merchant and Assistant at Ganjam. 1776: Senior Merchant and Third in Council at Ganjam. 1780: *Out of the service.*

EDEN, HENRY.—1764: Writer. *No trace after* 1768.

EDEN, ROBERT.—1819: Writer. 1823: Employed under the Commissioner in the Deccan. 1826: *At home on absentee allowance.* 1830: *Returned to India, per "Duke of Roxburgh;"* Canarese Translator to Government; Sheriff of Madras. 1831: Collector and Magistrate of Ganjam. 1832: Collector and Magistrate of Tinnevelly; Acting Principal Collector and Magistrate, afterwards Principal Collector and Magistrate of Northern Arcot. 1837: Principal Collector and Magistrate of Tinnevelly. 1841: *Out of employ.* 1842: *Proceeded on furlough.* 1843: *Resigned the service, 20th September, in England.* (*Annuitant on the Fund,* 1847.) *Died, 23d April* 1879, *in England.*

ELLIOTT, HON. JOHN E.—1805: Writer. 1806: *Removed to the Bengal Establishment, 23d July.*

ELLIOTT, HUGH MAXIMILIAN. — 1814: Writer. 1816: *Resigned, 1st April, in India.*

ELLIOTT, DANIEL.—1817: Writer. 1819: Register of the Zillah of Chingleput. 1821: Register of the Provincial Court, Centre Division. 1822: Deputy Tamil Translator to Government. 1823: Junior Deputy Secretary to the Board of Revenue, and Mahratti Translator to Government. 1826: Mahratti Translator to the Tanjore Commissioners. 1827: Secretary to the Board of Revenue. 1832: Member of the Board for the College and for Public Instruction; Acting Member of the Board of Revenue;

Register to the Sudder and Foujdarry Adawlut; Temporary Member of the Board of Revenue. 1833 : Mahratti Translator to Government. 1836: Third Member of the Board of Revenue. 1837 : Second Member of the Board of Revenue. 1838 : Member of the Indian Law Commission, Calcutta. 1839: Mahratti Translator to Government; Second Member of the Board of Revenue; Member of the College Board; Member of the Indian Law Commission. 1847 : Member of the Indian Law Commission, and Provisional Member of Council. 1848 : Member of Council, and President of the Revenue, Marine, and College Boards. 1855 : Member of the Legislative Council of India. 1858 : *Proceeded on furlough ; Resigned the service, 1st May, in India.* (*Annuitant on the Fund,* 1859.)

ELLIOTT, WALTER.—1821 : Writer. 1824: Employed under the Commissioner in the Deccan. 1833 : *At home.* 1837 : *Returned to India ;* Private Secretary to the Governor ; Canarese Translator to Government ; Member of the College Board ; Acting Persian Translator to Government ; and Third Member of the Board of Revenue. 1844 : Third Member of the Board of Revenue ; Member of the College Board and Mint Committee ; and Canarese Translator to Government. 1848 : Second Member of Board of Revenue, Member of College Board, and Canarese Translator to Government. 1851: First Member of Board of Revenue. 1855 : Member of Council and President of the Revenue and Marine Boards. 1856 : *Proceeded on furlough.* 1857 : *Returned to India ;* Member of Council, and President of the Revenue and Marine Boards. 1859 : *Resigned the service, 27th December, in India.* (*Annuitant on the Fund,* 1860.) *Knight Commander of the Star of India, 25th May* 1866.

ELLIOT, WILLIAM. — 1828 : Writer. 1831 : Assistant to Secretary in Revenue Department. 1832 : Commissioner for Government Lotteries, and Acting Canarese Translator. 1833 : Acting Head Assistant to Principal Collector and Magistrate, Nellore ; Assistant and Acting Head Assistant to Principal Collector and Magistrate, North Arcot ; Acting Register to the Zillah Court, and Acting First Assistant to the Principal Collector, of Nellore. 1834 : Head Assistant to Principal Collector and Magistrate, Salem. 1837 : Acting Sub-Collector and Joint Magistrate, Salem. 1838 : Acting Sub-Collector and Joint Magistrate at Nellore ; Acting Sub-Collector and Joint Magistrate at Salem ; and Acting Judge and Criminal Judge, Madura. 1840:

D

Acting Sub-Collector and Joint Magistrate, Salem. 1841 : Sub-Collector and Joint Magistrate, Madura. 1842 : Acting Judge and Criminal Judge, Madura. 1847 : Acting Collector and Magistrate, Trichinopoly. 1849 : Civil and Sessions Judge, Cuddapah. 1860 : Civil and Sessions Judge, Tinnevelly ; (*Proceeded to Europe on medical certificate.*) 1861 : Civil and Sessions Judge, Honore. 1862 : Civil and Sessions Judge, Cuddapah, and at Guntoor. 1865 : *Resigned the service, 24th January.* (*Annuitant.*) *Died, 19th March* 1872.

ELLIS, FRANCIS W.—1796 : Writer. 1798 : Assistant under the Secretary to the Board of Revenue. 1801 : Deputy Secretary to the Board of Revenue. 1802 : Secretary to the Board of Revenue. 1806 : Judge and Magistrate of the Zillah of Masulipatam. 1809 : Collector of Land Customs. 1810 : Collector of Madras. *Died, 10th March* 1819, *at Ramnad.*

ELLIS, CHARLES JOHN ROBERT.—1801 : Writer. 1802 : Assistant to the Secretary in the Revenue and Judicial Department ; Assistant to the Collector of Dindigul. 1803 : Assistant to the Collector of the Northern Division of Arcot. 1807 : Assistant to the Register of the Court of Appeal and Circuit, Northern Division. 1811 : Register to the Provincial Court, Northern Division. 1816 : Judge and Criminal Judge of the Zillah of Canara. 1819 : *Suspended.* 1820 : *At home.* 1822 : *Dismissed the service, 4th December.*

ELLIS, GEORGE HENRY.—1839 : Writer. 1841 : Assistant to Chief Secretary to Government, and Assistant to Collector and Magistrate, South Arcot. 1842 : Acting Head Assistant to Collector and Magistrate, Trichinopoly. 1843 : Head Assistant to Collector and Magistrate, Trichinopoly. 1844 : Head Assistant to Collector and Magistrate, Tanjore. 1847 : Acting Sub-Collector and Joint Magistrate, Tanjore. 1850 : Acting Sub-Judge, Madura. 1851 : *Proceeded to Europe on furlough.* 1854 : Acting Collector and Magistrate, Chingleput ; Additional Sub-Collector and Joint Magistrate, Canara ; Sub-Judge, Mangalore ; and Acting Civil and Sessions Judge, Combaconum. 1855 : Register to the Court of Sudder and Foujdarry Adawlut. 1857 : Acting Civil and Sessions Judge, Cuddalore. 1859 : Civil and Sessions Judge, Cuddalore. 1863 : Collector of Sea Customs, Madras. 1866 : Acting Judge of the High Court of Judicature, Madras. 1867 : Acting Commissioner for Inquiring into the Debts of Prince Azeem Jah Bahadoor ; also Acting Judge of the High Court. 1869 : Acting

Civil and Sessions Judge, Coimbatore, and Acting Collector and Magistrate and Agent to the Governor in Ganjam. 1870 : Civil and Sessions Judge, Cuddalore, and at Coimbatore. 1873 : District and Sessions Judge, Coimbatore. 1874 : *Resigned the service, 15th August. (Annuitant.)*

ELTON, FREDERICK BAYARD.—1830 : Writer. 1832 : Register of the Zillah of Bellary. 1838 : *At home on absentee allowance.* 1840 : *Returned to India.* 1841 : *Out of employ.* 1844 : Special Assistant to Collector and Magistrate, Tinnevelly. 1845 : Sub-Collector and Joint Magistrate, Tinnevelly. 1850 : *Proceeded on furlough.* 1853 : *Returned to India.* 1854 : Collector and Magistrate, Nellore. 1860 : *Proceeded on furlough ; Resigned the service, 30th April, in India. (Annuitant on the Fund, 1860.) Died, 4th October 1878, in England.*

ERSKINE, JOHN.—1779 : Writer. 1790 : Senior Merchant. 1792 : Senior Merchant and Collector in the Ongole and Palnaud Districts. *Died in 1793.*

FALCONER, ALEXANDER.—1789 : Writer. 1790 : Assistant under the Secretary in the Public and Revenue Department, and Deputy Persian Translator. 1792 : Examiner and Head Assistant to the Secretary in the Public, Commercial, and Revenue Department. 1794 : Gentoo Translator to the Board of Revenue, Deputy Secretary in the Public, Commercial, and Revenue Department, and Persian Translator to Government. 1800 : Junior Member of the Board of Revenue. 1803 : Second Member of the Board of Revenue. 1806 : Senior Member of the Board of Revenue. 1809 : Acting Chief Secretary to Government. 1811 : *Out of the service.*

FALLOFIELD, ERNEST WILLIAM. — 1767 : Writer. 1774 : Factor and Assistant at Cuddalore. 1776 : Junior Merchant, and Fifth in Council at Cuddalore. 1778 : Senior Merchant. 1791 : Resident at Nagore. 1792 : Collector at Tanjore. 1793 : Member of Council of the Governor. 1800 : Member of Council of the Governor, and President of the Board of Trade. 1806 : President of the Court of Judicature at Pondicherry, and Collector of Revenues there and of Cuddalore. 1807 : Senior Member of the Board of Revenue. 1808 : Third Member of the Board of Revenue. 1809 : Third Member of the Board of Revenue, and Acting Judge of Court of Judicature, Pondicherry. 1810 : *Without employ. Died, 5th June 1816, at Pondicherry.*

FANE, Edward George Robert.—1839 : Writer. 1840 : Assistant to Collector and Magistrate, Tinnevelly. 1842 : Acting Head Assistant to Principal Collector and Magistrate, Madura. 1843 : Head Assistant to Principal Collector and Magistrate, Madura. 1845 : Senior Assistant to Collector and Magistrate, and Agent to the Governor, in Vizagapatam. 1846 : Acting Principal Assistant to Collector and Magistrate, and Agent to the Governor, in Vizagapatam. 1850 : Acting Sub-Collector and Joint Magistrate, Rajahmundry. 1851 : Acting, afterwards Principal Assistant to the Collector and Magistrate, and Agent to the Governor, in Vizagapatam. 1855 : *Proceeded to England.* 1858 : *Without employ for 6 months.* 1859 : Acting Postmaster-General ; Collector and Magistrate, and Agent to the Governor, in Vizagapatam. 1862 : *On medical leave for 15 months, extended to 24 months.* 1864 : Collector and Magistrate of the Madras District. 1866 : Acting Member of the Board of Revenue. 1867 : *On 6 months' special leave to Europe.* 1868 : *On medical leave to the Cape of Good Hope.* 1869 : Acting Third Member of the Board of Revenue. 1870 : Collector and Magistrate, Madras District ; *Resigned the service, 20th March.* (*Annuitant.*)

FARQUHAR, Sir Robert Townsend, Bart.—1793 : Writer. 1796 : Assistant under the Accountant to the Board of Revenue. 1797 : Assistant under the Resident at Amboyna and Banda, and Dutch Translator to the Expedition under Admiral Rainier. 1798 : Deputy Commercial Resident at Amboyna and Banda, and Dutch Interpreter ; afterwards Commercial Resident at Amboyna and Banda. 1802 : *Out of employ.* 1804 : Lieutenant-Governor of Prince of Wales' Island. 1806 : *At home.* 1810 : *Returned to India ;* Employed on the Expedition to Bourbon ; Appointed Governor of the Mauritius, Bourbon, and its Dependencies. 1823 : *At home.* 1826 : *Elected a Director of the East India Company, 1st March. Died, 16th March 1830, in London.*

FARQUHAR, M. W. T.—1857 : Writer. 1860 : *Proceeded on furlough.* 1861 : *Resigned the service, 22d May, in England.*

FEATHERSTONE, Henry.—1818 : Writer. 1820 : Assistant to the Collector and Magistrate of Chingleput. 1822 : Assistant to the Collector and Magistrate of Trichinopoly. 1824 : Register of the Zillah of Combaconum. 1826 : Head Assistant to the Accountant-General. *Died, on his passage to England, 3d July 1826, on board the "Barossa."*

FIRTH, GIDEON.—1766: Writer. 1771: Factor. 1774: Junior Merchant. 1780: Senior Merchant. *No trace after* 1780.

FISHER, WILLIAM.—1836: Writer. 1838: Assistant to Principal Collector and Magistrate, North Arcot. 1839: Acting Head Assistant to Principal Collector and Magistrate, Bellary. 1842: Head Assistant to Collector and Magistrate, Bellary. 1844: Acting Sub-Judge of the Zillah of Bellary. 1845: *Proceeded to Europe.* 1848: Acting Sub-Judge of the Zillah of Chittoor; Acting Head Assistant to Collector and Magistrate, North Arcot; Acting Head Assistant to Collector and Magistrate, Canara. 1849: Head Assistant to Collector and Magistrate, and Acting Additional Sub-Collector and Joint Magistrate, Canara. 1851: Acting Sub-Judge, Mangalore. 1852: Sub-Judge, Combaconum. 1854: At first Additional, and subsequently Sub-Collector and Joint Magistrate, Canara. 1855: Acting Collector and Magistrate, Canara. 1856: Collector and Magistrate, Canara. 1859: Collector and Magistrate, South Canara. 1860: Collector and Magistrate, North Canara. 1862: Resident of Travancore and Cochin. 1864: *Resigned the service, 4th April.* (*Annuitant.*)

FITZHUGH, VALENTINE.—1774: Writer. 1782: Factor. *No trace after* 1782.

FLOYER, CHARLES (1st). — 1754: Writer. 1771: Senior Merchant. 1776: Member of the Council of the Governor. 1777: *Recalled by order of the General Court of Proprietors, 9th May, and suspended.* 1782: Appointed Chief of the Guntoor Circars. *No trace after* 1782.

FLOYER, CHARLES (2d).—1781: Writer. 1782: Assistant to the Secretary to the Select Committee. 1783: Clerk to the Committee of Stores; Assistant to the Committee of Circuit. 1786: Paymaster at Samalcottah. 1790: Collector in the Southern Division of Arcot. 1793: *Out of employ. Died, 1st May* 1794.

FORBES, MICHIE.—1796: Writer. 1799: Assistant in the Public, Commercial, and Revenue Department. 1800: Assistant to the Accountant in the Commercial and Revenue Department; Assistant under the Collector of the Polygar Peishcush. 1802: Deputy Revenue Accountant. 1804: *On leave to Bombay on private affairs.* 1813: *At home.* 1815: *Out of the service.*

FORBES, SIR JOHN, Bart.—1802: Writer. 1804: Assistant to the Secretary in the Revenue and Judicial Department. 1805: Assistant under the Collector of Nellore and Ongole. 1806:

Register of the Zillah of the Southern Division of Arcot. 1813 : Assistant Judge at Salem. 1818 : Judge and Criminal Judge of South Malabar. 1823 : Judge and Criminal Judge of the Zillah of Combaconum. 1824 : *At home. (Annuitant on the Fund from 1st January, 1827.)*

FORBES, Charles Henry.—1827 : Writer. 1830 : Second Assistant to the Principal Collector and Magistrate of Madura. 1831 : *At home.* 1837 : *Out of the service.*

FORBES, Henry.—1830 : Writer. 1832 : Doing Duty in Secretary's Office, Revenue and Judicial Department. 1833 : Assistant to the Principal Collector, Coimbatore. 1835 : Acting Head Assistant to the Principal Collector, Coimbatore ; Acting Head Assistant and afterwards Assistant to the Principal Collector, Tanjore. 1839 : Acting Sub - Collector and Joint Magistrate, Tinnevelly and Tanjore. 1840 : Sub-Collector and Joint Magistrate, Tanjore. 1842 : *Proceeded to Europe on furlough.* 1845 : Acting Civil and Sessions Judge, Chingleput ; Officiating Civil and Sessions Judge, Masulipatam ; Sub-Collector and Joint Magistrate, Rajahmundry. 1850 : Commissioner to Inquire into the Post Office System of the Presidency. 1851 : Collector and Magistrate, Cuddapah. 1853 : Acting Collector and Magistrate, afterwards Resident, at Tanjore. 1856 : Acting Member of the Board of Revenue. 1857 : Acting Secretary to Government in Revenue and Public Works Department. 1858 : Member of the Legislative Council of India. 1862 : *Resigned the service, 10th May. (Annuitant.)*

FORBES, Alexander Penrose.—1837 : Writer. 1838 : Assistant to the Collector and Magistrate of Rajahmundry. 1839 : Acting Head Assistant to the Sudder and Foujdarry Adawlut. 1840 : Assistant to Collector and Magistrate, Rajahmundry ; *Proceeded on furlough.* 1844 : *Resigned the service, 5th June, in England.*

FORBES, Gordon Sullivan.—1838 : Writer. 1839 : Assistant to Principal Collector and Magistrate, Guntoor. 1840 : Acting Head Assistant to Collector and Magistrate, Guntoor. 1841 : Register of the Zillah Court of Combaconum. 1843 : Extra Assistant to Collector and Magistrate, Tinnevelly. 1844 : Acting Head Assistant to Collector and Magistrate, Canara. 1845 : Acting Assistant Judge of the Zillah of Mangalore. 1846 : Acting Head Assistant to Collector and Magistrate, Canara. 1847 : Head Assistant to Collector and Magistrate, Canara. 1849 : *Proceeded* *to Europe on furlough*. 1852 : Acting Deputy Collector of Sea Customs, Madras : Acting Sub-Collector and Joint Magistrate, Malabar ; Additional Acting Sub-Collector and Joint Magistrate, South Arcot. 1854 : Acting Sub-Collector and Joint Magistrate, South Arcot. 1855 : Acting Secretary to Board of Revenue ; Sub-Collector and Magistrate, South Arcot, and at Nellore. 1856 : Secretary to the Board of Revenue ; *On medical leave to Europe for 15 months*. 1858 : Collector and Magistrate, and Agent to the Governor of Madras, in Ganjam. 1864 : *On special leave, extended to 12 months' medical leave to Europe*. 1867 : Third Member of the Board of Revenue ; Member of the Committee for the Examination of Assistants. 1869 : Additional Member of the Governor-General of India in Council ; Second Member of the Board of Revenue ; and Acting Commissioner for the Uncovenanted Civil Service Examination. 1870 : First Member of Board of Revenue, and Additional Member of Legislative Council of India. 1873 : *Resigned the service, 13th December*. (*Annuitant*.)

FORSTER, GEORGE.—1770 : Writer. 1776 : Factor. 1778 : Junior Merchant. 1782 : Senior Merchant. 1790 : *In Bengal, where he died*.

FORSYTH, WILLIAM ALEXANDER.—1826 : Writer. 1829 : Assistant to the Principal Collector of Coimbatore. 1830 : Head Assistant to the Collector of Guntoor. 1831 : Register of the Zillah of Malabar. 1835 : Sub-Collector and Joint Magistrate of Nellore ; Acting Assistant Judge of Malabar. 1836 : Acting Assistant Judge and Joint Criminal Judge of Salem. 1837 : Sub-Collector and Joint Magistrate of Canara ; Re-appointed Acting Assistant Judge and Joint Criminal Judge of Salem ; Assistant Judge and Joint Criminal Judge of Madura ; Acting Assistant Judge and Joint Criminal Judge of Salem. 1838 : *At home on absentee allowance*. 1841 : *Returned to India*. 1842 : Sub-Collector and Joint Magistrate of Canara. 1845 : Civil and Sessions Judge, Tellicherry. 1852 : Civil and Sessions Judge, Salem. 1854 : Civil and Sessions Judge, Nellore ; *Resigned the service, 1st May, in India*. (*Annuitant on the Fund*, 1854.) *Died, 24th October* 1867, *in London*.

FOSTER, HENRY.—1781 : Writer. *No trace after* 1782.

FRASER, THOMAS.—1794 : Writer. 1797 : Assistant under the Secretary in the Public, Revenue, and Commercial Department. 1799 : Accountant and Civil Auditor at Ceylon. 1802 : *Out of employ*. 1803 : Head Assistant to the Collector of Government

Customs; Deputy Accountant-General.   1806: Collector of the Zillah of Masulipatam.   1809: Accountant-General, and Accountant to the Supreme Court of Judicature; Collector of Nellore. *Died, 1st September 1823, at Madras.*

FRASER, WILLIAM A.—1806: Writer; Assistant under the Collector of Nellore and Ongole.   1810: *At home.*   1813: *Returned to India;* Head Assistant to the Collector of Malabar. 1815: Deputy Commercial Resident at Maddepollam and Masulipatam.   1823: *Out of the service.*

FRASER, JAMES.—1821: Writer.   1824: Assistant to the Principal Collector of the Southern Division of Arcot.   1826: *At home on absentee allowance.*   1828: *Returned to India, per " Wellington."*   1829: Additional Sub-Collector of Cuddapah.   1830: Sub-Collector of Ganjam.   1835: *At home.*   *Died, 22d July 1835, at Lymington.*

FRASER, JAMES BURNETT.—1828: Writer.   1830: Head Assistant to the Collector of Ganjam.   1832: Commissioner for Drawing Government Lotteries; Acting Deputy Telugoo Translator to Government.   *Died, 31st October 1832, at Madras.*

FREEMAN, CHARLES.—1771: Writer.   1776: Factor and Assistant at Ingeram.   1780: Junior Merchant.   1782: Senior Merchant.   1791: *At home.*   1792: *Out of the service.*

FREESE, ARTHUR.—1821: Writer.   1824: Employed under the Commissioner in the Deccan.   1826: Second Assistant to the Principal Collector in the Southern Mahratta Country.   1827: Third Assistant to the Principal Collector in the Southern Mahratta Dooab.   1828: Additional Sub-Collector and Joint Magistrate of Cuddapah.   1829: Sub-Collector and Joint Magistrate of Cuddapah.   1832: *At home on absentee allowance.*   1835: *Returned to India, per "Asia;"* Collector and Magistrate of Vizagapatam.   1837: Acting Judge and Criminal Judge of Chicacole. 1838: Judge and Criminal Judge of Chicacole; Acting Collector and Magistrate, afterwards Collector and Magistrate of Chingleput. 1839: Judge and Criminal Judge, Chicacole; Collector and Magistrate of Chingleput.   1851: Collector and Magistrate, Cuddapah. 1852: *Resigned the service, 30th June, in India.   (Annuitant on the Fund, 1851.)   Died, 3d January 1882, in England.*

FRENCH, WILLIAM.—1814: Writer.   1817: Second Assistant to the Collector at Madura.   1820: Head Assistant to the Collector and Magistrate of the Southern Division of Arcot.   *Died, 1st April 1823, at Cuddalore.*

FRERE, HATLEY.—1829 : Writer. 1832 : *At home on absentee allowance.* 1836 : Assistant and Acting Head Assistant to Principal Collector and Magistrate, Malabar ; Acting Head Assistant, afterwards Head Assistant to Principal Collector and Magistrate, Coimbatore. 1837 : Officiating Assistant Judge and Joint Criminal Judge, Salem. 1838 : Acting Sub-Collector and Joint Magistrate, Coimbatore ; Acting Assistant Judge and Joint Criminal Judge, Salem. 1839 : Acting Sub-Secretary to the Board of Revenue. 1840 : Assistant Judge and Joint Criminal Judge, Salem. 1843 : Sub-Judge, Salem. 1849 : Acting Civil and Sessions Judge, Tinnevelly. 1851 : Civil and Sessions Judge, Tellicherry. 1859 : Officiating Judge of the Court of Sudder and Foujdarry Adawlut. 1860 : Puisne Judge of the Court of Sudder and Foujdarry Adawlut. 1862 : Judge of the High Court of Judicature at Madras. 1866 : *Resigned the service,* 30*th January.* (*Annuitant.*)

FROUD, EDWARD.—1764 : Writer. 1771 : Factor. 1774 : Junior Merchant. 1776 : Senior Merchant and Paymaster at Vellore. *No trace after* 1780.

FULLERTON, ROBERT.—1789 : Writer. 1790 : Assistant under the Military Secretary. 1791 : Assistant at Masulipatam. 1797 : Assistant under the Commercial Resident at the Presidency. 1798 : Deputy Commercial Resident at Ingeram. 1802 : Commercial Resident at Ingeram. 1805 : General Agent for Managing the Monopoly and Sale of Salt. 1806 : Third Judge of the Provincial Court, Northern Division. 1809 : Third Member of the Board of Trade, and General Superintendent of Investments. 1812 : Superintendent of Government Lotteries. 1814 : Second Member of Council, and President of the Board of Trade. *Died in* 1830.

FULLERTON, JAMES.—1794 : Writer. 1797 : Assistant under the Secretary in the Military, Secret, and Political Department. 1799 : Assistant under the Commercial Resident at Maddepollam. 1800 : Deputy Commercial Resident at Maddepollam. *Died,* 25*th October* 1808, *at Maddepollam.*

FULLERTON, CHARLES. —1804 : Writer. 1805 : Assistant under the Collector of the Zillah of Rajahmundry. 1807 : Register of the Zillah of Cuddapah. 1809 : Register of the Zillah of Masulipatam. 1815 : Assistant Judge of the Zillah of Madura ; Assistant Judge of the Zillah of Chittoor. 1816 : Judge and Criminal Judge of the Zillah of Chingleput. *Died,* 17*th September* 1824, *at Madras.*

FULLERTON, WILLIAM ELPHINSTONE.—1817 : Writer. 1820 :

At home. 1824 : *Returned to India ;* Assistant to the Secretary to the Board of Revenue. 1826 : *Out of employ.* 1827 : Employed under the Penang Government. 1831 : *At home on absentee allowance.* 1835 : *Out of the service.*

FULLERTON, George F.—1843 : Writer. 1846 : Assistant to Collector and Magistrate, Chingleput. 1852 : Head Assistant to Collector and Magistrate, Chingleput. 1855 : *Proceeded on furlough.* 1857 : *Returned to India.* 1858 : Subordinate Judge, Mangalore. 1859 : Deputy Register of Court of Sudder and Foujdarry Adawlut. *Died, 5th July* 1861; *in London.*

GAHAGAN, Frederick.—1796 : Writer. 1798 : Assistant in the Public Revenue and Commercial Department ; Assistant under the Commercial Resident at the Presidency. 1799 : Assistant under the Governor of Ceylon. 1801 : Head Assistant in the Revenue and Judicial Department. 1802 : Deputy Postmaster-General. 1803 : Subordinate Collector in the Ceded Districts. 1807 : Collector of the Zillah of Bellary. 1809 : Secretary in the Revenue and Judicial Department ; French Translator to Government. 1810 : Superintendent of Stamps. 1812 : Third Judge of the Provincial Court, Centre Division. *Died, 19th May* 1815, *at Nellore.*

GAHAGAN, Thomas.—1804 : Writer. 1806 : Assistant under the Secretary in the Revenue and Judicial Department. 1808 : Assistant to the Register of the Zillah of Mangalore ; Fixed Examiner under the Secretary to the Board of Revenue. 1809 : Deputy Secretary to the Board of Revenue. 1812 : Head Assistant to the Collector of Malabar. 1813 : Register of the Zillah of Canara. 1815 : Register of the Zillah of Masulipatam. 1816 : Register to the Provincial Court, Northern Division. 1817 : Head Assistant to the Collector and Assistant Magistrate of Chingleput. 1820 : Judge and Criminal Judge of the Zillah of Nellore. 1823 : *At home.* 1828 : *Returned to India ;* Judge and Criminal Judge of Malabar. 1830 : Second Judge of the Provincial Court, Centre Division. *Died, 28th November* 1833, *at Chittoor.*

GAMBIER, Cornish.—1779 : Writer. 1790 : Senior Merchant. 1795 : Senior Merchant, and Collector at Muglatore. *No trace after* 1799.

GARDINER, Robert.—1767 : Writer. 1771 : Assistant at Vizagapatam. 1774 : Factor and Assistant at Vizagapatam. 1776 : Junior Merchant and Assistant, Vizagapatam. 1778 : Senior Mer-

chant. 1790 : *At home.* 1795 : Chief of Masulipatam. 1800 :
At home. 1801 : *Out of the service.*

GARDINER, HENRY.—1811 : Writer. 1814 : Register and
Assistant Collector of the Zillah of Seringapatam. 1821 : *At home.*
1826 : *Returned to India ;* Acting Collector and Magistrate of
Rajahmundry ; Acting Collector and Magistrate of Vizagapatam.
1833 : *At home.* (*Annuitant on the Fund from 1st January* 1836.)

GARDINER, RICHARD.—1824 : Writer. 1827 : Assistant to the
Principal Collector and Magistrate of Tanjore. 1828 : Head Assistant to the Principal Collector and Magistrate of North Arcot.
1829 : Head Assistant to the Principal Collector and Magistrate
of Salem. 1832 : Acting Sub-Collector and Joint Magistrate,
afterwards Sub-Collector and Joint Magistrate of South Arcot.
1835 : *At home on absent allowance.* 1840 : *Absent from India
five years.*

GARRATT, ROBERT SUDLOW.—1840 : Writer. 1843 : Assistant to Principal Collector and Magistrate, Malabar. 1845 : Assistant to Principal Collector and Magistrate, Canara. 1846 : Assistant to Principal Collector and Magistrate, Tanjore. 1847 :
Head Assistant to Principal Collector and Magistrate, Tanjore.
1848 : *Proceeded on furlough.* 1850 : *Returned to India.* 1851 :
*Proceeded on furlough ; Resigned the service, 3d September, in
England.*

GARROW, EDWARD.—1769 : Writer. 1771 : Assistant at
Cuddalore. 1774 : Factor and Assistant at Cuddalore. 1778 :
Junior Merchant. 1780 : Senior Merchant. 1792 : Senior Mer-
chant, and Paymaster and Storekeeper at Trichinopoly. 1795 :
At home. 1799 : *Out of the service.*

GARROW, JOSEPH.—1779 : Writer. 1790 : Senior Merchant.
Died in 1791.

GARROW, GEORGE.—1794 : Writer. 1797 : Assistant under
the Secretary in the Public, Revenue, and Commercial Department. 1798 : Assistant in the Revenue and Commercial Department at Ceylon. 1799 : *Out of employ ;* Deputy Secretary to the
Board of Revenue. 1800 : Superintendent of the Company's
Land in Black Town. 1801 : Secretary to the Board of Revenue.
1802 : Collector in the Division of Arcot south of the River
Palar. 1803 : *Out of employ.* 1805 : *At home.* 1807 : *Returned
to India ;* Acting Superintendent of Police. 1808 : Collector of
Trichinopoly. 1809 : Accountant-General, and Accountant-General
to the Supreme Court. 1827 : Judge and Criminal Judge of

Combaconum.   1829: First Judge of the Provincial Court, Northern Division.   1832 : First Judge of the Provincial Court, Southern Division.   1836 : Acting Civil Auditor and Superintendent of Stamps.   *Died, 4th August 1838, at Trichinopoly.*

GARROW, WILLIAM.—1796 : Writer.   1799 : Assistant under the Public, Commercial, and Revenue Department.   1800 : Assistant to the Sea Customer, and Collector of Government Customs ; Deputy Secretary to the Board of Trade.   1801 : Head Assistant under the Collector of Dindigul.   1803 : Collector of Coimbatore. 1805 : Principal Collector of Coimbatore.   *Died, 17th July 1815, at Fort St George.*

GIBBES, GEORGE S.—1830 : Writer.   *Died, 16th July 1833, at Kamptee.*

GLASS, EDWARD BINNEY.—1822 : Writer.   1823 : *At home.* 1826 : *Returned to India ;* Acting Head Assistant to the Collector and Magistrate of Masulipatam.   1828 : Head Assistant to the Collector and Magistrate of Bellary.   1831 : Sub-Collector and Joint Magistrate of Bellary.   1832 : Assistant Judge and Joint Criminal Judge of Salem.   1833 : *At home.*   1835 : *Returned to India.*   1836 : Acting Judge and Criminal Judge of Combaconum ; Acting Judge and Criminal Judge of Cuddapah ; Acting Collector and Magistrate of Guntoor.   1837 : Assistant Judge and Joint Criminal Judge of Guntoor; Acting Judge and Criminal Judge of Madura.   1838 : Acting Assistant Judge and Joint Criminal Judge of Chingleput ; Acting Assistant Judge and Joint Criminal Judge of Chicacole ; Judge and Criminal Judge of Chicacole. 1840 : Judge and Criminal Judge, Vizagapatam.   1842 : Third Judge of the Provincial Court of Appeal, Northern Division. 1844 : Civil and Sessions Judge, Chicacole.   1859 : *Proceeded on furlough ; Returned to India the same year ;* Civil and Sessions Judge, Chicacole.   1860: *Resigned the service in India.   (Annuitant on the Fund, 1860.)   Died, 17th December 1872.*

GLEIG, JONATHAN DUNCAN.—1812 : Writer.   1819 : Head Assistant to the Collector and Magistrate of Cuddapah ; (*At home.*) 1822 : *Returned to India.*   1823 : Register at Salem.   1824 : Sub-Collector and Assistant Magistrate of Madura ; (*At home.*)   1826 : *Returned to India ;* Sub-Collector of Madura.   1828 : Sub-Collector and Magistrate of Madura.   1829 : *At home on absentee allowance.* 1832 : *Returned to India ;* Acting Judge and Criminal Judge of Chittoor.   1833 : Collector and Magistrate of Masulipatam, and in Charge of the Treasury there.   1835 : Principal Collector and

Magistrate of Cuddapah. 1838 : Principal Collector and Magistrate of Salem. 1844: *Resigned the service, 3d December, in India.* (*Annuitant on the Fund*, 1845.) *Died, 20th January* 1852.

GODDARD, WALTER.—1762 : Writer. 1768 : Factor and Assistant at Masulipatam. *No trace after* 1771.

GOLDIE, JOHN HENRY.—1839 : Writer. 1841 : Assistant to Principal Collector and Magistrate, Coimbatore. 1843 : Acting Head Assistant to Collector and Magistrate, Malabar. 1844 : Acting Head Assistant to Register of the Court of Sudder and Foujdarry Adawlut ; Acting Head Assistant to Principal Collector and Magistrate, Coimbatore. 1845 : Head Assistant to Collector and Magistrate, Bellary ; (*Proceeded to Europe on furlough*). 1848 : Assistant to Collector and Magistrate, North Arcot ; Acting Head Assistant to Collector and Magistrate, Rajahmundry. 1849 : Acting Sub-Judge, Rajahmundry. 1850 : Head Assistant to Collector and Magistrate, Cuddapah ; Head Assistant to Collector and Magistrate, Rajahmundry ; Acting Sub-Collector and Magistrate, North Arcot. 1852 : Acting Sub-Judge, Chittoor. 1853 : Sub-Judge, Chittoor. 1857 : Acting Civil and Sessions Judge, Chittoor. 1858 : Acting Civil and Sessions Judge, Bellary. 1861 : Civil and Sessions Judge, Tinnevelly. 1863 : *On medical leave to Europe for* 18 *months.* 1865 : *Resigned the service,* 13*th September.* (*Annuitant.*)

GOLDINGHAM, JOHN.—1820 : Writer. 1821 : Assistant to the Collector and Magistrate of Nellore. 1825 : Assistant to the Secretary to the Board of Revenue. 1826 : Deputy Tamil Translator to Government ; Officiating Junior Deputy Secretary to the Board of Revenue. 1827 : Junior Deputy Secretary to the Board of Revenue. 1828 : Sub-Collector and Joint Magistrate of Tanjore. 1832 : *At home on absentee allowance.* 1835 : *Returned to India ;* Acting Judge and Criminal Judge of Salem. 1836 : Acting Collector and Magistrate of Masulipatam. 1837 : Acting Judge and Criminal Judge of Nellore ; Assistant Judge and Joint Criminal Judge of Chingleput ; Acting Collector and Magistrate of Guntoor. 1838 : Collector and Magistrate of Guntoor. 1843 : Collector and Magistrate of Northern Division, Arcot. 1849 : Third Member of the Board of Revenue. 1851 : Second Member of the Board of Revenue. 1852 : Second Member of the Board of Revenue, and Member of the College Board. 1855 : First Member of the Board of Revenue. 1860 : *Resigned the service in March, in India.* (*Annuitant on the Fund*, 1860.)

GOMONDE, EDWARD THOMAS.—1806 : Writer.   1807 : Assistant to the Secretary in the Revenue and Judicial Department. 1809 : Assistant to the Collector of Bellary.   1812 : Student at the College of Fort St. George ; Register of Seringapatam. *Died, 16th December* 1813, *at Seringapatam.*

GOODLAD, WILLIAM MARTIN.—1762 : Writer.   1768 : Factor. 1771 : Junior Merchant. *No trace after* 1771.

GOODWYN, THOMAS W.—1831 : Writer.   1832 : Second Assistant to the Principal Collector of Tanjore.   1833 : Register of the Zillah of Madura.   1834 : Register of the Zillah of Rajahmundry.   1835 : Acting Assistant to the Principal Collector of Madura.   1837 : Head Assistant to the Principal Collector and Magistrate of Madura, and Acting Head Assistant to the Principal Collector and Magistrate of Malabar ; Officiating Judge and Joint Criminal Judge of Malabar.   1838 : Acting Head Assistant to the Principal Collector and Magistrate of Malabar ; Acting Sub-Collector and Joint Magistrate of Malabar.   1839 : Head Assistant to the Principal Collector and Magistrate of Madura.   1841 : Sub-Collector and Joint Magistrate of Madura.   1842 : *Proceeded on furlough.*   1845 : *Returned to India ;* Assistant Judge, Calicut. 1846 : Subordinate Judge, Calicut.   1851 : Sub-Collector and Joint Magistrate, Tanjore.   1854: Civil and Sessions Judge, Salem. 1855 : *Proceeded on furlough.*   1856 : *Returned to India.*   1857 : Civil and Sessions Judge, Salem.   1859 : *Proceeded on furlough.* 1861 : *Resigned the service in England.* (*Annuitant on the Fund,* 1861.)

GORDON, WILLIAM.—1778 : Writer.   1790 : Senior Merchant and Assistant, Vizagapatam.   1795 : Senior Merchant and Assistant, Ganjam.   1800 : Paymaster and Garrison Storekeeper at Masulipatam.   1803 : First Judge of the Court of Circuit and Appeal for the Centre Division.   1806 : *At home.*   1809 : *Out of the service.*

GORDON, WILLIAM HESSE.—1791 : Writer ; Assistant under the Secretary to the Board of Revenue.   1792 : Under Searcher at the Sea Gate.   1796 : *At home.*   1797 : *Returned to India.* 1799 : Paymaster and Garrison Storekeeper at Seringapatam. 1806 : *At home.*   1809 : *Returned to India.*   1810 : *At home. Died,* 30th June 1813, *in England.*

GORDON, WILLIAM COLIN.—1816: Writer. *Died,* 8th February 1820, *at Coimbatore.*

GORDON, JAMES RICHARD.—1847 : Writer.   1849 : Assistant to Collector and Magistrate, Coimbatore. 1851: Assistant to Collector and Magistrate, Trichinopoly. 1854: Assistant to Collector and Magistrate, Guntoor. 1855: Head Assistant to Collector and Magistrate, Guntoor. *Died, 5th December* 1857, *at Vellore.*

GOSLING, GEORGE ROBERT.—1818: Writer. 1820: Assistant to the Collector and Magistrate of Bellary. 1821: Acting Head Assistant to the Collector and Magistrate of Bellary. *Died, 20th December* 1825, *at Anantapore.*

GOSTLING, CHARLES PHILIP.—1848: Writer. 1851: Assistant to Collector and Magistrate, Rajahmundry. 1854: Assistant to Collector and Magistrate, Chingleput. 1855: Head Assistant to Collector and Magistrate, Chingleput; Third Assistant to Accountant-General. 1857: *Proceeded on furlough. Died, 1st April* 1857, *at Exeter.*

GOWAN, GEORGE.—1796: Writer. 1798: Assistant under the Secretary in the Public, Revenue, and Commercial Department. 1800: Assistant under the Secretary in the Military, Political, and Secret Department; Assistant Collector of Canara. 1804: Register in the Northern Division of Arcot. 1805: Subordinate Collector of Canara. 1808: *At home.* 1814: *Returned to India;* Judge and Magistrate of the Zillah of Verdachellum. 1821: Second Judge of the Provincial Court, Southern Division. 1823: Second Puisne Judge of the Sudder and Foujdarry Adawlut. 1826: *At home.* 1827: *Out of the service.*

GRÆME, HENRY SULIVAN.—1796: Writer. 1798: Second Assistant under the Collector of the Polygar Peishcush. 1799: Head Assistant under the Collector of the Polygar Peishcush. 1800: Subordinate Collector in the Ceded Districts. 1803: Collector in the Southern Division of Coimbatore. 1804: Collector in the Northern Division of Arcot. 1818: Third Judge of the Provincial Court, Southern Division. 1820: Third Judge of the Provincial Court, Central Division; Third Member of the Board of Revenue. 1821: Second Puisne Judge of the Sudder and Foujdarry Adawlut. 1823: Member of Council and President of the Sudder Court and Board of Revenue. 1828: *Vacated Council agreeably to the Regulations.* 1830: Resident at Nagpore. 1834: *At home on absentee allowance. (Annuitant on the Fund from 1st May* 1837.)

GRAHAM, DAVID.—1773: Writer. 1778: Factor. 1782: Junior Merchant. *No trace after* 1782.

GRAHAM, JOHN.—1818: Writer. 1820: *At home.* 1825: *Out of the service.*

GRANT, ALEXANDER.—1789: Writer; Assistant under the Secretary in the Secret Department. *No trace after* 1789.

GRANT, FRANCIS ALEXANDER.—1789: Writer. 1790: Assistant to the Secretary to the Board of Revenue. 1791: Assistant under one of the Collectors of Tanjore. 1793: Assistant under the Resident at Nagpore. 1796: Collector in the Mayavaram Districts of the Tanjore Country. 1799: Resident at Nagpore. 1801: *At home.* 1806: *Returned to India.* 1809: Judge and Magistrate of the Zillah of Rajahmundry; Third Judge of the Provincial Court, Southern Division. 1811: Second Judge of the Provincial Court, Southern Division. 1821: Senior Judge of the Provincial Court, Southern Division. 1824: First Puisne Judge of the Sudder and Foujdarry Adawlut. (*Annuitant on the Fund from 1st May* 1832.)

GRANT, PATRICK.—1817: Writer. 1819: Assistant to the Secretary to the Board of Revenue'; Register of the Zillah of Nellore. 1820: Assistant to the Collector and Magistrate of the Northern Division of Arcot. 1823: Head Assistant to the Principal Collector and Magistrate of the Southern Division of Arcot. 1828: *At home on absentee allowance.* 1831: *Returned to India.* 1832: Sheriff of Madras. 1833: Judge and Criminal Judge of Canara. 1835: Collector and Magistrate of Guntoor, and Acting Collector of Rajahmundry. 1836: Collector and Magistrate of Rajahmundry. 1838: Collector and Magistrate of Masulipatam. *Died, 25th May* 1842, *at Masulipatam.*

GRANT, ROBERT.—1817: Writer. 1820: Assistant to the Collector and Magistrate of Guntoor. 1824: Head Assistant to the Collector and Magistrate of Trichinopoly. 1828: Sub-Collector and Joint Magistrate of the Northern Division of Arcot. 1831: *At home on absentee allowance.* 1834: *Returned to India, per* "*Amelia Thompson;*" Judge and Criminal Judge of Nellore. 1844: *Proceeded on furlough; Resigned the 'service, 4th June, in India.* (*Annuitant on the Fund,* 1844.) *Died, 1st December* 1870, *in England.*

GREENHILL, JOSEPH.—1781: Writer. 1783: Assistant to the Secretary to the Select Committee. 1784: Assistant to the Secretary in the Civil Department. 1786: Assistant to the Secretary in the Military Department, Deputy Garrison Storekeeper, Acting Secretary to the Committee for Revising, Correcting, and

Re-publishing the Book of Military Regulations, and Surveyor of the Company's Grounds. 1787 : Assistant to the Board of Trade. 1788 : Under Searcher at the Sea Gate. 1790 : Upper Searcher at the Sea Gate ; Deputy Sea Customer, and Deputy Controller-General. 1791 : Garrison Storekeeper. 1796 : Import Warehouse-keeper. 1797 : Commercial Resident at Ceylon. 1801 : *At home.* 1803 : *Returned to India ;* Commercial Resident in the Ceded Districts. 1805 : Military Paymaster at the Presidency and of Extraordinaries. 1807 : Garrison Storekeeper. 1811 : Paymaster to the King's Troops. *Died, 18th June 1811, at Madras.*

GREENWAY, EDWARD CROFT.—1796 : Writer. 1798 : Assistant under the Secretary in Public, Revenue, and Commercial Department ; Assistant to the Collector in the Jaghire. 1799 : First Assistant to the Collector in the Jaghire. 1801 : Collector in the Jaghire ; Collector of the Pulicat and the District of Setwadoo. 1803 : Secretary in the Revenue and Judicial Department. 1809 : Acting Junior Puisne Judge of the Sudder Adawlut, and Sudder Foujdarry Adawlut. 1811 : Junior Puisne Judge of the Sudder Adawlut and Sudder Foujdarry Adawlut. 1821 : *At home.* 1826 : *Returned to India ;* Judge and Criminal Judge of the Zillah of Bellary. *Died, 27th March 1828, at Mangalore.*

GREENWAY, GEORGE S.—1829 : Writer ; Assistant to the Collector of Trichinopoly. 1831 : Second Assistant, afterwards Head Assistant to the Collector and Magistrate of Chingleput. 1832 : Junior Deputy Secretary to the Board of Revenue. 1833 : Special Assistant to the Collector and Magistrate of Chingleput. 1835 : Register of the Zillah of Malabar. 1837 : Acting Assistant Judge and Joint Criminal Judge of Malabar ; Assistant Judge and Joint Criminal Judge of Cochin. 1844 : Assistant Judge and Joint Criminal Judge of Canara. 1844 : Assistant Judge of Mangalore. 1846 : Subordinate Judge of Mangalore. 1848 : Civil and Sessions Judge, Trichinopoly. 1854 : *Proceeded on furlough. Died, 10th March 1857, in London.*

GREGORY, ARTHUR WILLIAM.—1773 : Writer. 1778 : Factor. 1782 : Junior Merchant. 1790 : Senior Merchant. 1791 : Senior Merchant and Paymaster at Chicacole. 1792 : Second in Council at Vizagapatam. 1795 : Second in Council at Vizagapatam, and Accountant ; also Collector of a Division of the Vizianagram Zemindary. 1800 : *At home.* 1802 : *Out of the service.*

GREGORY, GEORGE.—1793: Writer. 1796: Assistant under the Export Warehouse-keeper, and Examiner in the Office of Commercial Accountant. 1797: Assistant under the Commercial Resident at Ceylon; Deputy Commercial Resident at Ceylon. 1801: Acting Commercial Agent at Ceylon. 1803: *Out of employ.* 1806: Judge and Magistrate of the Zillah of Ramnad. 1809: Collector of Cuddapah. 1810: Judge and Magistrate of the Zillah of Salem. 1816: Judge of the Zillah of Guntoor. 1818: Judge and Criminal Judge of the Zillah of Ganjam. 1821: Judge and Criminal Judge of the Zillah of Chicacole. 1824: *At home.* 1828: *Out of the service.*

GRENFELL, ST. LEGER MURRAY.—1850: Writer. 1853: Assistant to Collector and Magistrate, Chingleput. 1855: Head Assistant to Collector and Magistrate of the Northern Division of Arcot. 1856: Head Assistant to Collector and Magistrate, Tanjore. *Died, 22d February* 1860, *at Cuddapah.*

GUY, RICHARD. — 1769: Writer. 1774: Factor. 1776: Assistant at Cuddalore. 1778: Junior Merchant. 1780: Senior Merchant. *No trace after* 1782.

GWATKIN, JOHN.—1806: Writer; Deputy Secretary to the Board of Trade. 1807: Acting Secretary to the Board of Trade. 1810: Secretary to the Board of Trade. 1812: Reporter of External Commerce. 1814: *At home.* 1815: *Returned to India;* Secretary to the Board of Trade. 1819: Superintendent of Investments, and in Charge of the Import Warehouse. 1820: Second Member of the Board of Trade. 1823: Export Warehouse-keeper. 1824: Commercial Superintendent and Warehouse-keeper. 1830: *At home on absentee allowance.* (*Annuitant on the Fund from* 1st *May* 1832.)

HADOW, GEORGE JOHN.—1804: Writer. 1807: Assistant to the Chief Secretary in the Secret, Political, and Foreign Department. 1808: Assistant Collector of Government Sea Customs. 1821: Collector of Government Sea Customs. 1830: *Resigned the service, in May. Died,* 5th *March* 1869, *in England.*

HAIG, JAMES.—1808: Writer. 1810: Assistant to the Superintendent of Stamps; Assistant to the Collector in the Northern Division. 1812: Student at the College of Fort St. George; Register of the Zillah of Salem. 1816: Register of the Zillah of Tinnevelly. 1822: Acting Register of the Zillah of Combaconum. 1824: Register of the Zillah of Combaconum; Judge and Criminal Judge of Cuddapah. 1832: Acting .Third

Judge of the Provincial Court, Southern Division; (*At home on absentee allowance.*) 1834: *Returned to India, per "Alberton."* 1836: Second Judge of Provincial Court, Northern Division, and Acting Second Judge of Provincial Court, Southern Division. 1837: Acting First Judge of Provincial Court, Southern Division. 1840: First Judge of the Provincial Court of Appeal and Circuit for the Northern Division. (*Annuitant on the Fund*, 1840.) *Died, 31st May* 1854, *in England.*

HAGGARD, John.—1843: Writer. 1845: Assistant to Collector and Magistrate, Nellore. *Died, 30th June* 1849, *at Tranquebar.*

HALIBURTON, David.—1770: Writer. 1776: Factor. 1778: Junior Merchant. 1782: Senior Merchant. 1790: Senior Merchant, and Paymaster at Chandergherry. 1792: Member of the Board of Revenue. 1795: Member of the Board of Revenue and Persian Translator; (*At home.*) 1800: *Out of the service.*

HALL, Henry.—1796: Writer. 1798: Assistant under the Secret, Military, and Political Department, Dutch Translator, and Deputy Commercial Resident at Banda. *Died,* 1799, *at Malacca.*

HALL, Frederick.—1825: Writer. 1827: Assistant to the Collector and Magistrate of Madura. 1828: Head Assistant to the Collector of Tinnevelly. 1830: *At home on absentee allowance.* 1832: *Returned to India, per " Claudine." Died at sea, 13th May* 1834, *on board the " Hero of Malown."*

HALL, Arthur.—1831: Writer. 1834: Assistant to Principal Collector and Magistrate, Canara. 1836: Assistant to Principal Collector and Magistrate, North Arcot. 1837: Acting Head Assistant to Principal Collector and Magistrate, North Arcot. 1839: Head Assistant to Principal Collector and Magistrate, North Arcot. 1842: Acting Sub-Collector and Joint Magistrate, North Arcot. 1843: *Proceeded to Europe on furlough.* 1846: Acting Head Assistant to the Accountant-General, and Acting Tamil Translator to Government; Member of the College Board; and Acting Sub-Secretary to the Board of Revenue. 1847: Sub-Collector and Joint Magistrate, Canara. 1849: Acting Civil and Sessions Judge, Honore. 1854: Collector and Magistrate, South Arcot. 1857: *On medical leave to England for* 24 *months.* 1859: Member of the Board of Revenue. 1860: President of the Commissioners of Income Tax. 1862:

On medical leave for 12 *months ; Resigned the service,* 25*th November.* (*Annuitant.*)

HALLETT, CHARLES HUGHES. — 1828 : Writer.   1830 : Assistant to the Accountant-General.   1832 : Acting Head Assistant, afterwards Senior Assistant, to the Accountant-General.   1834 : Register to the Provincial Court, Centre Division ; Acting Sub-Collector and Joint Magistrate of North Arcot.   1836 : Sub-Collector and Joint Magistrate of North Arcot.   1838 : *At home on private affairs.*   1839 : *Returned to India, per " Thomas Grenville."*   1840 : *Out of employ.*   1842 : Head Assistant to Accountant-General ; Collector and Magistrate, Southern Division of Arcot.   *Died, 4th November* 1843, *at the Cape of Good Hope.*

HAMILTON, WILLIAM (of Edinburgh).—1766 : Writer.   1771 : Factor, and Assistant at Vizagapatam ; Junior Merchant, and Assistant at Vizagapatam.   1778 : Senior Merchant.   1790 : *At home.*   1795 : *Out of the service.*

HAMILTON, WILLIAM (of Kinghorn).—1766 : Writer.   1771 : Factor.   1774 : Junior Merchant.   1778 : Senior Merchant. 1790 : *Out of the service.*

HAMILTON, THOMAS.—1768 : Factor.   *No trace after* 1768.

HAMILTON, ROBERT.—1789 : Writer.   1791 : Assistant under the Secretary in the Public and Revenue Department.   1792 : Assistant under the Resident at Cuddalore.   1796 : Assistant to the Collector of Baramahal.   *Died, 12th April* 1797.

HAMILTON, JOHN.—1792 : Writer.   *Died,* 1794, *at sea.*

HAMILTON, SACKVILLE ROBERT.—1800 : Writer ; *Resigned,* 9*th August.*

HAMILTON, TERRICK.—1800 : Writer.   1804 : Register of the Zillah of Chingleput.   1805 : Register under the Collector of the Northern Division of Arcot.   1806 : Register of the Court of Appeal and Circuit, Centre Division.   1808 : *At home.*   1813 : *Resigned, 6th August, in England.*

HAMILTON, ARCHIBALD.—1839 : Writer.   1842 : Assistant to Principal Collector and Magistrate of Salem.   1844 : Head Assistant to Principal Collector and Magistrate of Salem.   *Died, 6th June* 1846, *in India* (*Shevaroy Hills*).

HAMMOND, ANTHONY. — 1771 : Writer.   1776 : Factor. 1778 : *At home.*   1780 : Junior Merchant.   1782 : *Out of the service.*

HANBURY, JOHN.—1804 : Writer.   1806 : Assistant under

the Secretary to the Board of Revenue ; Assistant to the Collector in the Zillah of Tinnevelly. 1813 : Secretary to the Board of Revenue. 1817 : Collector and Magistrate of Cuddapah. 1824 : Collector and Magistrate of Rajahmundry. 1827 : *At home on absentee allowance.* 1832 : *Returned to India ;* Acting Cashier to the Government Bank, and Superintendent of Lotteries. *Died, 18th April* 1834, *at Madras.*

HANKEY, THOMSON.—1792 : Writer. 1793 : Assistant under the Commercial Resident at Salem. 1794 : *At home.* 1795 : *Returned to India.* 1797 : Deputy Commercial Resident at Salem. 1800 : *Resigned, 28th March, in India.*

HARDING, THOMAS.—1802 : Writer. 1805 : *Transferred from the Bencoolen Establishment ;* Assistant to the Commercial Resident at Ramnad ; First Assistant to the Collector in the Zillah of Dindigul. 1806 : Register to the Zillah of the Southern Division of Tanjore. 1807 : *At home.* 1812 : *Out of the service.*

HARE, EDWARD.—1778 : Writer. 1790 : Senior Merchant, and Assistant at Ganjam. 1802 : *Out of the service.*

HARGRAVE, EDWARD ROBERT.—1793 : Writer. 1797 : Assistant under the Secretary in the Secret, Military, and Political Department ; Assistant to the Collector of Guntoor. 1799 : Assistant under the Collector in the Mayavaram District of Tanjore. 1801 : *At home.* 1803 : *Returned to India ;* Collector of the Zillah of Salem. 1823 : *At home.* 1828 : *Returned to India ;* Cashier of the Government Bank. *Died, 1st March* 1830, *at Salem.*

HARINGTON, WILLIAM, Sen.—1783 : Writer. 1785 : Assistant to the Secretary to the Select Committee. 1786 : Assistant to the Secretary in the Military Department, and Assistant at Tanjore. 1787 : Under the Secretary in the Secret Department. 1789 : Deputy Secretary to the Board of Revenue. 1790 : Secretary to the Board of Revenue. 1796 : Junior Member of the Board of Revenue. 1799 : *Out of employ.* 1806 : *At home.* 1813 : *Restored to the service.* 1814 : *Returned to India ;* Acting Postmaster-General. 1815 : Postmaster-General and Superintendent of Lotteries. 1818 : Collector of Government Sea Customs. *Died, 14th December* 1821, *at Fort St George.*

HARINGTON, WILLIAM, Jun.—1815 : Writer. 1817 : Assistant to the Register of the Provincial Court, Centre Division. 1819 : Assistant to the Secretary to the Board of Revenue. 1821 :

Head Assistant to the Collector and Magistrate of Northern Division of Arcot. 1825 : Sub-Collector and Assistant Magistrate of Northern Division of Arcot. 1827 : *At home on absentee allowance.* 1829 : *Returned to India, per " Neptune."* 1830 : Senior Deputy Register of the Sudder Adawlut. 1831 : Sub-Collector and Joint Magistrate of Salem ; Assistant Judge and Joint Criminal Judge of Chingleput. 1832 : Judge and Criminal Judge of Chicacole ; Acting Judge and Criminal Judge of Salem. 1834 : Acting Judge and Criminal Judge of Chittoor. 1835 : Acting Judge and Criminal Judge of Salem ; Acting Third Judge of the Provincial Court, Southern Division. 1836 : Acting Second Judge of the Provincial Court, Southern Division. 1837 : Third Judge of the Provincial Court, Southern Division ; Acting First Judge of the Provincial Court, Southern Division ; Acting Second Judge of the Provincial Court, Southern Division. 1838 : Third Judge of the Provincial Court of Appeal and Circuit for the Southern Division. 1842 : Second Judge, afterwards First Judge, of the Provincial Court of Appeal and Circuit for the Southern Division. 1844 : Civil and Sessions Judge, Trichinopoly. 1848 : Civil and Sessions Judge, Coimbatore. *Died, 28th June* 1849, *at Coimbatore.*

HARKER, ROBERT.—1776 : Writer. 1782 : Factor. *No trace after* 1782.

HARRIS, CHARLES.—1789 : Writer. 1790 : Assistant under the Military Secretary. 1791 : Assistant under the Collector in the Centre Division of Arcot. 1793 : Assistant under the Secretary to the Board of Revenue. 1794 : Assistant under the Collector in the Southern Division of the Jaghire. 1796 : *At home.* 1797 : *Returned to India ;* Senior Assistant to the Collector of the Polygar Peishcush. 1798 : Second Member of the Tanjore Commission. 1799 : *Out of employ.* 1800 : Collector in the Tanjore Country. 1804 : *Out of employ.* 1805 : Sub-Director and Treasurer of the Government Bank. 1806 : General Agent for the Salt Monopoly. 1807 : Acting Member of the Board of Revenue ; Second Judge of the Central Provincial Court. 1809 : First Judge of the Central Provincial Court. 1821 : First Puisne Judge of the Sudder and Foujdarry Adawlut. 1824 : *At home.* 1827 : *Returned to India.* 1828 : First Judge of the Provincial Court, Centre Division. 1829 : Member of Council and President of the Sudder Court. 1831 : President of the Revenue and Marine Boards. 1834 : Quitted Council agreeably to the Regulations, and appointed Senior Member of the Board of Revenue. (*Annuitant on the Fund*, 1835.)

HARRIS, STEPHEN.—1794 : Writer. 1795 : Assistant under the Accountant to the Board of Revenue. 1796 : Assistant under the Accountant-General ; Head Assistant under the Resident at Cuddalore. 1802 : Assistant to the Military Paymaster-General ; Second Assistant to the Manager for the Supply of Beetle, &c., and Collector of Revenues derived from the Sale of Arrack, &c. 1804 : Assistant to the Collector of the Home Farms ; (*At home.*) 1809 : *Returned to India ;* Commercial Resident at Cuddalore. 1812 : *At home.* 1817 : *Out of the service.*

HARRIS, HON. MICHAEL THOMAS.—1799 : Writer. 1802 : Assistant to the Collector of Ramnad and Tinnevelly. 1803 : Assistant to the Collector of the Zillah of Ramnad. 1805 : *At home.* 1807 : *Returned to India ;* Deputy Revenue Accountant. 1810 : *Out of employ.* 1811 : Deputy Collector of Madras. 1815 : Superintendent of Police. 1816 : Collector of Canara. 1822 : Principal Collector and Magistrate of Canara. *Died, 17th May* 1824, *at Mangalore.*

HARRIS, GEORGE ANSTRUTHER.—1830 : Writer. 1831 : Assistant to the Chief Secretary. 1832 : Second Assistant to Principal Collector and Magistrate, North Arcot ; Acting Assistant to the Chief Secretary. 1833 : Acting Register of the Zillah Court of Cuddapah ; Second Assistant to the Collector and Magistrate, Vizagapatam ; Officiating Assistant to Principal Collector and Magistrate, North Arcot. 1836 : Acting Register of the Zillah Court of Bellary ; Acting Head Assistant to Collector and Magistrate, Rajahmundry, and of Guntoor. 1838 : Head Assistant to Collector and Magistrate, Bellary ; Acting Assistant Judge and Joint Criminal Judge, Malabar. 1839 : Acting Assistant Judge and Joint Criminal Judge, Cochin, and at Malabar. 1842 : Assistant Judge and Joint Criminal Judge, Malabar. 1843 : Sub-Judge, Mangalore. 1846 : Assistant Judge at Mangalore. 1848 : Officiating Civil and Sessions Judge, and Acting Sub-Judge, at Mangalore. 1849 : *Proceeded to Europe on furlough.* 1852 : Acting Register to the Court of Sudder and Foujdarry Adawlut. 1853 : Acting Civil and Sessions Judge, Cuddalore ; Civil and Sessions Judge, Calicut. 1856 : Acting Civil and Sessions Judge, Mangalore ; Acting Puisne Judge of the Court of Sudder and Foujdarry Adawlut. 1857 : Civil and Sessions Judge, Chittoor. 1862 : *On medical leave for* 15 *months.* 1863 : Civil and Sessions

Judge, Ootacamund ; Civil and Sessions Judge, Coimbatore. 1866 : *Resigned the service, 25th July.* (*Annuitant.*)

HARRIS, Thomas Inglis Parish.—1830 : Writer. 1833 : Assistant under the Principal Collector of Tanjore ; Assistant under the Principal Collector and Magistrate, Madura. 1835 : Assistant under the Principal Collector and Magistrate, Coimbatore. 1837 : Acting Head Assistant to Principal Collector and Magistrate, Madura. 1838 : Register of the Provincial Court, Southern Division. 1839 : Acting Assistant Judge and Joint Criminal Judge, and Acting Sub-Collector and Magistrate, Salem. 1840 : Acting Assistant Judge, and Acting Register of the Zillah Court, Canara. 1842 : Assistant Judge and Joint Criminal Judge, Cochin. 1843 : Sub-Judge, Bellary. 1847 : Acting Civil and Sessions Judge, Bellary. 1849 : *Proceeded to Europe on furlough.* 1851 : Acting Deputy Collector of Sea Customs, Madras. 1852 : Acting Civil and Sessions Judge, Cuddalore. 1853 : Civil and Sessions Judge, Trichinopoly. 1858 : *On medical leave to Europe for 18 months.* 1860 : Resumed Charge of Office. 1866 : *Resigned the service, in February.* (*Annuitant.*)

HARRISON, John.—1808 : Writer ; Assistant under the Collector of Tinnevelly. 1811 : Deputy Commercial Resident at Tinnevelly. *Died, 11th May 1812, at Tinnevelly.*

HARRISON, Benjamin, Sen.—1807 : Writer. 1810 : Assistant to the Secretary to the Board of Revenue. 1811 : Assistant to the Collector of Malabar. 1813 : Head Assistant to the Collector of Madura. 1814 : *At home.* 1819 : *Out of the service.*

HARRISON, Benjamin, Jun.—1845 : Writer. 1847 : Assistant to Collector and Magistrate, Guntoor. *Died, 25th December 1847, at Guntoor.*

HASLEWOOD, Thomas.—1778 : Writer. *No trace after 1780.*

HATHWAY, Arthur.—1839 : Writer. 1840 : Assistant to Principal Collector and Magistrate, Nellore. 1841 : Acting Head Assistant to Principal Collector and Magistrate, Guntoor. 1842 : Head Assistant to Principal Collector and Magistrate, Masulipatam. 1845 : *Proceeded to Europe on furlough.* 1847 : Assistant to Collector and Magistrate, North Arcot. 1848 : Head Assistant to Collector and Magistrate, Trichinopoly. 1850 : Acting Sub-Collector and Joint Magistrate, Cuddapah. 1851 : Acting Sub-Judge, afterwards Sub-Judge, Cuddapah. 1852 : Acting Civil and Sessions Judge, Chittoor. 1857 : Acting Civil and Sessions

Judge, Tinnevelly. 1858 : Acting Collector and Magistrate, Madura ; Additional Sub-Collector and Joint Magistrate, Canara ; Acting Collector and Magistrate, Salem. 1859 : Collector and Magistrate, Bellary. 1863 : *On medical leave to England for 12 months. Died, 17th April 1866, in India.*

HAWKINS, WILLIAM.—1776 : Writer. 1782 : Factor. 1790 : Senior Merchant, and Paymaster at Poonamallee. 1795 : Paymaster at Trichinopoly. 1800 : Paymaster at Trichinopoly, and Garrison Storekeeper. 1805 : *At home.* 1808 : *In India without employ.* 1810 : Collector in the Zillah of Masulipatam. 1813 : *No employ.* 1815 : Third Judge of the Court of Appeal, Centre Division. 1819 : Second Judge of the Court of Appeal, Centre Division. 1820 : *At home.* 1823 : Agent to the East India Company at the Cape of Good Hope. 1831 : *Out of the service.*

HAWKINS, WILLIAM BROWN.—1832 : Writer. 1834 : Assistant under the Principal Collector of North Arcot. 1836 : Assistant to the Principal Collector and Magistrate of Bellary. 1837 : Acting Register, afterwards Register, of the Zillah of Bellary. 1838 : Assistant to Principal Collector and Magistrate, Bellary ; Register to the Zillah Court of Bellary. 1840 : Register to the Court of Appeal and Circuit, Centre Division. 1844 : Extra Assistant to Collector and Magistrate, Bellary. 1845 : Subordinate Judge, Cuddapah. 1847 : *Proceeded on furlough. Died, 3d July 1848, in London.*

. **HAY**, JAMES.—1756 : Writer. 1768 : Senior Merchant. 1771 : Senior Merchant, and Paymaster at Trichinopoly. 1774 : *At home.* 1776 : *Resigned the service.*

HEATH, JOSIAH MARSHALL.—1806 : Writer. 1808 : Assistant to the Secretary to the Board of Revenue. 1809 : Fixed Examiner under the Secretary to the Board of Trade. 1811 : Register to the Zillah of Chingleput. 1812 : Deputy Commercial Resident at Salem. 1820 : *Out of employ.* 1825 : *At home. (Annuitant on the Fund from 1st January 1829.)*

HEPBURN, SAMUEL.—1792 : Writer. *Died at sea in 1794.*

HEPBURN, JAMES.—1796 : Writer. 1798 : Assistant under the Secretary in the Public, Revenue, and Commercial Department ; Head Assistant under the Collector in the Jaghire. 1801 : Assistant to the Principal Collector in Coimbatore ; Head Assistant to the Collector in the Jaghire. 1802 : Collector in the Zillah Caragoody. 1806 : Collector of Tinnevelly. 1813 : Collector of Tanjore. 1820 : *At home.* 1824 : *Out of the service.*

HEYWOOD, EDMUND CULLING.—1838 : Writer.   *Died, 8th July* 1839, *at Madras.*

HICHENS, ROBERT.—1838 : Writer.   1840 : Assistant to Collector and Magistrate, Nellore ; Assistant to Collector and Magistrate, Rajahmundry.   1841 : Assistant to Collector and Magistrate, Masulipatam.   *Died, 2d November* 1841, *at Rajahmundry.*

HIGGINSON, GEORGE JOSEPH.—1776 : Junior Merchant and Sub-Accountant.   1790 : *Out of the service.*

HIGGINSON, CHARLES H.—1799 : Writer.   1803 : Head Assistant to the Secretary in the General and Commercial Department. 1804 : Deputy Revenue Accountant.   1807 : Register to Provincial Court, Northern Division.   1811 : Register to Provincial Court, Southern Division ; Judge and Magistrate of the Zillah of Trichinopoly.   1821 : Third Judge of the Provincial Court, Southern Division.   1824 : First Judge of the Provincial Court, Southern Division.   *Died, 18th July* 1824, *at Trichinopoly.*

HILL, DAVID.—1804 : Writer.   1806 : Assistant to the Collector of the Zillah of Tinnevelly.   1807 : Assistant to the Principal Collector of Malabar.   1809 : Head Assistant to the Chief Secretary to Government ; Deputy Postmaster.   1810 : Sub-Secretary to Government.   1812 : Acting Secretary in the Revenue and Judicial Department ; Paymaster of Carnatic Stipends ; Secretary to Government.   1820 : Paymaster of Carnatic Stipends at the Presidency.   1824 : Chief Secretary to Government.   1828 : *At home.*   1829 : *Returned to India ;* Chief Secretary to Government. 1831 : *At home on absentee allowance.* (*Annuitant on the Fund from* 1st *May* 1832.)   1832 : Appointed (*27th July*) an Assistant in Examiner's Office of the Home Establishment of the East India Company.   1836 : Assistant Examiner. (*Retired on pension,* 28th *March* 1856.)   *Died, 16th October* 1866, *in England.*

HIPPESLEY, JOHN COXE.—1782 : Writer.   1786 : Paymaster at Tanjore.   1787 : Member of the Committee of Inspection, Tanjore.   *No trace after* 1787.

HOARE, GEORGE.—1771 : Writer.   1776 : Factor.   1780 : Junior Merchant.   1782 : Senior Merchant.   1792 : Senior Merchant, and Paymaster to the Army.   1795 : *At home.*   1800 : *Out of the service.*

HODGES, JAMES.—1764 : Writer.   1771 : Factor.   1774 : Junior Merchant.   1776 : Senior Merchant, and Fourth in Council at Masulipatam.   1791 : Second in Council at Masulipatam. 1792 : *At home.*   1795 : *Out of the service.*

HODGSON, John.—1792 : Writer.   1794 : Assistant under the Secretary in the Public, Commercial, and Revenue Department, and Assistant to the Accountant to the Board of Revenue.   1796 : Assistant under the Collector in the Jaghire.   1799 : Collector in the Jaghire.   1800: Secretary in the Judicial and Revenue Department.   1802 : Secretary to the Special Commission.   1803 : Junior Member of the Board of Revenue.   1806 : Second Member of the Board of Revenue.   1808 : *At home.*   1812 : *Returned to India ;* Second Member of the Board of Revenue.   1813 : Senior Member of the Board of Revenue.   1819 : Fourth Member of Council and President of the Board of Revenue.   1821 : *At home.* 1823 : *Out of the service.*

HOISSARD, George Isaac.—1771 : Writer.   1776 : Factor. 1780 : Junior Merchant.   1782 : Senior Merchant.   1791 : Senior Merchant, and Assistant to Resident at Nagore, but to reside at Negapatam.   *Died in* 1791.

HOLLAND, Francis.—1806 : Writer.   1810 : Assistant to the Secretary in the Military Department ; Assistant to the Collector in the Zillah of Salem.   1811 : Fixed Examiner in the Revenue and Judicial Department.   1813 : Register to the Circuit Court, Western Division.   1821 : Sub-Collector and Assistant to the Magistrate of Malabar.   1824 : Judge and Criminal Judge of Malabar.   *Died on his passage to England, in* 1828, *on board the* " *Valleyfield.*"

HOLLIER, Henry.—1773 : Writer.   1778 : Factor.   1782 : Junior Merchant.   *No trace after* 1782.

HOLLOND, John.— 1761 : Writer.   1768 : Factor.   1771 : Junior Merchant.   1774 : Senior Merchant.   1782 : Member of Council of the Governor.   1790 : *Out of the service.*

HOLLOND, Edward John.—1769 : Writer.   1774 : Factor. 1778 : Junior Merchant.   1780 : Senior Merchant.   1790 : *Suspended from the service.*   1792 : *At home.*   1795 : *Out of the service.*

HOLLOND, Edward.—1789 : Writer.   1790 : Assistant under the Secretary to the Board of Revenue.   1791 : *Out of employ.* 1793 : Assistant to the Secretary in the Public, Commercial, and Revenue Department ; Assistant under the Secretary to the Board of Trade, and at the Import Warehouse.   1794 : Deputy Secretary to the Board of Trade.   1797 : Assistant to the Board of Trade. 1798 : *At home.*   1801 : *Returned to India.*   1802 : *At home.* 1808 : *Out of the service.*

HOME, Sir James, Bart., Sen.—1808: Writer. 1809: Assistant to the Secretary to the Board of Revenue. 1812: *At home.* 1815: *Resigned, 6th September, in England.*

HOME, Sir James, Bart., Jun. — 1819: Writer. 1820: Assistant to the Collector of Sea Customs in Malabar and Canara. 1824: Assistant to the Principal Collector and Magistrate of Malabar. 1825: Register of the Zillah of Salem. 1827: Deputy Accountant-General in the Military Department. 1828: Malyalum Translator to Government. 1830: Mint-Master. 1833: *At home.* 1836: *Returned to India, and died, 12th March, at Madras.*

HOME, William Gosset.—1828: Writer. 1831: *At home on absentee allowance. Died, 31st October* 1831, *at Madeira.*

HONEYMAN, Richard Bempde Johnstone.—1806: Writer. 1807: Assistant under the Chief Secretary in the Secret and Foreign Department; Assistant to the Collector of Coimbatore. 1809: Deputy Commercial Resident at Ramnad. 1811: *At home.* 1816: *Out of the service.*

HOOPER, George Stanley.—1817: Writer. 1819: *At home.* 1823: *Returned to India;* Assistant to the Collector and Magistrate of Tinnevelly. 1826: Register of the Zillah of Malabar. 1827: Head Assistant to the Principal Collector of Canara. 1828: Assistant Judge and Joint Criminal Judge of Salem. 1830: Judge and Joint Criminal Judge of Salem. 1832: Acting Collector and Magistrate of Masulipatam. 1833: Judge and Criminal Judge of Madura. 1836: Acting Third Judge of the Provincial Court, Southern Division. 1837: Judge and Criminal Judge of Madura. 1841: Third Judge of the Provincial Court of Appeal and Circuit, Western Division. 1842: Third Judge, afterwards Second Judge, of the Provincial Court of Appeal and Circuit, Southern Division. 1844: Civil and Sessions Judge, Madura. 1847: First Puisne Judge of the Sudder Dewannee and Sudder Foujdarry Adawlut. 1855: Puisne Judge of the Sudder Dewannee and Sudder Foujdarry Adawlut. 1860: *Resigned the service, May, in India. (Annuitant on the Fund,* 1860.)

HOOPER, Edward Pulteney Stanley.—1844: Writer. *Died, 26th July* 1846, *at Ramnad.*

HORNBY, John.—1789: Writer. 1790: Assistant under the Accountant and Import Warehouse-keeper. 1793: *At home; No trace after this date.*

HORNE, Benjamin.—1814: Writer. 1817: Second Assistant

to the Collector of Trichinopoly. *Died, 19th May 1819, near Trichinopoly.*

HORSLEY, JOHN.—1817 : Writer. 1821 :~*At home.* '1824 : *Returned to India ;* Register to the Zillah of Madura. 1826 : Head Assistant to the Principal Collector and Magistrate of Tanjore. 1828 : Sub-Collector and Joint Magistrate of Tinnevelly. 1829 : Assistant Judge and Joint Criminal Judge of Madura. 1832 : Judge and Criminal Judge of Chingleput. 1842 : Judge and Criminal Judge, Madura ; Second Judge of the Provincial Court of Appeal and Circuit, Northern Division. 1844 : Civil and Sessions Judge, Guntoor. 1850 : Civil and Sessions Judge, Cuddalore. *Died, 12th June 1851, at Madras.*

HORSLEY, RALPH.—1851 : Writer. 1853 : Assistant to Collector and Magistrate, Bellary. *Died, 4th July 1856, at Bellary.*

HOUSTOUN, GEORGE.—1805 : Writer. *Died, 16th September 1806.*

HOWDEN, ROBERT.—1781 : Writer. 1783 : Assistant to the Secretary to the Select Committee. 1784 : Secretary to General Ogle. 1786 : Assistant to the Secretary in the Military Department and Superintendent of Godown. 1787 : Deputy Commercial Storekeeper. *Died, 26th June 1788.*

HUDDLESTON, JOHN.—1766 : Writer. 1771 : Factor. 1774 : Junior Merchant. 1776 : Junior Merchant, and Fifth in Council at Ganjam. 1778 : Senior Merchant. 1790 : *Out of the service.*

HUDDLESTON, ANDREW FLEMING.—1812 : Writer. 1817 : Assistant to the Collector of Sea Customs at Malabar and Canara. 1821 : *At home.* 1825 : *Returned to India ;* Assistant to the Secretary in the Revenue and Judicial Department. 1826 : Sub-Collector and Assistant Magistrate of Canara. 1831 : Principal Collector and Magistrate of Malabar. 1832 : Third Judge of the Provincial Court, Western Division. 1833 : *At home on absentee allowance.* 1838 : *Absent five years, and out of the service. (Annuitant on the Fund,* 1841.) *Died, 2d September 1861, in England.*

HUDLESTON, JOHN BURLAND.—1804 : Writer. 1806 : Acting Register of the Zillah of Tinnevelly. 1807 : Register of the Zillah of Tinnevelly. 1812 : Register of the Provincial Court, Southern Division. 1818 : Justice of the Peace. 1820 : Judge and Criminal Judge of the Zillah of Tinnevelly ; Collector and Magistrate of Tinnevelly. *Died, 6th June 1823.*

HUDLESTON, WILLIAM. — 1808 : Writer. 1814 : First

Assistant to the Register of the Sudder and Foujdarry Adawlut. 1815: *Leave to the Cape, and eventually to Europe.* 1817: *Returned to India;* Assistant to the Register of the Sudder and Foujdarry Adawlut. 1818: First Assistant to the Register of the Sudder and Foujdarry Adawlut. 1819: Junior Deputy Register of the Sudder and Foujdarry Adawlut. 1821: Secretary to the Trustees of the Civil Fund. 1824: Register to the Sudder and Foujdarry Adawlut, and Persian Secretary to Government. 1826: *At home on absentee allowance.* 1830: *Returned to India, per "Minerva;"* Secretary to the Marine Board. 1831: Register to the Sudder and Foujdarry Adawlut. 1832: Third Judge, afterwards Officiating Second Judge, of the Sudder and Foujdarry Adawlut. 1838: Second Puisne Judge of the Sudder and Foujdarry Adawlut. (*Annuitant on the Fund,* 1840.) *Died, 29th June* 1855, *in England.*

HUDLESTON, JOSIAH ANDREW. — 1817: Writer. 1820: Second Assistant to the Collector and Magistrate of Tinnevelly. 1824: Head Assistant to the Register of the Sudder and Foujdarry Adawlut. 1826: Acting Deputy Register of the Sudder Court. 1828: Deputy Collector of Madras. 1831: Superintendent of Stationery. 1836: Acting Collector of Madras. 1837: Deputy Collector of Madras and Superintendent of Stationery. 1844: Collector of Madras. 1855: *Resigned the service, 1st May, in India.* (*Annuitant on the Fund,* 1856.)

HUDSON, MARK GILBERT. — 1796: Writer. 1798: *On leave to the Cape.* 1799: *Returned to India;* Assistant in the Public, Revenue, and Commercial Department. 1800: Assistant under the Collector of Guntoor. 1803: Deputy Postmaster at Guntoor. 1807: Deputy Commercial Resident at Ganjam. 1810: Commercial Resident at Ganjam. *Died, 19th July* 1812, *at Ganjam.*

HUGHES, ROBERT. — 1766: Writer. 1771: Factor and Assistant at Masulipatam. 1774: Junior Merchant. 1776: Junior Merchant, and Fourth in Council at Ganjam. 1778: Senior Merchant. 1791: Senior Merchant, and Collector of Revenue in Guntoor Circar. 1795: Paymaster in the Burramehal and Salem. 1800: Paymaster and Garrison Storekeeper at Madura. *Died, 17th April* 1803, *in England.*

HUNTER, JOHN ALEXANDER. — 1840: Writer. 1842: Assistant to Collector and Magistrate, Rajahmundry. 1846: Assistant to Collector and Magistrate, and Agent to the Governor, Vizagapatam. *Died, 9th July* 1848, *at Vizianagram.*

HURDIS, THOMAS BOWER.—1792 : Writer ; Assistant under the Accountant to the Board of Revenue. 1793 : Assistant under the Secretary in the Secret, Political, and Military Department. 1794 : Assistant to the Military Paymaster-General, and Assistant to the Collector in the Burramehal. 1796 : Head Assistant under the Collector of Ramnad. 1798 : Acting Collector of Dindigul. 1799 : Collector of Dindigul. 1801 : Collector of Madura and Dependent Polygars. 1803 : Register of the Sudder and Foujdarry Adawlut. 1806 : Puisne Judge of the Sudder and Foujdarry Adawlut. *Died, 16th November 1808, at Madras.*

HUTT, JOHN.—1813 : Writer. 1817 : Register of the Zillah of Nellore. 1818 : Register of the Provincial Court, Centre Division. 1821 : *At home.* 1826 : *Out of the service.*

HYDE, CHARLES.—1797 : Writer. 1799 : Assistant under the Secretary to the Board of Revenue. 1800 : Assistant under the Commercial Resident at Salem. 1801 : Assistant under the Collector of Burramehal and Salem. 1803 : Assistant to the Collector of the Southern Division of Arcot. 1805 : Subordinate Collector of the Northern Division of Arcot. 1808 : Head Assistant to the Collector of the Northern Division of Arcot. 1809 : Collector in the Zillah of Chingleput. 1811 : Collector in the Zillah of Vizagapatam. 1813 : Collector in the Southern Division of Arcot. 1821 : Principal Collector and Magistrate in the Southern Division of Arcot. 1826 : *At home on absentee allowance. (Annuitant on the Fund from 1st May 1831.)*

IBBETSON, SAMUEL.—1802 : Writer. 1804 : Assistant to the Collector of Tinnevelly. 1806 : Register of the Zillah of the Northern Division of Malabar. 1808 : Register of the Zillah of Tellicherry. 1810 : Register of the Zillah of Rajahmundry. 1812 : Register of the Zillah of Southern Malabar. 1815 : *At home.* 1819 : *Returned to India ;* Sheriff of Madras. 1820 : Judge and Criminal Judge of Bellary. *Died, 5th April 1826, at Bellary.*

INCE, DANIEL.—1781 : Writer. 1783 : Assistant at Ganjam. 1787 : Assistant to the Secretary in the Public and Revenue Department. 1788 : Deputy Secretary in the Military Department. 1790 : Secretary in the Military Department. 1793 : Deputy Secretary in the Military, Political, and Secret Department. 1797 : Collector in the First Division of the Masulipatam Districts. 1800 : *Resigned, 8th April, in India.*

INGLIS, WILLIAM ARTHUR DAVID.—1827 : Writer. 1828 :

Assistant to the Principal Collector of Nellore. 1830 : Head
Assistant to the Principal Collector and Magistrate of Cuddapah.
1833 : Head Assistant to the Principal Collector and Magistrate of Bellary.   1835 : Sub-Collector of Ganjam.   1838 : *At
home on absentee allowance.*   1842 : *Returned to India.*   1843 :
Out of employ.   1845 : Civil and Sessions Judge, Cuddapah.
1848 : Civil and Sessions Judge, Chingleput.   1853 : Civil and
Sessions Judge, Chingleput, and Member of the College Board.
1855 : *Proceeded on furlough.*   1856 : *Resigned the service, 1st
May, in India.   (Annuitant on the Fund, 1857.)*

IRVINE, PATRICK.—1832 : Writer.   1834 : Assistant to Prin-
cipal Collector of Salem.   1836 : Assistant to Collector and
Magistrate, Vizagapatam.   1837 : Assistant to Principal Collector
and Magistrate, Salem.   1838 : Acting Head Assistant to Principal
Collector and Magistrate, Madura.   1840 : Head Assistant to
Principal Collector and Magistrate, Madura ; (*Proceeded to Europe
on furlough.*)   1844 : Acting Sub-Judge, Calicut.   1845 : Acting
Sub-Judge, Mangalore.   1846 : Acting Assistant Judge, and
Acting Sub-Judge, Mangalore ; Head Assistant to Collector and
Magistrate, Bellary.   1847 : Sub-Judge, Rajahmundry.   1848 :
Acting Civil and Sessions Judge, Chicacole.   1849 : Acting Civil
and Sessions Judge, Masulipatam, and at Guntoor.   1850 : Acting
Civil and Sessions Judge, Masulipatam.   1851 : *Proceeded to
Europe on furlough.*   1853 : Acting Civil and Sessions Judge,
Nellore ; and Acting Sub-Judge, Rajahmundry.   1854 : Sub-
Judge, Rajahmundry.   1855 : Civil and Sessions Judge, Guntoor.
1856 : Civil and Sessions Judge, Bellary.   1859 : *On medical
leave to Europe for* 24 *months.*   1862 : *Resigned the service,
23d April.   (Annuitant.)   Died, 13th June* 1876, *in England.*

IRWIN, EYLES.—1767 : Writer.   1774 : Factor.   1776 : Junior
Merchant.   1778 : Senior Merchant.   1780 : *At home.*   1782 : *In
India.   No trace after this date.*

IRWIN, WILLIAM ROBERT.—1795 : Writer.   1798 : Assistant
under the Secretary to the Board of Revenue ; Assistant under the
Resident at Tanjore ; Assistant to the Collector at Tanjore.   1802 :
Register to the Court of Circuit and Appeal, Northern Division.
1806 : Judge and Magistrate of Madura.   *Died, 2d September* 1810,
at sea, near Malacca.

JACKSON, WILLIAM.—1770 : Writer.   1776 : Factor.   1778 :
Junior Merchant.   1782 : Senior Merchant.   1790 : *Out of the
service.*

JACKSON, WILLIAM COLLINS.—1781 : Writer. 1783 : Assistant to the Secretary to the Select Committee. 1785 : Deputy Secretary to the Select Committee. 1786 : Deputy Secretary in the Military and Political Department; Dutch, Spanish, and Portuguese Translator. 1790 : Secretary in the Military, Political, and Secret Department, and Judge Advocate-General. 1797 : Collector of the Southern Polygar Peishcush, and of Ramnad. 1799 : *At home.* 1812 : *Resigned, 18th March, in England.*

JACKSON, THOMAS SCOTT.—1789 : Writer. 1790 : Assistant under the Secretary in the Political and Revenue Department. 1791 : Assistant under Collector of Tinnevelly. 1793 : Assistant under Manager for supplying Beetle Tobacco and Ganja. 1794 : *At home.* 1797 : *Returned to India.* 1798 : Paymaster and Garrison Storekeeper at Kistnagherry and its Dependency. 1799 : *Out of employ; At home.* 1806 : *Returned to India.* 1807 : Paymaster and Garrison Storekeeper at Vizagapatam. *Died, 7th June 1807, at Vizagapatam.*

JARRETT, THOMAS.—1790 : Writer on the Bencoolen Establishment. 1805 : *Transferred to Madras Presidency.* 1806 : Commercial Resident at Masulipatam. 1807 : Collector in the Zillah of Guntoor. 1811 : Collector in the Zillah of Chingleput. 1814 : Sub-Treasurer. (*Annuitant on the Fund from December* 1832.) *Died, 11th September* 1837, *at Groombridge, near Tunbridge Wells.*

JELLICOE, WILLIAM EDWARD.—1830 : Writer. 1831 : Doing Duty under the Principal Collector and Magistrate of Nellore. 1837 : Acting Register of the Zillah Court of Rajahmundry. 1838 : Assistant to the Principal Collector and Magistrate of Nellore ; Acting Head Assistant to the Collector and Magistrate of Guntoor; Acting Register in the Provincial Court, Northern Division. 1839 : Acting Register, afterwards Register of the Zillah of Rajahmundry ; Acting Assistant Judge and Joint Criminal Judge of Guntoor. 1843 : Register of the Zillah Court of Chittoor. 1844 : *Proceeded on furlough.* 1846 : *Resigned the service, 30th September.*

JERVIS, JOHN.—1789 : Writer; Assistant under the Secretary in the Secret Department. 1790 : Assistant under the Accountant. 1791 : Assistant under one of the Collectors of Ganjam. 1793 : Assistant under the Sea Customer. 1796 : Assistant under the Collector of Jaffnapatam. 1797 : Assistant to the Resident at Ceylon. *Died, December* 1797.

F

JESSUP, George Kilby.—1807 : Writer.   1809 : Assistant to the Chief Secretary in the Secret, Political, and Foreign Department.   1812 : Head Assistant to the Collector of Madura.   *Died, 30th January* 1813.

JOHNSON, Samuel, Sen.—1754 : Writer.   1768 : Senior Merchant, and Second in Council at Masulipatam.   1774 : Member of Council of the Governor.   1776 : Member of Council of the Governor, and Chief of Vizagapatam.   1790 : *Out of the service.*

JOHNSON, Samuel, Jun.—1781 : Writer.   1782 : Paymaster at Madura.   1787 : Paymaster at Trichinopoly.   1790 : *Suspended, and dismissed from the service.*

JONES, Charles Edward.—1767 : Writer.   1774 : Factor. 1776 : Junior Merchant.   1778 : Senior Merchant.   1782 : *At home.   No trace after* 1782.

JONES, William.—1779 : Writer.   1790 : Senior Merchant ; Inspector of Godowns, and Deputy Civil Storekeeper ; Postmaster-General.   1800 : Commercial Resident at Amboyna and Banda.   1801 : Sub-Treasurer and Mint-Master.   1806 : *At home.* 1809 : *Out of the service.*

JOURDAN, Francis.—1759 : Writer.   1768 : Junior Merchant. 1771 : Senior Merchant.   1774 : Senior Merchant, and Third in Council at Masulipatam.   1776 : Member of Council of the Governor.   1777 : *Recalled by order of the General Court, 9th May.*   1780 : *Suspended from service.*

KAYE, Charles Turton.—1831 : Writer.   1832 : Assistant to the Principal Collector and Magistrate of Madura.   1834 : Acting Register of the Zillah of Malabar.   1835 : Acting Head Assistant to the Principal Collector.   1836 : Second Assistant and Acting First Assistant to the Accountant-General.   1838 : First Assistant to the Accountant-General, and Acting Assistant Judge and Joint Criminal Judge of Chingleput.   1839 : First Assistant to the Accountant-General.   1841 : Assistant Judge and Joint Criminal Judge, Chingleput.   1843 : *Proceeded on furlough.* 1846 : *Returned to India.   Died, 24th August* 1846, *at Madras.*

KEATE, Charles Robert Henry.—1832 : Writer.   *Died, 5th January* 1835, *at Tanjore.*

KEATING, Michael.—1776 : Writer.   1782 : Factor.   1790 : Senior Merchant ; In Council at Vizagapatam, and Paymaster of the Troops.   1792 : Manager of the Havellies, Vizagapatam. 1800 : *At home.*   1805 : *Out of the service.*

KEBLE, George Gilbert.—1794 : Writer. 1796 : Assistant under the Secretary in the Public, Commercial, and Revenue Department. 1798 : Senior Assistant under the Superintendent of the Export Warehouse ; Head Assistant in the Public Department, and French Translator. 1801 : Secretary to Government in the Public and Commercial Department. 1809 : Sub-Treasurer and Postmaster-General. *Died, 26th August* 1811, *at Cuddalore.*

KEENE, George Henry.—1801 : Writer. 1804 : Assistant to the Register to the Sudder and Foujdarry Adawlut. 1805 : *At home.* 1809 : *Returned to India ;* Register of the Zillah of Rajahmundry. 1810 : Second Assistant under the Register of the Sudder and Foujdarry Adawlut. 1811 : *At home.* 1816 : *Out of the service.*

KELSO, Alexander Hamilton. — 1800 : Writer. 1802 : Assistant to the Collector of the Western Polygar Peishcush and of Arcot, North of the River Palar. 1805 : Subordinate Collector of Coimbatore. 1807 : Judge and Magistrate of the Zillah of Mangalore. 1808 : Commissioner at Tranquebar. 1811 : *At home ; Out of the service.*

KENNAWAY, Richard.—1806 : Writer. *Died, 30th May* 1807, *at Rewarri.*

KENSINGTON, Henry Warner. — 1808 : Writer. 1810 : Assistant to the Secretary to the Board of Revenue. 1811 : Assistant to the Collector of Cuddapah. 1814 : Register of the Zillah of Vizagapatam. 1815 : Register of the Zillah of Chingleput. 1819 : Assistant to the Mint-Master. 1820 : Assistant to the Collector and Magistrate of Malabar. 1822 : Register to the Provincial Court, Southern Division. *Died, 12th May* 1825, *at Cuddalore.*

KENWORTHY, John.—1770 : Writer. 1776 : Factor. 1778 : Junior Merchant. 1782 : Senior Merchant. 1790 : *At home.* 1795 : Resident at Cuddalore. 1800 : Commercial Resident at Tinnevelly and Ramnad. 1803 : Garrison Storekeeper. 1806 : Garrison Storekeeper and Postmaster-General. 1808 : Postmaster-General. 1809 : Postmaster-General and Sub-Treasurer. 1810 : Second Member of the Board of Trade. *Died, 24th July* 1812, *at Fort St. George.*

KINCHANT, Richard.—1769 : Writer. 1774 : Factor and Assistant at Cuddalore. 1778 : Junior Merchant. 1780 : Senior Merchant. 1791 : Senior Merchant and Resident at Ragapore. 1795 : *At home.* 1800 : Commercial Resident at Cuddalore. 1809 : Commercial Resident at Cuddalore, and in Charge of the

Revenues of Pondicherry and Cuddalore. *Died, 24th August,* 1809, *at Cuddalore.*

KINDERSLEY, NATHANIEL EDWARD.—1779: Writer. 1790: Senior Merchant, and Member of the Board of Trade; also Assistant to Persian Translator. 1792: Collector in Southern Division of Arcot. 1800: *At home.* 1805: *Out of the service.*

KINDERSLEY, NATHANIEL WILLIAM.—1814: Writer. 1817: Second Assistant to the Collector and Magistrate of Coimbatore. 1818: *At home.* 1822: *Returned to India;* Head Assistant to the Collector and Magistrate of Nellore. 1824: Sub-Collector and Assistant Magistrate of Canara. 1825: Sub-Collector of Tinnevelly. 1828: Principal Collector and Magistrate of Tanjore. 1837: Principal Collector and Magistrate of Tanjore. 1843: Second Member of the Board of Revenue. 1844: *Proceeded on furlough; Resigned the service,* 1st *June, in India.* (*Annuitant on the Fund,* 1843.) *Died,* 3d *December* 1844, *in England.*

KINDERSLEY, EDWARD COCKBURN.—1815: Writer. 1817: *Resigned,* 28th *May, in England.*

KING, PHILIP STEVENS.—1781: Writer. *Lost on his passage to Bengal in* 1783.

KING, JAMES.—1807: Writer. 1809: Assistant to the Secretary in the Military Department. 1810: Fixed Examiner to the Military Department. 1812: Acting Register of the Zillah of Verdachellum. 1813: Register of the Zillah of Verdachellum. *Died,* 10th *May* 1814, *at Pondicherry.*

KINGSCOTE, THOMAS.—1773: Writer. 1778: Factor. 1782: Junior Merchant. 1790: Senior Merchant, and Agent for Clothing Company's Troops. 1792: Commissary of Grain and Provisions to the Army. 1793: *At home.* 1799: *Out of the service.*

KINLOCK, PEREGRINE.—1797: Writer. 1798: Assistant under the Secretary to the Board of Revenue. 1799: Assistant under the Collector of Ramnad. 1801: Assistant under the Collector of Trichinopoly. 1804: Acting Collector to the Register of Trichinopoly. 1805: Register of the Southern Division of Arcot. 1806: Collector of the Zillah of Ramnad. *Lost,* 20th *November* 1808, *in the ship "Lord Nelson," on his passage home.*

KNOX, WILLIAM.—1834: Writer. 1837: Assistant to Collector and Magistrate, Rajahmundry. 1838: Acting Head Assistant to Collector and Magistrate, Cuddapah. 1839: Head Assistant to Collector and Magistrate, Cuddapah. 1840: At first Acting

Assistant, afterwards Head Assistant to Collector and Magistrate, Rajahmundry. 1843: Acting Assistant Judge and Joint Criminal Judge, Vizagapatam; Acting Sub-Collector and Magistrate, Cuddapah. 1845: Sub-Collector and Joint Magistrate, Cuddapah; *Proceeded to Europe on furlough.* 1849: Acting Sub-Collector and Joint-Magistrate, Madura; also Head Assistant to Collector and Magistrate, Madura. 1850: Principal Assistant to Collector and Magistrate, and Agent to the Governor of Madras, Ganjam. 1854: Acting Collector and Magistrate, and Agent to the Governor in Ganjam. 1857: Collector and Magistrate, Masulipatam. 1859: Collector and Magistrate, Kistna. 1860: *On medical leave for* 15 *months.* 1861: *Resigned the service,* 27th *December, in England.* (*Annuitant.*) *Died,* 27th *October* 1867.

KNOX, THOMAS JOHN.—1839: Writer. 1840: Assistant to Collector and Magistrate, Rajahmundry. 1841: Acting Register of the Zillah Court of Rajahmundry. 1843: Register of the Zillah Court of Rajahmundry; Acting Head Assistant, afterwards Head Assistant, to the Collector and Magistrate, Rajahmundry. 1846: Acting Sub-Judge of the Zillah of Rajahmundry. 1848: *Proceeded to Europe on furlough.* 1853: Acting Deputy Collector of Sea Customs, Madras, and Sub-Collector and Joint Magistrate, Malabar. 1855: Principal Assistant to Collector and Magistrate, and Agent to the Governor of Madras, in Vizagapatam; Acting Civil and Sessions Judge, Masulipatam. 1857: Acting Collector and Magistrate, Masulipatam. 1858: Acting Collector and Magistrate, and Agent to the Governor of Madras, in Ganjam. 1859: Acting Collector and Magistrate, Masulipatam; Acting Collector and Magistrate at Salem. 1860: Civil and Sessions Judge, Chicacole. 1864: *On medical leave to Europe for* 15 *months.* 1865: *Resigned the service,* 28th *October, in England.* (*Annuitant.*) *Died,* 3d *October,* 1877.

LACON, HENRY.—1807: Writer. 1810: Assistant to the Register of the Sudder and Foujdarry Adawlut. 1811: Assistant to the Collector of Ganjam. 1813: Register of the Zillah of Northern Malabar. 1819: *At home.* 1823: *Returned to India;* Commissioner for Small Claims on the Carnatic Fund. 1827: Judge and Criminal Judge of the Zillah of Chicacole. 1830: Collector and Magistrate of Ganjam. 1831: Principal Collector and Magistrate of Cuddapah. (*Annuitant on the Fund from* 1st *January* 1835.) *Died,* 1st *February* 1864, *in England.*

LANDON, JAMES.—1777 : Writer. 1782 : Factor. 1790 : Senior Merchant; Upper Searcher at Sea Gate; Deputy Customer and Assay Master. 1792 : Collector in the Centre Division of Arcot. *Died, 22d June* 1794.

LANE, RICHARD. — 1777 : Writer. *Died, August* 1777, *in Bengal*.

LANE, JOHN FRASER.—1804 : Writer. 1807 : Assistant to the Collector of the Zillah of Chittoor. 1809 : Head Assistant to the Collector of the Zillah of Bellary. 1814 : Head Assistant to the Collector of the Zillah of Chingleput. 1815 : French Translator to Government. 1816 : Deputy Collector of Madras. 1820 : Secretary to the Mint Committee; Superintendent of the Issue and Custody of Stationery. 1821 : Collector and Magistrate of Masulipatam, and in Charge of the Treasury there. *Died, 2d January* 1824, *at Madras*.

LARKING, WILLIAM FLEETE.—1807 : Writer. 1810 : Assistant to the Chief Secretary in the Secret, Political, and Foreign Department. *Drowned, 30th April* 1812, *while bathing at Vizagapatam*.

LASCELLES, FRANCIS.—1815 : Writer. 1818 : Second Assistant to the Collector and Magistrate of Cuddapah. 1820 : Register of the Zillah of Cuddapah. 1826 : Register of the Provincial Court, Centre Division. 1827 : *At home on absentee allowance*. 1829 : *Returned to India*. 1831 : Acting Judge and Criminal Judge of Combaconum. 1832 : Acting Third Judge of Provincial Court, Southern Division. 1833 : Judge and Criminal Judge of Chittoor; *Out of employ for seven months*. 1835 : Judge and Criminal Judge of Chittoor. 1839 : Judge and Criminal Judge of Cuddapah. 1840 : Judge and Criminal Judge of Rajahmundry. 1843 : *Out of employ*. 1845 : Civil and Sessions Judge, Second Class, Honore. 1856 : *Proceeded on furlough; Resigned the service, 20th December, in India. (Annuitant on the Fund,* 1858.) *Died, 15th July* 1882, *at Brighton*.

LATHOM, RICHARD.—1756 : Writer. 1768 : Junior Merchant. 1771 : Senior Merchant and Resident at Ingeram. 1776 : Member of Council of the Governor. 1777 : *Recalled by order of the General Court, 9th May*. 1780 : Chief at Cuddalore. *No trace after* 1782.

LATHOM, ROBERT GEORGE.—1776 : Writer. 1782 : Factor. *Taken prisoner by Hyder Ally. No trace after* 1782.

LATHOM, RICHARD HENRY.—1794 : Writer. 1797 : Assistant

under the Secretary to the Board of Revenue. 1798: Senior Assistant under the Accountant-General. 1799: *Out of employ.* 1800: Assistant under the Collector in the Third Division of Vizagapatam District. 1802: Register of the Court of Circuit and Appeal, Northern Division. 1803: Judge of the Zillah of Ramnad. 1807: Judge and Magistrate of Trichinopoly. *Died, 8th October* 1810, *at Trichinopoly.*

LAUTOUR, JAMES.—1806: Writer. 1808: *At home.* 1816: *Out of the service.*

LAVIE, WILLIAM.—1824: Writer; Assistant to the Collector and Magistrate of Madura. 1826: Register of the Zillah of Combaconum. 1828: Head Assistant to the Principal Collector of Canara. 1831: Sub-Collector and Joint Magistrate of Canara. 1832: Acting Assistant Judge and Joint Criminal Judge of Canara. 1834: Assistant Judge and Joint Criminal Judge of Guntoor. 1835: Sub-Collector and Joint Magistrate of Canara. 1836: *At home on absentee allowance.* 1839: *Returned to India.* 1840: *Out of employ.* 1841: Judge and Criminal Judge of Canara. 1842: Second Judge of the Provincial Court of Appeal and Circuit, Centre Division. 1844: Civil and Sessions Judge, Cuddapah; Civil and Sessions Judge, Chittoor. 1848: *Resigned the service,* 15*th April.* (*Annuitant on the Fund,* 1848.) *Died,* 28*th April* 1862, *in England.*

LENNOX, JOHN.—1778: Writer. 1782: *At home.* 1790: Senior Merchant and Assistant at Maddepollam. 1792: Paymaster at Aska and Ganjam. 1795: Paymaster at Ongole and in the Palnaud. 1800: *At home.* 1805: *Out of the service.*

LEVINGE, VERE HENRY.—1839: Writer. 1841: Assistant to Principal Collector and Magistrate, Madura, and at Tanjore. 1842: Acting Register of the Zillah Court of Madura. 1843: Acting Head Assistant to Collector and Magistrate, Tinnevelly. 1845: Head Assistant to Collector and Magistrate, Tinnevelly. 1851: Acting Sub-Collector and Joint Magistrate, Madura; *Proceeded to Europe on furlough.* 1854: Acting Sub-Judge, Combaconum; and Sub-Collector and Joint Magistrate, Tinnevelly. 1856: Acting Civil and Sessions Judge, Tinnevelly. 1858: Acting Collector and Magistrate, Tinnevelly. 1859: Collector and Magistrate, North Canara. 1860: Collector and Magistrate, Madura. 1867: *Resigned the service,* 8*th April.* (*Annuitant.*)

LEWIN, THOMAS. — 1770: Writer. 1776: Factor. 1778:

Junior Merchant.   1782: Senior Merchant; *At home; Returned to India.*   1790: *At home.*   1792: *In India without employment.*   1800: *Out of the service.*

LEWIN, MALCOLM.—1815: Writer.   1818: Third Assistant to the Collector and Magistrate of Malabar.   1819: Register of the Zillah of Malabar.   1824: Acting Register of the Zillah of Canara.   1825: Head Assistant to the Collector and Magistrate of Canara.   1826: Acting Additional Sub-Collector of Canara.   1828: Additional Sub-Collector of Canara.   1830: *At home on absentee allowance.*   1834: *Returned to India;* Collector and Magistrate of Guntoor.   1835: Collector and Magistrate of Rajahmundry, and Acting Second Judge of Provincial Court, Northern Division.   1836: Principal Collector and Magistrate of Canara.   1838: Acting Second Judge of the Provincial Court, Centre Division.   1839: Principal Collector and Magistrate of Bellary.   1840: Second Judge of the Provincial Court of Appeal and Circuit, Centre Division.   1842: Third Judge of the Sudder Dewannee and Sudder Foujdarry Adawlut.   1845: Judge of the Sudder Dewannee and Sudder Foujdarry Adawlut.   1846: Second Judge of the Sudder Dewannee and Sudder Foujdarry Adawlut, and appointed Provisional Member of Council of the Governor; *Resigned the service, 10th December.*   (*Annuitant on the Fund,* 1848.)   *Died,* 5th *March* 1869, *in England.*

LEWIN, FREDERICK MORTIMER. — 1818: Writer.   1821: Assistant to the Collector and Magistrate of the Southern Division of Arcot.   1824: Register and Assistant Collector of Seringapatam.   1827: Assistant Judge and Joint Criminal Judge of Salem.   1828: Judge and Criminal Judge of Salem.   1831: *At home on absentee allowance.*   1833: *Returned to India, per " Horatio."*   1835: Acting Zillah Judge of Combaconum; afterwards Judge and Criminal Judge of Combaconum.   1844: Civil and Sessions Judge of Combaconum.   1847: *Resigned the service.*   (*Annuitant on the Fund,* 1847.)   *Died,* 17th *June* 1877, *in England.*

LEWIN, RICHARD COTTON. — 1846: Writer.   Assistant to Collector and Magistrate, Canara.   1851: *Proceeded on furlough.*   1852: *Returned to India;* Assistant to Collector and Magistrate, Northern Division of Arcot.   1855: Assistant to Collector and Magistrate, Trichinopoly.   1857: Additional Sub-Collector and Joint Magistrate, Canara.   *Died,* 28th *July* 1858, *at Bellary.*

LEWIS, JOHN WALTER.—1808 : Writer. 1814: Acting Assistant to the Register of the Sudder and Foujdarry Adawlut. 1816: Register of the Zillah of Masulipatum. 1819: *At home.* 1823: *Returned to India;* Register of the Zillah of Carnatic. 1824: Deputy Collector of Government Sea Customs at Madras. 1827: *At home on absentee allowance.* (*Annuitant on the Fund from 1st January 1829, and died, 20th October 1836, at Foxdown, near Wellington, Somersetshire.*)

LIGHT, WILLIAM.—1765 : Writer. 1768 : Assistant at Cuddalore. 1771 : Factor. 1774 : Junior Merchant. 1776 : Senior Merchant. *No trace after* 1782.

LIMOND, DAVID ROUSE.—1831 : Writer. 1833 : Assistant to the Collector of Tinnevelly. 1836 : Acting Register, afterwards Register of the Zillah of Madura. 1838 : Acting Assistant Judge and Joint Criminal Judge of Madura ; and in Charge of Auxiliary Court at Tinnevelly ; also Register of the Zillah Court of Madura. 1844: Extra Assistant to Collector and Magistrate, Madura. 1845 : Subordinate Judge, Madura. *Died, 18th November 1846, at Madura.*

LIND, FRANCIS.—1771 : Writer. 1776 : Factor. 1780 : Junior Merchant. 1782 : Senior Merchant and Military Storekeeper. 1792 : *At home.* 1800 : *Out of the service.*

LINLEY, WILLIAM. — 1790 : Writer; Assistant under the Military Secretary. 1791: Assistant under the Collector of Madura and Dindigul. 1793: Deputy Secretary to the Military Board. 1796 : *At home.* 1800 : *Returned to India.* 1801 : Paymaster and Garrison Storekeeper, at Nellore and Dependencies. 1805 : Sub-Treasurer and Mint-Master. 1806 : *At home.* 1810 : *Out of the service.*

LLOYD, HUGH.—1795 : Writer. *Not to be traced.*

LOCKART, ROBERT.—1781 : Writer. 1783 : Assistant to the Secretary of the Select Committee. *No trace after* 1786.

LOCKHART, WALTER ELLIOTT.—1826 : Writer. 1829 : Register to the Zillah of Nellore. 1832 : Acting Judge and Criminal Judge of Chingleput ; Junior Deputy Secretary to the Board of Revenue ; Additional Sub-Collector and Joint Magistrate of Cuddapah. 1835 : Sub-Collector and Joint Magistrate of Madura. 1837 : Re-appointed Joint Magistrate of Madura. 1838 : *At home on absentee allowance.* 1843 : *Returned to India.* 1844 : *Out of employ.* 1845 : Collector and Magistrate, Salem. *Died, 30th January 1850, at Ossoor.*

LONG, JOHN.—1796 : Writer on the Bencoolen Establishment. 1803 : *Transferred to Madras Presidency ;* Assistant to the Register of the Sudder and Foujdarry Adawlut; Register of the Zillah of Guntoor. 1805: Collector in the Zillah of Rajahmundry. 1810 : Judge and Magistrate of Madura. 1813 : Judge and Criminal Judge of Rajahmundry. 1823 : *Out of the service.*

LORD, HUGH.—1796 : Writer. 1797 : Assistant under the Secretary in the Public, Revenue, and Commercial Department ; Assistant under the Commercial Resident at Amboyna. 1801 : Paymaster and Garrison Storekeeper at Amboyna. 1802 : Acting Commercial Resident at Amboyna. 1804 : *Out of employ.* 1806 : Register to the Court of Appeal and Circuit, Northern Division ; Acting Judge and Magistrate of Nellore. 1807 : Judge and Magistrate of the Zillah of Nellore. 1820 : Third Judge of Provincial Court, Northern Division. 1821 : Second Judge of Provincial Court, Northern Division. 1825 : Acting Judge of the Sudder and Foujdarry Adawlut. 1828 : First Judge of the Provincial Court, Northern Division. *Died, 9th April 1829, at Mysore.*

LOVELL, EDMUND CHARLES.—1827 : Writer. 1829 : Assistant to the Secretary in the Military Department. 1832 : Acting Malayalum Translator, and First Assistant to the Secretary to Government in the Revenue and Judicial Department; First Assistant to the Chief Secretary to Government ; Acting Deputy Secretary in the Military Department. 1833 : Head Assistant to the Collector and Magistrate of Rajahmundry ; Head Assistant to the Principal Collector and Magistrate of Cuddapah. 1837 : Sub-Collector and Joint Magistrate of the Northern Division of Arcot. 1838 : *At home on absentee allowance.* 1842 : *Returned to India.* 1843 : Sub-Collector and Joint Magistrate, Northern Division of Arcot. 1848 : Civil and Sessions Judge, Chittoor. *Died, 1st September 1851, at Madras.*

LUSHINGTON, STEPHEN RUMBOLD.—1790 : Writer. 1792 : Assistant under the Secretary in the Military, Political, and Secret Department. 1793 : Assistant under the Translator to the Board of Revenue. 1794 : Deputy Persian Translator to Government, and Persian Translator to the Board of Revenue. 1796 : Deputy Secretary to the Board of Revenue ; Under Searcher at the Sea Gate. 1798 : Secretary and Persian Translator to the Board of Revenue. 1799 : Collector of the Southern Polygar Peishcush at Ramnad. 1801 : Collector of Tinnevelly. 1803 : Register of the Sudder and Foujdarry Adawlut; *At home.* 1807: *Out of the service.*

LUSHINGTON, CHARLES MAY.—1801 : Writer. 1803 : Assistant to the Register of the Sudder and Foujdarry Adawlut. 1804 : Register of the Zillah of Rajahmundry. 1808 : *Out of employ.* 1809 : Second Assistant to the Register of the Sudder and Foujdarry Adawlut; Assistant Judge of Rajahmundry. 1813 : Assistant Judge of Combaconum. 1815 : Collector and Magistrate of Trichinopoly. 1823 : Third Judge of the Provincial Court, Southern Division. 1824 : Second Judge of the Provincial Court, Southern Division. 1828 : First Judge of the Provincial Court, Southern Division. 1830 : Third Puisne Judge of the Sudder and Foujdarry Adawlut. 1831 : Second Puisne Judge of the Sudder and Foujdarry Adawlut. 1832 : First Puisne Judge of the Sudder and Foujdarry Adawlut. 1838 : Chief Puisne Judge of the Sudder and Foujdarry Adawlut, and Member of Council of the Governor. 1841 : Member of Council, and President of the Revenue, Marine, and College Boards. 1843 : *Resigned the service, 24th January, in India.* (*Annuitant on the Fund,* 1843.) *Died, 8th March 1844, in England.*

LUSHINGTON, THOMAS DAVIES.—1832 : Writer; Doing Duty as Assistant in the Chief Secretary's Office. 1834 : Assistant under the Principal Collector and Magistrate of Malabar. 1836 : Acting Head Assistant to the Principal Collector and Magistrate of Canara. 1837 : Head Assistant to the Principal Collector and Magistrate of Canara. 1842 : Additional Sub-Collector and Magistrate of Canara. 1845 : *Proceeded on furlough.* 1849 : *Returned to India.* 1850 : Principal Assistant to Collector and Magistrate, Ganjam ; Sub-Collector and Joint Magistrate, Salem. 1851 : Agent to the Governor at Kurnool. 1852 : Collector and Magistrate, Masulipatam. 1857 : *Proceeded on furlough.* 1858 : *Returned to India ;* Collector, Magistrate, and Agent to Governor, Ganjam. *Died at sea, 17th June 1858, on board the " Hydaspes."*

LUSHINGTON, FRANKLYN.—1838 : Writer. 1839 : Under the Principal Collector, Malabar ; Assistant to Collector and Magistrate, Chingleput. 1841 : Acting Second Assistant to the Accountant-General. 1842 : Second Assistant to the Accountant-General. 1843 : *Proceeded to Europe on furlough.* 1845: Assistant to Collector and Magistrate, South Arcot. 1846 : Head Assistant to Collector and Magistrate, South Arcot. 1847 : Acting Senior Deputy Register to the Court of Sudder and Foujdarry Adawlut. 1849 : Senior Deputy Register to the Court of Sudder and Foujdarry Adawlut. 1852 : At first Acting Register, afterwards

Register, to the Court of Sudder and Foujdarry Adawlut. 1855: Civil Auditor, and Superintendent of Stamps. 1859: Accountant, North-Western Provinces; and Accountant to the Government of Bengal. 1860: Officiating Accountant-General, Madras. 1861: Officiating Deputy Auditor and Accountant-General to the Governor of Fort St. George. 1862: *On medical leave for 12 months.* 1863: Deputy Auditor and Accountant-General, Madras. 1871: *On furlough.* 1873: Accountant-General, Madras; *Resigned the service, 16th August.* (*Annuitant.*)

MACDONALD, Charles Edward.—1826: Writer. 1828: Assistant to the Principal Collector of South Arcot. 1829: Head Assistant to the Principal Collector of North Arcot. 1832: Additional Sub-Collector and Joint Magistrate of Cuddapah. *Died, 15th June 1832, at Cuddapah.*

MACDONELL, Æneas R.—1807: Writer. 1808: Assistant to the Secretary in the Revenue and Judicial Department; Assistant under the Register of the Sudder and Foujdarry Adawlut. 1809: Assistant under the Assay Master; Head Assistant to the Collector of Cuddapah. 1816: Head Assistant to the Magistrate at Cuddapah. 1818: Secretary to the Honourable Mountstuart Elphinstone, Sole Commissioner for the Settlement of the Peishwah Territories. 1820: Private Secretary to Sir Thomas Munro, the Governor of Madras. 1822: Third Member of the Board of Revenue. 1824: Second Member of the Board of Revenue. 1832: Member of the Marine Board. 1836: First Member of the Board of Revenue. 1838: *At home on absentee allowance.* (*Annuitant on the Fund in* 1839.) *Died, 24th October 1868, in England.*

MACDOUALL, John.—1792: Writer. 1794: Assistant under the Secretary to the Board of Revenue, and Assistant to the Accountant-General. 1796: Paymaster to the Expedition against Trincomallee. 1798: Paymaster to the Expedition at Columbo. 1799: Collector of Columbo; *Out of Employ.* 1802: *At home.* 1806: *Returned to India.* 1809: Civil Auditor. 1810: Dutch Translator to Government. *Died, 5th August 1814, at Madras.*

MACKAY, George.—1766: Appointed Senior Merchant and Member of Council of the Governor. 1777: *Recalled by the order of the General Court of Proprietors, 9th May.* 1780: *At home, and suspended from the service.*

MACKENZIE, Alexander.—1789: Writer. 1790: Assistant under the Secretary in the Political and Revenue Department 1791: Assistant under the Board of Assumed Revenue. 1793:

Assistant to the Commercial Resident at Vizagapatam. 1796: Deputy Commercial Resident at Ganjam. 1798: *At home.* 1801: *Returned to India.* 1802: Secretary to the Board of Trade; Commercial Resident at Vizagapatam and Ganjam. 1805: Senior Judge of the Court of Circuit and Appeal, Southern Division. 1807: *At home.* 1811: *Out of the service.*

M'KERRELL, JOHN.—1804: Writer. 1806: Assistant under the Principal Collector in Canara; Register of the Zillah of the Northern Division of Canara. 1811: *At home.* 1812: *Returned to India ;* Gentoo and Teloogoo Translator to Government. 1815: Reporter of External Commerce, and Sheriff of Madras. 1816: Superintendent of Police. 1817: Canarese Translator to Government. 1820: Mint-Master. (*Annuitant on the Fund, from 12th May* 1830.) *Died in November* 1835.

MACKLIN, JOHN CHARLES.—1769: Writer. *No trace after* 1771.

MACKONOCHIE, ROBERT.—1800: Writer. 1803: Assistant to the Collector of Ramnad and Tinnevelly; *At home for his health.* 1809: *Returned to India ;* Deputy Mint-Master. 1811: Deputy Accountant in the Military Accounts Department. 1812: *Out of employ.* 1819: Mint-Master. 1820: *At home.* 1826: *Out of the service.* (*Annuitant on the Fund in* 1842.) *Died,* 19th *February* 1858, *in England.*

MACLEAN, ALEXANDER.—1817: Writer. 1821: Assistant to the Collector and Magistrate of Chingleput. 1825: Head Assistant to the Collector and Magistrate of Malabar. 1826: Acting Head Assistant to the Register of the Sudder Court, and Sanscrit Examiner to the College Board. 1828: Sub-Collector and Joint Magistrate of Malabar. 1830: Sub-Collector and Joint Magistrate of Canara; Judge and Criminal Judge of Combaconum. 1831: Judge and Criminal Judge of Malabar. 1833: Collector and Magistrate of Chingleput. 1835: Acting Malayalum Translator to Government. 1836: Malayalum Translator to Government. 1838: Acting Temporary Member of the Board of Revenue; Third Member of the Board of Revenue. 1839: Collector and Magistrate of Chingleput; Temporary Member of the Board of Revenue; and Malayalum Translator to Government. 1845: Collector and Magistrate, Cuddapah, and Malayalum Translator to Government. 1848: Third Member of the Board of Revenue, and Malayalum Translator to Government. 1850: *Retired from the service,* 1st *May, in India.* (*Annuitant on the Fund,* 1850.) *Died,* 28th *November* 1872, *in England.*

MACLEOD, ALEXANDER.—1777 : Writer. 1780 : *At home.*
1782 : Factor. 1790 : Senior Merchant, and one of the Collectors
of the Jaghire Revenue. 1792 : Collector in the Madura and
Nellore Districts, and Peishcash of the Marwars. 1795 : Collector
in the Dindigul Districts. 1800 : Resident at Negapatam, and
Revenue Assistant under the Resident at Nagore. 1801 : *At
home.* 1803 : *Out of the service.*

MACLEOD, JOHN M'PHERSON.—1811 : Writer. 1814 : Second
Assistant, afterwards First Assistant to Secretary to Government in
the several Civil Departments. 1816 : Member and Secretary of
the Committee for Revising the Customs Laws. 1820 : *At home
on account of health.* 1823 : *Returned to India ;* Acting Secretary
to Government in Financial and General Departments. 1824 :
Secretary to Government in Financial and General Departments.
1825 : Tamil Translator to Government, Member of the College
Board, of the Board of Public Instruction, and of the Mint Committee. 1826 : Persian Translator to Government. 1827 : Secretary
in the Revenue and Judicial Departments. 1829 : Temporary
Member, afterwards Third Member of the Board of Revenue. 1832 :
Commissioner for the Government of Mysore. 1834 : Deputed to
Hyderabad on Special Duty by the Governor-General. 1835 :
Member of the Indian Law Commission. 1836 : Member of the
Committee for Revising the System of Prison Discipline through-
out India. 1838 : *At home on absentee allowance.* 1841 : *Retired
from the service.* (*Annuitant on the Fund,* 1841.) *Died, 1st March
1881, in England.*

MAIDMAN, GEORGE.—1793 : Writer. 1796 : Assistant under
the Collector in the Jaghire. 1798 : *Out of employ ;* Assistant under
the Commercial Resident at Ingeram. 1802 : Deputy Commercial
Resident at Ingeram. 1807 : Commercial Resident in the Ceded
Districts ; Commercial Resident at Masulipatam. *Died, 8th April
1810, at Masulipatam.*

MAIDMAN, CHARLES.—1801 : Writer. 1803 : Assistant to
the Commercial Resident at Ingeram. 1807 : Deputy Commercial Resident at Ingeram. *Died, 29th August 1824, at
Ingeram.*

MAINWARING, WILLIAM.—1794 : Writer. 1796 : Assistant
to the Secretary in Public, Commercial, and Revenue Department.
1797 : Assistant to the Secretary in Military, Political, and
Secret Department, and French Translator. 1798 : Assistant to
the Collector of the First Division of Masulipatam. 1800 : Assis-

tant to the Collector of Muglatore. 1802 : Collector in the Zillah of Guntoor. 1803 : *Out of employ.* 1804 : Paymaster and Garrison Storekeeper at Trichinopoly. 1806 : Paymaster and Garrison Storekeeper at Madura. 1810 : *Out of employ. Died, 5th February 1812, at Tinnevelly.*

MAITLAND, WILLIAM.—1763 : Writer. 1768 : Factor and Assistant at Cuddalore. 1771 : Junior Merchant and Fourth in Council at Cuddalore. 1774 : Senior Merchant and Fourth in Council at Cuddalore. 1776 : Third in Council at Cuddalore. *No trace after* 1782.

MAITLAND, ADAM.—1824 : Writer. 1827 : Employed in the Mahratta Country under the Bombay Government. *Died, 26th May* 1828, *at Dharwar.*

MAJENDIE, ANDREW.—1766 : Writer. 1771 : Factor. 1774 : Junior Merchant. 1778 : Senior Merchant. 1782 : *At home. Died in* 1793, *in England.*

MALCOLM, ROBERT. — 1781 : Writer. 1783 : Assistant at Masulipatam. 1796 : Assistant to the Collector in the Fifth Division of Masulipatam District ; Commercial Resident at Vizagapatam. 1802 : Second Judge of the Court of Circuit and Appeal, Northern Division. 1808 : *At home.* 1809 : *Out of the service.*

MALTBY, EDWARD.—1828 : Writer. 1831 : Second Assistant to the Principal Collector, Canara. 1833 : Acting Head Assistant, afterwards Head Assistant, to the Principal Collector and Magistrate, Canara. 1835 : Acting Additional Sub-Collector and Joint Magistrate, Canara. 1837 : Additional, and afterwards Sub-Collector and Joint Magistrate, Canara. 1839 : Acting Principal Collector and Magistrate, Canara. 1841 : *Proceeded on furlough to Europe.* 1844 : Acting Deputy Collector, Madras ; and Acting Sub-Collector and Joint Magistrate, Nellore. 1845 : Sub-Collector and Joint Magistrate, Nellore ; Acting Collector and Magistrate, Chingleput. 1848 : Civil and Sessions Judge, Cuddapah. 1849 : Collector and Magistrate, Trichinopoly. 1851 : Collector and Magistrate, South Arcot. 1854 : Third Member of the Board of Revenue ; and Member of the Board of Examiners. 1857 : Acting Chief Secretary to Government. 1858 : Provincial Member of Council. 1859 : Member of Council of the Governor, and President of the Revenue and Marine Boards. 1864 : *Resigned the service, 16th December. (Annuitant.)*

MALTBY, FRANCIS NEWCOMBE.—1830 : Writer. 1832 : Register to the Zillah Court of Canara.   1834: Acting Assistant Judge and Joint Criminal Judge, Malabar.   1835: Acting Assistant Judge and Joint Criminal Judge, Canara; Acting Head Assistant to Principal Collector and Magistrate, Canara.   1836: Register to the Zillah Court of Canara.   1837: Additional Sub-Collector and Joint Magistrate, Canara.   1841: Sub-Collector and Joint Magistrate, Canara; *Proceeded to Europe on furlough.*   1845: Acting Assistant Judge, Mangalore.   1846: Sub-Collector and Joint Magistrate, Salem.   1850: Agent to the Governor of Madras, at Kurnool; Collector and Magistrate, Canara.   1855: Acting Member of the Board of Revenue.   1856: Financial and Judicial Commissioner of the Hyderabad Assigned Territories.   1858: *On medical leave to Europe.*   1859: Resident at Travancore and Cochin.   1861: *On medical leave for 6 months.*   1862: *Resigned the service, 1st May.   (Annuitant.)   Died, 27th August 1877, in North Britain.*

MARRIOTT, WILLIAM.—1795: Writer.   1798: Assistant under the Collector of Burramchal.   1799: Head Assistant under the Collector of Kistnagherry.   1801: *At home for his health.   Died, 18th February* 1805, *in England.*

MARTIN, GEORGE SULLIVAN.—1781: Writer.   1783: Assistant to the Secretary to the Select Committee in Bengal.   1784: Under the Resident at Tanjore.   1787: Assistant under the Resident at Negapatam.   1788: Under the Secretary, Secret Department; Deputy Postmaster-General; and Sheriff.   1789: Secretary to the Board of Trade.   1790: Paymaster at Palamcottah.   1794: Commercial Resident in the Southern Provinces.   1796: Commercial Resident at Ramnad and Tinnevelly.   1799: *At home.   No trace after* 1799.

MARTINDALE, JOSEPH.—1779: Writer.   *No trace after* 1782.

MASON, JOHN GEORGE.—1812: Writer.   1815: Second Assistant to the Collector of Tanjore.   1816: Head Assistant to the Collector of Ganjam; Assistant Magistrate of Ganjam.   *Died, 18th December* 1817, *in camp, at Itchapore.*

MASON, WILLIAM.—1813: Writer.   1817: Second Assistant to the Collector of Malabar, and Assistant Magistrate.   1821: Head Assistant to the Collector of Malabar, and Magistrate of Malabar.   1825: Sub-Collector and Assistant Magistrate of Malabar.   1826: Sub-Collector and Assistant Magistrate of Bellary.   1831: Collector and Magistrate of Guntoor.   1832: Collector and Magistrate of Vizagapatam.   *Died, 2d July* 1834, *at Vizagapatam.*

MASON, Wheeler Hood George. — 1832 : Writer. 1834 : Assistant to the Collector and Magistrate of Masulipatam. 1835 : Assistant to the Collector and Magistrate of Chingleput. 1837 : Acting Head Assistant Collector and Magistrate of Chingleput. 1838 : Head Assistant to Collector and Magistrate of Chingleput. 1839 : Assistant to Collector and Magistrate of Vizagapatam. 1840 : Assistant to Agent of the Governor, Collector, and Magistrate, Vizagapatam. *Died, 2d August* 1842, *at Madras.*

MATHISON, Archibald Stirling. —1830 : Writer. 1832 : Assistant to the Collector and Magistrate of Rajahmundry. 1833 : Head Assistant to the Collector and Magistrate of Guntoor. 1836 : Officiating Joint Criminal Judge of Guntoor. 1838 : Acting Sub-Collector and Joint Magistrate of Nellore. 1839 : Sub-Collector and Joint Magistrate of Nellore. 1843 : *Proceeded on furlough.* 1846 : *Returned to India.* 1847 : Principal Assistant to Agent of the Governor, Collector, and Magistrate, Vizagapatam. 1852 : Civil and Sessions Judge, Chittoor. 1856: *Proceeded on furlough.* 1859 : *Resigned the service,* 19th *February, in India. (Annuitant.)*

MAUNSELL, Robert. — 1763 : Writer. 1768 : Factor. 1771 : Junior Merchant and Paymaster at Itchapore. 1774 : Senior Merchant, and Assistant at Ganjam. 1776 : Senior Merchant, and Second in Council at Ganjam. 1790 : *At home.* 1792 : *Out of the service.*

MAXTONE, Charles. — 1769 : Writer. 1774 : Factor and Assistant at Vizagapatam. 1778 : Junior Merchant. 1780 : Senior Merchant. 1790 : *At home.* 1793 : Senior Merchant without Employ. 1800 : Commercial Resident at Ingeram. 1803 : Postmaster-General and Military Paymaster at the Presidency, and of Extraordinaries. 1806 : First Judge of the Court of Circuit and Appeal, Centre Division. 1808 : First Judge of the Court of Circuit and Appeal, Centre Division, and Acting Judge of the Sudder and Foujdarry Adawlut Courts. *Died, 24th February* 1809.

MAXWELL, Hugh. —1773 : Writer. 1778 : Factor. 1782 : Junior Merchant. 1790: Senior Merchant, and Manager of the Ganjam Havelly. 1792 : Member of the Revenue Board. *Died in* 1793.

MAYNAND, Josias. —1767 : Writer. 1771 : *At home.* 1774 : Factor (*but still at home*). 1776 : Junior Merchant; *At home ; Resigned the service.*

MAYNE, Dawson. —1837 : Writer. 1838 : Assistant to the Principal Collector and Magistrate of Bellary. 1841 : Head Assistant to Principal Collector and Magistrate, Cuddapah. 1850 :

G

Subordinate Judge, Cuddapah. 1852 : *Proceeded on furlough.* 1855 : *Returned to India;* Subordinate Judge, Bellary. 1858 : Civil and Sessions Judge, Madura. *Died, 23d November 1858, at Tutticorin.*

MEGGISON, ROBERT.—1804 : Writer. 1808 : Assistant under the Collector of Cuddapah. *Died, 20th May 1808, at Cuddapah.*

MELLOR, ABEL.—1824 : Writer. 1828 : Head Assistant to the Principal Collector at Madura. 1832 : Sub-Collector and Joint Magistrate of Tinnevelly. 1835 : *At home on absentee allowance.* 1838 : *Returned to India overland.* 1839 : Acting Civil Auditor and Superintendent of Stamps. 1840 : Collector and Magistrate, Bellary. 1850 : *Resigned the service, 5th November, in India.* (*Annuitant on the Fund,* 1851.) *Died, 16th July 1878, England.*

MICHELL, WILLIAM.—1773 : Writer. 1778 : Factor. 1782 : Junior Merchant. 1790 : Senior Merchant, and Assistant at Tanjore. 1792 : Resident at Nagore. 1794 : *At home.* 1800 : *Out of the service.*

MICHELL, HENRY CHICKLEY.—1777 : Writer. 1782 : Factor. 1790 : Senior Merchant, and Member of the Board of Trade ; Rental General and Scavenger. 1792 : Member of the Board of Trade and Export Warehouse-keeper. 1795 : *In England.* 1796 : *Dismissed by order of the Court of Directors, dated 30th March.*

MICROP, ISAAC VAN.—1776 : Writer. 1782 : Factor. *No trace after* 1782.

MITCHELL, JOHN.—1829 : Writer. 1831 : Second Assistant to the Collector and Magistrate of Tinnevelly. 1833 : Register of the Zillah of Combaconum. *Died, 1st March 1834.*

MITFORD, JOHN.—1771 : Writer. 1776 : Factor. 1780 : Junior Merchant. 1782 : Senior Merchant and Export Warehouse-keeper. 1795 : *At home.* 1801 : Member of the Board of Trade. 1806 : *At home.* 1809 : *Out of the service.*

MOLE, FREDERICK.—1830 : Writer. 1833 : Assistant to the Principal Collector and Magistrate of Salem. 1834 : Register of Salem. 1836 : Acting Head Assistant to the Principal Collector and Magistrate of Salem. 1837 : Register of the Zillah Court of Salem. *Died, 1st December 1842, at Salem.*

MOLLE, WILLIAM MACQUARIE.—1832 : Writer. 1833 : Assistant to the Principal Collector of South Arcot. 1834 : Assistant to the Collector of Tinnevelly. 1838 : Head Assistant to the Collector and Magistrate of Tinnevelly. 1841 : *Out of employ.* 1844 : Head Assistant to Collector and Magistrate of Tanjore.

1845 : Head Assistant to Collector and Magistrate of Trichinopoly. 1846: Sub-Collector and Joint Magistrate, Cuddapah. 1847 : *Proceeded on furlough.* 1850 : *Returned to India ;* Sub-Collector and Joint Magistrate, Coimbatore. 1856 : Civil and Sessions Judge, Honore. 1861 : *Proceeded on furlough; Resigned the service, 8th June, in England.* (*Annuitant in* 1861.)

MONCKTON, EDWARD.—1762 : Writer. 1768 : Factor. 1771 : Junior Merchant. 1774 : Senior Merchant. 1780 : *Out of the service.*

MONCKTON, GEORGE PACKENHAM.—1837 : Writer. 1839 : Assistant to the Collector and Magistrate of Malabar. 1844 : Assistant to Collector and Magistrate, Northern Division of Arcot. 1845 : *Proceeded on furlough.* 1848 : *Pensioned, 30th August.*

MONEY, SEPTIMUS.—1802 : Writer. 1805 : Assistant to the Secretary in the Revenue and Judicial Department. 1806: Register of the Zillah of Chittoor. 1813 : Judge and Magistrate of Cochin. 1817 : Judge and Criminal Judge of Dharapooram, afterwards of Coimbatore. 1821 : Judge and Criminal Judge of Cuddapah. 1824: *At home.* 1826: *Returned to India ;* Acting Additional Judge of Provincial Court, Northern Division. 1828 : Third Judge of Provincial Court, Northern Division. *Died, 14th August 1830, at Masulipatam.*

MONK, WILLIAM GARROW.—1804 : Writer. 1805 : Assistant under the Principal Collector of Coimbatore. 1806 : Register of the Zillah of Coimbatore. 1811 : *At home.* 1814 : *Returned to India ;* Register of the Zillah of Coimbatore. 1820 : Judge and Criminal Judge of Tinnevelly. 1822: Judge and Criminal Judge of Chicacole. 1827: *At home on absentee allowance.* (*Annuitant on the Fund from 1st January* 1829.) *Died, 3d March* 1859, *in England.*

MONTGOMERIE, WILLIAM.—1804 : Writer. 1806 : Assistant under the Register of the Sudder and Foujdarry Adawlut. 1807 : Assistant to the Register of the Zillah of Vizagapatam. 1809 : Register of the Zillah of Ganjam. 1811 : Deputy Commercial Resident at Vizagapatam. 1818 : Deputy Commercial Resident at Maddepollam and Masulipatam. 1823 : Assistant to the Commercial Resident at the General Factory at Ingeram. 1824 : Deputy Commercial Resident at the General Factory at Ingeram. 1826 : Commercial Resident at Tinnevelly. 1831 : *Out of employ.* 1832 : *At home on absentee allowance.* (*Annuitant on the Fund from 1st May* 1834.) *Died, 23d October* 1852, *in England.*

MONTGOMERIE, HUGH.—1812 : Writer. 1816 : Head Assistant to the Collector and Magistrate of Vizagapatam ; Assistant Magistrate at Vizagapatam.   1826 : Deputy Commercial Resident at the Factory of Ingeram.   1830 : Sub-Collector and Joint Magistrate of Tinnevelly.   1832 : Judge and Criminal Judge of Nellore.   1833 : *At home on absentee allowance.*   1835 : *Returned to India, per " Mary Ann."*   1836 : Acting Third Judge of the Provincial Court, Northern Division ; Acting Judge and Criminal Judge of Rajahmundry.   1838 : Acting Second Judge of the Provincial Court, Northern Division ; Judge and Criminal Judge of Cuddapah ; Third Judge of the Provincial Court, Northern Division. 1840 : Second Judge of the Provincial Court of Appeal and Circuit, Northern Division.   1841 : First Judge of the Provincial Court of Appeal and Circuit, Northern Division.   1842: *Resigned the service,* 12th *May.   (Annuitant on the Fund, 1842.)   Died, 24th February* 1864, *in England.*

MONTGOMERY, Sir HENRY CONYNGHAM, Bart. — 1825 : Writer.   1827 : Assistant to the Principal Collector and Magistrate of Nellore.   1828 : Head Assistant to the Principal Collector of Nellore ; Head Assistant to the Principal Collector of Tanjore. 1830 : Acting Additional Sub Collector of Salem ; Additional Sub-Collector and Joint Magistrate of Tanjore.   1832 : Sub-Collector and Joint Magistrate of Tanjore.   1836 : *At home for his health.* 1838 : *Returned to India, per " Windsor."*   1839 : Acting Principal Collector and Magistrate of Bellary.   1840 : Sub-Collector and Joint Magistrate, Tanjore.   1841 : Principal Collector and Magistrate of Tinnevelly.   1843 : Collector and Magistrate of Tanjore. 1847 : Secretary to Government in Revenue and Judicial Department.   1850: Chief Secretary to Government.   1855 : Chief Secretary to Government ; Provisional Member of Council ; afterwards Member of Council, and Chief Judge of the Sudder Dewannee and Sudder Foujdarry Adawluts.   1857 : *Resigned the service,* 29th *October, in India.   (Annuitant on the Fund, 1859.)   Died, 24th June* 1878, *in England.*

MOORE, GEORGE.—1796: Writer.   1799 : Assistant in the Military, Secret, and Political Department.   1802 : Register of Passports.   1804 : Head Assistant to the Secretary in the Revenue and Judicial Department, and Postmaster-General.   1806 : Deputy Accountant-General and Commercial.   1812 : Superintendent of Stamps.   1814 : Civil Auditor.   *Died,* 12th *December* 1834, *at Madras.*

MOORE, THOMAS PERRING.—1806 : Writer.   1808 : Assistant to the Secretary to the Board of Revenue. *Lost on his passage home, 14th March 1809, in the ship "Jane Duchess of Gordon."*

MOORE, MARK.—1831 : Writer. 1834 : Assistant to the Principal Collector and Magistrate of Salem. *Died, 26th November 1835, at Madras.*

MORDAUNT, CHARLES.—1765 : Writer and Assistant at Cuddalore. 1771 : Factor and Assistant at Cuddalore. 1774 : Junior Merchant. 1776 : Senior Merchant. 1778 : *At home ; Returned to India. Died, April 1780.*

MOREHEAD, WILLIAM AMBROSE. — 1824 : Writer. 1828 : Assistant to the Principal Collector, North Arcot; subsequently appointed Register of the Zillah of Chingleput. 1830 : Head Assistant to the Principal Collector and Magistrate, Chingleput. 1832 : Sub-Collector and Joint Magistrate, Cuddapah ; afterwards Acting Judge and Criminal Judge, Cuddapah. 1833 : Acting Assistant Judge and Joint Criminal Judge, Chingleput. 1834 : Acting Sub-Collector and Joint Magistrate, North Arcot ; Officiating Sub-Collector and Magistrate, South Arcot ; Acting Assistant Judge and Joint Criminal Judge, Chingleput. 1836 : Assistant Judge and Joint Criminal Judge, Chingleput ; (*Proceeded to Europe on private affairs.*) 1840 : Acting Deputy Collector, Madras ; Acting Secretary to the College Board ; and Acting Judge and Criminal Judge at Chingleput. 1841 : Acting Judge and Criminal Judge, Canara ; Acting Judge and Criminal Judge at Madura ; and Judge and Criminal Judge, Chingleput. 1843 : Acting Principal Collector and Magistrate, Madura ; and Civil and Sessions Judge, Chingleput. 1846 : Officiating Puisne Judge of the Court of Sudder and Foujdarry Adawlut. 1847 : Third Puisne Judge of the Court of Sudder and Foujdarry Adawlut ; also Member of the College Board. 1851 : *Absent on medical leave.* 1854 : President of the Board of Examiners. 1855 : Provisional Member of Council. 1856 : *Proceeded to Europe on medical leave.* 1857 : Member of Council, and Chief Judge of the Court of Sudder and Foujdarry Adawlut. 1859 : Commissioner for Inquiring into the System of Judicature in the Presidency. 1860 : Governor and President in Council. 1862 : *Resigned the service, 29th October. (Annuitant.)*

MORRIS, JOHN CARNAC.—1818 : Writer. 1820 : Assistant to the Chief Secretary to Government. 1821 : Head Assistant to the Collector and Magistrate of Masulipatam. 1822 : Senior Deputy Secretary to the Board of Revenue. 1823 : Deputy

Teloogoo Translator to Government. 1824 : Secretary to the College Board ; Secretary to the Civil Fund. 1825 : Assistant to the Collector of Sea Customs at the Presidency. 1829 : *At home on absentee allowance.* 1831 : *Returned to India, per " Duke of Buccleuch ;"* Acting Secretary to the Board of Revenue. 1832 : Secretary to the Board of Revenue and Teloogoo Translator to Government ; Acting Register of the Sudder and Foujdarry Adawlut ; Trustee to St. George's Church. 1833 : Register to the Sudder and Foujdarry Adawlut. 1834 : Acting Secretary and Treasurer to the Government Bank ; Acting Sub-Treasurer. 1835 : Superintendent and Treasurer of the Government Bank, and Sub-Treasurer. 1837 : Member of the Mint Committee. 1838 : Acting Temporary Member of the Board of Revenue. 1839 : Civil Auditor and Superintendent of Stamps, Member of the College Board and Mint Committee, also Teloogoo Translator to Government. 1843 : Civil Auditor and Superintendent of Stamps, Member of the College Board, and Teloogoo Translator to Government. 1846 : *Resigned the service, 1st July. (Annuitant on the Fund, 1846.) Died, 2d August 1858, in England.*

MORRIS, HENRY.—1823 : Writer. 1825 : Assistant to the Collector and Magistrate of Nellore. 1826 : Head Assistant to the Principal Collector and Magistrate of Northern Division of Arcot. 1828 : Head Assistant to the Principal Collector and Magistrate of South Arcot. 1829 : Sub-Collector and Joint Magistrate of Madura. 1830 : Sub-Collector and Joint Magistrate of Coimbatore. 1835 : Acting Assistant Judge of Salem ; Acting Deputy Collector of Madras. 1836 : Commissioner for Drawing Lotteries ; Officiating Police Magistrate. 1837 : *At home on absentee allowance.* 1841 : *Returned to India.* 1842 : Third Judge of the Provincial Court of Appeal and Circuit, Western Division. 1844 : Civil and Sessions Judge, Calicut. 1852 : *Resigned the service, 30th July. (Annuitant on the Fund, 1852.)*

MORTLOCK, HENRY.—1808 : Writer. 1810 : Assistant to the Register of the Sudder and Foujdarry Adawlut ; Fixed Examiner to the Sudder and Foujdarry Adawlut. 1811 : Deputy Persian Translator to Government ; First Assistant to the Sudder Adawlut. 1813 : Deputy Register to the Sudder and Foujdarry Adawlut. 1816 : *At home.* 1818 : *Returned to India;* Cashier to the Government Bank. 1819 : Deputy Persian Translator to Government. 1820 : Deputy Register of the Sudder Adawlut ; Secretary to the

College Board. 1823 : *At home.* 1824 : *Resigned, 1st September, in England. (Accepted an Annuity from the Civil Fund from 1st January* 1828.) *Died, 13th February* 1837, *in England.*

MOWBRAY, GEORGE.—1771 : Senior Merchant, with fixed Appointment as Accountant. 1791 : Member of the Board of Revenue. 1793 : *At home ; Retired from service.*

MUNRO, ROBERT DUNCAN.—1765 : Writer. 1771 : Factor. 1774 : Junior Merchant. 1776 : Senior Merchant ; Paymaster at Chingleput. 1791 : Second in Council at Ganjam. 1792 : *At home. Died,* 1795, *in India.*

MUNRO, JAMES A.—1806 : Writer. 1807 : Assistant to the Collector of the Northern Division of Arcot. 1808 : *Out of employ ;* Acting Register of the Zillah of Salem. 1809 : Register of the Zillah of Salem. 1812 : Register of the Zillah of Coimbatore. 1821 : Sub-Collector and Magistrate of Coimbatore. 1823 : Collector and Magistrate of Tinnevelly. *Died, 23d May* 1827, *at Palamcottah.*

MUNRO, JOHN COLLINS.—1817 : Writer. 1819 : Employed in the late Peishwah's Dominions. *Died, 11th December* 1824, *at Kittoor.*

MURRAY, The HON. LEVESTON GRANVILLE KEITH.—1792 : Writer. 1793 : Assistant under the Secretary in the Public, Revenue, and Commercial Department. 1796 : Deputy Commercial Resident at Salem. 1797 : Assistant under the Collector in the First Division of Masulipatam. 1798 : Paymaster and Garrison Storekeeper at Innacondah and its Dependencies. 1799 : Paymaster and Garrison Storekeeper at Vizagapatam and its Dependencies. 1803 : Collector of the Zillah of Vizagapatam. 1805 : *Out of Employ.* 1806 : Collector of Madras. 1807 : General Agent for the Monopoly of Salt. 1809 : Military Paymaster-General. 1810 : Collector of Rajahmundry. 1812 : *Out of employ.* 1814 : Superintendent of Investments and in Charge of the Import Warehouse. 1819 : Second Member of the Board of Trade. 1820 : Collector of Madras. 1828 : Superintendent of Stationery. 1830 : Collector of Sea Customs at Madras. (*Annuitant on the Fund, 9th May* 1831.) *Died, 6th January* 1837.

MURRAY, MACKENZIE.—1832 : Writer. 1833 : Assistant under the Principal Collector and Magistrate of Salem. 1836 : Acting Register of the Zillah of Canara ; Register of the Zillah of Cuddapah. 1838 : Acting Head Assistant to the Principal Collector and Magistrate of Nellore. 1839 : Register of the Zillah

Court of Cuddapah. 1840 : Sub-Collector and Joint Magistrate, Southern Division of Arcot. 1844 : *Proceeded on furlough.* 1846 : *Returned to India.* 1847 : Sub-Collector and Joint Magistrate, Cuddapah. 1854 : Collector and Magistrate, Cuddapah. 1860 : *Proceeded on furlough.* 1861 : *Resigned the service in England. (Annuitant on the Fund, 1861.) Died, 14th February 1876, in England.*

NAPIER, FRANCIS.—1796 : Writer. 1797 : Assistant under the Secretary to the Board of Trade. *Died, 19th July 1797.*

NEAVE, WILLIAM AUGUSTUS.—1821 : Writer. 1825 : Assistant to the Principal Collector and Magistrate of the Northern Division of Arcot. 1826 : Head Assistant to the Collector and Magistrate of Salem. 1827 : Head Assistant to the Collector and Magistrate of Chingleput. 1828 : Head Assistant to the Principal Collector of Coimbatore. 1830 : Sub-Collector and Joint Magistrate of Malabar. 1832 : Deputy Accountant-General ; Acting Mint-Master ; Assistant Judge and Joint Criminal Judge of Chingleput. 1836 : *At home on absentee allowance.* 1839 : *Returned to India ;* Acting Judge and Criminal Judge of Salem. 1840 : Judge and Joint Criminal Judge of Salem. 1842 : Third Judge of the Provincial Court of Appeal and Circuit, Southern Division. 1844 : Civil and Sessions Judge, Rajahmundry. *Died on his passage to Europe, 3d October 1844, on board the " Samarang."*

NELSON, ROBERT.—1816 : Writer. 1818 : Second Assistant to the Collector and Magistrate of Salem. 1821 : Head Assistant to the Collector and Magistrate of Salem ; *Leave to St. Helena, and eventually to England.* 1824 : *Returned to India ;* Head Assistant to the Collector and Magistrate of Madura. 1827 : Sub-Collector and Joint Magistrate of Tanjore. 1831 : Acting Collector and Magistrate of Trichinopoly. 1832 : Acting Collector and Magistrate of Masulipatam ; Acting Zillah Judge of Salem ; Acting Third Judge of Provincial Court, Centre Division. 1833 : Judge and Criminal Judge of Malabar. 1836 : Acting Third Judge of the Provincial Court, Southern Division. 1837 : *At home on absentee allowance.* 1842 : *Absent five years from India.*

NEWBERY, EDWARD.—1829 : Writer. 1831 : Second Assistant to the Collector of Masulipatam. 1833 : Register of the Zillah of Chicacole. 1834: Assistant Judge of Rajahmundry. 1837 : Acting Assistant Judge and Joint Criminal Judge of Guntoor. 1838: Assistant Judge and Joint Criminal Judge of Guntoor. 1839:

Acting Judge and Criminal Judge of Cuddapah. 1840: Assistant Judge and Joint Criminal Judge of Guntoor. 1841: *Proceeded on furlough.* *Died, 27th August 1842, in England.*

NEWBOLT, JOHN DIGBY.—1814: Writer. 1816: Assistant to the Collector of Chingleput; Register of the Zillah of Chittoor. 1818: *At home.* 1822: *Returned to India;* Head Assistant to the Collector and Magistrate of Masulipatam. 1824: Head Assistant to the Collector and Magistrate of Ganjam. *Died, 12th September* 1826.

NEWNHAM, THOMAS.—1799: Writer. 1800: Assistant under the Secretary in the Revenue and Judicial Department. 1803: Register of the Zillah Court of Ramnad. 1805: Officiating Judge and Magistrate of Ramnad. 1806: Judge and Magistrate of the Zillah of Arnee. 1808: British Agent for Captured Property at Tranquebar; Commissioner at Tranquebar; Judge, Magistrate, and Collector of Seringapatam. 1809: Register of the Sudder and Foujdarry Adawlut; Commissioner to Receive Depositions at Madras; Judge and Magistrate of the Zillah of Cuddapah. 1816: Judge and Criminal Judge of Cuddapah. 1821: Acting Judge in Circuit, Centre Division; Judge and Criminal Judge of Cuddapah; Third Judge of Provincial Court of Appeal and Circuit, Northern Division, and Acting Third Judge of Provincial Court of Appeal, Centre Division. 1822: Third Judge of Provincial Court, Centre Division, and Acting in Northern Division. 1824: Second Judge of Provincial Court, Centre Division. 1828: Acting Judge, afterwards Senior Judge of Provincial Court, Western Division, and Acting in Centre Division. 1830: Acting First Judge of Provincial Court, Centre Division; Permitted as First Judge, Western Division, to leave Chittoor for Madras. 1831: Resumed at Tellicherry the Duties of First Judge of Provincial Court, Western Division. 1833: *Resigned the service; Annuitant from 1st May. Died, 29th September 1861, in England.*

NICHOLLS, SOLOMON.—1806: Writer. 1807: Assistant under the Chief Secretary in the Foreign, Political, and Secret Department; Assistant to the Collector of Tinnevelly. 1808: Deputy Commercial Resident at Tinnevelly. 1811: Deputy Commercial Resident at Salem. 1812: *At home.* 1817: *Returned to India;* Deputy Accountant-General in the Military Department. 1822: Deputy Accountant-General in the Military Department, Commercial Accountant, and Auditor. 1826: Judge and Criminal Judge of Madura. 1830: Third Judge, Provincial Court, Southern Division.

1831 : *At home on absentee allowance.*   1833 : *Returned to India, per "Orient."*   1834 : Second Judge of Provincial Court, Northern Division.   1836 : *Retired from service.   (Annuitant on the Fund.)*

NISBET, JOSIAH.—1807 : Writer.   1810 : Assistant to the Chief Secretary in the Secret, Political, and Foreign Department. 1811 : Assistant to the Collector of Bellary.   1814 : Head Assistant to the Collector of Bellary.   1816 : Assistant Magistrate of Bellary.   1819 : Employed in the late Peishwah's Dominions. 1822 : *At home.*   1824 : *Returned to India.*   1825 : Principal Collector and Magistrate of the Northern Division of Arcot.   1827 : Principal Collector and Political Agent at Dharwar, under the Bombay Government.   *Died, 5th August 1834, at Dharwar.*

NORMAN, MARTIN.—1852 : Writer.   1853 : Assistant to Collector and Magistrate, Madura.   1857 : Deputy Secretary to Government, Revenue Department.   *Died, 16th October 1859, at Chiselhurst.*

NORRIS, HENRY.—1769 : Writer.   1774 : Factor and Assistant at Vizagapatam.   1778 : Junior Merchant.   1780 : Senior Merchant.   *No trace after 1782.*

OAKELEY, CHARLES.—1767 : Writer.   1774 : Factor.   1776 : Junior Merchant.   1778 : Senior Merchant.   1790 : *Created a Baronet, 5th June ;* Appointed Member of Council of the Governor. 1792 : Succeeded as Governor of Madras ; *Assumed charge of office, 1st August.*   1794 : *Embarked for England, 29th September.*

OAKES, THOMAS.—1770 : Writer.   1776 : Factor and Assistant at Ganjam.   1778 : Junior Merchant.   1782 : Senior Merchant.   1792 : Senior Merchant and Member of the Board of Revenue.   1795 : *At home.*   1802 : *In India without employ.* 1803 : Second Member of the Board of Revenue.   1804 : Senior Member of the Board of Revenue.   1806 : *Out of the service.*

OAKES, THOMAS ALEXANDER.—1802 : Writer ; Assistant to the Secretary in the Revenue and Judicial Department, and Acting Assistant to the Special Commission.   1805 : Assistant to the Register in the Zillah of Vizagapatam.   1806 : Register of the Zillah of the Eastern Division of the Ceded District.   1808 : Subordinate Collector at Coimbatore ; First Assistant to the Collector of Nellore.   1811 : Collector of Vizagapatam.   1812 : Collector and Magistrate of Guntoor.   1823 : *At home.*   1828 : *Returned to India ;* Second Judge of the Provincial Court, Centre Division.   1830 : First Judge of the Provincial Court, Centre Division.   1832 : Officiating Third Judge of the Sudder and Foujdarry Adawlut. 1838 : Officiating Second Judge of the Sudder and Foujdarry Adawlut. 1839 : First Judge of the Provincial Court of Appeal and Circuit, Centre Division. 1840 : *Proceeded on furlough. Died, 12th September 1840, in London.*

OAKES, HENRY ROBERT.—1804 : Writer; Assistant under the Secretary to the Board of Revenue. 1806 : Register of the Zillah of Manar Goody. 1808 : Acting Register of the Zillah of Madura ; Register of the Zillah of Madura. 1809 : Register of the Zillah of Vizagapatam. 1811 : Assistant Judge of Combaconum. 1813 : Collector of Rajahmundry. 1817 : *At home.* 1819 : *Returned to India ;* Commercial Resident at the Ceded Districts. 1820 : *Dismissed the service, 25th October, in England.*

OAKES, CHARLES E.—1822 : Writer. 1825 : Assistant to the Collector and Magistrate of Tinnevelly. 1828 : Register of the Zillah of Nellore ; Register to the Provincial Court, Northern Division. 1831 : *At home on absentee allowance.* 1833 : *Returned to India, per " Vansittart ;"* Acting Judge and Criminal Judge of Chittoor. 1836 : Assistant Judge and Criminal Judge of Guntoor. *Died, 20th August* 1837, *at Ootacamund.*

OGILVIE, THOMAS.—1771 : Writer. 1776 : Factor. 1780 : Junior Merchant. 1782 : Senior Merchant. 1790 : *Out of the service.*

OGILVIE, JOHN HUGH DONALD.— 1789 : Writer. 1790 : Assistant under the Secretary in the Military, Political, and Secret Department. 1793 : Assistant under the Resident at Ingeram and Maddepollam. 1796 : Deputy Commercial Resident at Ingeram. 1798 : Deputy Commercial Resident at Ganjam. 1802 : Head Assistant to the Manager for the Supply of Beetle, and Collector of Revenue derived from the Sale of Arrack, &c.; Collector of Madras, and Superintendent of Revenue of Home Farm Villages, Arrack and Toddy Quit Rent, and Company's Lands in Black Town. 1806 : Second Judge of the Provincial Court, Centre Division. 1807 : Collector of Madras. 1809 : Mint-Master. 1819 : Third Judge of the Sudder and Foujdarry Adawlut. 1820 : Fourth Member of Council and President of the Sudder Adawlut. 1821 : Senior Member of the Board of Trade. 1824 : Member of Council. 1830 : *At home on absentee allowance. (Annuitant on the Fund from 1st May* 1831.) *Died, 10th March,* 1851, *in England.*

OGILVIE, GEORGE MACARTNEY.—1812: Writer. 1816: Second Assistant to the Collector and Magistrate of the Southern Division of Arcot. 1818 : Head Assistant to the Collector and Magistrate of Tanjore. 1823 : Sub-Collector and Assistant Magistrate of Cuddapah. 1828 : *At home on absentee allowance.* 1832 : *Returned to India;* Collector and Magistrate of Ganjam. 1835 : Principal Collector and Magistrate of Canara ; Third Judge of the Provincial Court, Southern Division. 1836 : Acting Principal Collector and Magistrate of the Northern Division of Arcot. 1837 : Principal Collector and Magistrate of North Arcot. 1842 : *Resigned the service. (Annuitant on the Fund,* 1842.) *Died, 5th February* 1878, *in England.*

OGILVIE, WILLIAM CECIL.—1825 : Writer. 1827 : Assistant to the Collector and Magistrate of Masulipatam. 1828 : Head Assistant to the Collector and Magistrate of Masulipatam ; Secretary to the Board of College and for Public Instruction ; and Deputy Teloogoo Translator to Government. 1829 : Head Assistant to the Secretary in the Revenue Department. 1831 : Additional Sub-Collector and Joint Magistrate of Canara. 1832 : Additional Sub-Collector and Joint Magistrate of Salem. 1833 : Sub-Collector and Joint Magistrate of Salem. 1838 : Acting Collector and Magistrate of Trichinopoly. 1839 : Acting Judge and Criminal Judge of Combaconum. 1842 : Judge and Criminal Judge, Bellary. 1844 : Civil and Sessions Judge, Bellary. 1845 : *Proceeded on furlough ; Resigned the service,* 17th *September, in England. (Annuitant on the Fund,* 1849.) *Died,* 24th *April* 1868, *in England.*

OGILVIE, ALEXANDER.—1845 : Writer. 1848 : Assistant to Collector and Magistrate, Chingleput. 1851 : *Proceeded on furlough.* 1856 : *Absent from India five years.*

OLIVER, WILLIAM.—1800 : Writer. 1805 : Second Assistant, afterwards First Assistant, to the Register of the Sudder and Foujdarry Adawlut. 1807 : Deputy Persian Translator to Government. 1811 : Secretary to the Board of Revenue ; Persian Translator to Government. 1813 : Register of the Sudder and Foujdarry Adawlut. 1824 : Second Judge, afterwards First Judge, of the Provincial Court, Southern Division. 1826 : Third Puisne Judge of the Sudder and Foujdarry Adawlut. 1830 : Second Puisne Judge of the Sudder and Foujdarry Adawlut. 1831 : Member of Council, and President of the Sudder Court. 1836 : *Retired from service. (Annuitant on the Fund.)*

ONSLOW, ARTHUR POOLEY.—1822 : Writer. 1826 : Assistant to the Principal Collector and Magistrate of Coimbatore. 1828 : *Leave to sea for his health.* 1830 : Head Assistant to the Collector of Masulipatam. 1831 : Head Assistant to the Collector and Magistrate of Bellary. 1832: Acting as Cashier to the Government Bank ; Acting Judge and Joint Criminal Judge of Chingleput. 1833 : Sub-Collector and Joint Magistrate of Bellary. 1835 : Secretary to the Board of Revenue. 1839: Collector and Magistrate of Trichinopoly. 1850 : Collector, Magistrate, and Agent to the Governor, Ganjam. 1854: *Proceeded on furlough.* 1855 : *Resigned the service, 1st January, in India. (Annuitant on the Fund, 1856.)*

ONSLOW, Thomas.—1831 : Writer. 1833 : Assistant to Principal Collector and Magistrate, Bellary. 1834 : Acting Register to the Zillah Court of Cuddapah. 1835 : At first Acting, and afterwards Register to the Zillah Court of Chittoor. 1840: Acting Deputy Collector of Land Customs, Madras. 1841 : Acting Assistant Judge and Joint Criminal Judge, Rajahmundry. 1842 : *Proceeded on furlough.* 1845 : Acting Assistant Judge of the Zillah of Calicut. 1846 : Acting Sub-Judge of the Zillah of Calicut. 1847 : Sub-Judge of the Zillah of Cuddapah, and Acting Civil and Sessions Judge of Cuddapah. 1850 : Sub-Judge of the Zillah of Calicut. 1852 : *Proceeded to England.* 1856 : Acting Civil and Sessions Judge, Guntoor. 1857 : Civil and Sessions Judge, Guntoor. 1862 : *On medical leave for 15 months ;* Civil and Sessions Judge, Masulipatam. 1863 : Civil and Sessions Judge of Nundial, and of Chittoor ; also Collector and Magistrate of South Canara. 1864: *Resigned the service, 1st April. (Annuitant.) Died, 2d July 1882, at Ootacamund.*

ORAM, William.—1772 : Writer. 1778 : Factor. 1780 : Junior Merchant. 1790 : Senior Merchant, and Manager of Part of the Havally, Masulipatam. 1792 : Member of the Revenue Board. 1793 : *At home.* 1800 : *Out of the service.*

ORPIN, Richard Thomas.—1778 : Writer. *No trace after* 1782.

ORR, John.—1815 : Writer. 1818 : Second Assistant to the Collector and Magistrate of Coimbatore. 1820 : Assistant to the Collector and Magistrate of Malabar; *At home.* 1824 : *Returned to India ;* Head Assistant to the Collector and Magistrate of Nellore. 1826 : Sub-Collector and Assistant Magistrate of Nellore. 1829 : Acting Secretary in the Public, Commercial, and Revenue Department ; Collector and Magistrate of Salem. 1832 : Principal Collector and Magistrate of Salem. 1838 : Principal Collector and Magistrate of Cuddapah ; Acting Civil Auditor and Superintendent of Stamps ; Civil Auditor and Superintendent of Stamps.

1839 : *At home on private affairs.*   1842 : *Returned to India.*
1843 : Accountant - General.   1844 : Accountant - General, and
Member of the Mint Committee.   1845 : *Resigned the service,
30th April.*

OSWELL, W. F.—1827 : Writer.   1829 : Assistant to the
Head Collector of South Arcot.   1831 : *At home on absentee
allowance.   No trace after this date.*

OSWELL, WILLIAM COTTON.—1837 : Writer.   1840 : Assistant
to Principal Collector and Magistrate, Southern Division of Arcot.
1842 : Head Assistant to Principal Collector and Magistrate,
Southern Division of Arcot.   1844 : Head Assistant to Principal
Collector and Magistrate, Coimbatore.   1848 : *Proceeded on furlough.*
1851 : *Resigned the service, 19th March, in England.*

OWEN, ARTHUR MOSTYN.—1832 : Writer.   1833 : Assistant
under the Principal Collector of South Arcot.   1834 : Assistant
to the Principal Collector of Malabar.   1839 : Acting Head Assistant to the Principal Collector and Magistrate of Bellary ; Acting
Second Assistant to the Accountant-General ; Commissioner for
Drawing Government Lotteries.   1840 : Assistant to Collector and
Magistrate, Malabar.   1841 : Head Assistant to Collector and
Magistrate, Madura.   1844 : *Proceeded on furlough.*   1848 : *Absent
from India five years.*

PALK, THOMAS.—1769 : Writer.   1774 : Factor.   1778 :
Junior Merchant.   1780 : Senior Merchant.   1790 : *At home.*
1793 : *Out of the service.*

PALMER, ARCHDALE.—1755 : Writer.   1768 : Senior Merchant.   1771 : Paymaster at Madura.   1774 : Second in Council
at Masulipatam.   1776 : Member of Council of the Governor.
1777 : *Recalled by order of the General Court of Proprietors, 9th
May.*   1780 : *Suspended from the service.*

PARISH, GEORGE.—1796 : Writer.   1799 : Assistant in the
Public, Revenue, and Commercial Department.   1800 : Assistant
to the Collector of Canara ; Head Assistant under the Collector of
the Polygar Peishcush.   1803 : Subordinate Collector in the
Ceded Districts ; Collector of the Zillah of Ramnad, and of the
Provinces of Dindigul and Madura.   1812 : *At home.*   1817 :
Out of the service.

PARKER, ROBERT DEANE.—1829 : Writer ; Assistant to the
Secretary in the Revenue Department.   1831 : Head Assistant to the
Collector of Trichinopoly.   1832 : Acting Deputy Persian Translator
to Government ; Head Assistant to the Register of the Sudder and

Foujdarry Adawlut; Deputy Persian Translator to Government. 1833 : Junior Deputy Secretary to the Board of Revenue. 1835 : Acting Sub-Collector of Cuddapah. 1836 : Acting Sub-Collector and Joint Magistrate of Nellore. 1837 : Sub-Collector and Joint Magistrate of Nellore ; Officiating Senior Deputy Secretary to the Board of Revenue. 1838 : Acting Sub-Secretary to the Board of Revenue ; Acting Principal Collector and Magistrate of Nellore. 1839 : Sub-Secretary to the Board of Revenue. 1842 : *Proceeded on furlough.* 1844 : *Returned to India ;* Additional Sub-Collector and Joint Magistrate, Canara. 1845 : Sub-Collector and Joint Magistrate, Canara. 1848 : Collector and Magistrate, Madura. 1858 : Collector and Magistrate, Malabar. 1859 : *Resigned the service, 1st May, in India. (Annuitant on the Fund, 1859.)*

PARRY, GEORGE.—1789 : Writer. 1790 : Acting Deputy Secretary in the Military, Political, and Secret Department. 1793 : Examiner and Head Assistant under the Secretary in the Military, Political, and Secret Department; Land Customer and Choultry Register. 1796 : Civil Paymaster-General. 1797 : Deputy Secretary in the Military, Political, and Secret Department. 1798 : *At home for his health.* 1801 : *Returned to India ;* Special Agent for Conducting the Department of Provision. *Died, 6th September 1801, in Bengal.*

PARRY, WILLIAM HENRY.—1816 : Writer. 1819 : Second Assistant to the Secretary to Government. 1820 : Assistant to the Secretary in the Military Department; Register of the Zillah of Nellore. 1828 : *At home on absentee allowance. Died, 11th April 1832, at Brighton.*

PARSONS, WILLIAM.—1779 : Writer. 1790 : Senior Merchant ; Assistant at Ingeram. 1793 : *At home.* 1800 : *Out of the service.*

PASKE, GEORGE.—1797 : Writer. 1798 : Assistant under the Political, Revenue, and Commercial Department. 1799 : Assistant under the Collector of Vizagapatam. 1800 : Assistant to the Collector of the Third Division of Vizagapatam ; Assistant under the Collector of Ganjam. 1802 : Assistant to the Collector of Nellore. 1805 : Register under the Collector of Nellore and Ongole. 1806 : Judge and Magistrate of the Zillah of Masulipatam. 1821 : Third Judge of the Provincial Court, Centre Division. *Died on his passage home, April 1822, on board the " Cambridge."*

PASKE, JOHN BENSLEY GRESHAM PAGE.—1806: Writer. 1807: Assistant to the Register of the Zillah of Vizagapatam. 1811 :

Register of the Zillah of Vizagapatam. 1814 : *At home.* 1817 : *Returned to India ;* Register to the Provincial Court, Northern Division. 1824 : Judge and Criminal Judge of Chingleput. 1830 : Third Judge of the Provincial Court, Centre Division. 1832 : First Judge of the Provincial Court, Northern Division. 1840 : *Retired from the service.* (*Annuitant on the Fund,* 1840.) *Died, 3d August* 1859, *in England.*

PATERNOSTER, JOHN. — 1815 : Writer. 1818 : Second Assistant to the Collector and Magistrate of Vizagapatam. 1820 : Register of the Zillah of Ganjam. 1821 : Register of the Zillah of Bellary. 1824 : Register of the Zillah of Masulipatam. 1827 : Register to the Zillah of Salem. 1828 : Register of the Zillah of Combaconum. 1831 : Register of the Zillah of Chingleput. 1833 : Register to the Provincial Court, Northern Division. 1834 : *At home on absentee allowance.* 1837 : *Returned to India, per "Sophia,"* Judge and Criminal Judge of Cuddapah. 1838 : Judge and Criminal Judge of Bellary. 1843 : *Out of employ.* 1844 : *Proceeded on furlough.* 1846 : *Resigned the service, 30th April.* (*Annuitant on the Fund,* 1846.)

PATERNOSTER, RICHARD.—1821 : Writer. 1824 : Assistant to the Collector and Magistrate of Bellary. 1825 : Assistant to the Principal Collector and Magistrate of Malabar. 1827 : *At home on absentee allowance. Pensioned, 6th January* 1830, *in England.*

PEARCE, THOMAS.—1783 : Writer; Assistant in the Select Office. 1785 : Clerk to the Court of Requests. 1786 : Assistant to the Secretary in the Revenue Department, and Deputy Import Warehouse-keeper. 1789 : Assistant to the Accountant-General ; Accountant-General in the Mayor's Court ; and Deputy Postmaster-General. 1790 : Deputy Accountant and Accountant-General in the Mayor's Office. 1792 : Provisional Paymaster at Tanjore. *Died, February* 1794.

PEILE, JOHN HENRY.—1796 : Writer. 1798 : Assistant in the Military, Political, and Secret Department. 1799 : Head Assistant under the Resident at Mysore. 1800 : Postmaster at Mysore. 1803 : Secretary to the Resident at Mysore. 1806 : Judge and Magistrate of Cuddapah. 1809 : Secretary to Government in Military Department, and Superintendent of Stamps. 1811 : Persian Translator to Government ; Third Judge of the Provincial Court, Southern Division. 1818 : *At home.* 1823 : *Out of the service.*

PELLY, CHARLES.—1830 : Writer. 1832 : Second Assistant to Principal Collector and Magistrate, Bellary. 1834 : Acting Head

Assistant to Principal Collector and Magistrate, Bellary. 1835: Head Assistant to Principal Collector and Magistrate, Bellary. 1837: Acting Sub-Collector and Joint Magistrate, Bellary. 1838: Sub-Collector and Joint Magistrate, Bellary. 1841 : Acting Judge and Criminal Judge, Bellary. 1844: *Proceeded to Europe on fur-lough.* 1848: Acting Collector and Magistrate, Bellary. 1850: Collector and Magistrate, Bellary. 1859 : Member of the Board of Revenue, and Acting President of the Board of Examiners. 1862 : Government Director of the Bank of Madras. 1863 : Acting President of Income Tax Commission, and Commissioner for the Un-covenanted Civil Service Examination. 1867 : *Resigned the service, 15th January.* (*Annuitant.*)

PERRING, Peter.—1759 : Writer. 1768 : Junior Merchant. 1771 : Senior Merchant, and Second in Council at Vizagapatam. 1778 : Member of the Council of the Governor. 1781 : *Dismissed the service.*

PERRING, Richard.—1779 : Writer. *No trace after* 1780.

PETER, Rous.—1801 : Writer. 1804 : Assistant under the Collector of Trichinopoly. 1805 : Register under the Principal Collector of Tanjore. 1806: Register of the Zillah of Trichinopoly. 1807: Assistant to the Collector of Dindigul and Madura. 1812 : Collector and Magistrate of Dindigul and Madura. 1825 : Principal Collector and Magistrate of Madura. *Died, 6th August* 1828, *at Madura.*

PETERS, Edward.—1837 : Writer. 1838 : Assistant to the Principal Collector and Magistrate of Tanjore. 1839 : Acting Head Assistant to the Collector and Magistrate of Masulipatam. 1840 : Second Assistant to Accountant-General. 1841 : Assistant to Collector and Magistrate of Chingleput. 1843 : Head Assistant to Collector and Magistrate of Coimbatore ; *Proceeded on furlough.* 1846: *Returned to India.* 1847 : *Proceeded on furlough.* 1851 : *Absent from India five years.*

PETRIE, William.—1765 : Writer. 1771 : Factor. 1774 : Junior Merchant. 1776 : Senior Merchant; *At home.* 1778 : *In India.* 1782 : *At home.* 1790 : Member of the Council of the Governor. 1793 : *At home.* 1800 : President of the Board of Revenue, and Member of the Council of the Governor. 1809 : Appointed Governor of the Prince of Wales Island. *Died,* 27*th October* 1816, *at Prince of Wales Island.*

PHILLIPS, George.—1812 : Writer. 1815 : Assistant to the Register of the Provincial Court, Centre Division. 1816 : Head Assistant to the Collector of Trichinopoly ; Assistant Magistrate of

H

Trichinopoly. 1823: Sub-Collector and Assistant Magistrate of Coimbatore. *Died, 5th April 1825, at Coimbatore.*

PHILLIPS, HENRY DOMINIC.—1830: Writer. 1832: Acting Second Assistant to Principal Collector and Magistrate, Nellore; Register of the Zillah of Nellore. 1835: Acting Head Assistant to Principal Collector and Magistrate, Nellore; and Register to the Zillah Court there. 1836: Acting Assistant Judge and Joint Criminal Judge, Guntoor. 1837: Junior Deputy Secretary to the Board of Revenue; Officiating Senior Deputy Secretary to the Board of Revenue; Acting Assistant Judge and Joint Criminal Judge, Salem; Acting Assistant Judge and Joint Criminal Judge at Madura. 1838: Assistant Judge and Joint Criminal Judge, Madura; Acting Second Assistant to the Accountant-General; Acting Sub-Secretary to the Board of Revenue; Acting Deputy Register of the Sudder and Foujdarry Adawlut. 1839: Assistant Judge and Joint Criminal Judge of the Auxiliary Court, Trichinopoly; Acting Senior Deputy Register to the Sudder and Foujdarry Adawlut; and Commissioner for Government Lotteries. 1842: Acting Register to the Sudder and Foujdarry Adawlut. 1843: Acting Register to the Sudder and Foujdarry Adawlut, and Sub-Judge, Combaconum. 1846: Sub-Judge, Madura. 1847: Agent to the Governor of Madras at Kurnool and Bunganapilly. 1850: Collector and Magistrate, Salem. 1853: *Proceeded to England.* 1856: *In India, and without employ.* 1857: Acting Collector and Magistrate, and Resident Commissioner at Tanjore; also Civil and Session Judge at Mangalore, and at Madura; 1858: Collector and Magistrate, and Resident Commissioner at Tanjore; also Puisne Judge of the Court of Sudder and Foujdarry Adawlut. 1859: President of the Board of Examiners; Commissioner for the Affairs of the late Rajah of Tanjore. 1862: Judge of the High Court of Judicature, Madras. 1864: Provisional, afterwards Member of Council of the Governor of Fort St. George. 1869: *Resigned the service, 12th November.* (*Annuitant.*)

PHILLIPS, ALEXANDER WILLIAM. — 1839: Writer. 1841: Assistant to Collector and Magistrate, Tanjore. 1842: Acting Register of the Zillah Court of Combaconum. 1843: Acting Head Assistant to Collector and Magistrate, Trichinopoly. 1845: Acting Head Assistant to Collector and Magistrate, North Arcot; Acting Sub-Judge of the Zillah of Chittoor; Acting Head Assistant to Collector and Magistrate, North Arcot. 1846: Head Assistant to Collector and Magistrate, Salem, and at Chingleput.

1850: *Proceeded to Europe on furlough.* 1853: Special Assistant to Collector and Magistrate, Tanjore. 1854: Acting Sub-Judge, Madura. 1855: Acting Civil and Sessions Judge, and Sub-Judge, at Madura. 1856: Acting Civil and Sessions Judge, Madura. 1859: Acting Civil and Sessions Judge, Tinnevelly, and at Salem. 1861: Civil and Sessions Judge of Chingleput. 1862: *On medical leave.* 1863: Collector and Magistrate of Godavery District. 1864: Acting Civil and Sessions Judge, Ootacamund. 1866: *On 3 months' special leave;* Civil and Sessions Judge, Ootacamund. 1867: *On medical leave to Europe for 27 months.* 1869: *Resigned the service, 27th April, in England. (Annuitant.) Died, 25th February 1883, at Southsea.*

PHIPPS, CONSTANTINE.—1791: Writer. 1792: Assistant under the Secretary in the Public, Commercial, and Revenue Department. 1793: Assistant under the Secretary to the Revenue Board. 1794: Assistant to the Accountant to the Revenue Board. *Died, 15th April 1794.*

PINDER, JAMES ROSE.—1790: Writer. 1791: Assistant under the Secretary to the Board of Trade. *Died, 21st February 1793.*

PLACE, LIONEL.—1783: Writer. 1785: Assistant to the Secretary to the Select Committee. 1786: Assistant to the Secretary in the Military Department, and Clerk to the Committee of Stores; Assistant at Cuddalore. 1788: Assistant to the Accountant to the Board of Revenue. 1789: Deputy to the Accountant to the Board of Revenue. 1790: Accountant to the Board of Assumed Revenue. 1791: Accountant to the Board of Revenue. 1796: Collector in the Jaghire. 1799: *At home.* 1802: *Returned to India;* Acting Second Member of the Board of Revenue. 1803: *At home.* 1807: *Out of the service.*

PLUMER, HALL.—1769: Writer. 1774: Factor. 1778: Junior Merchant. 1780: Senior Merchant. *No trace after 1782.*

POPHAM, STRACHAN IRVINE.—1828: Writer. 1829: Assistant to the Collector of Tinnevelly. 1830: Assistant to the Collector of Salem. 1831: Second Assistant to the Collector and Magistrate of Tinnevelly. 1832: Acting Assistant Judge and Joint Criminal Judge of Salem; Head Assistant to the Principal Collector of Salem. 1834: Superintendent of a Division in Mysore. 1839: *At home on absentee allowance.* 1844: *Absent from India five years.*

PORCHER, JOSIAS DU PRÉ.—1778: Writer. 1790: Senior Merchant, Member of the Board of Trade, and Clerk to the Committee of Works. 1792: Member of the Board of Trade, Mayor of Madras, and Military Storekeeper. 1800 : *At home, and retired from the service.*

PORTER, RICHARD TINDAL.—1825 : Writer. 1827 : Assistant to the Principal Collector and Magistrate of Coimbatore. 1828 : Head Assistant to the Principal Collector and Magistrate of Coimbatore ; Head Assistant to the Principal Collector of Chingleput. 1829 : Deputy Tamil Translator to Government. 1830 : Junior Deputy Secretary to the Board of Revenue. 1831 : Senior Deputy Secretary to the Board of Revenue. 1837 : *At home on absentee allowance.* 1840 : *Returned to India.* 1841 : Sub-Secretary to the Board of Revenue. 1843 : Collector and Magistrate, Masulipatam. 1852 : *Out of employ.* 1854 : Civil Auditor and Superintendent of Stamps. 1855 : *Resigned the service, 1st May, in India. (Annuitant on the Fund, 1856.) Died, 9th December 1879, in England.*

PORTIS, GEORGE.—1781 : Writer. 1783 : Assistant to the Secretary to the Select Committee ; *At home. No trace after 1783.*

POWNEY, GEORGE.—1779 : Writer. 1790 : Senior Merchant. 1791 : Resident at Travancore, and Paymaster of Troops there. 1800 : *At home, and retired from the service.*

POWNEY, HENRY SAVERNE.—1781 : Writer. 1783 : Assistant at Vizagapatam. *No trace after 1785.*

POWNEY, EDWARD.— 1797 : Writer. 1799 : Assistant under the Secretary in the Military, Political, and Secret Department. 1800 : Assistant Collector of Tanjore. 1803 : Register to the Adawlut of the Zillah of Salem. 1806 : Register to the Court of Appeal and Circuit, Southern Division. 1810 : Judge and Magistrate of the Zillah of Combaconum. 1823 : *At home. (Retired on the Annuity Fund, 8th January 1828.) Died, 3d January 1855, in England.*

PRENDERGAST, THOMAS.—1826 : Writer. 1828 : Assistant to the Principal Collector of Tanjore. 1829 : Acting Head Assistant to the Principal Collector of Nellore. 1830 : Head Assistant to the Principal Collector of Nellore. 1831 : Acting Sub-Collector and Joint Magistrate of Nellore. 1833 : Acting Assistant Judge and Joint Criminal Judge at Guntoor. 1834 : Assistant Judge and Joint Criminal Judge of Tinnevelly. 1838 : *At home on absentee allowance.* 1841 : *Returned to India.* 1842 : Sub-Collector and Joint Magistrate, Salem. 1844 : Collector and Magistrate, Rajahmundry. 1855 : Collector and Magistrate, and Agent to Governor, in Ganjam ; *Proceeded on furlough.* 1858 : *Retired from the service, 27th March, in India. (Annuitant on the Fund, 1859.)*

PRENDERGAST, GUY LUSHINGTON.—1827 : Writer. 1829 :

Assistant to the Secretary in the Revenue Department. 1830 : Assistant to the Resident at Mysore ; Senior Assistant to the Register of the Sudder and Foujdarry Adawlut; Superintendent of Government Lotteries. 1832 : Senior Deputy Register of the Sudder and Foujdarry Adawlut. 1838 : *At home on absentee allowance.* 1839 : *Returned to India per " General Kyd."* 1840 : Assistant Judge and Joint Criminal Judge, Malabar; Deputy Accountant-General. 1857 : Accountant-General and Member of the Mint Committee. 1859 : *Dismissed the service, 3d September, in India.*

PRINGLE, ALEXANDER. — 1766 : Writer. 1771 : Factor. 1774 : Junior Merchant, and Assistant at Masulipatam. 1778 : Senior Merchant. 1790 : *Out of the service.*

PRINGLE, JOHN ROBERT.—1835 : Writer. 1837 : Doing Duty as an Assistant under the Collector of Chingleput. 1838 : Assistant to the Collector and Magistrate of Tinnevelly. 1841 : Head Assistant to the Collector and Magistrate of Tinnevelly. 1846 : Head Assistant to the Collector and Magistrate of Madura. 1847 : Head Assistant to the Collector and Magistrate of Nellore. *Died, 5th September 1847, on board the " Mary Ann."*

PROCTOR, GEORGE.—1767: Writer. 1774 : Factor. 1776 : Junior Merchant. 1778 : Senior Merchant. 1790 : *At home.* 1795 : *Out of the service.*

PURVIS, ARTHUR.—1831 : Writer. 1834 : Assistant to Principal Collector, Nellore. 1835 : Assistant to Principal Collector and Magistrate, Nellore. 1837 : Acting Assistant to Collector and Magistrate, Cuddapah, and Acting Head Assistant to Principal Collector and Magistrate, Nellore. 1838 : Head Assistant to Principal Collector and Magistrate, Masulipatam. 1839 : Head Assistant to Principal Collector and Magistrate, Nellore. 1840 : Acting Register of the Zillah Court of Nellore. 1842 : Acting Sub-Collector and Joint Magistrate, Nellore. 1843 : Sub-Collector and Joint Magistrate, Nellore. 1845 : *Proceeded to Europe on furlough.* 1848 : Acting Sub-Collector and Joint Magistrate, Nellore. 1849 : Sub-Collector and Joint Magistrate, Nellore. 1851 : Acting Collector and Magistrate, Guntoor. 1854 : Collector and Magistrate, Rajahmundry. 1859 : Collector and Magistrate, Godavari. 1863 : *Resigned the service, 1st June. (Annuitant.) Died, 1st June 1877, in England.*

PYBUS, JOHN.—1742 : Writer. 1768 : Member of Council of the Governor. 1768 : *Arrived in England, in the " Hector."*

PYBUS, JOHN BRYAN.—1807 : Writer. 1810 : Assistant to the Secretary in the Revenue and Judicial Department ; Assistant to the Superintendent of Stamps. 1811 : Fixed Examiner in the Office of Secretary to the Board of Revenue. 1814 : Deputy Secretary to the Board of Revenue ; Head Assistant to the Superintendent of Stamps. *Died, 27th January 1820, at Madras.*

PYCROFT, THOMAS.—1828 : Writer. 1831 : Second Assistant to Principal Collector, South Arcot. 1832 : Acting Assistant Judge and Joint Criminal Judge, Chingleput ; Acting Head Assistant to Principal Collector and Magistrate, South Arcot. 1833 : Head Assistant to Principal Collector and Magistrate, South Arcot. 1837 : Acting Sub-Collector and Joint Magistrate, and Sub-Collector and Joint Magistrate, South Arcot. 1839 : *Proceeded to Europe on furlough.* 1843 : Acting Sub-Secretary to the Board of Revenue ; Commissioner for Government Lotteries ; and Deputy Collector, Madras. 1845 : Assistant Judge, Calicut ; Secretary to the Board of Revenue ; and Acting Tamil Translator. 1850 : Secretary to Government in Revenue and Judicial Departments. 1855 : Chief Secretary to Government. 1857 : *Proceeded to Europe on private affairs.* 1862 : Additional, afterwards Provisional, and then Member of Council of the Governor of Fort St. George. 1866 : *Knight Commander of the Star of India, 25th May* 1867 : *Resigned the service, 29th October.* (*Annuitant.*)

PYNE, GEORGE.—1753 : Writer. 1768 : Senior Merchant. 1771 : Resident at Bandermallee. 1774 : *Out of the service.*

RADDAN, EDWARD.—1755 : Writer. 1768 : Senior Merchant, and Third in Council at Masulipatam. 1774 : *Out of the service.*

RAITT, CHARLES.—1763 : Writer. 1768 : Factor. *No trace after* 1768.

RAM, GEORGE ANDREW.—1767 : Writer. 1774 : Factor. 1776 : Junior Merchant. 1778 : Senior Merchant. 1791 : Resident at Tanjore. 1795 : Collector of Guntoor. 1801 : *At home.* 1802 : *Out of the service.*

RANDAL, BENJAMIN.—1797 : Writer. 1798 : Assistant in the Public, Revenue, and Commercial Department. 1799 : Second Assistant under the Collector of Dindigul. 1800 : Assistant under the Commercial Resident at Cuddalore. 1802 : Assistant to the Commercial Resident at Nagore. 1804 : Deputy Commercial Resident at Nagore. 1811 : Commercial Resident in the Ceded Districts. *Died, 10th July* 1819, *at Cuddapah.*

RATLIFF, JOHN.—1839 : Writer. 1840 : Assistant to Collector and Magistrate, Bellary. 1841 : Register of the Zillah Court of Bellary. 1843 : Assistant to Collector and Magistrate, North Arcot. 1844 : Acting Head Assistant to Principal Collector and Magistrate, Nellore. 1845 : Assistant to Collector and Magistrate, and Agent to the Governor of Madras, in Vizagapatam ; afterwards Head Assistant to Principal Collector and Magistrate, Madura. 1846 : Assistant to the Collector and Magistrate, afterwards Head Assistant to Collector and Magistrate, Cuddapah. 1847 : Acting Sub-Judge of the Zillah of Cuddapah. 1848 : Head Assistant to Collector and Magistrate, Madura. 1849 : Acting Sub-Judge, Madura. 1850: *Proceeded to Europe on furlough.* 1853 : Acting Sub-Collector and Joint Magistrate, Nellore. 1854 : Additional Sub-Collector and Magistrate, Canara ; Acting Collector and Magistrate, Nellore. 1855 : At first Acting, afterwards Sub-Judge, Cuddapah. 1857 : Acting Civil and Sessions Judge, and Acting Sub-Judge, Rajahmundry. 1858 : Acting Collector and Magistrate, South Arcot. 1859 : Acting Civil and Sessions Judge, Nellore. 1860 : Civil and Sessions Judge, Cuddapah. 1861 : Officiating Civil and Sessions Judge, Honore. 1862 : Civil and Sessions Judge, Bellary. 1864 : Civil and Sessions Judge, Nundial. 1865 : *On medical leave to Europe for* 15 *months.* 1866 : *Resigned the service,* 14th *October.* (*Annuitant.*) *Died,* 18th *May* 1877, *in England.*

RAVENSHAW, JOHN GOLDSBOROUGH.—1796 : Writer. 1797 : Assistant under the Secretary to the Board of Trade. 1798 : Assistant under the Secretary to the Board of Revenue, and Assistant to the Accountant-General. 1799 : Head Assistant to the Collector of Dindigul. 1800 : Collector in the Southern Division of the Canara Districts. 1805 : Principal Collector of the Southern Division of Arcot. 1809 : In Charge of the Revenues of Cuddalore and Pondicherry. 1813 : *At home.* 1818 : *Out of the service. Elected a Director of the East India Company,* 14th *July* 1819. *Died,* 6th *June* 1840, *at Crawley, Sussex.*

READ, JOHN.—1789 : Writer. 1790 : Assistant under the Military Secretary. 1791 : Acting Deputy Secretary to the Board of Revenue. 1793 : Deputy Secretary to the Board of Revenue. 1796 : *At home.* 1797 : *Returned to India;* Head Assistant to the Collector of the Fourth Division of Masulipatam. 1799 : Collector of the Fourth Division of Masulipatam. 1802 : Collector of the Third Division of Masulipatam ; Second Judge of the Court of Circuit and Appeal, Southern Division. 1809 : Acting Puisne Judge of the Sudder and Foujdarry Adawlut. 1811 : First Judge of the Court of Appeal and Circuit, Southern Division. 1815 : *At home.* 1820 : *Out of the service.*

READ, GEORGE.—1790 : Writer. 1791 : Assistant under the Secretary to the Military and Political Department. 1792 : Assistant under the Secretary to the Board of Trade. 1793: Assistant under the Accountant to the Board of Revenue. 1796: Deputy Accountant and Malabar Translator to the Board of Revenue. 1798: Accountant to the Board of Revenue. 1800: Deputy Accountant in the Revenue and Commercial Department, and Malabar Translator. 1801: Subordinate Collector under Major M'Leod's Authority. 1802: Third Judge of the Provincial Court, Centre Division. 1809: Second Judge of the Provincial Court, Centre Division. 1812: *At home.* 1816: *Out of the service.*

READ, ALEXANDER.—1796: Writer. 1797: Assistant under the Secretary to the Board of Trade. 1798: Assistant under the Board of Revenue, Assistant under the Collector in Burramehal. 1799: Head Assistant under the Collector in the Canara District. 1800: Collector in the Northern Division of Canara and Soondah. 1805: Principal Collector in Canara. 1816: *At home.* 1820: *Out of the service.*

READE, CHARLES WILLIAM.—1835: Writer. 1836: Under Principal Collector of Canara. 1837: Doing Duty as Assistant to Principal Collector of Canara. 1838: Assistant to Principal Collector and Magistrate, Canara. 1839: Acting Head Assistant to Principal Collector and Magistrate, Canara; and Acting Register to the Zillah Court of Chittoor. 1841: Register to the Zillah Court of Bellary; and Acting Head Assistant, subsequently Head Assistant to Principal Collector and Magistrate, Canara. 1842: Acting Register to the Zillah Court of Canara. 1846: Acting additional Sub-Collector and Joint Magistrate of Canara. 1848: *Proceeded to Europe on furlough.* 1852: Acting Civil and Sessions Judge, Chingleput. 1853: Sub-Judge at Salem. 1856: Acting Civil and Sessions Judge, Salem. 1857: Acting Civil and Sessions Judge, Cuddalore; Collector, Magistrate, and Agent to the Governor of Madras, in Vizagapatam. 1859: *Without employ. On private affairs to England for 6 months.* 1861: Acting Collector and Magistrate of Madras. 1862: Collector and Magistrate of South Arcot. 1871: *Resigned the service, 26th March. (Annuitant.) Died, 27th April* 1884, *in England.*

RENTON, JOHN.—1763: Junior Merchant, with Fixed Appointment as Sub-Accountant. *No trace after* 1774.

RENTON, WILLIAM.—1771: Junior Merchant, with Fixed Appointment as Sub-Accountant. *Died, 8th November* 1775.

REVELL, JOSEPH.—1769: Writer. 1774: Factor. 1778: Junior Merchant. 1780: Senior Merchant. 1791: Manager of the Muglatore Zemindary. 1793: *At home.* 1800: *Out of the service.*

RICE, John Adamson.—1796 : Writer. 1799 : Second Assistant under the Collector of Canara. *Died,* 21*st October* 1799.

RICHARDSON, William.—1777 : Writer. *No trace after* 1780.

RICHARDSON, John.—1779 : Writer. *No trace after* 1782.

RICHARDSON, Francis.—1793: Writer. 1796: Assistant under the Resident at the Presidency. 1797 : *At home for his health.* 1799 : *Returned to India ;* Assistant under the Commercial Resident at Nagore ; Deputy Commercial Resident at Nagore. 1801 : Commercial Resident at Nagore. 1817 : *At home.* 1822 : *Out of the service.*

RICKARDS, Richard.—1827 : Writer. 1829 : Assistant to the Principal Collector of South Arcot. 1830 : Head Assistant to the Collector of Vizagapatam. 1832 : Head Assistant to the Collector and Magistrate of Trichinopoly. 1833 : Register of the Zillah of Salem. *Died,* 26*th November* 1834, *at Amboorpatt.*

RIDDLE, John.—1797 : Writer. 1799 : Assistant under the Secretary to the Board of Revenue. 1801 : Assistant under the Collector of Salem. 1803 : Assistant to the Collector of Coimbatore. 1805 : Subordinate Collector of Coimbatore. 1808 : Head Assistant to the Collector of Coimbatore. 1811 : Acting Judge and Magistrate of the Zillah of Dharapooram ; Judge, Magistrate, and Collector of Seringapatam. 1813 : Judge and Magistrate of the Zillah of Madura. *Died, on his passage to England,* 7*th February* 1815, *on board the "Europe."*

ROBERTS, Charles.—1807 : Writer; Assistant to the Collector of the Northern Division of Arcot. 1810 : Head Assistant to the Collector of Chittoor. 1816 : Assistant Magistrate of Chittoor. 1821 : Sub-Collector and Assistant Magistrate of Tanjore. 1822 : Sub-Collector and Assistant Magistrate of Madura. 1824 : Collector and Magistrate of Masulipatam, and in Charge of the Treasury there. 1827 : Principal Collector and Magistrate of the Northern Division of Arcot. 1832 : Acting Second Member of the Board of Revenue ; Third Member of the Board of Revenue. 1837 : *At home on absentee allowance.* (*Retired on Annuity Fund from* 8*th May* 1838.) *Died,* 31*st July* 1850, *in London.*

ROBERTSON, Francis William. — 1806 : Writer. 1807 : Assistant under the Secretary to the Board of Revenue. 1808 : Deputy Commercial Resident at Masulipatam ; Assistant under the Collector of Masulipatam. 1811 : Register of the Zillah of Canara. 1812 : Assistant to the Collector of Guntoor. 1814 : Head Assistant to the Collector of Masulipatam. 1816 : Assistant

Magistrate of Masulipatam. 1819 : Collector and Magistrate of Rajahmundry. 1824 : Collector and Magistrate of Bellary. 1826 : Principal Collector and Magistrate of Bellary. *Died, 16th December 1838, at Anantapoor.*

ROBERTSON, ANDREW.—1817 : Writer. 1819 : Assistant to the Collector and Magistrate of Chittoor. 1820 : *At home.* 1825 : *Returned to India ;* Junior Deputy Secretary to the Board of Revenue. 1826 : Tamil Translator to Government. 1827 : Senior Deputy Secretary to the Board of Trade. 1830 : Secretary and Treasurer to the Government Bank. 1833 : Collector of Madras, Tamil Translator, and Member of the College Board. 1844 : Second Member of the Board of Revenue ; Member of the College Board ; and Tamil Translator to Government. 1847 : *Proceeded on furlough.* 1850 : *Returned to India.* 1851 : Collector, Magistrate, and Agent to the Governor, Vizagapatam. 1855 : *Resigned the service, 1st May, in India.* (*Annuitant on the Fund,* 1856.) *Died, 11th January* 1868, *in England.*

ROBINSON, THOMAS.—1796 : Writer. 1799 : Assistant under the Deputy Commercial Resident at Ganjam. 1802 : Head Assistant under the Secretary to the Board of Trade ; Assistant to the Collector in the Second Division of Masulipatam. 1805 : *At home for his health.* 1808 : *Returned to India.* 1811 : Deputy Commercial Resident at Ramnad ; Deputy Commercial Resident at Nagore. 1814 : Deputy Commercial Resident at Ramnad. *Died in* 1816, *in Madras.*

ROBSON, FRANCIS AUGUSTUS.—1795 : Writer. 1797 : Assistant under the Collector of Vizagapatam. 1799 : Assistant under the Collector of Ganjam. 1800 : Assistant under the Collector, Second Division of Vizagapatam. 1802 : Assistant to the Collector of Ganjam, &c. 1804 : Collector of Ganjam, &c. 1807 : Paymaster and Garrison Storekeeper in the Ceded Districts. 1812 : Commercial Resident at Ganjam. 1818 : *Out of employ.* 1821 : Deputy Collector of Madras ; Superintendent of Stationery. 1823 : Treasurer and Secretary to the Government Bank. 1828 : Judge and Criminal Judge of Guntoor. 1831 : *Out of employ.* 1832 : Acting as Judge and Criminal Judge of Rajahmundry. *Died, 3d September* 1833, *at Rajahmundry.*

ROEBUCK, BENJAMIN.—1776 : Writer. 1782 : Factor. 1790 : Senior Merchant. 1791 : Land Customer, and Deputy Military Storekeeper. 1792 : Civil and Military Paymaster-General ; A Member of the Committee for Investigating the King's Army Accounts, and Assay Master. 1801 : Assay Master. 1802 : Assay

Master, and Military Paymaster-General. 1809: Mint Master. *Died, 13th August 1809, at Vizagapatam.*

ROGERS, REGINALD.—1806: Writer. 1809: Assistant to the Chief Secretary in the Secret and Political Department. 1810: Assistant under the Collector of the Zillah of Chingleput. 1812: Deputy Commercial Resident at Tinnevelly. 1821: Register and Assistant to the Collector of Seringapatam. 1822: *At home.* 1825: *Returned to India;* Register of the Provincial Court, Southern Division. 1827: Assistant Judge and Joint Criminal Judge of Salem. (*Retired on the Annuity Fund from 1st January* 1828.) *Died, 23d December 1855, in England.*

ROHDE, JOHN.—1829: Writer. 1832: Second Assistant to Collector and Magistrate, Ganjam. 1835: Acting Register of the Zillah of Rajahmundry, and Acting Assistant Judge and Joint Criminal Judge, Chicacole. 1836: Officiating Assistant Judge, &c., at Chicacole. 1837: Register of the Zillah of Rajahmundry. 1838: Acting Assistant Judge and Joint Criminal Judge, Rajahmundry. 1839: Head Assistant to Collector and Magistrate, Masulipatam. 1840: Assistant Judge and Joint Criminal Judge, Rajahmundry. 1843: Sub-Judge at Rajahmundry. 1844: Acting Civil and Sessions Judge, Masulipatam, and at Rajahmundry. 1847: *Proceeded to Europe on furlough.* 1850: *In India, and without employ for 7 months;* Acting Civil and Sessions Judge, Trichinopoly. 1851: Acting Civil and Sessions Judge at Guntoor, Appointment subsequently confirmed. 1855: Inspector-General of Jails. 1866: *Resigned the service, 21st February.* (*Annuitant.*)

ROOKE, HARRY.—1808: Writer. *Died in 1813.*

ROSS, JOHN.—1765: Writer. 1771: Factor and Assistant at Cuddalore. 1774: Junior Merchant. *No trace after 1774.*

ROSS, JAMES.—1770: Writer. *No trace after 1771.*

ROSS, WILLIAM.—1770: Writer. 1776: Factor. 1778: Junior Merchant. 1782: Senior Merchant. *No trace after 1782.*

ROSS, ROBERT CHARLES.—1800: Writer. 1804: Register of the Southern Division of Arcot. 1805: Sub-Collector in the Southern Division of Arcot. 1808: Head Assistant to the Collector in Arcot. 1810: Collector of Cuddapah. *Died, 26th November 1816, at Masulipatam.*

ROUPELL, THOMAS BOONE.—1830: Writer. 1832: Assistant to the Principal Collector and Magistrate of Coimbatore. 1835: Head Assistant to the Principal Collector and Magistrate of Coimbatore. 1836: *At home on absentee allowance.* 1841: *Returned to India.* 1842: *Out of employ.* 1843: Sub-Secretary to the

Board of Revenue. 1850 : Civil and Sessions Judge, Coimbatore. 1857 : Civil and Sessions Judge, Cuddalore. 1858 : *Proceeded on furlough.* 1859 : *Resigned the service, 13th June, in India. (Annuitant on the Fund,* 1859.)

ROWLEY, JOHN.—1777 : Writer. 1782 : Factor. 1790 : Senior Merchant. 1791 : Muster-Master in Masulipatam, and Assistant at Maddepollam. 1795 : Resident at Maddepollam. 1800 : Postmaster-General. 1801 : Postmaster-General and Military Paymaster-General. 1803 : First Judge of the Court of Circuit and of Appeal for the Southern Division. *Died, 14th September* 1805, *at Pondicherry.*

RUSSEL, DANIEL.—1776 : Writer. 1782 : Factor. *No trace after* 1782.

RUSSELL, CLAUD.—1752 : Writer. 1771 : Member of Council of the Governor. 1777 : *Recalled by order of the General Court of Proprietors, 9th May.* 1780 : *At home.* 1782 : Chief of Vizagapatam. *No trace after* 1782.

RUSSELL, GEORGE EDWARD.—1802 : Writer. 1803 : Assistant to the Secretary in the Revenue and Judicial Department. 1804 : Assistant under the Register of the Zillah of Chingleput. 1805 : Register of the Zillah of Chingleput. 1812 : Collector and Magistrate of Masulipatam. 1815 : In Charge of the General Treasury at Masulipatam. 1822 : Second Member of the Board of Revenue. 1824 : At first Acting, then Senior Member of the Board of Revenue. 1832 : Officiating as Resident at the Court of H. H. the Rajah of Mysore ; Commissioner to Inquire into the State of Affairs at Ganjam and Vizagapatam. 1834 : Member of Council of the Governor, and President of the Revenue and Marine Boards. 1836 : Chief Judge of the Sudder and Foujdarry Adawlut. *(Retired on the Annuity Fund in* 1838.) *Died,* 20*th October* 1863, *in England.*

RUSSELL, JOHN WILLIAM.—1807 : Writer. 1809 : Assistant to the Collector of the Southern Division of Arcot. 1813 : Assistant to the Secretary to the Board of Revenue ; Secretary to the Native Fund, and to the Civil Fund Committee. 1817 : Deputy Secretary to the Board of Revenue. 1819 : *Leave to the Cape of Good Hope, and eventually to Europe.* 1822 : *Returned to India;* Private Secretary to the Governor. 1824 : Third Judge of Provincial Court, Centre Division. 1826 : Principal Collector and Magistrate of Cuddapah. 1828 : *At home on absentee allowance.* 1830 : *Returned to India, per "Lord Hungerford." Died,* 21*st August* 1831, *on board the "Claudine."*

RUTHERFORD, ROBERT.—1769: Writer. 1774: Factor and Assistant at Vizagapatam. 1778: Junior Merchant. 1780: Senior Merchant. *No trace after* 1782.

SADLEIR, ANTHONY.—1760: Writer. 1768: Factor. 1771: Senior Merchant. 1774: Resident at Madura. 1776: Resident at Ingeram. 1782: *Out of the service.*

SANDEMAN, ALEXANDER STUART.—1845: Writer. 1848: Assistant to Collector and Magistrate, Guntoor. 1850: *Proceeded on furlough.* 1852: *Returned to India;* Assistant to Collector and Magistrate, Malabar. 1855: Head Assistant to Collector and Magistrate, Malabar. *Died, 29th January* 1855, *at Cannanore.*

SAUNDERS, EDWARD.—1762: Writer. 1768: Factor. 1771: Junior Merchant and Paymaster, Chingleput and Wandi. 1774: Senior Merchant. 1776: Second in Council at Cuddalore. 1791: Member of the Board of Revenue. 1792: *At home.* 1795: *Out of the service.*

SAUNDERS, WILLIAM.—1800: Writer. 1805: Assistant to the Collector of Tinnevelly. 1806: Register of the Zillah of Ramnad. 1808: Acting Assistant to the Collector of Government Customs; Assistant to the Collector of Land Customs. 1810: Gentoo Translator to Government; Assistant to the Collector of Madras. *Died, 22d May* 1811, *on his passage to the Mauritius.*

SAUNDERS, GEORGE WILLIAM. — 1806: Writer. 1807: Assistant to the Secretary in the Revenue and Judicial Department; Register of the Zillah of Nellore. 1817: Assistant to the Accountant-General. 1818: Register to the Provincial Court, Southern Division. 1822: Sub-Collector and Assistant Magistrate of Canara. 1823: Collector and Magistrate of Trichinopoly. 1826: Judge and Criminal Judge of Nellore. 1828: Third Judge of the Provincial Court, Centre Division. *Died, 31st July* 1830, *at Cuddapah.*

SAVAGE, GEORGE.—1765: Writer. 1771: Factor. 1774: Junior Merchant. 1776: *At home.* 1780: *In India. No trace after* 1782.

SAVAGE, FRANCIS ARCHIBALD. — 1790: Writer; Assistant under the Secretary in the Revenue and Judicial Department, and Under Searcher of the Sea Gate. 1792: Assistant under the Collector of Muglatore. 1796: Assistant to the Collector in the Second Division of Masulipatam. 1800: Assistant to the Collector in the Third Division of Masulipatam; Paymaster and Garrison Storekeeper in the Ceded Districts. 1803: Deputy Postmaster at Bellary. 1807: Commercial Resident at Maddepollam;

Paymaster and Garrison Storekeeper at Masulipatam. 1812 : Commercial Resident at Ingeram. 1820 : Commercial Resident at the General Factory at Ingeram. 1830 : *Out of employ. Died, 23d June* 1831, *at Madras.*

SAVORY, James Scott.—1796 : Writer. 1798: Assistant under the Secretary to the Board of Revenue. 1799 : Second Assistant under the Collector of Kistnagherry. 1801 : Assistant under the Collector of Arcot, South of the River Palar. 1802 : Register to the Court of Circuit and Appeal, Centre Division. 1806 : Judge and Magistrate of Dharapooran in Coimbatore. 1817 : *At home.* 1821 : *Resigned the service, 24th October, in England.*

SCOTNEY, Bryan.—1777 : Appointed Military Storekeeper on the First Vacancy. *No trace after* 1782.

SCOTT, Andrew. — 1773: Writer. 1778 : Factor. 1782 : Junior Merchant. 1790 : Senior Merchant, and Manager of the Southern Division of the Masulipatam Havelly, and Assistant there. 1795 : Second in Council at Masulipatam, and Collector in Southern Division of Masulipatam Havelly. 1800 : Collector of the Third Division of Vizagapatam District. 1801 : Collector of Guntoor and of the Palnaud. 1803 : First Judge of the Court of Circuit and of Appeal for the Northern Division. 1808 : First Judge of the Court of Sudder and Foujdarry Adawlut. 1822 : *Without employ. Died, 21st January* 1825, *at Fort St George.*

SCOTT, John Corse.—1822 : Writer. 1825 : Assistant to the Principal Collector and Magistrate of Malabar. 1826 : Register of the Zillah of Canara. 1828 : *At home on absentee allowance.* 1832 : *Returned to India ;* Acting Assistant, afterwards Assistant Judge and Joint Criminal Judge of Madura. 1834 : Assistant Judge and Joint Criminal Judge of Canara. 1835 : Acting Zillah Judge of Madura ; Assistant Judge and Joint Criminal Judge of Chicacole. 1837 : Acting Judge and Criminal Judge of Malabar. 1839 : *At home for his health.* 1844 : *Resigned the service, 3d January, in England. (Annuitant on the Fund,* 1849.) *Died, 17th January* 1870, *in England.*

SCOTT, Septimus.—1829 : Writer. 1830 : Assistant under the Principal Collector of Coimbatore. 1832 : Acting Assistant Judge and Joint Criminal Judge of Salem ; Head Assistant to the Principal Collector and Magistrate of Tanjore. 1836 : Acting, afterwards Sub-Collector and Joint Magistrate of Tanjore. 1840 : *Proceeded on furlough.* 1842 : *Returned to India.* 1844 : Agent to the Governor of Fort St. George at Kurnool and Bunganapilly. 1848 : Civil and Sessions Judge, Combaconum. 1855 : *Proceeded* *on furlough.* 1857 : *Resigned the service,* 12*th August, in Eng-land.* (*Annuitant on the Fund,* 1859.)

SEDGLEY, WILLIAM. — 1770 : Writer. 1776 : Factor, and Assistant at Masulipatam. 1778 : Junior Merchant. 1782 : Senior Merchant. *Died in* 1782.

SEWELL, HENRY.—1807 : Writer; Assistant to the Collector of Rajahmundry. 1816 : Assistant to the Magistrate of Rajah-mundry. *Died,* 6*th June* 1823, *at Rajahmundry.*

SEWELL, ROBERT BROWNRIGG.—1831 : Writer. 1834 : Assis-tant to the Collector of Chingleput. 1836 : Acting Secretary to the Board of College and for Public Instruction ; Acting Deputy Secretary in the Chief Secretary's Department. 1837 : Deputy Secretary in the Chief Secretary's Department ; Commissioner for Drawing Government Lotteries ; Acting Secretary to the College Board. 1838 : *At home on absentee allowance. Died,* 4*th June* 1840, *at Carlsbad, Germany.*

SHAKESPEAR, WILLIAM OLIVER. — 1800 : Writer. 1803 : Assistant to the Commercial Resident at Vizagapatam and Gan-jam. 1806 : Assistant to the Register of the Zillah of Masulipatam. 1807 : Register of the Zillah of Trichinopoly. 1810 : Assistant Judge of Madura. 1815 : Judge and Magistrate of Madura. 1826 : Third Judge of the Provincial Court, Western Division. 1830 : Second Judge of the Provincial Court, Western Division. 1832: First Judge of the Provincial Court, Western Division. *Died,* 10*th August* 1838, *at Cannanore.*

SHAW, THOMAS.—1778 : Writer. *Dead in* 1780.

SHAW, JOSEPH.—1781 : Writer. 1783 : Assistant to the Sec-retary to the Select Committee. 1784 : Assistant to the Secretary in the Civil Department. 1785 : Register of the Choultry Court and Deputy Land Customer. 1786 : Assistant in the Military Department ; Assistant to the Sea Customer. 1787 : Assistant in the Secret Department. 1788 : One of the Contractors for Repairs. 1789 : Examiner in the Mayor's Court. 1792 : *At home. No trace after* 1795.

SHAW, HECTOR.—1801 : Writer. 1803 : Assistant to the Principal Collector in the Ceded Districts. 1807 : Subordinate Collector in the Ceded Districts. *Died,* 11*th February* 1808, *at Bellary.*

SHEFFIELD, WILLIAM.—1800 : Writer on the Bencoolen Establishment. 1804 : *Transferred to the Madras Presidency.* 1805 : Assistant to the Principal Collector of the Southern Division of Arcot. 1806 : Register of the Zillah of Combaconum. 1814 : Assistant Judge of the Zillah of South Malabar. 1817 : Head Assistant to the Collector and Magistrate of Malabar. 1820 : Judge and Criminal Judge of Malabar. 1826 : Principal Collector and Magistrate of Malabar. 1831 : *At home on absentee allowance.* (*Retired on the Annuity Fund from 1st May 1832.*) *Died, 24th February 1859, in England.*

SHERIDAN, RICHARD BRINSLEY. — 1825 : Writer. 1828 : Head Assistant to the Secretary to the Board of Revenue. 1830 : Superintendent of Government Lotteries ; Temporary Additional Sub-Collector and Joint Magistrate of Salem. 1831 : Assistant to the Commissioners for the Government of Mysore. 1832 : *At home on absentee allowance.* 1837 : *Out of the service.*

SHERSON, ROBERT.—1793 : Writer. 1795 : Assistant under the Secretary in the Public, Commercial, and Revenue Department. 1796 : Assistant to the Sea Customer. 1798 : Deputy Sea Customer. 1800 : *At home.* 1801 : *Returned to India ;* Deputy Collector of Government Customs. 1802 : Reporter of External Commerce of Madras Territories. 1807 : Joint Assay Master. 1808 : *Under temporary suspension from his different employments ; At home.* 1816 : *Returned to India ;* Third Member of the Board of Trade. 1818 : Collector and Magistrate of Chittoor. 1819 : Postmaster-General. 1821 : Treasurer and Secretary to the Government Bank. 1824 : *At home.* 1827 : *Out of the service.*

SHUBRICK, CHARLES JOHN.—1831 : Writer. 1834 : Assistant to Principal Collector and Magistrate, Bellary. 1838 : *Proceeded to Europe on absentee allowance.* 1841 : Acting Register to the Zillah Court of Canara. 1842 : Acting Additional Sub-Collector and Joint Magistrate ; and Acting Head Assistant to Sub-Collector and Joint Magistrate, Canara. 1843 : Register to the Zillah Court of Salem ; Acting Sub-Collector and Joint Magistrate, North Arcot ; and Extra Assistant to Principal Collector and Magistrate, Salem. 1844 : Acting Principal Assistant to Collector and Magistrate, and Agent to the Governor of Madras, in Vizagapatam. 1845 : Principal Assistant to Collector and Magistrate, and Agent to the Governor of Madras, in Ganjam. 1847 : Acting Collector and Magistrate, and Agent to the Governor in Ganjam. 1849 : *Proceeded to Europe on furlough.* 1853 : Acting Civil and Sessions Judge, Chingleput. 1855 : At first Acting, afterwards Collector and Magistrate, Chingleput. 1859 : *On medical leave to Europe for 15 months.* 1860 : Civil and Sessions Judge of Chingleput ; *On* *medical certificate to Europe for* 21 *months.* 1861 : Collector of Sea Customs, Madras. 1862 : Member and Commissioner for the Presidency Town, for Income Tax Acts for 1862–63. 1863 : *Resigned the service,* 27*th July.* (*Annuitant.*)

SILVER, JAMES.—1832 : Writer. 1834 : Assistant to Principal Collector and Magistrate, Madura. 1836 : Assistant to Collector and Magistrate, Tinnevelly. 1838 : Officiating Assistant Judge and Joint Criminal Judge, Madura ; Acting Head Assistant to Principal Collector and Magistrate, Malabar. 1839 : Head Assistant to Principal Collector and Magistrate, Malabar ; Acting Assistant Judge and Joint Criminal Judge, Cochin. 1843 : Special Assistant to Collector, Tinnevelly. 1844 : *Proceeded to Europe on furlough.* 1848 : *Without employ for* 10 *months, after which* Additional Sub-Collector and Joint Magistrate, Canara. 1849 : Acting Sub-Collector and Joint Magistrate, Canara. 1851 : Acting Civil and Sessions Judge, Honore. 1854 : At first Sub-Judge, then Acting Civil and Sessions Judge, Combaconum. 1855 : Acting Collector and Magistrate, Tinnevelly. 1856 : Collector and Magistrate, Tinnevelly. 1858 : *On medical certificate to Europe for* 21 *months.* 1859 : Resumed Charge of the Collectorate of Tinnevelly. 1865 : *Permitted to retire from the service,* 31*st January.* (*Annuitant.*) *Died,* 8*th July* 1870, *in England.*

SIMPSON, JAMES.—1778 : Writer. *No trace after* 1782.

SINCLAIR, ALEXANDER.—1812 : Writer. 1816 : Assistant under the Chief Secretary in the Secret, Political, and Foreign Department. 1817 : Register of the Zillah of Cuddapah. 1820 : *At home.* 1824 : *Returned to India ;* Sub-Collector and Assistant Magistrate of Tanjore. 1827 : *At home on absentee allowance.* 1832 : *Out of the service.*

SKARDON, JOHN HUMPHREY.—1771 : Writer. 1776 : Factor, and Assistant at Cuddalore. 1780 : Junior Merchant. 1782 : Senior Merchant. 1791 : Secretary to the Military Board, and Inspector of the Jaghire Accounts. 1792 : At Permacoil. 1795 : Paymaster at Pondicherry. 1800 : Paymaster and Garrison Store-keeper at Nellore and its Dependencies. 1803 : *At home.* 1806 : *Out of the service.*

SKELTON, GEORGE HOUGHAM.—1829 : Writer. 1832 : Acting Register of the Zillah of Cuddapah ; *At home on absentee allowance.* 1836 : *Returned to India.* 1837 : Register of the Zillah of Nellore. 1838 : Acting Assistant Judge and Joint Criminal Judge of Cochin. 1841 : Sub-Collector and Joint Magistrate, Cuddapah.   1842 : *Out of employ.*   1843 : *Proceeded on furlough.*   1845 : *Resigned the service, 9th July, in England.*

SKELTON, CHARLES PITMAN.—1830 : Writer.   1833 : Register to the Zillah of Cuddapah.   *Died, 21st February 1836, at Sydney.*

SKINNER, SAMUEL.—1791 : Writer.   1792 : Assistant under the Secretary in the Public, Commercial, and Revenue Department.   1794 : Assistant under the Superintendent of the Noozeed Zemindary.   1796 : Assistant Collector of the Third Division of Masulipatam.   1799 : Assistant Collector of the Second Division of Masulipatam.   1803 : Judge of the Zillah of Rajahmundry. 1806 : Judge of the Zillah of Ganjam.   1808 : Acting Judge of the Centre Circuit Court.   1809 : Third Judge of the Centre Circuit Court.   1812 : Second Judge of the Centre Circuit Court. 1820 : *At home.*   1825 : *Out of the service.*

SLINGSBY, ANDREW.—1793 : Writer.   1795 : Assistant under the Secretary to the Board of Trade.   1796 : Assistant under the Secretary in the Public, Commercial, and Revenue Department. 1797 : Assistant under the Commercial Resident at Masulipatam. 1804 : Assistant to the Commercial Resident at Cuddalore.   1806 : *Out of employ.   Died, 6th October 1809, at Vepery.*

SMALLEY, EDWARD.—1806 : Writer.   1808 : Assistant under the Collector of Tanjore.   1812 : Head Assistant to the Collector of Coimbatore ; Assistant to the Secretary in the Political, Revenue, and Judicial Department.   1815 : Secretary to the Board of Trade ; Assistant Judge of Combaconum.   1817 : Acting Collector and Magistrate of Rajahmundry.   1818 : Acting Collector of Bellary. 1820 : Collector and Magistrate of Chingleput.   1823 : Collector and Magistrate of Nellore.   1826 : Principal Collector and Magistrate of Nellore.   1830 : Collector of Madras.   1832 : Acting Senior Member of the Board of Revenue ; Temporary Member, afterwards Member, of the Board of Revenue.   1833 : *At home on absentee allowance.   (Annuitant on the Fund, 1836.)   Died, 4th April 1873, in England.*

SMITH, JOHN LEWIN.—1752 : Writer.   1768 : Senior Merchant, and First in Council at Masulipatam ; also Member of the Council of the Governor.   1771 : *Out of the service.*

SMITH, JOHN.—1752 : Writer.   1768 : Senior Merchant, and First in Council at Vizagapatam ; also Member of Council of the Governor.   1776 : *Out of the service.*

SMITH, CHARLES.—1753 : Writer.   1768 : Senior Merchant.

1774: Member of the Council of the Governor.   1782: *Out of the service.*

SMITH, CECIL.—1789: Writer.   1790: Assistant under the Accountant and Assistant to the Import Warehouse-keeper.   1793: Examiner and Head Assistant under the Accountant.   1794: Deputy Accountant-General.   1796: Superintendent of the Company's Lands.   1798: Deputy Accountant-General.   1799: Secretary to the Committee of Reform, and Secretary and Accountant to the Commissioners of the Sinking Fund.   1800: Deputy Accountant-General and Civil Auditor.   1801: Accountant-General to the Supreme Court of Judicature.   1802: Accountant-General and Civil Auditor.   1809: Third Judge of the Northern Provincial Court; *At home.*   1812: *Returned to India.*   1813: Senior Member of the Board of Trade.   *Died, 8th December 1813, at the Cape of Good Hope.*

SMITH, JOHN STUART. — 1789: Writer.   1790: Assistant under the Secretary in the Public and Revenue Department.   1791: Assistant under the Collector in the Northern Division of Arcot.   1793: Assistant under the Secretary in the Military, Political, and Secret Department.   1796: Assistant under the Military Paymaster-General and Choultry Register.   1797: Register of Native Alienations.   1799: Deputy Commercial Resident at Cuddalore.   1804: Paymaster and Garrison Storekeeper at Vellore and its Dependencies.   *Died, 10th July 1806, at Vellore.*

SMITH, HENRY.—1793: Writer.   1794: Assistant under the Secretary to the Board of Revenue.   *No trace after 1796.*

SMITH, JOHN.—1795: Writer on the Bencoolen Establishment.   1803: *Transferred to the Madras Presidency;* Assistant to the Chief Secretary to Government.   1804: Secretary to the Committee of Audit for Captured Dutch Settlements.   1806: Paymaster and Garrison Storekeeper at Seringapatam.   1813: Collector of Vizagapatam.   *Died, 20th June 1824, at Vizagapatam.*

SMITH, HOTHAM PITCHES.—1797: Writer.   1798: Assistant under the Military, Political, and Secret Department.   1799: Deputy Secretary to the Board of Trade.   1800: *Resigned the service, 7th February.*

SMITH, FRANCIS CURWEN.—1805: Writer.   1807: *Removed to the Bengal Establishment, 7th April.*

SMITH, CHARLES M.—1805: Writer.   1809: Assistant under the Judge and Collector of Seringapatam.   1812: *At home.*   1815: *Out of the service.*

SMITH, Samuel.— 1812 : Writer. 1814 : Head Assistant to the Collector of Salem. 1816 : Assistant Magistrate of Salem. 1821 : Head Assistant to the Principal Collector and Magistrate of Coimbatore. 1822 : *At home.* 1827 : *Returned to India ;* Sub-Collector and Assistant Magistrate of Ganjam. 1830 : Judge and Criminal Judge of Malabar. *Died, 1st June* 1831, *at Calicut.*

SMITH, George Anthony.—1820 : Writer. 1822 : Assistant to the Collector and Magistrate of Rajahmundry. 1824 : Head Assistant to the Collector and Magistrate of Masulipatam. 1826 : Head Assistant to the Collector and Magistrate of Rajahmundry. 1832 : Acting Collector and Magistrate of Vizagapatam. 1833 : *At home on absentee allowance.* 1836 : *Returned to India, per* " *Royal William ;*" Acting Judge and Criminal Judge of Rajahmundry. 1837 : Acting Collector and Register of Rajahmundry. 1838 : Collector and Magistrate of Rajahmundry. 1845 : *Proceeded on furlough.* 1846 : *Returned to India.* 1847 : Collector and Magistrate, Nellore. *Died, 1st June* 1849, *at Nellore.*

SMITH, Edmund.—1827 : Writer. 1829 : Assistant to the Chief Secretary to Government, and Deputy Persian Translator. 1831 : Assistant to the Commissioners for the Government of Mysore. 1832 : Junior Deputy Secretary to the Board of Revenue, and Secretary to the Board for the College, and for Public Instruction ; Sub-Collector and Joint Magistrate of Malabar ; Acting Private Secretary to the Governor. 1838 : Acting Deputy Register to the Sudder and Foujdarry Adawlut. 1839 : *At home on absentee allowance.* 1847 : *Not traced after being on furlough.* *Died,* 16th *August* 1873, *in England.*

SMOLLET, Patrick Boyle.—1825 : Writer. 1828 : Head Assistant to the Collector of Guntoor. 1830 : Head Assistant to the Secretary to the Board of Revenue. 1832 : Assistant to the Commissioners for the Government of Mysore. 1833 : Acting Assistant to the Chief Secretary in the Public and Secret Department. 1834 : Assistant Judge and Joint Criminal Judge of Madura ; Head Assistant to the Principal Collector and Magistrate of Nellore. 1835 : Acting Junior Deputy Secretary to the Board of Revenue. 1836 : Commissioner for Drawing Lotteries. 1837 : Assistant to the Judge and Criminal Judge of Chicacole ; Acting Senior Deputy Secretary to the Board of Revenue ; Officiating Secretary to the Board of Revenue. 1838 : Assistant Judge and Joint Criminal Judge of Rajahmundry ; Sub-Secretary to the Board of Revenue, and Acting Secretary. 1839 : Secretary to the Board of

Revenue. 1843: Register to the Courts of Sudder and Sudder Foujdarry Adawlut. 1845: Principal Assistant to Collector, Magistrate, and Agent to Governor, Vizagapatam. 1847: Collector, Magistrate, and Agent to Governor, Vizagapatam. 1851: *Proceeded on furlough.* 1854: *Returned to India.* 1855: Collector and Magistrate, Chingleput. 1856: Collector, Magistrate, and Agent to Governor, Vizagapatam. 1857: *Proceeded on furlough ; Resigned the service, from 28th December. (Annuitant on the Fund,* 1859.)

SMYTH, JAMES.—1801: Writer. *No trace after this date.*

SNEYD, GEORGE.—1789: Writer. 1790: Assistant under the Secretary in the Public and Revenue Department, and Under Searcher at the Sea Gate. 1791: *At home for his health. No trace after* 1791.

SNODGRASS, THOMAS.—1777: Writer. 1782: Factor. 1790: Senior Merchant and Assistant at Ganjam. 1795: Resident at Ganjam. 1800: Collector at Ganjam. 1801: *Without employ.* 1804: *Out of the service.*

SNOW, JOHN.—1776: Writer. 1782: Factor. 1790: Senior Merchant. 1791: Third in Council at Vizagapatam. 1795: Second in Council at Vizagapatam, and Collector of the Vizianagram Zemindary. 1800: *At home.* 1805: *Out of the service.*

SPALDING, JOHN.—1781: Writer. 1783: Assistant to the Secretary to the Select Committee ; Assistant to the Auditor of Accounts. 1785: Assistant to the Secretary in the Revenue Department. 1787: Agent for Half-mounting and Clothing the Revenue Battalions. 1789: *At home for his health. No trace after* 1789.

SPARKES, GEORGE.—1828: Writer. 1829: Register of the Zillah of Canara. 1832: Head Assistant to the Principal Collector and Magistrate of Malabar ; Acting Sub-Collector and Joint Magistrate of Malabar. 1834: Acting Assistant Judge of Malabar. 1836: Additional Sub-Collector and Joint Magistrate of Canara. 1837: *At home on absentee allowance.* 1840: *Resigned the service, 29th January.*

SPOTTISWOODE, HUGH.—1801: Writer. 1804: Acting Register of the Zillah of Vizagapatam. 1806: Register of the Zillah of Ganjam. 1809: Collector of Ganjam. 1819: Collector and Magistrate of the Northern Division of Arcot ; Collector of Madras ; Superintendent of Stationery. *Died, 4th April* 1820, *on his passage to the Cape.*

STATHAM, SAMUEL. — 1771: Writer. 1776: Factor, and

Assistant at Masulipatam.   1780: Junior Merchant.   1782:
Senior Merchant.   1791: Supernumerary Councillor at Masulipatam, and Resident at Nezampatam.   *Dead in* 1793.

STEPHENS, PHILIP.—1780: Writer.   *No trace after* 1782.

STEVENSON, JAMES ARTHUR ROBERT.—1819: Writer.   1823:
Employed under the Commissioners in the Deccan.   1831: *At
home on absentee allowance.*   1833: *Returned to India, per " Eliza."*
1834: Acting Mint Master.   1835: Collector and Magistrate of
Ganjam.   1837: Acting Commissioner in Goomsur and Sooradah,
under the Provisions of the Act of No. 23 of 1836.   *Died, 20th
June* 1837, *at Chatterpore.*

STODART, ALEXANDER. — 1789: Writer.   1790: Assistant
under the Secretary in the Public and Revenue Department.   1792:
Assistant under the Commercial Resident at Vizagapatam.   1796:
Assistant under the Collector of Dindigul.   1797: *Out of employ.*
1798: Assistant to the Collector in the Third Division of Vizagapatam.   1800: Subordinate Collector in the Ceded Districts.   1801:
Out of employ.   1803: *At home for his health.*   1807: *Returned
to India ;* Deputy Commercial Resident at Ganjam.   *Died, 16th
May* 1807, *at Madras.*

STOKES, JOHN. — 1807: Writer.   1809: Assistant to the
Register of the Sudder and Foujdarry Adawlut.   1811: Assistant
to the Collector of Trichinopoly.   1812: Fixed Examiner to the
Secretary to the Board of Revenue, and Assistant to the Superin-
tendent of Stamps ; Assistant to the Secretary in the Military and
Political Department.   1813: French Translator to Government.
1815: Deputy Collector of Sea Customs in Malabar and Canara.
1823: Sub-Collector of Canara.   1824: Secretary in the Revenue
and Judicial Department.   1827: Third Member of the Board of
Revenue.   1832: Employed as Commissioner in Canara.   1833:
*At home on absentee allowance. (Annuitant on the Fund from 1st
May* 1835.)   *Died, 17th June* 1876, *in England.*

STOKES, HUDLESTON.—1826: Writer.   1828: Assistant to the
Collector of Tinnevelly.   1830: Head Assistant to the Collector of
Tinnevelly.   1831: Head Assistant to the Principal Collector and
Magistrate of Canara.   1832: Under the Orders of the Commissioners for the Government of Mysore.   1834: Superintendent
of a Division in Mysore.   1838: *At home on absentee allowance.*
1841: *Returned to India.*   1842: Assistant to Commissioner,
Kurnool.   1843: Collector and Magistrate, Guntoor.   1854: Collector and Magistrate, Guntoor, and Member of the College Board.

1855 : Collector and Magistrate, Guntoor. 1856 : Collector of Land Customs, Madras. 1856 : *Resigned the service, 15th February, in India.* (*Annuitant on the Fund,* 1857.)

STONE, JOHN MAXWELL. — 1755 : Writer. 1768 : Senior Merchant. 1774 : Member of Council of the Governor. 1777 : *Recalled by order of the General Court of Proprietors,* 9th May 1782 : Chief at Ganjam. *No trace after* 1782.

STONE, JOHN TROTTER.—1779 : Writer. *No trace after* 1782.

STONEHOUSE, TIMOTHY VANSITTART.—1816 : Writer. 1819 : Assistant to the Secretary to the Board of Revenue. 1820 : Assistant to the Collector and Magistrate of Nellore. 1826 : Head Assistant to the Principal Collector and Magistrate of Nellore. 1828 : *At home on absentee allowance.* 1830 : *Returned to India, per " Duke of Bedford."* 1831 : Acting Collector and Magistrate of Masulipatam. 1832 : Collector and Magistrate of Masulipatam, and in Charge of Treasury there ; Acting Collector and Magistrate of Tinnevelly ; Acting Secretary in the Revenue and Judicial Department ; Member of the Mint Committee ; Acting Mint Master. 1833 : Mint Master and Malyalum Translator to Government. 1835 : Principal Collector and Magistrate of Nellore. 1845 : Accountant - General and Member of the Mint Committee. 1847 : Accountant-General and Member of the College Board. 1850 : Accountant-General and Member of the Mint Committee. 1851 : Accountant-General and Provisional Member of Council. 1855 : Accountant-General and Member of the Mint Committee. 1856 : *Resigned the service, 20th December, in India.* (*Annuitant on the Fund,* 1858.) *Died, 29th January* 1866, *in England.*

STORY, EDMUND. — 1829 : Writer. 1833 : Assistant under Principal Collector, Nellore. 1834 : Second Assistant to Principal Collector and Magistrate, Cuddapah. 1835 : Acting Register to the Zillah Courts of Cuddapah, and of Bellary. 1836 : Acting Register to the Zillah Court, Chicacole. 1838 : Register to the Zillah Court, Chicacole. 1839 : Acting Assistant Judge and Joint Criminal Judge, Chicacole ; Register to the Zillah Court, Vizagapatam. 1840 : Acting Register to the Northern Provincial Court ; Assistant Judge and Joint Criminal Judge, Guntoor. 1843 : Sub-Judge, Cuddapah ; Acting Sub-Judge at Salem. 1845 : *Proceeded to Europe on furlough.* 1847 : Acting Civil and Sessions Judge, Trichinopoly. 1849 : Acting Civil and Sessions Judge, Salem ; Sub-Judge at Bellary. 1850 : Acting Civil and Sessions Judge, Cuddapah. 1851 : Acting Civil and Sessions Judge,

Bellary.   1856 : Civil and Sessions Judge, at Guntoor and at Tinnevelly.   1859 : *On medical certificate to England.*   1860 : Civil and Sessions Judge, Nellore.   1865 : *Permitted to retire from the service, 1st February.*   (*Annuitant.*)   *Died, 17th April 1874, in England.*

STRACEY, EDWARD.—1758 : Writer.   1768 : Junior Merchant.   1771 : Senior Merchant.   1774 : Member of Council of the Governor.   1776 : *Resigned the service.*

STRACHAN, FRANCIS. — 1796 : Writer on the Bencoolen Establishment.   1804 : *Transferred to the Madras Presidency ;* Assistant to the Commercial Resident at Salem.   1806 : Register of the Zillah of Nellore ; Register of the Zillah of Salem.   *Died, on his passage to the Cape of Good Hope, 20th April 1808, on the "Brunswick" transport.*

STRACHEY, GEORGE.—1796 : Writer.   1798 : Assistant in the Military, Secret, and Political Department.   1800 : Secretary and Accountant to the Commissioners of the Sinking Fund.   1803 : Secretary in the Military Department.   1805 : Secretary to the Finance Committee.   1807 : Joint Assay Master.   1808 : Private Secretary to the Governor.   1809 : Judge and Magistrate of the Zillah of Cuddapah.   1810 : *Out of employ.*   1811 : Secretary in the Military Department.   1812 : Junior Secretary to Government.   1813 : Chief Secretary to Government.   1821 : *At home.*   1824 : *Out of the service.*

STRANGE, JAMES.—1773 : Writer.   1778 : Factor.   1782 : Junior Merchant.   1790 : Senior Merchant.   1791 : Paymaster at Tanjore.   1795 : *At home.*   1800 : *Out of the service.*

STRANGE, THOMAS LUMSDEN.—1825 : Writer.   1829 : Register of the Zillah of Malabar.   1831 : Assistant Judge and Joint Criminal Judge, Malabar.   1839 : *Proceeded to Europe on furlough.*   1842 : Acting Judge and Criminal Judge, Malabar.   1843 : Sub-Judge at Calicut, and Acting Civil and Sessions Judge, Tellicherry.   1845 : Civil and Sessions Judge, Tellicherry ; Civil and Sessions Judge, Bellary.   1851 : Acting Judge, subsequently Puisne Judge of the Court of Sudder and Foujdarry Adawlut.   1852 : Special Commissioner for Inquiring into the Moplah Disturbances in Malabar.   1856 : *Proceeded on medical certificate to Europe.*   1859 : Commissioner for Inquiring into the System of Judicature in the Presidency.   1862 : Judge of the High Court of Judicature.   1863 : *Resigned the service, 2d May.*   (*Annuitant.*)   *Died, 3d September 1884, in England.*

STRATTON, GEORGE. — 1751 : Writer. 1768 : Member of Council of the Governor. 1777 : *Recalled by order of the General Court of Proprietors, 9th May.* 1780 : *Suspended from the service.*

STRATTON, GEORGE.—1793 : Writer. 1796 : Assistant to the Beetle and Tobacco Manager, and to the Secretary to the Board of Revenue. 1797 : Assistant to the Superintendent of the Court of Cutcherry. 1799 : Head Assistant under the Collector of Salem. 1800 : *Out of employ ;* Collector of the Western Polygar Peishcush. 1801 : Collector of Arcot, North of the River Palar. 1803 : Judge of the Zillah of Carangooly. 1806 : Judge of the Zillah of Tinnevelly. 1810 : *At home.* 1815 : *Returned to India ;* Second Commissioner for the Revision of the Judicial System ; Third Judge of the Sudder Adawlut Court. 1819 : Third Member of the Board of Revenue. 1820 : Member of Council, and President of the Sudder Court and Board of Trade. 1824 : *At home.* 1829 : *Out of the service.*

STROMBOM, PETER HENRY.—1816 : Writer. 1818 : Secretary to the Commissioner for Conducting the Restitution of the Dutch Settlements ; French Translator to Government. 1820 : Register of the Zillah of Vizagapatam. 1821 : Assistant to the Collector and Magistrate of Cuddapah. 1830 : Register of the Zillah of Rajahmundry. 1832 : Judge and Criminal Judge of Cuddapah. 1837 : Judge and Criminal Judge of Chicacole. 1838 : Acting, afterwards Judge and Criminal Judge of Cuddapah. 1839 : Judge and Criminal Judge of Chittoor. 1840 : Third Judge of the Provincial Court of Appeal and Circuit, Northern Division. *Died, 28th August* 1841, *at Guntoor.*

STUART, CHARLES EDWARD.—1804 : Writer. 1807 : Assistant under the Principal Collector in the Ceded Districts ; Assistant to the Principal Collector in the Ceded Districts, Malabar. *Died on his passage home, 3d April* 1809, *on board the " Huddart."*

SULIVAN, JOHN.—1765 : Writer. 1771 : Factor. 1774 : Junior Merchant, and Fifth in Council at Masulipatam. 1776 : Senior Merchant, and Fourth in Council at Masulipatam. 1778 : *At home.* 1782 : *In India. No trace after* 1782.

SULIVAN, RICHARD JOSEPH.—1770 : Writer. 1776 : Factor ; *At home.* 1778 : Junior Merchant (*still at home*). 1782 : Senior Merchant. *No trace after* 1782.

SULIVAN, STEPHEN.—1778 : Persian Translator and Secretary. 1780 : Resident at Tanjore. *No trace after* 1780.

SULIVAN, JOHN STEWART.—1795 : Writer. 1798 : Assistant

under the Secretary in the Public, Commercial, and Revenue Department. 1799 : Assistant under the Commercial Resident at Tinnevelly. 1800 : Deputy Commercial Resident at Tinnevelly. 1801 : Deputy Commercial Resident at Ramnad. 1809 : Commercial Resident at Ramnad. 1814 : Commercial Resident at Tinnevelly. 1821 : *Out of employ.* 1823 : Commercial Resident at Tinnevelly. 1826 : *At home. (Annuitant on the Fund from 9th May 1826.) Died, 14th December 1837, in England.*

SULLIVAN, John.—1804 : Writer. 1805 : Assistant under the Secretary in the Revenue and Judicial Department. 1806 : Register of the Zillah of Chittaput. 1807 : Assistant to the Chief Secretary in the Secret, Political, and Foreign Department. 1809 : Acting Assistant to the Resident at Mysore. 1811 : *At home.* 1814 : *Returned to India;* Collector of Chingleput. 1815 : Collector of Coimbatore. 1821 : Principal Collector and Magistrate of Coimbatore. 1830 : *At home on absentee allowance.* 1835 : *Returned to India;* Senior Member of the Board of Revenue. 1836 : President of the Revenue, Marine, and College Boards. 1839 : Member of Council of the Governor, and President of the Revenue, Marine, and College Boards. *(Annuitant on the Fund, 1841.) Died, 16th January 1858, in England.*

SULLIVAN, Edward R.—1806 : Writer. 1809 : Assistant under the Collector of Malabar. 1811 : Acting Assistant to the Resident at Mysore. 1813 : Head Assistant to the Resident at Mysore. 1815 : Postmaster-General and Superintendent of Government Lotteries. 1819 : *At home.* 1822 : *Returned to India;* Assistant to the Chief Secretary to Government ; Secretary and Treasurer of the Government Bank. 1824 : *Out of the service.*

SULLIVAN, Richard James.—1838 : Writer. 1840 : Assistant to Collector and Magistrate, Trichinopoly. 1843 : *Proceeded on furlough.* 1845 : *Returned to India;* Assistant to Collector and Magistrate, Trichinopoly. 1846 : Head Assistant to Collector and Magistrate, Trichinopoly. 1847 : Head Assistant to Collector and Magistrate, Coimbatore. 1850 : Head Assistant to Collector and Magistrate, Northern Division of Arcot. 1851 : Head Assistant to Collector and Magistrate, Coimbatore. 1852 : *Proceeded on furlough.* 1854 : *Returned to India.* 1855 : *Out of employ.* 1856 : Subordinate Judge, Mangalore. *Died, 5th February 1858, at Ryde, Isle of Wight.*

SUTHERLAN, Alexander Milford.—1837 : Writer. 1838 : Assistant to the Principal Collector and Magistrate of Nellore.

1839: Acting Head Assistant to the Collector and Magistrate of Rajahmundry. 1840: Assistant to Collector, Magistrate, and Agent to Governor, Ganjam. 1844: *Proceeded on furlough.* 1847: *Returned to India.* 1848: Head Assistant to Collector and Magistrate, Nellore. 1850: Head Assistant to Accountant-General. 1851: *Proceeded on furlough.* 1853: *Returned to India.* 1854: *Proceeded on furlough.* 1857: *Resigned the service,* 26th *August, in England.*

SWINTON, George Melville.—1833: Writer. 1835: Assistant to the Principal Collector and Magistrate of Cuddapah. 1837: Acting, afterwards Assistant to the Collector and Magistrate of Chingleput. 1838: Acting, afterwards Head Assistant to the Collector and Magistrate of Chingleput. 1841: Second Assistant to Accountant-General. 1842: Head Assistant to Accountant-General. 1848: *Proceeded on furlough.* 1850: *Returned to India;* Assistant Judge, Mangalore. 1852: Assistant Judge, Combaconum. *Died, 24th October* 1853, *at the Cape of Good Hope.*

TANNER, Theodore Ivey.—1769: Writer. 1774: Factor. 1778: Junior Merchant. 1780: Senior Merchant. *No trace after* 1782.

TASWELL, William.—1794: Writer. 1796: Assistant under the Secretary in the Military, Political, and Secret Department. 1798: Assistant to the Import Warehouse-keeper. 1799: Deputy Sea Customer. 1800: *Resigned the service, 12th April.*

TAYLOR, James.—1764: Writer. 1771: Factor. 1774: Junior Merchant. 1776: Senior Merchant. 1790: *Suspended from the service.* 1792: *At home.* 1800: *Out of the service.*

TAYLOR, Harry.—1777: Writer. 1782: Factor. 1790: Senior Merchant. 1791: Senior Merchant and Paymaster at Ellore. 1800: Collector of the Cuddalore and Pondicherry Revenues. 1801: *At home.* 1805: *In India, without employ. Died, on his way to England, 5th December* 1806, *on board the ship "Glory."*

TAYLOR, James.—1794: Writer. 1796: Assistant under the Secretary in the Military, Political, and Secret Department. 1797: Assistant under the Accountant-General. 1798: Deputy Secretary, afterwards Secretary to the Board of Trade. 1800: In Charge of the Import Warehouse. 1802: Superintendent of the Quality of Investment. 1814: Third Member of the Board of Trade. 1816: Second Member of the Board of Trade. 1825: Acting Third Judge of the Provincial Court, Northern Division.

1826: First Judge of the Provincial Court, Southern Division. 1828: Member of Council of the Governor, and President of the Revenue and Marine Boards. 1831: *At home on absentee allowance. (Annuitant on the Fund from 1st May 1833.) Died, 9th September* 1852.

TAYLOR, HENRY.—1796: Writer. 1799: Assistant under the Secretary to the Board of Trade. 1800: Assistant under the Commercial Resident at Vizagapatam. 1805: Deputy Commercial Resident at Vizagapatam and Ganjam. 1810: Commercial Resident at Vizagapatam. 1819: Commercial Resident at Maddepollam and Masulipatam. 1821: *Out of employ.* 1823: *At home.* 1827: *Returned to India;* Commercial Resident at Vizagapatam. 1830: *Out of employ. Died, 2d October* 1832, *at Vizagapatam.*

TAYLOR, WILLIAM RAYNSFORD.—1814: Writer; Assistant Commercial Resident at Vizagapatam. 1815: *At home.* 1819: *Returned to India;* Assistant to the Secretary to the Board of Trade; Assistant to the Superintendent of the Import Warehouse; Assistant to the Superintendent of Stamps. 1820: Register of the Zillah of Trichinopoly. 1823: Second Assistant to the Accountant-General. 1825: *At home.* 1827: *Returned to India;* Assistant Judge and Joint Criminal Judge of the Zillah of Madura. 1829: Judge and Criminal Judge of Combaconum. 1830: Judge and Criminal Judge of Chingleput. 1832: Third Judge of the Provincial Court, Southern Division. 1833: *At home on absentee allowance.* 1836: *Returned to India;* Acting Judge and Criminal Judge of Nellore; Acting Judge and Criminal Judge of Chingleput. 1837: Acting Second Judge of the Provincial Court, Southern Division; Acting, afterwards Postmaster-General. 1838: Second Judge of the Provincial Court, Southern Division. 1841: First Judge of the Provincial Court of Appeal and Circuit, Centre Division. 1844: Civil and Session Judge, Chittoor; *Resigned the service, 3d December, in India. (Annuitant on the Fund,* 1845.) *Died, 10th January* 1864, *in England.*

TAYLOR, JAMES CORBETT.—1831: Writer. 1832: Assistant to the Collector and Magistrate of Nellore. 1833: Assistant to the Principal Collector and Magistrate of Nellore. 1835: Acting Register of the Zillah of Nellore. 1837: Head Assistant to the Principal Collector and Magistrate of Nellore. 1838: Acting Sub-Collector and Joint Magistrate of Salem. 1839: Acting Head Assistant to the Principal Collector and Magistrate of Salem. *Died, 4th February* 1839, *at Salem.*

TEMPLE, GRENVILLE TEMPLE.—1818: Writer. 1820: *Resigned, 14th June, in England.*

TERRY, EDWARD.—1796: Writer. 1799: Assistant in the Public Revenue and Commercial Department. 1800: Assistant to the Accountant to the Board of Revenue. 1801: Assistant to the Commercial Resident at Tinnevelly. *Lost on his passage home, December* 1801, *in the ship " Generous."*

THACKERAY, WILLIAM.—1793: Writer. 1797: Assistant under the Secretary in the Public, Commercial, and Revenue Department. 1798: Assistant under the Commercial Resident at Vizagapatam. 1799: Assistant under the Collector of Peddapore. 1800: Gentoo Translator to Government; Subordinate Collector in the Ceded Districts. 1803; Judge of the Adawlut in the Zillah of Masulipatam. 1806: Junior Member of the Board of Revenue. 1810: Chief Secretary to Government. 1813: *At home.* 1817: *Returned to India ;* Acting Collector of Coimbatore. 1818: Collector and Magistrate of Bellary. 1820: Third Judge of the Sudder Adawlut Court; Member of Council of the Governor, and President of the Board of Revenue. *Died on his passage to the Cape of Good Hope,* 11th January 1823, *on board the " Nancy."*

THACKERAY, WEBB.—1806: Writer. 1807: Assistant to the Judge and Magistrate of the Zillah of Bellary. *Died,* 1st *September* 1807, *at Gundloor.*

THACKERAY, ST. JOHN.—1806: Writer. 1809: Assistant under the Secretary to the Board of Revenue. 1812: Head Assistant to the Collector of Trichinopoly. 1814: Head Assistant to the Collector of Tanjore. 1816: Assistant Magistrate of Tanjore. 1819: Employed in the late Peishwah's Dominions. *Killed,* 23d *October* 1824, *at Kittoo.*

THOMAS, JAMES.—1812: Writer. 1817: Second Assistant to the Collector of Tinnevelly. 1819: Head Assistant to the Collector and Magistrate of Tinnevelly. 1821: *At home.* 1825: *Returned to India ;* Junior Assistant to the Accountant-General. 1826: Senior Deputy Accountant-General, Commercial Accountant, and Auditor. 1828: Sub-Collector and Joint Magistrate of Coimbatore. 1830: Principal Collector and Magistrate of Coimbatore. 1832: Third Judge of the Provincial Court, Centre Division. 1833: *At home on absentee allowance.* 1836: *Returned to India.* 1837: Acting Deputy Accountant-General; Judge and Criminal Judge of Rajahmundry. *Died,* 6th January 1840, *at Madras.*

THOMAS, JOHN FRYER.—1816: Writer. 1818: Assistant to

the Register of the Sudder and Foujdarry Adawlut. 1819: Sanscrit Examiner to the College; Head Assistant to the Register of
the Sudder Adawlut. 1824: Senior Deputy to the Register of
the Sudder Adawlut. 1827: *At home on absentee allowance.*
1831: *Returned to India;* Judge and Criminal Judge of Combaconum. 1832: Acting Principal Collector and Magistrate of
Coimbatore. 1834: Register of the Sudder and Foujdarry Adawlut.
1835: Additional Government Commissioner for Carnatic Claims.
1836: Acting Third Judge of the Provincial Court, Northern
Division. 1837: Additional Government Commissioner for Carnatic Claims. 1838: Sole Commissioner for Final Adjustments of
Small Claims drawn from the Carnatic Fund. 1839: Sole Government Commissioner for Small Claims withdrawn from the Carnatic Fund, and Member of the College Board. 1842: *Proceeded
on furlough.* 1843: *Returned to India;* Secretary to Government,
Civil Department. 1844: Secretary to Government, Civil Department, and Member of the Mint Committee. 1845: Chief
Secretary to Government. 1849: Chief Secretary to Government,
and Provisional Member of Council. 1850: Member of Council,
and Chief Judge of the Sudder Dewannee and Sudder Foujdarry
Adawlut. 1855: *Proceeded on furlough; Resigned the service,
31st December, in India.* (*Annuitant on the Fund,* 1857.) *Died,
7th April* 1877, *in England.*

THOMAS, THOMAS J. W.—1824: Writer. 1826: *At home on
absentee allowance.* 1830: *Returned to India, per "Alfred;"*
Register of the Zillah of Chicacole. 1832: Acting Head Assistant
to the Collector and Magistrate of Masulipatam. 1833: Head
Assistant to the Collector of Masulipatam. 1838: Acting Deputy
Collector of Sea Customs at Madras; Assistant Judge and Joint
Criminal Judge of Rajahmundry. 1841: Assistant Judge and Joint
Criminal Judge, Vizagapatam. 1844: Subordinate Judge, Madura.
Died, 17th *March* 1845, *at Madras.*

THOMAS, EDWARD BROWN.—1824: Writer. 1827: Assistant
to the Principal Collector and Magistrate, North Arcot. 1828:
Head Assistant to the Collector and Magistrate, Trichinopoly.
1830: Head Assistant to the Principal Collector, Coimbatore.
1833: Acting Sub-Collector and Joint Magistrate, Coimbatore.
1834: Acting Assistant Judge and Joint Criminal Judge at Salem;
Acting Sub-Collector and Joint Magistrate, South Arcot. 1835:
Sub-Collector and Joint Magistrate, South Arcot. 1837: *At home.*
1840: Acting Judge and Criminal Judge, Malabar. 1841: Judge

and Criminal Judge, Malabar. 1842 : Acting Collector and Magistrate, Tinnevelly. 1843 : Collector and Magistrate, Tinnevelly. 1848 : Officiating Secretary to Government. 1849 : Acting Principal Collector and Magistrate, Coimbatore. 1851 : Collector and Magistrate, Coimbatore. 1858 : *Proceeded to Europe in April, on medical certificate.* 1862 : *Resigned the service, 1st May.* (*Annuitant.*)

THOMPSON, GEORGE.—1776 : Writer. 1782 : Factor. 1790 : Senior Merchant. 1791 : Senior Merchant and Assistant at Nagore. 1800 : Resident at Negapatam, and Revenue Assistant under the Resident at Nagore. 1802 to 1804 : *Without employ.* 1805 : *Out of the service.*

THOMPSON, CHRISTOPHER ANSTEY.—1816 : Writer. 1819 : Register of the Zillah of Bellary. 1820 : Register of the Zillah of Combaconum. 1824 : Junior Deputy Register of the Sudder and Foujdarry Adawlut. 1828 : Secretary in the Public, Revenue, and Commercial Department ; Collector of Chingleput. 1829 : Principal Collector and Magistrate of Nellore. *Died, 11th June 1831, at Madras.*

THOMPSON, EDWARD PENTON.—1822 : Writer. 1826 : Assistant to the Collector and Magistrate of Vizagapatam. 1827 : Head Assistant to the Principal Collector of Cuddapah. 1828 : Acting Assistant to the Resident at Mysore. 1830 : Sub-Collector and Assistant Magistrate of Salem ; Assistant Judge and Joint Criminal Judge of Salem. 1832 : Acting, afterwards Judge and Criminal Judge of Canara. 1835 : Acting Zillah Judge of Canara. 1836 : Acting Judge and Criminal Judge of Malabar ; Acting Judge and Criminal Judge of Madura. 1837 : Acting Collector and Criminal Magistrate of Tinnevelly. 1838 : Assistant Judge and Joint Criminal Judge of Salem. 1840 : Principal Collector and Magistrate of Tinnevelly. 1841 : *Proceeded on furlough.* 1844 : *Returned to India.* 1845 : Secretary to Government, Civil Department. 1846 : Secretary to Government, Revenue, and Judicial Department. 1847 : Second Puisne Judge of the Sudder Dewannee and Sudder Foujdarry Adawlut. 1852 : *Resigned the service, 1st January, in India.* (*Annuitant on the Fund*, 1852.)

THORP, SAMUEL.—1789 : Writer. *Died, 15th July* 1791.

THURESBY, JOHN WILLIAM.—1789 : Writer. 1790 : Assistant under the Secretary to the Board of Trade. 1791 : Assistant under the Collector of the Southern Division of Arcot. 1793 : Assistant to the Resident at Cuddapah. 1794 : Assistant under the Accountant at Cuddalore and Pondicherry. 1797 : Assistant under the Collector of Cuddalore and Pondicherry. 1800 : *Out of employ.* 1801 : Paymaster and Garrison Storekeeper at Madura. *No trace after* 1801.

TIMBRELL, JAMES.—1823 : Writer. *Died, 25th January 1825, on his passage to England.*

TOD, JAMES OGILVIE.—1798 : Writer on the Bencoolen Estabishment. 1805 : *Transferred to the Madras Presidency ;* Assistant under the Chief Secretary in Secret, Political, and Foreign Department : Assistant under the Subordinate Collector of Trichinopoly. 1806 : Register of the Zillah of Masulipatam. 1809 : Judge and Criminal Judge of Masulipatam. 1822 : Third Judge of the Provincial Court, Northern Division. 1825 : Acting Judge of the Provincial Court, Northern Division. 1828 : Second Judge of the Provincial Court, Northern Division. (*Annuitant on the Fund from 9th May* 1831.) *Died, 6th January* 1837, *in England.*

TORIN, BENJAMIN.—1779 : Writer. 1790 : Senior Merchant. 1791 : Paymaster at Pallamcottah. 1792 : Collector in the Tinnevelly Districts. 1795 : *At home.* 1800 : Resident at Tanjore. 1803 : *At home.* 1805 : *Out of the service.*

TORIN, CHARLES BEAUVOIR.—1794 : Writer. 1796 : Assistant under the Secretary in the Public, Commercial, and Revenue Department. 1798 : Assistant to the Commercial Resident at Tanjore. 1799 : *At home for his health.* 1801 : *Returned to India, and out of employ. No trace after* 1811.

TORRIANO, WILLIAM HARCOURT. — 1766 : Writer. 1771 : Factor. 1774 : Junior Merchant. 1778 : Senior Merchant. 1791 : Paymaster at Vellore. 1795 : Resident at Nagore. 1800 : Sea Customer and Boat Master. 1801 : *At home.* 1803 : *In India, and without employ.* 1808 : *Out of the service.*

TORRIANO, LIONEL AUGUSTUS.—1769 : Writer. 1774 : Factor and Assistant at Cuddalore. *Dead in* 1776.

TOWNSEND, THOMAS. — 1792 : Writer. 1793 : Assistant under the Secretary in the Political, Military, and Secret Department. 1794 : Assistant to the Commercial Resident at Salem. 1796 : Assistant under the Collector of the Southern Division of the Vizianagram Zemindary. 1800 : Assistant under the Collector in the First Division of Vizagapatam. 1801 : Assistant under the Collector of Nellore and Ongole. 1802 : Judge of the Zillah of Guntoor. 1806 : Judge and Magistrate of the Zillah of Manargoody. 1808 : *Out of employ.* 1809 : Judge and Magistrate of the Zillah of Masulipatam ; Third Judge of the Provincial

Court, Northern Division. 1815: *At home.* 1817: *Out of the service.*

TRACEY, HON. WILLIAM HANBURY.—1829: Writer. 1831: Assistant under the Principal Collector of Coimbatore. 1832: Register to the Zillah of Combaconum. 1833: Register of the Zillah of Chittoor. 1834: Register of the Zillah of Combaconum. 1838: *At home.* 1839: *Returned to India.* 1840: *Out of employ.* 1841: Assistant Judge and Joint Criminal Judge, Cochin. 1843: *Proceeded on furlough.* 1846: *Name removed, 19th August, in England.*

TRAVERS, JOHN BENWARD.—1792: Writer. 1793: Assistant under the Accountant-General. 1794: Assistant to the Collector in the Northern Division of Jaghire. 1796: Assistant under the Collector in the Southern Division of the Vizianagram Zemindary. 1797: Deputy Secretary to the Board of Revenue. 1799: Secretary to the Board of Revenue. 1801: Collector of Nellore and Ongole. 1809: Acting Judge, afterwards Second Judge of the Provincial Court, Northern Division. 1816: *At home.* 1817: *Returned to India.* 1819: Third Judge of the Provincial Court, Northern Division. 1820: Second Judge of the Provincial Court, Centre Division. *Died in 1820, in Madras.*

TRAVERS, GEORGE FRANCIS.—1794: Writer. 1797: Assistant under the Secretary in the Military, Political, and Secret Department. 1798: Assistant to the Commercial Resident at Vizagapatam. 1799: Assistant under the Accountant-General. 1801: Deputy Accountant in the Commercial and Revenue Departments. 1802: Deputy General and Commercial Accountant. 1803: Subordinate Collector in the Ceded Districts. 1806: Judge and Magistrate of Kodicondah. 1808: Collector of the Zillah of Kodicondah; Collector of the Zillah of Ganjam. 1809: Collector of the Zillah of Trichinopoly. 1815: Judge and Magistrate of the Zillah of Guntoor; Third Judge of the Provincial Court, Northern Division. 1819: *At home.* 1822: *Out of the service.*

TRAVERS, OCTAVIUS.—1851: Writer. 1853: *Proceeded on furlough.* 1855: *Resigned the service 18th April, in England.*

TREMAMONDO, ANTHONY EDWARD A.—*See* ANGELO, ANTHONY EDWARD.

TUDOR, MATTHEW.—1770: Writer. 1776: Factor. 1778: Junior Merchant. 1782: Senior Merchant. 1791: Paymaster at Aska. 1792: Collector of the Northern and Centre Divisions of the Masulipatam Havelly. *Dead in 1795.*

TULLOH, ROBERT HENRY.—1804: Writer. 1807: Assistant

K

to the Register of the Sudder and Foujdarry Adawlut; *Removed to the Bengal Establishment, 30th July* 1807.

. **TURING,** JOHN.—1762: Writer. 1768: Factor. 1771: Junior Merchant. 1774: Senior Merchant, and Third in Council at Cuddalore. 1791: Civil and Military Paymaster-General, and Garrison Storekeeper. 1792: *At home.* 1795: *Out of the service.*

TURING, WILLIAM.—1769: Writer. 1774: Factor. 1778: Junior Merchant. 1780: Senior Merchant. 1790: *Out of the service.*

TURING, JOHN.—1795: Writer. 1798: Assistant in the Military, Political, and Secret Department. 1799: *At home for his health.* 1800: *Returned to India;* Assistant to the Secretary in the Public, Revenue, and Commercial Department; Head Assistant in the Military Department; Deputy Postmaster-General. 1802: *At home.* 1808: *Out of the service.*

TURNBULL, JOHN GEORGE.—1804: Writer. 1807: Assistant under the Principal Collector of Tanjore and Trichinopoly. 1808: Assistant under the Collector of Salem. 1810: Register of the Zillah of Northern Malabar. 1812: Register of the Zillah of Tinnevelly; Deputy Accountant in the Military Department. 1814: Deputy Accountant-General. 1815: Commercial Accountant and Auditor. 1822: Accountant-General. (*Retired upon Annuity Fund,* 1840.) *Died, 2d January* 1872, *in England.*

TWEEDIE, ALEXANDER GEORGE. — 1842: Writer. 1845: Assistant to Collector and Magistrate, Bellary. 1852: Head Assistant to Collector and Magistrate, Guntoor; Head Assistant to Collector and Magistrate, Masulipatam. 1854: *Proceeded on furlough. Died, 27th August* 1855, *at Dover.*

TYLER, GEORGE.—1777: Writer. 1782: Factor. 1790: Senior Merchant. 1791: *In Bengal, and continued there till* 1822; *employment not specified, though stated to be in the service.* 1823: *At home.* 1827: *In Madras without employ.* 1830: Cashier of the Government Bank. *Died, 18th October* 1834, *at Fort St. George.*

UNDERWOOD, WILLIAM ELPHINSTONE. — 1823: Writer. 1826: Assistant to the Collector and Magistrate of Guntoor. 1828: Register of the Zillah of Chingleput; Register to the Provincial Court, Centre Division. 1830: Secretary to the Marine Board; Acting Boat Paymaster. 1831: Acting Magistrate on the Beach. 1832: Deputy Collector of Sea Customs at Madras; Secretary to the Marine Board. 1837: Commissioner for Drawing

Government Lotteries. 1838: Acting Deputy Secretary to Government in the Chief Secretary's Department. 1839: Acting Principal Collector and Magistrate of Malabar; Deputy Collector of Sea Customs, Madras. 1841: Collector of Sea Customs, Madras. 1860: *Resigned the service in India.* (*Annuitant on the Fund, May* 1860.) *Died,* 19*th January* 1874, *in England.*

UTHOFF, EDWARD.—1812: Writer. 1806: Assistant to the Register of the Provincial Court, Southern Division; Assistant Magistrate of Tinnevelly. 1817: Head Assistant to the Collector of Tinnevelly. 1819: Deputy Malabar and Tamul Translator to Government; Junior Deputy Secretary to the Board of Revenue. *Died,* 21*st August* 1822, *at Madras.*

VANSITTART, GEORGE. — 1777: Writer. *No trace after* 1778.

VAUGHAN, HUGH.—1771: Writer. 1776: Factor. 1780: Junior Merchant. 1782: Senior Merchant. 1791: Senior Merchant, and Paymaster at Madura. 1800: *At home.* 1801: *Out of the service.*

VAUGHAN, JAMES.—1802: Writer. 1803: Assistant to the Collector of Nellore. 1806: Register of the Zillah of the Northern Division of Malabar. 1808: Register of the Zillah of the Augadeeporam. 1811; Deputy Collector of Sea Customs at Malabar and Canara. 1815: Head Assistant to the Collector of Malabar. 1816: Collector and Magistrate of Malabar. 1822: Principal Collector and Magistrate of Malabar. 1826: Second Judge of the Provincial Court, Western Division. 1830: *At home on absentee allowance.* (*Annuitant on the Fund from* 1*st May* 1830.) *Died,* 4*th January* 1833, *in England.*

VAUGHAN, JOHN.—1808: Writer. 1814: Register of the Zillah of Bellary. 1816: Register of the Zillah of Guntoor. 1817: ¦Head Assistant to the Collector, and Assistant to the Magistrate of Nellore. 1822: Sub-Collector and Assistant Magistrate of Cochin. 1823: Sub-Collector and Assistant Magistrate of Malabar. 1826: Judge and Criminal Judge of Canara. 1830: Third Judge of the Provincial Court, Western Division. 1832: Second Judge of the Provincial Court, Western Division. 1838: First Judge of the Provincial Court, Western Division. 1842: *Proceeded on furlough. Died,* 5*th October* 1842, *in Shropshire, England.*

VIBART, HENRY.—1804: Writer. 1807: Assistant to the Secretary to the Board of Revenue; Assistant to the Collector of the Zillah of Ganjam. 1811 : Register of the Zillah of Rajah-mundry. 1822 : Register and Assistant Collector of the Zillah of Seringapatam. 1824 : Judge and Criminal Judge of the Zillah of Masulipatam. (*Annuitant on the Fund from December* 1832.) *Died, 5th November* 1839, *in England.*

VINES, GOODSON.—1792 : Writer. 1793 : Assistant under the Secretary to the Board of Revenue. 1796 : Assistant under the Commercial Resident at Masulipatam. 1797 : Assistant under the Commercial Resident at Palamcottah. 1800 : *Out of employ.* 1803 : *Suspended the service and ordered home.* 1806 : *Out of the service.*

VIVEASH, HARRY (now BASKERVILLE.)—1811 : Writer. 1815 : Head Assistant to the Collector of Madras. 1817 : Mahratta Translator to Government. 1822 : Sub-Collector and Assistant Magistrate of Bellary. 1826 : Collector and Magistrate of Chingle-put. 1828 : Principal Collector and Magistrate of Madura. 1833 : Principal Collector and Magistrate of Canara. 1835 : Third Member of the Board of Revenue. 1836 : Second Member of the Board of Revenue. 1838 : *At home on absentee allowance.* (*Annuitant on the Fund from* 30th *April* 1838.) *Died, 6th February* 1877, *in England.*

WALKER, JOHN.—1823 : Writer. 1826 : Assistant to the Collector of Tinnevelly ; Register of the Zillah of Madura. 1828 : Junior Deputy Register of the Sudder Adawlut ; Assistant Judge of the Zillah of Canara. 1834 : *At home on absentee allowance.* 1837 : *Returned to India, per " General Kyd ; "* Police Magistrate. 1838 : Acting Deputy Collector of Madras, and Superintendent of Stationery ; Canarese Translator to Government. 1839 : Assistant Judge and Joint Criminal Judge of Madura, and Acting Judge and Criminal Judge of Malabar. 1840 : Judge and Criminal Judge of Cuddapah. 1844 : Civil and Session Judge, Nellore. 1853 : *Resigned the service, 1st May, in India.* (*Annuitant on the Fund.*) *Died, 24th July* 1862, *in England.*

WALLACE, JOHN, sen.—1789 : Writer. 1790 : Assistant under the Accountant. 1794 : Assistant at Masulipatam. 1796 : Deputy Commercial Resident at Nagore. 1799 : Commercial Resident at Nagore. 1800 : *Leave to the Cape of Good Hope, and eventually to Europe.* 1805 : *Returned to India ;* Commercial Resident at Ingeram. 1808 : *At home for his health.* 1811 : *Out of the service.*

WALLACE, THOMAS.—1790 : Writer. 1791 : Assistant under

the Secretary in the Military Department. 1792: Assistant at Ganjam. 1796: Deputy Secretary in the Military Department. 1797: *At home for his health. No trace after* 1797.

WALLACE, JOHN, jun.—1792: Writer. 1794: Assistant under the Secretary in the Military, Political, and Secret Department, and Assistant to the Accountant to the Board of Revenue. 1795: Assistant to the Accountant to the Board of Trade. 1796: Assistant under the Secretary to the Board of Trade, and to the Import Warehouse-keeper and Deputy Postmaster-General. 1798: Assistant under the Resident at Nagore. 1799: Assistant to the Collector of Nagore. 1800: Head Assistant to the Collector of Tanjore. 1801: Collector of Trichinopoly and its Dependent Polygars. 1805: Principal Collector of Tanjore and Trichinopoly. 1813: Second Member of the Board of Revenue. *Died, 7th August* 1814, *at Madras.*

WARD, SAMUEL NEVILL.—1831: Writer. 1833: Assistant to Collector and Magistrate, Trichinopoly. 1834: Acting Register to the Zillah Courts of Combaconum and of Chittoor. 1837: Acting Head Assistant to Collector and Magistrate, Ganjam; and Register of the Zillah Court of Canara. 1842: Acting Assistant Judge and Joint Criminal Judge, Cochin; Acting Register of the Zillah Court of Malabar; Acting Assistant Judge and Joint Criminal Judge, Malabar; and Acting Assistant Judge of the Zillah Court of Canara. 1843: Extra Assistant to Principal Collector and Magistrate, and Acting Sub-Collector and Joint Magistrate, Canara. 1844: Acting Additional Sub-Collector and Sub-Judge, Mangalore. 1845: Additional Sub-Collector and Joint Magistrate, Canara. 1847: *Proceeded to Europe on furlough.* 1850: Acting Civil and Sessions Judge, Madura; Acting Civil and Sessions Judge, Cuddapah; and Acting Collector and Magistrate, South Arcot. 1851: Sub-Collector and Joint Magistrate, Salem. 1852: At first Acting, then Civil and Sessions Judge, Calicut. 1853: Civil and Sessions Judge, Cuddalore. 1855: Acting Civil Auditor and Superintendent of Stamps. 1857: Civil and Sessions Judge, Coimbatore. *Resigned the service,* 27th October 1863. *(Annuitant.)*

WARD, EDWARD EYRE.—1834: Writer. 1836: Assistant to the Principal Collector and Magistrate of Salem. 1837: Assistant to the Principal Collector and Magistrate of Canara. 1838: Assistant to the Principal Collector and Magistrate of Coimbatore; Assistant to the Principal Collector and Magistrate of South Arcot. 1841: Head Assistant to Collector and Magistrate, Masulipatam.

1843 : Head Assistant to Collector and Magistrate, Coimbatore. *Died, 5th March* 1843, *at Ootacamund.*

WARE, THOMAS STEPHEN.—1793 : Writer.   1796 : Assistant under the Secretary to the Board of Revenue.   1797 : Assistant under the Accountant to the Board of Revenue.   1798 : Deputy Accountant to the Board of Revenue.   1799 : Acting Persian Translator to the Board of Revenue.   *Died, 5th November* 1799.

WARRICKER, JOHN.—1777 : Writer.   1782 : Factor.   1790 : Senior Merchant and Assistant at Vizagapatam.   1800 : Assistant to the Collector at Ganjam.   *No trace after* 1800.

WASEY, WILLIAM GEORGE.—1778 : Writer.   *No trace after* 1782.

WATERS, GEORGE JENKINS.—1808 : Writer.   1814 : Register of the Zillah of Canara.   1821 : *At home.*   1823 : *Returned to India ;* Acting Judge and Criminal Judge of Chittoor.   1825 : Acting Judge of the Zillah of Cuddapah.   1826 : Judge and Criminal Judge of the Zillah of Chittoor.   1832 : Officiating Mint-Master ; Third Judge of the Provincial Court, Northern Division. 1836 : *At home on absentee allowance.*   1837 : *Returned to India, per "Barretto Junior."*   1838 : Acting First Judge of the Provincial Court, Centre Division.   1839 : Acting Civil Auditor and Superintendent of Stamps ; Acting First Judge, Provincial Court, Southern Division.   1840 : Judge and Criminal Judge of Cuddapah ; First Judge of the Provincial Court of Appeal and Circuit for the Southern Division.   1842 : First Judge of the Provincial Court of Appeal and Circuit for the Western Division.   1844 : Civil and Session Judge, Second Class, Tellicherry.   1845 : Puisne Judge of the Sudder Dewannee and Sudder Foujdarry Adawlut. 1846 : First Puisne Judge of the Sudder Dewannee and Sudder Foujdarry Adawlut.   1847 : Civil and Session Judge, Coimbatore. *Resigned the service, 4th December.   (Annuitant on the Fund,* 1848.)   *Died, 12th February* 1882, *in England.*

WATTS, JOHN NICHOLSON.—1796 : Writer.   1799 : Assistant under the Secretary in Public, Revenue, and Commercial Department.   1800 : Head Assistant in the Revenue and Judicial Department.   1801 : Assistant under the Commercial Resident at Tinnevelly ; Deputy Commercial Resident at Tinnevelly.   1802 : Head Assistant to the Collector of Dindigul.   1804 : Register of Tanjore.   1805 : Subordinate Collector of Tanjore.   1808 : *At home.*   1814 : *Returned to India.   Died, 28th July* 1815, *at Fort St George.*

WATTS, THOMAS.—1806: Writer; Assistant to the Secretary to the Board of Revenue. 1807: Assistant to the Principal Collector of Tanjore, &c. 1808: Second Assistant to the Collector of Trichinopoly. 1811: Register of the Zillah of Dharapooram. *Died, May* 1811, *at Dharapooram.*

WAYTE, WILLIAM.—1797: Writer. 1800: Assistant under the Secretary in the Military, Political, and Secret Department. 1802: Deputy Secretary to the Board of Revenue. 1806: Secretary to the Board of Revenue. 1810: Third Member of the Board of Revenue. 1819: Second Member of the Board of Revenue. 1822: *At home.* 1827: *Out of the service.* (*Annuitant on the Fund from 1st January* 1827.) *Died,* 17*th December* 1860, *in England.*

WEBB, WILLIAM. — 1770: Writer. 1776: Factor. 1778: Junior Merchant. 1782: Senior Merchant. 1791: Import Warehouse-keeper at Cutwal, and Member of the Committee of Regulations. 1795: Member of the Board of Trade, and Import Warehouse-keeper. 1800: Agent for Supplies. 1801: *Without employ. Died,* 14*th August* 1807, *in Madras.*

WEBB, NATHANIEL.—1778: Writer. 1790: Senior Merchant. 1791: Collector of the Guntoor Circar. 1792: Manager of the Ganjam Havelly. 1800: Collector in the Second Division of the Vizagapatam Districts. 1803: Second Judge of the Court of Circuit and of Appeal for the Centre Division. 1808: Senior Judge of the Court of Circuit and for Appeal for the Northern Division. 1829: Postmaster-General. (*Annuitant on the Fund in* 1838.) *Died,* 5*th August* 1838.

WEBBE, JOSIAH.—1783: Writer; Assistant to the Secretary to the Select Committee. 1786: Assistant to the Secretary in the Military Department, Mahratta Translator, and Deputy Commissary-General. 1787: Under the Secretary in the Public and Revenue Department. 1790: Secretary to the Board of Assumed Revenue. 1792: Temporary Member of the Board of Assumed Revenue. 1793: Deputy Secretary in the Public, Commercial, and Revenue Department. 1796: Secretary in the Public and Commercial Department, Clerk to the Court of Appeal, and to the Committee of Treasury. 1797: Secretary to Government, and Mahratta Translator. 1800: Chief Secretary to Government, and Mahratta Translator. 1801: Resident at the Durbar of the Rajah of Mysore. 1803: Resident at Nagpore. 1804: Resident at the Court of Dowlut Rao Scindia. *Died,* 9*th November* 1804, *at Mussingabad, on the banks of the Nerbudda.*

WEBSTER, GEORGE.—1778 : Writer.   1790 : Senior Merchant. 1791 : Sepoy Paymaster.   *Died, 3d July* 1794, *in Madras.*

WEDDERBURN, JAMES A.—1848 : Writer.   1852 : Assistant to Collector and Magistrate, Coimbatore.   1853 : Assistant to Collector and Magistrate, Chingleput.   *Died, 19th May* 1854, *at Chingleput.*

WELCH, THOMAS. — 1771 : Writer.   1776 : Factor.   1780 : Junior Merchant.   1782 : Senior Merchant.   1790 : *At home.* 1793 : *Out of the service.*

WEST, FRANCIS ALEXANDER.—1826 : Writer.   1829 : Register of the Zillah of Bellary ; Register of the Zillah of Cuddapah. *Died, 26th September* 1832, *at Arcot.*

WESTCOTT, GEORGE. — 1764 : Writer.   1771 : Factor and Assistant at Masulipatam.   1774 : Junior Merchant.   1776 : Senior Merchant and Paymaster at Ellore.   1790 : *At home ; Returned to India.*   1801 : Senior Member of the Board of Trade.   *Died, 8th May* 1809, *at Fort St. George.*

WETHERELL, CHARLES.—1792 : Writer.   1794 : Assistant under the Secretary in the Public, Commercial, and Revenue Department.   1795 : Assistant to the Collector in the Burramchal. 1797 : Assistant under the Commercial Resident at Ingeram. 1799 : *Out of employ ;* Paymaster at Khistnagherry.   1802 : Paymaster and Garrison Storekeeper at Madura.   1806 : Paymaster and Garrison Storekeeper at Trichinopoly.   1811 : *At home.* 1816 : *Out of the service.*

WHEATLEY, THOMAS RUNDALL. — 1817 : Writer.   1819 : Assistant to the Register of the Zillah of Bellary ; Head Assistant to the Collector and Magistrate of Cuddapah.   1826 : Acting Deputy Accountant-General in the Military Department.   1827 : Sub-Collector and Joint Magistrate of Malabar.   1828 : *At home on absentee allowance.*   1832 : *Returned to India ;* Secretary in the Revenue and Judicial Department.   1835 : *At home.*   1840 : *Absent from India five years.*

WHISH, JOHN CLINTON.—1807 : Writer.   1809 : Assistant to the Chief Secretary in the General, Commercial, and Law Department.   1810 : Assistant to the Superintendent of Stamps.   1811 : Fixed Examiner in the Office of Sub-Secretary in the Commercial and Law Department.   1812 : Head Assistant to the Collector of Coimbatore.   1816 : Assistant Magistrate of Coimbatore.   1821 : Sub-Collector and Assistant Magistrate of Coimbatore ; Collector and Magistrate of Guntoor.   1831 : Principal Collector and Magistrate of Nellore. 1835: *At home on absentee allowance. (Annui-tant on the Fund, from 1st July 1837.) Died, 22d November 1837, at Mortimer House, near Reading.*

WHISH, CHARLES MATTHEW.—1813: Writer. 1815: Register of the Zillah of South Malabar. 1823: Register of the Zillah of Malabar. 1826: Sub-Collector and Joint Magistrate of Malabar. 1827: Assistant Judge and Joint Criminal Judge of Malabar. 1830: Assistant Judge and Joint Criminal Judge of Cuddapah. 1831: *Out of employ.* 1832: Acting Judge and Criminal Judge of Cuddapah. *Died, 14th April 1833, at Cud-dapah.*

WHITE, CHARLES NICHOLAS.—1776: Writer. 1782: Factor. 1790: Senior Merchant. 1791: Secretary in Public and Revenue Department, and Clerk of Appeals, and to Treasury. 1795: Member of the Revenue Board. 1800: Senior Member of the Board of Revenue. 1801: *At home.* 1805: *Out of the service.*

WHITE, EVAN MARSH.—1790: Writer. 1793: Assistant under the Secretary in the Military, Political, and Secret Depart-ment. 1794: Assistant to the Collector of Guntoor. 1796: Acting Paymaster at Ongole. *Died, 17th August 1796.*

WHITE, DANIEL.—1829: Writer. 1831: Assistant to the Principal Collector of Malabar. 1832: Acting Head Assistant to the Principal Collector and Magistrate of Malabar. 1835: Assis-tant to the Principal Collector and Magistrate of Malabar; Acting Sub-Collector, Malabar. 1836: Head Assistant to the Principal Collector and Magistrate of Malabar. 1837: Acting Assistant Judge and Joint Criminal Judge of Salem; Acting Additional Sub-Collector and Joint Magistrate of Canara; Head Assistant to the Principal Collector and Magistrate of Malabar (Resumed); Acting Assistant Judge and Joint Criminal Judge of Malabar. 1838: Acting Assistant Judge and Joint Criminal Judge of Cochin; Acting Assistant Judge and Joint Criminal Judge of Malabar. 1839: Assistant Judge and Joint Criminal Judge of Malabar. 1840: *Proceeded on furlough.* 1843: *Returned to India;* Sub-Collector and Joint Magistrate, Southern Division of Arcot. 1850: Collector and Magistrate, Nellore. *Died, 31st March 1853, at Pointe de Galle, Ceylon.*

WHITEHILL, JOHN.—1752: Writer. 1768: Senior Merchant and Member of the Council of the Governor. 1780: *Dismissed from Council and service.*

WHITTINGHAM, CHARLES. — 1830: Writer. 1834: Assis-

tant to Principal Collector and Magistrate, South Arcot. 1836 :
Acting Register to the Zillah Court of Combaconum ; Acting Head
Assistant to Principal Collector and Magistrate, South Arcot ;
Officiating Joint Criminal Judge, Chingleput.   1837 : Head Assis-
tant to Principal Collector and Magistrate, South Arcot ; Officiat-
ing Junior Deputy Secretary to the Board of Revenue.   1838 :
Head Assistant to Collector and Magistrate, South Arcot.   1839 :
Acting Sub-Collector and Joint Magistrate, South Arcot.   1840 :
Acting Head Assistant to the Accountant-General ; Commissioner
for Government Lotteries.   1841 : Acting, afterwards Sub-Collector
and Joint Magistrate, Tinnevelly.   1845 : *Proceeded to Europe on
furlough.*   1848 : Acting Sub-Collector and Joint Magistrate,
Tinnevelly.   1849 : Sub-Collector and Joint Magistrate, Tinne-
velly.   1854 : Collector and Magistrate, North Arcot.   1859 :
On medical certificate to England for 30 months.   1861 : *Resigned
the service, 18th December, in England.*   *(Annuitant.)   Died, 10th
November 1879, in London.*

WHITTINGHAM, ANTHONY. — 1837 : Writer.   1840 : *Proceeded on furlough.   Pensioned in England, 2d August 1843.*

WHITTINGTON, WILLIAM.—1804 : Writer.   *Died, 17th September 1806, in Madras.*

WILLIAMS, MORGAN.—1760 : Writer.   1768 : Junior Merchant.   1771 : Senior Merchant, and Third in Council at Vizagapatam.   1782 : Member of the Council of the Governor.   *Died
in 1790.*

WILLIAMS, HENRY.—1820 : Writer ; *At home.*   1826 : *Returned to India ;* Assistant to the Principal Collector and Magistrate of Canara ; Head Assistant to the Collector and Magistrate
of Chingleput.   1827 : Head Assistant to the Collector and
Magistrate of Salem.   1828 : Head Assistant to the Collector
and Magistrate of Cuddapah.   *Died, 29th March 1830, at
Cuddapah.*

WILLIAMSON, ROBERT HUDLESTON.—1828 : Writer.   1832 :
Register of the Zillah of Madura ; Acting Assistant to the
Accountant-General.   1833 : Register to the Zillah Court of Rajah-
mundry.   1834 : Register to the Zillah Court of Madura.   1836 :
Proceeded to Europe on furlough.   1841 : Acting Deputy Collector
of Sea Customs, Madras.   1842 : Deputy Collector of Sea Customs,
Madras ; Commissioner for Government Lotteries.   1845 : Acting
Collector of Sea Customs, Madras.   1853 : Acting Postmaster-
General.   1854 : Postmaster-General.   1859 : Officiating Director-

General of Post Offices in India. 1860: Resumed Charge of Office of Postmaster - General, Madras. 1862: *Proceeded to Europe on furlough; Resigned the service, 25th November 1862. (Annuitant.)*

WILLIS, RICHARD LEGGE. — 1778: Writer. 1790: Senior Merchant. 1791: Paymaster in Guntoor Circar. 1792: *Suspended from service.*

WILLOCK, ARTHUR.—1817: Writer. 1823: Assistant to the Secretary to the Board of Revenue. *Died, 18th September 1824, at Madras.*

WILMOT, ARTHUR.—1824: Writer. 1827: Assistant to the Principal Collector and Magistrate of Bellary. *Died, 1827, at Anantapoor.*

WILSON, GEORGE.—1781: Writer. 1782: Assistant to the Secretary in the Civil Department. 1783: Assistant at Vizagapatam. 1790: Paymaster at Chicacole. 1798: Paymaster and Garrison Storekeeper at Vizagapatam and its Dependencies. *Died, 24th August 1799, at Vizagapatam.*

WILSON, HENRY.—1789: Writer; Assistant under the Secretary in the Secret Department, and Assistant to the Secretary to the Board of Revenue. 1791: Assistant to the Collector in the Northern and Central Division of Masulipatam Havelly. 1796: Assistant to the Collector in the First Division of the Masulipatam District. 1797: *At home for his health.* 1799: *Returned to India;* Paymaster and Garrison Storekeeper at Jumacondah and its Dependencies. 1800: Deputy Paymaster at Guntoor. 1802: *Out of employ.* 1803: Paymaster and Garrison Storekeeper at Vizagapatam. 1808: *At home.* 1810: *Out of the service.*

WILSON, ALEXANDER.—1797: Writer. 1799: Assistant under the Secretary to the Board of Revenue. 1801: Assistant under the Collector of the Northern Division of Canara. 1803: Register of the Zillah of Rajahmundry. 1805: Subordinate Collector of Canara. 1807: Judge and Magistrate of the Zillah of Honore. 1809: Judge and Magistrate of the Zillah of Canara. 1814: Judge and Magistrate of the Zillah of Malabar. 1823: Judge and Criminal Judge of the Zillah of Malabar. 1824: Third Judge of the Provincial Court, Western Division. 1826: *Annuitant from 1st May. Died, 28th November 1863, in England.*

WILSON, WILLIAM.—1830: Writer. 1832: Assistant to the Principal Collector and Magistrate of the Southern Division of

Arcot. 1833 : Register of the Zillah of Chingleput. 1834 :
Register of the Zillah of Chittoor. 1835 : *At home.* 1840 :
Absent from India five years.

WISSETT, ROBERT.—1793 : Writer. 1795 : Assistant under
the Secretary to the Board of Trade. 1796 : Assistant under the
Resident at Vizagapatam. 1797 : Assistant under the Resident
at the Presidency. *Died at sea in* 1798.

WISSETT, THOMAS.—1795 : Writer. 1797 : Assistant under
the Secretary in the Military, Secret, and Political Department.
1798 : Assistant under the Commercial Resident at Vizagapatam.
1800 : Deputy Commercial Resident at Ganjam. *Died,* 11*th
December* 1806, *at Ganjam.*

WOOD, JOHN.—1772 : Writer. 1778 : Factor. *No trace
after* 1778.

WOOD, EDWARD.—1800 : Writer. 1803 : Persian Translator
to the Sudder and Foujdarry Adawlut. 1804 : Deputy Register
to the Sudder and Foujdarry Adawlut. 1806 : Acting Register
to the Sudder and Foujdarry Adawlut. 1807 : Register to the
Sudder and Foujdarry Adawlut. 1809 : Judge and Magistrate of
Seringapatam ; Register to the Sudder and Foujdarry Adawlut.
1813 : Senior Secretary to Government. 1815 : Paymaster of
Stipends at the Presidency. 1820 : Chief Secretary to Government. *Died,* 28*th May* 1824, *at Madras.*

WOOD, HENRY.—1832 : Writer. 1834 : Assistant to Principal
Collector, Cuddapah. 1835 : Assistant to Principal Collector, South
Arcot. 1837 : Assistant to Principal Collector and Magistrate,
South Arcot. 1838 : Acting Second Assistant to Accountant-
General. 1839 : *Proceeded to Europe on furlough.* 1841 : Acting
Register of the Provincial Court of the Northern Division, and
Assistant Collector and Magistrate, Chingleput. 1842 : Acting
Assistant Judge and Joint Criminal Judge, Guntoor. 1843 :
Acting Head Assistant to Collector and Magistrate, Chingleput.
1844 : Head Assistant to Collector and Magistrate, Chingleput.
1845 : Acting Sub-Collector and Joint Magistrate, South Arcot.
1846 : Head Assistant to Collector and Magistrate, Salem. 1847 :
Acting Sub-Collector and Joint Magistrate, South Arcot. 1849 :
Sub-Collector and Joint Magistrate, South Arcot. 1854 : Acting
Collector and Magistrate, Guntoor. 1855 : Collector and Magistrate, Guntoor. 1859 : *Leave to England, on private affairs, for*
6 *months ;* Collector and Magistrate, South Arcot. 1862 : *Proceeded to Europe on furlough.* 1865 : *Extension of* 6 *months on*

private affairs; Resigned the service, 14th December, in England.
(Annuitant.) Died, 10th October 1873, in England.

WOODCOCK, CHARLES. — 1796 : Writer. 1798 : Assistant under the Accountant to the Board of Revenue ; Senior Assistant under the Accountant to the Board of Revenue ; Deputy Postmaster-General. 1800 : Deputy Accountant to the Board of Revenue, and Head Assistant to the Accountant-General in the Revenue and Commercial Department. 1801 : *At home.* 1806 : *Returned to India ;* Register of the Zillah of Tinnevelly. 1807 : Judge and Magistrate of the Zillah of Combaconum. 1810 : Judge and Magistrate of the Zillah of Ganjam. 1818 : Judge and Criminal Judge of the Zillah of Guntoor ; *Out of employ.* 1820 : *At home.* (*Annuitant on the Fund in* 1834.) *Died, 25th May 1852, in England.*

WOODCOCK, EDWARD H.—1806 : Writer. 1807 : Assistant to the Secretary in the Revenue and Judicial Department ; Assistant to the Register to the Sudder and Foujdarry Adawlut. 1808 : Fixed Examiner under the Secretary in the Revenue and Judicial Department. 1809 : Register of the Zillah of Cuddapah. 1812 : Register of the Zillah of Tinnevelly. 1816 : Register of the Zillah of Salem. 1822 : Sub-Collector of Tanjore. 1824 : Judge and Criminal Judge of the Zillah of Cuddapah. 1825 : Judge and Criminal Judge of the Zillah of Salem. 1828 : Third Judge of the Provincial Court, Southern Division. 1830 : Second Judge of the Provincial Court, Southern Division. 1831 : *At home on absentee allowance.* (*Annuitant on the Fund from 1st May* 1834.) *Died, 30th October 1870, in England.*

WOODGATE, CHARLES HENRY.—1832 : Writer. 1833 : Assistant to the Principal Collector and Magistrate of North Arcot. 1835 : Acting Head Assistant to the Collector and Magistrate of Trichinopoly. 1836 : Acting Head Assistant to the Collector and Magistrate of Coimbatore. 1838 : Head Assistant to the Collector and Magistrate of Trichinopoly. 1844 : *Proceeded on furlough.* 1847 : *Returned to India.* 1848 : Subordinate Judge, Madura. 1855 : Civil and Sessions Judge, Tinnevelly. *Died, 30th October 1856, on board the "Alma."*

WOOLF, ROBERT. — 1779 : Writer. 1790 : Senior Merchant. 1791 : Auditor of Civil Accounts, Deputy Accountant, and Contractor for Repairs. 1795 : Accountant-General. 1803 : *At home.* 1805 : *Out of the service.*

WORDSWORTH, FAVEL.—1777 : Writer. 1782 : Factor. *No trace after* 1782.

WRANGHAM, John. — 1783: Writer.   1785: *In Bengal.*
1787: Assistant to the Secretary in the Public Department.   1788:
Assistant at Tanjore.   1790: Deputy Paymaster and Deputy
Import Warehouse-keeper, and Member of the Committee for
Investigating the King's Army Accounts.   1791: Assistant to
the Collector of Madura and Dindigul.   1793: Member of the
Committee of Investigation at Noozeed.   1796: Collector of
the Fourth Division of the Masulipatam Districts.   1798: *Out
of employ.*   1800: *At home.   Died, 4th November* 1804, *at Tunbridge Wells.*

WREY, Edward Bourchier.—1811: Writer.   1815: Assistant
to the Accountant-General.   1819: Secretary to the Native Pension
Fund Committee.   1822: Assistant to the Accountant-General.
1825: Register to the Provincial Court, Northern Division.   1827:
Assistant Judge and Joint Criminal Judge of Masulipatam.
1830: *At home on absentee allowance.*   1833: *Returned to India.*
1834: Judge and Criminal Judge of Nellore; Judge and Criminal
Judge of Rajahmundry.   (*Annuitant on the Fund in* 1839.)   *Died,
30th May* 1840, *in England.*

WRIGHT, William Evatt.—1794: Writer.   1797: Assistant
under the Secretary to the Board of Revenue.   1799: Acting
Deputy Secretary to the Board of Revenue.   1800: *At home.*
1803: *Returned to India;* Deputy Secretary to the Board of
Trade.   1805: Malabar Translator to Government.   1806: Judge
and Magistrate of Chittoor.   1808: Third Judge of the Provincial
Court, Centre Division.   1821: *At home.*   1824: *Out of the
service.*

WROUGHTON, John Chardin.—1817: Writer.   1823: Assistant to the Collector and Magistrate of Bellary.   1824: Assistant
to the Collector and Magistrate of Cuddapah; *At home.*   1827:
Returned to India; Head Assistant to the Principal Collector and
Magistrate of Madura.   1828: Sub-Collector and Joint Magistrate
of Cuddapah.   1829: Sub-Collector and Joint Magistrate of Tinnevelly.   1830: Sub-Collector and Joint Magistrate of Madura.
1835: Collector and Magistrate of Masulipatam, and in Charge of
the Treasury there.   1836: Acting Collector of Sea Customs at
Madras, and Member of the Marine Board.   1838: Collector of
Sea Customs at Madras, and Member of the Marine Board.   1841:
Principal Collector and Magistrate of Coimbatore.   1851: *Proceeded on furlough.*   1852: *Resigned the service, 30th April, in
India.*   (*Annuitant on the Fund,* 1852.)   *Died, 30th November*
1854, *in England.*

WYLIE, GEORGE.—1849: Writer. 1851: Assistant to Collector and Magistrate, Chingleput. 1853: *Proceeded on furlough.* 1854: *Returned to India;* Assistant to Collector and Magistrate, Guntoor. 1855: Head Assistant to Collector and Magistrate, Guntoor. 1857: Head Assistant to Collector and Magistrate, Rajahmundry; *Proceeded on furlough.* 1859: *Resigned the service, 12th April, in England.*

WYNCH, WILLIAM. — 1767: Writer. 1774: Factor and Assistant at Masulipatam. 1776: Junior Merchant and Paymaster at Trichinopoly. 1778: *At home. Returned to India after 1782, became Senior Merchant, and was at home in 1790.* 1793: *Out of the service.*

WYNCH, ALEXANDER.—1768: Member of the Council of the Governor. 1774: Governor of the Presidency. *Resigned before 1775.*

WYNCH, GEORGE.—1772: Writer. 1778: Factor. 1780: Junior Merchant. 1790: Senior Merchant. 1791: Third in Council at Ganjam. 1792: Collector at Caroor. 1795: *Without employ. Suspended from the service, and at home in 1800.* 1805: *Out of the service.*

WYNCH, JOHN.—1777: Writer. 1782: Factor; *At home.* 1790: Senior Merchant. 1791: Deputy Export Warehouse-keeper. 1792: Paymaster to the Western Army. 1795: Paymaster at Walajabad and at Arnee. *Died in 1795.*

WYNOX, CHARLES.—1789: Writer. 1790: Assistant to the Secretary to the Board of Revenue. 1793: Assistant under the Resident at Ingeram. 1794: *Out of employ.* 1796: Collector in the Fourth Division of the Masulipatam District. 1798: *Out of employ.* 1803: Secretary to the Board of Trade. 1807: Acting Member of the Board of Trade. 1811: *At home.* 1815: *Returned to India. Died, January 1818.*

YEATES, MATTHEW.—1767: Writer. 1774: Factor. 1776: Junior Merchant and Assistant at Ingeram. 1778: Senior Merchant. 1791: Senior Merchant and Resident at Ingeram. 1800: *Without employ. Died, 13th November 1808, at St. Thomé, Madras.*

YOUNG, SAMUEL.—1781: Writer. 1783: Assistant to the Secretary to the Select Committee in Bengal; Assistant to the Secretary in the Civil Department. 1786: Assistant at Masulipatam. 1787: Paymaster at Ongole and at the Palnaud. 1793: *At home.* 1801: *Returned to India.* 1802: Paymaster and Garrison Storekeeper at Masulipatam and its Dependencies.   1808 : *At home.*   1812 : *Out of the service.*

YOUNG, ROBERT HERRIES.—1797 : Writer on the Bencoolen Establishment.   1803 : *Transferred to the Madras Presidency ;* Acting Assistant to the Secretary in the Military Department; Assistant to the Collector in the Southern Division of Arcot. 1805 : Subordinate Collector of Trichinopoly.   1808 : Head Assistant to the Collector of Trichinopoly.   1810 : Judge and Criminal Judge of Tinnevelly.   1820 : Collector and Magistrate of Tinnevelly.   *Died, 9th May 1820, at Trichindoor.*

YOUNG, STUART JOHNSON.—1833 : Writer.   1835 : Assistant to the Collector and Magistrate of Chingleput.   1837 : Assistant to the Principal Collector and Magistrate at Canara.   1838 : Acting Head Assistant to the Collector and Magistrate of Tinnevelly. 1840 : Head Assistant to Collector and Magistrate, Tinnevelly. *Died, 2d June 1840, at Satoor.*

SUPPLEMENTARY LIST

OF

MADRAS CIVIL SERVANTS.

AGNEW, GEORGE VANS.—1852 : Writer and Student at the College. 1854 : Assistant to Collector and Magistrate, Tanjore. 1856 : Acting Assistant to Collector and Magistrate, Trichinopoly ; Acting Special Assistant, afterwards Special Assistant at Tanjore. 1859 : Acting Sub-Judge, Combaconum ; Acting Principal Assistant to Collector and Magistrate, and Agent to the Governor of Fort St. George, in Vizagapatam ; Acting Sub-Collector and Joint Magistrate, Godavari. 1860 : Sub-Collector and Joint Magistrate, Godavari. 1861 : *On medical leave to Europe for 15 months ;* Sub-Collector and Joint Magistrate, Tinnevelly. 1863 : Sub-Collector and Joint Magistrate, Madura. 1864 : *On special leave to Europe for 5 months.* 1866 : Acting Collector and Magistrate, Trichinopoly ; Sub-Collector and Joint Magistrate, Tanjore. 1867 : Acting Collector and Magistrate, Trichinopoly. 1868 : Acting Collector and Magistrate, North Arcot ; also of Cuddapah. 1869 : Collector and Magistrate, Cuddapah. 1870 : Collector and Magistrate, Nellore. 1876 : *On furlough to Europe.* 1877 : *Retired from service, 15th January. (Annuitant on the Fund.)*

ALDERSEY, WILLIAM.—1754 : Arrived on the Coromandel Coast 8th June as Writer and under the Secretary to the Secret Committee at Fort St. George. 1759 : Factor ; and Secretary in the Secret Department and Translator. 1761 : Secretary, Solicitor, and Clerk of Appeals. 1762 : Junior Merchant, and Secretary, Solicitor, and Clerk of Appeals. 1766 : *Services transferred to Bengal.* 1767 : Senior Merchant, appointed Eighth Member of Council of the Governor of Fort William in Bengal : Import Warehouse-keeper and Buxey. (*See Bengal Volume.*)

AMES, CHARLES HERBERT.—1851 : Writer and Student at the

L

College. 1854: Assistant to Collector and Magistrate, Tinnevelly. 1856: *On medical leave for* 15 *months.* 1857: Assistant and Acting Head Assistant to Collector and Magistrate, Tinnevelly. 1858: Acting Sub-Collector and Magistrate, and Head Assistant to the Collector and Magistrate, Tinnevelly. 1859: Acting Sub-Collector and Magistrate, Canara, afterwards at Madura. 1860: Sub-Collector and Magistrate, Madura. 1862: *On furlough to Europe.* 1864: *Retired from service, 8th February.* (*Invalid Annuitant.*) 1878: *Died, 19th January, at Henley-on-Thames.*

ARBUTHNOTT, Hon. David.—1841: Writer. 1843: Assistant to Collector and Magistrate, Bellary. 1845: Acting Head Assistant to Collector and Magistrate, Bellary. 1847: Head Assistant to Collector and Magistrate, Bellary. 1848: Acting Sub-Collector and Joint Magistrate, Bellary. 1849: Acting Sub-Judge, Bellary. 1854: Sub-Collector and Joint Magistrate, Bellary. 1858: Collector and Magistrate of the District of Kurnool. 1860: *On medical leave to Europe for* 24 *months.* 1862: Assumed Charge of Office of Collector and Magistrate, Kurnool; afterwards Collector and Magistrate, Salem. 1867: Acting Collector and Magistrate, afterwards Collector and Magistrate, Madura. 1869: *On furlough to Europe for* 18 *months.* 1871: Acting Collector and Magistrate of Sea Customs and of the Madras District, and Acting Protector of Emigrants, Madras. 1873: Acting Collector and Magistrate, and Agent, Tanjore. 1874: Acting Third Member of the Revenue Board. 1875: Acting Second Member, afterwards Acting First Member of the Revenue Board. 1878: *Retired from service, 1st January.* (*Annuitant on the Fund.*)

ARBUTHNOT, Sir Alexander John, K.C.S.I., C.I.E.—1842: Writer. 1843: Acting Assistant to the Collector and Magistrate, Chingleput. 1844: Assistant to the Principal Collector and Magistrate, Nellore. 1845: Head Assistant to the Register to the Court of Sudder and Foujdarry Adawlut. 1846: Officiating Secretary to the College Board and University, Madras. 1848: Acting Head Assistant to Collector and Magistrate, Cuddapah; afterwards Acting Malayum Translator to Government. 1849: Malayum Translator to Government. 1851: Acting Secretary, afterwards Secretary to the College and University Boards, Madras. 1852: Acting, afterwards Deputy Register to the Court of Sudder and Foujdarry Adawlut. 1853: Acting Register to the aforesaid Court. 1854: Member of, and Secretary to, the Board of Examiners. 1855: Director of Public Instruction. 1861: Commissioner for the Uncovenanted Civil Service Examination. 1862 : Acting Chief Secretary, afterwards Chief Secretary to Government; Fellow of the University of Madras. 1864 : Additional Member of Council of Fort St. George, for the purpose of making Law and Regulations. 1867 : Member of Council. 1872 : *On furlough to Europe for 2 years.* 1873 : *Made a K.C.S.I. 24th January.* 1874 : *Retired from service, 29th October.* 1878 : *Made a Companion of the Order of the Indian Empire 1st January.* (*Annuitant on the Fund.*)

ARBUTHNOT, WILLIAM HENRY.—1855 : Writer and Student at the College. 1856 : Assistant to Collector and Magistrate, North Arcot; afterwards Acting Head Assistant at Tinnevelly. 1857 : Acting Second Assistant to the Accountant-General, Madras. 1858 : Officiating Second Assistant to the Accountant-General; *On medical leave to Europe for 3 years and 9 months.* 1862 : *On medical leave to Europe, forfeiting appointment.* 1865 : *Retired from service, 16th February.* (*Invalid Annuitant.*)

ARBUTHNOTT, JOHN ROBERT.—1857 : Writer and Student at the College. 1859 : Assistant to Collector and Magistrate, Kurnool. 1861 : Officiating Head Assistant, Kurnool. 1862 : Head Assistant at Kurnool. 1863 : Acting Civil and Sessions Judge, Nundyal. 1865 : *On furlough to Europe for 16 months.* 1866 : Acting Sub-Collector, Malabar; also Head Assistant Collector, Tinnevelly, Sub-Collector, Bellary, and Sub-Collector, Madura. 1868 : Acting Collector and Magistrate, Madura; also in South Arcot. 1869 : Acting Collector and Magistrate, Madura. 1870 : Acting Collector and Magistrate, Tinnevelly. 1871 : *On furlough to Europe for 12 months.* 1872 : *Died, 30th April, in England.*

BALLARD, GEORGE ALEXANDER. — 1845 : Writer. 1847 : Assistant to Collector and Magistrate, Tinnevelly. 1851 : Acting Head Assistant to Collector and Magistrate, Tinnevelly. 1853 : In the same capacity at Madura; afterwards Special Assistant to Collector and Magistrate, Masulipatam. 1854 : Acting Principal Assistant to Collector and Magistrate, and Agent to the Governor of Fort St. George, in Vizagapatam. 1855 : Head Assistant to Collector and Magistrate, Madura; Acting Sub-Collector and Joint Magistrate, Masulipatam; Sub-Collector and Joint Magistrate, Madura; *On furlough to Europe for 3 years.* 1857 : Acting Sub-Judge, Chittoor. 1858 : Additional Sub-Collector and Joint Magistrate, Bellary; Deputy Director of Revenue Settlement. 1860 : *On furlough for the un-*

expired portion of leave granted in 1855, *with* 3 *months in addition for time occupied on his passage to and from India.* 1861 : *Returned to Madras.* 1862 : Acting Collector and Magistrate, Tanjore ; Sub-Collector of Madura ; Collector and Magistrate, Malabar. 1869 : At first Acting, afterwards Resident in Travancore and Cochin. 1870 : *On furlough to Europe for* 14 *months.* 1871 : Resumed Office as Resident in Travancore and Cochin. 1875 : Acting Second Member, afterwards Acting Third Member, of the Revenue Board. 1876 : Third Member of the Revenue Board ; *On furlough to Europe for* 1 *year and* 4 *months.* 1877 : Acting Second Member of the Revenue Board. 1878 : First Member of the Revenue Board ; Services placed at the Disposal of the Government of India on Appointment as Member of the Famine Commission. 1879 : *Retired from service,* 28*th January.* (*Annuitant on the Fund.*)

BANBURY, George.—1848 : Writer. 1849 : Student at the College. 1850 : Assistant to Collector and Magistrate, South Arcot. 1853 : Acting Head Assistant, South Arcot. 1855 : Head Assistant, South Arcot. 1856 : Acting Additional Sub-Collector and Joint Magistrate, North Arcot. 1858 : Deputy Director of Revenue Settlement. 1859 : *On furlough to Europe for* 3 *years and* 4 *months.* 1862 : Acting Collector and Magistrate, Kurnool. 1863 : Acting Sub-Collector and Joint Magistrate, North Arcot ; Acting Civil and Sessions Judge, Cuddalore ; Sub-Collector and Joint Magistrate, afterwards Acting Collector and Magistrate, Madras District. 1864 : Acting Collector and Magistrate, North . Arcot. 1865 : Acting Collector and Magistrate, Tinnevelly, afterwards of South Arcot ; Acting Civil and Sessions Judge, Rajahmundry ; Acting Sub-Secretary to the Revenue Board. 1866 : Collector and Magistrate, Trichinopoly, afterwards Acting at Tanjore. 1867 : *On medical leave for* 19 *months.* 1870 : Acting Director of Revenue Settlement. 1872 : Director of Revenue Settlement. 1873 : Second Member of the Revenue Board. 1874 : *On furlough to Europe for* 15 *months.* 1876 : *Retired from service,* 21*st March.* (*Annuitant on the Fund.*)

BARLOW, Richard Wellesley.—1855 : Writer and Student at the College. 1857 : Assistant to Collector and Magistrate, Guntoor. 1858 : Assistant at South Arcot ; *On medical leave to Europe for* 21 *months.* 1860 : Assistant to Collector and Magistrate, Nellore. 1861 : Officiating Head Assistant, Nellore ; Acting Head Assistant, North Arcot. 1862 : Head Assistant, North Arcot ; Acting Sub-Collector there, with full Powers of a Magistrate.

1864 : Justice of the Peace ; Acting Sub-Collector, North Arcot ; *On special leave for 6 months;* Acting Sub-Collector and Joint Magistrate, North Arcot. 1865 : Sub-Collector and Joint Magistrate, North Arcot. 1866 : In Charge of the Collector's Office, North Arcot. 1867 : Sub-Collector, North Arcot ; *On medical leave to Europe for 2 years and 6 months.* 1869 : Acting Judge of Small Cause Court, Tellicherry. 1870 : Acting Civil and Sessions Judge, Chingleput. 1871 : Acting Collector and Magistrate, Chingleput. 1872 : Collector and Magistrate, Kistna. 1873 : Collector and Magistrate, Godavari; also at Chingleput. 1875 : *On furlough to Europe for 12 months.* 1876 : Collector, Chingleput. 1878 : Acting Commissioner, Nilgiri Hills ; Government Member of the Lawrence Asylum Committee ; appointed Commissioner, Nilgiri Hills. 1880 : Acting Third Member of the Revenue Board ; Acting Collector of Sea Customs, and Protector of Emigrants, Madras. 1881 : Acting Third Member of the Revenue Board, and in Charge of the Settlement Department; Acting Collector of Sea Customs, and Protector of Emigrants, Madras ; Commissioner, Nilgiri Hills. 1882 : Collector and Magistrate, and Additional Sessions Judge of the Nilgiri District. 1883 : Collector of Sea Customs and Protector of Emigrants, Madras ; *On furlough to Europe for 4 months, and 6 weeks in India.* 1884 : Resumed Collector of Sea Customs, Madras District; Appointed Acting Resident in Travancore and Cochin ; Returned to Madras as Collector of Sea Customs, and Protector of Emigrants.

BIRD, EDWARD WHELER.—1842 : Writer. 1843 : Assistant to the Collector and Magistrate, Masulipatam. 1845 : Acting Head Assistant to the Collector and Magistrate, Masulipatam. 1846 : *Proceeded to Europe.* 1847 : Assistant to Collector and Magistrate, Chingleput ; afterwards Officiating Government Agent at Chepauk, and Paymaster of Carnatic Stipends. 1848 : Acting Head Assistant to the Register to the Court of Sudder and Foujdarry Adawlut ; afterwards Assistant to Collector and Magistrate, and Agent to the Governor of Fort St. George, Vizagapatam. 1850 : Acting Head Assistant to Collector and Magistrate, Nellore. 1851 : Special Assistant to Collector and Magistrate, Masulipatam. 1853 : Acting Assistant Judge, afterwards Assistant Judge, Combaconum. 1856 : Acting Civil and Sessions Judge, Combaconum. 1857 : Acting Sub-Judge, Combaconum. 1858 : Sub-Judge, Octacamund. 1859 : Acting Civil and Sessions Judge, Coimbatore. 1861 : Officiating, afterwards Acting Civil and Sessions Judge, Negapatam ;

Civil and Sessions Judge, Tanjore. 1866 : *On medical leave to Europe.* 1868 : *Retired from service, 28th September.* (*Annuitant on the Fund.*)

BLAIR, JOHN HUNTER.—1845 : Writer. 1846 : Under the Principal Collector of Coimbatore. 1847 : Assistant to Collector and Magistrate, Madura. 1848 : In the same capacity at Tinnevelly. 1851 : Acting Head Assistant to Collector and Magistrate, Tinnevelly. 1852 : *Absent in England.* 1853 : Assistant to Collector and Magistrate, Rajahmundry ; Acting Assistant, afterwards Assistant to Collector and Magistrate, and Agent to the Governor of Fort St. George, in Vizagapatam. 1855 : Acting Principal Assistant, and Agent to the Governor, in Vizagapatam. 1856 : Acting Sub-Collector and Joint Magistrate, Masulipatam ; Acting Sub-Judge, afterwards Sub-Judge, Rajahmundry. 1859 : Acting Civil and Sessions Judge, Masulipatam ; *Proceeded on furlough to Europe for* 3 *years.* 1863 : Acting Civil and Sessions Judge, Cuddalore; afterwards at Tinnevelly; Sub-Collector and Joint Magistate, Tinnevelly, but Acting Collector of Sea Customs, Madras. 1864 : Collector of Sea Customs, Madras. 1865 : Member of the Income-Tax Commission. 1866 : On Special Duty at Calcutta. 1868 : Protector of Emigrants, Madras. 1869 : On Special Duty at Bangalore. 1870 : Collector of the Town of Madras. 1871 : Acting Third Member of the Revenue Board ; *On furlough to Europe for* 2 *years.* 1873 : Resumed Acting Third Member of the Revenue Board. 1876 : *On furlough to Europe for* 6 *months.* 1877 : *Retired from service, 14th March.* (*Annuitant on the Fund.*) *Died, 27th March* 1885, *in England.*

BLAIR, WILLIAM THOMAS.—1848 : Writer. 1849 : Assistant to Collector and Magistrate, North Arcot. 1850 : Acting Head Assistant, North Arcot. 1851 : Acting Head Assistant to Collector and Magistrate, Cuddapah. 1852 : Acting Sub-Judge, Cuddapah. 1853 : Head Assistant to Collector and Magistrate, Cuddapah. 1856 : Acting Sub-Judge, Cuddapah. 1857 : Sub-Collector and Magistrate, Cuddapah. 1858 : *On medical leave to Europe for* 24 *months.* 1860 : Sub-Collector and Joint Magistrate, North Arcot. 1862 : Acting Inam Commissioner. 1863 : Acting Civil and Sessions Judge, Chittoor ; Acting Civil and Sessions Judge, Rajahmundry, but continuing to Act as Inam Commissioner at Madras. 1865 : Acting Civil and Sessions Judge, Coimbatore. 1866 : Civil and Sessions Judge, Cuddapah, but still Acting as Inam Commissioner ; Civil and Sessions Judge, Chingleput, and continuing to

Act as Inam Commissioner. 1868 : Civil and Sessions Judge, Berhampore, and Inam Commissioner; Member of the Committee for the Examination of Assistants. 1869 : Civil and Sessions Judge, Vizagapatam ; Acting Collector, Madras District. 1870 : Secretary to the Revenue Board, with Previous Office ; Acting Collector and Magistrate, Chingleput. 1871 : *On furlough to Europe for 2 years.* 1872 : Civil and Sessions Judge, Mangalore. 1873 : *Retired from service, 15th January, in England. (Annuitant on the Fund.)* 1877 : *Died, 21st December, in England.*

BOSWELL, JOHN ALEXANDER CORRIE.—1855 : Writer and Student at the College. 1856 : Assistant, afterwards Acting Head Assistant, to Collector and Magistrate, Coimbatore. 1858 : Assistant to Collector and Magistrate, and Agent to the Governor of Fort St. George, in Vizagapatam ; Acting Head Assistant to Collector and Magistrate, Coimbatore. 1859 : Head Assistant to Collector and Magistrate, Salem ; officiating Subordinate Judge, Combaconum. 1860 : *On medical leave to Europe for 3 years and 9 months.* 1863 : Acting Sub-Collector and Joint Magistrate, Madras. 1864 : Acting Principal Assistant to Collector and Magistrate, and Agent to the Governor, in Vizagapatam ; also Head Assistant at Nellore. 1865 : Principal Assistant at Vizagapatam ; Sub - Collector and Joint Magistrate, Nellore. 1867 : Acting Collector and Magistrate, Nellore. 1868 : Acting Collector and Magistrate, South Canara. 1869 : In the same capacity at Kistna. 1870 : Collector and Magistrate, Kistna. 1871 : *On furlough to Europe for 12 months.* 1872 : *Died, 6th January, in England.*

BREEKS, JAMES WILLIAMSON.—1849 : Writer and Student at the College. 1852 : Assistant to Collector and Magistrate, Bellary. 1855 : Acting Third Assistant to the Accountant-General, Madras. 1856 : Second Assistant, afterwards Acting First Assistant to the Accountant-General. 1857 : Canarese Translator to Government. 1858 : Civil Auditor for the Punjab Government. 1859 : Officiating Sub-Judge, Madura ; Sub-Collector and Joint Magistrate, afterwards Acting Subordinate Judge, Bellary ; *Proceeded to Europe on furlough for 3 years.* 1861 : Private Secretary to the Governor of Fort St. George. 1864 : Judge of Small Cause Court, Combaconum, continuing to Act as Private Secretary to the Governor ; *On medical leave to Europe for 3 years.* 1868 : Acting Civil and Sessions Judge, Chittoor ; Acting Commissioner, afterwards Commissioner, Nilgiri Hills. 1872 : *Died, 6th June, in India.*

CADELL, WILLIAM MOLLE.—1840 : Writer. 1841 : Assistant

to the Principal Collector and Magistrate, Canara. 1842 : Acting Register of the Zillah Court of Canara; afterwards Assistant to the Collector and Magistrate, Chingleput. 1845 : Assistant, afterwards Acting Head Assistant to the Collector and Magistrate, Chingleput. 1846 : Acting Head Assistant to the Collector and Magistrate, Masulipatam; afterwards Head Assistant to Collector and Magistrate, Trichinopoly. 1847 : *On furlough to Europe.* 1850 : *Returned to Madras;* Assistant to Collector and Magistrate, Nellore; and Acting Head Assistant of that District; *Proceeded to Europe.* 1851 : *Without employ on return.* 1852 : Acting Sub-Judge, Combaconum. 1853 : Head Assistant to Collector and Magistrate, afterwards Acting Sub-Collector and Joint Magistrate, then Sub-Collector and Joint Magistrate, Tanjore. 1858 : Collector and Magistrate, Tanjore. 1862 : *On medical leave for* 15 *months.* 1865 : Collector and Magistrate, South Canara. 1867 : Acting Civil and Sessions Judge, Cuddapah; afterwards at Trichinopoly. 1870 : Acting Collector and Magistrate, Trichinopoly; Civil and Sessions Judge, Tellicherry, continuing to Act as before; Acting Collector and Magistrate and Political Agent at Tanjore. 1872 : Civil and Sessions Judge, Nellore, but continuing to Act as before at Tanjore; also Civil and Sessions Judge, Madura, continuing to Act at Tanjore. 1873 : *Retired from service,* 31*st March.* (*Annuitant on the Fund.*)

CARMICHAEL, DAVID FREEMANTLE (SMITH).—1851 : Writer and Student at the College; Assistant to Collector and Magistrate, North Arcot. 1852 : Justice of the Peace. 1854 : Acting Head Assistant and Register to the Court of Sudder and Foujdarry Adawlut. 1855 : Head Assistant and Register to the aforesaid Court; *On medical leave to Europe for* 20 *months.* 1856 : Deputy Secretary to Government in Chief Secretary's Departments, and Secretary to the Board of Examiners. 1859 : Private Secretary to Sir C. E. Trevelyan, K.C.B., Governor of Fort St. George. 1860 : *On medical leave to Europe for* 17 *months.* 1861 : Acting Sub-Judge, Chicacole; Principal Assistant to Collector and Magistrate, and Agent to the Governor of Fort St. George, in Ganjam. 1862 : Acting Collector and Magistrate, and Agent to the Governor, in Vizagapatam. 1863 : Collector and Magistrate, and Agent, Vizagapatam. 1867 : Acting, afterwards Collector and Magistrate, and Agent to the Governor, Ganjam. 1869 : Acting Judge of the High Court of Judicature; *On furlough to Europe for* 23 *months.* 1871 : Acting Secretary to Government, Revenue Department;

Acting Third Member of the Revenue Board; President of the Committee for Examination of Assistants; Inam Commissioner. 1872: Acting Secretary to Government, Revenue Department; Acting Second Member of the Revenue Board; on Special Duty as President of the Committee inquiring into the Action of Officials during the Cyclone; Acting Third Member, afterwards Second Member, and again Third Member of the Revenue Board: Assistant Secretary, afterwards Secretary, to Government, Revenue Department. 1873: *On furlough to Europe for 8 months;* resumed Secretary to Government, Revenue Department. 1874: Acting Chief Secretary to Government; additional Member of Council for making Laws and Regulations. 1876: On special duty with Government at the Imperial Assemblage at Delhi. 1877: Chief Secretary to Government. 1878: At first Temporary, afterwards Ordinary Member of Council, *took his seat 10th December.* 1883: Vacated Seat in Council; *On furlough to Europe for* 18 *months.*

CARR-GOMM, FRANCIS CULLING (*Barrister-at-Law*).—1855: Writer and Student at the College. 1857: Assistant to Collector and Magistrate, Salem. 1858: Acting Head Assistant at Salem. 1859: Acting Head Assistant, afterwards Head Assistant to Collector and Magistrate, Coimbatore; officiating Subordinate Judge, Salem. 1860: Acting Sub-Collector and Joint Magistrate, Salem. 1861: Officiating Sub-Collector and Joint Magistrate, Coimbatore. 1865: Judge of Small Cause Court, Cuddalore. 1866: *On furlough to Europe for* 3 *years and* 3 *months.* 1870: Acting Civil and Sessions Judge, Calicut; Acting Civil and Sessions Judge, Vizagapatam. 1871: Acting Collector and Magistrate, and Agent to the Governor, Ganjam; Acting Civil and Sessions Judge, Tinnevelly. 1872: District and Sessions Judge, Tinnevelly. 1874: *On special leave to Europe for* 6 *months;* Resumed his Previous Duties on Return to Madras. 1878: *On furlough to Europe for* 2 *years and* 7 *months. (Took the name of Gomm on marriage.)* 1880: District and Sessions Judge, Coimbatore. 1882: *Retired from the service* 10*th June. (Annuitant on the Fund.)*

CHAMIER, CHARLES FREDERIC. — 1843: Writer. 1844: Assistant to the Principal Collector and Magistrate, Coimbatore. 1847: Acting Head Assistant to the Register to the Court of Sudder and Foujdarry Adawlut, and Acting Secretary to the Madras University and to the College Board; afterwards Acting Head Assistant to Collector and Magistrate, Trichinopoly. 1850: Acting Head Assistant to Collector and Magistrate, Canara.   1852 : Head Assistant to Collector and Magistrate, Canara ; afterwards Acting Sub-Judge, Mangalore.   1855 : Officiating Special Assistant to the Collector, Madras; afterwards Deputy Register to the Court of Sudder and Foujdarry Adawlut, and Tamil Translator to Government.   1857 : Acting Register to the Court of Sudder and Foujdarry Adawlut.   1859 : Register to the High Court of Judicature, Appellate side.   1864 : *On medical leave to Europe for 16 months.* 1865 : Civil and Sessions Judge, Salem.   1869 : *Died, 20th April, in India.*

CHASE, MORGAN CHARLES.—1847 : Writer.   1848 : Assistant to Collector and Magistrate, Canara.   1854 : Acting Head Assistant to Collector and Magistrate, Canara ; afterwards Head Assistant at Bellary.   1856 : Acting Sub-Judge, Cuddapah; afterwards at Chittoor; also Sub-Collector and Joint Magistrate, Masulipatam. 1857 : Assistant to Collector and Magistrate, and Agent to the Governor of Fort St. George, in Vizagapatam.   1858 : Senior Assistant to Collector and Magistrate, and Agent to the Governor in Ganjam ; Acting Sub-Collector and Joint Magistrate, Masulipatam ; *Proceeded on furlough to Europe for 12 months.*   1863 : *Retired from service, 5th January, in England. (Annuitant on the Fund.)*   1874 : *Died, 21st December, in England.*

CHASE, THOMAS ALEXANDER NICHOLLS.—1850 : Writer and Student at the College.   1851 : Assistant to Collector and Magistrate, Masulipatam.   1855 : Acting Head Assistant at Masulipatam ; afterwards Head Assistant to Collector and Magistrate, Rajahmundry ; then Head Assistant at Masulipatam.   1859 : Acting Sub-Collector and Magistrate, Masulipatam ; afterwards Head Assistant and Acting Sub-Collector and Magistrate, Kistna.   1860 : *On furlough to Europe for 2 years.*   1862 : Acting Sub-Collector and Joint Magistrate, Godavari.   1863 : Sub-Collector and Joint Magistrate, Kistna, but continuing to Act as before ; Acting Civil and Sessions Judge, Rajahmundry.   1865 : Sub-Collector and Joint Magistrate, Godavari ; Acting Collector and Magistrate, Kistna.   1866 : Acting Civil and Sessions Judge, Cuddapah ; Acting Collector and Magistrate, Kistna, afterwards at Nellore, then at Kurnool.   1867 : Collector and Magistrate, Kurnool. 1873 : *On furlough to Europe for 2 years.*   1875 : *Retired from service, 8th April. (Annuitant on the Fund.)*

CHILD, FREDERICK SAMUEL.—1844 : Writer.   1846 : Assistant to Collector and Magistrate, South Arcot.   1847 : Assistant to

Collector and Magistrate, Tinnevelly. 1849 : Assistant to Collector and Magistrate, Nellore ; afterwards at Tinnevelly. 1851 : Acting Head Assistant, afterwards Head Assistant, to Collector and Magistrate, Tinnevelly. 1855 : Acting Sub-Judge, Madura ; afterwards Sub-Collector and Joint Magistrate, Madura. 1855 : *On furlough to Europe.* 1857 : Resumed Acting Sub-Judge at Madura. 1858 : Sub-Collector and Joint Magistrate, Malabar. 1859 : *On furlough to Europe for the unexpired portion of his leave obtained in* 1855 ; *Granted* 12 *months' extension on medical certificate in* 1859 *and* 1861. 1861 : *Returned to Madras,* 25*th October.* 1862 : Acting Sub - Collector and Joint Magistrate, afterwards Sub-Collector, South Arcot; Acting Civil and Sessions Judge, afterwards Civil Judge, Guntoor ; Civil and Sessions Judge, Cuddapah. 1865 : Civil and Sessions Judge, Tinnevelly. 1867 : *On medical leave for* 4 *months.* 1869 : *On furlough to Europe for* 12 *months.* 1871 : *Retired from service,* 22*d July.* (*Annuitant on the Fund.*) 1873 : *Died,* 1*st October, in England.*

COCKERELL, JOHN RENNIE.—1850 : Writer and Student at the College. 1852 : Assistant to Collector and Magistrate, Madura. 1855 : Acting Head Assistant, afterwards Head Assistant at Madura. 1856 : Acting Sub-Judge, Madura ; Acting Sub-Collector and Joint Magistrate, Madura. 1859 : Acting Sub-Judge, Combaconum ; Sub-Collector and Joint Magistrate, Tinnevelly. 1860 : Acting Sub-Collector and Joint Magistrate, South Arcot. 1861 : Officiating Collector and Magistrate, South Arcot ; *On furlough for* 3 *years.* 1865 : Acting Sub-Collector and Joint Magistrate, Kistna ; Acting Collector of Sea Customs, Madras ; Acting Collector and Magistrate, Cuddapah ; Acting Sub-Collector and Joint Magistrate, Madras. 1866 : Sub-Collector and Joint Magistrate, afterwards Acting Collector and Magistrate, Madras. 1867 : Sub-Secretary, afterwards Acting Secretary of the Revenue Board ; Civil and Sessions Judge, Nellore. 1872 : Commissioner, Nilgiri Hills. 1878 : *Retired from service,* 30*th September.* (*Annuitant on the Fund.*)

COLLETT, CHARLES.—1845 : Writer. 1846 : Assistant to the Collector and Magistrate, Nellore. 1847 : Assistant to Collector and Magistrate, Malabar. 1851 : Acting Head Assistant to Collector and Magistrate, Malabar. 1855 : Acting Sub-Judge, Calicut ; afterwards Sub-Collector and Joint Magistrate, Malabar. 1856 : Acting Deputy Collector of Sea Customs, Madras ; *Proceeded to Europe on furlough.* 1857 : Resumed Acting Deputy Collectorship of Sea

Customs, Madras; afterwards Additional Sub-Collector and Joint Magistrate, Bellary. 1858: Sub-Collector and Joint Magistrate, Bellary. 1859: *On furlough to Europe for the unexpired portion of his leave granted in* 1856. 1861: *Permitted extension of 2 months and 6 days on account of time occupied on his passage to and from India;* Officiating Collector of Sea Customs, Madras; afterwards Member of Central Committee at Madras for the London Exhibition of 1862; also Commissioner for the Assessment of Income-Tax; and Sub-Judge, Calicut. 1862: Acting Civil and Sessions Judge, Chittoor; Judge of the Small Cause Court, Cuddalore. 1863: Acting Civil and Sessions Judge, Nundyal; Civil and Sessions Judge, Vizagapatam. 1866: Judge of the High Court of Judicature, Madras. 1871: *Retired from service,* 30th *July.* (*Annuitant on the Fund.*)

DALYELL, ROBERT ANSTRUTHER, C.S.I.—1850: Writer and Student at the College. 1853: Assistant to Collector and Magistrate, Salem. 1855: *On medical leave to Europe for* 39 *months.* 1859: Assistant Collector and Magistrate, South Arcot; Senior Assistant to Collector and Magistrate, and Agent to the Governor of Fort St. George, in Vizagapatam; Acting Sub-Collector, South Arcot. 1860: Principal Assistant to Collector and Magistrate, and Agent to the Governor, in Vizagapatam; to Act as Sub-Collector, South Arcot; Acting Subordinate Judge at Chicacole. 1861: Officiating Sub-Secretary, afterwards Sub-Secretary to the Revenue Board; Commissioner for the Assessment of Income-Tax. 1862: *On special leave for* 6 *months.* 1864: Member of the Income-Tax Commission. 1865: Acting Secretary to the Revenue Board; Officiating President of the Income-Tax Commission; Acting Secretary to the Board of Examiners. 1866: Secretary to the Board of Examiners; Acting Secretary to the Revenue Board; Acting Inam Commissioner; Acting Collector of Sea Customs, Madras. 1867: Secretary, Board of Revenue; and Acting Collector of Sea Customs. 1868: Acting Secretary to Government, Revenue Department. 1870: Collector and Magistrate, Madras District, as well as Secretary to Government; Collector and Magistrate, Chingleput; *On furlough to Europe for* 12 *months.* 1872: Acting Third Member of the Revenue Board; On Special Duty in Mysore. 1873: Additional Member of the Governor-General's Council for Making Laws and Regulations; Acting Secretary to Government, Revenue Department; Acting Chief Secretary to Government; Third Member of the Revenue

Board. 1875: Officiating Chief Commissioner of Mysore and Coorg. 1876: Second Member of the Revenue Board. 1877: *Proceeded on furlough to Europe ;* appointed Member of Council of the Secretary of State for India, and took his seat 6th November, with permission to be considered still in the service of the Madras Government. 1879: *Retired from the service, 12th March ; made a C.S.I., 29th July* 1879. (*Annuitant on the Fund.*)

DAVIDSON, ROBERT, C.S.I.—1852: Writer and Student at the College. 1853: Assistant to Collector and Magistrate, Salem. 1854: Acting Assistant, afterwards Assistant, to Collector and Magistrate, and Agent to the Governor of Fort St. George, in Ganjam. 1856: Acting Principal Assistant, and Agent to the Governor, in Ganjam. 1857: *On medical leave to Europe for* 21 *months.* 1858: Head Assistant to Collector and Magistrate, Malabar. 1859: Acting Sub-Judge, Rajahmundry; Head Assistant to Collector and Magistrate, Trichinopoly; afterwards Head Assistant at Malabar; Acting Principal Assistant to Collector and Magistrate, and Agent to the Governor of Fort St. George, in Vizagapatam. 1860: Officiating Collector and Magistrate, and Agent to the Governor, Ganjam; Subordinate Judge, Cuddapah. 1861: Acting Civil and Sessions Judge, Cuddapah. 1862: Sub-Judge, Cuddapah; Judge of the Court of Small Causes, Chittoor; Acting Civil and Sessions Judge, Madura; Acting Judge of Small Cause Court, Madura. 1863: Judge of Small Cause Court, Chittoor; Acting Civil and Sessions Judge, Nundyal. 1864: Justice of the Peace; Acting Civil and Sessions Judge, Bellary. 1866: Judge of Small Cause Court, Chittoor; Acting Civil and Sessions Judge, Tanjore. 1867: Civil and Sessions Judge, Trichinopoly. 1868: *On furlough to Europe for* 15 *months.* 1869: Resumed Civil and Sessions Judge, Trichinopoly. 1870: Acting Commissioner, Nilgiri Hills. 1873: *On special leave to Europe for 6 months.* 1874: District and Sessions Judge, Cuddapah; Acting Collector and Magistrate, and Agent to the Governor, in Ganjam. 1876: District and Sessions Judge, Chingleput; Acting Collector and Magistrate, Kurnool. 1878: *On furlough to Europe for 22 months ;* appointed while on furlough Third Member of the Revenue Board; *Made a C.S.I. 25th May,* 1878. 1880: Chief Secretary to Government; Additional Member of the Legislative Council. 1881: Provisional Member of Council; Chief Secretary to Government. 1882: Acting First Member of the Revenue Board; In Charge of the Settlement Department; First Member of the Revenue Board; In Charge of the Inam Depart-

ment.   1883 : *On furlough to Europe for 9 months and 12 days.*
1884 : *Retired from service 1st July.*   (*Annuitant on the Fund.*)

DYKES, James William Ballantyne.—1842 : Writer.   1844 :
Assistant to the Principal Collector and Magistrate, Salem.   1847 :
Acting Head Assistant to the Collector and Magistrate, Salem.
1849 : Head Assistant to Collector and Magistrate, Salem.   1851 :
Acting Sub-Judge of the Zillah of Madura.   1852 : Acting Sub-
Judge of the Zillah of Chittoor ; *On furlough to Europe.*   1857 :
Acting, afterwards Sub-Collector and Joint Magistrate, Salem.
1858 : On Special Duty in Rajahmundry and Masulipatam ; Act-
ing Sub-Collector and Joint Magistrate, Cuddapah ; afterwards
Sub-Collector and Joint Magistrate, Rajahmundry.   1859 : Acting
Collector and Magistrate, Guntoor ; afterwards at Nellore ; then
Sub-Collector and Joint Magistrate, Godavari.   1860 : Collector
and Magistrate, Nellore.   1867 : *On medical leave to Europe for
18 months.*   1869 : *Resigned the service, 4th September, in India.*
(*Annuitant on the Fund.*)

ELLIOT, Edward Frederick.—1854 : Writer and Student at
the College.   1855 : Assistant to Collector and Magistrate, Cudda-
pah ; afterwards at North Arcot.   1856 : Acting Head Assistant
at South Arcot.   1857 : Returned to North Arcot as Acting Head
Assistant.   1859 : Head Assistant to Collector and Magistrate,
North Arcot ; Acting Subordinate Judge, Chittoor ; Officiating Sub-
Collector and Joint Magistrate, Bellary, and at North Arcot.   1860 :
Officiating Sub-Collector and Joint Magistrate, Madras.   1862 :
Sub-Collector of Nellore ; Acting Civil and Sessions Judge, Nel-
lore.   1864 : *On furlough to Europe for 3 years.*   1867 : Sub-
Collector and Joint Magistrate, Kistna ; Acting Civil and Sessions
Judge, Tranquebar.   1868 : Acting Civil and Sessions Judge,
Chittoor.   1869 : Sub-Collector and Joint Magistrate, Tanjore,
with Duties as before ; Civil and Sessions Judge, Salem.   1873 :
Died, 27th October, in India.

ELLIS, Robert Staunton, C.B.—1844 : Writer.   1846 : Under
the Principal Collector, Coimbatore ; afterwards Assistant to Collector and Magistrate, Tanjore.   1848 : *On furlough to Europe.*
1851 : Assistant to the Collector of Land Customs, Madras.   1852 :
Head Assistant to the Register to the Court of Sudder and Foujdarry Adawlut.   1853 : Acting Deputy Register to the aforesaid
Court.   1854 : Deputy Commissioner of the Second Class, Nagpore
Commission.   1858 : *On medical leave to Europe for 21 months.*
1860 : Officiating Collector and Magistrate, Chingleput ; afterwards

Sub-Collector, Madras, and Joint Magistrate, Chingleput; *Made a C.B. 19th May;* Special Commissioner for the Assessment of Income-Tax. 1862 : Acting Superintendent of Stamps ; Acting Deputy Secretary to Government in Chief Secretary's Departments ; Member and Commissioner for the Assessment of Income-Tax ; Services placed temporarily at the Disposal of the Government of India ; Additional Member of Governor-General's Council for Making Laws and Regulations. 1863 : Acting Collector and Magistrate, afterwards Collector and Magistrate, Madras District ; on Special Duty as Member of Governor-General's Council. 1864 : President of the Sanitary Commission. 1865 : *On special leave to Europe for* 12 *months.* 1867 : Chief Secretary to Government. 1869 : Officiating Member of Council. 1872 : Appointed Member of Council. 1873 : *On furlough to Europe for* 12 *months.* 1875 : Member of Council. 1877 : *Retired from service, 12th March; Appointed Member of Council of the Secretary of State for India ; Died,* 9th *October* 1877, *in London.*

FLOYER, CHARLES.—1755 : Arrived on the Coromandel Coast 9th June ; Writer and under the Secretary to the Secret Committee at Fort St. George. 1759 : Commissary to the Troops in the Field. 1760 : Factor, and under the Military Paymaster. 1761 : Resident at Tranquebar ; afterwards under the Import Warehouse-keeper. 1764 : Junior Merchant, and Paymaster at Trichinopoly. 1766 : *Services transferred to Bengal.* 1767 : Senior Merchant ; appointed Tenth Member of Council of the Governor of Fort William in Bengal, and Military Storekeeper. (*See Bengal Volume.*)

FOORD, EDWARD BROMLEY.—1844 : Writer. 1846 : Assistant to Collector and Magistrate, Masulipatam. 1851 : Acting Senior Assistant to Collector and Magistrate, and Agent to the Governor of Fort St. George in Vizagapatam. 1853 : Assistant to Collector and Magistrate, and Agent to the Governor, in Vizagapatam. 1854 : Acting Principal Assistant to Collector and Magistrate, and Agent to the Governor, in Ganjam. 1856 : Sub-Judge, Rajahmundry ; *Proceeded to Europe on furlough.* 1859 : Acting Subordinate Judge, Chittoor. 1860 : Sub-Collector and Joint Magistrate, Bellary. 1861 : Officiating Civil and Sessions Judge, Chingleput ; *On medical leave for* 10 *months.* 1862 : Acting Collector and Magistrate, Bellary ; afterwards at Kistna. 1864 : Acting Civil and Sessions Judge, Chicacole ; Acting Collector and Magistrate, and Agent to the Governor, in Ganjam. 1865 : Civil and Sessions Judge, Bellary ; afterwards at Berhampore. 1868 :

District and Sessions Judge, Chingleput. 1870: *On furlough to Europe for* 12 *months.* 1871: Resumed District and Sessions Judge, Chingleput. 1874: *On furlough to Europe for* 13 *months.* 1876: *Retired from service,* 15*th July. (Annuitant on the Fund.)*

FORBES, Louis.—1850: Writer and Student at the College. 1853: Assistant to Collector and Magistrate, Nellore. 1854: Acting Head Assistant at Nellore. 1855: Acting Head Assistant to the Register to the Court of Sudder and Foujdarry Adawlut. 1856: Acting Assistant Judge, Combaconum; Head Assistant to Collector and Magistrate, Nellore; Acting Sub-Secretary to the Revenue Board. 1858: Acting Additional Sub-Collector, Bellary; afterwards Acting Deputy Collector of Sea Customs, Madras. 1859: Deputy Secretary to Government in Chief-Secretary's Departments, and Secretary to the Board of Examiners. 1861: *On furlough for* 3 *years and* 8 *months.* 1865: Acting Civil and Sessions Judge, Nundyal; Sub-Collector and Joint Magistrate, Bellary. 1866: Judge of the Small Cause Court, Madura; and Civil and Sessions Judge, Nundyal. 1869: *On furlough to Europe for* 12 *months.* 1871: Acting Civil and Sessions Judge, Bellary. 1872: *On special leave to Europe for* 6 *months.* 1873: Resumed Acting Civil and Sessions Judge, Bellary. 1874: District and Sessions Judge, Coimbatore, continuing to Act as before mentioned. 1875: Acting Judge of the High Court of Judicature, Madras. 1877: District and Sessions Judge, Bellary. 1878: Again Acting Judge of the High Court, Madras. 1880: *On furlough to Europe for* 12 *months.* 1881: Additional Member of the Governor-General's Legislative Council. 1882: *Retired from service,* 4*th April. (Annuitant on the Fund.)*

FRASER, James.—1840: Writer. 1841: Assistant to the Collector and Magistrate, Bellary; afterwards at Rajahmundry. 1842: In the same Capacity at Masulipatam. 1843: Acting Assistant to the Collector and Magistrate, and Agent to the Governor of Fort St. George, in Ganjam. 1845: Acting Principal Assistant to the Collector and Magistrate, and Agent to the Governor, in Ganjam. 1854: Sub-Collector and Joint Magistrate, Masulipatam. 1855: Acting Collector and Joint Magistrate, Masulipatam. 1856: Acting Collector and Magistrate, Masulipatam. 1857: *On medical leave to Europe for* 15 *months.* 1859: Acting Collector and Magistrate, Cuddapah; afterwards Sub-Collector and Joint Magistrate, Kistna. 1860: Collector and Magistrate, South Canara. 1861: *On medical leave for* 3 *months.* 1862: Acting Collector and Magistrate, North

Arcot.   1863 : Collector and Magistrate, Trichinopoly, but to continue to act as before.   1864 : Acting Collector and Magistrate, Godavari.   1868 : *On special leave for 6 months.*   1869 : Collector and Magistrate, Godavari.   1871 : *On furlough to Europe for 2 years.*   1873 : *Retired from service, 1st August.   (Annuitant on the Fund.)*

GARSTIN, JOHN HENRY, C.S.I.—1857 : Writer and Student at the College.   1859 : *Leave on private affairs to Calcutta for 6 months;* Assistant to the Collector and Magistrate, Tinnevelly.   1860 : Officiating Head Assistant, afterwards Head Assistant at Tinnevelly.   1863 : Acting Sub-Collector and Joint Magistrate, Malabar ; Justice of the Peace.   1864 : Head Assistant, Malabar ; Acting Sub-Collector there.   1866 : Private Secretary to H. E. Lord Napier.   1871 : Acting Collector of Sea Customs, and Protector of Emigrants, Madras ; Acting Collector and Magistrate, South Arcot ; afterwards Collector and Magistrate, and Special Agent of the French Settlement and Political Agent for Pondicherry.   1872 : *On furlough to Europe for 21 months.*   1874 : Collector, South Arcot.   1875 : On Special Duty at Madras.   1876 : Collector, South Arcot ; Acting Secretary to Government, Revenue Department.   1877 : Temporary Additional Secretary to Government, Revenue Department.   1878 : Collector, District Magistrate, and Agent to the Governor, in Vizagapatam ; *Made a C.S.I. 25th May.*   1879 : Acting Secretary to Government, Revenue Department.   1880 : On Duty in the Government Secretariat ; Collector, Magistrate, and Agent to the Governor, in Vizagapatam.   1881 : Collector, Vizagapatam.   *On furlough to Europe for 20 months.*   1882 : Appointed Third Member of the Revenue Board.   1883 : Acting Second Member, afterwards Acting First Member, of the Revenue Board ; Also intrusted with the Duty of Revising the Establishments of Collectors and Divisional Officers in the Presidency.   1884 : Second Member, afterwards Acting First Member, of the Revenue Board ; Also Magistrate of the First Class with ordinary and special Powers, in Tinnevelly District.

GOLDINGHAM, JOHN DALRYMPLE.—1853 : Writer and Student at the College.   1855 : Assistant to Collector and Magistrate, Salem.   1856 : Acting Head Assistant at Cuddapah ; afterwards at Bellary.   1857 : Head Assistant to Collector and Magistrate, Bellary.   1858 : Officiating Sub-Judge, Bellary.   1859 : Officiating Sub-Judge, Madura.   1861 : Head Assistant Collector and Magistrate, South Canara ; Sub-Judge, Madura ; Officiating Civil and Sessions Judge, Tinnevelly; Officiating Sub-Collector and Joint Magistrate, Madura. 1862 : Sub-Judge, Madura ; *On special leave to Europe for 6 months.* 1862 : Judge of the Court of Small Causes, Madura. 1864: Justice of the Peace; Acting Civil and Sessions Judge, afterwards Judge of the Small Cause Court, Madura. 1865 : *On furlough to Europe for 3 years.* 1868 : Resumed Acting Civil and Sessions Judge, Madura. 1869 : Civil and Sessions Judge, Madura. 1872 : District and Sessions Judge, Nellore. 1874: *On furlough to Europe for 2 years.* 1876 : District Judge, Nellore. 1880: *On furlough to Europe for 8 months ;* Resumed District Judge, Nellore. 1881 : Acting District and Sessions Judge, Bellary. 1882 : District and Sessions Judge, Bellary.

   GRÆME, Henry Munro Showers.—1848 : Writer and Student at the College. 1851: Assistant to Collector and Magistrate, Salem ; afterwards at Cuddapah. 1854: Acting Head Assistant to Collector and Magistrate, Salem. 1856: Acting Sub-Judge, Salem ; Head Assistant to Collector and Magistrate, Trichinopoly. 1857 : Acting Additional Sub-Collector and Joint Magistrate, Canara. 1859 : *On furlough to Europe for 3 years and 9 months.* 1863 : Acting Civil and Sessions Judge, Salem ; Acting Sub-Collector and Joint Magistrate, South Arcot, also at Kistna; Sub-Collector and Joint Magistrate, Tinnevelly. 1864 : *On medical leave to Europe.* 1868 : *Resigned the service, 2d February, in England.* (*Invalid Annuitant.*) 1884 : *Died, 28th August, in England.*

   GRANT, Patrick.—1842 : Writer. 1844 : Assistant to the Collector and Magistrate, Tinnevelly. 1845 : Assistant to Collector and Magistrate, Tanjore. 1846 : Special Assistant to Collector and Magistrate, Tanjore. 1852 : Acting Sub-Collector and Joint Magistrate, Tanjore. 1853 : *Proceeded to Europe.* 1856 : *Without employ.* 1857 : Additional Sub-Collector and Joint Magistrate, South Arcot; afterwards Sub-Collector and Joint Magistrate, Salem. 1858 : Acting Collector and Magistrate, Malabar. 1859 : Collector and Magistrate, Malabar. 1862 : Collector and Magistrate, Coimbatore. 1862 : *Resigned the service, 21st March, in India.* (*Annuitant on the Fund.*)

   HANNYNGTON, John Child.—1857 : Writer and Student at the College. 1859 : *On leave to Bengal for 6 months ;* Assistant to Collector and Magistrate, Trichinopoly. 1861 : Officiating Head Assistant at Malabar ; Justice of the Peace. 1862 : Invested with Full Powers of a Magistrate. 1863 : Special Assistant to Collector and Magistrate, and Acting Head Assistant, Malabar ;

Special Assistant to Collector and Magistrate, Coimbatore. 1866 : Acting Judge of Small Cause Court, Tellicherry. 1867 : Sub-Collector, Bellary ; Acting Collector and Magistrate, Malabar ; Judge of Small Cause Court, Tellichery. 1868 : Acting Civil and Sessions Judge, Tellicherry ; afterwards at Calicut. 1869 : *On furlough to Europe for 2 years.* 1871 : Resumed Judge of Small Cause Court, Tellicherry ; Acting Collector and Magistrate, Malabar ; also at Kistna. 1872 : Acting Civil and Sessions Judge, Guntoor. 1873 : Judge of Small Cause Court, Vellore ; District and Sessions Judge, Guntoor ; afterwards at Salem. 1876 : *On furlough to Europe for 2 years.* 1878 : Acting Resident, Travancore and Cochin. 1879 : District and Sessions Judge, Salem. 1880 : On Special Duty as Arbitrator of Boundary Disputes between Travancore and Cochin. 1881 : Acting Resident, Travancore and Cochin. 1882 : Resident at Travancore and Cochin. 1883 : *On furlough to Europe for* 15 *months.* 1884 : Resumed Resident at Travancore and Cochin.

HATHAWAY, WILLIAM FREDERICK.—1858 : Writer and Student at the College. 1859 : Assistant to Collector and Magistrate, Salem. 1860 : Acting Head Assistant at Salem. 1862 : Head Assistant at Salem. 1864 : Acting Sub-Collector and Joint Magistrate, Madras ; afterwards at North Arcot. 1865 : *On furlough to Europe for* 16 *months.* 1866 : Acting Sub-Collector, North Arcot ; also Head Assistant to Collector and Magistrate, Kurnool. 1867 : Acting Sub-Collector, South Arcot ; Sub-Collector, Tinnevelly ; Sub-Collector and Joint Magistrate, South Arcot. 1868 : Sub-Collector and Joint Magistrate, Tanjore. 1870 : Acting Collector and Magistrate, Tanjore ; *On furlough to Europe for* 18 *months.* 1871 : *Retired from service,* 15*th November.*

HODGSON, WILLIAM.—1840 : Writer. 1841 : Under the Principal Collector of Malabar. 1843 : Assistant to the Principal Collector and Magistrate, Nellore. 1844: *Absent in Europe.* 1848 : Assistant to Collector and Magistrate, Rajahmundry ; *Proceeded to Europe.* 1851 : Assistant to Collector and Magistrate, South Arcot. 1852 : Acting Head Assistant to Collector and Magistrate, South Arcot ; afterwards Head Assistant at Salem. 1853 : Acting Sub-Judge, Salem. 1855 : Acting Sub-Judge, Mangalore ; *Proceeded to Europe.* 1857 : Acting Sub-Judge, Salem. 1859 : Sub-Judge, Bellary ; afterwards at Salem. 1861 : Acting Civil and Sessions Judge, Chittoor ; afterwards at Salem. 1862 : Assistant to Collector and Magistrate, Coimbatore. 1863 :

Acting Civil and Sessions Judge, Tinnevelly.   1864: Sub-Collector
and Joint Magistrate, Nellore ; Acting Sub-Collector and Joint
Magistrate, Tinnevelly.   1865 : Civil and Sessions Judge, Gun-
toor.   1867 : *On medical leave to Europe for* 10 *months.*   1868 :
Civil and Sessions Judge, Cuddapah ; Acting Civil and Sessions
Judge, Cuddalore.   1870 : District and Sessions Judge, South
Arcot.   1872 : *On furlough to Europe for* 2 *years.*   1874 : *Retired
from service,* 19*th February.*   (*Annuitant on the Fund.*)

   HODGSON, Arthur Pemberton.—1844: Writer.   1845 : Per-
mitted to Pursue his Studies under the Collector of Salem.   1847 :
Assistant to Collector and Magistrate, Madura.   1847 : Acting
Head Assistant to Collector and Magistrate, Madura.   1851 :
Head Assistant to Collector and Magistrate, Madura.   1855 :
Acting Sub-Judge, Madura ; *Proceeded to Europe.*   1857: *Without
employ for* 5 *months.*   1858 : Acting Sub-Collector and Joint
Magistrate, afterwards Sub-Collector and Joint Magistrate,
Madura.   1859 : *On medical leave to Europe for* 2 *years.*   1861 :
Sub-Collector and Joint Magistrate, Cuddapah ; Acting Collector
and Magistrate, South Canara.   1862 : Sub-Collector and Joint
Magistrate, Kistna.   1863 : Acting Sub-Collector and Joint
Magistrate, Coimbatore ; *on furlough to Europe.*   1866 : *Resigned
the service,* 16*th February, in England.*   (*Invalid Annuitant.*)

   HOLLOWAY, William, C.S.I. — 1848 : Writer.   1849 :
Student at the College.   1851 : Assistant to Collector and Magis-
trate, Tanjore.   1852 : Acting Head Assistant to Collector and
Magistrate, Tanjore.   1853 : Acting Deputy Register, afterwards
Acting Head Assistant to the Register to the Court of Sudder and
Foujdarry Adawlut.   1854 : Head Assistant to Collector and Magis-
trate, Masulipatam.   1855 : Acting Sub-Judge ; Head Assistant
to Collector and Magistrate, Rajahmundry : afterwards Acting
Sub-Judge, Calicut.   1856 : Head Assistant to Collector and
Magistrate, Trichinopoly ; Special Assistant to Collector and Magis-
trate, Tanjore ; and Assistant to Collector and Magistrate, and
Agent to the Governor of Fort St. George, in Vizagapatam.   1857 :
Sub-Judge, Calicut.   1859 : Secretary to the Commission for
Inquiring into the System of Judicature in the Madras Presidency;
afterwards Acting Civil and Sessions Judge, Tellicherry.   1861 :
Civil and Sessions Judge, Tellicherry.   1863 : Acting Puisne
Judge, afterwards Judge of the High Court of Judicature, Madras.
1868 : *On medical leave to Europe for* 1 *year and* 8 *months.*
1870 : Resumed Judge of the High Court.   1873 : Acting Chief

Justice, Madras. 1875 : *On furlough to Europe ; made a C.S.I.,* 31*st December.* 1877 : *Retired from service, 29th January.* (*Annuitant on the Fund.*)

HOOPER, WILLIAM STANLEY.—1855 : Writer and Student at the College. 1857 : Assistant to Collector and Magistrate, Nellore. 1858 : Acting Head Assistant at Nellore. 1859 : Acting Head Assistant at Tanjore. 1860 : Senior Assistant to Collector and Magistrate, and Agent to the Governor of Fort St. George, in Ganjam ; afterwards Principal Assistant, Ganjam. 1862 : Acting Sub-Collector, Madras. 1863 : *On medical leave to Europe for* 15 *months.* 1864 : Principal Assistant to Collector and Magistrate, and Agent to the Governor of Fort St. George, in Ganjam. 1865 : *Died, 24th February, in India.*

HORSLEY, WILLIAM DOWDESWELL.—1855 : Writer and Student at the College. 1856 : Assistant to Collector and Magistrate, Rajahmundry. 1859 : Assistant at Godavari. 1860 : Acting Head Assistant at Godavari. 1862 : Invested with Full Powers of a Magistrate ; Head Assistant to Collector and Magistrate, Cuddapah, also at Godavari, at Kurnool, and at Madura ; Acting Sub-Collector, afterwards Acting Sub-Collector and Joint Magistrate, Kistna. 1864 : Justice of the Peace ; *On special leave in India for* 4 *months.* 1865 : Acting Sub-Collector, Kistna ; Sub-Collector and Joint Magistrate, Cuddapah. 1866 ; Acting Civil and Sessions Judge, afterwards Sub-Collector, Cuddapah. 1870 : *On furlough in India for* 8 *months.* 1871 : Acting Collector and Magistrate, Cuddapah. 1872 : Collector and Magistrate, Cuddapah. 1876: *On furlough to Europe for* 2 *years.* 1878: Collector at Cuddapah ; Acting Third Member of the Revenue Board. 1879 : Acting Collector, District Magistrate, and Agent to the Governor in Ganjam. 1881 : Acting Collector and Magistrate, Godavari ; Acting Third Member, afterwards Acting Second Member of the Revenue Board. 1882 : Collector and Magistrate, Cuddapah. 1883 : *On furlough to Europe for* 2 *years.* 1884 : *Retired from service,* 31*st December.*

HUDDLESTON, WILLIAM, C.S.I. — 1845 : Writer. 1847 : Assistant to Collector and Magistrate, Canara. 1852 : Acting Head Assistant to Collector and Magistrate, Canara. 1854 : Acting Head Assistant to the Register to the Court of Sudder and Foujdarry Adawlut ; Head Assistant to Collector and Magistrate, Chingleput ; Acting Deputy Register to the Court of Sudder and Foujdarry Adawlut ; Acting Deputy Secretary to Government in the Departments under the Chief Secretary. 1855 : Deputy Secretary to Government under the Chief Secretary; afterwards Secretary to the Board of Examiners. 1856 : *On furlough to Europe.* 1857 : Acting Deputy Secretary to Government in the Revenue and Public Works Departments. 1858 : Acting Deputy Collector of Sea Customs, Madras ; afterwards Sub-Secretary to the Revenue Board. 1860 : Acting Secretary to the Revenue Board. 1861 : Secretary to the Revenue Board. 1865 : Acting Secretary to Government, Revenue Department. 1867 : Secretary to Government, Revenue Department. 1868 : *On furlough to Europe for 23 months.* 1871 : Acting Chief Secretary to Government. 1872 : Chief Secretary to Government. 1873 : Temporary Member of Council. 1874 : *On furlough to Europe for 12 months.* 1875 : Resumed Temporary Member of Council. 1877 : Appointed Member of Council. 1881 : Acting Governor of Fort St. George and President in Council. 1882 : *Made a C.S.I. 23rd May ; Retired from service, 12th June. (Annuitant on the Fund.)*

HUTCHINS, ARTHUR ROBERT.—1857 : Writer and Student at the College. 1858 : Assistant to Collector and Magistrate, Trichinopoly. 1859 : *On medical leave to Europe for 15 months.* 1861 : Assistant to Collector and Magistrate, South Arcot. 1862 : Acting Head Assistant, Tanjore. 1864 : Head Assistant at Tanjore, and at Madura ; Acting Judge of Small Cause Court, Madura ; Acting Sub-Collector, South Arcot ; Acting Sub-Collector and Joint Magistrate, Madura. 1865 : Acting Sub-Collector and Joint Magistrate, Kistna. 1866 : Acting Sub-Collector, Tanjore ; Head Assistant to Collector and Joint Magistrate, South Arcot ; Sub-Collector, Tanjore ; *On furlough to Europe for 14 months.* 1867 : Assistant and Acting Head Assistant to Collector and Magistrate, Tanjore. 1868 : Acting Principal Assistant to Collector and Magistrate, and Agent to the Governor, in Vizagapatam ; Junior Assistant, afterwards Senior Assistant, in Ganjam ; Sub-Collector and Magistrate, Godavari. 1869 : *On furlough to Europe for 12 months.* 1870 : *Retired from service, 6th October. (Invalid Annuitant.)*

HUTCHINS, PHILIP PERCIVAL.—1858 : Writer and Student at the College. 1859 : Assistant to Collector and Magistrate, South Arcot. 1860 : Head Assistant, South Arcot. 1862 : Acting Sub-Collector and Joint Magistrate, South Arcot ; Acting Deputy Secretary to Government, Revenue Department, afterwards under the Chief Secretary. 1863 : Acting Secretary to the Board of Examiners, also Acting Deputy Secretary to Government, Revenue Department ; Acting Judge of Small Cause Court, Chittoor ; Acting

Sub-Collector and Joint Magistrate, Madras; Private Secretary to
H.E. the Governor, the Hon. E. Maltby.   1864: Head Assistant
to Collector and Magistrate, South Arcot, and Acting Sub-Collector
and Joint Magistrate, Madras; Acting Registrar to the High
Court, Appellate Side.   1865: Registrar to the High Court,
Appellate Side.   1867: *On medical leave to Europe for 19 months.*
1868: Resumed Registrar, High Court.   1869: Acting Civil and
Sessions Judge, Nundyal.   1870: Acting Civil and Sessions Judge,
Tanjore.   1871: Acting Civil and Sessions Judge, Cuddapah.
1872: Acting Civil and Sessions Judge, Bellary, afterwards at
Madura.   1873: District and Sessions Judge, Madura.   1874:
On furlough to Europe for 20 months.   1875: District Judge,
Madura.   1881: Acting Judge of the High Court, Madras; *On
special leave to Europe, urgent private affairs, for 6 months.*   1882:
District and Sessions Judge, Madura; Member of the Rent Law
Committee; Acting Secretary to Government, Revenue Depart-
ment.   1883: On Special Duty connected with Reorganisation of
Judicial Establishments; Member of the Board of Examiners;
Acting Judge of the High Court, Madras; appointed Judge of the
High Court, Madras.   1884: Fellow of the Madras University.

INNES, Lewis Charles.—1844: Writer.   1846: Assistant to
Collector and Magistrate, Canara.   1847: Assistant to Collector
and Magistrate, Trichinopoly; afterwards Assistant to Collector and
Magistrate, Salem.   1849: *On furlough to Europe.*   1852: Assis-
tant and Acting Head Assistant to Collector and Magistrate, Salem.
1853: Acting Head Assistant, afterwards Head Assistant to
Collector and Magistrate, Tanjore.   1855: Acting Sub-Judge,
Combaconum.   1856: Sub-Judge, Combaconum.   1858: Civil and
Sessions Judge at Nundyal.   1862: Civil and Sessions Judge,
Rajahmundry.   1863: Civil and Sessions Judge, Coimbatore, after-
wards at Ootacamund.   1865: Judge of the High Court of Judi-
cature, Madras.   1867: *On medical leave to Europe for 21 months-*
1869: Resumed Judge of the High Court, Madras.   1875: *On
medical leave to Europe for 5 months.*   1877: Acting Chief Justice,
Madras.   1880: *On furlough to Europe for 8 months.*   1882:
Acting Chief Justice, Madras.   1883: *Retired from service, 9th
September.* (*Annuitant on the Fund.*)

IRVINE, Octavius Butler.—1856: Writer.   1857: Student
at the College.   1858: Assistant to Collector and Magistrate,
Coimbatore.   1861: Officiating Head Assistant at Coimbatore;
Head Assistant, Kistna.   1862: *On medical leave for 2 years and*

6 *months*.   1865 : Assistant, afterwards Acting Head Assistant to Collector and Magistrate, South Arcot.   1866 : Head Assistant, North Arcot, and at South Arcot; Acting Sub-Collector, South Arcot; Sub-Collector, Bellary.   1867 : Acting Judge of Small Cause Court, afterwards Sub-Judge, Vellore ; Acting Civil and Sessions Judge, Chittoor.   1868 : Acting Civil and Sessions Judge, Bellary.   1871 : *On furlough to Europe for* 18 *months.*   1873 : District and Sessions Judge, Godavari, also of North Arcot. 1874 : Acting District and Sessions Judge, Chittoor; District and Sessions Judge, South Arcot.   1879 : Acting Collector and Magistrate, and Agent to the Governor of Fort St. George, Vizagapatam.   1880 : *Died, 14th May, at Vizagapatam.*

KELSALL, Thomas.— 1755 : Arrived on the Coromandel Coast 9th June, as Writer, and placed under the Secretary at Fort St. George.   1756 : Under the Accountant at Fort St. David.   1759 : Under the Secretary in the Secret Department at Fort St. George. 1760 : Factor and Paymaster at Arcot.   1761 : Secretary in the Secret Department, and Translator at Fort St. George.   1762 : Clerk to the Committee of Treasury and Accounts.   1764 : Register of the Sea Gate, and Clerk to the Committee of Treasury and Accounts.   1765 : Junior Merchant and Assistant at Masulipatam. 1766 : *Services transferred to Bengal.*   1767 : Appointed Ninth Member of Council of the Governor of Fort William in Bengal; Military Paymaster-General and Custom Master.   (*See Bengal Volume.*)

KERR, William Hobart.— 1856 : Writer and Student at the College.   1857 : Assistant to Collector and Magistrate, Tanjore. 1859 : Acting Special Assistant at Tanjore.   1860 : Head Assistant at Madura.   1861 : Head Assistant at Tanjore ; Deputy Secretary to Government in Chief Secretary's Departments ; *On medical leave to Europe for* 2 *years.*   1864 : Superintendent of Coorg.   1865 : *On special leave to Europe for 6 months ;* resumed Superintendentship of Coorg.   1866 : *On medical leave to Europe for* 12 *months.*   1867 : *Retired from service, 11th March.* (*Invalid Annuitant.*)

KINDERSLEY, John Robert.— 1847 : Writer.   1849 : Assistant to Collector and Magistrate, Salem.   1851 : Acting Head Assistant at Salem.   1852 : Assistant to Collector and Magistrate, Masulipatam ; *On medical leave to Europe.*   1855 : Assistant to Collector and Magistrate, Chingleput ; afterwards Acting Head Assistant at Trichinopoly ; then Head Assistant at Malabar ; and Acting Sub-Judge, Mangalore.   1856 : Head Assistant to Collector

and Magistrate, Chingleput. 1857 : Assistant Judge, after-
wards Acting Civil and Sessions Judge, Mangalore. 1858 : Acting
Sub-Judge, Bellary. 1859 : Senior Assistant to Collector and
Magistrate, and Agent to the Governor of Fort St. George, in
Ganjam ; Acting Civil and Sessions Judge, Nundyal. 1860 :
Officiating Civil and Sessions Judge, Bellary ; *Proceeded on
furlough to Europe for* 3 *years.* 1864 : Acting Civil and Sessions
Judge, Rajahmundry. 1865 : Civil and Sessions Judge, Rajah-
mundry. 1866 : Civil and Sessions Judge, Bellary ; Officiating
Judicial Commissioner, Mysore. 1870 : Acting Judge of the
High Court of Judicature, Madras; Officiating Judicial Com-
missioner, Mysore ; Resumed Acting Judge of the High Court,
Madras. 1877 : Appointed Judge of the High Court, Madras ;
Fellow of the Madras University. 1878 : *On furlough to Europe
for* 15 *months.* 1879 : Resumed Judge of the High Court, Madras.
1884 : *Retired from service, 6th January. (Annuitant on the Fund.)*

KINDERSLEY, Francis Marten.—1855 : Writer and Student
at the College. 1857 : Assistant to Collector and Magistrate,
South Arcot. 1859 : Acting Head Assistant, South Arcot. 1860 :
Head Assistant at Tanjore ; Officiating Sub-Collector and Joint
Magistrate, Tinnevelly. 1863 : Acting Civil and Sessions Judge,
Tinnevelly. 1864 : Acting Judge of Small Cause Court, Tanjore.
1865 : Sub-Collector and Joint Magistrate, Tanjore. 1866 :
Judge of Small Cause Court, Combaconum. 1867 : Acting Civil
and Sessions Judge, Trichinopoly ; *On furlough to Europe for*
2 *years.* 1869 : Acting Civil and Sessions Judge, Coimbatore.
1871 : District and Sessions Judge, Tanjore. 1872 : *On furlough
for* 7 *months.* 1874 : Acting District and Sessions Judge, Coimbatore. 1877 : District and Sessions Judge, Coimbatore. 1878 :
On furlough to Europe for 1 *year.* 1880 : *Retired from service,
24th December, in India. (Annuitant on the Fund.)*

LEMAN, George Downton.—1857 : Writer and Student at
the College. 1859 : Assistant to Collector and Magistrate, North
Arcot. 1861 : *On medical leave for* 3 *months;* Officiating Head
Assistant, North Arcot ; *On medical leave to Europe for* 21 *months.*
1863 : Assistant Collector, North Arcot ; Acting Head Assistant
to Collector and Magistrate ; Invested with Full Powers of a Magis-
trate. 1864 : Justice of the Peace ; Acting Head Assistant,
Trichinopoly ; Senior Assistant to Collector and Magistrate, and
Agent to the Governor in Ganjam. 1865 : Acting Principal
Assistant, and Agent, in Ganjam. 1866 : Principal Assistant and

Agent, Ganjam.   1867 : Acting Collector and Magistrate, Kistna.
1868 : Acting Civil and Sessions Judge, Guntoor ; Acting Collector
of Sea Customs, and Protector of Emigrants, Madras ; Acting
Civil and Sessions Judge, Tellicherry.   1869 : Acting Inam Commissioner ; on Special Duty connected with the Quit Rent Department, Madras.   1870 : *On furlough to Europe for 21 months.*
1872 : Acting Collector and Magistrate, Kistna.   1873 : Collector
and Magistrate, Kistna.   1875 : On Special Duty at Madras ; Acting Collector of Sea Customs, and Protector of Emigrants, Madras.
1877 : Collector and Magistrate, Kistna ; Collector, Magistrate,
and Agent to the Governor in Ganjam.   1879 : *On furlough to
Europe for 15 months.*   1880 : Resumed Collector, Magistrate, and
Agent, Ganjam.   1881 : Acting Collector and Magistrate, Coimbatore ; Acting Collector of Sea Customs, and Protector of Emigrants, Madras.   1882 : Collector and Magistrate, Coimbatore.
1884 : *Special leave to Europe on urgent private affairs for 6
months ;* resumed Collector and Magistrate, Coimbatore.

LONGLEY, Charles Thomas.—1853 : Writer and Student at
the College.   1855 : Assistant to Collector and Magistrate, Madura.
1856 : Acting Head Assistant at Madura.   1858 : Head Assistant
to Collector and Magistrate, Kurnool ; *On medical leave to Europe
for 24 months.*   1860 : Officiating Sub-Judge, Chicacole ; Senior
Assistant to Collector and Magistrate, and Agent to the Governor
of Fort St. George, in Vizagapatam.   1861 : Principal Assistant
at Vizagapatam.   1862 : Acting Collector and Magistrate, Ganjam.   1864 : Acting Judge of Small Cause Court, Chittoor.   1866 :
On furlough to Europe for 23 months and 11 days.   1867 :
Acting Collector and Magistrate, Trichinopoly.   1868 : Acting
Collector and Magistrate, Tinnevelly.   1869 : Collector and Magis-
trate, Nellore.   1870 : Collector and Magistrate, Salem.   1873 :
On furlough to Europe for 15 months.   1874 : Resumed Duties
at Salem.   1878 : Acting Second Member of the Revenue
Board.   1879 : Acting First Member of the Board of Revenue,
and Commissioner for Examinations of Uncovenanted Civil
Servants ; Acting Third Member of the Revenue Board.   1880 :
Acting Second Member, afterwards Third Member, and again
Second Member, of the Revenue Board ; In Charge of the Inam
Department.   1881 : Acting Second Member, appointed Third
Member, and Acting First Member, of the Revenue Board ; *On
furlough to Europe for 9 months and 14 days.*   1882 : *Retired
from service, 15th July, in England.*   (*Annuitant on the Fund.*)

LUSHINGTON, James Law.—1841 : Writer. 1843 : Assistant to Principal Collector and Magistrate, Tanjore. 1844: In the same Capacity at Nellore. 1845: Acting Head Assistant to Collector and Magistrate, Nellore. 1847 : Head Assistant to Collector and Magistrate, Trichinopoly ; afterwards Second Assistant to the Accountant-General, Madras. 1848: Acting Head Assistant to the Accountant-General. 1850 : Head Assistant to the Accountant-General, and Canarese Translator to Government. 1854 : Acting First Assistant to the Accountant-General. 1856 : First Assistant to the Accountant-General ; afterwards Acting Sub-Treasurer, Secretary to the Savings Bank, Member of the Mint Committee, and Director of the Incorporated Bank of Madras. 1858 : Acting Civil Auditor and Superintendent of Stamps. 1859 : Civil Auditor ; afterwards Accountant, North - Western Provinces. 1861 : *On medical leave to Europe for* 15 *months.* 1863 : Acting Deputy at Madras, afterwards Deputy Auditor and Accountant-General, Bengal, and officiating Auditor-General and Accountant-General to the Government of India. 1864 : Acting Deputy Auditor and Accountant-General, Madras. 1865 : Accountant-General, Bombay. 1868: *On private affairs to Europe for* 6 *months ;* on duty in England. 1869 : *On furlough to Europe for* 2 *years.* 1871 : Resumed Accountant-General, Bombay. 1876 : *Retired from service,* 24*th December, in India.* (*Annuitant on the Fund.*)

MACGREGOR, Atholl.—1855: Writer and Student at the College. 1857: Assistant to Collector and Magistrate, Madura. 1859: Acting Head Assistant at Tinnevelly. 1860: Special Assistant to Collector and Magistrate, Malabar. 1861 : Acting Sub-Collector, Malabar. 1863 : *On furlough to Europe for* 20 *months.* 1865 : Acting Sub-Collector and Joint Magistrate, Tinnevelly ; Head Assistant at Coimbatore ; Sub-Collector, Nellore. 1866 : Principal Assistant to Collector, and Agent to the Governor of Fort St. George, Ganjam ; also Sub-Collector, Tinnevelly ; Acting Collector and Magistrate, Coimbatore. 1867 : Sub-Collector and Joint Magistrate, Madras District ; Acting Resident, Travancore ; *Leave on private affairs for* 6 *months.* 1868 : Resumed Sub-Collector and Joint Magistrate, Madras District ; Acting Secretary to the Revenue Board. 1869 : Acting Collector of Sea Customs, and Protector of Emigrants, Madras. 1870: Secretary to the Revenue Board ; Collector and Magistrate, Malabar ; Agent for French Settlement of Mahé. 1875: Acting Secretary to Government, Revenue

Department; Acting Resident of Travancore and Cochin. 1876: Resident of Travancore and Cochin. 1877: *On furlough to Europe for 2 years, with extension for another year.* 1882: *Retired from service, 13th April, in England. (Annuitant on the Fund.)*

MASTER, ROBERT EDWARD.—1845: Writer. 1846: Assistant to Collector and Magistrate, Rajahmundry. 1849: Acting Head Assistant to Collector and Magistrate, Rajahmundry. 1850: Acting Sub-Judge, Rajahmundry. 1853: Head Assistant to Collector and Magistrate, Rajahmundry. 1855: Sub-Judge, Rajahmundry. 1856: *On furlough to Europe.* 1857: Acting Second Assistant to the Accountant-General. 1858: Deputy Director of Revenue Settlement. 1861: Acting Sub-Collector and Joint Magistrate, Godavari, without prejudice to previous Appointment; Acting Director of Revenue Settlement. 1862: Officiating Director. 1868: Director of Revenue Settlement. 1870: *On furlough to Europe for 2 years.* 1872: *Retired from service, 30th April. (Annuitant on the Fund.)*

MASTER, JOHN HENRY.—1852: Writer and Student at the College. 1853: Assistant to Collector and Magistrate, Rajahmundry. 1854: Assistant Commissioner, Third Class, Nagpur Commission. 1858: Officiating Deputy Commissioner, Chindwara, Central Provinces. 1859: Deputy Secretary to Government in the Revenue and Public Works Departments. 1860: Deputy Commissioner, Third Class, Chindwara. 1862: Deputy Commissioner, Second Class, Bhundara. 1864: *On furlough to Europe for 3 years.* 1867: Sub-Collector, Bellary; Acting Collector and Magistrate, and Agent to the Governor, in Vizagapatam. 1868: Acting Collector and Magistrate, afterwards Sub-Collector and Joint Magistrate, Godavari; Acting Civil and Sessions Judge, Berhampore; Civil and Sessions Judge, Tellicherry. 1869: Acting Civil and Sessions Judge, Vizagapatam; Acting Collector and Magistrate, Bellary. 1870: Civil and Sessions Judge, Cuddapah. 1873: Collector and Magistrate, Bellary; Political Agent at Sundur. 1878: *On furlough to Europe.* 1880: *Retired from service, 30th April, in England. (Annuitant on the Fund.)*

MASTER, CHARLES GILBERT.—1854: Writer and Student at the College. 1855: Assistant to Collector and Magistrate, Masulipatam. 1856: Acting Head Assistant at Guntoor. 1859: Head Assistant to the Collector, Guntoor; afterwards Head Assistant to Collector and Magistrate, North Canara; Deputy Secretary to

Government in the Revenue and Public Works Departments.
1860: Commissioner for the Assessment of Income-Tax. 1861:
Officiating Secretary, afterwards Secretary, to the Board of
Examiners. 1862: Acting Sub-Secretary to the Revenue Board.
1866: *On furlough to Europe for* 3 *years.* 1869: Acting Civil
and Sessions Judge, Calicut; Justice of the Peace; on Special Duty
on Irrigation Works, Godavari and Kistna; Acting Collector and
Magistrate, Nellore. 1870: Collector and Magistrate, Kistna,
afterwards at Cuddapah. 1871: Acting Collector and Magistrate,
Ganjam. 1872: Collector and Magistrate, Vizagapatam. 1873:
Collector and Magistrate, Ganjam. 1874: Acting Secretary to
Government, Revenue Department. 1875: *On furlough to Europe
for* 14 *months.* 1876: Collector and Magistrate, Ganjam. 1877;
Acting Secretary, afterwards Secretary, to Government, Revenue
Department. 1878: Acting Chief Secretary to Government.
1881: Chief Secretary to Government. 1882: Additional Mem-
ber of the Legislative Council. 1883: Temporary Member of
Council. 1884: Ordinary Member of Council; *took his seat 8th
January.*

M'DONELL, ÆNEAS RANALD.—1843: Writer. 1844: *Absent
in Europe.* 1846: Assistant to the Collector and Magistrate,
Chingleput; afterwards Head Assistant to the Accountant-General,
Madras. 1847: Acting Head Assistant to Collector and Magistrate, South Arcot. 1849: Head Assistant to Collector and
Magistrate, South Arcot. 1852: Acting Sub-Judge, Salem.
1853: Acting Additional Sub-Collector and Joint Magistrate,
South Arcot. 1854: Acting Sub-Judge, Combaconum; Acting
Additional Sub-Collector and Joint Magistrate, South Arcot.
1855: Sub-Judge, Cuddapah; Acting, afterwards Sub-Collector
and Joint Magistrate, South Arcot. 1859: Acting Collector
and Magistrate, South Arcot; Officiating Civil and Sessions
Judge, Combaconum. 1860: Collector and Magistrate, Trichinopoly. 1863: *On medical leave to Europe for* 10 *months;* Collector
and Magistrate, South Canara; Civil and Sessions Judge, Rajahmundry. 1864: Acting Collector and Magistrate, Madura, also
at Trichinopoly. 1865: Collector and Magistrate, Trichinopoly.
1866: Civil and Sessions Judge, Trichinopoly. 1867: *Died, 2d
February, in India.*

M'QUHAE, WILLIAM.—1857: Writer and Student at the College. 1858: Assistant to Collector and Magistrate, Salem. 1859:
Acting Head Assistant at Cuddapah. 1861: Head Assistant to

Collector and Magistrate, Kurnool.   1862 : Head Assistant, Cuddapah.   1864 : Acting Sub-Collector and Joint Magistrate, Coimbatore.   1866 : Acting Sub-Collector, Coimbatore, and at Salem ; Acting Sub-Secretary, Revenue Board ; Sub-Collector, Coimbatore. 1867 : Acting Civil and Sessions Judge, Trichinopoly.   1868 : Acting Collector and Magistrate, Kistna ; *On furlough to Europe for* 1 *year and* 11 *months.*   1870 : Acting Collector and Magistrate, Trichinopoly.   1871 : Acting Collector and Magistrate, Madura. 1873 : Collector and Magistrate, Madura.   1875 : *On furlough to Europe for* 13 *months.*   1876 : Resumed Duties at Madura. 1878 : *On furlough to Europe for* 1 *year.*   1879 : *Retired from service, 28th July.   (Invalid Annuitant.)*

MELVILLE, Robertson John.—1856 : Writer. 1857 : Student at the College.   1858 : Assistant to Collector and Magistrate, Masulipatam.   1859 : Acting Head Assistant at Masulipatam ; afterwards Assistant and Acting Head Assistant to the Collector and Magistrate, Kistna.   1862 : Acting Judge of Small Cause Court, Madura, also at Chittoor ; Head Assistant to Collector and Magistrate, Madura.   1863 : Acting Judge of Small Cause Court, Chittoor ; Head Assistant to Collector and Magistrate, Godavari. 1864 : Officiating Director of Revenue Settlement.   1866 : Principal Assistant to Collector and Magistrate, and Agent to the Governor, Ganjam; Deputy Director of Revenue Settlement; Sub-Collector, Malabar.   1867 : *On furlough to Europe for* 2 *years.* 1869 : Acting Judge of Small Cause Court, Vellore ; Acting Collector and Magistrate, Nellore ; Sub-Collector, Nellore.   1870 : Acting Collector and Magistrate, and Agent to the Governor, Vizagapatam.   1873 : *On furlough to Europe for* 18 *months.*   1875 : Acting Collector and Magistrate, Chingleput.   1876 : Acting Collector of Sea Customs and of Madras Town, and Protector of Emigrants. 1880 : *On furlough to Europe for* 14 *months.*   1882 : *Retired from service, 31st December, in India.   (Annuitant on the Fund.)*

MINCHIN, James Innes.—1844 : Writer.   1845 : Assistant to Collector and Magistrate, Tanjore.   1847 : Acting Head Assistant to Collector and Magistrate, Tanjore.   1849 : Acting Special Assistant to Collector and Magistrate, Tanjore.   1850 : Acting Head Assistant to Collector and Magistrate, Tanjore.   1851 : Head Assistant to Collector and Magistrate, Tanjore.   1853 : Head Assistant to Collector and Magistrate, Nellore.   1854 : Acting Sub-Judge, Cuddapah ; afterwards Acting Sub-Collector and Joint Magistrate, Nellore.   1856 : Sub-Collector and Joint Magistrate,

Nellore. 1859: Officiating Civil and Sessions Judge, Masuli-patam. 1860: Officiating Collector and Magistrate, Kurnool. 1862: Collector and Magistrate, Kurnool. 1866: *On medical leave to Europe for* 19 *months.* 1867: On Special Duty at Calcutta; Collector and Magistrate, and Agent to the Governor of Fort St. George, Vizagapatam. 1869: Acting Chief Secretary to Government. 1870: Acting Third Member of the Revenue Board; Acting Resident in Travancore and Cochin. 1871: *On furlough to Europe for* 2 *years.* 1873: *Retired from service,* 1st *April.* (*Annuitant on the Fund.*)

MOLONY, FREDERICK BERESFORD. — 1853: Writer. 1854: Student at the College. 1855: Assistant to Collector and Magistrate, Rajahmundry. 1856: Acting Head Assistant, Rajahmundry. 1857: Head Assistant to Collector and Magistrate, Cuddapah. *On medical leave to Europe for* 15 *months.* 1858: Acting Sub-Collector and Joint Magistrate, Cuddapah. 1862: Sub-Collector and Joint Magistrate, Kistna, but continuing to act as Sub-Collector at Cuddapah. 1865: *On furlough to Europe for* 3 *years.* 1868: *Died, in India,* 13th *November.*

MORRIS, GEORGE LEE.—1847: Writer. 1848: Under the Collector of Malabar. 1850: Assistant to Collector and Magistrate, Tanjore. 1852: Acting Special Assistant to Collector and Magistrate, Tanjore. 1855: Special Assistant at Tanjore; Officiating Special Assistant to Collector and Magistrate, Coimbatore. 1856: Acting Sub-Collector and Joint Magistrate, afterwards Sub-Collector and Joint Magistrate, Malabar. 1857: *On medical leave to Europe for* 24 *months.* 1858: Sub-Collector and Joint Magistrate, Madura; afterwards at Tanjore. 1862: Acting Collector at Tanjore. 1863: Acting Collector and Magistrate, South Canara. 1864: Collector and Magistrate, South Canara. 1865: Collector and Magistrate, and Political Agent at Tanjore. 1866: *On special leave for* 6 *months.* 1870: Acting Third Member of the Revenue Board. 1871: Acting Second Member of the Revenue Board; *On furlough to Europe.* 1873: *Retired from service,* 15th *May.* (*Annuitant on the Fund.*)

MORRIS, HENRY.—1848: Writer and Student at the College. 1850: Assistant to Collector and Magistrate, Nellore. 1855: Acting Head Assistant at Nellore. 1856: Head Assistant at Nellore; Inspector of Schools, Madras. 1857: Acting Sub-Collector and Joint Magistrate, Rajahmundry; Head Assistant to Collector and Magistrate, Guntoor. 1859: *On* *furlough to Europe for* 3 *years and* 7 *months.* 1863 : Acting Judge of the Small Cause Court, Chittoor; Acting Civil and Sessions Judge, Nundyal; Acting Collector and Magistrate, Godavari. 1864: Acting Sub-Collector and Joint Magistrate, Nellore; Sub-Collector and Joint Magistrate, Tanjore, with Duties as before ; Acting Civil and Sessions Judge, Chicacole. 1865: Sub-Collector and Joint Magistrate, Nellore ; Principal Assistant to Collector and Magistrate, and Agent to the Governor of Fort St. George in Ganjam ; Acting Civil and Sessions Judge, Rajahmundry. 1866 : District and Sessions Judge, Godavari. 1873 : *On furlough to Europe for* 2 *years.* 1875 : *Retired from service,* 20*th July.* (*Annuitant on the Fund.*)

MORRIS, FREDERICK WILLIAM.—1854 : Writer and Student at the College. 1856 : Assistant to Collector and Magistrate, afterwards Acting Head Assistant, at Nellore. 1858 : Acting Assistant to Collector and Magistrate, and Agent to the Governor of Fort St. George, in Ganjam. 1859 : Senior Assistant and Agent to the Governor, afterwards Officiating Principal Assistant, Ganjam. 1860 : Deputy Director of Revenue Settlement. 1863 : *Died,* 15*th October, in India.*

NESBITT, WILLIAM SMITH.—1845 : Writer. 1848 : Assistant to Collector and Magistrate, Guntoor. 1851 : Acting Head Assistant to Collector and Magistrate, Masulipatam ; *On medical leave to Europe.* 1857 : Acting Sub-Judge, Cuddapah. 1858 : Acting Deputy Collector of Sea Customs, Madras ; Acting Subordinate Judge, Chittoor. 1859 : Acting Sub-Judge, Ootacamund ; Assistant to Collector and Magistrate, Coimbatore. 1861: Acting Sub-Judge, Ootacamund. 1862 : Sub-Judge, Ootacamund. 1866 : *On furlough to Europe.* 1869: *Resigned the service,* 1*st February, in England.* (*Invalid Annuitant.*)

NEWILL, HENRY.—1840 : Writer. 1841 : Assistant to the Collector and Magistrate, Guntoor. 1842 : Acting Register to the Zillah Court of Cuddapah. 1843 : Acting Head Assistant to the Collector and Magistrate, Guntoor. 1845 : Head Assistant to the Collector and Magistrate, Guntoor. 1850 : Acting Collector and Magistrate, Guntoor. 1851 : *Proceeded on furlough to Europe.* 1853 : *Returned to Madras.* 1854 : Assistant to the Commissioner for the Northern Circars. 1855 : Acting Collector and Magistrate, Guntoor. 1857 : Director of Revenue Settlement. 1862 : *On medical leave for* 1 *year.* 1863 : Collector and Magistrate, Godavari. 1864 : Acting Resident, and in 1865 Resident of Travancore and Cochin. 1869 : *Died,* 25*th April, in India.*

NISBET, WALTER.—1855 : Writer and Student at the College. 1856: Assistant to Collector and Magistrate, Tanjore. 1857 : *On medical leave to Europe for* 30 *months.* 1859 : Assistant to Collector and Magistrate, Chingleput. 1860 : Head Assistant at Trichinopoly. 1862 : Acting Sub-Collector, Madura. 1864 : *On medical leave to Europe, forfeiting appointment.* 1865 : *Retired from service* 24*th August. (Invalid Annuitant.)*

PAUNCEFOTE, BERNARD.—1845 : Writer. 1847 : Assistant to Collector and Magistrate, South Arcot. 1851 : Acting Head Assistant to Collector and Magistrate, Nellore. 1853 : Acting Assistant to the Accountant-General, Madras. 1854 : Head Assistant to Collector and Magistrate, Trichinopoly ; afterwards at Chingleput. 1855 : Acting Sub-Collector and Joint Magistrate, Madura. 1856 : Additional Sub-Collector and Joint Magistrate, North Arcot ; *Proceeded to Europe on medical certificate for* 27 *months.* 1861 : Officiating Civil and Sessions Judge, Chingleput ; Acting Sub-Collector, South Arcot. 1862 : Sub-Collector, South Arcot ; *On furlough for* 3 *years.* 1865 : *Retired from service,* 27*th January. (Invalid Annuitant.)*

PELLY, CHARLES RAYMOND.—1847 : Writer. 1848 : Assistant to Collector and Magistrate, Bellary. 1850 : Acting Head Assistant at Bellary. 1854 : Acting Head Assistant to Collector and Magistrate, Canara. 1855 : Head Assistant to Collector and Magistrate, Malabar, and again at Canara ; Acting Sub-Judge, Mangalore. 1856 : Acting Sub-Collector and Joint Magistrate, Rajahmundry. 1857 : Acting Principal Assistant to Collector and Magistrate, and Agent to the Governor of Fort St. George, in Vizagapatam. 1858 : Senior Assistant, and Acting Principal Assistant to Collector and Magistrate, and Agent to the Governor, Vizagapatam. 1859: Sub-Judge, Chicacole. 1860 : Acting Civil and Sessions Judge, Masulipatam. 1863 : Judge of the Small Cause Court, Cuddalore ; but acting as Civil and Sessions Judge, Nundyal ; *On special leave for* 6 *months.* 1864 : Acting Civil and Sessions Judge, Madura. 1865 : Civil and Sessions Judge, Nellore. 1867 : *On furlough to Europe for* 1 *year and* 11 *months.* 1869 : Civil and Sessions Judge, Calicut. 1870 : Civil and Sessions Judge, Tanjore, but acting at Tranquebar. 1871 : Civil and Sessions Judge, Tranquebar. 1872 : *On furlough to Europe for* 12 *months.* 1873 : *Retired from service,* 6*th June. (Annuitant on the Fund.)*

PLUMER, CHARLES GEORGE.—1856 : Writer and Student at

N

the College. 1857 : Assistant to Collector and Magistrate, Tinne-velly.   1858 : Acting Head Assistant Collector, Tinnevelly.
1859 : Acting Head Assistant to Collector and Magistrate, Chingle-put ; *On medical leave to Europe for 25 months.*   1861 : Acting
Head Assistant, Tanjore ; Assistant to Collector, Madura.   1862 :
Head Assistant to Collector, Salem, and at Tanjore ; Sub-Collector
at Tanjore ; Head Assistant at Malabar.   1863 : Head Assistant,
Madura ; Sub-Collector and Joint Magistrate, Tanjore.   1864 :
Justice of the Peace ; Head Assistant to Collector, Trichinopoly,
and Sub-Collector, Tanjore.   1866 : Sub-Collector and Joint
Magistrate, Nellore ; Acting Judge of Small Cause Court, Vellore ;
Sub-Collector and Joint Magistrate, Kistna.   1867 : *On furlough
to Europe for 2 years.*   1869 : Acting Civil and Sessions Judge,
Calicut ; also at Salem and at Chittoor.   1872 : District and
Sessions Judge, North Arcot.   1874 : *On furlough to Europe for
12 months.*   1875 : Resumed District and Sessions Judge, North
Arcot ; In Charge of Small Cause Court, Vellore.   1882 : Member
of the Board of Examiners ; District and Sessions Judge, North
Arcot ; Officiating Chief Judge and Inspector-General of Prisons,
Mysore ; Judicial Commissioner of Coorg.   1884 : *Retired from
service, 1st June.*   (*Annuitant on the Fund.*)

POCHIN, CHARLES NORMAN.—1848 : Writer and Student at
the College. 1850 : Assistant to Collector and Magistrate, Madura ;
1852 : Officiating Head Assistant to the Register to the Court of
Sudder and Foujdarry Adawlut ; afterwards Assistant to Collector
and Magistrate, Coimbatore.   1854 : Acting Head Assistant to
Collector and Magistrate, Tanjore.   1856 : Head Assistant to Col-lector and Magistrate, North Arcot.   1857 : Acting Additional
Sub-Collector and Joint Magistrate, Canara.   1859 : Additional
Sub-Collector and Joint Magistrate, Canara ; afterwards Acting
Collector and Magistrate, North Canara.   1860 : Acting Civil
and Sessions Judge, afterwards Subordinate Judge, Mangalore ;
Officiating Collector and Magistrate, North Canara.   1861 : *On
furlough to Europe for 3 years.* 1864 : Acting Sub-Collector and
Joint Magistrate, Madras.   1865 : Sub-Collector and Joint Magis-trate, Tanjore, but acting as Collector of Salem ; Acting Civil
and Sessions Judge, Madura ; Judge of the Small Cause Court,
Madura.   1866 : Acting Collector and Magistrate, Trichinopoly ;
Civil and Sessions Judge, Calicut ; Acting Collector and Magis-trate, Kurnool.   1867 : Acting Collector and Magistrate, Salem,

afterwards Collector and Magistrate there. 1870: *Died, 26th August, in India.*

PUCKLE, RICHARD KAYE, C.I.E.—1851: Writer and Student at the College. 1853: Assistant to Collector and Magistrate, South Arcot. 1855: Acting Head Assistant to Collector and Magistrate, Chingleput. 1856: Head Assistant to Collector and Magistrate, Malabar. 1857: Acting Assistant to the Agent to the Governor of Fort St. George, Vizagapatam; afterwards Acting Head Assistant to Collector and Magistrate, South Arcot. 1858: Head Assistant at South Arcot. 1859: Acting Deputy Director of Revenue Settlement; afterwards Deputy Director. 1860: *On medical leave to Europe for* 15 *months.* 1862: Deputy Director of Revenue Settlement; Special Assistant to Collector and Magistrate, Trichinopoly; Deputy Director of Revenue Settlement, Tinnevelly; and at Salem in 1863. 1866: Collector and Magistrate, Tinnevelly. 1869: On Special Duty at the Office of the Board of Revenue; *On furlough to Europe for* 16 *months.* 1874: Acting Director of Revenue Settlement. 1875: Director of Revenue Settlement; *On furlough to Europe for* 12 *months.* 1876: Acting Additional Member of the Revenue Board. 1877: Acting Third Member of the Revenue Board. 1878: *Made C.I.E. 1st January; On furlough to Europe.* 1881: *Retired from service, 16th June, in England.* (*Annuitant on the Fund.*)

REID, JOHN WILLIAM (*Barrister-at-Law*).—1855: Writer and Student at the College. 1856: Assistant, afterwards Acting Head Assistant, to Collector and Magistrate, Cuddapah. 1859: Head Assistant at Rajahmundry, and Acting Subordinate Judge, Cuddapah; Head Assistant to Collector and Magistrate, Godavari. 1860: Acting Sub-Collector and Joint Magistrate, Bellary; Acting Sub-Collector and Joint Magistrate, Kistna. 1861: Acting Sub-Collector, Bellary. 1863: Head Assistant Collector, Malabar; Acting Sub-Collector and Joint Magistrate, Bellary; Justice of the Peace. 1864: Head Assistant, Tinnevelly; Sub-Collector, Bellary. 1866: Sub-Collector, Kistna; Acting Sub-Collector, Bellary; *On furlough to Europe for* 3 *years.* 1869: Acting Civil and Sessions Judge, Calicut; afterwards at Tellicherry. 1872: District and Sessions Judge, North Malabar. 1873: *On special leave to Europe for* 6 *months;* District and Sessions Judge, Tellicherry. 1877: Additional Sessions Judge at Nellore, and at Coimbatore. 1878: *On furlough to Europe for* 12 *months.* 1879: District and Sessions Judge, North Malabar. 1882: *On furlough to Europe for* 18 *months.* 1884: Resumed District and Sessions Judge, North Malabar; afterwards at Coimbatore.

ROBERTS, CLARENCE ARMSTRONG.—1844: Writer and Student at the College. 1845: Permitted to Pursue his Studies under the Collector of Salem. 1847: Assistant to Collector and Magistrate, South Arcot. 1848: Acting Second Assistant to the Accountant-General, Madras. 1849: Acting Head Assistant to Collector and Magistrate, Tanjore. 1850: Second Assistant to the Accountant-General. 1852: Secretary to the Mint Committee. 1853: Acting Head Assistant to the Accountant-General, and Acting Canarese Translator to Government. 1854: Member of the Board of Examiners; Acting First Assistant to the Accountant-General. 1855: *Proceeded to Europe on furlough.* 1858: *Without employ for 3 months;* Secretary to the Mint Committee; Acting First Assistant to the Accountant-General; Acting Collector of Sea Customs, Madras; Acting Sub-Collector and Joint Magistrate, Tinnevelly. 1859: Sub-Collector and Joint Magistrate, Coimbatore; Officiating Postmaster-General, Madras. 1861: *On medical leave to Europe for* 20 *months.* 1863: Acting Collector and Magistrate, Madras District; Acting Collector of Sea Customs, Madras; Acting Civil and Sessions Judge, afterwards Civil and Sessions Judge, Chittoor. 1867: Commissioner for the Debts of H.H. Prince Azeem Jah, Bahadur. 1871: *On furlough to Europe for* 16 *months.* 1872: *Retired from service, 12th July. (Annuitant on the Fund.)*

ROBINSON, JAMES DOUGLAS.—1840: Writer. 1842: Assistant to the Collector and Magistrate, Bellary. 1844: Acting Head Assistant to the Collector and Magistrate, Bellary. 1845: In the same capacity at Coimbatore. 1846: Head Assistant to the Principal Collector and Magistrate, Madura. 1847: Acting Sub-Judge of the Zillah of Madura. 1848: *Proceeded to Europe on furlough.* 1851: *Returned to Madras.* 1852: Acting Additional Sub-Collector and Joint Magistrate, Canara; Acting Sub-Collector and Joint Magistrate, Malabar; Head Assistant to the Collector and Magistrate, Malabar. 1854: Acting Sub-Judge of the Zillah of Mangalore; Additional Sub-Collector and Joint Magistrate, Canara. 1856: Sub-Collector and Joint Magistrate, Canara. 1857: Acting Collector and Magistrate, Canara. 1858: On Special Duty in Connection with the Disturbances on the Frontier of Canara District. 1859: Acting Collector and Magistrate, North Arcot. 1860: Sub-Collector and Joint Magistrate, Kistna. 1861: Col-

lector and Magistrate, North Arcot. 1862 : *On medical leave for*
10 *months.* 1864 : *On special leave for* 12 *months.* 1866 : Resumed Collector and Magistrate, North Arcot. 1868 : *On medical
leave to Europe for 6 months.* 1869 : Resumed his previous duties.
1870 : *On furlough to Europe.* 1873 : *Resigned the service,* 3d
March, in England. (*Annuitant on the Fund.*)

ROBINSON, Sir WILLIAM ROSE, K.C.S.I.—1842 : Writer.
1843 : Assistant to the Collector and Magistrate, Canara. 1847 :
Acting Head Assistant to Collector and Magistrate, Malabar.
1848 : Head Assistant to Collector and Magistrate, Malabar.
1849 : Officiating Sub-Judge, Calicut. 1851 : Acting Sub-Col-
lector and Joint Magistrate, Malabar. 1852 : *On furlough to
Europe.* 1856 : Sub-Collector and Joint Magistrate, Madura ;
Acting Sub-Collector and Joint Magistrate, Rajahmundry ; Acting
Collector and Magistrate, Malabar. 1858 : Inspector-General of
Police for the Madras Presidency. 1866 : *Made a C.S.I.* 1867 :
Acting Third Member of the Revenue Board. 1868 : *On special
leave to Europe for 6 months ;* resumed Acting Third Member of
the Revenue Board. 1869 : Third Member and Acting Second
Member of the Revenue Board ; afterwards Acting First Member ;
Inam Commissioner. 1870 : Second Member, and Acting First
Member of the Revenue Board ; Additional Member of Council of
the Governor-General for making Laws and Regulations. 1872 :
On furlough to Europe for 9 *months.* 1873 : Member of Council.
1875 : Acting Governor of Fort St. George for 7 months ; *made a
K.C.S.I.* 31*st December.* 1878 : *Retired from service,* 5*th Decem-
ber.* (*Annuitant on the Fund.*)

RUSSELL, CLAUD.—1752 : Arrived on the Coromandel Coast
17th June ; Writer and under the Secretary at Fort St. George.
1754 : Sub-Secretary and Accountant-General of the Mayor's
Court. 1759 : Factor and Sub-Import Warehouse-keeper. 1760 :
Junior Merchant and Commissary at Camp. 1762 : Senior
Merchant and Under Searcher at the Sea Gate and Assistant to
Mint Master. 1764 : Under Searcher and Assay Master. 1765 :
*Absent by desire of the Select Committee at Fort William in
Bengal.* 1767 : Appointed Sixth Member of Council of the
Governor of Fort William ; Accountant and Collector-General.
(*See Bengal Volume.*)

SHARPE, GEORGE ROBINSON.—1855 : Writer and Student
at the College. 1856 : Assistant to Collector and Magistrate,
South Arcot. 1857 : Acting Head Assistant at Salem ; after-

wards at Malabar.   1859 : Head Assistant at Malabar ; Acting
Subordinate Judge, Calicut.   1862 : Judge of the Small Cause
Court, Tellicherry.   1864 : *On special leave to Europe for 6
months.*   1866 : Acting Civil and Sessions Judge, Calicut.   1867 :
Civil and Sessions Judge, Calicut.   1868 : Civil and Sessions
Judge, Madura ; *On furlough to Europe for 2 years.*   1870 :
District and Sessions Judge, Malabar.   1874 : *On furlough to
Europe.*   1876 : *Forfeited appointment.*   1877 : *Retired from
service, 24th October. (Invalid Annuitant.)*

SIM, JAMES DUNCAN, C.S.I.—1842 : Writer.   1843 : Acting
Head Assistant to the Register to the Court of Sudder and Foujdarry Adawlut.   1844 : *Proceeded to Europe.*   1849 : Assistant,
afterwards Head Assistant, to Collector and Magistrate, Nellore.
1850 : Acting Deputy Secretary to Government.   1851 : Acting,
afterwards Deputy Secretary under the Chief Secretary to Government.   1853 : Acting Teloogoo Translator to Government.   1854 :
Teloogoo Translator to Government ; Member of the Board of
Examiners ; Acting Sub-Secretary to the Revenue Board.   1855 :
Sub-Secretary to the Revenue Board.   1856 : Acting Secretary to
the Revenue Board.   1858 : Secretary to the Revenue Board.
1860 : Acting Secretary to Government, Revenue, and Public
Works Department.   1861 : Secretary to Government, Revenue,
and Public Works Department.   1865 : *On special leave to Europe
for 6 months.*   1866 : Acting Chief Secretary to Government.
1867 : Third Member of the Revenue Board ; Commissioner for
the Examination of Uncovenanted Civil Servants.   1867 : Director
of the Incorporated Bank of Madras ; Second Member of the
Revenue Board.   1868 : *Made a C.S.I. 22d December.*   1869 : *On
furlough to Europe for* 10 *months.*   1870 : Member of Council.
1875 : *Retired from service, 7th March. (Annuitant on the Fund.)*

SIM, WILLIAM CLULOW.—1852 : Writer.   1853 : Student at the
College.   1854 : Acting Third Assistant to the Accountant-General,
Madras.   1855 : Assistant to Collector and Magistrate, North
Arcot ; *Medical leave to Europe for 16 months.*   1857 : Acting
Head Assistant to Collector and Magistrate, Trichinopoly.   1858 :
Acting Head Assistant at Chingleput.   1859 : Head Assistant to
Collector and Magistrate, Salem ; Acting Deputy Secretary to
Government in the Revenue and Judicial Departments ; Head
Assistant at South Arcot ; Acting Canarese Translator to Govern-
ment.   1861 : *On furlough to Europe for 3 years.*   1864 : *Retired
from service, 5th May, in England. (Invalid Annuitant.)*

SMITH, Henry George.—1844: Writer. 1846: Assistant to the Collector and Magistrate, Cuddapah. 1850: Acting Head Assistant to Collector and Magistrate, Trichinopoly. 1851: Head Assistant to Collector and Magistrate, Trichinopoly. 1852: Acting Assistant Judge, Combaconum. 1854: *On furlough to Europe.* 1857: Acting Sub-Collector and Joint Magistrate, Malabar. 1858: Acting Sub-Collector and Joint Magistrate, Salem. 1859: Sub-Collector and Joint Magistrate, Salem. 1862: Acting Collector and Magistrate, South Arcot. 1863: Acting Collector and Magistrate, Cuddapah; Civil and Sessions Judge, Nundyal, but continuing to act as before at Cuddapah. 1864: Civil and Sessions Judge, Bellary. 1865: Collector and Magistrate, Cuddapah. 1868: *On medical leave to Europe.* 1869: *Died, in India, 27th April.*

ST. CLAIR, Hon. James Chisholme.—1856: Writer. 1857: Student at the College. 1858: Assistant to Collector and Magistrate, Bellary. 1859: Acting Head Assistant at Bellary. 1861: Head Assistant at Bellary. 1862: Acting Sub-Collector, Coimbatore. 1864: Acting Sub-Collector and Joint Magistrate, Nellore. 1866: Sub-Collector and Joint Magistrate, Nellore. 1867: Sub-Collector and Joint Magistrate, North Arcot; Acting Civil and Sessions Judge, Mangalore. 1869: *On furlough to Europe for 2 years.* 1871: Acting Collector and Magistrate, Bellary: Sub-Collector and Joint Magistrate, Chingleput; Acting Civil and Sessions Judge, Nundyal. 1873: District and Sessions Judge, South Canara; and at Kurnool. 1874: District and Sessions Judge, Kurnool. 1880: *On furlough to Europe for 2 years.* 1882: *Retired from service, 25th March.* (*Annuitant on the Fund.*)

SULLIVAN, Augustus William.—1844: Writer. 1845: Assistant to Collector and Magistrate, Trichinopoly; Second Assistant to the Accountant-General, Madras. 1846: Assistant to Collector and Magistrate, North Arcot. 1847: Acting Head Assistant to Collector and Magistrate, North Arcot. 1850: Head Assistant to Collector and Magistrate, North Arcot. 1853: Acting Sub-Collector and Joint Magistrate, North Arcot. 1856: Sub-Collector and Joint Magistrate, North Arcot. 1859: Officiating Collector, Madras. 1860: *Without employ for 11 months.* 1861: Officiating Civil and Sessions Judge, Rajahmundry; Sub-Collector and Joint Magistrate, Kistna. 1862: Civil and Sessions Judge, Nundyal. 1863: Acting Civil and Sessions Judge, afterwards Civil and Sessions Judge, Tellicherry.   1868 : *Died, 31st August, in India.*

SULLIVAN, HENRY EDWARD.—1850 : Writer and Student at the College.   1852 : Assistant to Collector and Magistrate, Trichinopoly ; Justice of the Peace.   1855 : Head Assistant to Collector and Magistrate, Malabar ; and at Coimbatore.   1856 : Acting Sub-Collector and Joint Magistrate, Coimbatore.   1857 : Acting Sub-Judge, Madura ; Head Assistant, Coimbatore ; Acting Sub-Collector and Joint Magistrate, Coimbatore ; and at Malabar.   1859 : Sub-Collector and Joint Magistrate, Malabar.   1861 : *On medical leave to Europe for* 23 *months.*   1863 : Sub-Collector, Malabar ; Acting Civil and Sessions Judge, Bellary ; Acting Judge of Small Cause Court, Tellicherry ; Acting Sub-Collector and Joint Magistrate, Coimbatore ; Sub-Collector, Coimbatore.   1865 : Acting Civil and Sessions Judge, Salem ; Sub-Collector, Coimbatore. 1866 : Acting Collector and Magistrate, Kurnool ; Judge of Small Cause Court, Cuddalore ; afterwards at Madura ; Acting Civil and Sessions Judge, Bellary ; Civil and Sessions Judge, Cuddapah. 1868 : Acting Collector and Magistrate, afterwards Collector and Magistrate, Bellary.   1869 : Acting Collector and Magistrate, Coimbatore.   1870 : On Special Duty at Bangalore ; Collector at Bellary.   1871 : *Special leave to Europe for* 6 *months.*   1872 : Acting Collector and Magistrate, Godavari ; and at South Arcot. 1873 : Collector and Magistrate, Trichinopoly.   1874 : Acting Collector, South Arcot ; Officiating Director of Revenue Settlement ; *On furlough to Europe for* 18 *months.*   1876 : Acting Third Member of the Revenue Board ; President of the Committee for Examination of Assistants ; In Charge of the Inam Department.   1877 : Acting Resident of Travancore and Cochin.   1878 : Resumed Third Member, afterwards Second Member of the Revenue Board ; In Charge of the Inam Department ; Acting First Member of the Revenue Board.   1879 : Member of the Famine Commission ; First Member of the Revenue Board ; Commissioner of Uncovenanted Civil Service Examinations ; On Special Duty in Godavari District in Connection with the Rumpa Disturbances ; Member of the Famine Commission in England. 1880 : *Privilege leave in England for* 3 *months, including voyage to India ;* resumed First Member of the Revenue Board.   1881 : Additional Member of the Legislative Council ; In Charge of Settlement Department ; Provisional Member of Council.   1882 : Ordinary Member of Council, *took his seat* 12*th June.*

SWINTON, ROBERT BLAIR.—1849 : Writer and Student at the College. 1851 : Assistant to Collector and Magistrate, Tinnevelly. 1855 : Acting Head Assistant, afterwards Head Assistant at Tinnevelly. 1856 : Acting Sub-Collector and Joint Magistrate, Tinnevelly ; Acting Head Assistant to Collector and Magistrate, Trichinopoly. 1857 : *On medical leave to Europe for* 15 *months.* 1858 : Acting Head Assistant, afterwards Head Assistant to Collector and Magistrate, Rajahmundry ; Acting Subordinate Judge, Cuddapah. 1859 : Sub-Collector and Joint Magistrate, Bellary ; Acting Sub-Judge, Madura, and at Ootacamund ; Subordinate Judge, Mangalore. 1860 : Subordinate Judge, Combaconum. 1862 : Judge of Small Cause Court, Tanjore. 1863 : Acting Civil and Sessions Judge, Tanjore ; and at Negapatam. 1864 : *On furlough to Europe for* 3 *years.* 1867 : *Out of employ for six months ;* Acting Judge of Small Cause Court, Madura ; Acting Civil and Sessions Judge, Tinnevelly. 1868 : District and Sessions Judge, Kistna. 1872 : Acting District and Sessions Judge, South Arcot. 1874 : *Retired from service,* 23d *June.* (*Annuitant on the Fund.*)

TAYLOR, GEORGE NOBLE.—1840 : Writer. 1841 : Assistant to the Collector and Magistrate, Masulipatam. 1842 : Assistant to the Principal Collector and Magistrate, Cuddapah ; Acting Assistant to the Collector and Magistrate, and Agent to the Governor of Fort St. George, in Ganjam. 1843 : In the same capacity at Vizagapatam. 1845 : Assistant to the Collector and Magistrate, and Agent to the Governor of Fort St. George, in Vizagapatam ; *Proceeded to Europe on furlough.* 1848 : *Returned to Madras.* 1849 : Assistant to the Collector and Magistrate, Chingleput ; Acting Secretary to the College and University Boards ; Assistant to the Collector of Land Customs, Madras. 1851 : Secretary to the College Board and to Madras University ; at first Acting, then Sub-Collector and Joint Magistrate, Rajahmundry. 1856 : Acting Deputy Secretary to Government, and Secretary to the Board of Examiners ; *Proceeded to Europe on furlough for* 6 *months.* 1857 : Acting Deputy Collector of Sea Customs, Madras ; Acting Collector and Magistrate, Nellore ; and at South Arcot. 1858 : Inam Commissioner for the Presidency. 1863 : Services placed temporarily at the Disposal of the Government of India. 1864 : Provisional Member of the Council of the Governor-General of India. 1865 : Member of Council of the Viceroy and Governor-General of India. 1869 : *On medical leave to Europe for* 6 *months.*

1870 : *Retired from service,* 11*th March.* (*Annuitant on the Fund.*)

THOMAS, EDWARD CROFT GREENWAY.—1851 : Writer and Student at the College. 1853 : Assistant to Collector and Magistrate, Coimbatore. 1855 : Acting Head Assistant to Collector and Magistrate, Malabar. 1856 : Special Assistant to Collector and Magistrate, Malabar. 1858 : Acting Sub-Judge, Calicut. 1859 : Deputy Director of Revenue Settlement for the Wynaad Talook in Malabar. 1860 : *On medical leave for* 4 *months;* Deputy Director of Revenue Settlement with the Salem Party. 1862 : *On furlough to Europe for* 9 *months.* 1865 : Sub-Collector and Joint Magistrate, Malabar; but to act as Civil and Sessions Judge, Cuddapah; Acting Collector and Magistrate, Kurnool. 1866 : Acting Civil and Sessions Judge at Chingleput, and at Cuddalore, also Civil and Sessions Judge at the latter place; Judge of Small Cause Court, Madura. 1867 : Civil and Sessions Judge, Madura. 1868 : Civil and Sessions Judge, Calicut; *On medical leave for* 6 *months.* 1869 : Acting Collector and Magistrate, afterwards Collector' and Magistrate, Malabar; District and Sessions Judge, Vizagapatam. 1870 : *On special leave for* 6 *months.* 1871 : Resumed District and Sessions Judge, Vizagapatam. 1878 : *On furlough to Europe for* 16 *months, with extension for another year.* 1882 : *Retired from service,* 21*st January, in England.* (*Annuitant on the Fund.*)

THOMAS, HENRY SULLIVAN.—1855 : Writer and Student at the College. 1857 : Assistant to Collector and Magistrate, Canara. 1858 : *On medical leave to the Nilgiri Hills for* 9 *months.* 1859 : Assistant to Collector and Magistrate, Madura. 1860 : Acting Head Assistant, Madura. 1861 : Head Assistant, Collector, and Magistrate, Madura; Officiating Sub-Collector and Joint Magistrate, Nellore. 1862 : Sub-Collector and Joint Magistrate, Madura; Sub-Collector, Madras; Acting Sub-Collector, Salem. 1863 : Sub-Collector, Madura; Acting Sub-Collector, Salem; Sub-Collector and Joint Magistrate, Salem. 1864 : Justice of the Peace. 1866 : Acting Collector of Sea Customs, Madras; Member of the Board of Examiners; Acting Civil and Sessions Judge, Ootacamund; and at Chingleput. 1867 : Acting Collector and Magistrate, South Canara. 1870 : *On furlough to Europe for* 2 *years.* 1872 : Collector and Magistrate, South Canara. 1874 : Acting Collector and Magistrate, and Agent to the Governor of Fort St. George, Tanjore, and Political Agent for French Settlement at Karikal. 1875 : Collector and Magistrate, Kurnool. 1878 : Acting Collector, Tanjore ; Acting Third Member of the Revenue Board, afterwards Acting Second Member : Acting Secretary to Government, Revenue Department. 1879 : Acting Second Member, afterwards Third Member of the Revenue Board ; In Charge of the Inam Department. 1880 : *On furlough to Europe for* 17 *months*. 1881 : Second Member of the Revenue Board, and acting as First Member ; President of the Board of Examiners. 1882 : Member of the Local Self-Government Committee ; proceeded to Calcutta as Additional Member of the Governor-General's Legislative Council. 1883 : Acting First Member of the Revenue Board, Madras ; again to Calcutta as Additional Member of the Governor-General's Legislative Council. 1884 : On Special Duty connected with the " Pearl Fisheries," Tuticorin ; on Deputation to Ceylon for the same purpose ; Acting First Member of the Revenue Board, Madras, afterwards First Member. 1885 : Additional Member of the Governor-General's Council for making Laws and Regulations.

THOMPSON, JOHN GEORGE.—1848 : Writer. 1850 : Assistant to the Principal Collector and Magistrate, Coimbatore. 1853 : Acting Head Assistant at Coimbatore. 1855 : Inspector of Schools. 1857 : Acting Sub-Judge, Mangalore ; Head Assistant to Collector and Magistrate, Salem. 1859 : Sub-Judge, Mangalore ; *Proceeded on furlough to Europe for* 3 *years and* 37 *days*. 1863 : Acting Civil and Sessions Judge, Tellicherry ; and at Mangalore ; Sub-Collector and Joint Magistrate, Malabar. 1864 : Acting Judge of Small Cause Court, Tellicherry. 1865 : Civil and Sessions Judge, Cuddapah, but acting as such at Chingleput. 1866 : Acting, afterwards, Civil and Sessions Judge, Vizagapatam. 1869 : District and Sessions Judge, Ganjam. 1875 : *On furlough to Europe for* 2 *years*. 1877 : *Retired from service, 30th September.* (*Annuitant on the Fund.*)

THOMPSON, STEWART.—1855 : Writer and Student at the College. 1857 : *On medical leave to Europe for* 21 *months*. 1860 : Assistant Collector, Bellary ; *On medical leave for* 15 *months*. 1862 : *Died, 26th December, in England*.

THORNHILL, GEORGE, C.S.I.—1842 : Writer. 1844 : Assistant to the Principal Collector and Magistrate, Coimbatore ; Assistant to Collector and Magistrate, Rajahmundry. 1845 : Acting Head Assistant to Collector and Magistrate, Rajahmundry, and at Cuddapah. 1846 : In the same capacity at Masulipatam.

1847 : Head Assistant to Collector and Magistrate, Masulipatam. 1852 : Head Assistant to Collector and Magistrate, Guntoor. 1853 : *On furlough to Europe.* 1856 : Acting Principal Assistant to Collector and Magistrate, and Agent to the Governor of Fort St. George, in Ganjam. 1857 : Principal Assistant, and Agent to the Governor, Ganjam. 1859 : Acting Collector and Magistrate, and Agent to the Governor, in Vizagapatam ; afterwards Acting Collector and Magistrate, Kurnool. 1860 : Acting Civil and Sessions Judge, Masulipatam ; Acting Collector and Magistrate, Kistna. 1861 : Collector and Magistrate, Kistna. 1862 : *On medical leave for* 15 *months.* 1865 : Acting Collector and Magistrate, and Agent to the Governor, Ganjam. 1867 : Acting Collector and Magistrate, Madras District. 1868 : On Special Duty. 1869 : Acting Third Member of the Revenue Board. 1870 : Acting Second Member, afterwards Third Member of the Revenue Board. 1873 : First Member of the Revenue Board. 1877 : *Made a C.S.I.,* 1*st January.* 1878 : *Retired from service,* 7*th April, in India.* (*Annuitant on the Fund.*)

TOD, George Boulderson.—1852 : Writer. 1853 : Student at the College. 1854 : Assistant to Collector and Magistrate, Malabar. 1856 : Acting Head Assistant at Chingleput. 1857 : Head Assistant at Chingleput. 1858 : *On medical leave to Europe for* 21 *months.* 1860 : Officiating Subordinate Judge, Cuddapah ; Head Assistant to Collector and Magistrate, Trichinopoly ; Acting Principal Assistant to Collector and Magistrate, and Agent to the Governor of Fort St. George, in Ganjam ; Assistant to Collector and Magistrate, Kistna ; Sub-Collector and Joint Magistrate, South Arcot. 1861 : *Died,* 14*th November, at Madras.*

WALHOUSE, Moreton John.—1843 : Writer. 1844 : Assistant to the Principal Collector and Magistrate, Coimbatore. 1846 : Acting Head Assistant to the Principal Collector and Magistrate, Coimbatore. 1851 : Acting Sub-Judge, Salem. 1852 : Head Assistant to Collector and Magistrate, Coimbatore. 1853 : Acting Sub-Collector and Joint Magistrate, Madura. 1854 : In the same capacity at Coimbatore. 1855 : Sub-Collector and Joint Magistrate, Coimbatore. 1856 : Acting Civil and Sessions Judge, Calicut ; and at Honore. 1858 : Acting Collector and Magistrate, Trichinopoly. 1859 : *On furlough to Europe for* 3 *years.* 1862 : Acting Civil and Sessions Judge, Tanjore. 1863 : Acting Collector and Magistrate, Trichinopoly ; Civil and Sessions Judge, Mangalore. 1864 : Acting Collector and Magistrate, Malabar.

1867 : *On medical leave to Europe for 2 years.* 1870 : Civil and Sessions Judge, Mangalore. 1872 : *Resigned the service, 11th March, in India.* (*Annuitant on the Fund.*)

WEBSTER, ALEXANDER M'CALLUM.—1857: Writer and Student at the College. 1859 : Assistant to Collector and Magistrate, Canara; Assistant at North Canara. 1860 : Acting Head Assistant at North Canara, afterwards Head Assistant. 1862 : Head Assistant, South Canara. 1865 : Acting Sub-Collector and Joint Magistrate, Madras District. 1866 : *On medical leave for 20 months.* 1867 : Head Assistant to Collector and Magistrate, South Canara; Sub-Collector and Joint Magistrate, Coimbatore ; Acting Principal Assistant to Collector and Magistrate, and Agent to the Governor, in Vizagapatam. 1868 : Acting Sub-Collector and Joint Magistrate, Coimbatore. 1869 : Sub-Collector and Joint Magistrate, Coimbatore ; Acting Collector and Magistrate, Coimbatore ; and at Malabar. 1870 : Acting Collector and Magistrate, South Canara. 1872 : Acting Collector and Magistrate, Trichinopoly ; Sub-Collector and Joint Magistrate, Chingleput ; *On furlough to Europe for 23 months.* 1873 : Collector and Magistrate, Godavari ; Acting Collector of Sea Customs, and Collector of Madras. 1874 : Acting Collector and Agent to the Governor of Fort St. George, Vizagapatam ; Acting Collector and Magistrate, South Canara. 1875 : Collector and Magistrate, South Canara ; *On special leave to Europe for 6 months.* 1876 : Acting Commissioner, Nilgiri Hills. 1877 : Collector, District Magistrate, and Agent to the Governor, Vizagapatam. 1879: *Died, 27th September, at Coimbatore.*

WEBSTER, EDMUND FOSTER (*Barrister-at-Law*). — 1857 : Writer. 1858: Student at the College. 1859 : Assistant to Collector and Magistrate, Tanjore. 1861 : Acting Head Assistant at Tanjore : *On medical leave to Europe for 2 years and 11 months.* 1864 : Assistant to Collector and Magistrate, Salem ; Acting Head Assistant at Salem, afterwards at Cuddapah. 1865 : Head Assistant at Kistna, and at Kurnool; Acting Sub-Collector and Joint Magistrate, Bellary ; Head Assistant at Salem ; Acting Sub-Collector and Joint Magistrate, Godavari. 1866 : Justice of the Peace ; Head Assistant, afterwards Acting Sub-Collector, Godavari. 1867 : Sub-Collector, Godavari ; Acting First Judge of Small Cause Court, Madras ; Judge of Small Cause Court, Madura, also at Cuddalore in 1868, afterwards Acting Civil and Sessions Judge at Coimbatore. 1869 : Judge of Small Cause Court,

Cuddalore; Acting Civil and Sessions Judge, Tinnevelly. 1871: Judge of Small Cause Court, Cuddalore; *On furlough to Europe for* 14 *months.* 1873: Acting District and Sessions Judge, Cuddapah; Appointment confirmed; District and Sessions Judge, Trichinopoly. 1878: Collector and Magistrate, and Agent to the Governor of Fort St. George, in Tanjore; on Special Duty as a Member of the Famine Committee on Questions of Irrigation. 1879: Resumed Collector and Magistrate, and Agent, Tanjore; *On special leave to Europe for* 5 *months.* 1880: Collector and Magistrate, Tanjore. 1881: Acting Secretary to Government, Revenue Department; Secretary to Famine Code Committee. 1882: Resumed Acting Secretary, afterwards Secretary, to Government, Revenue Department; Member of the Forest Draft Bill Committee; Member of Local Self - Government Committee. 1883: Acting Chief Secretary to Government; Additional Member of Council for making Laws and Regulations. 1884: Chief Secretary to Government; Fellow of the Madras University.

WEDDERBURN, MAXWELL ANDREW.—1841: Writer. 1843: Assistant to Collector and Magistrate, South Arcot. 1845: Assistant to Collector and Magistrate, Malabar. 1846: Acting Head Assistant to Collector and Magistrate, North Arcot. 1847: *Proceeded to Europe.* 1848: Assistant to Collector and Magistrate, North Arcot; Acting Head Assistant to Collector and Magistrate, Cuddapah. 1850: Head Assistant to Collector and Magistrate, Cuddapah. 1851: Acting Sub-Collector and Joint Magistrate, Cuddapah. 1853: Sub-Collector and Magistrate, Cuddapah. 1857: *On furlough to Europe.* 1860: Acting Collector and Magistrate, Cuddapah. 1861: Collector and Magistrate, Cuddapah. 1863: Acting Collector and Magistrate, Bellary. 1864: *On medical leave to Europe for* 16 *months.* 1865: Collector and Magistrate, Tinnevelly. 1866: Collector and Magistrate, Bellary. 1868: Acting Collector and Magistrate, afterwards Collector and Magistrate, Coimbatore. 1869: *On furlough to Europe for* 20 *months.* 1872: Resumed Collector and Magistrate, Coimbatore. 1878: *Retired from service,* 2d *April, in India.* (*Annuitant on the Fund.*)

WHITESIDE, WILLIAM SOUTHEY.—1855: Writer and Student at the College. 1857: Assistant to Collector and Magistrate, North Arcot. 1858: Acting Head Assistant at Tanjore. 1859: Head Assistant to Collector and Magistrate, Nellore. 1860: Officiating Sub-Collector and Joint Magistrate, Nellore. 1861: Officiating Deputy Secretary to Government in Chief-Secretary's Departments. 1862 : Sub-Collector and Joint Magistrate, South Arcot; Deputy Secretary to Government; Acting Civil and Sessions Judge, Chingleput ; Sub-Collector, South Arcot. 1863 : Justice of the Peace. 1864 : *On special leave for 4 months.* 1866 : Acting Judge, afterwards Judge, of Small Cause Court, Cuddalore. 1867 : Acting Collector and Magistrate, South Canara ; Acting Civil and Sessions Judge, Chingleput. 1868 : Judge of Small Cause Court, Madura; Acting Civil and Sessions Judge, Tanjore. 1870 : Acting Collector and Magistrate, North Arcot. 1871 : Acting Collector and Magistrate, Trichinopoly. 1872 : On Duty at Madras ; Acting Collector and Magistrate, North Arcot ; Collector of Trichinopoly. 1873 : Collector and Magistrate, North Arcot. 1882 : Acting Collector and Magistrate, and Agent to the Governor of Fort St. George, Tanjore ; Collector and Magistrate, North Arcot; on Special Duty as Member of the Forest Draft Bill Committee, Ootacamund ; Collector and Magistrate, and Agent, Tanjore ; Acting Second Member of the Revenue Board ; In Charge of the Inam Department ; Acting President of the Board of Examiners. 1884 : Acting Third Member of the Revenue Board ; Director of Revenue Settlement and Agriculture ; Acting Inam Commissioner ; Third Member of the Revenue Board, and President of the Board of Examiners.

WILLIAMS, DERING.—1856 : Writer and Student at the College. 1858 : Assistant to Collector and Magistrate, Malabar. 1859 : Acting Head Assistant, South Canara. 1861 : Head Assistant, South Canara. 1862 : Head Assistant at Nellore. 1864 : *On furlough to Europe for 1 year and 8 months.* 1865 : Assistant to Collector and Magistrate, Madras District ; Acting Sub-Collector and Joint Magistrate, North Arcot. 1866 : *Died, 4th April, in India.*

ADDENDUM.

—-+—

o

					PAGE
Cotton, J. J. . . .	Annuitant,	1862.	Died	Dec. 20, 1867 .	36
Cunliffe, E. W. .	„	1836.	„	Dec. 20, 1866 .	39
Cunliffe, Brooke, Sen. .	„	1835.	„	Dec. 11, 1857 .	39
Dalzell, J. A. . .	„	1839.	„	Dec. 30, 1877 .	40
Daniel, Thos. . .	„	1837.	„	Aug. 25, 1842 .	41
Darvall, Roger . .	„	1806.	„	Oct. 28, 1813 .	41
Dick, Mungo . . .	„	1809.	„	March 31, 1833	44
Dillon, Richard . .	„	1807.	„	Aug. 21, 1818 .	45
Dodwell, Wm. . .	„	1825.	„	Nov. 30, 1859 .	45
Elliott, Daniel (Sir) .	„	1859.	„	Oct. 30, 1872 .	49
Falconer, Alex. . .	„	1812.	„	Dec. 10, 1847 .	51
Forbes, Michie	„	1828.	„	Aug. 24, 1839 .	53
Forbes, Sir J. . . .	„	1827.	„	Feb. 16, 1846 .	54
Frere, Hatley . .	„	1866.	„	Nov. 3, 1868 .	57
Gardiner, H. . . .	„	1836.	„	Aug. 8, 1843 .	59
Gordon, Wm. . . .	„	1806.	„	Oct. 13, 1833 .	62
Gowan, Geo. . .	„	1826.	„	May 25, 1856 .	63
Græme, H. S. .	„	1837.	„	July 14, 1850 .	63
Grant, F. A. . .	„	1832.	„	March 20, 1843	64
Gwatkin, J. . .	„	1832.	„	July 10, 1855 .	66
Hankey, Thompson	„	1827.	„	Oct. 26, 1855 .	69
Harris, Charles	„	1835.	„	Jan. 12, 1840 .	71
Harris, T. J. P. .	„	1866.	„	June 28, 1867 .	72
Hawkins, W. .	„	1820.	„	July 31, 1836 .	73
Heath, J. M. . .	„	1829.	„	Jan. 28, 1851 .	73
Hepburn, Jas. . .	„	1824.	„	May 27, 1845 .	73
Hodgson, J. . .	„	1820.	„	Dec. 29, 1857 .	75
Honeyman, R. B. J.	„	1836.	„	Feb. 23, 1842 .	76
Hooper, G. S. .	„	1860.	„	May 21, 1867 .	76
Hudleston, J. A.	„	1855.	„	Aug. 19, 1865 .	78
Hyde, Chas. .	„	1831.	„	Jan. 13, 1862 .	79
Ince, Daniel . .	„	1807.	„	July 13, 1822 .	79
Inglis, W. A. D. . .	„	1856.	„	Oct. 18, 1873 .	80
Jones, W. . . .	„	1806.	„	March 16, 1812	82
Keene, G. H. . . .	„	1836.	„	Jan. 29, 1864 .	83
Kelso (Hamilton), A. H. .	„	1834.	„	June 11, 1853 .	83
Kindersley, N. E. . .	„	1806.	„	Feb. 16, 1831 .	84
Lacon, H. . . .	„	1835.	„	Feb. 1, 1864 .	85
Lascelles, F. . . .	„	1858.	„	July 15, 1882 .	86
Linley, W. . . .	„	1825.	„	May 6, 1839 .	89

					PAGE
Lushington, C. M.	Annuitant,	1843.	Died March 8, 1864	.	91
Macdonell, Æ. R.	„	1839.	„ Oct. 24, 1866	.	92
Mackenzie, Alex.	„	1810.	„ April 14, 1852	.	93
Mackonochie, R.	„	1842.	„ Feb. 19, 1858	.	93
Malcolm, R.	„	1806.	„ Oct. 2, 1813	.	95
Mathison, A. S.	„	1859.	„ April 18, 1882	.	97
Mitford, J.	„	1805.	„ Oct. 9, 1834	.	98
Monk, W. G.	„	1829.	„ March 3, 1859	.	99
Montgomerie, W.	„	1834.	„ Oct. 23, 1852	.	99

Montgomery, Sir H. C. . Appointed Member of Council of the Secretary of State, September 2, 1858, on transfer of Government from the East India Company to the Crown. Retired from Council, November 13, 1876 100

Morehead, W. A.	Annuitant,	1862.	Died Dec. 1, 1863	.	101
Mortlock, H.	„	1828.	„ Feb. 13, 1837	.	103
Newnham, Thos.	„	1833.	„ Sept. 29, 1861	.	105
Nicholls, Solomon	„	1836.	„ Aug. 22, 1857	.	106
Oakes, Thos.	„	1815.	„ Dec. 29, 1834	.	106
Ogilvie, J. H. D.	„	1831.	„ March 10, 1851	.	107
Oliver, W.	„	1836.	„ Aug. 2, 1846	.	108
Orr, John	„	1844.	„ in 1845	.	110
Parish, G.	„	1828.	„ April 7, 1839	.	110
Parker, R. D.	„	1859.	„ Sept. 20, 1873	.	111
Read, John	„	1816.	„ July 7, 1843	.	119
Read, George	„	1815.	„ Sept. 28, 1825	.	120
Read, Alex.	„	1825.	„ Oct. 8, 1849	.	120
Reade, C. W.	„	1871.	„ April 27, 1884	.	120
Richardson, Francis	„	1821.	„ Sept. 25, 1856	.	121
Savory, J. S.	„	1821.	„ June 22, 1857	.	126
Sherson, Robt.	„	1823.	„ March 23, 1843	.	128
Skardon, J. H.	„	1803.	„ April 24, 1810	.	129
Skinner, Samuel	„	1819.	„ May 21, 1854	.	130
Snodgrass, Thos.	„	1805.	„ Aug. 28, 1834	.	133
Strachey, Geo.	„	1820.	„ in 1849	.	136
Strange, Jas.	„	1816.	„ Oct. 6, 1840	.	136
Stratton, Geo.	„	1824.	„ Aug. 30, 1853	.	137
Taswell, W.	„	1830.	„ Aug. 24, 1857	.	139
Thompson, G.	„	...	„ in 1804 (*India*)	.	143
Torin, Benjamin	„	1805.	„ May 11, 1839	.	144
Torriano, W. H.	„	1808.	„ Nov. 16, 1828	.	144

PRINTED BY BALLANTYNE, HANSON, AND CO.
EDINBURGH AND LONDON.

A

CATALOGUE OF IMPORTANT WORKS,

PUBLISHED BY

TRÜBNER & CO.

57 AND 59 LUDGATE HILL.

———•———

ABEL.—LINGUISTIC ESSAYS. By Carl Abel. CONTENTS: Language as the Expression of National Modes of Thought—The Conception of Love in some Ancient and Modern Languages—The English Verbs of Command—The Discrimination of Synonyms—Philological Methods—The Connection between Dictionary and Grammar—The Possibility of a Common Literary Language for the Slav Nations—Coptic Intensification—The Origin of Language—The Order and Position of Words in the Latin Sentence. Post 8vo, pp. xii. and 282, cloth. 1882. 9s.

ABEL.—SLAVIC AND LATIN. Ilchester Lectures on Comparative Lexicography. Delivered at the Taylor Institution, Oxford. By Carl Abel, Ph.D. Post 8vo, pp. vi.–124, cloth. 1883. 5s.

ABRAHAMS.—A MANUAL OF SCRIPTURE HISTORY FOR USE IN JEWISH SCHOOLS AND FAMILIES. By L. B. Abrahams, B.A., Principal Assistant Master, Jews' Free School. With Map and Appendices. Third Edition. Crown 8vo, pp. viii. and 152, cloth. 1883. 1s. 6d.

AGASSIZ.—AN ESSAY ON CLASSIFICATION. By Louis Agassiz. 8vo, pp. vii. and 381, cloth. 1859. 12s.

AHLWARDT.—THE DIVANS OF THE SIX ANCIENT ARABIC POETS, ENNÁBIGA, 'ANTARA, THARAFA, ZUHAIR, 'ALQUAMA, and IMRUULQUAIS; chiefly according to the MSS. of Paris, Gotha, and Leyden, and the Collection of their Fragments, with a List of the various Readings of the Text. Edited by W. Ahlwardt, Professor of Oriental Languages at the University of Greifswald. Demy 8vo, pp. xxx. and 340, sewed. 1870. 12s.

AHN.—PRACTICAL GRAMMAR OF THE GERMAN LANGUAGE. By Dr. F. Ahn. A New Edition. By Dr. Dawson Turner, and Prof. F. L. Weinmann. Crown 8vo, pp. cxii. and 430, cloth. 1878. 3s. 6d.

AHN.—NEW, PRACTICAL, AND EASY METHOD OF LEARNING THE GERMAN LANGUAGE. By Dr. F. Ahn. First and Second Course. Bound in 1 vol. 12mo, pp. 86 and 120, cloth. 1866. 3s.

AHN.—KEY to Ditto. 12mo, pp. 40, sewed. 8d.

AHN.—MANUAL OF GERMAN AND ENGLISH CONVERSATIONS, or Vade Mecum for English Travellers. 12mo, pp. x. and 137, cloth. 1875. 1s. 6d.

A

AHN.—New, Practical, and Easy Method of Learning the French Language. By Dr. F. Ahn. First Course and Second Course. 12mo, cloth. Each 1s. 6d. The Two Courses in 1 vol. 12mo, pp. 114 and 170, cloth. 1865. 3s.

AHN.—New, Practical, and Easy Method of Learning the French Language. Third Course, containing a French Reader, with Notes and Vocabulary. By H. W. Ehrlich. 12mo, pp. viii. and 125, cloth. 1866. 1s. 6d.

AHN.—Manual of French and English Conversations, for the use of Schools and Travellers. By Dr. F. Ahn. 12mo, pp. viii. and 200, cloth. 1862. 2s. 6d.

AHN.—New, Practical, and Easy Method of Learning the Italian Language. By Dr. F. Ahn. First and Second Course. 12mo, pp. 198, cloth. 1872. 3s. 6d.

AHN.—New, Practical, and Easy Method of Learning the Dutch Language, being a complete Grammar, with Selections. By Dr. F. Ahn. 12mo, pp. viii. and 166, cloth. 1862. 3s. 6d.

AHN.—Ahn's Course. Latin Grammar for Beginners. By W. Ihue, Ph.D. 12mo, pp. vi. and 184, cloth. 1864. 3s.

ALABASTER.—The Wheel of the Law : Buddhism illustrated from Siamese Sources by the Modern Buddhist, a Life of Buddha, and an Account of the Phra Bat. By Henry Alabaster, Esq., Interpreter of Her Majesty's Consulate-General in Siam. Demy 8vo, pp. lviii. and 324, cloth. 1871. 14s.

ALI.—The Proposed Political, Legal, and Social Reforms in the Ottoman Empire and other Mohammedan States. By Moulaví Cherágh Ali, H.H. the Nizam's Civil Service. Demy 8vo, pp. liv. and 184, cloth. 1883. 8s.

ALLAN-FRASER.—Christianity and Churchism. By Patrick Allan-Fraser. 2d (revised and enlarged) Edition. Crown 8vo, pp. 52, cloth. 1884. 1s.

ALLEN.—The Colour Sense. See English and Foreign Philosophical Library, Vol. X.

ALLIBONE.—A Critical Dictionary of English Literature and British and American Authors (Living and Deceased). From the Earliest Accounts to the latter half of the 19th century. Containing over 46,000 Articles (Authors), with 40 Indexes of subjects. By S. A. Allibone. In 3 vols. royal 8vo, cloth. £5, 8s.

ALTHAUS.—The Spas of Europe. By Julius Althaus, M.D. 8vo, pp. 516, cloth. 1862. 7s. 6d.

AMATEUR Mechanic's Workshop (The). A Treatise containing Plain and Concise Directions for the Manipulation of Wood and Metals ; including Casting, Forging, Brazing, Soldering, and Carpentry. By the Author of "The Lathe and its Uses." Sixth Edition. Demy 8vo, pp. vi. and 148, with Two Full-Page Illustrations, on toned paper and numerous Woodcuts, cloth. 1880. 6s.

AMATEUR MECHANICAL SOCIETY.—Journal of the Amateur Mechanical Society. 8vo. Vol. i. pp. 344 cloth. 1871-72. 12s. Vol. ii. pp. vi. and 290, cloth. 1873-77. 12s. Vol. iii. pp. iv. and 246, cloth. 1878-79. 12s. 6d.

AMERICAN Almanac and Treasury of Facts, Statistical, Financial, and Political. Edited by Ainsworth R. Spofford, Librarian of Congress. Crown 8vo, cloth. Published yearly. 1878-1884. 7s. 6d. each.

AMERY.—Notes on Forestry. By C. F. Amery, Deputy Conservator N.|W. Provinces, India. Crown 8vo, pp. viii. and 120, cloth. 1875. 5s.

AMBERLEY.—An Analysis of Religious Belief. By Viscount Amberley. 2 vols. demy 8vo, pp. xvi. and 496 and 512, cloth. 1876. 30s.

AMONGST MACHINES. A Description of Various Mechanical Appliances used in the Manufacture of Wood, Metal, and other Substances. A Book for Boys, copiously Illustrated. By the Author of "The Young Mechanic." Second Edition. Imperial 16mo, pp. viii. and 336, cloth. 1878. 7s. 6d.

ANDERSON.—PRACTICAL MERCANTILE CORRESPONDENCE. A Collection of Modern Letters of Business, with Notes, Critical and Explanatory, and an Appendix, containing a Dictionary of Commercial Technicalities, pro forma Invoices, Account Sales, Bills of Lading, and Bills of Exchange; also an Explanation of the German Chain Rule. 24th Edition, revised and enlarged. By William Anderson. 12mo, pp. 288, cloth. 5s.

ANDERSON and TUGMAN.—MERCANTILE CORRESPONDENCE, containing a Collection of Commercial Letters in Portuguese and English, with their translation on opposite pages, for the use of Business Men and of Students in either of the Languages, treating in modern style of the system of Business in the principal Commercial Cities of the World. Accompanied by pro forma Accounts, Sales, Invoices, Bills of Lading, Drafts, &c. With an Introduction and copious Notes. By William Anderson and James E. Tugman. 12mo, pp. xi. and 193, cloth. 1867. 6s.

APEL.—PROSE SPECIMENS FOR TRANSLATION INTO GERMAN, with copious Vocabularies and Explanations. By H. Apel. 12mo, pp. viii. and 246, cloth. 1862. 4s. 6d.

APPLETON (Dr.)—LIFE AND LITERARY RELICS. See English and Foreign Philosophical Library, Vol. XIII.

ARAGO.—LES ARISTOCRATIES. A Comedy in Verse. By Etienne Arago. Edited, with English Notes and Notice on Etienne Arago, by the Rev. E. P. H. Brette, B.D., Head Master of the French School, Christ's Hospital, Examiner in the University of London. Fcap. 8vo, pp. 244, cloth. 1868. 4s.

ARMITAGE.—LECTURES ON PAINTING : Delivered to the Students of the Royal Academy. By Edward Armitage, R.A. Crown 8vo, pp. 256, with 29 Illustrations, cloth. 1883. 7s. 6d.

ARNOLD.—INDIAN IDYLLS. From the Sanskrit of the Mahâbhârata. By Edwin Arnold, C.S.I., &c. Crown 8vo, pp. xii. and 282, cloth. 1883. 7s. 6d.

ARNOLD.—PEARLS OF THE FAITH ; or, Islam's Rosary : being the Ninety-nine beautiful names of Allah. With Comments in Verse from various Oriental sources as made by an Indian Mussulman. By Edwin Arnold, C.S.I., &c. Third Edition. Crown 8vo, pp. xvi. and 320, cloth. 1884. 7s. 6d.

ARNOLD.—THE LIGHT OF ASIA ; or, THE GREAT RENUNCIATION (Mahâbhinishkramana). Being the Life and Teaching of Gautama, Prince of India, and Founder of Buddhism (as told in verse by an Indian Buddhist). By Edwin Arnold, C.S.I., &c. Crown 8vo, pp. xiii. and 238, limp parchment. 1884. 2s. 6d. Library Edition. 1883. 7s. 6d. Illustrated Edition. Small 4to, pp. xx.-196, cloth. 1884. 21s.

ARNOLD.—THE SECRET OF DEATH : Being a Version, in a popular and novel form, of the Katha Upanishad, from the Sanskrit. With some Collected Poems. By Edwin Arnold, M.A., Author of "The Light of Asia," &c., &c. Crown 8vo. pp. viii.-406, cloth. 1885. 7s. 6d.

ARNOLD.—THE ILIAD AND ODYSSEY OF INDIA. By Edwin Arnold, M.A., F.R.G.S., &c., &c. Fcap. 8vo, pp. 24, sewed. 1s.

ARNOLD.—A SIMPLE TRANSLITERAL GRAMMAR OF THE TURKISH LANGUAGE. Compiled from Various Sources. With Dialogues and Vocabulary. By Edwin Arnold, M.A., C.S.I., F.R.G.S. Post 8vo, pp. 80, cloth. 1877. 2s. 6d.

ARNOLD.—INDIAN POETRY. See Trübner's Oriental Series.

ARTHUR.—THE COPARCENERS : Being the Adventures of two Heiresses. By F. Arthur. Crown 8vo, pp. iv.-312, cloth. 1885. 10s. 6d.

ARTOM.—SERMONS. By the Rev. B. Artom, Chief Rabbi of the Spanish and Portuguese Congregations of England. First Series. Second Edition. Crown 8vo, pp. viii. and 314, cloth. 1876. 6s.

ASIATIC SOCIETY OF BENGAL. List of Publications on application.

ASIATIC SOCIETY.—JOURNAL OF THE ROYAL ASIATIC SOCIETY OF GREAT BRITAIN AND IRELAND, from the Commencement to 1863. First Series, complete in 20 Vols. 8vo, with many Plates. £10, or in parts from 4s. to 6s. each.

ASIATIC SOCIETY.—JOURNAL OF THE ROYAL ASIATIC SOCIETY OF GREAT BRITAIN AND IRELAND. New Series. 8vo. Stitched in wrapper. 1864-84.

Vol. I., 2 Parts, pp. iv. and 490, 16s.—Vol. II., 2 Parts, pp. 522, 16s.—Vol. III., 2 Parts, pp. 516, with Photograph, 22s.—Vol. IV., 2 Parts. pp. 521, 16s.—Vol. V., 2 Parts, pp. 463, with 10 full-page and folding Plates, 18s. 6d.—Vol. VI., Part 1, pp. 212, with 2 Plates and a Map, 8s. —Vol. VI. Part 2, pp. 272, with Plate and Map, 8s.—Vol. VII., Part 1, pp. 194, with a Plate. 8s.—Vol. VII., Part 2, pp. 204, with 7 Plates and a Map, 8s.—Vol. VIII., Part 1, pp. 156, with 3 Plates and a Plan, 8s.—Vol. VIII., Part 2, pp. 152, 8s.—Vol. IX., Part 1, pp. 154, with a Plate, 8s.—Vol. IX., Part 2, pp. 292, with 3 Plates, 10s. 6d.—Vol. X., Part 1, pp. 156, with 2 Plates and a Map, 8s.—Vol. X., Part 2, pp. 146, 6s.—Vol. X., Part 3, pp. 204, 8s.—Vol. XI., Part 1, pp. 128, 5s.—Vol. XI., Part 2, pp. 158, with 2 Plates, 7s. 6d.—Vol. XI., Part 3, pp. 250, 8s.—Vol. XII., Part 1, pp. 152, 5s.—Vol. XII., Part 2, pp. 182, with 2 Plates and Map, 6s.— Vol. XII., Part 3, pp. 100, 4s.—Vol. XII., Part 4, pp. x., 152., cxx., 16, 8s.—Vol. XIII., Part 1, pp. 120, 5s.—Vol. XIII., Part 2, pp. 170, with a Map, 8s.—Vol. XIII., Part 3, pp. 178, with a Table, 7s. 6d.—Vol. XIII., Part 4, pp. 282, with a Plate and Table, 10s. 6d.—Vol. XIV., Part 1, pp. 124, with a Table and 2 Plates, 5s.—Vol. XIV., Part 2, pp. 164, with 1 Table, 7s. 6d.—Vol. XIV., Part 3, pp. 206, with 6 Plates, 8s.—Vol. XIV., Part 4, pp. 492, with 1 Plate, 14s.—Vol. XV., Part 1, pp. 136, 6s. ; Part 2, pp. 158, with 3 Tables, 5s. : Part 3, pp. 192, 6s. ; Part 4, pp. 140, 5s.—Vol. XVI., Part 1, pp. 138, with 2 Plates, 7s. Part 2, pp. 184, with 1 Plate, 9s. Part 3, July 1884, pp. 74-clx., 10s. 6d. Part 4, pp. 132, 8s.—Vol. XVII., Part 1, pp. 144, with 6 Plates, 10s. 6d.

ASPLET.—THE COMPLETE FRENCH COURSE. Part II. Containing all the Rules of French Syntax, &c., &c. By Georges C. Asplet, French Master, Frome. Fcap. 8vo, pp. xx. and 276, cloth. 1880. 2s. 6d.

ASTON.—A Short Grammar of the Japanese Spoken Language. By W. G. Aston, M.A. Third Edition. Crown 8vo, pp. 96, cloth. 1873. 12s.

ASTON.—A GRAMMAR OF THE JAPANESE WRITTEN LANGUAGE. By W. G. Aston, M.A., Assistant Japanese Secretary H.B.M.'s Legation, Yedo, Japan. Second Edition. 8vo, pp. 306, cloth. 1877. 28s.

ASTONISHED AT AMERICA. BEING CURSORY DEDUCTIONS, &c., &c. By Zigzag. Fcap. 8vo, pp. xvi.-108, boards. 1880. 1s.

AUCTORES SANSCRITI.

Vol. I. THE JAIMINÎYA-NYÂYA-MÂLÂ-VISTARA. Edited for the Sanskrit Text Society, under the supervision of Theodor Goldstücker. Large 4to, pp. 582, cloth. £3, 13s. 6d.

Vol. II. THE INSTITUTES OF GAUTAMA. Edited, with an Index of Words, by A. F. Stenzler, Ph.D., Prof. of Oriental Languages in the University of Breslau. 8vo, pp. iv. and 78, cloth. 1876. 4s. 6d. Stitched, 3s. 6d.

Vol. III. VAITÂNA SUTRA : THE RITUAL OF THE ATHARVA VEDA. Edited, with Critical Notes and Indices, by Dr. R. Garbe. 8vo, pp. viii. and 120, sewed. 1878. 5s.

Vols. IV. and V.—VARDHAMANA'S GANARATNAMAHODADHI, with the Author's Commentary. Edited, with Critical Notes and Indices, by Julius Eggeling, Ph.D. 8vo. Part I., pp. xii. and 240, wrapper. 1879. 6s. Part II., pp. 240, wrapper. 1881. 6s.

AUGIER.—DIANE. A Drama in Verse. By Émile Augier. Edited with English Notes and Notice on Augier. By T. Karcher, LL.B., of the Royal Military Academy and the University of London. 12mo, pp. xiii. and 146, cloth. 1867. 2s. 6d.

AUSTIN.—A PRACTICAL TREATISE on the Preparation, Combination, and Application of Calcareous and Hydraulic Limes and Cements. To which is added many useful Recipes for various Scientific, Mercantile, and Domestic Purposes. By James G. Austin, Architect. 12mo, pp. 192, cloth. 1862. 5s.

AUSTRALIA.—THE YEAR BOOK OF AUSTRALIA for 1885. Demy 8vo, pp.   . 5s.

AXON.—THE MECHANIC'S FRIEND. A Collection of Receipts and Practical Suggestions relating to Aquaria, Bronzing, Cements, Drawing, Dyes, Electricity, Gilding, Glass-working, &c. Numerous Woodcuts. Edited by W. E. A. Axon, M.R.S.L., F.S.S. Crown 8vo, pp. xii. and 339, cloth. 1875. 4s. 6d.

BABA.—An Elementary Grammar of the Japanese Language, with Easy Progressive Exercises. By Tatui Baba. Crown 8vo, pp. xiv. and 92, cloth. 1873. 5s.

BACON.—THE LIFE AND TIMES OF FRANCIS BACON. Extracted from the Edition of his Occasional Writings by James Spedding. 2 vols. post 8vo, pp. xx., 710, and xiv., 708, cloth. 1878. 21s.

BADEN-POWELL.—PROTECTION AND BAD TIMES, with Special Reference to the Political Economy of English Colonisation. By George Baden-Powell, M.A., F.R.A.S., F.S.S., Author of "New Homes for the Old Country," &c., &c. 8vo, pp. xii.-376, cloth. 1879. 6s. 6d.

BADER.—THE NATURAL AND MORBID CHANGES OF THE HUMAN EYE, AND THEIR TREATMENT. By C. Bader. Medium 8vo, pp. viii. and 506, cloth. 1868. 16s.

BADER.—PLATES ILLUSTRATING THE NATURAL AND MORBID CHANGES OF THE HUMAN EYE. By C. Bader. Six chromo-lithographic Plates, each containing the figures of six Eyes, and four lithographed Plates, with figures of Instruments. With an Explanatory Text of 32 pages. Medium 8vo, in a portfolio. 21s. Price for Text and Atlas taken together, £1, 12s.

BADLEY.—INDIAN MISSIONARY RECORD AND MEMORIAL VOLUME. By the Rev. B. H. Badley, of the American Methodist Mission. 8vo, pp. xii. and 280, cloth. 1876. 10s. 6d.

BALFOUR.—WAIFS AND STRAYS FROM THE FAR EAST; being a Series of Disconnected Essays on Matters relating to China. By Frederick Henry Balfour. Demy 8vo, pp. 224, cloth. 1876. 10s. 6d.

BALFOUR.—THE DIVINE CLASSIC OF NAN-HUA; being the Works of Chuang Tsze, Taoist Philosopher. With an Excursus, and Copious Annotations in English and Chinese. By F. H. Balfour. 8vo, pp. xlviii. and 426, cloth. 1881. 14s.

BALFOUR.—TAOIST TEXTS, Ethical, Political, and Speculative. By F. H. BALFOUR, Editor of the *North-China Herald;* Author of "The Divine Classic of Nanhua," &c. Imp. 8vo, pp. vi.-118, cloth. 10s. 6d.

BALL.—THE DIAMONDS, COAL, AND GOLD OF INDIA; their Mode of Occurrence and Distribution. By V. Ball, M.A., F.G.S., of the Geological Survey of India. Fcap. 8vo, pp. viii. and 136, cloth. 1881. 5s.

BALL.—A MANUAL OF THE GEOLOGY OF INDIA. Part III. Economic Geology. By V. Ball, M.A., F.G.S. Royal 8vo, pp. xx. and 640, with 6 Maps and 10 Plates, cloth. 1881. 10s. (For Parts I. and II. see MEDLICOTT.)

BALLAD SOCIETY—Subscriptions, small paper, one guinea; large paper, two guineas per annum. List of publications on application.

BALLANTYNE.—ELEMENTS OF HINDI AND BRAJ BHAKHA GRAMMAR. Compiled for the use of the East India College at Haileybury. By James R. Ballantyne. Second Edition. Crown 8vo, pp. 38, cloth. 1868. 5s.

BALLANTYNE.—FIRST LESSONS IN SANSKRIT GRAMMAR; together with an Introduction to the Hitopadeśa. Fourth Edition. By James R. Ballantyne, LL.D., Librarian of the India Office. 8vo, pp. viii. and 110, cloth. 1884. 3s. 6d.

BALLANTYNE.—THE SANKHYA APHORISMS OF KAPILA. See Trübner's Oriental Series.

BARANOWSKI.—VADE MECUM DE LA LANGUE FRANÇAISE, rédigé d'après les Dictionnaires classiques avec les Exemples de Bonnes Locutions que donne l'Académie Française, on qu'on trouve dans les ouvrages des plus célèbres auteurs. Par J. J. Baranowski, avec l'approbation de M. E. Littré, Sénateur, &c. Second Edition. 32mo, pp. 224. 1883. Cloth, 2s. 6d.

BARANOWSKI.—ANGLO-POLISH LEXICON. By J. J. Baranowski, formerly Under-Secretary to the Bank of Poland, in Warsaw. Fcap. 8vo, pp. viii. and 492, cloth. 1883. 6s.

BARANOWSKI.—SLOWNIK POLSKO-ANGIELSKI. (Polish-English Lexicon.) By J. J. Baranowski. Fcap. 8vo, pp. iv.-402, cloth. 1884. 6s. 6d.

BARENTS' RELICS.—Recovered in the summer of 1876 by Charles L. W. Gardiner, Esq., and presented to the Dutch Goverment. Described and explained by J. K. J. de Jonge, Deputy Royal Architect at the Hague. Published by command of His Excellency, W. F. Van F.R.P. Taelman Kip. Minister of Marine. Translated, with a Preface, by S. R. Van Campen. With a Map, Illustrations, and a fac-simile of the Scroll. 8vo, pp. 70, cloth. 1877. 5s.

BARRIÈRE and CAPENDU.—LES FAUX BONSHOMMES, a Comedy. By Théodore Barrière and Ernest Capendu. Edited, with English Notes and Notice ou Barrière, by Professor Ch. Cassal, LL.D., of University College, London. 12mo, pp. xvi. and 304, cloth. 1868. 4s.

BARTH.—THE RELIGIONS OF INDIA. See Trübner's Oriental Series.

BARTLETT.—DICTIONARY OF AMERICANISMS. A Glossary of Words and Phrases colloquially used in the United States. By John Russell Bartlett. Fourth Edition, cousiderably enlarged and improved. 8vo, pp. xlvi. aud 814, cloth. 1877. 20s.

BATTYE.—WHAT IS VITAL FORCE? or, a Short and Comprehensive Sketch, including Vital Physics, Animal Morphology, and Epidemics; to which is added an Appendix upon Geology, IS THE DENTRITAL THEORY OF GEOLOGY TENABLE? By Richard Fawcett Battye. 8vo, pp. iv. and 336, cloth. 1877. 7s. 6d.

BAZLEY.—NOTES ON THE EPICYCLODIAL CUTTING FRAME of Messrs. Holtzapffel & Co. With special reference to its Compensation Adjustment, and with numerous Illustrations of its Capabilities. By Thomas Sebastian Bazley, M.A. 8vo, pp. xvi. and 192, cloth. Illustrated. 1872. 10s. 6d.

BAZLEY.—THE STARS IN THEIR COURSES: A Twofold Series of Maps, with a Catalogue, showing how to identify, at any time of the year, all stars down to the 5.6 magnitude, inclusive of Heis, which are clearly visible in English latitudes. By T. S. Bazley, M.A., Author of "Notes on the Epicycloidal Cutting Frame." Atlas folio, pp. 46 and 24, Folding Plates, cloth. 1878. 15s.

BEAL.—A CATENA OF BUDDHIST SCRIPTURES FROM THE CHINESE. By S. Beal, B.A., Trinity College, Cambridge; a Chaplain in Her Majesty's Fleet, &c. 8vo, pp. xiv. and 436, cloth. 1871. 15s.

BEAL.—THE ROMANTIC LEGEND OF SAKYA BUDDHA. From the Chinese-Sanskrit. By the Rev. Samuel Beal. Crown 8vo, pp. 408, cloth. 1875. 12s.

BEAL.—DHAMMAPADA. See Trübner's Oriental Series.

BEAL.—BUDDHIST LITERATURE IN CHINA: Abstract of Four Lectures, Delivered by Samuel Beal, B.A., Professor of Chinese at University College, London. Demy 8vo, pp. xx. and 186, cloth. 1882. 10s. 6d.

BEAL.—SI-YU-KI. Buddhist Records of the Western World. See Trübner's Oriental Series.

BEAMES.—OUTLINES OF INDIAN PHILOLOGY. With a Map showing the Distribution of Indian Languages. By John Beames, M.R.A.S., B.C.S., &c. Second enlarged and revised Edition. Crown 8vo, pp. viii. and 96, cloth. 1868. 5s.

BEAMES.—A COMPARATIVE GRAMMAR OF THE MODERN ARYAN LANGUAGES OF INDIA, to wit, Hindi, Panjabi, Sindhi, Gujarati, Marathi, Oriya, and Bengali. By John Beames, B.C.S., M.R.A.S., &c., &c. Demy 8vo. Vol. I. On Sounds. Pp. xvi. and 360, cloth. 1872. 16s.—Vol. II. The Noun and the Pronoun. Pp. xii. aud 348, cloth. 1875. 16s.—Vol. III. The Verb. Pp. xii. and 316, cloth. 1879. 16s.

BELLEW.—FROM THE INDUS TO THE TIGRIS. A Narrative of a Journey through Balochistan, Afghanistan, Khorassan, and Iran in 1872; together with a Synoptical Grammar and Vocabulary of the Brahoe Language, and a Record of the Meteorological Observations on the March from the Indus to the Tigris. By Henry Walter Bellew, C.S.I., Surgeon, B.S.C. 8vo, pp. viii. and 496, cloth. 1874. 14s.

BELLEW.—KASHMIR AND KASHGHAR: a Narrative of the Journey of the Embassy to Kashghar in 1873-74. By H. W. Bellew, C.S.I. Demy 8vo, pp. xxxii. and 420, cloth. 1875. 16s.

BELLEW.—THE RACES OF AFGHANISTAN. Being a Brief Account of the Principal Nations Inhabiting that Country. By Surgeon-Major H. W. Bellew, C.S.I., late on Special Political Duty at Kabul. 8vo, pp. 124, cloth. 1880. 7s. 6d.

BELLOWS.—ENGLISH OUTLINE VOCABULARY for the use of Students of the Chinese, Japanese, and other Languages. Arranged by John Bellows. With Notes on the Writing of Chinese with Roman Letters, by Professor Summers, King's College, London. Crown 8vo, pp. vi. and 368, cloth. 1867. 6s.

BELLOWS.—OUTLINE DICTIONARY FOR THE USE OF MISSIONARIES, EXPLORERS, AND STUDENTS OF LANGUAGE. By Max Müller, M.A., Taylorian Professor in the University of Oxford. With an Introduction on the proper use of the ordinary English Alphabet in transcribing Foreign Languages. The Vocabulary compiled by John Bellows. Crown 8vo, pp. xxxi. and 368, limp morocco. 1867. 7s. 6d.

BELLOWS.—TOUS LES VERBES. Conjugations of all the Verbs in the French and English Languages. By John Bellows. Revised by Professor Beljame, B.A., LL.B., of the University of Paris, and Official Interpreter to the Imperial Court, and George B. Strickland, late Assistant French Master, Royal Naval School, London. Also a New Table of Equivalent Values of French and English Money, Weights, and Measures. 32mo, 76 Tables, sewed. 1867. 1s.

BELLOWS.—FRENCH AND ENGLISH DICTIONARY FOR THE POCKET. By John Bellows. Containing the French-English and English-French divisions on the same page; conjugating all the verbs; distinguishing the genders by different types; giving numerous aids to pronunciation; indicating the *liaison* or *non-liaison* of terminal consonants; and translating units of weight, measure, and value, by a series of tables differing entirely from any hitherto published. The new edition, which is but six ounces in weight, has been remodelled, and contains many thousands of additional words and renderings. Miniature maps of France, the British Isles. Paris, and London, are added to the Geographical Section. Second Edition. 32mo, pp. 608, roan tuck, or persian without tuck. 1877. 10s. 6d.; morocco tuck, 12s. 6d.

BENEDIX.—DER VETTER. Comedy in Three Acts. By Roderich Benedix. With Grammatical and Explanatory Notes by F. Weinmann, German Master at the Royal Institution School, Liverpool, and G. Zimmermann, Teacher of Modern Languages. 12mo, pp. 128, cloth. 1863. 2s. 6d.

BENFEY.—A PRACTICAL GRAMMAR OF THE SANSKRIT LANGUAGE, for the use of Early Students. By Theodor Benfey, Professor of Sanskrit in the University of Göttingen. Second, revised, and enlarged Edition. Royal 8vo, pp. viii. and 296, cloth. 1868. 10s. 6d.

BENTHAM.—THEORY OF LEGISLATION. By Jeremy Bentham. Translated from the French of Etienne Dumont by R. Hildreth. Fourth Edition. Post 8vo, pp. xv. and 472, cloth. 1882. 7s. 6d.

BETTS.—*See* VALDES.

BEVERIDGE.—THE DISTRICT OF BAKARGANJ. Its History and Statistics. By H. Beveridge, B.C.S., Magistrate and Collector of Bakarganj. 8vo, pp. xx. and 460, cloth. 1876. 21s.

BHANDARKAR.—EARLY HISTORY OF THE DEKKAN DOWN TO THE MAHOMEDAN CONQUEST. By Ramkrishna Gopal Bhandarkar, M.A., Hon. M.R.A.S., Professor of Oriental Languages, Dekkan College. Written for the *Bombay Gazette*. Royal 8vo, pp. 128, wrapper. 1884. 5s.

BICKNELL.—*See* HAFIZ.

BIERBAUM.—HISTORY OF THE ENGLISH LANGUAGE AND LITERATURE.—By F. J. Bierbaum, Ph.D. Crown 8vo, pp. viii. and 270, cloth. 1883. 3s.

BIGANDET.—THE LIFE OF GAUDAMA. See Trübner's Oriental Series.

BILLINGS.—THE PRINCIPLES OF VENTILATION AND HEATING, and their Practical Application. By John S. Billings, M.D., LL.D. (Edinb.), Surgeon U.S. Army. Demy 8vo, pp. x. and 216, cloth. 1884. 15s.

BIRCH.—FASTI MONASTICI ÆVI SAXONICI ; or, An Alphabetical List of the Heads of Religious Houses in England previous to the Norman Conquest, to which is prefixed a Chronological Catalogue of Contemporary Foundations. By Walter de Gray Birch. 8vo, pp. vii. and 114, cloth. 1873. 5s.

BIRD.—PHYSIOLOGICAL ESSAYS. Drink Craving, Differences in Men, Idiosyncrasy, and the Origin of Disease. By Robert Bird, M.D. Demy 8vo, pp. 246, cloth. 1870. 7s. 6d.

BIZYENOS.—ΑΤΘΙΔΕΞ ΑΥΡΑΙ. Poems. By George M. Bizyenos. With Frontispiece Etched by Prof. A. Legros. Royal 8vo, pp. viii.-312, printed on hand-made paper, and richly bound. 1883. £1, 11s. 6d.

BLACK.—YOUNG JAPAN, YOKOHAMA AND YEDO. A Narrative of the Settlement and the City, from the Signing of the Treaties in 1858 to the Close of the Year 1879; with a Glance at the Progress of Japan during a Period of Twenty-one Years. By John R. Black, formerly Editor of the "Japan Herald" and the 'Japan Gazette." Editor of the "Far East." 2 vols. demy 8vo, pp. xviii. and 418 ; xiv. and 522, cloth. 1881. £2, 2s.

BLACKET.—RESEARCHES INTO THE LOST HISTORIES OF AMERICA ; or, The Zodiac shown to be an Old Terrestrial Map, in which the Atlantic Isle is delineated ; so that Light can be thrown upon the Obscure Histories of the Earthworks and Ruined Cities of America. By W. S. Blacket. Illustrated by numerous Engravings. 8vo, pp. 336, cloth. 1883. 10s. 6d.

BLADES.—SHAKSPERE AND TYPOGRAPHY. Being an Attempt to show Shakspere's Personal Connection with, and Technical Knowledge of, the Art of Printing ; also Remarks upon some common Typographical Errors, with especial reference to the Text of Shakspere. By William Blades. 8vo, pp. viii. and 78, with an Illustration, cloth. 1872. 3s.

BLADES.—THE BIOGRAPHY AND TYPOGRAPHY OF WILLIAM CAXTON, England's First Printer. By William Blades. Founded to a great extent upon the Author's "Life and Typography of William Caxton." Brought up to the Present Date, and including all Discoveries since made. Elegantly and appropriately printed in demy 8vo, on hand-made paper, imitation old bevelled binding. 1877. £1, 1s. Cheap Edition. Crown 8vo, cloth. 1881. 5s.

BLADES.—THE ENEMIES OF BOOKS. By William Blades, Typograph. Crown 8vo, pp. xvi. and 112, parchment wrapper. 1880.

BLAKEY.—MEMOIRS OF DR. ROBERT BLAKEY, Professor of Logic and Metaphysics, Queen's College, Belfast. Edited by the Rev. Henry Miller. Crown 8vo, pp. xii. and 252, cloth. 1879. 5s.

BLEEK.—REYNARD THE FOX IN SOUTH AFRICA ; or, Hottentot Fables and Tales, chiefly Translated from Original Manuscripts in the Library of His Excellency Sir George Grey, K.C.B. By W. H. I. Bleek, Ph.D. Post 8vo, pp. xxvi. and 94, cloth. 1864. 3s. 6d.

BLEEK.—A BRIEF ACCOUNT OF BUSHMAN FOLK LORE, and other Texts. By W. H. I. Bleek. Ph.D. Folio, pp. 21, paper. 2s. 6d.

BLUMHARDT.—See CHARITABALI.

BOEHMER.—*See* VALDES, and SPANISH REFORMERS.

BOJESEN.—A GUIDE TO THE DANISH LANGUAGE. Designed for English Students. By Mrs. Maria Bojesen. 12mo, pp. 250, cloth. 1863. 5s.

BOLIA.—THE GERMAN CALIGRAPHIST: Copies for German Handwriting. By C. Bolia. Oblong 4to, sewed. 1s.

BOOLE.—MESSAGE OF PSYCHIC SCIENCE TO MOTHERS AND NURSES. By Mary Boole. Crown 8vo, pp. xiv. and 266, cloth. 1883. 5s.

BOTTRELL.—Stories and Folk-Lore of West Cornwall. By William Bottrell. With Illustrations by Joseph Blight. Third Series. 8vo, pp. viii. and 200, cloth. 1884. 6s.

BOY ENGINEERS.—See under Lukin.

BOYD.—Nágánanda ; or, the Joy of the Snake World. A Buddhist Drama in Five Acts. Translated into English Prose, with Explanatory Notes, from the Sanskrit of Sá-Harsha-Deva. By Palmer Boyd, B.A., Cambridge. With an Introduction by Professor Cowell. Crown 8vo, pp. xvi. and 100, cloth. 1872. 4s. 6d.

BRADSHAW.—B. Bradshaw's Dictionary of Bathing Places and Climatic Health Resorts. Much Revised and Considerably Enlarged. With a Map in Eleven Colours. Third Edition. Small Crown 8vo, pp. lxxviii. and 364, cloth. 1884. 2s. 6d.

BRENTANO.—On the History and Development of Gilds, and the Origin of Trade-Unions. By Lujo Brentano, of Aschaffenburg, Bavaria, Doctor Juris Utriusque et Philosophiæ. 1. The Origin of Gilds. 2. Religious (or Social) Gilds. 3. Town-Gilds or Gild-Merchants. 4. Craft-Gilds. 5. Trade-Unions. 8vo, pp. xvi. and 136, cloth. 1870. 3s. 6d.

BRETSCHNEIDER.—Early European Researches into the Flora of China. By E. Bretschneider, M.D., Physician of the Russian Legation at Peking. Demy 8vo, pp. iv. and 194, sewed. 1881. 7s. 6d.

BRETSCHNEIDER.—Botanicon Sinicum. Notes on Chinese Botany, from Native and Western Sources. By E. Bretschneider, M.D. Crown 8vo, pp. 228, wrapper. 1882. 10s. 6d.

BRETTE.—French Examination Papers set at the University of London from 1839 to 1871. Arranged and edited by the Rev. P. H. Ernest Brette, B.D. Crown 8vo, pp. viii. and 278, cloth. 3s. 6d.; interleaved, 4s. 6d.

BRITISH MUSEUM.—List of Publications of the Trustees of the British Museum, on application.

BROWN.—The Dervishes ; or, Oriental Spiritualism. By John P. Brown, Secretary and Dragoman of the Legation of the United States of America at Constantinople. Crown 8vo, pp. viii. and 416, cloth, with 24 Illustrations. 1868. 14s.

BROWN.—Sanskrit Prosody and Numerical Symbols Explained. By Charles Philip Brown, M.R.A.S., Author of a Telugu Dictionary, Grammar, &c., Professor of Telugu in the University of London. 8vo, pp. viii. and 56, cloth. 1869. 3s. 6d.

BROWNE.—How to use the Ophthalmoscope ; being Elementary Instruction in Ophthalmoscopy. Arranged for the use of Students. By Edgar A. Browne, Surgeon to the Liverpool Eye and Ear Infirmary, &c. Second Edition. Crown 8vo, pp. xi. and 108, with 35 Figures, cloth. 1883. 3s. 6d.

BROWNE.—A Bángálí Primer, in Roman Character. By J. F. Browne, B.C.S. Crown 8vo, pp. 32, cloth. 1881. 2s.

BROWNE.—A Hindi Primer in Roman Character. By J. F. Browne, B.C.S. Crown 8vo, pp. 36, cloth. 1882. 2s. 6d.

BROWNE.—An Uriyá Primer in Roman Character. By J. F. Browne, B.C.S. Crown 8vo, pp. 32, cloth. 1882. 2s. 6d.

BROWNING SOCIETY'S PAPERS.—Demy 8vo, wrappers. 1881-84. Part I., pp. 116. 10s. Bibliography of Robert Browning from 1833-81. Part II., pp. 142. 10s. Part III., pp. 168. 10s. Part IV., pp. 148. 10s. Part V. 10s.

BROWNING'S POEMS, Illustrations to. 4to, boards. Parts I. and II. 10s. each.

BRUNNOW.—*See* Scheffel.

BRUNTON.—Map of Japan. See under Japan.

BUDGE.—ARCHAIC CLASSICS. Assyrian Texts; being Extracts from the Annals of Shalmaneser II., Sennacherib, and Assur-Bani-Pal. With Philological Notes. By Ernest A. Budge, B.A., M.R.A.S., Assyrian Exhibitioner, Christ's College, Cambridge. Small 4to, pp. viii. and 44, cloth. 1880. 7s. 6d.

BUDGE.—HISTORY OF ESARHADDON. See Trübner's Oriental Series.

BUNYAN.—SCENES FROM THE PILGRIM'S PROGRESS. By. R. B. Rutter. 4to, pp. 142, boards, leather back. 1882. 5s.

BURGESS :- ·
  ARCHÆOLOGICAL SURVEY OF WESTERN INDIA :—
    REPORT OF THE FIRST SEASON'S OPERATIONS IN THE BELGÂM AND KALADI DISTRICTS. January to May 1874. By James Burgess, F.R.G.S. With 56 Photographs and Lithographic Plates. Royal 4to, pp. viii. and 45; half bound. 1875. £2, 2s.
    REPORT ON THE ANTIQUITIES OF KÂTHIÂWÂD AND KACHH, being the result of the Second Season's Operations of the Archæological Survey of Western India, 1874-75. By James Burgess, F.R.G.S. Royal 4to, pp. x. and 242, with 74 Plates; half bound. 1876. £3, 3s.
    REPORT ON THE ANTIQUITIES IN THE BIDAR AND AURANGABAD DISTRICTS, in the Territories of His Highness the Nizam of Haiderabad, being the result of the Third Season's Operations of the Archæological Survey of Western India, 1875-76. By James Burgess, F.R.G.S., M.R.A.S., Archæological Surveyor and Reporter to Government, Western India. Royal 4to, pp. viii. and 138, with 63 Photographic Plates ; half bound. 1878. £2, 2s.
    REPORT ON THE BUDDHIST CAVE TEMPLES AND THEIR INSCRIPTIONS; containing Views, Plans, Sections, and Elevation of Façades of Cave Temples ; Drawings of Architectural and Mythological Sculptures ; Facsimiles of Inscriptions, &c. ; with Descriptive and Explanatory Text, and Translations of Inscriptions, &c., &c. By James Burgess, LL.D., F.R.G.S., &c. Royal 4to, pp. x. and 140, with 86 Plates and Woodcuts ; half-bound.
    REPORT ON ELURA CAVE TEMPLES, AND THE BRAHMANICAL AND JAINA CAVES IN WESTERN INDIA. By James Burgess, LL.D., F.R.G.S., &c. Royal 4to, pp. viii. and 90, with 66 Plates and Woodcuts ; half-bound. } 2 Vols. 1883. £6, 6s.

BURMA.—THE BRITISH BURMA GAZETTEER. Compiled by Major H. R. Spearman, under the direction of the Government of India. 2 vols. 8vo, pp. 764 and 878, with 11 Photographs, cloth. 1880. £2, 10s.

BURMA.—HISTORY OF. See Trübner's Oriental Series, page 70.

BURNE.—SHROPSHIRE FOLK-LORE. A Sheaf of Gleanings. Edited by Charlotte S. Burne, from the Collections of Georgina F. Jackson. Part I. Demy 8vo, pp. xvi.-176, wrapper. 1883. 7s. 6d.

BURNELL.—ELEMENTS OF SOUTH INDIAN PALÆOGRAPHY, from the Fourth to the Seventeenth Century A.D., being an Introduction to the Study of South Indian Inscriptions and MSS. By A. C. Burnell. Second enlarged and improved Edition. 4to, pp. xiv. and 148, Map and 35 Plates, cloth. 1878. £2, 12s. 6d.

BURNELL.—A CLASSIFIED INDEX TO THE SANSKRIT MSS. IN THE PALACE AT TANJORE. Prepared for the Madras Government. By A. C. Burnell, Ph.D., &c., &c. 4to, stiff wrapper. Part I., pp. iv.-80, Vedic and Technical Literature. Part II., pp. iv.-80, Philosophy and Law. Part III., Drama, Epics, Purānas, and Zantras ; Indices. 1879. 10s. each.

BURNEY.—THE YOUNG SEAMAN'S MANUAL AND RIGGER'S GUIDE. By Commander C. Burney, R.N., F.R.G.S. Sixth Edition. Revised and corrected. Approved by the Lords Commissioners of the Admiralty. Crown 8vo. pp. xxxviii. and 592, cloth. With 200 Illustrations and 16 Sheets of Signals. 1878. 7s. 6d.

BURTON.—HANDBOOK FOR OVERLAND EXPEDITIONS ; being an English Edition of the "Prairie Traveller," a Handbook for Overland Expeditions. With Illustrations and Itineraries of the Principal Routes between the Mississippi and the Pacific, and a Map. By Captain R. B. Marcy (now General and Chief of the Staff, Army of the Potomac). Edited, with Notes, by Captain Richard F. Burton. Crown 8vo, pp. 270, numerous Woodcuts, Itineraries, and Map, cloth. 1863. 6s. 6d.

BUTLER.—EREWHON ; or, Over the Range. By Samuel Butler. Seventh Edition. Crown 8vo, pp. xii. and 244, cloth. 1884. 5s.

BUTLER.—THE FAIR HAVEN. A Work in Defence of the Miraculous Element in Our Lord's Ministry upon Earth, both as against Rationalistic Impugners and certain Orthodox Defenders. By the late John Pickard Owen. With a Memoir of the Author by William Bickersteth Owen. By Samuel Butler. Second Edition. Demy 8vo, pp. x. and 248, cloth. 1873. 7s. 6d.

BUTLER.—LIFE AND HABIT. By Samuel Butler. Second Edition. Crown 8vo, pp. x. and 308, cloth. 1878. 7s. 6d.

BUTLER.—EVOLUTION, OLD AND NEW ; or, The Theories of Buffon, Dr. Erasmus Darwin, and Lamarck, as compared with that of Mr. Charles Darwin. By Samuel Butler. Second Edition, with an Appendix and Index. Crown 8vo, pp. xii. and 430, cloth. 1882. 10s. 6d.

BUTLER.—UNCONSCIOUS MEMORY : A Comparison between the Theory of Dr. Ewald Hering, Professor of Physiology at the University of Prague, and the "Philosophy of the Unconscious" of Dr. Edward von Hartmann. With Translations from these Authors, and Preliminary Chapters bearing on "Life and Habit," "Evolution, New and Old," and Mr. Charles Darwin's edition of Dr. Krause's "Erasmus Darwin." By Samuel Butler. Crown 8vo, pp. viii. and 288, cloth. 1880. 7s. 6d.

BUTLER.—ALPS AND SANCTUARIES OF PIEDMONT AND THE CANTON TICINO. Profusely Illustrated by Charles Gogin, H. F. Jones, and the Author. By Samuel Butler. Foolscap 4to, pp. viii. and 376, cloth. 1882. 21s.

BUTLER.—SELECTIONS FROM HIS PREVIOUS WORKS, with Remarks on Mr. G. J. Romanes' recent work, "Mental Evolution in Animals," and "A Psalm of Montreal." By Samuel Butler. Crown 8vo, pp. viii. and 326, cloth. 1884. 7s. 6d.

BUTLER.—THE SPANISH TEACHER AND COLLOQUIAL PHRASE-BOOK. An Easy and Agreeable Method of acquiring a Speaking Knowledge of the Spanish Language. By Francis Butler. Fcap. 8vo, pp. xviii. and 240, half-roan. 2s. 6d.

BUTLER.—HUNGARIAN POEMS AND FABLES FOR ENGLISH READERS. Selected and Translated by E. D. Butler. of the British Museum ; with Illustrations by A. G. Butler. Foolscap, pp. vi. and 88, limp cloth. 1877. 2s.

BUTLER.—THE LEGEND OF THE WONDROUS HUNT. By John Arany. With a few Miscellaneous Pieces and Folk-Songs. Translated from the Magyar by E. D. Butler, F.R.G.S. Crown 8vo, pp. viii. and 70. Limp cloth. 2s. 6d.

CAITHNESS.—LECTURES ON POPULAR AND SCIENTIFIC SUBJECTS. By the Earl of Caithness, F.R.S. Delivered at various times and places. Second enlarged Edition. Crown 8vo, pp. 174, cloth. 1879. 2s. 6d.

CALCUTTA REVIEW.—SELECTIONS FROM Nos. I.-XXXVII. 5s. each.

CALDER.—THE COMING ERA. By A. Calder, Officer of the Legion of Honour, and Author of "The Man of the Future." 8vo, pp. 422, cloth. 1879. 10s. 6d.

CALDWELL.—A COMPARATIVE GRAMMAR OF THE DRAVIDIAN OR SOUTH INDIAN FAMILY OF LANGUAGES. By the Rev. R. Caldwell, LL.D. A second, corrected, and enlarged Edition. Demy 8vo, pp. 804, cloth. 1875. 28s.

CALENDARS OF STATE PAPERS. List on application.

CALL.—REVERBERATIONS. Revised. With a chapter from My Autobiography. By W. M. W. Call, M.A., Cambridge, Author of "Lyra Hellenica" and "Golden Histories." Crown 8vo, pp. viii. and 200, cloth. 1875. 4s. 6d.

CALLAWAY.—Nursery Tales, Traditions, and Histories of the Zulus. In their own words, with a Translation into English, and Notes. By the Rev. Canon Callaway, M.D. Vol. I., 8vo, pp. xiv. and 378, cloth. 1868. 16s.

CALLAWAY.—The Religious System of the Amazulu.

> Part I.—Unkulunkulu ; or, The Tradition of Creation as existing among the Amazulu and other Tribes of South Africa, in their own words, with a Translation into English, and Notes. By the Rev. Canon Callaway, M.D. 8vo, pp. 128, sewed. 1868. 4s.

> Part II.—Amatongo ; or, Ancestor-Worship as existing among the Amazulu, in their own words, with a Translation into English, and Notes. By the Rev. Canon Callaway, M.D. 8vo, pp. 127, sewed. 1869. 4s.

> Part III.—Izinyanga Zokubula ; or, Divination, as existing among the Amazulu, in their own words, with a Translation into English, and Notes. By the Rev. Canon Callaway, M.D. 8vo, pp. 150, sewed. 1870. 4s.

> Part IV.—On Medical Magic and Witchcraft. 8vo, pp. 40, sewed, 1s. 6d.

CAMBRIDGE PHILOLOGICAL SOCIETY (Transactions). Vol. I., from 1872-1880. 8vo, pp. xvi.-420, wrapper. 1881. 15s. Vol. II., for 1881 and 1882. 8vo, pp. viii.-286, wrapper. 1883. 12s.

CAMERINI.—L'Eco Italiano ; a Practical Guide to Italian Conversation. By E. Camerini. With a Vocabulary. 12mo, pp. 98, cloth. 1860. 4s. 6d.

CAMPBELL.—The Gospel of the World's Divine Order. By Douglas Campbell. New Edition. Revised. Crown 8vo, pp. viii. and 364, cloth. 1877. 4s. 6d.

CANDID Examination of Theism. By Physicus. Post 8vo, pp. xviii. and 198, cloth. 1878. 7s. 6d.

CANTICUM CANTICORUM, reproduced in facsimile, from the Scriverius copy in the British Museum. With an Historical and Bibliographical Introduction by I. Ph. Berjeau. Folio, pp. 36, with 16 Tables of Illustrations. vellum. 1860. £2, 2s.

CAREY.—The Past, the Present, and the Future. By H. C. Carey. Second Edition. 8vo, pp. 474, cloth. 1856. 10s. 6d.

CARLETTI.—History of the Conquest of Tunis. Translated by J. T. Carletti. Crown 8vo, pp. 40, cloth. 1883. 2s. 6d.

CARNEGY.—Notes on the Land Tenures and Revenue Assessments of Upper India. By P. Carnegy. Crown 8vo, pp. viii. and 136, and forms, cloth. 1874. 6s.

CATHERINE II., Memoirs of the Empress. Written by herself. With a Preface by A. Herzen. Trans. from the French. 12mo, pp. xvi. and 352, bds. 1859. 7s. 6d.

CATLIN.—O-Kee-Pa. A Religious Ceremony ; and other Customs of the Mandans. By George Catlin. With 13 coloured Illustrations. Small 4to, pp. vi. and 52, cloth. 1867. 14s.

CATLIN.—The Lifted and Subsided Rocks of America, with their Influence on the Oceanic, Atmospheric, and Land Currents, and the Distribution of Races. By George Catlin. With 2 Maps. Cr. 8vo, pp. xii. and 238, cloth. 1870. 6s. 6d.

CATLIN.—Shut your Mouth and Save your Life. By George Catlin, Author of "Notes of Travels amongst the North American Indians," &c., &c. With 29 Illustrations from Drawings by the Author. Eighth Edition, considerably enlarged. Crown 8vo, pp. 106, cloth. 1882. 2s. 6d.

CAXTON.—The Biography and Typography of. See Blades.

CAXTON CELEBRATION, 1877.—CATALOGUE OF THE LOAN COLLECTION OF ANTI-QUITIES, CURIOSITIES, AND APPLIANCES CONNECTED WITH THE ART OF PRINTING. Edited by G. Bullen, F.S.A. Post 8vo, pp. xx. and 472, cloth, 3s. 6d.

CAZELLES.—OUTLINE OF THE EVOLUTION-PHILOSOPHY. By Dr. W. E. Cazelles. Translated from the French by the Rev. O. B. Frothingham. Crown 8vo, pp. 156, cloth. 1875. 3s. 6d.

CESNOLA.—SALAMINIA (Cyprus). The History, Treasures, and Antiquities of Salamis in the Island of Cyprus. By A. Palma di Cesnola, F.S.A., &c. With an Introduction by S. Birch, Esq., D.C.L., LL.D., Keeper of the Egyptian and Oriental Antiquities in the British Museum. Royal 8vo, pp. xlviii. and 325, with upwards of 700 Illustrations and Map of Ancient Cyprus, cloth. 1882. 31s. 6d.

CHALMERS.—STRUCTURE OF CHINESE CHARACTERS, under 300 Primary Forms after the Shwoh-wan, 100 A.D., and the Phonetic Shwoh-wan, 1833. By J. Chalmers, M.A., LL.D., A.B. Demy 8vo, pp. x. and 200, with two plates, limp cloth. 1882. 12s. 6d.

CHAMBERLAIN.—THE CLASSICAL POETRY OF THE JAPANESE. By Basil Hall Chamberlain, Author of "Yeigo Henkaku, Ichiran." Post 8vo, pp. xii. and 228, cloth. 1880. 7s. 6d.

CHAPMAN.—CHLOROFORM AND OTHER ANÆSTHETICS : Their History and Use during Childbirth. By John Chapman, M.D. 8vo, pp. 51, sewed. 1859. 1s.

CHAPMAN.—DIARRHŒA AND CHOLERA : Their Nature, Origin, and Treatment through the Agency of the Nervous System. By John Chapman, M.D., M.R.C.P., M.R.C.S. 8vo, pp. xix. and 248, cloth. 7s. 6d.

CHAPMAN.—MEDICAL CHARITY : its Abuses, and how to Remedy them. By John Chapman, M.D. 8vo, pp. viii. and 108, cloth. 1874. 2s. 6d.

CHAPMAN.—SEA-SICKNESS, AND HOW TO PREVENT IT. An Explanation of its Nature and Successful Treatment, through the Agency of the Nervous System, by means of the Spinal Ice Bag ; with an Introduction on the General Principles of Neuro-Therapeutics. By John Chapman, M.D., M.R.C.P., M.R.C.S. Second Edition. 8vo, pp. viii. and 112, cloth. 1868. 3s.

CHAPTERS ON CHRISTIAN CATHOLICITY. By a Clergyman. 8vo, pp. 282, cloth. 1878. 5s.

CHARITABALI (THE), or, Instructive Biography. By Isvarachandra Vidyasagara. With a Vocabulary of all the Words occurring in the Text. By J. F. Blumhardt, Bengal Lecturer at the University College, London ; and Teacher of Bengali for the Cambridge University. 12mo, pp. 174, cloth. 1884. 5s. The Vocabulary only, 2s. 6d.

CHARNOCK.—A GLOSSARY OF THE ESSEX DIALECT. By Richard Stephen Charnock, Ph.D., F.S.A. Fcap., pp. xii. and 64, cloth. 1880. 3s. 6d.

CHARNOCK.—PRŒNOMINA ; or, The Etymology of the Principal Christian Names of Great Britain and Ireland. By R. S. Charnock, Ph.D., F.S.A. Crown 8vo, pp. xvi. and 128, cloth. 1882. 6s.

CHATTOPADHYAYA.—THE YÀTRÀS ; or, The Popular Dramas of Bengal. By N. Chattopadhyaya. Post 8vo, pp. 50, wrapper. 1882. 2s.

CHAUCER SOCIETY.—Subscription, two guineas per annum. List of Publications on application.

CHILDERS.—A PALI-ENGLISH DICTIONARY, with Sanskrit Equivalents, and with numerous Quotations, Extracts, and References. Compiled by Robert Cæsar Childers, late of the Ceylon Civil Service. Imperial 8vo, double columns, pp. 648, cloth. 1875. £3, 3s.

CHILDERS.—THE MAHAPARINIBBANASUTTA OF THE SUTTA PITAKA. The Pali Text. Edited by the late Professor R. C. Childers. 8vo, pp. 72, limp cloth. 1878. 5s.

CHINTAMON.—A Commentary on the Text of the Bhagavad-Gítá ; or, The Discourse between Khrishna and Arjuna of Divine Matters A Sanskrit Philosophical Poem. With a few Introductory Papers. By Hurrychund Chintamon, Political Agent to H. H. the Guicowar Mulhar Rao Maharajah of Baroda. Post 8vo, pp. 118, cloth. 1874. 6s.

CHRONICLES and Memorials of Great Britain and Ireland during the Middle Ages. List on application.

CLARK.—Meghaduta, the Cloud Messenger. Poem of Kalidasa. Translated by the late Rev. T. Clark, M.A. Fcap. 8vo, pp. 64, wrapper. 1882. 1s.

CLARK.—A Forecast of the Religion of the Future. Being Short Essays on some important Questions in Religious Philosophy. By W. W. Clark. Post 8vo, pp. xii. and 238, cloth. 1879. 3s. 6d.

CLARKE.—Ten Great Religions : An Essay in Comparative Theology. By James Freeman Clarke. Demy 8vo, pp. x. and 528, cloth. 1871. 15s.

CLARKE.—Ten Great Religions. Part II., A Comparison of all Religions. By J. F. Clarke. Demy 8vo, pp. xxviii.- 414, cloth. 1883. 10s. 6d.

CLARKE.—The Early History of the Mediterranean Populations, &c., in their Migrations and Settlements. Illustrated from Autonomous Coins, Gems, Inscriptions, &c. By Hyde Clarke. 8vo, pp. 80, cloth. 1882. 5s.

CLAUSEWITZ.—On War. By General Carl von Clausewitz. Translated by Colonel J. J. Graham, from the third German Edition. Three volumes complete in one. Fcap 4to, double columns, pp. xx. and 564, with Portrait of the author, cloth. 1873. 10s. 6d.

COKE.—Creeds of the Day : or, Collated Opinions of Reputable Thinkers. By Henry Coke. In Three Series of Letters. 2 vols. Demy 8vo, pp. 302-324, cloth. 1883. 21s.

COLEBROOKE.—The Life and Miscellaneous Essays of Henry Thomas Colebrooke. The Biography by his Son, Sir T. E. Colebrooke, Bart., M.P. 3 vols. Vol. I. The Life. Demy 8vo, pp. xii. and 492, with Portrait and Map, cloth. 1873. 14s. Vols. II. and III. The Essays. A new Edition, with Notes by E. B. Cowell, Professor of Sanskrit in the University of Cambridge. Demy 8vo, pp. xvi. and 544, and x. and 520, cloth. 1873. 28s.

COLENSO.—Natal Sermons. A Series of Discourses Preached in the Cathedral Church of St Peter's, Maritzburg. By the Right Rev. John William Colenso, D.D., Bishop of Natal. 8vo, pp. viii. and 373, cloth. 1866. 7s. 6d. The Second Series. Crown 8vo, cloth. 1868. 5s.

COLLINS.—A Grammar and Lexicon of the Hebrew Language, Entitled Sefer Hassoham. By Rabbi Moseh Ben Yitshak, of England. Edited from a MS. in the Bodleian Library of Oxford, and collated with a MS. in the Imperial Library of St. Petersburg, with Additions and Corrections, by G. W. Collins, M.A. Demy 4to, pp. 112, wrapper. 1882. 7s. 6d.

COLYMBIA.—Crown 8vo, pp. 260, cloth. 1873. 5s.

" The book is amusing as well as clever."—*Athenæum.*   " Many exceedingly humorous passages."—*Public Opinion.*   " Deserves to be read."—*Scotsman.*   " Neatly done."—*Graphic.* " Very amusing."—*Examiner.*

COMTE.—The Catechism of Positive Religion : Translated from the French of Auguste Comte. By Richard Congreve. Second Edition. Revised and Corrected. and conformed to the Second French Edition of 1874. Crown 8vo, pp. 316, cloth, 1883. 2s. 6d.

COMTE.—The Eight Circulars of Auguste Comte. Translated from the French, under the auspices of R. Congreve. Fcap. 8vo, pp. iv. and 90, cloth. 1882. 1s. 6d.

COMTE.—PRELIMINARY DISCOURSE ON THE POSITIVE SPIRIT. Prefixed to the "Traité Philosophique d'Astronomie Populaire." By M. Auguste Comte. Translated by W. M. W. Call, M.A., Camb. Crown 8vo, pp. 154, cloth. 1883. 2s. 6d.

COMTE.—THE POSITIVE PHILOSOPHY OF AUGUSTE COMTE. Translated and condensed by Harriet Martineau. 2 vols. Second Edition. 8vo, cloth. Vol. I., pp. xxiv. and 400; Vol. II., pp. xiv. and 468. 1875. 25s.

CONGREVE.—THE ROMAN EMPIRE OF THE WEST. Four Lectures delivered at the Philosophical Institution, Edinburgh, February 1855, by Richard Congreve, M.A. 8vo, pp. 176, cloth. 1855. 4s.

CONGREVE.—ELIZABETH OF ENGLAND. Two Lectures delivered at the Philosophical Institution, Edinburgh, January 1862. By Richard Congreve. 18mo, pp. 114, sewed. 1862. 2s. 6d.

CONTOPOULOS.—A LEXICON OF MODERN GREEK-ENGLISH AND ENGLISH MODERN GREEK. By N. Contopoulos. Part I. Modern Greek-English. Part II. English Modern Greek. 8vo, pp. 460 and 582, cloth. 1877. 27s.

CONWAY.—THE SACRED ANTHOLOGY : A Book of Ethnical Scriptures. Collected and Edited by Moncure D. Conway. Fifth Edition. Demy 8vo, pp. viii. and 480, cloth. 1876. 12s.

CONWAY.—IDOLS AND IDEALS. With an Essay on Christianity. By Moncure D. Conway, M.A., Author of "The Eastern Pilgrimage," &c. Crown 8vo, pp. 352, cloth. 1877. 4s.

CONWAY.—EMERSON AT HOME AND ABROAD. See English and Foreign Philosophical Library.

CONWAY.—TRAVELS IN SOUTH KENSINGTON. By M. D. Conway. Illustrated. 8vo, pp. 234, cloth. 1882. 12s.
CONTENTS.—The South Kensington Museum—Decorative Art and Architecture in England —Bedford Park.

COOMARA SWAMY.—THE DATHAVANSA ; or, The History of the Tooth Relic of Gotama Buddha, in Pali verse. Edited, with an English Translation, by Mutu Coomara Swamy, F.R.A.S. Demy 8vo, pp. 174, cloth. 1874. 10s. 6d. English Translation. With Notes. pp. 100. 6s.

COOMARA SWAMY.—SUTTA NIPATA ; or, Dialogues and Discourses of Gotama Buddha (2500 years old). Translated from the original Pali. With Notes and Introduction. By Mutu Coomara Swamy, F.R.A.S. Crown 8vo, pp. xxxvi. and 160, cloth. 1874. 6s.

COPARCENERS (THE): Being the Adventures of Two Heiresses. Crown 8vo.

CORNELIA. A Novel. Post 8vo, pp. 250, boards. 1863. 1s. 6d.

COTTA.—GEOLOGY AND HISTORY. A Popular Exposition of all that is known of the Earth and its Inhabitants in Pre-historic Times. By Bernhard Von Cotta, Professor of Geology at the Academy of Mining, Freiberg, in Saxony. 12mo, pp. iv. and 84, cloth. 1865. 2s.

COUSIN.—THE PHILOSOPHY OF KANT. Lectures by Victor Cousin. Translated from the French. To which is added a Biographical and Critical Sketch of Kant's Life and Writings. By A. G. Henderson. Large post 8vo, pp. xciv. and 194, cloth. 1864. 6s.

COUSIN.—ELEMENTS OF PSYCHOLOGY : included in a Critical Examination of Locke's Essay on the Human Understanding, and in additional pieces. Translated from the French of Victor Cousin, with an Introduction and Notes. By Caleb S. Henry, D.D. Fourth improved Edition, revised according to the Author's last corrections. Crown 8vo, pp. 568, cloth. 1871. 8s.

COWELL.—A SHORT INTRODUCTION TO THE ORDINARY PRAKRIT OF THE SANSKRIT DRAMAS. With a List of Common Irregular Prâkrit Words. By E. B. Cowell, Professor of Sanskrit in the University of Cambridge, and Hon. LL.D. of the University of Edinburgh. Crown 8vo, pp. 40, limp cloth. 1875. 3s. 6d.

COWELL.—PRAKRITA-PRAKASA; or, The Prakrit Grammar of Vararuchi, with the Commentary (Manorama) of Bhamaha; the first complete Edition of the Original Text, with various Readings from a collection of Six MSS. in the Bodleian Library at Oxford, and the Libraries of the Royal Asiatic Society and the East India House; with Copious Notes, an English Translation, and Index of Prakrit Words, to which is prefixed an Easy Introduction to Prakrit Grammar. By Edward Byles Cowell, of Magdalen Hall, Oxford, Professor of Sanskrit at Cambridge. New Edition, with New Preface, Additions, and Corrections. Second Issue. 8vo, pp. xxxi. and 204, cloth. 1868. 14s.

COWELL.—THE SARVADARSANA SAMGRAHA. See Trübner's Oriental Series.

COWLEY.—POEMS. By Percy Tunnicliff Cowley. Demy 8vo, pp. 104, cloth. 1881. 5s.

CRAIG.—THE IRISH LAND LABOUR QUESTION, Illustrated in the History of Rala-hine and Co-operative Farming. By E. T. Craig. Crown 8vo, pp. xii. and 202, cloth. 1882. 2s. 6d. Wrappers, 2s.

CRANBROOK.—CREDIBILIA; or, Discourses on Questions of Christian Faith. By the Rev. James Cranbrook, Edinburgh. Reissue. Post 8vo, pp. iv. and 190, cloth. 1868. 3s. 6d.

CRANBROOK.—THE FOUNDERS OF CHRISTIANITY; or, Discourses upon the Origin of the Christian Religion. By the Rev. James Cranbrook, Edinburgh. Post 8vo, pp. xii. and 324. 1868. 6s.

CRAVEN.—THE POPULAR DICTIONARY IN ENGLISH AND HINDUSTANI, AND HINDU-STANI AND ENGLISH. With a Number of Useful Tables. Compiled by the Rev. T. Craven, M.A. 18mo, pp. 430, cloth. 1881. 3s. 6d.

CRAWFORD.—RECOLLECTIONS OF TRAVEL IN NEW ZEALAND AND AUSTRALIA. By James Coutts Crawford, F.G.S., Resident Magistrate, Wellington, &c., &c. With Maps and Illustrations. 8vo, pp. xvi. and 468, cloth. 1880. 18s.

CROSLAND.—APPARITIONS; An Essay explanatory of Old Facts and a New Theory. To which are added Sketches and Adventures. By Newton Crosland. Crown 8vo, pp. viii. and 166, cloth. 1873. 2s. 6d.

CROSLAND.—PITH: ESSAYS AND SKETCHES GRAVE AND GAY, with some Verses and Illustrations. By Newton Crosland. Crown 8vo, pp. 310, cloth. 1881. 5s.

CROSLAND.—THE NEW PRINCIPIA; or, The Astronomy of the Future. An Essay Explanatory of a Rational System of the Universe. By N. Crosland, Author of " Pith," &c. Foolscap 8vo, pp. 88, cloth limp elegant, gilt edges. 1884. 2s. 6d.

CROSS.—HESPERIDES. The Occupations, Relaxations, and Aspirations of a Life. By Launcelot Cross, Author of " Characteristics of Leigh Hunt," " Brandon Tower," " Business," &c. Demy 8vo, pp. iv.–486, cloth. 1883. 10s. 6d.

CUMMINS.—A GRAMMAR OF THE OLD FRIESIC LANGUAGE. By A. H. Cummins, A.M. Crown 8vo, pp. x. and 76, cloth. 1881. 3s. 6d.

CUNNINGHAM.—THE ANCIENT GEOGRAPHY OF INDIA. I. The Buddhist Period, including the Campaigns of Alexander and the Travels of Hwen-Thsang. By Alexander Cunningham, Major-General, Royal Engineers (Bengal Retired). With 13 Maps. 8vo, pp. xx. and 590, cloth. 1870. £1, 8s.

CUNNINGHAM.—THE STUPA OF BHARHUT: A Buddhist Monument ornamented with numerous Sculptures illustrative of Buddhist Legend and History in the Third Century B.C. By Alexander Cunningham, C.S.I., C.I.E., Maj.-Gen., R.E. (B.R.), Dir.-Gen. Archæol. Survey of India. Royal 8vo, pp. viii. and 144, with 57 Plates, cloth. 1879. £3, 3s.

CUNNINGHAM.—ARCHÆOLOGICAL SURVEY OF INDIA, Reports from 1862-80. By A. Cunningham, C.S.I., C.I.E., Major-General, R.E. (Bengal Retired), Director-General, Archæological Survey of India. With numerous Plates, cloth, Vols. I.-XI. 10s. each. (Except Vols. VII., VIII., and IX., and also Vols. XII. to XVIII., which are 12s. each.)

CUSHMAN.—CHARLOTTE CUSHMAN: Her Letters and Memories of her Life. Edited by her friend, Emma Stebbins. Square 8vo, pp. viii. [and 308, cloth. With Portrait and Illustrations. 1879. 12s. 6d.

CUST.—LANGUAGES OF THE EAST INDIES. See Trübner's Oriental Series.

CUST.—LINGUISTIC AND ORIENTAL ESSAYS. See Trübner's Oriental Series.

CUST.—LANGUAGES OF AFRICA. See Trübner's Oriental Series.

CUST.—PICTURES OF INDIAN LIFE, Sketched with the Pen from 1852 to 1881. By R. N. Cust, late I.C.S., Hon. Sec. Royal Asiatic Society. Crown 8vo, pp. x. and 346, cloth. With Maps. 1881. 7s. 6d.

DANA.—A TEXT-BOOK OF GEOLOGY, designed for Schools and Academies. By James D. Dana, LL.D., Professor of Geology, &c., at Yale College. Illustrated. Crown 8vo, pp. vi. and 354, cloth. 1876. 10s.

DANA.—MANUAL OF GEOLOGY, treating of the Principles of the Science, with special Reference to American Geological History; for the use of Colleges, Academies, and Schools of Science. By James D. Dana, LL.D. Illustrated by a Chart of the World, and over One Thousand Figures. 8vo, pp. xvi. and 800, and Chart, cl. 21s.

DANA.—THE GEOLOGICAL STORY BRIEFLY TOLD. An Introduction to Geology for the General Reader and for Beginners in the Science. By J. D. Dana, LL.D. Illustrated. 12mo, pp. xii. and 264, cloth. 7s. 6d.

DANA.—A SYSTEM OF MINERALOGY. Descriptive Mineralogy, comprising the most Recent Discoveries. By J. D. Dana, aided by G. J. Brush. Fifth Edition, re-written and enlarged, and illustrated with upwards of 600 Woodcuts, with three Appendixes and Corrections. Royal 8vo, pp. xlviii. and 892, cloth. £2, 2s.

DANA.—A TEXT BOOK OF MINERALOGY. With an Extended Treatise on Crystallo-graphy and Physical Mineralogy. By E. S. Dana, on the Plan and with the Co-operation of Professor J. D. Dana. Third Edition, revised. Over 800 Wood-cuts and 1 Coloured Plate. 8vo, pp. viii. and 486, cloth. 1879. 18s.

DANA.—MANUAL OF MINERALOGY AND LITHOLOGY; Containing the Elements of the Science of Minerals and Rocks, for the Use of the Practical Mineralogist and Geologist, and for Instruction in Schools and Colleges. By J. D. Dana. Fourth Edition, rearranged and rewritten. Illustrated by numerous Woodcuts. Crown 8vo, pp. viii. and 474, cloth. 1882. 7s. 6d.

DATES AND DATA RELATING TO RELIGIOUS ANTHROPOLOGY AND BIBLICAL ARCHÆ-OLOGY. (Primæval Period.) 8vo, pp. viii. and 106, cloth. 1876. 5s.

DAUDET.—LETTERS FROM MY MILL. From the French of Alphonse Daudet, by Mary Corey. Fcap. 8vo, pp. 160. 1880. Cloth, 3s.; boards, 2s.

DAVIDS.—BUDDHIST BIRTH STORIES. See Trübner's Oriental Series.

DAVIES.—HINDU PHILOSOPHY. 2 vols. See Trübner's Oriental Series.

DAVIS.—NARRATIVE OF THE NORTH POLAR EXPEDITION, U.S. SHIP *Polaris*, Cap-tain Charles Francis Hall Commanding. Edited under the direction of the Hon. G. M. Robeson, Secretary of the Navy, by Rear-Admiral C. H. Davis, U.S.N. Third Edition. With numerous Steel and Wood Engravings, Photolithographs, and Maps. 4to, pp. 696, cloth. 1881. £1, 8s.

DAY.—THE PREHISTORIC USE OF IRON AND STEEL; with Observations on certain matter ancillary thereto. By St. John V. Day, C.E., F.R.S.E., &c. 8vo, pp. xxiv. and 278, cloth. 1877. 12s.

DE FLANDRE.—MONOGRAMS OF THREE OR MORE LETTERS, DESIGNED AND DRAWN ON STONE. By C. De Flandre, F.S.A. Scot., Edinburgh. With Indices, showing the place and style or period of every Monogram, and of each individual Letter. 4to, 42 Plates, cloth. 1880. Large paper, £7, 7s.; small paper, £3, 3s.

DELBRUCK.—INTRODUCTION TO THE STUDY OF LANGUAGE: A Critical Survey of the History and Methods of Comparative Philology of the Indo-European Languages. By B. Delbrück. Authorised Translation, with a Preface by the Author. 8vo, pp. 156, cloth. 1882. 5s. Sewed, 4s.

B

DELEPIERRE.—HISTOIRE LITTERAIRE DES FOUS. Par Octave Delepierre. Crown 8vo, pp. 184, cloth. 1860. 5s.

DELEPIERRE.—MACARONEANA ANDRA ; overum Nouveaux Mélanges de Litterature Macaronique. Par Octave Delepierre. Small 4to, pp. 180, printed by Whittingham, and handsomely bound in the Roxburghe style. 1862. 10s. 6d.

DELEPIERRE.—ANALYSE DES TRAVAUX DE LA SOCIETE DES PHILOBIBLON DE LONDRES. Par Octave Delepierre. Small 4to, pp. viii. and 134, bound in the Roxburghe style. 1862. 10s. 6d.

DELEPIERRE.—REVUE ANALYTIQUE DES OUVRAGES ÉCRITS EN CENTONS, depuis les Temps Anciens, jusqu'au xix^{ieme} Siècle. Par un Bibliophile Belge. Small 4to, pp. 508, stiff covers. 1868. £1, 10s.

DELEPIERRE.—TABLEAU DE LA LITTÉRATURE DU CENTON, CHEZ LES ANCIENS ET CHEZ LES MODERNES. Par Octave Delepierre. 2 vols, small 4to, pp. 324 and 318. Paper cover. 1875. £1, 1s.

DELEPIERRE.—L'ENFER : Essai Philosophique et Historique sur les Légendes de la Vie Future. Par Octave Delepierre. Crown 8vo, pp. 160, paper wrapper. 1876. 6s. Only 250 copies printed.

DENNYS.—A HANDBOOK OF THE CANTON VERNACULAR OF THE CHINESE LANGUAGE. Being a Series of Introductory Lessons for Domestic and Business Purposes. By N. B. Dennys, M.R.A.S., &c. Royal 8vo, pp. iv. and 228, cloth. 1874. 30s.

DENNYS.—A HANDBOOK OF MALAY COLLOQUIAL, as spoken in Singapore, being a Series of Introductory Lessons for Domestic and Business Purposes. By N. B. Dennys, Ph.D., F.R.G.S., M.R.A.S. Impl. 8vo, pp. vi. and 204, cloth. 1878. 21s.

DENNYS.—THE FOLK-LORE OF CHINA, AND ITS AFFINITIES WITH THAT OF THE ARYAN AND SEMITIC RACES. By N. B. Dennys, Ph.D., F.R.G.S., M.R.A.S. 8vo, pp. 166, cloth. 1876. 10s. 6d.

DE VALDES.—See VALDES.

DE VINNE.—THE INVENTION OF PRINTING : A Collection of Texts and Opinions. Description of Early Prints and Playing Cards, the Block-Books of the Fifteenth Century, the Legend of Lourens Janszoon Coster of Haarlem, and the Works of John Gutenberg and his Associates. Illustrated with Fac-similes of Early Types and Woodcuts. By Theo. L. De Vinne. Second Edition. In royal 8vo, elegantly printed, and bound in cloth, with embossed portraits, and a multitude of Fac-similes and Illustrations. 1877. £1 1s.

DICKSON.—WHO WAS SCOTLAND'S FIRST PRINTER? Ane Compendious and breue Tractate, in Commendation of Androw Myllar. Compylit be Robert Dickson, F.S.A. Scot. Fcap. 8vo, pp. 24, parchment wrapper. 1881. 1s.

DOBSON.—MONOGRAPH OF THE ASIATIC CHIROPTERA, and Catalogue of the Species of Bats in the Collection of the Indian Museum, Calcutta. By G. E. Dobson, M.A., M.B., F.L.S., &c. 8vo, pp. viii. and 228, cloth. 1876. 12s.

D'ORSEY.—A PRACTICAL GRAMMAR OF PORTUGUESE AND ENGLISH, exhibiting in a Series of Exercises, in Double Translation, the Idiomatic Structure of both Languages, as now written and spoken. Adapted to Ollendorff's System by the Rev. Alexander J. D. D'Orsey, of Corpus Christi College, Cambridge, and Lecturer on Public Reading and Speaking at King's College, London. Third Edition. 12mo, pp. viii. and 298, cloth. 1868. 7s.

DOUGLAS.—CHINESE-ENGLISH DICTIONARY OF THE VERNACULAR OR SPOKEN LANGUAGE OF AMOY, with the principal variations of the Chang-Chew and Chin-Chew Dialects. By the Rev. Carstairs Douglas, M.A., LL.D., Glasg., Missionary of the Presbyterian Church in England. High quarto, double columns, pp. 632, cloth. 1873. £3, 3s.

DOUGLAS.—CHINESE LANGUAGE AND LITERATURE. Two Lectures delivered at the Royal Institution, by R. K. Douglas, of the British Museum, and Professor of Chinese at King's College. Crown 8vo, pp. 118, cloth. 1875. 5s.

DOUGLAS.—THE LIFE OF JENGHIZ KHAN. Translated from the Chinese. With an Introduction. By Robert K. Douglas, of the British Museum, and Professor of Chinese at King's College. Crown 8vo, pp. xxxvi. and 106, cloth. 1877. 5s.

DOUGLAS.—POEMS : Lyrical and Dramatic. By Evelyn Douglas. Fcap. 8vo.

DOUSE.—GRIMM'S LAW. A Study ; or, Hints towards an Explanation of the so-called "Lautverschiebung ;" to which are added some Remarks on the Primitive Indo-European K, and several Appendices. By T. Le Marchant Douse. 8vo, pp. xvi. and 232, cloth. 1876. 10s. 6d.

DOWSON.—DICTIONARY OF HINDU MYTHOLOGY, &c. See Trübner's Oriental Series.

DOWSON.—A GRAMMAR OF THE URDŪ OR HINDŪSTĀNĪ LANGUAGE. By John Dowson, M.R.A.S., Professor of Hindūstānī, Staff College, Sandhurst. Crown 8vo, pp. xvi. and 264, with 8 Plates, cloth. 1872. 10s. 6d.

DOWSON.—A HINDŪSTĀNĪ EXERCISE BOOK ; containing a Series of Passages and Extracts adapted for Translation into Hindūstānī. By John Dowson, M.R.A.S., Professor of Hindūstānī, Staff College, Sandhurst. Crown 8vo, pp. 100, limp cloth. 1872. 2s. 6d.

DUNCAN.—GEOGRAPHY OF INDIA, comprising a Descriptive Outline of all India, and a Detailed Geographical, Commercial, Social, and Political Account of each of its Provinces. With Historical Notes. By George Duncan. Tenth Edition (Revised and Corrected to date from the latest Official Information). 18mo, pp. viii. and 182, limp cloth. 1880. 1s. 6d.

DUSAR.—A GRAMMAR OF THE GERMAN LANGUAGE; with Exercises. By P. Friedrich Dusar, First German Master in the Military Department of Cheltenham College. Second Edition. Crown 8vo, pp. viii. and 208, cloth. 1879. 4s. 6d.

DUSAR.—A GRAMMATICAL COURSE OF THE GERMAN LANGUAGE. By P. Friedrich Dusar. Third Edition. Crown 8vo, pp. x. and 134, cloth. 1883. 3s. 6d.

DYMOCK.—THE VEGETABLE MATERIA MEDICA OF WESTERN INDIA. By W. Dymock, Surgeon-Major Bombay Army, &c. &c. To be completed in four parts. 8vo, Part I., pp. 160 ; Part II., pp. 168 ; wrappers, 4s. each.

EARLY ENGLISH TEXT SOCIETY.—Subscription, one guinea per annum. *Extra Series.* Subscriptions—Small paper, one guinea ; large paper, two guineas, per annum. List of publications on application.

EASTWICK.—KHIRAD AFROZ (the Illuminator of the Understanding). By Maulaví Hafizu'd-dín. A New Edition of the Hindūstání Text, carefully revised, with Notes, Critical and Explanatory. By Edward B. Eastwick, F.R.S., F.S.A., M.R.A.S., Professor of Hindūstání at Haileybury College. Imperial 8vo, pp. xiv. and 319, cloth. Reissue, 1867. 18s.

EASTWICK.—THE GULISTAN. See Trübner's Oriental Series.

EBERS.—THE EMPEROR. A Romance. By Georg Ebers. Translated from the German by Clara Bell. In two volumes, 16mo, pp. iv. 319 and 322, cloth. 1881. 7s. 6d.

EBERS.—A QUESTION : The Idyl of a Picture by his friend, Alma Tadema. Related by Georg Ebers. From the German, by Mary J. Safford. 16mo, pp. 125, with Frontispiece, cloth. 1881. 4s.

ECHO (DEUTSCHES). THE GERMAN ECHO. A Faithful Mirror of German Conversation. By Ludwig Wolfram. With a Vocabulary. By Henry P. Skelton. Post 8vo, pp. 130 and 70, cloth. 1863. 3s.

ECHO FRANÇAIS. A PRACTICAL GUIDE TO CONVERSATION. By Fr. de la Fruston. With a complete Vocabulary. By Anthony Maw Border. Post 8vo, pp. 120 and 72, cloth. 1860. 3s.

ECO ITALIANO (L'). A PRACTICAL GUIDE TO ITALIAN CONVERSATION. By Eugene Camerini. With a complete Vocabulary. By Henry P. Skelton. Post 8vo, pp. vi., 128, and 98, cloth. 1860. 4s. 6d.

ECO DE MADRID. THE ECHO OF MADRID. A Practical Guide to Spanish Conversation. By J. E. Hartzenbusch and Henry Lemming. With a complete Vocabulary, containing copious Explanatory Remarks. By Henry Lemming. Post 8vo, pp. xii., 144, and 83, cloth. 1860. 5s.

ECKSTEIN.—PRUSIAS: A Romance of Ancient Rome under the Republic. By Ernst Eckstein. From the German by Clara Bell. Two vols. 16mo, pp. 356 and 336, cloth. 1884. 7s. 6d. ; paper, 5s.

ECKSTEIN. — QUINTUS CLAUDIUS. A Romance of Imperial Rome. By Ernst Eckstein. From the German by Clara Bell, Two vols. 16mo, pp. 314 and 304, cloth. 1884. 7s. 6d. ; paper, 5s.

EDDA SÆMUNDAR HINNS FRODA. The Edda of Sæmund the Learned. Translated from the Old Norse, by Benjamin Thorpe. Complete in 1 vol. fcap. 8vo, pp. viii. and 152, and pp. viii. and 170, cloth. 1866. 7s. 6d.

EDKINS.— CHINA'S PLACE IN PHILOLOGY. An attempt to show that the Languages of Europe and Asia have a common origin. By the Rev. Joseph Edkins. Crown 8vo, pp. xxiii. and 403, cloth. 1871. 10s. 6d.

EDKINS.—INTRODUCTION TO THE STUDY OF THE CHINESE CHARACTERS. By J. Edkins, D.D., Peking, China. Royal 8vo, pp. 340, paper boards. 1876. 18s.

EDKINS.—RELIGION IN CHINA. See English and Foreign Philosophical Library, Vol. VIII., or Trübner's Oriental Series.

EDKINS.—CHINESE BUDDHISM. See Trübner's Oriental Series.

EDWARDS.— MEMOIRS OF LIBRARIES, together with a Practical Handbook of Library Economy. By Edward Edwards. Numerous Illustrations. 2 vols. royal 8vo, cloth. Vol. i. pp. xxviii. and 841 ; Vol. ii. pp. xxxvi. and 1104. 1859. £2, 8s.

DITTO, large paper, imperial 8vo, cloth. £4, 4s.

EDWARDS.— CHAPTERS OF THE BIOGRAPHICAL HISTORY OF THE FRENCH ACADEMY. 1629-1863. With an Appendix relating to the Unpublished Chronicle "Liber de Hyda." By Edward Edwards. 8vo, pp. 180, cloth. 1864. 6s.

DITTO, large paper, royal 8vo. 10s. 6d.

EDWARDS.— LIBRARIES AND FOUNDERS OF LIBRARIES. By Edward Edwards. 8vo, pp. xix. and 506, cloth. 1865. 18s.

DITTO, large paper, imperial 8vo, cloth. £1, 10s.

EDWARDS. — FREE TOWN LIBRARIES, their Formation, Management, and History in Britain, France, Germany, and America. Together with Brief Notices of Book Collectors, and of the respective Places of Deposit of their Surviving Collections. By Edward Edwards. 8vo, pp. xvi. and 634, cloth. 1869. 21s.

EDWARDS.— LIVES OF THE FOUNDERS OF THE BRITISH MUSEUM, with Notices of its Chief Augmentors and other Benefactors. 1570-1870. By Edward Edwards. With Illustrations and Plans. 2 vols. 8vo, pp. xii. and 780, cloth. 1870. 30s.

EDWARDES.—See ENGLISH AND FOREIGN PHILOSOPHICAL LIBRARY, Vol. XVII.

EGER AND GRIME.—An Early English Romance. Edited from Bishop Percy's Folio Manuscripts, about 1650 A.D. By John W. Hales, M.A., Fellow and late Assistant Tutor of Christ's College, Cambridge, and Frederick J. Furnivall, M.A., of Trinity Hall, Cambridge. 4to, large paper, half bound, Roxburghe style, pp. 64. 1867. 10s. 6d.

EGERTON.—SUSSEX FOLK AND SUSSEX WAYS. Stray Studies in the Wealden Formation of Human Nature. By the Rev. J. Coker Egerton, M.A., Rector of Burwash. Crown 8vo, pp. 140, cloth. 1884. 2s.

EGGELING.—See AUCTORES SANSKRITI, Vols. IV. and V.

EGYPTIAN GENERAL STAFF PUBLICATIONS :—

GENERAL REPORT ON THE PROVINCE OF KORDOFAN. Submitted to General C. P. Stone, Chief of the General Staff Egyptian Army. By Major H. G. Prout, Corps of Engineers, Commanding Expedition of Reconnaissance. Made at El-Obeiyad (Kordofan), March 12th, 1876. Royal 8vo, pp. 232, stitched, with 6 Maps. 1877. 10s. 6d.

EGYPTIAN GENERAL STAFF PUBLICATIONS—*continued.*

PROVINCES OF THE EQUATOR : Summary of Letters and Reports of the Governor-General. Part 1. 1874. Royal 8vo, pp. viii. and 90, stitched, with Map. 1877. 5s.

REPORT ON THE SEIZURE BY THE ABYSSINIANS of the Geological and Mineralogical Reconnaissance Expedition attached to the General Staff of the Egyptian Army. By L. H. Mitchell, Chief of the Expedition. Containing an Account of the subsequent Treatment of the Prisoners and Final Release of the Commander. Royal 8vo, pp. xii. and 126, stitched, with a Map. 1878. 7s. 6d.

EGYPTIAN CALENDAR for the year 1295 A.H. (1878 A.D.) : Corresponding with the years 1594, 1595 of the Koptic Era. 8vo, pp. 98, sewed. 1878. 2s. 6d.

EHRLICH.—FRENCH READER : With Notes and Vocabulary. By H. W. Ehrlich. 12mo, pp. viii. and 125, limp cloth. 1877. 1s. 6d.

EITEL.—BUDDHISM : Its Historical, Theoretical, and Popular Aspects. In Three Lectures. By E. J. Eitel, M.A., Ph.D. Second Edition. Demy 8vo, pp. 130. 1873. 5s.

EITEL.—FENG-SHUI ; or, The Rudiments of Natural Science in China. By E. J. Eitel, M.A., Ph.D. Royal 8vo, pp. vi. and 84, sewed. 1873. 6s.

EITEL.—HANDBOOK FOR THE STUDENT OF CHINESE BUDDHISM. By the Rev. E. J. Eitel, of the London Missionary Society. Crown 8vo, pp. viii. and 224, cloth. 1870. 18s.

ELLIOT. —MEMOIRS ON THE HISTORY, FOLK-LORE, AND DISTRIBUTION OF THE RACES OF THE NORTH-WESTERN PROVINCES OF INDIA. By the late Sir Henry M. Elliot, K.C.B. Edited, revised, and rearranged by John Beames, M.R.A.S., &c., &c. In 2 vols. demy 8vo, pp. xx., 370, and 396, with 3 large coloured folding Maps, cloth. 1869. £1 16s.

ELLIOT.—THE HISTORY OF INDIA, as told by its own Historians. The Muhammadan Period. Edited from the Posthumous Papers of the late Sir H. M. Elliot, K.C.B., East India Company's Bengal Civil Service. Revised and continued by Professor John Dowson, M.R.A.S., Staff College, Sandhurst. 8vo. Vol. I.—Vol. II., pp. x. and 580, cloth. Vol. III., pp. xii. and 627, cloth. 24s.—Vol. IV., pp. xii. and 564, cloth. 1872. 21s.—Vol. V.. pp. x. and 576, cloth. 1873. 21s.—Vol. VI., pp. viii. 574, cloth. 21s.—Vol. VII., pp. viii.–574. 1877. 21s. Vol. VIII., pp. xxxii.–444. With Biographical, Geographical, and General Index. 1877. 24s. Complete sets, £8, 8s. Vols. I. and II. not sold separately.

ELLIS.—ETRUSCAN NUMERALS. By Robert Ellis, B.D., late Fellow of St. John's College, Cambridge. 8vo, pp. 52, sewed. 1876. 2s. 6d.

ELY.—FRENCH AND GERMAN SOCIALISM IN MODERN TIMES. By R. T. Ely, Ph.D., Associate Professor of Political Economy in the Johns Hopkins University, Baltimore ; and Lecturer on Political Economy in Cornell University, Ithaca, N. Y. Crown 8vo, pp. viii.–274, cloth. 1884. 3s. 6d.

EMERSON AT HOME AND ABROAD. See English and Foreign Philosophical Library, Vol. XIX.

EMERSON.—INDIAN MYTHS ; or, Legends, Traditions, and Symbols of the Aborigines of America, compared with those of other Countries, including Hindostan, Egypt, Persia, Assyria, and China. By Ellen Russell Emerson. Illustrated. Post 8vo, pp. viii.–678, cloth. 1884. £1, 1s.

ENGLISH DIALECT SOCIETY.—Subscription, 10s. 6d. per annum. List of publications on application.

ENGLISH AND FOREIGN PHILOSOPHICAL LIBRARY (THE).
Post 8vo, cloth, uniformly bound.

I. to III.—A HISTORY OF MATERIALISM, and Criticism of its present Importance. By Professor F. A. Lange. Authorised Translation from the German by Ernest C. Thomas. In three volumes. Vol. I. Second Edition. pp. 350. 1878. 10s. 6d.—Vol. II., pp. viii. and 298. 1880. 10s. 6d. —Vol. III., pp. viii. and 376. 1881. 10s. 6d.

ENGLISH AND FOREIGN PHILOSOPHICAL LIBRARY—*continued.*

IV.—NATURAL LAW: an Essay in Ethics. By Edith Simcox. Second Edition. Pp. 366. 1878. 10s. 6d.

V. and VI.—THE CREED OF CHRISTENDOM; its Foundations contrasted with Super-structure. By W. R. Greg. Eighth Edition, with a New Introduction. In two volumes, pp. cxiv.-154 and vi.-282 1883. 15s.

VII.—OUTLINES OF THE HISTORY OF RELIGION TO THE SPREAD OF THE UNIVERSAL RELIGIONS. By Prof. C. P. Tiele. Translated from the Dutch by J. Estlin Carpenter, M.A., with the author's assist-ance. Third Edition. Pp. xx. and 250. 1884. 7s. 6d.

VIII.—RELIGION IN CHINA; containing a brief Account of the Three Religions of the Chinese; with Observations on the Prospects of Christian Conversion amongst that People. By Joseph Edkins, D.D., Peking. Third Edition. Pp. xvi. and 260. 1884. 7s. 6d.

IX.—A CANDID EXAMINATION OF THEISM. By Physicus. Pp. 216. 1878. 7s. 6d.

X.—THE COLOUR-SENSE; its Origin and Development; an Essay in Com-parative Psychology. By Grant Allen, B.A., author of "Phy-siological Æsthetics." Pp. xii. and 282. 1879. 10s. 6d.

XI.—THE PHILOSOPHY OF MUSIC; being the substance of a Course of Lectures delivered at the Royal Institution of Great Britain in February and March 1877. By William Pole, F.R.S., F.R.S.E., Mus. Doc., Oxon. Pp. 336. 1879. 10s. 6d.

XII.—CONTRIBUTIONS TO THE HISTORY OF THE DEVELOPMENT OF THE HUMAN RACE: Lectures and Dissertations, by Lazarus Geiger. Translated from the German by D. Asher, Ph.D. Pp. x. and 156. 1880. 6s.

XIII.—DR. APPLETON: his Life and Literary Relics. By J. H. Appleton, M.A., and A. H. Sayce, M.A. Pp. 350. 1881. 10s. 6d.

XIV.—EDGAR QUINET: His Early Life and Writings. By Richard Heath. With Portraits, Illustrations, and an Autograph Letter. Pp. xxiii. and 370. 1881. 12s. 6d.

XV.—THE ESSENCE OF CHRISTIANITY. By Ludwig Feuerbach. Translated from the German by Marian Evans, translator of Strauss's "Life of Jesus." Second Edition. Pp. xx. and 340. 1881. 7s. 6d.

XVI.—AUGUSTE COMTE AND POSITIVISM. By the late John Stuart Mill, M.P. Third Edition. Pp. 200. 1882. 3s. 6d.

XVII.—ESSAYS AND DIALOGUES OF GIACOMO LEOPARDI. Translated by Charles Edwardes. With Biographical Sketch. Pp. xliv. and 216. 1882. 7s. 6d.

XVIII.—RELIGION AND PHILOSOPHY IN GERMANY: A Fragment. By Hein-rich Heine. Translated by J. Snodgrass. Pp. xii. and 178, cloth. 1882. 6s.

XIX.—EMERSON AT HOME AND ABROAD. By M. D. Conway. Pp. viii. and 310. With Portrait. 1883. 10s. 6d.

XX.—ENIGMAS OF LIFE. By W. R. Greg. Fifteenth Edition, with a Postscript. CONTENTS: Realisable Ideals—Malthus Notwithstand-ing—Non-Survival of the Fittest—Limits and Directions of Human Development—The Significance of Life—De Profundis—Elsewhere—Appendix. Pp. xx. and 314, cloth. 1883. 10s. 6d.

XXI.—ETHIC DEMONSTRATED IN GEOMETRICAL ORDER AND DIVIDED INTO FIVE PARTS, which treat (1) Of God, (2) Of the Nature and Origin of the Mind, (3) Of the Origin and Nature of the Affects, (4) Of Human Bondage, or of the Strength of the Affects, (5) Of the Power of the Intellect, or of Human Liberty. By Benedict de Spinoza. Trans-lated from the Latin by William Hale White. Pp. 328. 1883. 10s. 6d.

XXII.—THE WORLD AS WILL AND IDEA. By Arthur Schopenhauer. Trans-lated from the German by R. B. Haldane, M.A., and John Kemp, M.A. 3 vols. Vol. I., pp. xxxii.-532. 1883. 18s.

ENGLISH AND FOREIGN PHILOSOPHICAL LIBRARY—*continued.*

XXV. to XXVII.—THE PHILOSOPHY OF THE UNCONSCIOUS. By Eduard Von
Hartmann. Speculative Results, according to the Inductive Method
of Physical Science. Authorised Translation, by William C. Coupland, M.A. 3 vols. pp. xxxii.-372; vi.-368; viii.-360. 1884. 31s. 6d.

XXVIII.—THE GUIDE OF THE PERPLEXED OF MAIMONIDES. Translated from
the Original Text and Annotated by M. Friedlander, Ph.D. 3
vols., pp.

Extra Series.

I. and II.—LESSING : His Life and Writings. By James Sime, M.A. Second
Edition. 2 vols., pp. xxii. and 328, and xvi. and 358, with portraits. 1879. 21s.

III. and VI.—AN ACCOUNT OF THE POLYNESIAN RACE: its Origin and Migrations,
and the Ancient History of the Hawaiian People to the Times of
Kamehameha I. By Abraham Fornander, Circuit Judge of the
Island of Maui, H.I. Vol. I., pp. xvi. and 248. 1877. 7s. 6d. Vol.
II., pp. viii. and 400, cloth. 1880. 10s. 6d.

IV. and V.—ORIENTAL RELIGIONS, and their Relation to Universal Religion—
India. By Samuel Johnson. In 2 vols., pp. viii. and 408; viii.
and 402. 1879. 21s.

VI.—AN ACCOUNT OF THE POLYNESIAN RACE. By A. Fornander. Vol.
II., pp. viii. and 400, cloth. 1880. 10s. 6d.

ER SIE ES.—FACSIMILE OF A MANUSCRIPT supposed to have been found in an Egyptian Tomb by the English soldiers last year. Royal 8vo, in ragged canvas covers,
with string binding, with dilapidated edges (? just as discovered). 1884. 6s. 6d.

ETHERINGTON.—THE STUDENT'S GRAMMAR OF THE HINDÍ LANGUAGE. By the Rev.
W. Etherington, Missionary, Benares. Second Edition. Crown 8vo, pp. xiv.,
255, and xiii., cloth. 1873. 12s.

EYTON.—DOMESDAY STUDIES : AN ANALYSIS AND DIGEST OF THE STAFFORDSHIRE
SURVEY. Treating of the Method of Domesday in its Relation to Staffordshire,
&c. By the Rev. R. W. Eyton. 4to, pp. vii. and 135, cloth. 1881. £1, 1s.

FABER.—THE MIND OF MENCIUS. See Trübner's Oriental Series.

FALKE.—ART IN THE HOUSE. Historical, Critical, and Æsthetical Studies on the
Decoration and Furnishing of the Dwelling. By J. von Falke, Vice-Director of
the Austrian Museum of Art and Industry at Vienna. Translated from the German.
Edited, with Notes, by C. C. Perkins, M.A. Royal 8vo, pp. xxx. 356, cloth.
With Coloured Frontispiece, 60 Plates, and over 150 Illustrations. 1878. £3.

FARLEY.—EGYPT, CYPRUS, AND ASIATIC TURKEY. By J. L. Farley, author of "The
Resources of Turkey," &c. 8vo, pp. xvi. and 270, cloth gilt. 1878. 10s. 6d.

FAUSBOLL.—See JATAKA.

FEATHERMAN.—THE SOCIAL HISTORY OF THE RACES OF MANKIND. Vol. V.
THE ARAMÆANS. By A. Featherman. Demy 8vo, pp. xvii. and 664, cloth.
1881. £1, 1s.

FENTON.—EARLY HEBREW LIFE: a Study in Sociology. By John Fenton. 8vo,
pp. xxiv. and 102, cloth. 1880. 5s.

FERGUSSON.—ARCHÆOLOGY IN INDIA. With especial reference to the works of
Babu Rajendralala Mitra. By James Fergusson, C.I.E., F.R.S., D.C.L., LL.D.,
V.-P.R.A.S., &c. Demy 8vo, pp. 116, with Illustrations, sewed. 1884. 5s.

FERGUSSON.—THE TEMPLE OF DIANA AT EPHESUS. With Especial Reference to
Mr. Wood's Discoveries of its Remains. By James Fergusson, C.I.E., D.C.L.,
LL.D., F.R.S., &c. From the Transactions of the Royal Institute of British
Architects. Demy 4to, pp. 24, with Plan, cloth. 1883. 5s.

FERGUSSON AND BURGESS.—THE CAVE TEMPLES OF INDIA. By James Fergusson,
D.C.L., F.R.S., and James Burgess, F.R.G.S. Impl. 8vo, pp. xx. and 536, with
98 Plates, half bound. 1880. £2, 2s.

FERGUSSON.—Chinese Researches. First Part. Chinese Chronology and Cycles. By Thomas Fergusson, Member of the North China Branch of the Royal Asiatic Society. Crown 8vo, pp. viii. and 274, sewed. 1881. 10s. 6d.

FEUERBACH.—The Essence of Christianity. See English and Foreign Philosophical Library, vol. XV.

FICHTE.—J. G. Fichte's Popular Works : The Nature of the Scholar—The Vocation of Man—The Doctrine of Religion. With a Memoir by William Smith, LL.D. Demy 8vo, pp. viii. and 564, cloth. 1873. 15s.

FICHTE.—Characteristics of the Present Age. By J. G. Fichte. Translated from the German by W. Smith. Post 8vo. pp. xi. and 271, cloth. 1847. 6s.

FICHTE.—Memoir of Johann Gottlieb Fichte. By William Smith. Second Edition. Post 8vo, pp. 168, cloth. 1848. 4s.

FICHTE.—On the Nature of the Scholar, and its Manifestations. By Johann Gottlieb Fichte. Translated from the German by William Smith. Second Edition. Post 8vo, pp. vii. and 131, cloth. 1848. 3s.

FICHTE.—New Exposition of the Science of Knowledge. By J. G. Fichte. Translated from the German by A. E. Krœger. 8vo, pp. vi. and 182, cloth. 1869. 6s.

FIELD.—Outlines of an International Code. By David Dudley Field. Second Edition. Royal 8vo, pp. iii. and 712, sheep. 1876. £2, 2s.

FIGANIERE.—Elva : A Story of the Dark Ages. By Viscount de Figanière, G.C. St. Anne, &c. Crown 8vo, pp. viii. and 194, cloth. 1878. 5s.

FINN.—Persian for Travellers. By Alexander Finn, F.R.G.S., &c., H.B.M. Consul at Resht. Oblong 32mo, pp. xxii.-232, cloth. 1884. 5s.

FISCHEL.—Specimens of Modern German Prose and Poetry : with Notes, Grammatical, Historical, and Idiomatical. To which is added a Short Sketch of the History of German Literature. By Dr. M. M. Fischel, formerly of Queen's College, Harley Street, and late German Master to the Stockwell Grammar School. Crown 8vo, pp. viii. and 280, cloth. 1880. 4s.

FISKE.—The Unseen World, and other Essays. By John Fiske, M.A., LL.B. Crown 8vo, pp. 350. 1876. 10s.

FISKE.—Myths and Myth-Makers ; Old Tales and Superstitions, interpreted by Comparative Mythology. By John Fiske, M.A., LL.B., Assistant Librarian, and late Lecturer on Philosophy at Harvard University. Crown 8vo, pp. 260, cloth. 1873. 10s.

FITZGERALD.—Australian Orchids. By R. D. Fitzgerald, F.L.S. Folio.—Part I. 7 Plates.—Part II. 10 Plates.—Part III. 10 Plates.—Part IV. 10 Plates.— Part V. 10 Plates.—Part VI. 10 Plates. Each Part, Coloured 21s.; Plain, 10s. 6d. —Part VII. 10 Plates. Vol. II., Part I. 10 Plates. Each, Coloured, 25s.

FITZGERALD.—An Essay on the Philosophy of Self-Consciousness. Comprising an Analysis of Reason and the Rationale of Love. By P. F. Fitzgerald. Demy 8vo, pp. xvi. and 196, cloth. 1882. 5s.

FORJETT.—External Evidences of Christianity. By E. H. Forjett. 8vo, pp. 114, cloth. 1874. 2s. 6d.

FORNANDER.—The Polynesian Race. See English and Foreign Philosophical Library, Extra Series, Vols. III. and VI.

FORSTER.—Political Presentments.—By William Forster, Agent-General for New South Wales. Crown 8vo, pp. 122, cloth. 1878. 4s. 6d.

FOULKES.—The Data Bhaga, the Law of Inheritance of the Sarasvati Vilasa. The Original Sanskrit Text, with Translation by the Rev. Thos. Foulkes, F.L.S., M.R.A.S., F.R.G.S., Fellow of the University of Madras, &c. Demy 8vo, pp. xxvi. and 194-162, cloth. 1881. 10s. 6d.

FOX.—Memorial Edition of Collected Works, by W. J. Fox. 12 vols. 8vo, cloth. £3.

FRANKLYN.—Outlines of Military Law, and the Laws of Evidence. By H. B. Franklyn, LL.B. Crown 16mo, pp. viii. and 152, cloth. 1874. 3s. 6d.

FREEMAN.—LECTURES TO AMERICAN AUDIENCES. By E. A. Freeman, D.C.L., LL.D., Honorary Fellow of Trinity College, Oxford. I. The English People in its Three Homes. II. The Practical Bearings of General European History. Post 8vo, pp. viii.-454, cloth. 1883. 8s. 6d.

FRIEDRICH.—PROGRESSIVE GERMAN READER, with Copious Notes to the First Part. By P. Friedrich. Crown 8vo, pp. 166, cloth. 1868. 4s. 6d.

FRIEDRICH.—A GRAMMATICAL COURSE OF THE GERMAN LANGUAGE. See under DUSAR.

FRIEDRICH.—A GRAMMAR OF THE GERMAN LANGUAGE, WITH EXERCISES. See under DUSAR.

FRIEDERICI.—BIBLIOTHECA ORIENTALIS, or a Complete List of Books, Papers, Serials, and Essays, published in England and the Colonies, Germany and France; on the History, Geography, Religions, Antiquities, Literature, and Languages of the East. Compiled by Charles Friederici. 8vo, boards. 1876, pp. 86, 2s. 6d. 1877, pp. 100, 3s. 1878, pp. 112, 3s. 6d. 1879, 3s. 1880, 3s.

FRŒMBLING.—GRADUATED GERMAN READER. Consisting of a Selection from the most Popular Writers, arranged progressively; with a complete Vocabulary for the first part. By Friedrich Otto Frœmbling. Eighth Edition. 12mo, pp. viii. and 306, cloth. 1883. 3s. 6d.

FRŒMBLING.—GRADUATED EXERCISES FOR TRANSLATION INTO GERMAN. Consisting of Extracts from the best English Authors, arranged progressively; with an Appendix, containing Idiomatic Notes. By Friedrich Otto Frœmbling, Ph.D., Principal German Master at the City of London School. Crown 8vo, pp. xiv. and 322, cloth. With Notes, pp. 66. 1867. 4s. 6d. Without Notes, 4s.

FROUDE.—THE BOOK OF JOB. By J. A. Froude, M.A., late Fellow of Exeter College, Oxford. Reprinted from the *Westminster Review*. 8vo, pp. 38, cloth. 1s.

FRUSTON.—ECHO FRANÇAIS. A Practical Guide to French Conversation. By F. de la Fruston. With a Vocabulary. 12mo, pp. vi. and 192, cloth. 3s.

FRYER.—THE KHYENG PEOPLE OF THE SANDOWAY DISTRICT, ARAKAN. By G. E. Fryer, Major, M.S.C., Deputy Commissioner, Sandoway. With 2 Plates. 8vo, pp. 44, cloth. 1875. 3s. 6d.

FRYER.—PÁLI STUDIES. No. I. Analysis, and Páli Text of the Subodhálankara, or Easy Rhetoric, by Sangharakkhita Thera. 8vo, pp. 35, cloth. 1875. 6d.

FURNIVALL.—EDUCATION IN EARLY ENGLAND. Some Notes used as forewords to a Collection of Treatises on "Manners and Meals in Olden Times," for the Early English Text Society. By Frederick J. Furnivall, M.A. 8vo, pp. 4 and lxxiv., sewed. 1867. 1s.

GALDOS.—TRAFALGAR: A Tale. By B. Perez Galdos. From the Spanish by Clara Bell. 16mo, pp. 256, cloth. 1884. 4s. Paper, 2s. 6d.

GALDOS.—MARIANELA. By B. Perez Galdos. From the Spanish, by Clara Bell. 16mo, pp. 264, cloth. 1883. 4s. Paper, 2s. 6d.

GALDOS.—GLORIA: A Novel. By B. Perez Galdos. From the Spanish, by Clara Bell. Two volumes, 16mo, pp. vi. and 318, iv. and 362, cloth. 1883. 7s. 6d. Paper, 5s.

GALLOWAY.—A TREATISE ON FUEL. Scientific and Practical. By Robert Galloway, M.R.I.A., F.C.S., &c. With Illustrations. Post 8vo, pp. x. and 136, cloth. 1880. 6s.

GALLOWAY.—EDUCATION: SCIENTIFIC AND TECHNICAL; or, How the Inductive Sciences are Taught, and How they Ought to be Taught. By Robert Galloway, M.R.I.A., F.C.S. 8vo, pp. xvi. and 462, cloth. 1881. 10s. 6d.

GAMBLE.—A MANUAL OF INDIAN TIMBERS: An Account of the Structure, Growth, Distribution, and Qualities of Indian Woods. By J. C. Gamble, M.A., F.L.S. 8vo, pp. xxx. and 522, with a Map, cloth. 1881. 10s.

GARBE.—See AUCTORES SANSKRITI, Vol. III.

GARFIELD.—The Life and Public Service of James A. Garfield, Twentieth President of the United States. A Biographical Sketch. By Captain F. H. Mason, late of the 42d Regiment, U.S.A. With a Preface by Bret Harte. Crown 8vo, pp. vi. and 134, cloth. With Portrait. 1881. 2s. 6d.

GARRETT.—A Classical Dictionary of India : Illustrative of the Mythology, Philosophy, Literature, Antiquities, Arts, Manners, Customs, &c., of the Hindus. By John Garrett, Director of Public Instruction in Mysore. 8vo, pp. x. and 794, cloth. With Supplement, pp. 160. 1871 and 1873. £1, 16s.

GAUTAMA.—The Institutes of. See Auctores Sanskriti, Vol. II.

GAZETTEER of the Central Provinces of India. Edited by Charles Grant, Secretary to the Chief Commissioner of the Central Provinces. Second Edition. With a very large folding Map of the Central Provinces of India. Demy 8vo, pp. clvii. and 582, cloth. 1870. £1, 4s.

GEIGER.—A Peep at Mexico ; Narrative of a Journey across the Republic from the Pacific to the Gulf, in December 1873 and January 1874. By J. L. Geiger, F.R.G.S. Demy 8vo, pp. 368, with Maps and 45 Original Photographs. Cloth, 24s.

GEIGER.—Contributions to the History of the Development of the Human Race : Lectures and Dissertations, by Lazarus Geiger. Translated from the Second German Edition, by David Asher, Ph.D. Post 8vo, pp. x.-156, cloth. 1880. 6s.

GELDART.—Faith and Freedom. Fourteen Sermons. By E. M. Geldart, M.A. Crown 8vo, pp. vi. and 168, cloth. 1881. 4s. 6d.

GELDART.—A Guide to Modern Greek. By E. M. Geldart, M.A. Post 8vo, pp. xii. and 274, cloth. 1883. 7s. 6d. Key, pp. 28, cloth. 1883. 2s. 6d.

GELDART.—Greek Grammar. See Trübner's Collection.

GEOLOGICAL MAGAZINE (The) : or, Monthly Journal of Geology. With which is incorporated "The Geologist." Edited by Henry Woodward, LL.D., F.R.S., F.G.S., &c., of the British Museum. Assisted by Professor John Morris, M.A., F.G.S., &c., and Robert Etheridge, F.R.S., L. & E., F.G.S., &c., of the Museum of Practical Geology. 8vo, cloth. 1866 to 1883. 20s. each.

GHOSE.—The Modern History of the Indian Chiefs, Rajas, Zamindars, &c. By Loke Nath Ghose. 2 vols. post 8vo, pp. xii. and 218, and xviii. and 612, cloth. 1883. 21s.

GILES.—Chinese Sketches.—By Herbert A. Giles, of H.B.M.'s China Consular Service. 8vo, pp. 204, cloth. 1875. 10s. 6d.

GILES.—A Dictionary of Colloquial Idioms in the Mandarin Dialect. By Herbert A. Giles. 4to, pp. 65, half bound. 1873. 28s.

GILES.—Synoptical Studies in Chinese Character. By Herbert A. Giles. 8vo, pp. 118, half bound. 1874. 15s.

GILES.—Chinese without a Teacher. Being a Collection of Easy and Useful Sentences in the Mandarin Dialect. With a Vocabulary. By Herbert A. Giles. 12mo, pp. 60, half bound. 1872. 5s.

GILES.—The San Tzu Ching ; or, Three Character Classic ; and the Ch'Jen Tsu Wen ; or, Thousand Character Essay. Metrically Translated by Herbert A. Giles. 12mo, pp. 28, half bound. 1873. 2s. 6d.

GLASS.—Advance Thought. By Charles E. Glass. Crown 8vo, pp. xxxvi. and 188, cloth. 1876. 6s.

GOETHE'S Faust.—See Scoones and Wysard.

GOETHE'S Minor Poems.—See Selss.

GOLDSTÜCKER.—A DICTIONARY, SANSKRIT AND ENGLISH, extended and improved from the Second Edition of the Dictionary of Professor H. H. Wilson, with his sanction and concurrence. Together with a Supplement, Grammatical Appendices, and an Index, serving as a Sanskrit-English Vocabulary. By Theodore Goldstücker. Parts I. to VI. 4to, pp. 400. 1856-63. 6s. each.

GOLDSTÜCKER.—See AUCTORES SANSKRITI, Vol. I.

GOOROO SIMPLE. Strange Surprising Adventures of the Venerable G. S. and his Five Disciples, Noodle, Doodle, Wiseacre, Zany, and Foozle : adorned with Fifty Illustrations, drawn on wood, by Alfred Crowquill. A companion Volume to "Münchhausen" and "Owlglass," based upon the famous Tamul tale of the Gooroo Paramartan, and exhibiting, in the form of a skilfully-constructed consecutive narrative, some of the finest specimens of Eastern wit and humour. Elegantly printed on tinted paper, in crown 8vo, pp. 223, richly gilt ornamental cover, gilt edges. 1861. 10s. 6d.

GORKOM.—HANDBOOK OF CINCHONA CULTURE. By K. W. Van Gorkom, formerly Director of the Government Cinchona Plantations in Java. Translated by B. D. Jackson, Secretary of the Linnæan Society of London. With a Coloured Illustration. Imperial 8vo, pp. xii. and 292, cloth. 1882. £2.

GOUGH.—The SARVA-DARSANA-SAMGRAHA. See Trübner's Oriental Series.

GOUGH.—PHILOSOPHY OF THE UPANISHADS. See Trübner's Oriental Series.

GOVER.—THE FOLK-SONGS OF SOUTHERN INDIA. By C. E. Gover, Madras. Contents : Canarese Songs ; Badaga Songs ; Coorg Songs ; Tamil Songs ; The Cural ; Malayalam Songs ; Telugu Songs. 8vo, pp. xxviii. and 300, cloth. 1872. 10s. 6d.

GRAY.—DARWINIANA : Essays and Reviews pertaining to Darwinism. By Asa Gray. Crown 8vo, pp. xii. and 396, cloth. 1877. 10s.

GRAY.—NATURAL SCIENCE AND RELIGION : Two Lectures Delivered to the Theological School of Yale College. By Asa Gray. Crown 8vo, pp. 112, cloth. 1880. 5s.

GREEN.—SHAKESPEARE AND THE EMBLEM-WRITERS : An Exposition of their Similarities of Thought and Expression. Preceded by a View of the Emblem-Book Literature down to A.D. 1616. By Henry Green, M.A. In one volume, pp. xvi. 572, profusely illustrated with Woodcuts and Photolith. Plates, elegantly bound in cloth gilt. 1870. Large medium 8vo, £1, 11s. 6d. ; large imperial 8vo. £2, 12s. 6d.

GREEN.—ANDREA ALCIATI, and his Books of Emblems : A Biographical and Bibliographical Study. By Henry Green, M.A. With Ornamental Title, Portraits, and other Illustrations. Dedicated to Sir William Stirling-Maxwell, Bart., Rector of the University of Edinburgh. Only 250 copies printed. Demy 8vo, pp. 360, handsomely bound. 1872. £1, 1s.

GREENE.—A NEW METHOD OF LEARNING TO READ, WRITE, AND SPEAK THE FRENCH LANGUAGE ; or, First Lessons in French (Introductory to Ollendorff's Larger Grammar). By G. W. Greene, Instructor in Modern Languages in Brown University. Third Edition, enlarged and rewritten. Fcap. 8vo, pp. 248, cloth. 1869. 3s. 6d.

GREENE.—THE HEBREW MIGRATION FROM EGYPT. By J. Baker Greene, LL.B., M.B., Trin. Coll., Dub. Second Edition. Demy 8vo, pp. xii. and 440, cloth. 1882. 10s. 6d.

GREG.—TRUTH VERSUS EDIFICATION. By W. R. Greg. Fcap. 8vo, pp. 32, cloth. 1869. 1s.

GREG.—WHY ARE WOMEN REDUNDANT? By W. R. Greg. Fcap. 8vo, pp. 40, cloth. 1869. 1s.

GREG.—LITERARY AND SOCIAL JUDGMENTS. By W. R. Greg. Fourth Edition, considerably enlarged. 2 vols. crown 8vo, pp. 310 and 288, cloth. 1877. 15s.

GREG.—MISTAKEN AIMS AND ATTAINABLE IDEALS OF THE ARTISAN CLASS. By W. R. Greg. Crown 8vo, pp. vi. and 332, cloth. 1876. 10s. 6d.

GREG.—ENIGMAS OF LIFE. By W. R. Greg. Fifteenth Edition, with a postscript. Contents: Realisable Ideals. Malthus Notwithstanding. Non-Survival of the Fittest. Limits and Directions of Human Development. The Significance of Life. De Profundis. Elsewhere. Appendix. Post 8vo, pp. xxii. and 314, cloth. 1883. 10s. 6d.

GREG.—POLITICAL PROBLEMS FOR OUR AGE AND COUNTRY. By W. R. Greg. Contents: I. Constitutional and Autocratic Statesmanship. II. England's Future Attitude and Mission. III. Disposal of the Criminal Classes. IV. Recent Change in the Character of English Crime. V. The Intrinsic Vice of Trade-Unions. VI. Industrial and Co-operative Partnerships. VII. The Economic Problem. VIII. Political Consistency. IX. The Parliamentary Career. X. The Price we pay for Self-government. XI. Vestryism. XII. Direct *v.* Indirect Taxation. XIII. The New Régime, and how to meet it. Demy 8vo, pp. 342, cloth. 1870. 10s. 6d.

GREG.—THE GREAT DUEL: Its True Meaning and Issues. By W. R. Greg. Crown 8vo, pp. 96, cloth. 1871. 2s. 6d.

GREG.—THE CREED OF CHRISTENDOM. See English and Foreign Philosophical Library, Vols. V. and VI.

GREG.—ROCKS AHEAD; or, The Warnings of Cassandra. By W. R. Greg. Second Edition, with a Reply to Objectors. Crown 8vo, pp. xliv. and 236, cloth. 1874. 9s.

GREG.—MISCELLANEOUS ESSAYS. By W. R. Greg. First Series. Crown 8vo, pp. iv.-268, cloth. 1881. 7s. 6d.
　　　CONTENTS :—Rocks Ahead and Harbours of Refuge. Foreign Policy of Great Britain. The Echo of the Antipodes. A Grave Perplexity before us. Obligations of the Soil. The Right Use of a Surplus. The Great Twin Brothers: Louis Napoleon and Benjamin Disraeli. Is the Popular Judgment in Politics more Just than that of the Higher Orders? Harriet Martineau. Verify your Compass. The Prophetic Element in the Gospels. Mr. Frederick Harrison on the Future Life. Can Truths be Apprehended which could not have been Discovered?

GREG.—MISCELLANEOUS ESSAYS. By W. R. Greg. Second Series. Pp. 294. 1884. 7s. 6d.
　　　CONTENTS :—France since 1848. France in January 1852. England as it is. Sir R. Peel's Character and Policy. Employment of our Asiatic Forces in European Wars.

GRIFFIN.—THE RAJAS OF THE PUNJAB. Being the History of the Principal States in the Punjab, and their Political Relations with the British Government. By Lepel H. Griffin, Bengal Civil Service. Acting Secretary to the Government of the Punjab, Author of "The Punjab Chiefs," &c. Second Edition. Royal 8vo, pp. xvi. and 630, cloth. 1873. £1, 1s.

GRIFFIN.—THE WORLD UNDER GLASS. By Frederick Griffin, Author of "The Destiny of Man," "The Storm King," and other Poems. Fcap. 8vo, pp. 204, cloth gilt. 1879. 3s. 6d.

GRIFFIN.—THE DESTINY OF MAN, THE STORM KING, and other Poems. By F. Griffin. Second Edition. Fcap. 8vo, pp. vii.-104, cloth. 1883. 2s. 6d.

GRIFFIS.—THE MIKADO'S EMPIRE. Book I. History of Japan, from 660 B.C. to 1872 A.D.—Book II. Personal Experiences, Observations, and Studies in Japan, 1870-1874. By W. E. Griffis, A.M. Second Edition. 8vo, pp. 626, cloth. Illustrated. 1883. 20s.

GRIFFIS.—JAPANESE FAIRY WORLD. Stories from the Wonder-Lore of Japan. By W. E. Griffis. Square 16mo, pp. viii. and 304, with 12 Plates. 1880. 7s. 6d.

GRIFFITH.—The Birth of the War God. See Trübner's Oriental Series.

GRIFFITH.—Yusuf and Zulaikha. See Trübner's Oriental Series.

GRIFFITH.—Scenes from the Ramayana, Meghaduta, &c. Translated by Ralph T. H. Griffith, M.A., Principal of the Benares College. Second Edition. Crown 8vo, pp. xviii. and 244, cloth. 1870. 6s.

CONTENTS.—Preface—Ayodhya—Ravan Doomed—The Birth of Rama—The Heir-Apparent—Manthara's Guile—Dasaratha's Oath—The Step-mother—Mother and Son—The Triumph of Love—Farewell ?—The Hermit's Son—The Trial of Truth—The Forest—The Rape of Sita—Rama's Despair—The Messenger Cloud—Khumbakarna—The Suppliant Dove—True Glory—Feed the Poor—The Wise Scholar.

GRIFFITH.—The Rámáyan of Válmíki. Translated into English Verse. By Ralph T. H. Griffith, M.A., Principal of the Benares College. Vol. I., containing Books I. and II., demy 8vo, pp. xxxii. and 440, cloth. 1870. —Vol. II., containing Book II., with additional Notes and Index of Names. Demy 8vo, pp. 504, cloth. 1871. —Vol. III., demy 8vo, pp. 390, cloth. 1872. —Vol. IV., demy 8vo, pp. viii. and 432, cloth. 1873. —Vol. V., demy 8vo, pp. viii. and 360, cloth. 1875. The complete work, 5 vols. £7, 7s.

GROTE.—Review of the Work of Mr. John Stuart Mill entitled "Examination of Sir William Hamilton's Philosophy." By George Grote, Author of the "History of Ancient Greece," "Plato, and the other Companions of Socrates," &c. 12mo, pp. 112, cloth. 1868. 3s. 6d.

GROUT.—Zulu-Land; or, Life among the Zulu-Kafirs of Natal and Zulu-Land, South Africa. By the Rev. Lewis Grout. Crown 8vo, pp. 352, cloth. With Map and Illustrations. 7s. 6d.

GROWSE.—Mathura : A District Memoir. By F. S. Growse, B.C.S., M.A., Oxon, C.I.E., Fellow of the Calcutta University. Second edition, illustrated, revised, and enlarged, 4to, pp. xxiv. and 520, boards. 1880. 42s.

GUBERNATIS.—Zoological Mythology; or, The Legends of Animals. By Angelo de Gubernatis, Professor of Sanskrit and Comparative Literature in the Instituto di Studii Superiori e di Perfezionamento at Florence, &c. 2 vols. 8vo, pp. xxvi. and 432, and vii. and 442, cloth. 1872. £1, 8s.

This work is an important contribution to the study of the comparative mythology of the Indo-Germanic nations. The author introduces the denizens of the air, earth, and water in the various characters assigned to them in the myths and legends of all civilised nations, and traces the migration of the mythological ideas from the times of the early Aryans to those of the Greeks, Romans, and Teutons.

GULSHAN I. RAZ : The Mystic Rose Garden of Sa'd ud din Mahmud Shabistari. The Persian Text, with an English Translation and Notes, chiefly from the Commentary of Muhammed Bin Yahya Lahiji. By E. H. Whinfield, M.A., Barrister-at-Law, late of H.M.B.C.S. 4to, pp. xvi., 94, 60, cloth. 1880. 10s. 6d.

GUMPACH.—Treaty Rights of the Foreign Merchant, and the Transit System in China. By Johannes von Gumpach. 8vo, pp. xviii. and 421, sewed. 10s. 6d.

HAAS.—Catalogue of Sanskrit and Pali Books in the British Museum. By Dr. Ernst Haas. Printed by permission of the Trustees of the British Museum. 4to, pp. viii. and 188, paper boards. 1876. 21s.

HAFIZ OF SHIRAZ.—Selections from his Poems. Translated from the Persian by Hermann Bicknell. With Preface by A. S. Bicknell. Demy 4to, pp. xx. and 384, printed on fine stout plate-paper, with appropriate Oriental Bordering in gold and colour, and Illustrations by J. R. Herbert, R.A. 1875. £2, 2s.

HAFIZ.—See Trübner's Oriental Series.

HAGEN.—Norica; or, Tales from the Olden Time. Translated from the German of August Hagen. Fcap. 8vo, pp. xiv. and 374. 1850. 5s.

HAGGARD.—Cetywayo and his White Neighbours; or, Remarks on Recent Events in Zululand, Natal, and the Transvaal. By H. R. Haggard. Crown 8vo, pp. xvi. and 294, cloth. 1882. 7s. 6d.

HAGGARD.—See "The Vazir of Lankuran."

HAHN.—Tsuni-‖Goam, the Supreme Being of the Khoi-Khoi. By Theophilus Hahn, Ph.D., Custodian of the Grey Collection, Cape Town, &c., &c. Post 8vo, pp. xiv. and 154. 1882. 7s. 6d.

HALDANE. — See Schopenhauer, or English and Foreign Philosophical Library, vol. xxii.

HALDEMAN.—Pennsylvania Dutch: A Dialect of South Germany with an Infusion of English. By S. S. Haldeman, A.M., Professor of Comparative Philology in the University of Pennsylvania, Philadelphia. 8vo, pp. viii. and 70, cloth. 1872. 3s. 6d.

HALL.—On English Adjectives in -Able, with Special Reference to Reliable. By FitzEdward Hall, C.E., M.A., Hon. D.C.L. Oxon; formerly Professor of Sanskrit Language and Literature, and of Indian Jurisprudence in King's College, London. Crown 8vo, pp. viii. and 238, cloth. 1877. 7s. 6d.

HALL.—Modern English. By FitzEdward Hall, M.A., Hon. D.C.L. Oxon. Crown 8vo, pp. xvi. and 394, cloth. 1873. 10s. 6d.

HALL.—Sun and Earth as Great Forces in Chemistry. By T. W. Hall, M.D., L.R.C.S.E. Crown 8vo, pp. xii. and 220, cloth. 1874. 3s.

HALL.—The Pedigree of the Devil. By F. T. Hall, F.R.A.S. With Seven Autotype Illustrations from Designs by the Author. Demy 8vo, pp. xvi. and 256, cloth. 1883. 7s. 6d.

HALL.—Arctic Expedition. See Nourse.

HALLOCK.—The Sportsman's Gazetteer and General Guide. The Game Animals, Birds, and Fishes of North America: their Habits and various methods of Capture, &c., &c. With a Directory to the principal Game Resorts of the Country. By Charles Hallock. New Edition. Crown 8vo, cloth. Maps and Portrait. 1883. 15s.

HAM.—The Maid of Corinth. A Drama in Four Acts. By J. Panton Ham. Crown 8vo, pp. 65, sewed. 2s. 6d.

HARLEY.—The Simplification of English Spelling, specially adapted to the Rising Generation. An Easy Way of Saving Time in Writing, Printing, and Reading. By Dr. George Harley, F.R.S., F.C.S. 8vo. pp. 128, cloth. 1877. 2s. 6d.

HARRISON.—Woman's Handiwork in Modern Homes. By Constance Cary Harrison. With numerous Illustrations and Five Coloured Plates, from designs by Samuel Colman, Rosina Emmet, George Gibson, and others. 8vo, pp. xii. and 242, cloth. 1881. 10s.

HARTMANN.—See English and Foreign Philosophical Library, vol. XXV.

HARTZENBUSCH and LEMMING.—Eco de Madrid. A Practical Guide to Spanish Conversation. By J. E. Hartzenbusch and H. Lemming. Second Edition. Post 8vo, pp. 250, cloth. 1870. 5s.

HASE.—Miracle Plays and Sacred Dramas: An Historical Survey. By Dr. Karl Hase. Translated from the German by A. W. Jackson, and Edited by the Rev. W. W. Jackson, Fellow of Exeter College, Oxford. Crown 8vo, pp. 288. 1880. 9s.

HAUG.—GLOSSARY AND INDEX of the Pahlavi Texts of the Book of Arda Viraf, the Tale of Gosht—J. Fryano, the Hadokht Nask, and to some extracts from the Dinkard and Nirangistan ; prepared from Destur Hoshangji Jamaspji Asa's Glossary to the Arda Viraf Namak, and from the Original Texts, with Notes on Pahlavi Grammar by E. W. West, Ph.D. Revised by M. Haug, Ph.D., &c. Published by order of the Bombay Government. 8vo, pp. viii. and 352, sewed. 1874. 25s.

HAUG.— THE SACRED LANGUAGE, &c., OF THE PARSIS. See Trübner's Oriental Series.

HAUPT.—THE LONDON ARBITRAGEUR ; or, The English Money Market, in connection with Foreign Bourses. A Collection of Notes and Formulæ for the Arbitration of Bills, Stocks, Shares, Bullion, and Coins, with all the Important Foreign Countries. By Ottomar Haupt. Crown 8vo, pp. viii. and 196, cloth. 1870. 7s. 6d.

HAWKEN.—UPA-SASTRĀ : Comments, Linguistic, Doctrinal, on Sacred and Mythic Literature. By J. D. Hawken. Crown 8vo, pp. viii. and 288, cloth. 1877. 7s. 6d.

HAZEN.—THE SCHOOL AND THE ARMY IN GERMANY AND FRANCE, with a Diary of Siege Life at Versailles. By Brevet Major-General W. B. Hazen, U.S.A., Col. 6th Infantry. 8vo, pp. 408, cloth. 1872. 10s. 6d.

HEATH.—EDGAR QUINET. See English and Foreign Philosophical Library, Vol. XIV.

HEATON—AUSTRALIAN DICTIONARY OF DATES AND MEN OF THE TIME. Containing the History of Australasia from 1542 to May 1879. By I. H. Heaton. Royal 8vo, pp. iv. and 554, cloth. 15s.

HEBREW LITERATURE SOCIETY.—Subscription, one guinea per annum. List of publications on application.

HECHLER.—THE JERUSALEM BISHOPRIC DOCUMENTS. With Translations, chiefly derived from "Das Evangelische Bisthum in Jerusalem," Geschichtliche Darlegung mit Urtunden. Berlin, 1842. Published by Command of His Majesty Frederick William IV., King of Prussia. Arranged and Supplemented by the Rev. Prof. William H. Hechler, British Chaplain at Stockholm. 8vo, pp. 212, with Maps, Portrait, and Illustrations, cloth. 1883. 10s. 6d.

HECKER.—THE EPIDEMICS OF THE MIDDLE AGES. Translated by G. B. Babington, M.D., F.R.S. Third Edition, completed by the Author's Treatise on Child-Pilgrimages. By J. F. C. Hecker. 8vo, pp. 384, cloth. 1859. 9s. 6d.

CONTENTS.—The Black Death—The Dancing Mania—The Sweating Sickness—Child Pilgrimages.

HEDLEY.—MASTERPIECES OF GERMAN POETRY. Translated in the Measure of the Originals, by F. H. Hedley. With Illustrations by Louis Wanke. Crown 8vo, pp. viii. and 120, cloth. 1876. 6s.

HEINE.—RELIGION AND PHILOSOPHY IN GERMANY. See English and Foreign Philosophical Library, Vol. XVIII.

HEINE.—WIT, WISDOM, AND PATHOS from the Prose of Heinrich Heine. With a few pieces from the "Book of Songs." Selected and Translated by J. Snodgrass. With Portrait. Crown 8vo, pp. xx. and 340, cloth. 1879. 7s. 6d.

HEINE.—PICTURES OF TRAVEL. Translated from the German of Henry Heine, by Charles G. Leland. 7th Revised Edition. Crown 8vo, pp. 472, with Portrait, cloth. 1873. 7s. 6d.

HEINE.—HEINE'S BOOK OF SONGS. Translated by Charles G. Leland. Fcap. 8vo, pp. xiv. and 240, cloth, gilt edges. 1874. 7s. 6d.

HEITZMANN.—MICROSCOPICAL MORPHOLOGY OF THE ANIMAL BODY IN HEALTH AND DISEASE. By C. Heitzmann, M.D. Royal 8vo, pp. xx.-850, cloth. 1884. 31s. 6d.

HENDRIK.—MEMOIRS OF HANS HENDRIK, THE ARCTIC TRAVELLER ; serving under Kane, Hayes, Hall, and Nares, 1853-76. Written by Himself. Translated from the Eskimo Language, by Dr. Henry Rink. Edited by Prof. Dr. G. Stephens, F.S.A. Crown 8vo, pp. 100, Map, cloth. 1878. 3s. 6d.

HENNELL.—Present Religion: As a Faith owning Fellowship with Thought. Vol. I. Part I. By Sara S. Hennell. Crown 8vo, pp. 570, cloth. 1865. 7s. 6d.

HENNELL.—Comparative Ethics—I. Sections II. and III. Moral Principle in Regard to Sexhood. Present Religion, Vol. III. By S. Hennell. Crown 8vo, pp. 92, wrapper. 1884. 2s.

HENNELL.—Present Religion: As a Faith owning Fellowship with Thought. Part II. First Division. Intellectual Effect: shown as a Principle of Metaphysical Comparativism. By Sara S. Hennell. Crown 8vo, pp. 618, cloth. 1873. 7s. 6d.

HENNELL.—Present Religion, Vol. III. Part II. Second Division. The Effect of Present Religion on its Practical Side. By S. S. Hennell. Crown 8vo, pp. 68, paper covers. 1882. 2s.

HENNELL.—Comparativism shown as Furnishing a Religious Basis to Morality. (Present Religion. Vol. III. Part II. Second Division: Practical Effect.) By Sara S. Hennell. Crown 8vo, pp. 220, stitched in wrapper. 1878. 3s. 6d.

HENNELL.—Thoughts in Aid of Faith. Gathered chiefly from recent Works in Theology and Philosophy. By Sara S. Hennell. Post 8vo, pp. 428, cloth. 1860. 6s.

HENWOOD.—The Metalliferous Deposits of Cornwall and Devon; with Appendices on Subterranean Temperature; the Electricity of Rocks and Veins; the Quantities of Water in the Cornish Mines; and Mining Statistics. (Vol. V. of the Transactions of the Royal Geographical Society of Cornwall.) By William Jory Henwood, F.R.S., F.G.S. 8vo, pp. x. and 515; with 113 Tables, and 12 Plates, half bound. £2, 2s.

HENWOOD.—Observations on Metalliferous Deposits, and on Subterranean Temperature. (Vol. VIII. of the Transactions of the Royal Geological Society of Cornwall.) By William Jory Henwood, F.R.S., F.G.S., President of the Royal Institution of Cornwall. In 2 Parts. 8vo, pp. xxx., vii. and 916; with 38 Tables, 31 Engravings on Wood, and 6 Plates. £1, 16s.

HEPBURN.—A Japanese and English Dictionary. With an English and Japanese Index. By J. C. Hepburn, M.D., LL.D. Second Edition. Imperial 8vo, pp. xxxii., 632, and 201, cloth. £8, 8s.

HEPBURN.—Japanese-English and English-Japanese Dictionary. By J. C. Hepburn, M.D., LL.D. Abridged by the Author. Square fcap., pp. vi. and 536, cloth. 1873. 18s.

HERNISZ.—A Guide to Conversation in the English and Chinese Languages, for the Use of Americans and Chinese in California and elsewhere. By Stanislas Hernisz. Square 8vo, pp. 274, sewed. 1855. 10s. 6d.

HERSHON.—Talmudic Miscellany. See Trübner's Oriental Series.

HERZEN.—Du Developpement des Idées Revolutionnaires en Russie. Par Alexander Herzen. 12mo, pp. xxiii. and 144, sewed. 1853. 2s. 6d.

HERZEN.—A separate list of A. Herzen's works in Russian may be had on application.

HILL.—The History of the Reform Movement in the Dental Profession in Great Britain during the last twenty years. By Alfred Hill, Licentiate in Dental Surgery, &c. Crown 8vo, pp. xvi. and 400, cloth. 1877. 10s. 6d.

HILLEBRAND.—France and the French in the Second Half of the Nineteenth Century. By Karl Hillebrand. Translated from the Third German Edition. Post 8vo, pp. xx. and 262, cloth. 1881. 10s. 6d.

HINDOO Mythology Popularly Treated. Being an Epitomised Description of the various Heathen Deities illustrated on the Silver Swami Tea Service presented, as a memento of his visit to India, to H.R.H. the Prince of Wales, K.G., G.C.S.I., by His Highness the Gaekwar of Baroda. Small 4to, pp. 42, limp cloth. 1875. 3s. 6d.

HITTELL.—The Commerce and Industries of the Pacific Coast of North America. By J. S. Hittell, Author of "The Resources of California." 4to, pp. 820. 1882. £1, 10s.

HODGSON.—Academy Lectures. By J. E. Hodgson, R.A., Librarian and Professor of Painting to the Royal Academy. Cr. 8vo, pp. viiii. and 312, cloth. 1884. 7s. 6d.

HODGSON.—Essays on the Languages, Literature, and Religion of Népal and Tibet. Together with further Papers on the Geography, Ethnology, and Commerce of those Countries. By B. H. Hodgson, late British Minister at the Court of Nepál. Royal 8vo, cloth, pp. xii. and 276. 1874. 14s.

HODGSON.— Essays on Indian Subjects. See Trübner's Oriental Series.

HODGSON.—The Education of Girls; and the Employment of Women of the Upper Classes Educationally considered. Two Lectures. By W. B. Hodgson, LL.D. Second Edition. Cr. 8vo, pp. xvi. and 114, cloth. 1869. 3s. 6d.

HODGSON.—Turgot: His Life, Times, and Opinions. Two Lectures. By W. B. Hodgson, LL.D. Crown 8vo, pp. vi. and 83, sewed. 1870. 2s.

HOERNLE.—A Comparative Grammar of the Gaudian Languages, with Special Reference to the Eastern Hindi. Accompanied by a Language Map, and a Table of Alphabets. By A. F. Rudolf Hoernle. Demy 8vo, pp. 474, cloth. 1880. 18s.

HOLBEIN SOCIETY.—Subscription, one guinea per annum. List of publications on application.

HOLMES-FORBES.—The Science of Beauty. An Analytical Inquiry into the Laws of Æsthetics. By Avary W. Holmes-Forbes, of Lincoln's Inn, Barrister-at-Law. Post 8vo, cloth, pp. vi. and 200. 1881. 6s.

HOLST.—The Constitutional and Political History of the United States. By Dr. H. von Holst. Translated by J. J. Lalor and A. B. Mason. Royal 8vo. Vol. I. 1750-1833. State Sovereignty and Slavery. Pp. xvi. and 506. 1876. 18s. —Vol. II. 1828-1846. Jackson's Administration—Annexation of Texas. Pp. 720. 1879. £1, 2s.—Vol. III. 1846-1850. Annexation of Texas—Compromise of 1850. Pp. x. and 598. 1881. 18s.

HOLYOAKE.—Travels in Search of a Settler's Guide-Book of America and Canada. By George Jacob Holyoake, Author of "The History of Co-operation in England." Post 8vo, pp. 148, wrapper. 1884. 2s. 6d.

HOLYOAKE.—The History of Co-operation in England: its Literature and its Advocates. By G. J. Holyoake. Vol. I. The Pioneer Period, 1812-44. Crown 8vo, pp. xii. and 420, cloth. 1875. 4s.—Vol. II. The Constructive Period, 1845-78. Crown 8vo, pp. x. and 504, cloth. 1878. 8s.

HOLYOAKE.—The Trial of Theism accused of Obstructing Secular Life. By G. J. Holyoake. Crown 8vo, pp. xvi. and 256, cloth. 1877. 2s. 6d.

HOLYOAKE.—Reasoning from Facts: A Method of Everyday Logic. By G. J. Holyoake. Fcap., pp. xii. and 94, wrapper. 1877. 1s. 6d.

HOLYOAKE.—Self-Help by the People. Thirty-three Years of Co-operation in Rochdale. In Two Parts. Part I., 1844-1857; Part II., 1857-1877. By G. J. Holyoake. Ninth Edition. Crown 8vo, pp. 174, cloth. 1883. 2s. 6d.

HOPKINS.—Elementary Grammar of the Turkish Language. With a few Easy Exercises. By F. L. Hopkins, M.A., Fellow and Tutor of Trinity Hall, Cambridge. Crown 8vo, pp. 48, cloth. 1877. 3s. 6d.

HORDER.—A Selection from "The Book of Praise for Children," as Edited by W. Garrett Horder. For the Use of Jewish Children. Fcap. 8vo, pp. 80, cloth. 1883. 1s. 6d.

HOSMER.—The People and Politics; or, The Structure of States and the Significance and Relation of Political Forms. By G. W. Hosmer, M.D. Demy 8vo, pp. viii. and 340, cloth. 1883. 15s.

HOWELLS.—A Little Girl among the Old Masters. With Introduction and Comment. By W. D. Howells. Oblong crown 8vo, cloth, pp. 66, with 54 plates. 1884. 10s.

C

HOWELLS.—Dr. Breen's Practice : A Novel. By W. D. Howells. English Copyright Edition. Crown 8vo, pp. 272, cloth. 1882. 6s.

HOWSE.—A Grammar of the Cree Language. With which is combined an Analysis of the Chippeway Dialect. By Joseph Howse, F.R.G.S. 8vo, pp. xx. and 324, cloth. 1865. 7s. 6d.

HULME.—Mathematical Drawing Instruments, and How to Use Them. By F. Edward Hulme, F.L.S., F.S.A., Art-Master of Marlborough College, Author of "Principles of Ornamental Art," &c. With Illustrations. Second Edition. Imperial 16mo, pp. xvi. and 152, cloth. 1881. 3s. 6d.

HUMBERT.—On "Tenant Right." By C. F. Humbert. 8vo, pp. 20, sewed. 1875. 1s.

HUMBOLDT.—The Sphere and Duties of Government. Translated from the German of Baron Wilhelm Von Humboldt by Joseph Coulthard, jun. Post 8vo, pp. xv. and 203, cloth. 1854. 5s.

HUMBOLDT.—Letters of William Von Humboldt to a Female Friend. A complete Edition. Translated from the Second German Edition by Catherine M. A. Couper, with a Biographical Notice of the Writer. 2 vols. crown 8vo, pp. xxviii. and 592, cloth. 1867. 10s.

HUNT.—The Religion of the Heart. A Manual of Faith and Duty. By Leigh Hunt. Fcap. 8vo, pp. xxiv. and 259, cloth. 2s. 6d.

HUNT.—Chemical and Geological Essays. By Professor T. Sterry Hunt. Second Edition. 8vo, pp. xxii. and 448, cloth. 1879. 12s.

HUNTER.—A Comparative Dictionary of the Non-Aryan Languages of India and High Asia. With a Dissertation, Political and Linguistic, on the Aboriginal Races. By W. W. Hunter, B.A., M.R.A.S., Hon. Fel. Ethnol. Soc., Author of the "Annals of Rural Bengal," of H.M.'s Civil Service. Being a Lexicon of 144 Languages, illustrating Turanian Speech. Compiled from the Hodgson Lists, Government Archives, and Original MSS., arranged with Prefaces and Indices in English, French, German, Russian, and Latin. Large 4to, toned paper, pp. 230, cloth. 1869. 42s.

HUNTER.—The Indian Musalmans. By W. W. Hunter, B.A., LL.D., Director-General of Statistics to the Government of India, &c., Author of the "Annals of Rural Bengal," &c. Third Edition. 8vo, pp. 219, cloth. 1876. 10s. 6d.

HUNTER.—Famine Aspects of Bengal Districts. A System of Famine Warnings. By W. W. Hunter, B.A., LL.D. Crown 8vo, pp. 216, cloth. 1874. 7s. 6d.

HUNTER.—A Statistical Account of Bengal. By W. W. Hunter, B.A., LL.D., Director-General of Statistics to the Government of India, &c. In 20 vols. 8vo, half morocco. 1877. £5.

HUNTER.—Catalogue of Sanskrit Manuscripts (Buddhist). Collected in Nepal by B. H. Hodgson, late Resident at the Court of Nepal. Compiled from Lists in Calcutta, France, and England, by W. W. Hunter, C.I.E., LL.D. 8vo, pp. 28, paper. 1880. 2s.

HUNTER.—The Imperial Gazetteer of India. By W. W. Hunter, C.I.E., LL.D., Director-General of Statistics to the Government of India In Nine Volumes. 8vo, pp. xxxiii. and 544, 539, 567, xix. and 716, 509, 513, 555, 537, and xii. and 478, half morocco. With Maps. 1881.

HUNTER.—The Indian Empire : Its History, People, and Products. By W. W. Hunter, C.I.E., LL.D. Post 8vo, pp. 568, with Map, cloth. 1882. 16s.

HUNTER.—An Account of the British Settlement of Aden, in Arabia. Compiled by Capt. F. M. Hunter, Assistant Political Resident, Aden. 8vo, pp. xii. and 232, half bound. 1877. 7s. 6d.

HUNTER.—A Statistical Account of Assam. By W. W. Hunter, B.A., LL.D., C.I.E., Director-General of Statistics to the Government of India, &c. 2 vols. 8vo, pp. 420 and 490, with 2 Maps, half morocco. 1879. 10s.

HUNTER.—A Brief History of the Indian People. By W. W. Hunter, C.I.E. LL.D. Fourth Edition. Crown 8vo, pp. 222, cloth. With Map. 1884. 3s. 6d.

HURST.—History of Rationalism: embracing a Survey of the Present State of Protestant Theology. By the Rev. John F. Hurst, A.M. With Appendix of Literature. Revised and enlarged from the Third American Edition. Crown 8vo, pp. xvii. and 525, cloth. 1867. 10s. 6d.

HYETT.—Prompt Remedies for Accidents and Poisons : Adapted to the use of the Inexperienced till Medical aid arrives. By W. H. Hyett, F.R.S. A Broadsheet, to hang up in Country Schools or Vestries, Workshops, Offices of Factories, Mines and Docks, on board Yachts, in Railway Stations, remote Shooting Quarters, Highland Manses, and Private Houses, wherever the Doctor lives at a distance. Sold for the benefit of the Gloucester Eye Institution. In sheets, 21½ by 17½ inches, 2s. 6d. ; mounted, 3s. 6d.

HYMANS.—Pupil *Versus* Teacher. Letters from a Teacher to a Teacher. Fcap. 8vo, pp. 92, cloth. 1875. 2s.

IHNE.—A Latin Grammar for Beginners. By W. H. Ihne, late Principal of Carlton Terrace School, Liverpool. Crown 8vo, pp. vi. and 184, cloth. 1864. 3s.

IKHWÁNU-S SAFÁ; or, Brothers of Purity. Translated from the Hindustani by Professor John Dowson, M.R.A.S., Staff College, Sandhurst. Crown 8vo, pp. viii. and 156, cloth. 1869. 7s.

INDIA.—Archæological Survey of Western India. See Burgess.

INDIA.—Publications of the Archæological Survey of India. A separate list on application.

INDIA.—Publications of the Geographical Department of the India Office, London. A separate list, also list of all the Government Maps, on application.

INDIA.—Publications of the Geological Survey of India. A separate list on application.

INDIA OFFICE PUBLICATIONS :—

Aden, Statistical Account of. 5s.
Assam, do. do. Vols. I. and II. 5s. each.
Baden Powell, Land Revenues, &c., in India. 12s.
    Do. Jurisprudence for Forest Officers. 12s.
Beal's Buddhist Tripitaka. 4s.
Bengal, Statistical Account of. Vols. I. to XX. 100s. per set.
    Do. do. do. Vols. VI. to XX. 5s. each.
Bombay Code. 21s.
Bombay Gazetteer. Vol. II., 14s. Vol. VIII., 9s. Vol. XIII. (2 parts), 16s.
    Do. do. Vols. III. to VII., and X., XI., XII., XIV., XVI. 8s. each.
    Do. do. Vols. XXI., XXII., and XXIII. 9s. each.
Burgess' Archæological Survey of Western India. Vols. I. and III. 42s. each.
    Do. do. do. Vol. II. 63s.
    Do. do. do. Vols. IV. and V. 126s.
Burma (British) Gazetteer. 2 vols. 50s.
Catalogue of Manuscripts and Maps of Surveys. 12s.
Chambers' Meteorology (Bombay) and Atlas. 30s.
Cole's Agra and Muttra. 70s.
Cook's Gums and Resins. 5s.
Corpus Inscriptionem Indicarum. Vol. I. 32s.
Cunningham's Archæological Survey. Vols. I. to XVIII. 10s. and 12s. each.
    Do. Stupa of Bharut. 63s.
Egerton's Catalogue of Indian Arms. 2s. 6d.
Ferguson and Burgess, Cave Temples of India. 42s.
    Do. Tree and Serpent Worship. 105s.
Finance and Revenue Accounts of the Government of India for 1882-3. 2s. 6d.
Gamble, Manual of Indian Timbers. 10s.
Hunter's Imperial Gazetteer. 9 vols.
Indian Education Commission, Report of the. 12s.

INDIA OFFICE PUBLICATIONS—*continued.*
Jaschke's Tibetan-English Dictionary. 30s.
King. Chinchona-Planting. 1s.
Kurz. Forest Flora of British Burma. Vols. I. and II. 15s. each.
Liotard's Materials for Paper. 2s. 6d.
Liotard's Silk in India. Part I. 2s.
Markham's Tibet. 21s.
    Do.   Memoir of Indian Surveys. 10s. 6d.
    Do.   Abstract of Reports of Surveys. 1s. 6d.
Mitra (Rajendralala), Buddha Gaya. 60s.
Moir, Torrent Regions of the Alps. 1s.
Mueller. Select Plants for Extra-Tropical Countries. 8s.
Mysore and Coorg Gazetteer. Vols. I. and II. 10s. each.
    Do.   do.   Vol. III. 5s.
N. W. P. Gazetteer. Vols. I. and II. 10s. each.
    Do.   do.   Vols. III. to VI. and IX., X.,XI., XIII., and XIV. 12s. each.
    Do.   do.   Vol. VII. 8s.
Oudh   do.   Vols. I. to III. 10s. each.
Pharmacopœia of India, The. 6s.
People of India, The. Vols. I. to VIII. 45s. each.
Raverty's Notes on Afghanistan and Baluchistan. Sections I. and II. 2s. Section III. 5s. Section IV. 3s.
Rajputana Gazetteer. 3 vols. 15s.
Saunders' Mountains and River Basins of India. 3s.
Sewell's Amaravati Tope. 3s.
Smith's (Brough) Gold Mining in Wynaad. 1s.
Taylor. Indian Marine Surveys. 2s. 6d.
Trigonometrical Survey, Synopsis of Great. Vols. I. to VI. 10s. 6d. each.
Trumpp's Adi Granth. 52s. 6d.
Watson's Cotton Gins. Boards, 10s. 6d. Paper, 10s.
    Do.   Rhea Fibre. 2s. 6d.
    Do.   Tobacco. 5s.
Wilson. Madras Army. Vols. I. and II. 21s.

INDIAN GAZETTEERS.—See GAZETTEER, and INDIA OFFICE PUBLICATIONS.

INGLEBY.—See SHAKESPEARE.

INMAN.—NAUTICAL TABLES. Designed for the use of British Seamen. By the Rev. James Inman, D.D., late Professor at the Royal Naval College, Portsmouth. Demy 8vo, pp. xvi. and 410, cloth. 1877. 15s.

INMAN.—HISTORY OF THE ENGLISH ALPHABET : A Paper read before the Liverpool Literary and Philosophical Society. By T. Inman, M.D. 8vo, pp. 36, sewed. 1872. 1s.

IN SEARCH OF TRUTH. Conversations on the Bible and Popular Theology, for Young People. By A. M. Y. Crown 8vo, pp. x. and 138, cloth. 1875. 2s. 6d.

INTERNATIONAL NUMISMATA ORIENTALIA (THE).—Royal 4to, in paper wrapper. Part I. Ancient Indian Weights. By E. Thomas, F.R.S. Pp. 84, with a Plate and Map of the India of Manu. 9s. 6d.—Part II. Coins of the Urtukí Turkumáns. By Stanley Lane Poole, Corpus Christi College, Oxford. Pp. 44, with 6 Plates. 9s.—Part III. The Coinage of Lydia and Persia, from the Earliest Times to the Fall of the Dynasty of the Achæmenidæ. By Barclay V. Head, Assistant-Keeper of Coins, British Museum. Pp. viii.-56, with 3 Autotype Plates. 10s. 6d.— Part IV. The Coins of the Tuluní Dynasty. By Edward Thomas Rogers. Pp. iv.-22, and 1 Plate. 5s.—Part V. The Parthian Coinage. By Percy Gardner, M.A. Pp. iv.-66, and 8 Autotype Plates. 18s.—Part VI. The Ancient Coins and Measures of Ceylon. By T. W. Rhys Davids. Pp. iv. and 60, and 1 Plate. 10s.—Vol. I., containing the first six parts, as specified above. Royal 4to, half bound. £3, 13s. 6d.

INTERNATIONAL NUMISMATA—*continued.*

Vol. II. COINS OF THE JEWS. Being a History of the Jewish Coinage and Money in the Old and New Testaments. By Frederick W. Madden, M.R.A.S., Member of the Numismatic Society of London, Secretary of the Brighton College, &c., &c. With 279 woodcuts and a plate of alphabets. Royal 4to, pp. xii. and 330, sewed. 1881. £2.

Vol. III. Part I. THE COINS OF ARAKAN, OF PEGU, AND OF BURMA. By Lieut.-General Sir Arthur Phayre, C.B., K.C.S.I., G.C.M.G., late Commissioner of British Burma. Also contains the Indian Balhara, and the Arabian Intercourse with India in the Ninth and following Centuries. By Edward Thomas, F.R.S. Royal 4to, pp. viii. and 48, with Five Autotype Illustrations, wrapper. 1882. 8s. 6d.

Part II. THE COINS OF SOUTHERN INDIA. By Sir W. Elliot. Royal 4to.

JACKSON.—ETHNOLOGY AND PHRENOLOGY AS AN AID TO THE HISTORIAN. By the late J. W. Jackson. Second Edition. With a Memoir of the Author, by his Wife. Crown 8vo, pp. xx. and 324, cloth. 1875. 4s. 6d.

JACKSON.—THE SHROPSHIRE WORD-BOOK. A Glossary of Archaic and Provincial Words, &c., used in the County. By Georgina F. Jackson. Crown 8vo, pp. civ. and 524, cloth. 1881. 31s. 6d.

JACOB.—HINDU PANTHEISM. See Trübner's Oriental Series.

JAGIELSKI.—ON MARIENBAD SPA, and the Diseases Curable by its Waters and Baths. By A. V. Jagielski, M.D., Berlin. Second Edition. Crown 8vo, pp. viii. and 186. With Map. Cloth. 1874. 5s.

JAMISON.—THE LIFE AND TIMES OF BERTRAND DU GUESCLIN. A History of the Fourteenth Century. By D. F. Jamison, of South Carolina. Portrait. 2 vols. 8vo, pp. xvi., 287, and viii., 314, cloth. 1864. £1, 1s.

JAPAN.—MAP OF NIPPON (Japan): Compiled from Native Maps, and the Notes of most recent Travellers. By R. Henry Brunton, M.I.C.E., F.R.G.S., 1880. Size, 5 feet by 4 feet. 20 miles to the inch. In 4 Sheets, £1, 1s.; Roller, varnished. £1, 11s. 6d.; Folded, in Case, £1, 5s. 6d.

JASCHKE.—A TIBETAN-ENGLISH DICTIONARY. With special reference to the Prevailing Dialects. To which is added an English-Tibetan Vocabulary. By H. A. Jäschke, late Moravian Missionary at Kyèlang, British Lahoul. Imperial 8vo, pp. xxiv.-672, cloth. 1881. £1, 10s.

JASCHKE.—TIBETAN GRAMMAR. By H. A. Jäschke. Crown 8vo, pp. viii.-104, cloth. 1883. 5s.

JATAKA (THE), together with its COMMENTARY : being tales of the Anterior Birth of Gotama Buddha. Now first published in Pali, by V. Fausboll. Text. 8vo. Vol. I., pp. viii. and 512, cloth. 1877. 28s.—Vol. II., pp. 452, cloth. 1879, 28s.—Vol. III., pp. viii. and 544, cloth. 1883. 28s. (For Translation see Trübner's Oriental Series, "Buddhist Birth Stories.")

JENKINS.—A PALADIN OF FINANCE : Contemporary Manners. By E. Jenkins, Author of "Ginx's Baby." Crown 8vo, pp. iv. and 392, cloth. 1882. 7s. 6d.

• **JENKINS.**—VEST-POCKET LEXICON. An English Dictionary of all except familiar Words, including the principal Scientific and Technical Terms, and Foreign Moneys, Weights and Measures; omitting what everybody knows, and containing what everybody wants to know and cannot readily find. By Jabez Jenkins. 64mo, pp. 564, cloth. 1879. 1s. 6d.

JOHNSON.—ORIENTAL RELIGIONS. India. See English and Foreign Philosophical Library, Extra Series, Vols. IV. and V.

JOHNSON.—ORIENTAL RELIGIONS AND THEIR RELATION TO UNIVERSAL RELIGION Persia. By Samuel Johnson. With an Introduction by O. B. Frothingham. Demy 8vo, pp. xliv. and 784, cloth. 1885. 18s.

JOLLY.—See NARADÍYA.

JOMINI.—The Art of War. By Baron de Jomini, General and Aide-de-Camp to the Emperor of Russia. A New Edition, with Appendices and Maps. Translated from the French. By Captain G. H. Mendell, and Captain W. O. Craighill. Crown 8vo, pp. 410, cloth. 1879. 9s.

JOSEPH.—Religion, Natural and Revealed. A Series of Progressive Lessons for Jewish Youth. By N. S. Joseph. Crown 8vo, pp. xii.-296, cloth. 1879. 3s.

JUVENALIS SATIRÆ. With a Literal English Prose Translation and Notes. By J. D. Lewis, M.A., Trin. Coll. Camb. Second Edition. Two vols. 8vo, pp. xii. and 230 and 400, cloth. 1882. 12s.

KARCHER.—Questionnaire Français. Questions on French Grammar, Idiomatic Difficulties, and Military Expressions. By Theodore Karcher, LL.B. Fourth Edition, greatly enlarged. Crown 8vo, pp. 224, cloth. 1879. 4s. 6d. Interleaved with writing paper, 5s. 6d.

KARDEC.—The Spirit's Book. Containing the Principles of Spiritist Doctrine on the Immortality of the Soul, &c., &c., according to the Teachings of Spirits of High Degree, transmitted through various mediums, collected and set in order by Allen Kardec. Translated from the 120th thousand by Anna Blackwell. Crown 8vo, pp. 512, cloth. 1875. 7s. 6d.

KARDEC.—The Medium's Book; or, Guide for Mediums and for Evocations. Containing the Theoretic Teachings of Spirits concerning all kinds of Manifestations, the Means of Communication with the Invisible World, the Development of Medianimity, &c., &c. By Allen Kardec. Translated by Anna Blackwell. Crown 8vo, pp. 456, cloth. 1876. 7s. 6d.

KARDEC.—Heaven and Hell; or, the Divine Justice Vindicated in the Plurality of Existences. By Allen Kardec. Translated by Anna Blackwell. Crown 8vo, pp. viii. and 448, cloth. 1878. 7s. 6d.

KEMP. See Schopenhauer.

KENDRICK.—Greek Ollendorff. A Progressive Exhibition of the Principles of the Greek Grammar. By Asahel C. Kendrick. 8vo, pp. 371, cloth. 1870. 9s.

KERMODE.—Natal: Its Early History, Rise, Progress, and Future Prospects as a Field for Emigration. By W. Kermode, of Natal. Crown 8vo, pp. xii. and 228, with Map, cloth. 1883. 3s. 6d.

KEYS OF THE CREEDS (The). Third Revised Edition. Crown 8vo, pp. 210, cloth. 1876. 5s.

KINAHAN.—Valleys and their Relation to Fissures, Fractures, and Faults. By G. H. Kinahan, M.R.I.A., F.R.G.S.I., &c. Dedicated by permission to his Grace the Duke of Argyll. Crown 8vo, pp. 256, cloth, illustrated. 7s. 6d.

KING'S STRATAGEM (The); Or, The Pearl of Poland; A Tragedy in Five Acts. By Stella. Second Edition. Crown 8vo, pp. 94, cloth. 1874. 2s. 6d.

KINGSTON.—The Unity of Creation. A Contribution to the Solution of the Religious Question. By F. H. Kingston. Crown 8vo, pp. viii. and 152, cloth. 1874. 5s.

KISTNER.—Buddha and his Doctrines. A Bibliographical Essay. By Otto Kistner. 4to, pp. iv. and 32, sewed. 1869. 2s. 6d.

KNOX.—On a Mexican Mustang. See under Sweet.

KLEMM.—Muscle Beating; or, Active and Passive Home Gymnastics, for Healthy and Unhealthy People. By C. Klemm. With Illustrations. 8vo, pp. 60, wrapper. 1878. 1s.

KOHL.—Travels in Canada and through the States of New York and Pennsylvania. By J. G. Kohl. Translated by Mrs. Percy Sinnett. Revised by the Author. Two vols. post 8vo, pp. xiv. and 794, cloth. 1861. £1, 1s.

KRAPF.—DICTIONARY OF THE SUAHILI LANGUAGE. Compiled by the Rev. Dr. L. Krapf, missionary of the Church Missionary Society in East Africa. With an Appendix, containing an outline of a Suahili Grammar. Medium 8vo, pp. xl. and 434, cloth. 1882. 30s.

KRAUS.—CARLSBAD AND ITS NATURAL HEALING AGENTS. from the Physiological and Therapeutical Point of View. By J. Kraus, M. D. With Notes Introductory by the Rev. J. T. Walters, M.A. Second Edition. Revised and enlarged. Crown 8vo, pp. 104, cloth. 1880. 5s.

KROEGER.—THE MINNESINGER OF GERMANY. By A. E. Kroeger. Fcap. 8vo, pp. 290, cloth. 1873. 7s.

KURZ.—FOREST FLORA OF BRITISH BURMA. By S. Kurz, Curator of the Herbarium. Royal Botanical Gardens, Calcutta. 2 vols. crown 8vo, pp. xxx., 550, and 614, cloth. 1877. 30s.

LACERDA'S JOURNEY TO CAZEMBE in 1798. Translated and Annotated by Captain R. F. Burton, F.R.G.S. Also Journey of the Pombeiros, &c. Demy 8vo, pp. viii. and 272. With Map, cloth. 1873. 7s. 6d.

LANARI.—COLLECTION OF ITALIAN AND ENGLISH DIALOGUES. By A. Lanari. Fcap. 8vo, pp. viii. and 200, cloth. 1874. 3s. 6d.

LAND.—THE PRINCIPLES OF HEBREW GRAMMAR. By J. P. N. Land, Professor of Logic and Metaphysics in the University of Leyden. Translated from the Dutch, by Reginald Lane Poole, Balliol College, Oxford. Part I. Sounds. Part II. Words. With Large Additions by the Author, and a new Preface. Crown 8vo, pp. xx. and 220, cloth. 1876. 7s. 6d.

LANE.—THE KORAN. See Trübner's Oriental Series.

LANGE.—A HISTORY OF MATERIALISM. See English and Foreign Philosophical Library, Vols. I. to III.

LANGE.—GERMANIA. A German Reading-book Arranged Progressively. By F. K. W. Lange, Ph.D. Part I. Anthology of German Prose and Poetry, with Vocabulary and Biographical Notes. 8vo, pp. xvi. and 216, cloth, 1881, 3s. 6d. Part II. Essays on German History and Institutions, with Notes. 8vo, pp. 124, cloth. Parts I. and II. together. 5s. 6d.

LANGE.—GERMAN PROSE WRITING. Comprising English Passages for Translation into German. Selected from Examination Papers of the University of London, the College of Preceptors, London, and the Royal Military Academy, Woolwich, arranged progressively, with Notes and Theoretical as well as Practical Treatises on themes for the writing of Essays. By F. K. W. Lange, Ph.D., Assistant German Master, Royal Academy. Woolwich : Examiner, Royal College of Preceptors London. Crown 8vo, pp. viii. and 176, cloth. 1881. 4s.

LANGE.—GERMAN GRAMMAR PRACTICE. By F. K. W. Lange, Ph.D. Crown 8vo, pp. viii. and 64, cloth. 1882. 1s. 6d.

LANGE.—COLLOQUIAL GERMAN GRAMMAR. With Special Reference to the Anglo-Saxon Element in the English Language. By F. K. W. Lange, Ph.D., &c. Crown 8vo, pp. xxxii. and 380, cloth. 1882. 4s. 6d.

LANMAN.—A SANSKRIT READER. With Vocabulary and Notes. By Charles Rockwell Lanman, Professor of Sanskrit in Harvard College. Imperial 8vo, pp. xx. and 294, cloth. 1884. 10s. 6d.

LARSEN.—DANISH-ENGLISH DICTIONARY. By A. Larsen. Crown 8vo, pp. viii. and 646, cloth. 1884. 7s. 6d.

LASCARIDES.—A Comprehensive Phraseological English-Ancient and Modern Greek Lexicon. Founded upon a manuscript of G. P. Lascarides, and Compiled by L. Myriantheus, Ph.D. 2 vols. 18mo, pp. xi. and 1338, cloth. 1882. £1, 10s.

LATHE (The) and its Uses; or, Instruction in the Art of Turning Wood and Metal, including a description of the most modern appliances for the Ornamentation of Plain and Curved Surfaces, &c. Sixth Edition. With additional Chapters and Index. Illustrated. 8vo, pp. iv. and 316, cloth. 1883. 10s. 6d.

LE-BRUN.—Materials for Translating from English into French; being a short Essay on Translation, followed by a Graduated Selection in Prose and Verse. By L. Le-Brun. Seventh Edition. Revised and corrected by Henri Van Laun. Post 8vo, pp. xii. and 204, cloth. 1882. 4s. 6d.

LEE.—Illustrations of the Physiology of Religion. In Sections adapted for the use of Schools. Part I. By Henry Lee, F.R.C.S., formerly Professor of Surgery, Royal College of Surgeons, &c. Crown 8vo, pp. viii. and 108, cloth. 1880. 3s. 6d.

LEES.—A Practical Guide to Health, and to the Home Treatment of the Common Ailments of Life : With a Section on Cases of Emergency, and Hints to Mothers on Nursing. &c. By F. Arnold Lees, F.L.S. Crown 8vo, pp. 334, stiff covers. 1874. 3s.

LEGGE.—The Chinese Classics. With a Translation, Critical and Exegetical, Notes, Prolegomena, and copious Indexes. By James Legge, D.D., of the London Missionary Society. In 7 vols. Royal 8vo. Vols. I.-V. in Eight Parts, published, cloth. £2, 2s. each Part.

LEGGE.—The Chinese Classics, translated into English. With Preliminary Essays and Explanatory Notes. Popular Edition. Reproduced for General Readers from the Author's work, containing the Original Text. By James Legge, D.D. Crown 8vo. Vol. I. The Life and Teachings of Confucius. Third Edition. Pp. vi. and 338, cloth. 1872. 10s. 6d.—Vol. II. The Works of Mencius. Pp. x. and 402, cloth, 12s.—Vol. III. The She-King; or, The Book of Poetry. Pp. vi. and 432, cloth. 1876. 12s.

LEGGE.—Confucianism in Relation to Christianity. A Paper read before the Missionary Conference in Shanghai, on May 11th, 1877. By Rev. James Legge, D.D., LL.D., &c. 8vo, pp. 12, sewed. 1877. 1s. 6d.

LEGGE.—A Letter to Professor Max Müller, chiefly on the Translation into English of the Chinese Terms *Tî* and *Shang Tî*. By James Legge, Professor of the Chinese Language and Literature in the University of Oxford. Crown 8vo, pp. 30, sewed. 1880. 1s.

LEIGH.—The Religion of the World. By H. Stone Leigh. 12mo, pp. xii. and 66, cloth. 1869. 2s. 6d.

LEIGH.—The Story of Philosophy. By Aston Leigh. Post 8vo, pp. xii. and 210, cloth. 1881. 6s.

LEÏLA-HANOUM.—A Tragedy in the Imperial Harem at Constantinople. By Leïla-Hanoum. Translated from the French, with Notes by General R. E. Colston. 16mo, pp. viii. and 300, cloth. 1883. 4s. Paper, 2s. 6d.

LELAND.—The Breitmann Ballads. The only authorised Edition. Complete in 1 vol., including Nineteen Ballads, illustrating his Travels in Europe (never before printed), with Comments by Fritz Schwackenhammer. By Charles G. Leland. Crown 8vo, pp. xxviii. and 292, cloth. 1872. 6s.

LELAND.—The Music Lesson of Confucius, and other Poems. By Charles G. Leland. Fcap. 8vo, pp. viii. and 168, cloth. 1871. 3s. 6d.

LELAND.—Gaudeamus. Humorous Poems translated from the German of Joseph Victor Scheffel and others. By Charles G. Leland. 16mo, pp. 176, cloth. 1872. 3s. 6d.

LELAND.—The Egyptian Sketch-Book. By C. G. Leland. Crown 8vo, pp. viii. and 316, cloth. 1873. 7s. 6d.

LELAND.—The English Gipsies and their Language. By Charles G. Leland. Second Edition. Crown 8vo, pp. xvi. and 260, cloth. 1874. 7s. 6d.

LELAND.—Fu-Sang; or, The Discovery of America by Chinese Buddhist Priests in the Fifth Century. By Charles G. Leland. Crown 8vo, pp. 232, cloth. 1875. 7s. 6d.

LELAND.—Pidgin-English Sing-Song; or, Songs and Stories in the China-English Dialect. With a Vocabulary. By Charles G. Leland. Crown 8vo, pp. viii. and 140, cloth. 1876. 5s.

LELAND.—The Gypsies. By C. G. Leland. Crown 8vo, pp. 372, cloth. 1882. 10s. 6d.

LEOPARDI.—See English and Foreign Philosophical Library, Vol. XVII.

LEO.—Four Chapters of North's Plutarch, Containing the Lives of Caius Marcius, Coriolanus, Julius Cæsar, Marcus Antonius, and Marcus Brutus, as Sources to Shakespeare's Tragedies; Coriolanus, Julius Cæsar, and Antony and Cleopatra; and partly to Hamlet and Timon of Athens. Photolithographed in the size of the Edition of 1595. With Preface, Notes comparing the Text of the Editions of 1579, 1595, 1603, and 1612; and Reference Notes to the Text of the Tragedies of Shakespeare. Edited by Professor F. A. Leo, Ph.D., Vice-President of the New Shakespeare Society; Member of the Directory of the German Shakespeare Society; and Lecturer at the Academy of Modern Philology at Berlin. Folio, pp. 22, 130 of facsimiles, half-morocco. Library Edition (limited to 250 copies), £1, 11s. 6d.; Amateur Edition (50 copies on a superior large hand-made paper), £3, 3s.

LERMONTOFF.—The Demon. By Michael Lermontoff. Translated from the Russian by A. Condie Stephen. Crown 8vo, pp. 88, cloth. 1881. 2s. 6d.

LESLEY.—Man's Origin and Destiny. Sketched from the Platform of the Physical Sciences. By. J. P. Lesley, Member of the National Academy of the United States, Professor of Geology, University of Pennsylvania. Second (Revised and considerably Enlarged) Edition, crown 8vo, pp. viii. and 142, cloth. 1881. 7s. 6d.

LESSING.—Letters on Bibliolatry. By Gotthold Ephraim Lessing. Translated from the German by the late H. H. Bernard, Ph.D. 8vo, pp. 184, cloth. 1862. 5s.

LESSING.—See English and Foreign Philosophical Library, Extra Series, Vols. I. and II.

LETTERS on the War between Germany and France. By Mommsen, Strauss, Max Müller, and Carlyle. Second Edition. Crown 8vo, pp. 120, cloth. 1871. 2s. 6d.

LEWES.—Problems of Life and Mind. By George Henry Lewes. First Series: The Foundations of a Creed. Vol. I., demy 8vo. Fourth edition, pp. 488, cloth. 1884. 12s.—Vol. II., demy 8vo, pp. 552, cloth. 1875. 16s.

LEWES.—Problems of Life and Mind. By George Henry Lewes. Second Series. The Physical Basis of Mind. 8vo, with Illustrations, pp. 508, cloth. 1877. 16s. Contents.—The Nature of Life; The Nervous Mechanism; Animal Automatism; The Reflex Theory.

LEWES.—Problems of Life and Mind. By George Henry Lewes. Third Series. Problem the First—The Study of Psychology: Its Object, Scope, and Method. Demy 8vo, pp. 200, cloth. 1879. 7s. 6d.

LEWES.—Problems of Life and Mind. By George Henry Lewes. Third Series. Problem the Second—Mind as a Function of the Organism. Problem the Third—The Sphere of Sense and Logic of Feeling. Problem the Fourth—The Sphere of Intellect and Logic of Signs. Demy 8vo, pp. x. and 500, cloth. 1879. 15s.

LEWIS.—See JUVENAL and PLINY.

LIBRARIANS, TRANSACTIONS AND PROCEEDINGS OF THE CONFERENCE OF, held in London, October 1877. Edited by Edward B. Nicholson and Henry R. Tedder. Imperial 8vo, pp. 276, cloth. 1878. £1, 8s.

LIBRARY ASSOCIATION OF THE UNITED KINGDOM, Transactions and Proceedings of the Annual Meetings of the. Imperial 8vo, cloth. FIRST, held at Oxford, October 1, 2, 3, 1878. Edited by the Secretaries, Henry R. Tedder, Librarian of the Athenæum Club, and Ernest C. Thomas, late Librarian of the Oxford Union Society. Pp. viii. and 192. 1879. £1, 8s.—SECOND, held at Manchester, September 23, 24, and 25, 1879. Edited by H. R. Tedder and E. C. Thomas. Pp. x. and 184. 1880. £1, 1s.—THIRD, held at Edinburgh, October 5, 6, and 7, 1880. Edited by E. C. Thomas and C. Welsh. Pp. x. and 202. 1881. £1, 1s.

LIEBER.—THE LIFE AND LETTERS OF FRANCIS LIEBER. Edited by T. S. Perry. 8vo, pp. iv. and 440, cloth, with Portrait. 1882. 14s.

LITTLE FRENCH READER (THE). Extracted from "The Modern French Reader." Third Edition. Crown 8vo, pp. 112, cloth. 1884. 2s.

LLOYD AND NEWTON.—PRUSSIA'S REPRESENTATIVE MAN. By F. Lloyd of the Universities of Halle and Athens, and W. Newton, F.R.G.S. Crown 8vo, pp. 648, cloth. 1875. 10s. 6d.

LOBSCHEID.—CHINESE AND ENGLISH DICTIONARY, arranged according to the Radicals. By W. Lobscheid. 1 vol. imperial 8vo, pp. 600, cloth. £2, 8s.

LOBSCHEID.—ENGLISH AND CHINESE DICTIONARY, with the Punti and Mandarin Pronunciation. By W. Lobscheid. Four Parts. Folio, pp. viii. and 2016, boards. £8, 8s.

LONG.—EASTERN PROVERBS. See Trübner's Oriental Series.

LOVETT.—THE LIFE AND STRUGGLES OF WILLIAM LOVETT in his pursuit of Bread, Knowledge, and Freedom ; with some short account of the different Associations he belonged to, and of the Opinions he entertained. 8vo, pp. vi. and 474, cloth. 1876. 5s.

LOVELY.—WHERE TO GO FOR HELP : Being a Companion for Quick and Easy Reference of Police Stations, Fire-Engine Stations, Fire-Escape Stations, &c., &c., of London and the Suburbs. Compiled by W. Lovely, R.N. Third Edition. 18mo, pp. 16, sewed. 1882. 3d.

LOWELL.—THE BIGLOW PAPERS. By James Russell Lowell. Edited by Thomas Hughes, Q.C. A Reprint of the Authorised Edition of 1859, together with the Second Series of 1862. First and Second Series in 1 vol. Fcap., pp. lxviii.-140 and lxiv.-190, cloth. 1880. 2s. 6d.

LUCAS.—THE CHILDREN'S PENTATEUCH : With the Haphtarahs or Portions from the Prophets. Arranged for Jewish Children. By Mrs. Henry Lucas. Crown 8vo, pp. viii. and 570, cloth. 1878. 5s.

LUDEWIG.—THE LITERATURE OF AMERICAN ABORIGINAL LANGUAGES. By Hermann E. Ludewig. With Additions and Corrections by Professor Wm. W. Turner. Edited by Nicolas Trübner. 8vo, pp. xxiv. and 258, cloth. 1858. 10s. 6d.

LUKIN.—THE BOY ENGINEERS : What they did, and how they did it. By the Rev. L. J. Lukin. Author of "The Young Mechanic," &c. A Book for Boys ; 30 Engravings. Imperial 16mo, pp. viii. and 344, cloth. 1877. 7s. 6d.

LUX E TENEBRIS; OR, THE TESTIMONY OF CONSCIOUSNESS. A Theoretic Essay. Crown 8vo, pp. 376, with Diagram, cloth. 1874. 10s. 6d.

MACCORMAC.—The Conversation of a Soul with God : A Theodicy. By Henry MacCormac, M.D. 16mo, pp. xvi. and 144, cloth. 1877. 3s. 6d.

MACHIAVELLI.—The Historical, Political, and Diplomatic Writings of Niccolo Machiavelli. Translated from the Italian by C. E. Detmold. With Portraits. 4 vols. 8vo, cloth, pp. xli., 420, 464, 488, and 472. 1882. £3, 3s.

MACKENZIE.—History of the Relations of the Government with the Hill Tribes of the North-East Frontier of Bengal. By Alexander Mackenzie, of the Bengal Civil Service ; Secretary to the Government of India in the Home Department, and formerly Secretary to the Government of Bengal. Royal 8vo, pp. xviii. and 586, cloth, with Map. 1884. 16s.

MADDEN.—Coins of the Jews. Being a History of the Jewish Coinage and Money in the Old and New Testaments. By Frederick W. Madden, M.R.A.S. Member of the Numismatic Society of London, Secretary of the Brighton College, &c., &c. With 279 Woodcuts and a Plate of Alphabets. Royal 4to, pp. xii. and 330, cloth. 1881. £2, 2s.

MADELUNG.—The Causes and Operative Treatment of Dupuytren's Finger Contraction. By Dr. Otto W. Madelung, Lecturer of Surgery at the University, and Assistant Surgeon at the University Hospital, Bonn. 8vo, pp. 24, sewed. 1876. 1s.

MAHAPARINIBBANASUTTA.—See Childers.

MAHA-VIRA-CHARITA ; or, The Adventures of the Great Hero Rama. An Indian Drama in Seven Acts. Translated into English Prose from the Sanskrit of Bhavabhūti. By John Pickford, M.A. Crown 8vo, cloth. 5s.

MAIMONIDES.—The Guide of the Perplexed of Maimonides. See English and Foreign Philosophical Library.

MALLESON.—Essays and Lectures on Indian Historical Subjects. By Colonel G. B. Malleson, C.S.I. Second Issue. Crown 8vo, pp. 348, cloth. 1876. 5s.

MANDLEY.—Woman Outside Christendom. An Exposition of the Influence exerted by Christianity on the Social Position and Happiness of Women. By J. G. Mandley. Crown 8vo, pp. viii. and 160, cloth. 1880. 5s.

MANIPULUS Vocabulorum. A Rhyming Dictionary of the English Language. By Peter Levins (1570). Edited, with an Alphabetical Index, by Henry B. Wheatley. 8vo, pp. xvi. and 370, cloth. 1867. 14s.

MANŒUVRES.—A Retrospect of the Autumn Manœuvres, 1871. With 5 Plans. By a Recluse. 8vo, pp. xii. and 133, cloth. 1872. 5s.

MARIETTE-BEY.—The Monuments of Upper Egypt: a translation of the "Itinéraire de la Haute Egypte" of Auguste Mariette-Bey. Translated by Alphonse Mariette. Crown 8vo, pp. xvi. and 262, cloth. 1877. 7s. 6d.

MARKHAM.—Quichua Grammar and Dictionary. Contributions towards a Grammar and Dictionary of Quichua, the Language of the Yncas of Peru. Collected by Clements R. Markham, F.S.A. Crown 8vo, pp. 223, cloth. £1, 11s. 6d.

MARKHAM.—Ollanta : A Drama in the Quichua Language. Text, Translation, and Introduction. By Clements R. Markham, C.B. Crown 8vo, pp. 128, cloth. 1871. 7s. 6d.

MARKHAM.—A Memoir of the Lady Ana de Osorio, Countess of Chincon, and Vice-Queen of Peru. A.D. 1629-39. With a Plea for the correct spelling of the Chinchona Genus. By Clements R. Markham, C.B., Member of the Imperial Academy Naturæ Curiosorum, with the Cognomen of Chinchon. Small 4to, pp. xii. and 100. With 2 Coloured Plates, Map, and Illustrations. Handsomely bound. 1874. 28s.

MARKHAM.—A MEMOIR ON THE INDIAN SURVEYS. By Clements R. Markham, C.B., F.R.S., &c., &c. Published by Order of H. M. Secretary of State for India in Council. Illustrated with Maps. Second Edition. Imperial 8vo, pp. xxx. and 481, boards. 1878. 10s. 6d.

MARKHAM.—NARRATIVES OF THE MISSION OF GEORGE BOGLE TO TIBET, and of the Journey of Thomas Manning to Lhasa. Edited with Notes, an Introduction, and Lives of Mr. Bogle and Mr. Manning. By Clements R. Markham, C.B., F.R.S. Second Edition. 8vo, pp. clxv. and 362, cloth. With Maps and Illustrations. 1879. 21s.

MARMONTEL.—BELISAIRE. Par Marmontel. Nouvelle Edition. 12mo, pp. xii. and 123, cloth. 1867. 2s. 6d.

MARSDEN.—NUMISMATA ORIENTALIA ILLUSTRATA. THE PLATES OF THE ORIENTAL COINS, ANCIENT AND MODERN, of the Collection of the late William Marsden, F.R.S., &c. &c. Engraved from Drawings made under his Directions. 4to, 57 Plates, cloth. 31s. 6d.

MARTIN AND TRÜBNER.—THE CURRENT GOLD AND SILVER COINS OF ALL COUNTRIES, their Weight and Fineness, and their Intrinsic Value in English Money, with Facsimiles of the Coins. By Leopold C. Martin, of Her Majesty's Stationery Office, and Charles Trübner. In 1 vol. medium 8vo, 141 Plates, printed in Gold and Silver, and representing about 1000 Coins, with 160 pages of Text, handsomely bound in embossed cloth, richly gilt, with Emblematical Designs on the Cover, and gilt edges. 1863. £2, 2s.

MARTIN.—THE CHINESE : THEIR EDUCATION, PHILOSOPHY, AND LETTERS. By W. A. P. Martin, D.D., LL.D., President of the Tungwen College, Pekin. 8vo, pp. 320, cloth. 1881. 7s. 6d.

MARTINEAU.—ESSAYS, PHILOSOPHICAL AND THEOLOGICAL. By James Martineau. 2 vols. crown 8vo, pp. iv. and 414—x. and 430, cloth. 1875. £1, 4s.

MARTINEAU.—LETTERS FROM IRELAND. By Harriet Martineau. Reprinted from the *Daily News.* Post 8vo, pp. viii. and 220, cloth. 1852. 6s. 6d.

MASON.—BURMA : ITS PEOPLE AND PRODUCTIONS ; or, Notes on the Fauna, Flora, and Minerals of Tenasserim, Pegu and Burma. By the Rev. F. Mason, D.D., M.R.A.S., Corresponding Member of the American Oriental Society, of the Boston Society of Natural History, and of the Lyceum of Natural History, New York. Vol. I. GEOLOGY, MINERALOGY AND ZOOLOGY. Vol. II. BOTANY. Rewritten and Enlarged by W. Theobald, late Deputy-Superintendent Geological Survey of India. Two Vols., royal 8vo, pp. xxvi. and 560; xvi. and 788 and xxxvi., cloth. 1884. £3.

MATHEWS.—ABRAHAM IBN EZRA'S COMMENTARY ON THE CANTICLES AFTER THE FIRST RECENSION. Edited from the MSS., with a translation, by H. J. Mathews, B.A., Exeter College, Oxford. Crown 8vo, pp. x., 34, and 24, limp cloth. 1874. 2s. 6d.

MAXWELL.—A MANUAL OF THE MALAY LANGUAGE. By W. E. Maxwell, of the Inner Temple, Barrister-at-Law; Assistant Resident, Perak, Malay Peninsula. With an Introductory Sketch of the Sanskrit Element in Malay. Crown 8vo, pp. viii. and 182, cloth. 1882. 7s. 6d.

MAY.—A BIBLIOGRAPHY OF ELECTRICITY AND MAGNETISM. 1860 to 1883. With Special Reference to Electro-Technics. Compiled by G. May. With an Index by O. Salle, Ph.D. Crown 8vo, pp. viii.-204, cloth. 1884. 5s.

MAYER.—ON THE ART OF POTTERY : with a History of its Rise and Progress in Liverpool. By Joseph Mayer, F.S.A., F.R.S.N.A., &c. 8vo, pp. 100, boards. 1873. 5s.

MAYERS.—TREATIES BETWEEN THE EMPIRE OF CHINA AND FOREIGN POWERS, together with Regulations for the conduct of Foreign Trade, &c. Edited by W. F. Mayers, Chinese Secretary to H.B.M.'s Legation at Peking. 8vo, pp. 246, cloth. 1877. 25s.

MAYERS.—The Chinese Government: a Manual of Chinese Titles, categorically arranged and explained, with an Appendix. By Wm. Fred. Mayers, Chinese Secretary to H.B.M.'s Legation at Peking, &c., &c. Royal 8vo, pp. viii. and 160, cloth. 1878. 30s.

M'CRINDLE.—Ancient India, as Described by Megasthenes and Arrian; being a translation of the fragments of the Indika of Megasthenes collected by Dr. Schwanbeck, and of the first part of the Indika of Arrian. By J. W. M'Crindle, M.A., Principal of the Government College, Patna, &c. With Introduction, Notes, and Map of Ancient India. Post 8vo, pp. xi. and 224, cloth. 1877. 7s. 6d.

M'CRINDLE.—The Commerce and Navigation of the Erythræan Sea. Being a Translation of the Periplus Maris Erythræi, by an Anonymous Writer, and of Arrian's Account of the Voyage of Nearkhos, from the Mouth of the Indus to the Head of the Persian Gulf. With Introduction, Commentary, Notes, and Index. By J. W. M'Crindle, M.A., Edinburgh, &c. Post 8vo, pp. iv. and 238, cloth. 1879. 7s. 6d.

M'CRINDLE.—Ancient India as Described by Ktesias the Knidian; being a Translation of the Abridgment of his "Indika" by Photios, and of the Fragments of that Work preserved in other Writers. With Introduction, Notes, and Index. By J. W. M'Crindle, M.A., M.R.S.A. 8vo, pp. viii. and 104, cloth. 1882. 6s.

MECHANIC (The Young). A Book for Boys, containing Directions for the use of all kinds of Tools, and for the construction of Steam Engines and Mechanical Models, including the Art of Turning in Wood and Metal. Fifth Edition. Imperial 16mo, pp. iv. and 346, and 70 Engravings, cloth. 1878. 6s.

MECHANIC'S Workshop (Amateur). A Treatise containing Plain and Concise Directions for the Manipulation of Wood and Metals, including Casting, Forging, Brazing, Soldering, and Carpentry. By the Author of "The Lathe and its Uses." Sixth Edition. Demy 8vo, pp. iv. and 148. Illustrated, cloth. 1880. 6s.

MEDITATIONS on Death and Eternity. Translated from the German by Frederica Rowan. Published by Her Majesty's gracious permission. 8vo, pp. 386, cloth. 1862. 10s. 6d.

    Ditto. Smaller Edition, crown 8vo, printed on toned paper, pp. 352, cloth. 1884. 6s.

MEDITATIONS on Life and its Religious Duties. Translated from the German by Frederica Rowan. Dedicated to H.R.H. Princess Louis of Hesse. Published by Her Majesty's gracious permission. Being the Companion Volume to "Meditations on Death and Eternity." 8vo, pp. vi. and 370, cloth. 1863. 10s. 6d.

    Ditto. Smaller Edition, crown 8vo, printed on toned paper, pp. 338. 1863. 6s.

MEDLICOTT.—A Manual of the Geology of India, chiefly compiled from the observations of the Geological Survey. By H. B. Medlicott, M.A., Superintendent, Geological Survey of India, and W. T. Blanford, A.R.S.M., F.R.S., Deputy Superintendent. Published by order of the Government of India. 2 vols. 8vo, pp. xviii.–lxxx.–818. with 21 Plates and large coloured Map mounted in case, uniform, cloth. 1879. 16s. (For Part III. see Ball.)

MEGHA-DUTA (The). (Cloud-Messenger.) By Kālidāsa. Translated from the Sanskrit into English Verse by the late H. H. Wilson, M.A., F.R.S. The Vocabulary by Francis Johnson. New Edition. 4to, pp. xi. and 180, cloth. 10s. 6d.

MEREDYTH.—Arca, a Repertoire of Original Poems, Sacred and Secular. By F. Meredyth, M.A., Canon of Limerick Cathedral. Crown 8vo, pp. 124, cloth. 1875. 5s.

METCALFE.—The Englishman and the Scandinavian. By Frederick Metcalfe, M.A., Fellow of Lincoln College, Oxford; Translator of "Gallus" ·and "Charicles;" and Author of "The Oxonian in Iceland." Post 8vo, pp. 512, cloth. 1880. 18s.

MICHEL.—Les Écossais en France, Les Français en Écosse Par Francisque Michel, Correspondant de l'Institut de France, &c. In 2 vols. 8vo, pp. vii., 547, and 551, rich blue cloth, with emblematical designs. With upwards of 100 Coats of Arms, and other Illustrations. Price, £1, 12s.—Also a Large-Paper Edition (limited to 100 Copies), printed on Thick Paper. 2 vols. 4to, half morocco, with 3 additional Steel Engravings. 1862. £3, 3s.

MICKIEWICZ.—Konrad Wallenrod. An Historical Poem. By A. Mickiewicz. Translated from the Polish into English Verse by Miss M. Biggs. 18mo, pp. xvi. and 100, cloth. 1882. 2s. 6d.

MILL.—Auguste Comte and Positivism. By the late John Stuart Mill, M.P. Third Edition. 8vo, pp. 200, cloth. 1882. 3s. 6d.

MILLHOUSE.—Manual of Italian Conversation. For the Use of Schools. By John Millhouse. 18mo, pp. 126, cloth. 1866. 2s.

MILLHOUSE.—New English and Italian Pronouncing and Explanatory Dictionary. By John Millhouse. Vol. I. English-Italian. Vol. II. Italian-English. Fourth Edition. 2 vols. square 8vo, pp. 654 and 740, cloth. 1867. 12s.

MILNE.—Notes on Crystallography and Crystallo-physics. Being the Substance of Lectures delivered at Yedo during the years 1876-1877. By John Milne, F.G.S. 8vo, pp. viii. and 70, cloth. 1879. 3s.

MINOCHCHERJI.—Pahlavi, Gujārati, and English Dictionary. By Jamashji Dastur Minochcherji. Vol. I., with Photograph of Author. 8vo, pp. clxxii. and 168, cloth. 1877. 14s.

MITRA.—Buddha Gaya: The Hermitage of Sákya Muni. By Rajendralala Mitra, LL.D., C.I.E., &c. 4to, pp. xvi. and 258, with 51 Plates, cloth. 1879. £3.

MOCATTA.—Moral Biblical Gleanings and Practical Teachings, Illustrated by Biographical Sketches Drawn from the Sacred Volume. By J. L. Mocatta. 8vo, pp. viii. and 446, cloth. 1872. 7s.

MODERN FRENCH READER (The). Prose. Junior Course. Tenth Edition. Edited by Ch. Cassal, LL.D., and Théodore Karcher, LL.B. Crown 8vo, pp. xiv. and 224, cloth. 1884. 2s. 6d.

Senior Course. Third Edition. Crown 8vo, pp. xiv. and 418, cloth. 1830. 4s.

MODERN FRENCH READER.—A Glossary of Idioms, Gallicisms, and other Difficulties contained in the Senior Course of the Modern French Reader; with Short Notices of the most important French Writers and Historical or Literary Characters, and hints as to the works to be read or studied. By Charles Cassal, LL.D., &c. Crown 8vo, pp. viii. and 104, cloth. 1881. 2s. 6d.

MODERN FRENCH READER.—Senior Course and Glossary combined. 6s.

MORELET.—Travels in Central America, including Accounts of some Regions unexplored since the Conquest. From the French of A. Morelet, by Mrs. M. F. Squier. Edited by E. G. Squier. 8vo, pp. 430, cloth. 1871. 8s. 6d.

MORFILL.—Simplified Polish Grammar. See Trübner's Collection.

MORFIT.—A PRACTICAL TREATISE ON THE MANUFACTURE OF SOAPS. By Campbell Morfit, M.D., F.C.S., formerly Professor of Applied Chemistry in the University of Maryland. With Illustrations. Demy 8vo, pp. xii. and 270, cloth. 1871. £2, 12s. 6d.

MORFIT.—A PRACTICAL TREATISE ON PURE FERTILIZERS, and the Chemical Conversion of Rock Guanos, Marlstones, Coprolites, and the Crude Phosphates of Lime and Alumina generally into various valuable Products. By Campbell Morfit, M.D., F.C.S., formerly Professor of Applied Chemistry in the University of Maryland. With 28 Plates. 8vo, pp. xvi. and 547, cloth. 1873. £4, 4s.

MORRIS.—A DESCRIPTIVE AND HISTORICAL ACCOUNT OF THE GODAVERY DISTRICT, IN THE PRESIDENCY OF MADRAS. By Henry Morris, formerly of the Madras Civil Service, author of "A History of India, for use in Schools," and other works. With a Map. 8vo, pp. xii. and 390, cloth. 1878. 12s.

MOSENTHAL.—OSTRICHES AND OSTRICH FARMING. By J. de Mosenthal, late Member of the Legistive Council of the Cape of Good Hope, &c., and James E. Harting, F.L.S., F.Z.S., Member of the British Ornithologist's Union, &c. Second Edition. With 8 full-page illustrations and 20 woodcuts. Royal 8vo, pp. xxiv. and 246, cloth. 1879. 10s. 6d.

MOTLEY.—JOHN LOTHROP MOTLEY: a Memoir. By Oliver Wendell Holmes. English Copyright Edition. Crown 8vo, pp. xii. and 275, cloth. 1878. 6s.

MUELLER.—THE ORGANIC CONSTITUENTS OF PLANTS AND VEGETABLE SUBSTANCES, and their Chemical Analysis. By Dr. G. C. Wittstein. Authorised Translation from the German Original, enlarged with numerous Additions, by Baron Ferd. von Mueller. K.C.M.G., M. & Ph. D., F.R.S. Crown 8vo, pp. xviii. and 332, wrapper. 1880. 14s.

MUELLER.—SELECT EXTRA-TROPICAL PLANTS READILY ELIGIBLE FOR INDUSTRIAL CULTURE OR NATURALISATION. With Indications of their Native Countries and some of their Uses. By F. Von Mueller, K.C.M.G., M.D., Ph.D., F.R.S. 8vo, pp. x., 394, cloth. 1880. 8s.

MUHAMMED.—THE LIFE OF MUHAMMED. Based on Muhammed Ibn Ishak. By Abd El Malik Ibn Hisham. Edited by Dr. Ferdinand Wüstenfeld. One volume containing the Arabic Text. 8vo, pp. 1026, sewed. £1, 1s. Another volume, containing Introduction, Notes, and Index in German. 8vo, pp. lxxii. and 266, sewed. 7s. 6d. Each part sold separately.

MUIR.—EXTRACTS FROM THE CORAN. In the Original, with English rendering. Compiled by Sir William Muir, K.C.S.I., LL.D., Author of "The Life of Mahomet." Crown 8vo, pp. viii. and 64, cloth. 1880. 3s. 6d.

MUIR.—ORIGINAL SANSKRIT TEXTS, on the Origin and History of the People of India, their Religion and Institutions. Collected, Translated, and Illustrated by John Muir, D.C.L., LL.D., Ph.D., &c. &c.

Vol. I. Mythical and Legendary Accounts of the Origin of Caste, with an Inquiry into its existence in the Vedic Age. Second Edition, rewritten and greatly enlarged. 8vo, pp. xx. and 532, cloth. 1868. £1, 1s.

Vol. II. The Trans-Himalayan Origin of the Hindus, and their Affinity with the Western Branches of the Aryan Race. Second Edition, revised, with Additions. 8vo, pp. xxxii. and 512, cloth. 1871. £1, 1s.

Vol. III. The Vedas: Opinions of their Authors, and of later Indian Writers, on their Origin, Inspiration, and Authority. Second Edition, revised and enlarged. 8vo, pp. xxxii. and 312, cloth. 1868. 16s.

Vol. IV. Comparison of the Vedic with the later representation of the principal Indian Deities. Second Edition, revised. 8vo, pp. xvi. and 524, cloth. 1873. £1, 1s.

MUIR.—ORIGINAL SANSKRIT TEXTS—*continued.*

Vol. V. Contributions to a Knowledge of the Cosmogony, Mythology, Religious Ideas, Life and Manners of the Indians in the Vedic Age. Third Edition. 8vo, pp. xvi. and 492, cloth. 1884. £1, 1s.

MUIR.—TRANSLATIONS FROM THE SANSKRIT. See Trübner's Oriental Series.

MULHALL.—HANDBOOK OF THE RIVER PLATE, Comprising the Argentine Republic, Uruguay, and Paraguay. With Six Maps. By M. G. and E. T. Mulhall, Proprietors and Editors of the Buenos Ayres *Standard.* Fifth Edition (Ninth Thousand), crown 8vo, pp. x. and 732, cloth. 1885. 7s. 6d.

MÜLLER.—OUTLINE DICTIONARY, for the Use of Missionaries, Explorers, and Students of Language. With an Introduction on the proper Use of the Ordinary English Alphabet in transcribing Foreign Languages. By F. Max Müller, M.A. The Vocabulary compiled by John Bellows. 12mo, pp. 368, morocco. 1867. 7s. 6d.

MÜLLER.—LECTURE ON BUDDHIST NIHILISM. By F. Max Müller, M.A. Fcap. 8vo, sewed. 1869. 1s.

MÜLLER.—THE SACRED HYMNS OF THE BRAHMINS, as preserved to us in the oldest collection of religious poetry, the Rig-Veda-Sanhita. Translated and explained, by F. Max Müller, M.A., Fellow of All Souls' College, Professor of Comparative Philology at Oxford, Foreign Member of the Institute of France, &c., &c. Vol. I. Hymns to the Maruts or the Storm-Gods. 8vo, pp. clii. and 264, cloth. 1869. 12s. 6d.

MÜLLER.—THE HYMNS OF THE RIG-VEDA, in the Samhita and Pada Texts. Reprinted from the Editio Princeps. By F. Max Müller, M.A., &c. Second Edition, with the two Texts on Parallel Pages. In two vols. 8vo, pp. 1704, sewed. £1, 12s.

MÜLLER.—A SHORT HISTORY OF THE BOURBONS. From the Earliest Period down to the Present Time. By R. M. Müller, Ph.D., Modern Master at Forest School, Walthamstow, and Author of "Parallèle entre 'Jules César,' par Shakespeare, et 'Le Mort de César,' par Voltaire," &c. Fcap. 8vo, pp. 30, wrapper. 1882. 1s.

MÜLLER.—ANCIENT INSCRIPTIONS IN CEYLON. By Dr. Edward Müller. 2 Vols. Text, crown 8vo, pp. 220, cloth, and Plates, oblong folio, cloth. 1883. 21s.

MÜLLER.—PALI GRAMMAR. See Trübner's Collection.

MULLEY.—GERMAN GEMS IN AN ENGLISH SETTING. Translated by Jane Mulley. Fcap., pp. xii. and 180, cloth. 1877. 3s. 6d.

NÁGÁNANDA; OR, THE JOY OF THE SNAKE WORLD. A Buddhist Drama in Five Acts. Translated into English Prose, with Explanatory Notes, from the Sanskrit of Sri-Harsha-Deva, by Palmer Boyd, B.A. With an Introduction by Professor Cowell. Crown 8vo, pp. xvi. and 100, cloth. 1872. 4s. 6d.

NAPIER.—FOLK LORE; or, Superstitious Beliefs in the West of Scotland within this Century. With an Appendix, showing the probable relation of the modern Festivals of Christmas, May Day, St. John's Day, and Hallowe'en, to ancient Sun and Fire Worship. By James Napier, F.R.S.E., &c. Crown 8vo, pp. vii. and 190, cloth. 1878. 4s.

NARADÍYA DHARMA-SASTRA; OR, THE INSTITUTES OF NARADA. Translated, for the first time, from the unpublished Sanskrit original. By Dr. Julius Jolly, University, Wurzburg. With a Preface, Notes, chiefly critical, an Index of Quotations from Narada in the principal Indian Digests, and a general Index. Crown 8vo, pp. xxxv. and 144, cloth. 1876. 10s. 6d.

NEVILL.—HAND LIST OF MOLLUSCA IN THE INDIAN MUSEUM, CALCUTTA. By Geoffrey Nevill, C.M.Z.S., &c., First Assistant to the Superintendent of the Indian Museum. Part I. Gastropoda, Pulmonata, and Prosobranchia-Neurobranchia. 8vo, pp. xvi. and 338, cloth. 1878. 15s.

NEWMAN.—THE ODES OF HORACE. Translated into Unrhymed Metres, with Introduction and Notes. By F. W. Newman. Second Edition. Post 8vo, pp. xxi. and 247, cloth. 1876. 4s.

NEWMAN.—THEISM, DOCTRINAL AND PRACTICAL; or, Didactic Religious Utterances. By F. W. Newman. 4to, pp. 184, cloth. 1858. 4s. 6d.

NEWMAN.—HOMERIC TRANSLATION IN THEORY AND PRACTICE. A Reply to Matthew Arnold. By F. W. Newman. Crown 8vo, pp. 104, stiff covers. 1861. 2s. 6d.

NEWMAN.—HIAWATHA: Rendered into Latin. With Abridgment. By F. W. Newman. 12mo, pp. vii. and 110, sewed. 1862. 2s. 6d.

NEWMAN.—A HISTORY OF THE HEBREW MONARCHY from the Administration of Samuel to the Babylonish Captivity. By F. W. Newman. Third Edition. Crown 8vo, pp. x. and 354, cloth. 1865. 8s. 6d.

NEWMAN.—PHASES OF FAITH; or, Passages from the History of my Creed. By F. W. Newman. New Edition; with Reply to Professor Henry Rogers, Author of the "Eclipse of Faith." Crown 8vo, pp. viii. and 212, cloth. 1881. 3s. 6d.

NEWMAN.—A HANDBOOK OF MODERN ARABIC, consisting of a Practical Grammar, with numerous Examples, Dialogues, and Newspaper Extracts, in European Type. By F. W. Newman. Post 8vo, pp. xx. and 192, cloth. 1866. 6s.

NEWMAN.—TRANSLATIONS OF ENGLISH POETRY INTO LATIN VERSE. Designed as Part of a New Method of Instructing in Latin. By F. W. Newman. Crown 8vo, pp. xiv. and 202, cloth. 1868. 6s.

NEWMAN.—THE SOUL: Her Sorrows and her Aspirations. An Essay towards the Natural History of the Soul, as the True Basis of Theology. By F. W. Newman. Tenth Edition. Post 8vo, pp. xii. and 162, cloth. 1882. 3s. 6d.

NEWMAN.—THE TEXT OF THE IGUVINE INSCRIPTIONS. With Interlinear Latin Translation and Notes. By F. W. Newman. 8vo, pp. 56, sewed. 1868. 2s.

NEWMAN.—MISCELLANIES; chiefly Addresses, Academical and Historical. By F. W. Newman. 8vo, pp. iv. and 356, cloth. 1869. 7s. 6d.

NEWMAN.—THE ILIAD OF HOMER, faithfully translated into Unrhymed English Metre, by F. W. Newman. Royal 8vo, pp. xvi. and 384, cloth. 1871. 10s. 6d.

NEWMAN.—A DICTIONARY OF MODERN ARABIC. 1. Anglo-Arabic Dictionary. 2. Anglo-Arabic Vocabulary. 3. Arabo-English Dictionary. By F. W. Newman. In 2 vols. crown 8vo, pp. xvi. and 376–464, cloth. 1871. £1, 1s.

NEWMAN.—HEBREW THEISM. By F. W. Newman. Royal 8vo, pp. viii. and 172. Stiff wrappers. 1874. 4s. 6d.

NEWMAN.—THE MORAL INFLUENCE OF LAW. A Lecture by F. W. Newman, May 20, 1860. Crown 8vo, pp. 16, sewed. 3d.

NEWMAN.—RELIGION NOT HISTORY. By F. W. Newman. Foolscap, pp. 58, paper wrapper. 1877. 1s.

NEWMAN.—MORNING PRAYERS IN THE HOUSEHOLD OF A BELIEVER IN GOD. By F. W. Newman. Second Edition. Crown 8vo, pp. 80, limp cloth. 1882. 1s. 6d.

NEWMAN.—REORGANIZATION OF ENGLISH INSTITUTIONS. A Lecture by Emeritus Professor F. W. Newman. Delivered in the Manchester Athenæum, October 15, 1875. Crown 8vo, pp. 28, sewed. 1880. 6d.

NEWMAN.—WHAT IS CHRISTIANITY WITHOUT CHRIST? By F. W. Newman. Emeritus Professor of University College, London. 8vo, pp. 28, stitched in wrapper. 1881. 1s.

NEWMAN.—LIBYAN VOCABULARY. An Essay towards Reproducing the Ancient Numidian Language out of Four Modern Languages. By F. W. Newman. Crown 8vo, pp. vi. and 204, cloth. 1882. 10s. 6d.

NEWMAN.—A CHRISTIAN COMMONWEALTH. By F. W. Newman. Crown 8vo, pp. 60, cloth. 1883. 1s.

NEWMAN.—CHRISTIANITY IN ITS CRADLE. By F. W. Newman, once Fellow of Balliol College, Oxford, now Emeritus Professor of University College, London. Crown 8vo, pp. iv. and 132, cloth. 1884. 2s.

D

NEWMAN.—COMMENTS ON THE TEXT OF ÆSCHYLUS. By F. W. Newman, Honorary Fellow of Worcester College, Oxford, and formerly Fellow of Balliol College. Demy 8vo, pp. xii. and 144, cloth. 1884. 5s.

NEWMAN.—REBILIUS CRUSO: Robinson Crusoe in Latin. A Book to Lighten Tedium to a Learner. By F. W. Newman, Emeritus Professor of Latin in University College, London; Honorary Fellow of Worcester College, Oxford. Post 8vo, pp. xii. and 110, cloth. 1884. 5s.

NEW SOUTH WALES, PUBLICATIONS OF THE GOVERNMENT OF. List on application.

NEW SOUTH WALES.—JOURNAL AND PROCEEDINGS OF THE ROYAL SOCIETY OF Published annually. Price 10s. 6d. List of Contents on application.

NEWTON.—PATENT LAW AND PRACTICE: showing the mode of obtaining and opposing Grants, Disclaimers, Confirmations, and Extensions of Patents. With a Chapter on Patent Agents. By A. V. Newton. Enlarged Edition. Crown 8vo, pp. xii. and 104, cloth. 1879. 2s. 6d.

NEWTON.—AN ANALYSIS OF THE PATENT AND COPYRIGHT LAWS: Including the various Acts relating to the Protection of Inventions, Designs, Trade Marks; Literary and Musical Compositions, Dramatic Performances; Engravings, Sculpture, Paintings, Drawings, and Photographs. By A. Newton, author of "Patent Law and Practice." Demy 8vo, pp. viii. and 70, cloth. 1884. 3s. 6d.

NEW ZEALAND INSTITUTE PUBLICATIONS:—

I. TRANSACTIONS AND PROCEEDINGS of the New Zealand Institute. Demy 8vo, stitched. Vols. I. to XVI., 1868 to 1883. £1, 1s. each.

II. AN INDEX TO THE TRANSACTIONS AND PROCEEDINGS of the New Zealand Institute. Vols. I. to VIII. Edited and Published under the Authority of the Board of Governors of the Institute. By James Hector, C.M.G., M.D., F.R.S. Demy, 8vo, 44 pp., stitched. 1877. 2s. 6d.

NEW ZEALAND.—GEOLOGICAL SURVEY. List of Publications on application.

NOIRIT.—A FRENCH COURSE IN TEN LESSONS. By Jules Noirit, B.A. Lessons I.-IV. Crown 8vo, pp. xiv. and 80, sewed. 1870. 1s. 6d.

NOIRIT.—FRENCH GRAMMATICAL QUESTIONS for the use of Gentlemen preparing for the Army, Civil Service, Oxford Examinations, &c., &c. By Jules Noirit. Crown 8vo, pp. 62, cloth. 1870. 1s. Interleaved, 1s. 6d.

NOURSE.—NARRATIVE OF THE SECOND ARCTIC EXPEDITION MADE BY CHARLES F. HALL. His Voyage to Repulse Bay; Sledge Journeys to the Straits of Fury and Hecla, and to King William's Land, and Residence among the Eskimos during the years 1864–69. Edited under the orders of the Hon. Secretary of the Navy, by Prof. J. E. Nourse, U.S.N. 4to, pp. l. and 644, cloth. With maps, heliotypes, steel and wood engravings. 1880. £1, 8s.

NUGENT'S IMPROVED FRENCH AND ENGLISH AND ENGLISH AND FRENCH POCKET DICTIONARY. Par Smith. 24mo, pp. 489 and 320, cloth. 1873. 3s.

NUTT.—TWO TREATISES ON VERBS CONTAINING FEEBLE AND DOUBLE LETTERS. By R. Jehuda Hayug of Fez. Translated into Hebrew from the original Arabic by R. Moses Gikatilia of Cordova, with the Treatise on Punctuation by the same author, translated by Aben Ezra. Edited from Bodleian MSS., with an English translation, by J. W. Nutt, M.A. Demy 8vo, pp. 312, sewed. 1870. 5s.

NUMISMATA ORIENTALIA ILLUSTRATA. See MARSDEN, and INTERNATIONAL.

NUTT.—A SKETCH OF SAMARITAN HISTORY, DOGMA, AND LITERATURE. An Introduction to "Fragments of a Samaritan Targum." By J. W. Nutt, M.A., &c., &c. Demy 8vo, pp. 180, cloth. 1874. 5s.

OEHLENSCHLÄGER.—AXEL AND VALBORG: a Tragedy, in Five Acts, and other Poems. Translated from the Danish of Adam Ochlenschläger by Pierce Butler, M.A., late Rector of Ulcombe, Kent. Edited by Professor Palmer, M.A., of St. John's Coll., Camb. With a Memoir of the Translator. Fcap. 8vo, pp. xii. and 164, cloth. 1874. 5s.

OERA LINDA BOOK (THE).—From a Manuscript of the 13th Century, with the permission of the proprietor, C. Over de Linden of the Helder. The Original Frisian Text as verified by Dr. J. O. Ottema, accompanied by an English Version of Dr. Ottema's Dutch Translation. By W. R. Sandbach. 8vo, pp. xxv. and 254, cloth. 1876. 5s.

OGAREFF.—ESSAI SUR LA SITUATION RUSSE. Lettres à un Anglais. Par N. Ogareff. 12mo, pp. 150, sewed. 1862. 3s.

OLCOTT.—A BUDDHIST CATECHISM, according to the Canon of the Southern Church. By Colonel H. S. Olcott, President of the Theosophical Society. 24mo, pp. 32. 1s.

OLCOTT.—THE YOGA PHILOSOPHY: Being the Text of Patanjali, with Bhojarajah's Commentary. A Reprint of the English Translation of the above, by the late Dr. Ballantyne and Govind Shastri Deva; to which are added Extracts from Various Authors. With an Introduction by Colonel H. S. Olcott, President of the Theosophical Society. The whole Edited by Tukaram Tatia, F.T.S. Crown 8vo, pp. xvi.-294, wrapper. 1882. 7s. 6d.

OLLENDORFF.—METODO PARA APRENDER A LEER, escribir y hablar el Inglés segun el sistema de Ollendorff. Por Ramon Palenzuela y Juan de la Carreño. 8vo, pp. xlvi. and 460, cloth. 1873. 7s. 6d.
KEY to Ditto. Crown 8vo, pp. 112, cloth. 1873. 4s.

OLLENDORFF.—METODO PARA APRENDER A LEER, escribir y hablar el Frances, segun el verdadero sistema de Ollendorff; ordenado en lecciones progresivas, consistiendo de ejercicios orales y escritos; enriquecido de la pronunciacion figurada como se estila en la conversacion; y de un Apéndice abrazando las reglas de la sintáxis, la formacion de los verbos regulares, y la conjugacion de los irregulares. Por Teodoro Simonné, Professor de Lenguas. Crown 8vo, pp. 342, cloth. 1873. 6s.
KEY to Ditto. Crown 8vo, pp. 80, cloth. 1873. 3s. 6d.

OPPERT.—ON THE CLASSIFICATION OF LANGUAGES: A Contribution to Comparative Philology. By Dr. Gustav Oppert, Ph.D., Professor of Sanskrit, Presidency College, Madras. 8vo, paper, pp. viii. and 146. 1883. 7s. 6d.

OPPERT.—LISTS OF SANSKRIT MANUSCRIPTS in Private Libraries of Southern India, Compiled, Arranged, and Indexed by Gustav Oppert, Ph.D., Professor of Sanskrit, Presidency College, Madras. Vol. I. 8vo, pp. vii. and 620, cloth. 1883. £1, 1s.

OPPERT.—ON THE WEAPONS, ARMY ORGANISATION, AND POLITICAL MAXIMS OF THE ANCIENT HINDUS; with special reference to Gunpowder and Firearms. By Dr. Gustav Oppert, Ph.D., Professor of Sanskrit, Presidency College, Madras. 8vo, paper, pp. vi. and 162. 1883. 7s. 6d.

ORIENTAL SERIES.—See TRÜBNER'S ORIENTAL SERIES.

ORIENTAL TEXT SOCIETY'S PUBLICATIONS. A list may be had on application.

ORIENTAL CONGRESS.—REPORT OF THE PROCEEDINGS OF THE SECOND INTERNATIONAL CONGRESS OF ORIENTALISTS HELD IN LONDON, 1874. Royal 8vo, pp. viii. and 68, sewed. 1874. 5s.

ORIENTALISTS.—TRANSACTIONS OF THE SECOND SESSION OF THE INTERNATIONAL CONGRESS OF ORIENTALISTS. Held in London in September 1874. Edited by Robert K. Douglas, Hon. Sec. 8vo, pp. viii. and 456, cloth. 1876. 21s.

OTTÉ.—HOW TO LEARN DANISH (Dano-Norwegian): a Manual for Students of Danish based on the Ollendorffian system of teaching languages, and adapted for self-instruction. By E. C. Otté. Second Edition. Crown 8vo, pp. xx. and 338, cloth. 1884. 7s. 6d.
Key to above. Crown 8vo, pp. 84, cloth. 3s.

OTTÉ.—SIMPLIFIED DANISH AND SWEDISH GRAMMARS. See TRÜBNER'S COLLECTION

OVERBECK.—CATHOLIC ORTHODOXY AND ANGLO-CATHOLICISM. A Word about the Intercommunion between the English and Orthodox Churches. By J. J. Overbeck, D.D. 8vo, pp. viii. and 200, cloth. 1866. 5s.

OVERBECK.—BONN CONFERENCE. By J. J. Overbeck, D.D. Crown 8vo, pp. 48, sewed. 1876. 1s.

OVERBECK.—A Plain View of the Claims of the Orthodox Catholic Church as Opposed to all other Christian Denominations. By J. J. Overbeck, D.D. Crown 8vo, pp. iv. and 138, wrapper. 1881. 2s. 6d.

OWEN.—Footfalls on the Boundary of Another World. With Narrative Illustrations. By R. D. Owen. An enlarged English Copyright Edition. Post 8vo, pp. xx. and 392, cloth. 1875. 7s. 6d.

OWEN.—The Debatable Land between this World and the Next. With Illustrative Narrations. By Robert Dale Owen. Second Edition. Crown 8vo, pp. 456, cloth. 1874. 7s. 6d.

OWEN.—Threading my Way: Twenty-Seven Years of Autobiography. By R. D. Owen. Crown 8vo, pp. 344, cloth. 1874. 7s. 6d.

OXLEY.—Egypt: And the Wonders of the Land of the Pharaohs. By William Oxley, author of "The Philosophy of Spirit." Illustrated by a New Version of the Bhagavat-Gita, an Episode of the Mahabharat, one of the Epic Poems of Ancient India. Crown 8vo, pp. viii.-328, cloth. 1884. 7s. 6d.

OYSTER (THE): Where, How, and When to Find, Breed, Cook, and Eat It. Second Edition, with a New Chapter, "The Oyster-Seeker in London." 12mo, pp. viii. and 106, boards. 1863. 1s.

PALESTINE.—Memoirs of the Survey of Western Palestine. Edited by W. Besant, M.A., and E. H. Palmer, M.A., under the Direction of the Committee of the Palestine Exploration Fund. Complete in seven volumes. Demy 4to, cloth, with a Portfolio of Plans, and large scale Map. Second Issue. Price Twenty Guineas.

PALMER.—A Concise English-Persian Dictionary; together with a simplified Grammar of the Persian Language. By the late E. H. Palmer, M.A., Lord Almoner's Reader, and Professor of Arabic, Cambridge, &c. Completed and Edited, from the MS. left imperfect at his death, by G. Le Strange. Royal 16mo, pp. 606, cloth. 1883. 10s. 6d.

PALMER.—A Concise Persian-English Dictionary. By E. H. Palmer, M.A., of the Middle Temple, Barrister-at-Law, Lord Almoner's Reader, and Professor of Arabic, and Fellow of St. John's College in the University of Cambridge. Second Edition. Royal 16mo, pp. 726, cloth. 1884. 10s. 6d.

PALMER.—The Song of the Reed, and other Pieces. By E. H. Palmer, M.A., Cambridge. Crown 8vo, pp. 208, cloth. 1876. 5s.

PALMER.—Hindustani, Arabic, and Persian Grammar. See Trübner's Collection.

PALMER.—The Patriarch and the Tsar. Translated from the Russ by William Palmer, M.A. Demy 8vo, cloth. Vol. I. The Replies of the Humble Nicon. Pp. xl. and 674. 1871. 12s.—Vol. II. Testimonies concerning the Patriarch Nicon, the Tsar, and the Boyars. Pp. lxxviii. and 554. 1873. 12s.—Vol. III. History of the Condemnation of the Patriarch Nicon. Pp. lxvi. and 558. 1873. 12s.—Vols. IV., V., and VI. Services of the Patriarch Nicon to the Church and State of his Country, &c. Pp. lxxviii. and 1 to 660; xiv.-661-1028, and 1 to 254; xxvi.-1029-1656, and 1-72. 1876. 36s.

PARKER.—Theodore Parker's Celebrated Discourse on Matters Pertaining to Religion. People's Edition. Cr. 8vo, pp. 351. 1872. Stitched, 1s. 6d.; cl., 2s.

PARKER.—Theodore Parker. A Biography. By O. B. Frothingham. Crown 8vo. pp. viii. and 588, cloth, with Portrait. 1876. 12s.

PARKER.—The Collected Works of Theodore Parker, Minister of the Twenty-eighth Congregational Society at Boston, U.S. Containing his Theological, Polemical, and Critical Writings; Sermons, Speeches, and Addresses; and Literary Miscellanies. In 14 vols. 8vo, cloth. 6s. each.

Vol. I. Discourse on Matters Pertaining to Religion. Preface by the Editor, and Portrait of Parker from a medallion by Saulini. Pp. 380.
Vol. II. Ten Sermons and Prayers. Pp. 360.
Vol. III. Discourses of Theology. Pp. 318.
Vol. IV. Discourses on Politics. Pp. 312.

PARKER.—COLLECTED WORKS—*continued.*

    Vol. V. Discourses of Slavery. I. Pp. 336.
    Vol. VI. Discourses of Slavery. II. Pp. 323.
    Vol. VII. Discourses of Social Science. Pp. 296.
    Vol. VIII. Miscellaneous Discourses. Pp. 230.
    Vol. IX. Critical Writings. I. Pp. 292.
    Vol. X. Critical Writings. II. Pp. 308.
    Vol. XI. Sermons of Theism, Atheism, and Popular Theology. Pp. 257.
    Vol. XII. Autobiographical and Miscellaneous Pieces. Pp. 356.
    Vol. XIII. Historic Americans. Pp. 236.
    Vol. XIV. Lessons from the World of Matter and the World of Man. Pp. 352.

PARKER.—MALAGASY GRAMMAR. See Trübner's Collection.

PARRY.—A SHORT CHAPTER ON LETTER-CHANGE, with Examples. Being chiefly an attempt to reduce in a simple manner the principal classical and cognate words to their primitive meanings. By J. Parry, B.A., formerly Scholar of Corpus Christi College, Cambridge. Fcap. 8vo, pp. 16, wrapper. 1884. 1s.

PATERSON.—NOTES ON MILITARY SURVEYING AND RECONNAISSANCE. By Lieut.-Colonel William Paterson. Sixth Edition. With 16 Plates. Demy 8vo, pp. xii. and 146, cloth. 1882. 7s. 6d.

PATERSON.—TOPOGRAPHICAL EXAMINATION PAPERS. By Lieut.-Col. W. Paterson. 8vo, pp. 32, with 4 Plates. Boards. 1882. 2s.

PATERSON.—TREATISE ON MILITARY DRAWING. With a Course of Progressive Plates. By Captain W. Paterson, Professor of Military Drawing at the Royal Military College, Sandhurst. Oblong 4to, pp. xii. and 31, cloth. 1862. £1, 1s.

PATERSON.—THE OROMETER FOR HILL MEASURING, combining Scales of Distances, Protractor, Clinometer, Scale of Horizontal Equivalents, Scale of Shade, and Table of Gradients. By Captain William Paterson. On cardboard. 1s.

PATERSON.—CENTRAL AMERICA. By W. Paterson, the Merchant Statesman. From a MS. in the British Museum, 1701. With a Map. Edited by S. Bannister, M.A. 8vo, pp. 70, sewed. 1857. 2s. 6d.

PATON.—A HISTORY OF THE EGYPTIAN REVOLUTION, from the Period of the Mamelukes to the Death of Mohammed Ali; from Arab and European Memoirs, Oral Tradition, and Local Research. By A. A. Paton. Second Edition. 2 vols. demy 8vo, pp. xii. and 395, viii. and 446, cloth. 1870. 7s. 6d.

PATON.—HENRY BEYLE (otherwise DE STENDAHL). A Critical and Biographical Study, aided by Original Documents and Unpublished Letters from the Private Papers of the Family of Beyle. By A. A. Paton. Crown 8vo, pp. 340, cloth. 1874. 7s. 6d.

PATTON.—THE DEATH OF DEATH; or, A Study of God's Holiness in Connection with the Existence of Evil, in so far as Intelligent and Responsible Beings are Concerned. By an Orthodox Layman (John M. Patton). Revised Edition, crown 8vo, pp. xvi. and 252, cloth. 1881. 6s.

PAULI.—SIMON DE MONTFORT, EARL OF LEICESTER, the Creator of the House of Commons. By Reinhold Pauli. Translated by Una M. Goodwin. With Introduction by Harriet Martineau. Crown 8vo, pp. xvi. and 340, cloth. 1876. 6s.

PETTENKOFER.—THE RELATION OF THE AIR TO THE CLOTHES WE WEAR, THE HOUSE WE LIVE IN, AND THE SOIL WE DWELL ON. Three Popular Lectures delivered before the Albert Society at Dresden. By Dr. Max Von Pettenkofer, Professor of Hygiene at the University of Munich, &c. Abridged and Translated by Augustus Hess, M.D., M.R.C.P., London, &c. Cr. 8vo, pp. viii. and 96, limp cl. 1873. 2s. 6d.

PETRUCCELLI.—PRELIMINAIRES DE LA QUESTION ROMAINE DE M. ED. ABOUT. Par F. Petruccelli de la Gattina. 8vo, pp. xv. and 364, cloth. 1860. 7s. 6d.

PEZZI.—ARYAN PHILOLOGY, according to the most recent researches (Glottologia Aria Recentissima). Remarks Historical and Critical. By Domenico Pezzi. Translated by E. S. Roberts, M.A. Crown 8vo, pp. xvi. and 200, cloth. 1879. 6s.

PHAYRE.—A History of Burma. See Trübner's Oriental Series.

PHAYRE.—The Coins of Arakan, of Pegu, and of Burma. By Sir Arthur Phayre, C.B., K.C.S.I., G.C.M.G., late Commissioner of British Burma. Royal 4to, pp. viii.-48, with Autotype Illustrative Plates. Wrapper. 1882. 8s. 6d.

PHILLIPS.—The Doctrine of Addai, the Apostle, now first edited in a complete form in the Original Syriac, with English Translation and Notes. By George Phillips, D.D., President of Queen's College, Cambridge. 8vo, pp. xv. and 52 and 53, cloth. 1876. 7s. 6d.

PHILOLOGICAL SOCIETY, Transactions of, published irregularly. List of publications on application.

PHILOSOPHY (THE) OF INSPIRATION AND REVELATION. By a Layman. With a preliminary notice of an Essay by the present Lord Bishop of Winchester, contained in a volume entitled "Aids to Faith." 8vo, pp. 20, sewed. 1875. 6d.

PICCIOTTO.—Sketches of Anglo-Jewish History. By James Picciotto. Demy 8vo, pp. xi. and 420, cloth. 1875. 12s.

PIESSE.—Chemistry in the Brewing-Room : being the substance of a Course of Lessons to Practical Brewers. With Tables of Alcohol, Extract, and Original Gravity. By Charles H. Piesse, F.C.S., Public Analyst. Fcap., pp. viii. and 62, cloth. 1877. 5s.

PIRY.—Le Saint Edit, Étude de Litterature Chinoise. Préparée par A. Théophile Piry, du Service des Douanes Maritimes de Chine. 4to, pp. xx. and 320, cloth. 1879. 21s.

PLAYFAIR.—The Cities and Towns of China. A Geographical Dictionary. By G. M. H. Playfair, of Her Majesty's Consular Service in China. 8vo, pp. 506, cloth. 1879. £1, 5s.

PLINY.—The Letters of Pliny the Younger. Translated by J. D. Lewis, M.A., Trinity College, Cambridge. Post 8vo, pp. vii. and 390, cloth. 1879. 5s.

PLUMPTRE.—King's College Lectures on Elocution ; on the Physiology and Culture of Voice and Speech and the Expression of the Emotions by Language, Countenance, and Gesture. To which is added a Special Lecture on the Causes and Cure of the Impediments of Speech. Being the substance of the Introductory Course of Lectures annually delivered by Charles John Plumptre, Lecturer on Public Reading and Speaking at King's College, London, in the Evening Classes Department. Dedicated by permission to H.R.H. the Prince of Wales. Fourth, greatly Enlarged Illustrated, Edition. Post 8vo, pp. xviii. and 494, cloth. 1883. 15s.

PLUMPTRE.—General Sketch of the History of Pantheism. By C. E. Plumptre. Vol. I., from the Earliest Times to the Age of Spinoza ; Vol. II., from the Age of Spinoza to the Commencement of the 19th Century. 2 vols. demy 8vo, pp. viii. and 395 ; iv. and 348, cloth. 1881. 18s.

POLE.—The Philosophy of Music. See English and Foreign Philosophical Library. Vol. XI.

PONSARD.—Charlotte Corday. A Tragedy. By F. Ponsard. Edited, with English Notes and Notice on Ponsard, by Professor C. Cassal, LL.D. 12mo, pp. xi. and 133, cloth. 1867. 2s. 6d.

PONSARD.—L'Honneur et L'Argent. A Comedy. By François Ponsard. Edited, with English Notes and Memoir of Ponsard, by Professor C. Cassal, LL.D. Fcap. 8vo, pp. xvi. and 172, cloth. 1869. 3s. 6d.

POOLE.—An Index to Periodical Literature. By W. F. Poole, LL.D., Librarian of the Chicago Public Library. Third Edition, brought down to January 1882. 1 vol. royal 8vo, pp. xxviii. and 1442, cloth. 1883. £3, 13s. 6d. Wrappers, £3, 10s.

PRACTICAL GUIDES :—
FRANCE, BELGIUM, HOLLAND, AND THE RHINE. 1s.—ITALIAN LAKES. 1s.—WINTERING PLACES OF THE SOUTH. 2s.—SWITZERLAND, SAVOY, AND NORTH ITALY. 2s. 6d.—GENERAL CONTINENTAL GUIDE. 5s.—GENEVA. 1s.—PARIS. 1s.—BERNESE OBERLAND. 1s.—ITALY. 4s.

PRATT.—A GRAMMAR AND DICTIONARY OF THE SAMOAN LANGUAGE. By Rev. George Pratt, Forty Years a Missionary of the London Missionary Society in Samoa. Second Edition. Edited by Rev. S. J. Whitmee, F.R.G.S. Crown 8vo, pp. viii. and 380, cloth. 1878. 18s.

PSYCHICAL RESEARCH, PROCEEDINGS OF THE SOCIETY FOR. Published irregularly. Vol. I. Post 8vo, pp. 338, cloth. 1884. 10s.

PURITZ.—CODE-BOOK OF GYMNASTIC EXERCISES. By Ludwig Puritz. Translated by O. Knofe and J. W. Macqueen. Illustrated. 32mo, pp. xxiv.-292, boards. 1883. 1s. 6d.

QUINET.—EDGAR QUINET. See English and Foreign Philosophical Library, Vol. XIV.

RAM RAZ.—ESSAY ON THE ARCHITECTURE OF THE HINDUS. By Ram Raz, Native Judge and Magistrate of Bangalore, Corr. Mem. R.A.S. With 48 Plates. 4to, pp. xiv. and 64, sewed. 1834. £2, 2s.

RAMSAY.—TABULAR LIST OF ALL THE AUSTRALIAN BIRDS AT PRESENT KNOWN TO THE AUTHOR, showing the distribution of the species. By E. P. Ramsay, F.L.S., &c.. Curator of the Australian Museum, Sydney. 8vo, pp. 36, and Map ; boards. 1878. 5s.

RASK.—GRAMMAR OF THE ANGLO-SAXON TONGUE, from the Danish of Erasmus Rask. By Benjamin Thorpe. Third Edition, corrected and improved, with Plate. Post 8vo, pp. vi. and 192, cloth. 1879. 5s. 6d.

RASK.—A SHORT TRACTATE on the Longevity ascribed to the Patriarchs in the Book of Genesis, and its relation to the Hebrew Chronology ; the Flood, the Exodus of the Israelites, the Site of Eden, &c. From the Danish of the late Professor Rask, with his manuscript corrections, and large additions from his autograph, now for the first time printed. With a Map of Paradise and the circumjacent Lands. Crown 8vo, pp. 134, cloth. 1863. 2s. 6d.

RAVENSTEIN.—THE RUSSIANS ON THE AMUR ; its Discovery, Conquest, and Colonization, with a Description of the Country, its Inhabitants, Productions, and Commercial Capabilities, and Personal Accounts of Russian Travellers. By E. G. Ravenstein, F.R.G.S. With 4 tinted Lithographs and 3 Maps. 8vo, pp. 500, cloth. 1861. 15s.

RAVENSTEIN AND HULLEY.—THE GYMNASIUM AND ITS FITTINGS. By E. G. Ravenstein and John Hulley. With 14 Plates of Illustrations. 8vo, pp. 32, sewed. 1867. 2s. 6d.

RAVERTY.—NOTES ON AFGHANISTAN AND PART OF BALUCHISTAN, Geographical, Ethnographical, and Historical, extracted from the Writings of little known Afghan, and Tajyik Historians, &c., &c., and from Personal Observation. By Major H. G. Raverty, Bombay Native Infantry (Retired). Foolscap folio. Sections I. and II., pp. 98, wrapper. 1880. 2s. Section III., pp. vi. and 218. 1881. 5s. Section IV. 1884. 3s.

READE.—THE MARTYRDOM OF MAN. By Winwood Reade. Eighth Edition. Crown 8vo, pp. viii. and 544, cloth. 1884. 7s. 6d.

RECORD OFFICE.—A SEPARATE CATALOGUE OF THE OFFICIAL PUBLICATIONS OF THE PUBLIC RECORD OFFICE, on sale by Trübner & Co., may be had on application.

RECORDS OF THE HEART. By Stella, Author of "Sappho," "The King's Stratagem," &c. Second English Edition. Crown 8vo, pp. xvi. and 188, with six steel-plate engravings, cloth. 1881. 3s. 6d.

REDHOUSE.—THE MESNEVI. See Trübner's Oriental Series.

REDHOUSE.—SIMPLIFIED OTTOMAN-TURKISH GRAMMAR. See Trübner's Collection.

REDHOUSE.—THE TURKISH VADE-MECUM OF OTTOMAN COLLOQUIAL LANGUAGE: Containing a Concise Ottoman Grammar; a Carefully Selected Vocabulary Alphabetically Arranged, in two Parts, English and Turkish, and Turkish and English; Also a few Familiar Dialogues and Naval and Military Terms. The whole in English Characters. the Pronunciation being fully indicated. By J. W. Redhouse, M.R.A.S. Third Edition. 32mo, pp. viii. and 372, cloth. 1882. 6s.

REDHOUSE.—ON THE HISTORY, SYSTEM, AND VARIETIES OF TURKISH POETRY. Illustrated by Selections in the Original and in English Paraphrase, with a Notice of the Islamic Doctrine of the Immortality of Woman's Soul in the Future State. By J. W. Redhouse, Esq., M.R.A.S. 8vo, pp. 62, cloth, 2s. 6d.; wrapper, 1s. 6d. 1879.

REEMELIN.—A CRITICAL REVIEW OF AMERICAN POLITICS. By C. Reemelin, of Cincinnati, Ohio. Demy 8vo, pp. xxiv. and 630, cloth. 1881. 14s.

RELIGION IN EUROPE HISTORICALLY CONSIDERED: An Essay in Verse. By the Author of "The Thames." Fcap. 8vo, pp. iv. and 152, cloth. 1883. 2s. 6d.

RENAN.—PHILOSOPHICAL DIALOGUES AND FRAGMENTS. From the French of Ernest Renan. Translated, with the sanction of the Author, by Ras Bihari Mukharji. Post 8vo, pp. xxxii. and 182, cloth. 1883. 7s. 6d.

RENAN.—AN ESSAY ON THE AGE AND ANTIQUITY OF THE BOOK OF NABATHÆAN AGRICULTURE. To which is added an Inaugural Lecture on the Position of the Shemitic Nations in the History of Civilisation. By Ernest Renan. Crown 8vo, pp. xvi. and 148, cloth. 1862. 3s. 6d.

RENAN.—THE LIFE OF JESUS. By Ernest Renan. Authorised English Translation. Crown 8vo, pp. xii. and 312, cloth. 2s. 6d.; sewed, 1s. 6d.

REPORT OF A GENERAL CONFERENCE OF LIBERAL THINKERS, for the discussion of matters pertaining to the religious needs of our time, and the methods of meeting them. Held June 13th and 14th, 1878, at South Place Chapel, Finsbury, London. 8vo, pp. 77, sewed. 1878. 1s.

RHODES.—UNIVERSAL CURVE TABLES FOR FACILITATING THE LAYING OUT OF CIRCULAR ARCS ON THE GROUND FOR RAILWAYS, CANALS, &c. Together with Table of Tangential Angles and Multiples. By Alexander Rhodes, C.E. Oblong 18mo, band, pp. ix. and 104, roan. 1881. 5s.

RHYS.—LECTURES ON WELSH PHILOLOGY. By John Rhys, M.A., Professor of Celtic at Oxford, Honorary Fellow of Jesus College, &c., &c. Second Edition, Revised and Enlarged. Crown 8vo, pp. xiv. and 467, cloth. 1879. 15s.

RICE.—MYSORE AND COORG. A Gazetteer compiled for the Government of India. By Lewis Rice, Director of Public Instruction, Mysore and Coorg. Vol. I. Mysore in General. With 2 Coloured Maps. Vol. II. Mysore, by Districts. With 10 Coloured Maps. Vol. III. Coorg. With a Map. 3 vols. royal 8vo, pp. xii. 670 and xvi.; 544 and xxii.; and 427 and xxvii., cloth. 1878. 25s.

RICE.—MYSORE INSCRIPTIONS. Translated for the Government by Lewis Rice. 8vo, pp. xcii. and 336–xxx., with a Frontispiece and Map, boards. 1879. 30s.

RIDLEY.—KÁMILARÓI, AND OTHER AUSTRALIAN LANGUAGES. By the Rev. William Ridley, B.A. Second Edition, revised and enlarged by the author; with comparative Tables of Words from twenty Australian Languages, and Songs, Traditions, Laws, and Customs of the Australian Race. Small 4to, pp. vi. and 172, cloth. 1877. 10s. 6d.

RIG-VEDA-SANHITA. A Collection of Ancient Hindu Hymns. Constituting the 1st to the 8th Ashtakas, or Books of the Rig-Veda; the oldest authority for the Religious and Social Institutions of the Hindus. Translated from the Original Sanskrit. By the late H. H. Wilson, M.A., F.R.S.. &c., &c.

     Vol. I. 8vo, pp. lii. and 348, cloth. 21s.

     Vol. II. 8vo, pp. xxx. and 346, cloth. 1854. 21s.

     Vol. III. 8vo, pp. xxiv. and 525, cloth. 1857. 21s.

     Vol. IV. Edited by E. B. Cowell, M.A. 8vo, pp. 214, cloth. 1866. 14s.

     Vols. V. and VI. in the Press.

RILEY.—MEDIÆVAL CHRONICLES OF THE CITY OF LONDON. Chronicles of the Mayors and Sheriffs of London, and the Events which happened in their Days, from the Year A.D. 1188 to A.D. 1274. Translated from the original Latin of the "Liber de Antiquis Legibus" (published by the Camden Society), in the possession of the Corporation of the City of London ; attributed to Arnold Fitz-Thedmar, Alderman of London in the Reign of Henry III.—Chronicles of London, and of the Marvels therein, between the Years 44 Henry III., A.D. 1260, and 17 Edward III., A.D. 1343. Translated from the original Anglo-Norman of the "Croniques de London," preserved in the Cottonian Collection (Cleopatra A. iv.) in the British Museum. Translated, with copious Notes and Appendices, by Henry Thomas Riley, M.A., Clare Hall, Cambridge, Barrister-at-Law. 4to, pp. xii. and 319, cloth. 1863. 12s.

RIOLA.—HOW TO LEARN RUSSIAN : a Manual for Students of Russian, based upon the Ollendorffian System of Teaching Languages, and adapted for Self-Instruction. By Henry Riola, Teacher of the Russian Language. With a Preface by W.R.S. Ralston, M.A. Second Edition. Crown 8vo, pp. 576, cloth. 1883. 12s. KEY to the above. Crown 8vo, pp. 126, cloth. 1878. 5s.

RIOLA.—A GRADUATED RUSSIAN READER, with a Vocabulary of all the Russian Words contained in it. By Henry Riola, Author of "How to Learn Russian." Crown 8vo, pp. viii. and 314, cloth. 1879. 10s. 6d.

RIPLEY.—SACRED RHETORIC ; or, Composition and Delivery of Sermons. By Henry I. Ripley. 12mo, pp. 234, cloth. 1858. 2s. 6d.

ROCHE.—A FRENCH GRAMMAR, for the use of English Students, adopted for the Public Schools by the Imperial Council of Public Instruction. By A. Roche. Crown 8vo, pp. xii. and 176, cloth. 1869. 3s.

ROCHE.—PROSE AND POETRY. Select Pieces from the best English Authors, for Reading, Composition, and Translation. By A. Roche. Second Edition. Fcap. 8vo, pp. viii. and 226, cloth. 1872. 2s. 6d.

ROCKHILL.—UDANAVARGA. See Trübner's Oriental Series.

ROCKHILL.—THE LIFE OF THE BUDDHA. See Trübner's Oriental Series.

RODD.—THE BIRDS OF CORNWALL AND THE SCILLY ISLANDS. By the late Edward Hearle Rodd. Edited, with an Introduction, Appendix, and Memoir, by J. E. Harting. 8vo, pp. lvi. and 320, with Portrait and Map, cloth. 1880. 14s.

ROGERS.—THE WAVERLEY DICTIONARY : An Alphabetical Arrangement of all the Characters in Sir Walter Scott's Waverley Novels, with a Descriptive Analysis of each Character, and Illustrative Selections from the Text. By May Rogers. 12mo, pp. 358, cloth. 1879. 10s.

ROSING.—ENGLISH-DANISH DICTIONARY. By S. Rosing. Crown 8vo, pp. x. and 722, cloth. 8s. 6d.

ROSS.—ALPHABETICAL MANUAL OF BLOWPIPE ANALYSIS ; showing all known Methods, Old and New. By Lieut.-Colonel W. A. Ross, late R.A., Member of the German Chemical Society (Author of "Pyrology, or Fire Chemistry"). Crown 8vo, pp. xii. and 148, cloth. 1880. 5s.

ROSS.—PYROLOGY, OR FIRE CHEMISTRY ; a Science interesting to the General Philosopher, and an Art of infinite importance to the Chemist, Metallurgist, Engineer, &c., &c. By W. A. Ross, lately a Major in the Royal Artillery. Small 4to, pp. xxviii. and 346, cloth. 1875. 36s.

ROSS.—CELEBRITIES OF THE YORKSHIRE WOLDS. By Frederick Ross, Fellow of the Royal Historical Society. 12mo, pp. 202, cloth. 1878. 4s.

ROSS.—THE EARLY HISTORY OF LAND HOLDING AMONG THE GERMANS. By Denman W. Ross, Ph.D. 8vo, pp. viii. and 274, cloth. 1883. 12s.

ROSS.—COREAN PRIMER : being Lessons in Corean on all Ordinary Subjects. Transliterated on the principles of the "Mandarin Primer," by the same author. By Rev. John Ross, Newchwang. 8vo, pp. 90, wrapper. 1877. 10s.

ROSS.—HONOUR OR SHAME? By R. S. Ross. 8vo, pp. 183. 1878. Cloth. 3s. 6d. ; paper, 2s. 6d.

ROSS.--REMOVAL OF THE INDIAN TROOPS TO MALTA. By R. S. Ross. 8vo, pp. 77, paper. 1878. 1s. 6d.

ROSS.—THE MONK OF ST. GALL. A Dramatic Adaptation of Scheffel's "Ekkehard." By R. S. Ross. Crown 8vo, pp. xii. and 218. 1879. 5s.

ROSS.—ARIADNE IN NAXOS. By R. S. Ross. Square 16mo, pp. 200, cloth. 1882. 5s.

ROTH.—NOTES ON CONTINENTAL IRRIGATION. By H. L. Roth. Demy 8vo, pp. 40, with 8 Plates, cloth. 1882. 5s.

ROUGH NOTES OF JOURNEYS made in the years 1868-1873 in Syria, down the Tigris, India, Kashmir, Ceylon, Japan, Mongolia, Siberia, the United States, the Sandwich Islands, and Australasia. Demy 8vo, pp. 624, cloth. 1875. 14s.

ROUSTAING.—THE FOUR GOSPELS EXPLAINED BY THEIR WRITERS. With an Appendix on the Ten Commandments. Edited by J. B. Roustaing. Translated by W. E. Kirby. 3 vols. crown 8vo, pp. 440-456-304, cloth. 1881. 15s.

ROUTLEDGE.—ENGLISH RULE AND NATIVE OPINION IN INDIA. From Notes taken in 1870-74. By James Routledge. 8vo, pp. x. and 338, cloth. 1878. 10s. 6d.

ROWE.—AN ENGLISHMAN'S VIEWS ON QUESTIONS OF THE DAY IN VICTORIA. By C. J. Rowe, M.A. Crown 8vo, pp. 122, cloth. 1882. 4s.

ROWLEY.— ORNITHOLOGICAL MISCELLANY. By George Dawson Rowley, M.A., F.Z.S. Vol. I. Part 1, 15s.—Part 2, 20s.—Part 3, 20s.—Part 4, 20s.
   Vol. II. Part 5, 20s.—Part 6, 20s.—Part 7, 10s. 6d.—Part 8, 10s. 6d.—Part 9, 10s. 6d.—Part 10, 10s. 6d.
   Vol. III. Part 11, 10s. 6d.—Part 12, 10s. 6d.—Part 13, 10s. 6d.—Part 14, 20s.

ROYAL SOCIETY OF LONDON (THE).—CATALOGUE OF SCIENTIFIC PAPERS (1800-1863), Compiled and Published by the Royal Society of London. Demy 4to, cloth, per vol. £1; in half-morocco, £1, 8s. Vol. I. (1867), A to Cluzel. pp. lxxix. and 960; Vol. II. (1863), Coaklay—Graydon. pp. iv. and 1012; Vol. III. (1869), Greatheed—Leze. pp. v. and 1002; Vol. IV. (1870), L'Héritier de Brutille—Pozzetti. pp. iv. and 1006; Vol. V. (1871), Praag—Tizzani. pp. iv. and 1000; Vol. VI. (1872), Tkalec—Zylius, Anonymous and Additions. pp. xi. and 763. Continuation of above (1864-1873): Vol. VII. (1877), A to Hyrtl. pp. xxxi. and 1047; Vol. VIII. (1879), Ibañez—Zwicky. pp. 1310. A List of the Publications of the Royal Society (Separate Papers from the Philosophical Transactions), on application.

RUNDALL.—A SHORT AND EASY WAY TO WRITE ENGLISH AS SPOKEN. Méthode Rapide et Facile d'Ecrire le Français comme on le Parle. Kurze und Leichte Weise Deutsch zu Schreiben wie man es Spricht. By J. B. Rundall, Certificated Member of the London Shorthand Writers' Association. 6d. each.

RUSSELL.—THE WAVE OF TRANSLATION IN THE OCEANS OF WATER, AIR, AND ETHER. By John Scott Russell, M.A., F.R.S.S. L. and E. Demy 8vo, pp. 318, with 10 Diagrams, cloth. 1885. 12s. 6d.

RUTHERFORD.—THE AUTOBIOGRAPHY OF MARK RUTHERFORD, Dissenting Minister. Edited by his friend, Reuben Shapcott. Crown 8vo, pp. xii. and 180, boards. 1881. 5s.

RUTHERFORD.—MARK RUTHERFORD'S DELIVERANCE: Being the Second Part of his Autobiography. Edited by his friend, Reuben Shapcott. Crown 8vo, pp. viii. and 210, boards. 1885. 5s.

RUTTER.—See BUNYAN.

SÂMAVIDHÂNABRÂHMANA (THE) (being the Third Brâhmana) of the Sâma Veda. Edited, together with the Commentary of Sâyana, an English Translation, Introduction, and Index of Words, by A. C. Burnell. Vol. I. Text and Commentary, with Introduction. Demy 8vo, pp. xxxviii. and 104, cloth. 1873. 12s. 6d.

SAMUELSON.—HISTORY OF DRINK. A Review, Social, Scientific, and Political. By James Samuelson, of the Middle Temple, Barrister-at-Law. Second Edition. 8vo, pp. xxviii. and 288, cloth. 1880. 6s.

SAND.—MOLIÈRE. A Drama in Prose. By George Sand. Edited, with Notes, by Th. Karcher, LL.B. 12mo, pp. xx. and 170, cloth. 1868. 3s. 6d.

SARTORIUS.—MEXICO. Landscapes and Popular Sketches. By C. Sartorius. Edited by Dr. Gaspey. With Engravings, from Sketches by M. Rugendas. 4to, pp. vi. and 202, cloth gilt. 1859. 18s.

SATOW.—AN ENGLISH JAPANESE DICTIONARY OF THE SPOKEN LANGUAGE. By Ernest Mason Satow, Japanese Secretary to H.M. Legation at Yedo, and Ishibashi Masakata of the Imperial Japanese Foreign Office. Second Edition. Imperial 32mo. pp. xv. and 416, cloth. 1879. 12s. 6d.

SAVAGE.—THE MORALS OF EVOLUTION. By M. J. Savage, Author of "The Religion of Evolution," &c. Crown 8vo, pp. 192, cloth. 1880. 5s.

SAVAGE.—BELIEF IN GOD; an Examination of some Fundamental Theistic Problems. By M. J. Savage. To which is added an Address on the Intellectual Basis of Faith. By W. H. Savage. 8vo, pp. 176, cloth. 1881. 5s.

SAVAGE.—BELIEFS ABOUT MAN. By M. J. Savage. Crown 8vo, pp. 130, cloth. 1882. 5s.

SAYCE.—AN ASSYRIAN GRAMMAR for Comparative Purposes. By A. H. Sayce, M.A., Fellow and Tutor of Queen's College, Oxford. Crown 8vo, pp. xvi. and 188. cloth. 1872. 7s. 6d.

SAYCE.—THE PRINCIPLES OF COMPARATIVE PHILOLOGY. By A. H. Sayce, M.A. Crown 8vo, pp. 384, cloth. 1874. 10s. 6d.

SCHAIBLE.—AN ESSAY ON THE SYSTEMATIC TRAINING OF THE BODY. By C. H. Schaible, M.D., &c., &c. A Memorial Essay, Published on the occasion of the first Centenary Festival of Frederick L. Jahn, with an Etching by H. Herkomer. Crown 8vo, pp. xviii. and 124, cloth. 1878. 5s.

SCHEFFEL.—MOUNTAIN PSALMS. By J. V. von Scheffel. Translated by Mrs. F. Brunnow. Fcap., pp. 62, with 6 Plates after designs by A. Von Werner. Parchment. 1882. 3s. 6d.

SCHILLER.—THE BRIDE OF MESSINA. Translated from the German of Schiller in English Verse. By Emily Allfrey. Crown 8vo, pp. viii. and 110, cloth. 1876. 2s.

SCHLAGINTWEIT.—BUDDHISM IN TIBET: Illustrated by Literary Documents and Objects of Religious Worship. By Emil Schlagintweit, LL.D. With a folio Atlas of 20 Plates, and 20 Tables of Native Print in the Text. Roy. 8vo, pp. xxiv. and 404. 1863. £2, 2s.

SCHLAU, SCHLAUER, AM SCHLÄUESTEN.—Facsimile of a Manuscript supposed to have been found in an Egyptian Tomb by the English Soldiers. Royal 8vo, in ragged canvas covers, with string binding, and dilapidated edges (? just as discovered). 1884. 6s.

SCHLEICHER.—A COMPENDIUM OF THE COMPARATIVE GRAMMAR OF THE INDO-EUROPEAN, SANSKRIT, GREEK, AND LATIN LANGUAGES. By August Schleicher. Translated from the Third German Edition, by Herbert Bendall, B.A., Chr. Coll., Camb. 8vo. Part I., Phonology. Pp. 184, cloth. 1874. 7s. 6d. Part II., Morphology. Pp. viii. and 104, cloth. 1877. 6s.

SCHOPENHAUER.—THE WORLD AS WILL AND IDEA. By Arthur Schopenhauer. Translated from the German by R. B. HALDANE, M.A., and J. KEMP, M.A. Vol. I., containing Four Books. Post 8vo, pp. xxxii.-532, cloth. 1883. 18s.

SCHULTZ.—UNIVERSAL DOLLAR TABLES (Complete United States). Covering all Exchanges between the United States and Great Britain, France, Belgium, Switzerland, Italy, Spain, and Germany. By C. W. H. Schultz. 8vo, cloth. 1874. 15s.

SCHULTZ.—UNIVERSAL INTEREST AND GENERAL PERCENTAGE TABLES. On the Decimal System. With a Treatise on the Currency of the World, and numerous examples for Self-Instruction. By C. W. H. Schultz. 8vo, cloth. 1874. 10s. 6d.

SCHULTZ.—ENGLISH GERMAN EXCHANGE TABLES. By C. W. H. Schultz. With a Treatise on the Currency of the World. 8vo. boards. 1874. 5s.

SCHWENDLER.—INSTRUCTIONS FOR TESTING TELEGRAPH LINES, and the Technical Arrangements in Offices. Written on behalf of the Government of India, under the Orders of the Director-General of Telegraphs in India. By Louis Schwendler. Vol. I., demy 8vo, pp. 248, cloth. 1878. 12s. Vol. II., demy 8vo, pp. xi. and 268, cloth. 1880. 9s.

SCOONES.—FAUST. A Tragedy. By Goethe. Translated into English Verse, by William Dalton Scoones. Fcap., pp. vi. and 230, cloth. 1879. 5s.

SCOTT.—THE ENGLISH LIFE OF JESUS. By Thomas Scott. Crown 8vo, pp. xxviii. and 350, cloth. 1879. 2s. 6d.

SCOTUS.—A NOTE ON MR. GLADSTONE'S "The Peace to Come." By Scotus. 8vo, pp. 106. 1878. Cloth, 2s. 6d. ; paper wrapper, 1s. 6d.

SELL.—THE FAITH OF ISLAM. By the Rev. E. Sell, Fellow of the University of Madras. Demy 8vo, pp. xiv. and 270, cloth. 1881. 6s. 6d.

SELL.—IHN-I-TAJWID ; OR, ART OF READING THE QURAN. By the Rev. E. Sell, B.D. 8vo, pp. 48, wrappers. 1882. 2s. 6d.

SELSS.—GOETHE'S MINOR POEMS. Selected, Annotated, and Rearranged. By Albert M. Selss, Ph.D. Crown 8vo, pp. xxxi. and 152, cloth. 1875. 3s. 6d.

SERMONS NEVER PREACHED. By Philip Phosphor. Crown 8vo, pp. vi. and 124, cloth. 1878. 2s. 6d.

SEWELL.—REPORT ON THE AMARAVATI TOPE, and Excavations on its Site in 1877. By Robert Sewell, of the Madras C.S., &c. With four plates. Royal 4to, pp. 70, boards. 1880. 3s.

SHADWELL.—POLITICAL ECONOMY FOR THE PEOPLE. By J. L. Shadwell, Author of "A System of Political Economy." Fcap., pp. vi. and 154, limp cloth. 1880. 1s. 6d.

SHAKESPEARE.—A NEW STUDY OF SHAKESPEARE : An Inquiry into the connection of the Plays and Poems, with the origins of the Classical Drama, and with the Platonic Philosophy, through the Mysteries. Demy 8vo, pp. xii. and 372, with Photograph of the Stratford Bust, cloth. 1884. 10s. 6d.

SHAKESPEARE'S CENTURIE OF PRAYSE ; being Materials for a History of Opinion on Shakespeare and his Works, culled from Writers of the First Century after his Rise. By C. M. Ingleby. Medium 8vo, pp. xx. and 384. Stiff cover. 1874. £1, 1s. Large paper, fcap. 4to, boards. £2, 2s.

SHAKESPEARE.—HERMENEUTICS ; OR, THE STILL LION. Being an Essay towards the Restoration of Shakespeare's Text. By C. M. Ingleby, M.A., LL.D., of Trinity College, Cambridge. Small 4to, pp. 168, boards. 1875. 6s.

SHAKESPEARE.—THE MAN AND THE BOOK. By C. M. Ingleby, M.A., LL.D. Small 4to. Part I., pp. 172, boards. 1877. 6s.

SHAKESPEARE.—OCCASIONAL PAPERS ON SHAKESPEARE ; being the Second Part of "Shakespeare : the Man and the Book." By C. M. Ingleby, M.A., LL.D., V.P.R.S.L. Small 4to, pp. x. and 194, paper boards. 1881. 6s.

SHAKESPEARE'S BONES.—The Proposal to Disinter them, considered in relation to their possible bearing on his Portraiture : Illustrated by instances of Visits of the Living to the Dead. By C. M. Ingleby, LL.D., V.P.R.S.L. Fcap. 4to, pp. viii. and 48, boards. 1883. 1s. 6d.

SHAKESPEARE.—A NEW VARIORUM EDITION OF SHAKESPEARE. Edited by Horace Howard Furness. Royal 8vo. Vol. I. Romeo and Juliet. Pp. xxiii. and 480, cloth. 1871. 18s.—Vol. II. Macbeth. Pp. xix. and 492. 1873. 18s.—Vols. III. and IV. Hamlet. 2 vols. pp. xx. and 474 and 430. 1877. 36s.—Vol. V. King Lear. Pp. vi. and 504. 1880. 18s.

SHAKESPEARE.—CONCORDANCE TO SHAKESPEARE'S POEMS. By Mrs. H. H. Furness. Royal 8vo, cloth. 18s.

SHAKSPERE SOCIETY (THE NEW).—Subscription, One Guinea per annum. List of Publications on application.

SHERRING.—THE SACRED CITY OF THE HINDUS. An Account of Benares in Ancient and Modern Times. By the Rev. M. A. Sherring, M.A., LL.D. ; and Prefaced with an Introduction by FitzEdward Hall, D.C.L. With Illustrations. 8vo, pp. xxxvi. and 388, cloth. 21s.

SHERRING.—HINDU TRIBES AND CASTES; together with an Account of the Mohamedan Tribes of the North-West Frontier and of the Aboriginal Tribes of the Central Provinces. By the Rev. M. A. Sherring, M.A., LL.B., Lond., &c. 4to. Vol. II. Pp. lxviii. and 376, cloth. 1879. £2, 8s.—Vol. III., with Index of 3 vols. Pp. xii. and 336, cloth. 1881. 32s.

SHERRING.—THE HINDOO PILGRIMS. By Rev. M. A. Sherring, M.A., LL.D. Crown 8vo, pp. 126, cloth. 1878. 5s.

SHIELDS.—THE FINAL PHILOSOPHY; or, System of Perfectible Knowledge issuing from the Harmony of Science and Religion. By Charles W. Shields. D.D., Professor in Princeton College. Royal 8vo, pp. viii. and 610, cloth. 1878. 18s.

SIBREE.—THE GREAT AFRICAN ISLAND. Chapters on Madagascar. A Popular Account of Recent Researches in the Physical Geography, Geology, and Exploration of the Country, and its Natural History and Botany; and in the Origin and Divisions, Customs and Language, Superstitions, Folk-lore, and Religious Beliefs and Practices of the Different Tribes. Together with Illustrations of Scripture and Early Church History from Native Habits and Missionary Experience. By the Rev. James Sibree, jun., F.R.G.S., Author of "Madagascar and its People," &c. 8vo, pp. xii. and 272, with Physical and Ethnological Maps and Four Illustrations, cloth. 1879. 12s.

SIBREE.—POEMS: including "Fancy," "A Resting Place," &c. By John Sibree, M.A., London. Crown 8vo, pp. iv. and 134, cloth. 1884. 4s.

SIMCOX.—EPISODES IN THE LIVES OF MEN, WOMEN, AND LOVERS. By Edith Simcox. Crown 8vo, pp. 312, cloth. 1882. 7s. 6d.

SIMCOX.—NATURAL LAW. See English and Foreign Philosophical Library, Vol. IV.

SIME.—LESSING. See English and Foreign Philosophical Library, Extra Series, Vols. I. and II.

SIMPSON-BAIKIE.—THE DRAMATIC UNITIES IN THE PRESENT DAY. By E. Simpson-Baikie. Third Edition. Fcap. 8vo, pp. iv. and 108, cloth. 1878. 2s. 6d.

SIMPSON-BAIKIE.—THE INTERNATIONAL DICTIONARY for Naturalists and Sportsmen in English, French, and German. By Edwin Simpson-Baikie. 8vo, pp. iv. and 284, cloth. 1880. 15s.

SINCLAIR.—THE MESSENGER: A Poem. By Thomas Sinclair, M.A. Foolscap 8vo, pp. 174, cloth. 1875. 5s.

SINCLAIR.—LOVES'S TRILOGY: A Poem. By Thomas Sinclair, M.A. Crown 8vo, pp. 150, cloth. 1876. 5s.

SINCLAIR.—THE MOUNT: Speech from its English Heights. By Thomas Sinclair, M.A. Crown 8vo, pp. viii. and 302, cloth. 1877. 10s.

SINCLAIR.—GODDESS FORTUNE: A Novel. By Thomas Sinclair, Author of "The Messenger," &c. Three vols., post 8vo, pp. viii.-302, 302, 274, cloth. 1884. 31s. 6d.

SINGER.—HUNGARIAN GRAMMAR. See Trübner's Collection.

SINNETT.—THE OCCULT WORLD. By A. P. Sinnett. Fourth Edition. With an Appendix of 20 pages, on the subject of Mr. Kiddle's Charge of Plagiarism. 8vo, pp. xx. and 206, cloth. 1884. 3s. 6d.

SINNETT.—ESOTERIC BUDDHISM. By A. P. Sinnett, Author of "The Occult World," President of the Simla Eclectic Philosophical Society. Fourth Edition. Crown 8vo, pp. xx.-216, cloth. 1885. 7s. 6d.

SMITH.—THE DIVINE GOVERNMENT. By S. Smith, M.D. Fifth Edition. Crown 8vo, pp. xii. and 276, cloth. 1866. 6s.

SMITH.—THE RECENT DEPRESSION OF TRADE. Its Nature, its Causes, and the Remedies which have been suggested for it. By Walter E. Smith, B.A., New College. Being the Oxford Cobden Prize Essay for 1879. Crown 8vo, pp. vi. and 108, cloth. 1880. 3s.

SMYTH.—THE ABORIGINES OF VICTORIA. With Notes relating to the Habits of the Natives of other Parts of Australia and Tasmania. Compiled from various sources for the Government of Victoria. By R. Brough Smyth, F.L.S., F.G.S., &c., &c. 2 vols. royal 8vo, pp. lxxii.-484 and vi.-456, Maps, Plates, and Woodcuts, cloth. 1878. £3, 3s.

SNOW—A Theologico-Political Treatise.   By G. D. Snow.   Crown 8vo, pp. 180, cloth.   1874.   4s. 6d.

SOLLING.—Diutiska: An Historical and Critical Survey of the Literature of Germany, from the Earliest Period to the Death of Goethe.   By Gustav Solling.   8vo, pp. xviii. and 368.   1863.   10s. 6d.

SOLLING.—Select Passages from the Works of Shakespeare.   Translated and Collected.   German and English.   By G. Solling.   12mo, pp. 155, cloth.   1866.   3s. 6d.

SOLLING.—Macbeth.   Rendered into Metrical German (with English Text adjoined).   By Gustav Solling.   Crown 8vo, pp. 160, wrapper.   1878.   3s. 6d.

SONGS of the Semitic in English Verse.   By G. E. W.   Crown 8vo, pp. iv. and 134, cloth.   1877.   5s.

SOUTHALL.—The Epoch of the Mammoth and the Apparition of Man upon Earth.   By James C. Southall, A.M., LL.D.   Crown 8vo, pp. xii. and 430, cloth.   Illustrated.   1878.   10s. 6d.

SPANISH REFORMERS of Two Centuries from 1520; Their Lives and Writing, according to the late Benjamin B. Wiffen's Plan, and with the Use of His Materials.   Described by E. Boehmer, D.D., Ph.D.   Vol. I.   With B. B. Wiffen's Narrative of the Incidents attendant upon the Republication of Reformistas Antiguos Españoles, and with a Memoir of B. B. Wiffen.   By Isaline Wiffen.   Royal 8vo, pp. xvi. and 216, cloth.   1874.   12s. 6d.   Roxburghe, 15s.—Vol. II.   Royal 8vo, pp. xii.-374, cloth.   1883.   18s.

SPEDDING.—The Life and Times of Francis Bacon.   Extracted from the Edition of his Occasional Writings, by James Spedding.   2 vols. post 8vo, pp. xx.-710 and xiv.-708, cloth.   1878.   21s.

SPIERS.—The School System of the Talmud.   By the Rev. B. Spiers.   8vo, pp. 48, cloth.   1882.   2s. 6d.

SPINOZA.—Benedict de Spinoza: his Life, Correspondence, and Ethics.   By R. Willis, M.D.   8vo, pp. xliv. and 648, cloth.   1870.   21s.

SPINOZA.—Ethic Demonstrated in Geometrical Order and Divided into Five Parts, which treat—I. Of God; II. Of the Nature and Origin of the Mind; III. Of the Origin and Nature of the Affects; IV. Of Human Bondage, or of the Strength of the Affects; V. Of the Power of the Intellect, or of Human Liberty.   By Benedict de Spinoza.   Translated from the Latin by W. Hale White.   Post 8vo, pp. 328, cloth.   1883.   10s. 6d.

SPIRITUAL EVOLUTION, An Essay on, considered in its bearing upon Modern Spiritualism, Science, and Religion.   By J. P. B.   Crown 8vo, pp. 156, cloth.   1879.   3s.

SPRUNER.—Dr. Karl Von Spruner's Historico-Geographical Hand-Atlas, containing 26 Coloured Maps.   Obl. cloth.   1861.   15s.

SQUIER.—Honduras; Descriptive, Historical, and Statistical.   By E. G. Squier, M.A., F.S.A.   Cr. 8vo, pp. viii. and 278, cloth.   1870.   3s. 6d.

STATIONERY OFFICE.—Publications of Her Majesty's Stationery Office.   List on application.

STEDMAN.—Oxford: Its Social and Intellectual Life.   With Remarks and Hints on Expenses, the Examinations, &c.   By Algernon M. M. Stedman, B.A., Wadham College, Oxford.   Crown 8vo, pp. xvi. and 309, cloth.   1878.   7s. 6d.

STEELE.—An Eastern Love Story.   Kusa Játakaya: A Buddhistic Legendary Poem, with other Stories.   By Th. Steele.   Cr. 8vo, pp. xii. and 260, cl.   1871.   6s.

STENT.—THE JADE CHAPLET. In Twenty-four Beads. A Collection of Songs, Ballads, &c. (from the Chinese). By G. C. Stent, M.N.C.B.R.A.S. Post 8vo, pp. viii. and 168, cloth. 1874. 5s.

STENZLER.—See AUCTORES SANSKRITI, Vol. II.

STOCK.—ATTEMPTS AT TRUTH. By St. George Stock. Crown 8vo, pp. **vi.** and 248, cloth. 1882. 5s.

STOKES.—GOIDELICA—Old and Early-Middle Irish Glosses: Prose and Verse. Edited by Whitley Stokes. 2d Edition. Med. 8vo, pp. 192, cloth. 1872. 18s.

STOKES.—BEUNANS MERIASEK. The Life of Saint Meriasek, Bishop and Confessor. A Cornish Drama. Edited, with a Translation and Notes, by Whitley Stokes. Med. 8vo, pp. xvi. and 280, and Facsimile, cloth. 1872. 15s.

STOKES.—TOGAIL TROY, THE DESTRUCTION OF TROY. Transcribed from the Facsimile of the Book of Leinster, and Translated, with a Glossarial Index of the Rarer Words, by Whitley Stokes. Crown 8vo, pp. xvi. and 188, paper boards. 1882. 18s.

STOKES.—THREE MIDDLE-IRISH HOMILIES ON THE LIVES OF SAINTS—PATRICK, BRIGIT, AND COLUMBA. Edited by Whitley Stokes. Crown 8vo, pp. xii. and 140, paper boards. 1882. 10s. 6d.

STRANGE.—THE BIBLE; is it "The Word of God"? By Thomas Lumisden Strange. Demy 8vo, pp. xii. and 384, cloth. 1871. 7s.

STRANGE.—THE SPEAKER'S COMMENTARY. Reviewed by T. L. Strange. Cr. 8vo, pp. viii. and 159, cloth. 1871. 2s. 6d.

STRANGE.—THE DEVELOPMENT OF CREATION ON THE EARTH. By T. L. Strange. Demy 8vo, pp. xii. and 110, cloth. 1874. 2s. 6d.

STRANGE.—THE LEGENDS OF THE OLD TESTAMENT. By T. L. Strange. Demy 8vo, pp. xii. and 244, cloth. 1874. 5s.

STRANGE.—THE SOURCES AND DEVELOPMENT OF CHRISTIANITY. By Thomas Lumisden Strange. Demy 8vo, pp. xx. and 256, cloth. 1875. 5s.

STRANGE.—WHAT IS CHRISTIANITY? An Historical Sketch. Illustrated with a Chart. By T. L. Strange. Foolscap 8vo, pp. 72, cloth. 1880. 2s. 6d.

STRANGE.—CONTRIBUTIONS TO A SERIES OF CONTROVERSIAL WRITINGS, issued by the late Mr. Thomas Scott, of Upper Norwood. By Thomas Lumisden Strange. Fcap. 8vo, pp. viii. and 312, cloth. 1881. 2s. 6d.

STRANGFORD.—ORIGINAL LETTERS AND PAPERS OF THE LATE VISCOUNT STRANGFORD UPON PHILOLOGICAL AND KINDRED SUBJECTS. Edited by Viscountess Strangford. Post 8vo, pp. xxii. and 284, cloth. 1878. 12s. 6d.

STRATMANN.—THE TRAGICALL HISTORIE OF HAMLET, PRINCE OF DENMARKE. By William Shakespeare. Edited according to the first printed Copies, with the various Readings and Critical Notes. By F. H. Stratmann. 8vo, pp. vi. and 120, sewed. 3s. 6d.

STRATMANN.—A DICTIONARY OF THE OLD ENGLISH LANGUAGE. Compiled from Writings of the Twelfth, Thirteenth, Fourteenth, and Fifteenth Centuries. By F. H. Stratmann. Third Edition. 4to, pp. x. and 662, sewed. 1878. 30s.

STUDIES OF MAN. By a Japanese. Crown 8vo, pp. 124, cloth. 1874. 2s. 6d.

SUMNER.—WHAT SOCIAL CLASSES OWE TO EACH OTHER. By W. G. Sumner, Professor of Political and Social Science in Yale College. 18mo, pp. 170, cloth. 1884. 3s. 6d.

SUYEMATZ.—GENJI MONOGATARI. The Most Celebrated of the Classical Japanese Romances. Translated by K. Suyematz. Crown 8vo, pp. xvi. and 254, cloth. 1882. 7s. 6d.

SWEET.—SPELLING REFORM AND ENGLISH LITERATURE. By Henry Sweet, M.A. 8vo, pp. 8, wrapper. 1884. 2d.

SWEET.—HISTORY OF ENGLISH SOUNDS, from the Earliest Period, including an Investigation of the General Laws of Sound Change, and full Word Lists. By Henry Sweet. Demy 8vo, pp. iv.-164, cloth. 1874. 4s. 6d.

SWEET.—ON A MEXICAN MUSTANG THROUGH TEXAS FROM THE GULF TO THE RIO GRANDE. By Alex. E. Sweet and J. Armoy Knox, Editors of "Texas Siftings." English Copyright Edition. Demy 8vo, pp. 672. Illustrated, cloth. 1883. 10s.

SYED AHMAD.—A SERIES OF ESSAYS ON THE LIFE OF MOHAMMED, and Subjects subsidiary thereto. By Syed Ahmad Khan Bahadur, C.S.I.   8vo, pp. 532, with 4 Tables, 2 Maps, and Plate, cloth. 1870. 30s.

TALBOT.—ANALYSIS OF THE ORGANISATION OF THE PRUSSIAN ARMY. By Lieutenant Gerald F. Talbot, 2d Prussian Dragoon Guards. Royal 8vo, pp. 78, cloth. 1871. 3s.

TAYLER.—A RETROSPECT OF THE RELIGIOUS LIFE OF ENGLAND; or, Church, Puritanism, and Free Inquiry. By J. J. Tayler, B.A. Second Edition. Reissued, with an Introductory Chapter on Recent Development, by James Martineau, LL.D., D.D. Post 8vo, pp. 380, cloth. 1876. 7s. 6d.

TAYLOR.—PRINCE DEUKALION: A Lyrical Drama. By Bayard Taylor. Small 4to, pp. 172. Handsomely bound in white vellum. 1878. 12s.

TECHNOLOGICAL DICTIONARY of the Terms employed in the Arts and Sciences; Architecture; Civil Engineering; Mechanics; Machine-Making; Shipbuilding and Navigation; Metallurgy; Artillery; Mathematics; Physics; Chemistry; Mineralogy, &c. With a Preface by Dr. K. Karmarsch. Second Edition. 3 vols.

     Vol. 1. German-English-French.   8vo, pp. 646. , 12s.
     Vol. II. English-German-French.   8vo, pp. 666. 12s.
     Vol. III. French-German-English.   8vo, pp. 618. 12s.

TECHNOLOGICAL DICTIONARY.—A POCKET DICTIONARY OF TECHNICAL TERMS USED IN ARTS AND MANUFACTURES. English-German-French, Deutsch-Englisch-Französisch, Français-Allemand-Anglais. Abridged from the above Technological Dictionary by Rumpf, Mothes, and Unverzagt. With the addition of Commercial Terms. 3 vols. sq. 12mo, cloth, 12s.

TEMPLE.—THE LEGENDS OF THE PUNJAB. By Captain R. C. Temple, Bengal Staff Corps, F.G.S., &c. Vol. I., 8vo, pp. xviii.-546, cloth. 1884. £1, 6s.

THEÁTRE FRANÇAIS MODERNE.—A Selection of Modern French Plays. Edited by the Rev. P. H. E. Brette, B.D., C. Cassal, LL.D., and Th. Karcher, LL.B.

     First Series, in 1 vol. crown 8vo, cloth, 6s., containing—

CHARLOTTE CORDAY. A Tragedy. By F. Ponsard. Edited, with English Notes and Notice on Ponsard, by Professor C. Cassal, LL.D. Pp. xii. and 134. Separately, 2s. 6d.

DIANE. A Drama in Verse. By Emile Augier. Edited, with English Notes and Notice on Augier, by Th. Karcher, LL.B. Pp. xiv. and 145. Separately, 2s. 6d.

LE VOYAGE À DIEPPE, A Comedy in Prose. By Wafflard and Fulgence. Edited, with English Notes, by the Rev. P. H. E. Brette, B.D. Pp. 104. Separately, 2s. 6d.

     Second Series, crown 8vo, cloth, 6s., containing—

MOLIÈRE. A Drama in Prose. By George Sand. Edited, with English Notes and Notice of George Sand, by Th. Karcher, LL.B. Fcap. 8vo, pp. xx. and 170, cloth. Separately, 3s. 6d.

LES ARISTOCRATIES. A Comedy in Verse. By Etienne Arago. Edited, with English Notes and Notice of Etienne Arago, by the Rev. P. H. E. Brette, B.D. 2d Edition. Fcap. 8vo, pp. xiv. and 236, cloth. Separately, 4s.

THEÁTRE FRANÇAIS MODERNE—*continued.*

Third Series, crown 8vo, cloth, 6s., containing—

LES FAUX BONSHOMMES. A Comedy. By Théodore Barrière and Ernest Capendu. Edited, with English Notes and Notice on Barrière, by Professor C. Cassal, LL.D. Fcap. 8vo, pp. xvi. and 304. 1868. Separately, 4s.

L'HONNEUR ET L'ARGENT. A Comedy. By François Ponsard. Edited, with English Notes and Memoir of Ponsard, by Professor C. Cassal, LL.D. 2d Edition. Fcap. 8vo, pp. xvi. and 171, cloth. 1869. Separately, 3s. 6d.

THEISM.—A CANDID EXAMINATION OF THEISM. By Physicus. Post 8vo, pp. xviii. and 198, cloth. 1878. 7s. 6d.

THEOSOPHY AND THE HIGHER LIFE; or, Spiritual Dynamics and the Divine and Miraculous Man. By G. W., M.D., Edinburgh. President of the British Theosophical Society. 12mo, pp. iv. and 138, cloth. 1880. 3s.

THOM.—ST. PAUL'S EPISTLES TO THE CORINTHIANS. An Attempt to convey their Spirit and Significance. By the Rev. J. H. Thom. 8vo, pp. xii. and 408, cloth. 1851. 5s.

THOMAS.—EARLY SASSANIAN INSCRIPTIONS, SEALS, AND COINS, illustrating the Early History of the Sassanian Dynasty, containing Proclamations of Ardeshir Babek, Sapor I., and his Successors. With a Critical Examination and Explanation of the celebrated Inscription in the Hájíábad Cave, demonstrating that Sapor, the Conqueror of Valerian, was a professing Christian. By Edward Thomas. Illustrated. 8vo, pp. 148, cloth. 7s. 6d.

THOMAS.—THE CHRONICLES OF THE PATHAN KINGS OF DEHLI. Illustrated by Coins, Inscriptions, and other Antiquarian Remains. By E. Thomas, F.R.A.S. With Plates and Cuts. Demy 8vo, pp. xxiv. and 467, cloth. 1871. 28s.

THOMAS.—THE REVENUE RESOURCES OF THE MUGHAL EMPIRE IN INDIA, from A.D. 1593 to A.D. 1707. A Supplement to "The Chronicles of the Pathán Kings of Delhi." By E. Thomas, F.R.S. 8vo, pp. 60, cloth. 3s. 6d.

THOMAS.—SASSANIAN COINS. Communicated to the Numismatic Society of London. By E. Thomas, F.R.S. Two Parts, 12mo, pp. 43, 3 Plates and a Cut, sewed. 5s.

THOMAS.—JAINISM; OR, THE EARLY FAITH OF ASOKA. With Illustrations of the Ancient Religions of the East, from the Pantheon of the Indo-Scythians. To which is added a Notice on Bactrian Coins and Indian Dates. By Edward Thomas, F.R.S. 8vo, pp. viii.-24 and 82. With two Autotype Plates and Woodcuts. 1877. 7s. 6d.

THOMAS.—THE THEORY AND PRACTICE OF CREOLE GRAMMAR. By J. J. Thomas. 8vo, pp. viii. and 135, boards. 12s.

THOMAS.—RECORDS OF THE GUPTA DYNASTY. Illustrated by Inscriptions, Written History, Local Tradition, and Coins. To which is added a Chapter on the Arabs in Sind. By Edward Thomas, F.R.S. Folio, with a Plate, pp. iv. and 64, cloth. 14s.

THOMAS.—THE INDIAN BALHARA, and the Arabian Intercourse with India in the Ninth and following Centuries. By Edward Thomas, F.R.S. (Contained in International Numismata Orientalia. Vol. III., Part I. Coins of Arakan.) Royal 4to, pp. viii.-48, wrappers. 1882. 8s. 6d.

THOMAS.—BOYHOOD LAYS. By William Henry Thomas. 18mo, pp. iv. and 74, cloth. 1877. 2s. 6d.

THOMPSON.—DIALOGUES, RUSSIAN AND ENGLISH. Compiled by A. R. Thompson, sometime Lecturer of the English Language in the University of St. Vladimir, Kieff. Crown 8vo, pp. iv. and 132, cloth. 1882. 5s.

E

THOMSON.—Evolution and Involution. By George Thomson, Author of "The World of Being," &c. Crown 8vo, pp. viii. and 206, cloth. 1880. 5s.

THORBURN.—Bannú; or, Our Afghan Frontier. By S. S. Thorburn, F.C.S., Settlement Officer of the Bannú District. 8vo, pp. x. and 480, cloth. 1876. 18s.

THORPE.—Diplomatarium Anglicum Ævi Saxonici. A Collection of English Charters, from the reign of King Æthelberht of Kent, A.D. DCV., to that of William the Conqueror. Containing: I. Miscellaneous Charters. II. Wills. III. Guilds. IV. Manumissions and Acquittances. With a Translation of the Anglo-Saxon. By the late Benjamin Thorpe, Member of the Royal Academy of Sciences at Munich, and of the Society of Netherlandish Literature at Leyden. 8vo, pp. xlii. and 682, cloth. 1865. £1, 1s.

THOUGHTS ON LOGIC; or, the S.N.I.X. Propositional Theory. Crown 8vo, pp. iv. and 76, cloth. 1877. 2s. 6d.

THOUGHTS ON THEISM, with Suggestions towards a Public Religious Service in Harmony with Modern Science and Philosophy. Ninth Thousand. Revised and Enlarged. 8vo, pp. 74, sewed. 1882. 1s.

THURSTON.—Friction and Lubrication. Determinations of the Laws and Co-efficients of Friction by new Methods and with new Apparatus. By Robert H. Thurston, A.M., C.E., &c. Crown 8vo, pp. xvi. and 212, cloth. 1879. 6s. 6d.

TIELE.—See English and Foreign Philosophical Library, Vol. VII. and Trübner's Oriental Series.

TOLHAUSEN.—A Synopsis of the Patent Laws of Various Countries. By A. Tolhausen, Ph.D. Third Edition. 12mo, pp. 62, sewed. 1870. 1s. 6d.

TONSBERG.—Norway. Illustrated Handbook for Travellers. Edited by Charles Tönsberg. With 134 Engravings on Wood, 17 Maps, and Supplement. Crown 8vo, pp. lxx., 482, and 32, cloth. 1875. 18s.

TOPOGRAPHICAL WORKS.—A List of the various Works prepared at the Topographical and Statistical Department of the War Office may be had on application.

TORCEANU.—Roumanian Grammar. See Trübner's Collection.

TORRENS.—Empire in Asia: How we came by it. A Book of Confessions. By W. M. Torrens, M.P. Med. 8vo, pp. 426. cloth. 1872. 14s.

TOSCANI.—Italian Conversational Course. A New Method of Teaching the Italian Language, both Theoretically and Practically. By Giovanni Toscani, Professor of the Italian Language and Literature in Queen's Coll., London, &c. Fourth Edition. 12mo, pp. xiv. and 300, cloth. 1872. 5s.

TOSCANI.—Italian Reading Course. By G. Toscani. Fcap. 8vo, pp. xii. and 160. With table. Cloth. 1875. 4s. 6d.

TOULON.—Its Advantages as a Winter Residence for Invalids and Others. By an English Resident. The proceeds of this pamphlet to be devoted to the English Church at Toulon. Crown 8vo, pp. 8, sewed. 1873. 6d.

TRADLEG.—A Son of Belial. Autobiographical Sketches. By Nitram Tradleg, University of Bosphorus. Crown 8vo, pp. viii.-260, cloth. 1882. 5s.

TRIMEN.—South-African Butterflies; a Monograph of the Extra-Tropical Species. By Roland Trimen, F.L.S., F.Z.S., M.E.S., Curator of the South African Museum, Cape Town. Royal 8vo. [*In preparation.*

TRÜBNER'S American, European, and Oriental Literary Record. A Register of the most Important Works published in America, India, China, and the British Colonies. With Occasional Notes on German, Dutch, Danish, French, Italian, Spanish, Portuguese, and Russian Literature. The object of the Publishers in issuing this publication is to give a full and particular account of every publication of importance issued in America and the East. Small 4to, 6d. per number. Subscription, 5s. per volume.

TRÜBNER.—TRÜBNER'S BIBLIOGRAPHICAL GUIDE TO AMERICAN LITERATURE: A Classed List of Books published in the United States of America, from 1817 to 1857. With Bibliographical Introduction, Notes, and Alphabetical Index. Compiled and Edited by Nicolas Trübner. In 1 vol. 8vo, half bound, pp. 750. 1859. 18s.

TRÜBNER'S CATALOGUE OF DICTIONARIES AND GRAMMARS OF THE PRINCIPAL LANGUAGES AND DIALECTS OF THE WORLD. Considerably Enlarged and Revised, with an Alphabetical Index. A Guide for Students and Booksellers. Second Edition, 8vo, pp. viii. and 170, cloth. 1882. 5s.

TRÜBNER'S COLLECTION OF SIMPLIFIED GRAMMARS OF THE PRINCIPAL ASIATIC AND EUROPEAN LANGUAGES. Edited by Reinhold Rost, LL.D., Ph.D. Crown 8vo, cloth, uniformly bound.

 I.—HINDUSTANI, PERSIAN, AND ARABIC. By E. H. Palmer, M.A. Second Edition. Pp. 112. 1885. 5s.
 II.—HUNGARIAN. By I. Singer. Pp. vi. and 88. 1882. 4s. 6d.
 III.—BASQUE. By W. Van Eys. Pp. xii. and 52. 1883. 3s. 6d.
 IV.—MALAGASY. By G. W. Parker. Pp. 66, with Plate. 1883. 5s.
 V.—MODERN GREEK. By E. M. Geldart, M.A. Pp. 68. 1883. 2s. 6d.
 VI.—ROUMANIAN. By R. Torceanu. Pp. viii. and 72. 1883. 5s.
 VII.—TIBETAN GRAMMAR. By H. A. JASCHKE. Pp. viii.-104. 1883. 5s.
 VIII.—DANISH. By E. C. Otté. Pp. viii. and 66. 1884. 2s. 6d.
 IX.—TURKISH. By J. W. Redhouse, M.R.A.S. Pp. xii. and 204. 1884. 10s.6d.
 X.—SWEDISH. By E. C. Otté. Pp. xii.-70. 1884. 2s. 6d.
 XI.—POLISH. By W. R. Morfill, M.A. Pp. viii.-64. 1884. 3s. 6d.
 XII.—PALI. By E. Müller. Pp. xvi.-144. 1884. 7s. 6d.
 XIII.—SANSKRIT. By H. Edgren. Pp. (.) 1885. (.)

TRÜBNER'S ORIENTAL SERIES :—
 Post 8vo, cloth, uniformly bound.

ESSAYS ON THE SACRED LANGUAGE, WRITINGS, AND RELIGION OF THE PARSIS. By Martin Haug, Ph.D., late Professor of Sanskrit and Comparative Philology at the University of Munich. Third Edition. Edited and Enlarged by E. W. West, Ph.D. To which is also added, A Biographical Memoir of the late Dr. Haug. By Professor E. P. Evans. Pp. xlviii. and 428. 1884. 16s.

TEXTS FROM THE BUDDHIST CANON, commonly known as Dhammapada. With Accompanying Narratives. Translated from the Chinese by S. Beal, B.A., Trinity College, Cambridge, Professor of Chinese, University College, London. Pp. viii. and 176. 1878. 7s. 6d.

THE HISTORY OF INDIAN LITERATURE. By Albrecht Weber. Translated from the German by J. Mann. M.A., and Dr. T. Zachariae, with the Author's sanction and assistance. 2d Edition. Pp. 368. 1882. 10s. 6d.

[A SKETCH OF THE MODERN LANGUAGES OF THE EAST INDIES. Accompanied by Two Language Maps, Classified List of Languages and Dialects, and a List of Authorities for each Language. By Robert Cust, late of H.M.I.C.S., and Hon. Librarian of R.A.S. Pp. xii. and 198. 1878. 12s.

THE BIRTH OF THE WAR-GOD: A Poem. By Kálidasá. Translated from the Sanskrit into English Verse, by Ralph T. H. Griffiths, M.A., Principal of Benares College. Second Edition. Pp. xii. and 116. 1879. 5s.

A CLASSICAL DICTIONARY OF HINDU MYTHOLOGY AND HISTORY, GEOGRAPHY AND LITERATURE. By John Dowson, M.R.A.S., late Professor in the Staff College. Pp. 432. 1879. 16s.

METRICAL TRANSLATIONS FROM SANSKRIT WRITERS; with an Introduction, many Prose Versions, and Parallel Passages from Classical Authors. By J. Muir, C.I.E., D.C.L., &c. Pp. xliv.-376. 1879. 14s.

MODERN INDIA AND THE INDIANS: being a Series of Impressions, Notes, and Essays. By Monier Williams, D.C.L., Hon. LL.D. of the University of Calcutta, Boden Professor of Sanskrit in the University of Oxford. Third Edition, revised and augmented by considerable additions. With Illustrations and Map, pp. vii. and 368. 1879. 14s.

TRÜBNER'S ORIENTAL SERIES—*continued.*

THE LIFE OR LEGEND OF GAUDAMA, the Buddha of the Burmese. With Annotations, the Ways to Neibban, and Notice on the Phongyies, or Burmese Monks. By the Right Rev. P. Bigandet, Bishop of Ramatha, Vicar Apostolic of Ava and Pegu. Third Edition. 2 vols. Pp. xx.-368 and viii.-326. 1880. 21s.

MISCELLANEOUS ESSAYS, relating to Indian Subjects. By B. H. Hodgson, late British Minister at Nepal. 2 vols., pp. viii.-408, and viii.-348. 1880. 28s.

SELECTIONS FROM THE KORAN. By Edward William Lane, Author of an "Arabic-English Lexicon," &c. A New Edition, Revised, with an Introduction. By Stanley Lane Poole. Pp. cxii. and 174. 1879. 9s.

CHINESE BUDDHISM. A Volume of Sketches, Historical and Critical. By J. Edkins, D.D., Author of "China's Place in Philology," "Religion in China," &c., &c. Pp. lvi. and 454. 1880. 18s.

THE GULISTAN; OR, ROSE GARDEN OF SHEKH MUSHLIU'D-DIN SADI OF SHIRAZ. Translated for the first time into Prose and Verse, with Preface and a Life of the Author, from the Atish Kadah, by E. B. Eastwick, F.R.S., M.R.A.S. 2d Edition. Pp. xxvi. and 244. 1880. 10s. 6d.

A TALMUDIC MISCELLANY; or, One Thousand and One Extracts from the Talmud, the Midrashim, and the Kabbalah. Compiled and Translated by P. J. Hershon. With a Preface by Rev. F. W. Farrar, D.D., F.R.S., Chaplain in Ordinary to Her Majesty, and Canon of Westminster. With Notes and Copious Indexes. Pp. xxviii. and 362. 1880. 14s.

THE HISTORY OF ESARHADDON (Son of Sennacherib), King of Assyria, B.C. 681–668. Translated from the Cuneiform Inscriptions upon Cylinders and Tablets in the British Museum Collection. Together with Original Texts, a Grammatical Analysis of each word, Explanations of the Ideographs by Extracts from the Bi-Lingual Syllabaries, and List of Eponyms, &c. By E. A. Budge, B.A., M.R.A.S., Assyrian Exhibitioner, Christ's College, Cambridge. Post 8vo, pp. xii. and 164, cloth. 1880. 10s. 6d.

BUDDHIST BIRTH STORIES; or, Jātaka Tales. The oldest Collection of Folk-Lore extant: being the Jātakatthavannanā, for the first time edited in the original Pali, by V. Fausböll, and translated by T. W. Rhys Davids. Translation. Vol. I. Pp. cxvi. and 348. 1880. 18s.

THE CLASSICAL POETRY OF THE JAPANESE. By Basil Chamberlain, Author of "Yeigio Henkaku, Ichiran." Pp. xii. and 228. 1880. 7s. 6d.

LINGUISTIC AND ORIENTAL ESSAYS. Written from the year 1846–1878. By R. Cust, Author of "The Modern Languages of the East Indies." Pp. xii. and 484. 1880. 18s.

INDIAN POETRY. Containing a New Edition of "The Indian Song of Songs," from the Sanskrit of the Gîta Govinda of Jayadeva; Two Books from "The Iliad of India" (Mahábhárata); "Proverbial Wisdom" from the Shlokas of the Hitopadésa, and other Oriental Poems. By Edwin Arnold, C.S.I., &c. Third Edition. Pp. viii. and 270. 1884. 7s. 6d.

THE RELIGIONS OF INDIA. By A. Barth. Authorised Translation by Rev. J. Wood. Pp. xx. and 310. 1881. 16s.

HINDŪ PHILOSOPHY. The Sānkhya Kārikā of Iswara Krishna. An Exposition of the System of Kapila. With an Appendix on the Nyaya and Vaiseshika Systems. By John Davies, M.A., M.R.A.S. Pp. vi. and 151. 1881. 6s.

TRÜBNER'S ORIENTAL SERIES—*continued*.

A MANUAL OF HINDU PANTHEISM. The Vedantasara. Translated with Copious Annotations. By Major G. A. Jacob, Bombay Staff Corps, Inspector of Army Schools. With a Preface by E. B. Cowell, M.A., Professor of Sanskrit in the University of Cambridge. Pp. x. and 130 1881. 6s.

THE MESNEVĪ (usually known as the Mesneviyi Sherīf, or Holy Mesnevī) of Mevlānā (Our Lord) Jelālu-'d-Dīn Muhammed, Er-Rūmī. Book the First. Together with some Account of the Life and Acts of the Author, of his Ancestors, and of his Descendants. Illustrated by a selection of Characteristic Anecdotes as collected by their Historian Mevlānā Shemsu-'d-Dīn Ahmed, El Eflākī El Arifī. Translated, and the Poetry Versified by James W. Redhouse, M.R.A.S., &c. Pp. xvi. and 136, vi. and 290. 1881. £1, 1s.

EASTERN PROVERBS AND EMBLEMS ILLUSTRATING OLD TRUTHS. By the Rev. J. Long, Member of the Bengal Asiatic Society, F.R.G.S. Pp. xv. and 280. 1881. 6s.

THE QUATRAINS OF OMAR KHAYYÁM. A New Translation. By E. H. Whinfield, late of H.M. Bengal Civil Service. Pp. 96. 1881. 5s.

THE QUATRAINS OF OMAR KHAYYÁM. The Persian Text, with an English Verse Translation. By E. H. Whinfield. Pp. xxxii.–335. 1883. 10s. 6d.

THE MIND OF MENCIUS ; or, Political Economy Founded upon Moral Philosophy. A Systematic Digest of the Doctrines of the Chinese Philosopher Mencius. The Original Text Classified and Translated, with Comments, by the Rev. E. Faber, Rhenish Mission Society. Translated from the German, with Additional Notes, by the Rev. A. B. Hutchinson, Church Mission, Hong Kong. Author in Chinese of " Primer Old Testament History," &c., &c. Pp. xvi. and 294. 1882. 10s. 6d.

YÚSUF AND ZULAIKHA. A Poem by Jami. Translated from the Persian into English Verse. By R. T. H. Griffith. Pp. xiv. and 304. 1882. 8s. 6d.

TSUNI- ‖ GOAM : The Supreme Being of the Khoi-Khoi. By Theophilus Hahn, Ph.D., Custodian of the Grey Collection, Cape Town, Corresponding Member of the Geographical Society, Dresden ; Corresponding Member of the Anthropological Society, Vienna, &c., &c. Pp. xii. and 154. 1882. 7s. 6d.

A COMPREHENSIVE COMMENTARY TO THE QURAN. To which is prefixed Sale's Preliminary Discourse, with Additional Notes and Emendations. Together with a Complete Index to the Text, Preliminary Discourse, and Notes. By Rev. E. M. Wherry, M.A., Lodiana. Vol. I. Pp. xii. and 392. 1882. 12s. 6d. Vol. II. Pp. xi. and 408. 1884. 12s. 6d.

HINDU PHILOSOPHY. THE BHAGAVAD GÎTÂ ; or, The Sacred Lay. A Sanskrit Philosophical Lay. Translated, with Notes, by John Davies, M.A. Pp. vi. and 208. 1882. 8s. 6d.

THE SARVA-DARSANA-SAMGRAHA ; or, Review of the Different Systems of Hindu Philosophy. By Madhava Acharya. Translated by E. B. Cowell, M.A., Cambridge, and A. E. Gough, M.A., Calcutta. Pp. xii. and 282. 1882. 10s. 6d.

TIBETAN TALES. Derived from Indian Sources. Translated from the Tibetan of the Kay-Gyur. By F. Anton von Schiefner. Done into English from the German, with an Introduction. By W. R. S. Ralston, M.A. Pp. lxvi. and 368. 1882. 14s.

LINGUISTIC ESSAYS. By Carl Abel, Ph.D. Pp. viii. and 265. 1882. 9s.

THE INDIAN EMPIRE : Its History, People, and Products. By W. W. Hunter, C.I.E., LL.D. Pp. 568. 1882. 16s.

HISTORY OF THE EGYPTIAN RELIGION. By Dr. C. P. Tiele, Leiden. Translated by J. Ballingal. Pp. xxiv. and 230. 1882. 7s. 6d.

TRÜBNER'S ORIENTAL SERIES—*continued.*

THE PHILOSOPHY OF THE UPANISHADS. By A. E. Gough, M.A., Calcutta. Pp. xxiv.–268. 1882. 9s.

UDANAVARGA. A Collection of Verses from the Buddhist Canon. Compiled by Dharmatrâta. Being the Northern Buddhist Version of Dhammapada. Translated from the Tibetan of Bkah-hgyur, with Notes, and Extracts from the Commentary of Pradjnavarman, by W. Woodville Rockhill. Pp. 240. 1883. 9s.

A HISTORY OF BURMA, including Burma Proper, Pegu, Taungu, Tenasserim, and Arakan. From the Earliest Time to the End of the First War with British India. By Lieut.-General Sir Arthur P. Phayre, G.C.M.G., K.C.S.I., and C.B. Pp. xii.–312. 1883. 14s.

A SKETCH OF THE MODERN LANGUAGES OF AFRICA. Accompanied by a Language-Map. By R. N. Cust, Author of "Modern Languages of the East Indies," &c. 2 vols., pp. xvi. and 566, with Thirty-one Autotype Portraits. 1883. 25s.

RELIGION IN CHINA; containing a brief Account of the Three Religions of the Chinese; with Observations on the Prospects of Christian Conversion amongst that People. By Joseph Edkins, D.D., Peking. Third Edition. Pp. xvi. and 260. 1884. 7s. 6d.

OUTLINES OF THE HISTORY OF RELIGION TO THE SPREAD OF THE UNIVERSAL RELIGIONS. By Prof. C. P. TIELE. Translated from the Dutch by J. Estlin Carpenter, M.A., with the Author's assistance. Third Edition. Pp. xx. and 250. 1884. 7s. 6d.

SI-YU-KI. BUDDHIST RECORDS OF THE WESTERN WORLD. Translated from the Chinese of Hiuen Tsiang (A.D. 629). By Samuel Beal, Professor of Chinese, University College, London. 2 vols., with a specially prepared Map. Pp. cviii.–242 and viii.–370. 1884. 24s. Dedicated by permission to H.R.H. the Prince of Wales.

THE LIFE OF THE BUDDHA, AND THE EARLY HISTORY OF HIS ORDER. Derived from Tibetan Works in the Bkah-Hgyur and the Bstan-Hgyur, followed by Notices on the Early History of Tibet and Khoten. By W. W. Rockhill. Pp. xii. and 274. 1884. 10s. 6d.

THE SANKHYA APHORISMS OF KAPILA. With Illustrative Extracts from the Commentaries. Translated and Edited by J. R. Ballantyne, LL.D., late Principal of Benares College. Third Edition, now entirely Re-Edited by Fitzedward Hall. Pp. viii. and 464. 1885. 16s.

THE ORDINANCES OF MANU. Translated from the Sanskrit. With an Introduction by the late A. C. Burnell, Ph.D., C.I.E. Completed and Edited by Edward W. Hopkins, Ph.D., of Columbia College, New York. Pp. xliv. and 400. 1884. 12s.

THE LIFE AND TRAVELS OF ALEXANDER CSOMA DE KÖRÖS between 1819 and 1842. With a Short Notice of all his Published and Unpublished Works and Essays. From Original and for the most part Unpublished Documents. By T. Duka, M.D., F.R.C.S. (Eng.), Surgeon-Major H.M.'s Bengal Medical Service, Retired, &c.

TURNER.—THE ENGLISH LANGUAGE. A Concise History of the English Language, with a Glossary showing the Derivation and Pronunciation of the English Words. By Roger Turner. In German and English on opposite pages. 18mo, pp. viii.–80, sewed. 1884. 1s. 6d.

UNGER.—A SHORT CUT TO READING : The Child's First Book of Lessons. Part I. By W. H. Unger. Fourth Edition. Cr. 8vo, pp. 32, cloth. 1873. 5d.

SEQUEL to Part I. and Part II. Fourth Edition. Cr. 8vo, pp. 64, cloth. 1873. 6d. Parts I. and II. Third Edition. Demy 8vo, pp. 76, cloth. 1873. 1s. 6d. In folio sheets. Pp. 44. Sets A to D, 10d. each ; set E, 8d. 1873. Complete, 4s.

UNGER.—W. H. UNGER'S CONTINUOUS SUPPLEMENTARY WRITING MODELS, designed to impart not only a good business hand, but correctness in transcribing. Oblong 8vo, pp. 40, stiff covers. 1874. 6d.

UNGER.—THE STUDENT'S BLUE BOOK: Being Selections from Official Correspondence, Reports, &c.; for Exercises in Reading and Copying Manuscripts, Writing, Orthography, Punctuation, Dictation, Précis, Indexing, and Digesting, and Tabulating Accounts and Returns. Compiled by W. H. Unger. Folio, pp. 100, paper. 1875. 2s.

UNGER.—TWO HUNDRED TESTS IN ENGLISH ORTHOGRAPHY, or Word Dictations. Compiled by W. H. Unger. Foolscap, pp. viii. and 200, cloth. 1877. 1s. 6d. plain, 2s. 6d. interleaved.

UNGER.—THE SCRIPT PRIMER: By which one of the remaining difficulties of Children is entirely removed in the first stages, and, as a consequence, a considerable saving of time will be effected. In Two Parts. By W. H. Unger. Part I. 12mo, pp. xvi. and 44, cloth. 5d. Part II., pp. 59, cloth. 5d.

UNGER.—PRELIMINARY WORD DICTATIONS ON THE RULES FOR SPELLING. By W. H. Unger. 18mo, pp. 44, cloth. 4d.

URICOECHEA.—MAPOTECA COLOMBIANA: Catalogo de Todos los Mapas, Planos, Vistas, &c., relativos a la América-Española, Brasil, e Islas adyacentes. Arreglada cronologicamente i precedida de una introduccion sobre la historia cartografica de América. Por el Doctor Ezequiel Uricoechea, de Bogóta, Nueva Granada. 8vo, pp. 232, cloth. 1860. 6s.

URQUHART.—ELECTRO-MOTORS. A Treatise on the Means and Apparatus employed in the Transmission of Electrical Energy and its Conversion into Motive-power. For the Use of Engineers and Others. By J. W. Urquhart, Electrician. Crown 8vo, cloth, pp. xii. and 178, illustrated. 1882. 7s. 6d.

VAITANA SUTRA.—See AUCTORES SANSKRITI, Vol. III.

VALDES.—LIVES OF THE TWIN BROTHERS, JUÁN AND ALFONSO DE VALDÉS. By E. Boehmer, D.D. Translated by J. T. Betts. Crown 8vo, pp. 32, wrappers. 1882. 1s.

VALDES.—SEVENTEEN OPUSCULES. By Juán de Valdés. Translated from the Spanish and Italian, and edited by John T. Betts. Crown 8vo, pp. xii. and 188, cloth. 1882. 6s.

VALDES.—JUÁN DE VALDÉS' COMMENTARY UPON THE GOSPEL OF ST. MATTHEW. With Professor Boehmer's "Lives of Juán and Alfonso de Valdés." Now for the first time translated from the Spanish, and never before published in English. By John T. Betts. Post 8vo, pp. xii. and 512–30, cloth. 1882. 7s. 6d.

VALDES.—SPIRITUAL MILK; or, Christian Instruction for Children. By Juán de Valdés. Translated from the Italian, edited and published by John T. Betts. With Lives of the twin brothers, Juán and Alfonso de Valdés. By E. Boehmer. D.D. Fcap. 8vo, pp. 60, wrappers. 1882. 2s.

VALDES.—SPIRITUAL MILK. Octaglot. The Italian original, with translations into Spanish, Latin, Polish, German, English, French, and Engadin. With a Critical and Historical Introduction by Edward Boehmer, the Editor of "Spanish Reformers." 4to, pp. 88, wrappers. 1884. 6s.

VALDES.—THREE OPUSCULES: an Extract from Valdés' Seventeen Opuscules. By Juán de Valdés. Translated, edited, and published by John T. Betts. Fcap. 8vo, pp. 58, wrappers. 1881. 1s. 6d.

VALDES.—JUÁN DE VALDÉS' COMMENTARY UPON OUR LORD'S SERMON ON THE MOUNT. Translated and edited by J. T. Betts. With Lives of Juán and Alfonso de Valdés. By E. Boehmer, D.D. Crown 8vo, pp. 112, boards. 1882. 2s. 6d.

VALDES.—JUÁN DE VALDÉS' COMMENTARY UPON THE EPISTLE TO THE ROMANS. Edited by J. T. Betts. Crown 8vo, pp. xxxii. and 296, cloth. 1883. 6s.

VALDES.—JUÁN DE VALDÉS' COMMENTARY UPON ST. PAUL'S FIRST EPISTLE TO THE CHURCH AT CORINTH. Translated and edited by J. T. Betts. With Lives of Juán and Alphonso de Valdés. By E. Boehmer. Crown 8vo, pp. 390, cloth. 1883. 6s.

VAN CAMPEN.—THE DUTCH IN THE ARCTIC SEAS.   By Samuel Richard Van Campen, author of "Holland's Silver Feast." 8vo. Vol. I. A Dutch Arctic Expedition and Route. Third Edition. Pp. xxxvii. and 263, cloth. 1877. 10s. 6d. Vol. II. *in preparation.*

VAN DE WEYER.—CHOIX D'OPUSCULES PHILOSOPHIQUES, HISTORIQUES, POLITIQUES ET LITTÉRAIRES de Sylvain Van de Weyer, Précédés d'Avant propos de l'Editeur. Roxburghe style. Crown 8vo. PREMIÈRE SÉRIE. Pp. 374. 1863. 10s. 6d.— DEUXIÈME SÉRIE. Pp. 502. 1869. 12s.—TROISIÈME SÉRIE. Pp. 391. 1875. 10s. 6d.—QUATRIÈME SÉRIE. Pp. 366. 1876. 10s. 6d.

VAN EYS.—BASQUE GRAMMAR.   See Trübner's Collection.

VAN LAUN.—GRAMMAR OF THE FRENCH LANGUAGE. By H. Van Laun. Parts I. and II. Accidence and Syntax. 13th Edition. Cr. 8vo, pp. 151 and 120, cloth. 1874. 4s. Part III. Exercises. 11th Edition. Cr. 8vo, pp. xii. and 285, cloth. 1873. 3s. 6d.

VAN LAUN.—LEÇONS GRADUÉES DE TRADUCTION ET DE LECTURE ; or, Graduated Lessons in Translation and Reading, with Biographical Sketches, Annotations on History, Geography, Synonyms and Style, and a Dictionary of Words and Idioms. By Henri Van Laun. 4th Edition. 12mo, pp. viii. and 400, cloth. 1868. 5s.

VAN PRAAGH.—LESSONS FOR THE INSTRUCTION OF DEAF AND DUMB CHILDREN, in Speaking, Lip-reading, Reading, and Writing. By W. Van Praagh, Director of the School and Training College for Teachers of the Association for the Oral Instruction of the Deaf and Dumb, Officier d'Academie, France. Fcap. 8vo, Part I., pp. 52, cloth. 1884. 2s. 6d. Part II., pp. 62, cloth. 1s. 6d.

VARDHAMANA'S GANARATNAMAHODADHI.   See AUCTORES SANSKRITI, Vol. IV.

VAZIR OF LANKURAN : A Persian Play.   A Text-Book of Modern Colloquial Persian. Edited, with Grammatical Introduction, Translation, Notes, and Vocabulary, by W. H. Haggard, late of H.M. Legation in Teheran, and G. le Strange. Crown 8vo, pp. 230, cloth. 1882. 10s. 6d.

VELASQUEZ AND SIMONNÉ'S NEW METHOD TO READ, WRITE, AND SPEAK THE SPANISH LANGUAGE. Adapted to Ollendorff's System. Post 8vo, pp. 558, cloth. 1882. 6s.
    KEY.   Post 8vo, pp. 174, cloth.   4s.

VELASQUEZ.—A DICTIONARY OF THE SPANISH AND ENGLISH LANGUAGES. For the Use of Young Learners and Travellers. By M. Velasquez de la Cadena. In Two Parts. I. Spanish-English. II. English-Spanish. Crown 8vo, pp. viii. and 846, cloth. 1883. 7s. 6d.

VELASQUEZ.—A PRONOUNCING DICTIONARY OF THE SPANISH AND ENGLISH LANGUAGES. Composed from the Dictionaries of the Spanish Academy, Terreos, and Salvá, and Webster, Worcester, and Walker. Two Parts in one thick volume. By M. Velasquez de la Cadena. Roy. 8vo, pp. 1280, cloth. 1873. £1, 4s.

VELASQUEZ.—NEW SPANISH READER : Passages from the most approved authors, in Prose and Verse. Arranged in progressive order. With Vocabulary. By M. Velasquez de la Cadena. Post 8vo, pp. 352, cloth. 1866. 6s.

VELASQUEZ.—AN EASY INTRODUCTION TO SPANISH CONVERSATION, containing all that is necessary to make a rapid progress in it. Particularly designed for persons who have little time to study, or are their own instructors. By M. Velasquez de la Cadena. 12mo, pp. 150, cloth. 1863. 2s. 6d.

VERSES AND VERSELETS.   By a Lover of Nature. Foolscap 8vo, pp. viii. and 88, cloth. 1876. 2s. 6d.

VICTORIA GOVERNMENT.—PUBLICATIONS OF THE GOVERNMENT OF VICTORIA. *List in preparation.*

VOGEL.—ON BEER. A Statistical Sketch. By M. Vogel. Fcap. 8vo, pp. xii. and 76, cloth limp. 1874. 2s.

WAFFLARD and FULGENCE.—LE VOYAGE À DIEPPE. A Comedy in Prose. By Wafflard and Fulgence. Edited, with Notes, by the Rev. P. H. E. Brette, B.D. Cr. 8vo, pp. 104, cloth. 1867. 2s. 6d.

WAKE.--THE EVOLUTION OF MORALITY. Being a History of the Development of Moral Culture. By C. Staniland Wake. 2 vols. crown 8vo, pp. xvi.-506 and xii.-474, cloth. 1878. 21s.

WALLACE.—ON MIRACLES AND MODERN SPIRITUALISM ; Three Essays. By Alfred Russel Wallace, Author of "The Malay Archipelago," "The Geographical Distribution of Animals," &c., &c. Second Edition, crown 8vo, pp. viii. and 236, cloth. 1881. 5s

WANKLYN and CHAPMAN.—WATER ANALYSIS. A Practical Treatise on the Examination of Potable Water. By J. A. Wanklyn, and E. T. Chapman. Sixth Edition. Entirely rewritten. By J. A. Wanklyn, M.R.C.S. Crown 8vo, pp. 192, cloth. 1884. 5s.

WANKLYN.—MILK ANALYSIS ; a Practical Treatise on the Examination of Milk and its Derivatives, Cream, Butter, and Cheese. By J. A. Wanklyn, M.R.C.S., &c. Crown 8vo, pp. viii. and 72, cloth. 1874. 5s.

WANKLYN.—TEA, COFFEE, AND COCOA. A Practical Treatise on the Analysis of Tea, Coffee, Cocoa, Chocolate, Maté (Paraguay Tea), &c. By J. A. Wanklyn, M.R.C.S., &c. Crown 8vo, pp. viii. and 60, cloth. 1874. 5s.

WAR OFFICE.— A LIST OF THE VARIOUS MILITARY MANUALS AND OTHER WORKS PUBLISHED UNDER THE SUPERINTENDENCE OF THE WAR OFFICE may be had on application.

WARD.—ICE : A Lecture delivered before the Keswick Literary Society, and published by request. To which is appended a Geological Dream on Skiddaw. By J. Clifton Ward, F.G.S. 8vo, pp. 28, sewed. 1870. 1s.

WARD.—ELEMENTARY NATURAL PHILOSOPHY ; being a Course of Nine Lectures, specially adapted for the use of Schools and Junior Students. By J. Clifton Ward, F.G.S. Fcap. 8vo, pp. viii. and 216, with 154 Illustrations, cloth. 1871. 3s. 6d.

WARD.—ELEMENTARY GEOLOGY : A Course of Nine Lectures, for the use of Schools and Junior Students. By J. Clifton Ward, F.G.S. Fcap. 8vo, pp. 292, with 120 Illustrations, cloth. 1872. 4s. 6d.

WATSON.—INDEX TO THE NATIVE AND SCIENTIFIC NAMES OF INDIAN AND OTHER EASTERN ECONOMIC PLANTS AND PRODUCTS, originally prepared under the authority of the Secretary of State for India in Council. By John Forbes Watson, M.D. Imp. 8vo, pp. 650, cloth. 1868. £1, 11s. 6d.

WATSON.—SPANISH AND PORTUGUESE SOUTH AMERICA DURING THE COLONIAL PERIOD. By R. G. Watson. 2 vols. post 8vo, pp. xvi.-308, viii.-320, cloth. 1884. 21s.

WEBER.—THE HISTORY OF INDIAN LITERATURE. By Albrecht Weber. Translated from the Second German Edition. by J. Mann, M.A., and T. Zachariae, Ph.D., with the sanction of the Author. Second Edition, post 8vo, pp. xxiv. and 360, cloth. 1882. 10s. 6d.

WEDGWOOD.—THE PRINCIPLES OF GEOMETRICAL DEMONSTRATION. reduced from the Original Conception of Space and Form. By H. Wedgwood, M.A. 12mo, pp. 48, cloth. 1844. 2s.

WEDGWOOD.—ON THE DEVELOPMENT OF THE UNDERSTANDING. By H. Wedgwood, A.M. 12mo, pp. 133, cloth. 1848. 3s.

WEDGWOOD.—THE GEOMETRY OF THE THREE FIRST BOOKS OF EUCLID. By Direct Proof from Definitions Alone. By H. Wedgwood, M.A. 12mo, pp. 104, cloth. 1856. 3s.

WEDGWOOD.—ON THE ORIGIN OF LANGUAGE. By H. Wedgwood, M.A. 12mo, pp. 165, cloth. 1866. 3s. 6d.

WEDGWOOD.—A DICTIONARY OF ENGLISH ETYMOLOGY. By H. Wedgwood. Third Edition, revised and enlarged. With Introduction on the Origin of Language. 8vo, pp. lxxii. and 746, cloth. 1878. £1, 1s.

WEDGWOOD.—CONTESTED ETYMOLOGIES IN THE DICTIONARY OF THE REV. W. W. SKEAT. By H. Wedgwood. Crown 8vo, pp. viii. and 194, cloth. 1882. 5s.

WEISBACH.—THEORETICAL MECHANICS : A Manual of the Mechanics of Engineering and of the Construction of Machines ; with an Introduction to the Calculus. Designed as a Text-book for Technical Schools and Colleges, and for the use of Engineers, Architects, &c. By Julius Weisbach, Ph.D., Oberbergrath, and Professor at the Royal Mining Academy at Freiberg, &c. Translated from the German by Eckley B. Coxe, A.M., Mining Engineer. Demy 8vo, with 902 woodcuts, pp. 1112, cloth. 1877. 31s. 6d.

WELLER.—AN IMPROVED DICTIONARY ; English and French, and French and English. By E. Weller. Royal 8vo, pp. 384 and 340, cloth. 1864. 7s. 6d.

WEST and BUHLER.—A DIGEST OF THE HINDU LAW OF INHERITANCE, PARTITION, AND ADOPTION ; embodying the Replies of the Sâstris in the Courts of the Bombay Presidency, with Introductions and Notes. By Raymond West and J. G. Bühler. Third Edition. Demy 8vo, pp. 1450, sewed. 1884. £1, 16s.

WETHERELL.—THE MANUFACTURE OF VINEGAR, its Theory and Practice; with especial reference to the Quick Process. By C. M. Wetherell, Ph.D., M.D. 8vo, pp. 30, cloth. 7s. 6d.

WHEELDON.—ANGLING RESORTS NEAR LONDON : The Thames and the Lea. By J. P. Wheeldon, Piscatorial Correspondent to "Bell's Life." Crown 8vo, pp. viii. and 218. 1878. Paper, 1s. 6d.

WHEELER.—THE HISTORY OF INDIA FROM THE EARLIEST AGES. By J. Talboys Wheeler. Demy 8vo, cloth. Vol. I. containing the Vedic Period and the Mahâ Bhârata. With Map. Pp. lxxv. and 576, cl. 1867, o. p. Vol. II. The Ramayana, and the Brahmanic Period. Pp. lxxxviii. and 680, with 2 Maps, cl. 21s. Vol. III. Hindu, Buddhist, Brahmanical Revival. Pp. xxiv.-500. With 2 Maps, 8vo, cl. 1874. 18s. This volume may be had as a complete work with the following title, "History of India ; Hindu, Buddhist, and Brahmanical." Vol IV. Part I. Mussulman Rule. Pp. xxxii.-320. 1876. 14s. Vol. IV. Part II. completing the History of India down to the time of the Moghul Empire. Pp. xxviii. and 280. 1881. 12s.

WHEELER.—EARLY RECORDS OF BRITISH INDIA : A History of the English Settlements in India, as told in the Government Records, the works of old Travellers, and other Contemporary Documents, from the earliest period down to the rise of British Power in India. By J. Talboys Wheeler, late Assistant Secretary to the Government of India in the Foreign Department. Royal 8vo, pp. xxxii. and 392, cloth. 1878. 15s.

WHEELER.—THE FOREIGNER IN CHINA. By L. N. Wheeler, D.D. With Introduction by Professor W. C. Sawyer, Ph.D. 8vo, pp. 268, cloth. 1881. 6s. 6d.

WHERRY.—A COMPREHENSIVE COMMENTARY TO THE QURAN. To which is prefixed Sale's Preliminary Discourse, with additional Notes and Emendations. Together with a complete Index to the Text, Preliminary Discourse, and Notes. By Rev. E. M. Wherry M.A., Lodiana. 3 vols. post 8vo, cloth. Vol. I. Pp. xii. and 392. 1882. 12s. 6d. Vol. II. Pp. vi. and 408. 1884. 12s. 6d.

WHINFIELD.—QUATRAINS OF OMAR KHAYYAM. See Trübner's Oriental Series.

WHINFIELD.—See GULSHAN I. RAZ.

WHIST.—SHORT RULES FOR MODERN WHIST, Extracted from the "Quarterly Review" of January 1871. Printed on a Card, folded to fit the Pocket. 1878. 6d.

WHITE.—SPINOZA. See English and Foreign Philosophical Library.

WHITNEY.—LANGUAGE AND THE STUDY OF LANGUAGE : Twelve Lectures on the Principles of Linguistic Science. By W. D. Whitney. Fourth Edition, augmented by an Analysis. Crown 8vo, pp. xii. and 504, cloth. 1884. 10s. 6d.

WHITNEY.—LANGUAGE AND ITS STUDY, with especial reference to the Indo-European Family of Languages. Seven Lectures by W. D. Whitney, Instructor in Modern Languages in Yale College. Edited with Introduction, Notes, Tables, &c., and an Index, by the Rev. R. Morris, M.A., LL.D. Second Edition. Crown 8vo, pp. xxii. and 318, cloth. 1880. 5s.

WHITNEY.—Oriental and Linguistic Studies. By W. D. Whitney. First Series. Crown 8vo, pp. x. and 420, cloth. 1874. 12s. Second Series. Crown 8vo, pp. xii. and 434. With chart, cloth. 1874. 12s.

WHITNEY.—A SANSKRIT GRAMMAR, including both the Classical Language and the older Dialects of Veda and Brahmana. By William Dwight Whitney, Professor of Sanskrit and Comparative Philology in Yale College, Newhaven, &c., &c. 8vo, pp. xxiv. and 486. 1879. Stitched in wrapper, 10s. 6d; cloth, 12s.

WHITWELL.—IRON SMELTER'S POCKET ANALYSIS BOOK. By Thomas Whitwell, Member of the Institution of Mechanical Engineers, &c. Oblong 12mo, pp. 152, roan. 1877. 5s.

WILKINSON.—THE SAINT'S TRAVEL TO THE LAND OF CANAAN. Wherein are discovered Seventeen False Rests short of the Spiritual Coming of Christ in the Saints, with a Brief Discovery of what the Coming of Christ in the Spirit is. By R. Wilkinson. Printed 1648; reprinted 1874. Fcap. 8vo, pp. 208, cloth. 1s. 6d.

WILLIAMS.—A SYLLABIC DICTIONARY OF THE CHINESE LANGUAGE; arranged according to the Wu-Fang Yuen Yin, with the pronunciation of the Characters as heard in Pekin, Canton, Amoy, and Shanghai. By S. Wells Williams, LL.D. 4to, pp. 1336. 1874. £5, 5s.

WILLIAMS.—MODERN INDIA AND THE INDIANS. See Trübner's Oriental Series.

WILSON.—WORKS OF THE LATE HORACE HAYMAN WILSON, M.A., F.R.S., &c.

Vols. I. and II. Essays and Lectures chiefly on the Religion of the Hindus, by the late H. H. Wilson, M.A., F.R.S., &c. Collected and Edited by Dr. Reinhold Rost. 2 vols. demy 8vo, pp. xiii. and 399, vi. and 416, cloth. 21s.

Vols. III., IV., and V. Essays Analytical, Critical, and Philological, on Subjects connected with Sanskrit Literature. Collected and Edited by Dr. Reinhold Rost. 3 vols. demy 8vo, pp. 408, 406, and 390, cloth. 36s.

Vols. VI., VII., VIII., IX., and X. (2 parts). Vishnu Puráná, a System of Hindu Mythology and Tradition. Translated from the original Sanskrit, and Illustrated by Notes derived chiefly from other Puránás. By the late H. H. Wilson. Edited by FitzEdward Hall, M.A., D.C.L., Oxon. Vols. I. to V. (2 parts). Demy 8vo, pp. cxl. and 200, 344, 346, 362, and 268, cloth. £3, 4s. 6d.

Vols. XI. and XII. Select Specimens of the Theatre of the Hindus. Translated from the original Sanskrit. By the late H. H. Wilson, M.A., F.R.S. Third corrected Edition. 2 vols. demy 8vo, pp. lxxi. and 384, iv. and 418, cloth. 21s.

WISE.—COMMENTARY ON THE HINDU SYSTEM OF MEDICINE. By T. A. Wise, M.D. 8vo, pp. xx. and 432, cloth. 1845. 7s. 6d.

WISE.—REVIEW OF THE HISTORY OF MEDICINE. By Thomas A. Wise. 2 vols. demy 8vo, cloth. Vol. I., pp. xcviii. and 397. Vol. II., pp. 574. 10s.

WISE.—HISTORY OF PAGANISM IN CALEDONIA. By T. A. Wise, M.D., &c. Demy 4to, pp. xxviii.–272, cloth, with numerous Illustrations. 1884. 15s.

WITHERS.—THE ENGLISH LANGUAGE AS PRONOUNCED. By G. Withers. Royal 8vo, pp. 84, sewed. 1874. 1s.

WOOD.—CHRONOS. Mother Earth's Biography. A Romance of the New School. By Wallace Wood, M.D. Crown 8vo, pp. xvi. and 334, with Illustration, cloth. 1873. 6s.

WOMEN.—THE RIGHTS OF WOMEN. A Comparison of the Relative Legal Status of the Sexes in the Chief Countries of Western Civilisation. Crown 8vo, pp. 104, cloth. 1875. 2s. 6d.

WRIGHT.—FEUDAL MANUALS OF ENGLISH HISTORY, a series of Popular Sketches of our National History compiled at different periods, from the Thirteenth Century to the Fifteenth, for the use of the Feudal Gentry and Nobility. Now first edited from the Original Manuscripts. By Thomas Wright, M.A., F.S.A., &c. Small 4to, pp. xxix. and 184, cloth. 1872. 15s.

WRIGHT.—THE HOMES OF OTHER DAYS. A History of Domestic Manners and Sentiments during the Middle Ages. By Thomas Wright, M.A., F.S.A. With Illustrations from the Illuminations in Contemporary Manuscripts and other Sources. Drawn and Engraved by F. W. Fairholt, F.S.A. Medium 8vo, 350 Woodcuts, pp. xv. and 512, cloth. 1871. 21s.

WRIGHT.—ANGLO-SAXON AND OLD ENGLISH VOCABULARIES. By Thomas Wright, M.A., F.S.A., Hon. M.R.S.L. Second Edition, Edited and Collated by Richard Paul Wulcker. 2 vols. demy 8vo, pp. xx.-408, and iv.-486, cloth. 1884. 28s. Illustrating the Condition and Manners of our Forefathers, as well as the History of the forms of Elementary Education, and of the Languages Spoken in this Island from the Tenth Century to the Fifteenth.

WRIGHT.—THE CELT, THE ROMAN, AND THE SAXON; a History of the Early Inhabitants of Britain down to the Conversion of the Anglo-Saxons to Christianity. Illustrated by the Ancient Remains brought to light by Recent Research. By Thomas Wright, M.A., F.S.A., &c., &c. Third Corrected and Enlarged Edition. Cr. 8vo, pp. xiv. and 562. With nearly 300 Engravings. Cloth. 1875. 14s.

WRIGHT.—THE BOOK OF KALILAH AND DIMNAH. Translated from Arabic into Syriac. Edited by W. Wright, LL.D., Professor of Arabic in the University of Cambridge. Demy 8vo, pp. lxxxii.-408, cloth. 1884. 21s.

WRIGHT.—MENTAL TRAVELS IN IMAGINED LANDS. By H. Wright. Crown 8vo, pp. 184, cloth. 1878. 5s.

WYLD.—CLAIRVOYANCE; or, the Auto-Noetic Action of the Mind. By George Wyld, M.D. Edin. 8vo, pp. 32, wrapper. 1883. 1s.

WYSARD.—THE INTELLECTUAL AND MORAL PROBLEM OF GOETHE'S FAUST. By A. Wysard. Parts I. and II. Fcap. 8vo, pp. 80, limp parchment wrapper. 1883. 2s. 6d.

YOUNG MECHANIC (THE).—See MECHANIC.

ZELLER.—STRAUSS AND RENAN. An Essay by E. Zeller. Translated from the German. Post 8vo, pp. 110, cloth. 1866. 2s. 6d.

PERIODICALS

PUBLISHED AND SOLD BY TRÜBNER & CO.

AMATEUR MECHANICAL SOCIETY'S JOURNAL.—Irregular.

ANTHROPOLOGICAL INSTITUTE OF GREAT BRITAIN AND IRELAND (JOURNAL OF).— Quarterly, 5s.

ARCHITECT (AMERICAN) AND BUILDING NEWS.—Contains General Architectural News, Articles on Interior Decoration, Sanitary Engineering, Construction, Building Materials, &c., &c. Four full-page Illustrations accompany each Number. Weekly. Annual Subscription, £1, 11s. 6d. Post free.

ASIATIC SOCIETY (ROYAL) OF GREAT BRITAIN AND IRELAND (JOURNAL OF).— Irregular.

www.ingramcontent.com/pod-product-compliance
Lightning Source LLC
Chambersburg PA
CBHW021212270326
41929CB00010B/1095